GENDERING **DISGUST**
IN MEDIEVAL RELIGIOUS
POLEMIC

GENDERING **DISGUST** IN MEDIEVAL RELIGIOUS POLEMIC

ALEXANDRA CUFFEL

University of Notre Dame Press
Notre Dame, Indiana

Notre Dame, Indiana 46556
www.undpress.nd.edu

Manufactured in the United States of America

Library of Congress Cataloging-in-Publication Data

Cuffel, Alexandra.
Gendering disgust in medieval religious polemic / Alexandra Cuffel.
p. cm.
Includes bibliographical references (p.) and index.
ISBN-13: 978-0-268-02367-6 (pbk. : alk. paper)
ISBN-10: 0-268-02367-0 (pbk. : alk. paper)
1. Women—Religious aspects—History of doctrines—Middle Ages, 600 to 1500—Comparative studies. 2. Body, Human—Religious aspects—History of doctrines—Middle Ages, 600 to 1500—Comparative studies. 3. Purity, Ritual—History of doctrines—Middle Ages, 600–1500—Comparative studies. 4. Aversion—History—To 1500. 5. Apologetics—History—Middle Ages, 600–1500. 6. Islam—Apologetic works—History and criticism. 7. Judaism—Apologetic works—History and criticism. 8. Religions—Relations. I. Title.
BL458.C84 2007
201'.50902—dc22

2007003387

♻ *This book is printed on recycled paper.*

Dedicated to my father,

KEITH D. CUFFEL
(1935–1998),

who first taught me to ask questions of a text

Contents

PART II

Twelfth–Fourteenth Centuries: Intensification and Collision of Jewish-Christian-Muslim Polemic

Acknowledgments

Menstruation as polemic. It started out as a joke over coffee at the International Congress of Medieval Studies at Kalamazoo. I had noted that in a twelfth-century literary text titled *Sefer Sha'ashu'im*, by an Iberian Jew, Joseph ibn Zabara, there is a curious passage: "They that understand the healing art have said, 'If one lie with his wife during her period, and she conceive of that seed, the offspring will ever be leprous. If it be the first day of her period it will be leprous in its childhood; if in the second day, in its youth; if the third, in its prime; and thereafter in old age." When I quoted this passage in my first conference presentation, John Victor Tolan, now at the Université de Nantes, asked if it was related to the medieval Jewish "anti-Gospels," known as the *Toledot Yesu* stories, in which Jesus is said to have been conceived while Mary was menstruating, and if Jesus was ever portrayed as a leper in Jewish texts. I did not know the answers then, but these questions and the playful urging of friends and colleagues to also explore all types of impurity and filth in medieval religious polemic began the adventure that has resulted in this book. I owe thanks to John Lamoreaux, Southern Methodist University; Tom Burman, University of Tennessee at Knoxville; Larry Simon, Western Michigan University; James T. Muldoon, J. Carter Brown Library; James Brundage, University of Kansas; Thomas Allsen and JoAnn Gross, the College of New Jersey; Shaun Marmon, Princeton University; Paul Freedman, Yale University; Rob Meens, Utrecht; Mark Pegg and Yechiel Goldberg, California State University, Long Beach; Joel Hecker, Reconstructionist Seminary of America; Joel Kenny; Justine Henning; and Elizabeth Hatcher. I also wish to thank Alan Gotthelf, formerly of The College of New Jersey's philosophy department for our many discussions of Aristotle's biology and the ancient world. I benefited immensely from the suggestions of Heinrich von Staden, Princeton Institute of Advanced Studies; and Carlin Barton, University of

Massachusetts, Amherst; as well as the comments of Moshe David Herr; Hava Lazarus Yafeh, Israel Yuval, and Daniel Lasker, Ben Gurion University of the Negev; and Tzvi Langerman, now at Bar-Ilan University, during my year at Hebrew University. I owe particular thanks to Susanne Borchers, who was completing research on women in *Sefer Hasidim* while we were both in Jerusalem, for sharing her insights (and bibliography) on medieval Jewish views of women and patiently listening to mine as we labored together over sticky passages in Hebrew and Latin. Willis Johnson at Hebrew Union College–Los Angeles, Susan Einbinder at Hebrew Union College–Cincinnati, and Chaviva Levin at New York University graciously shared their work before it was published. David Burr, Elizabeth Struthers Malbon, and Brian Britt, all at Virginia Tech, read or discussed earlier chapters of this book with me. I am especially grateful to David Burr for our many discussions and his suggestions regarding the Immaculate Conception. Irven Resnick shared his sources and wisdom about "menstruating" Jewish men and then later on Jews and Saturn. Sahar Amer at the University of North Carolina at Chapel Hill has not only been a longtime source of support and good advice, but she read and critiqued an earlier version of chapter 6. Sahar, Joel Hecker, and Irven Resnick proofread the Arabic, Hebrew, and Latin respectively in the final versions of my notes (all errors are my own). William Chester Jordan at Princeton University has been a kind friend and an endless font of wicked humor, sanity, and insight. I also wish to thank Barbara Hanrahan, director of the University of Notre Dame Press and my editor, for her support, advice, and patience.

Perhaps one of the greatest debts a person can incur is to former teachers. Thus I wish to thank Elliot Wolfson, New York University, for his stimulating discussions on gender and mysticism; Robert Chazan, New York University, who pushed me to deal with multiple types of impurity; and especially Penelope Johnson for discussion on this project as it evolved from idea to dissertation to book. I also owe a debt of thanks to Anna Sapir Abulafia, whose research and careful supervision when I was completing an M. Phil. at the University of Cambridge inspired me to pursue Jewish studies, and to Clifford Flanagan, who was a staunch supporter for my fascination of even the most esoteric aspects of medieval culture when I was an undergraduate at Indiana University.

Along with friends and colleagues, I am indebted to the history department at the University of Massachusetts for having me as a guest for two years and allowing me to work free of committee obligations; to Virginia Polytechnic Institute and State University for awarding me a humanities grant to spend a summer examining manuscripts and cathedrals for chapter 6; and to the National Women's Studies Association Jewish Caucus and the International University Fellowship Foundation and the State Department (F.L.A.S.) program for financial support for this project.

My parents, Victoria and Keith Cuffel; my in-laws, Nathan and Lois Knobler; and my brother and his family, Chris Martin, Laura Chaiken, and Autum Martin, endured my studious and sometimes antisocial behavior with grace. However, my greatest thanks and debt of intellectual exchange, expertise, and love goes to my partner in all things, Adam Knobler, The College of New Jersey, who was there from the very beginning.

Abbreviations

AHR	*American Historical Review*
Aschkenas	*Aschkenas: Zeitschraft für Geschichte und Kultur der Juden*
BHM	*Bulletin of the History of Medicine*
BT	Babylonian Talmud
Byzantion	*Byzantion: Revue Internationale des Études Byzantines*
CCCM	*Corpus Christianorum continuatio mediaevalis*
CCSL	*Corpus Christianorum series Latina*
CSCO	Corpus Scriptorum Christianorum Orientalium
CSM	*Corpus Scriptorum Muzarabicorum*, 2 vols., ed. Johannes Gil (Madrid, 1973)
DSST	*Dead Sea Scrolls Translated: The Qumran Texts in English*, ed. and trans. Florentino García Martínez, trans. Wilfred G. E. Watson (Leiden, 1994)
HAR	*Hebrew Annual Review*
HN	*Historia Naturalis*

HTR	*Harvard Theological Review*
JHS	*Jewish Historical Studies*
JJS	*Journal of Jewish Studies*
JMEMS	*Journal of Medieval and Early Modern Studies*
JMH	*Journal of Medieval History*
JQR	*Jewish Quarterly Review*
JSQ	*Jewish Studies Quarterly*
JT	Jerusalem Talmud
MGH	*Monumenta Germaniae Historica*
Nat. D.	*De Natura Deorum*
PAAJR	*Proceedings of the American Academy for Jewish Research*
PG	*Patrologia Graeca*
PL	*Patrologia Latina*
PO	*Patrologia Orientalis*
REI	*Revue des Études Islamiques*
REJ	*Revue des Études Juives*
RHC	*Recueil des Historiens des Croisades*
RSR	*Revue des Sciences Réligieuses*

Illustrations

Transliteration

Arabic - English

أ	'
ب	b
ت	t
ث	th
ج	j
ح	ḥ
خ	ch
د	d
ذ	dh
ر	r
ز	z
س	s
ش	sh
ص	ṣ
ض	ḍ
ط	ṭ
ظ	ẓ
ع	'
غ	gh
ف	f
ق	q
ك	k
ل	l
م	m

ن	n
ه	h
و	w/ū
ي	y/ī

Hebrew - English

א	’
ב	b/v
ג	g
ד	d
ה	h
ו	w/v
וּ	u
וֹ	o
ז	z
ח	ḥ
ט	ṭ
י	y/i
ך	k/kh
ל	l
מ	m
נ	n
ס	s
ע	‘
פ	p/f
צ	ẓ
ק	q
ר	r
שׁ	sh
שׂ	s
ת	t

Introduction

Problems and Theories

By its very nature, an examination of late antique and medieval polemical evocations of impurity and filth as a form of religious attack focuses on unsavory imagery. This imagery was disturbing to premodern readers; the discomfort, indeed revulsion, provoked by accusations of uncleanness was what gave the polemic that employed it its very power. Modern readers will no doubt cringe at detailed descriptions of the filthy, smelly impurity used to characterize human existence, in particular the existence of "undesirables." This reaction was probably shared by the audience for whom the polemical texts were originally intended. In this book I seek to uncover the relationships between accusations of filthy corporeality in medieval religious polemic and the shifting paradigms of Jewish, Christian, and Muslim views of the body, especially the female body. I explore how categories of filth and ritual pollution functioned during late antiquity and the Middle Ages to define and denigrate the religious "other" and why this type of polemic was so powerful, or at least so favored by some authors and artists.[1]

Studying ritual pollution, dirt, and the male and female bodies as part of religious polemic in medieval Islam presents difficulties because of the relative paucity of research on the subject compared to what is available for Judaism and Christianity. Studies of polemic between Muslims and other religions have tended to focus on issues of transmission, specific authors, or philosophically oriented texts.[2] Although some scholars have dealt with the incarnation as a subject, so far much of the work has been narrowly focused on individual tractates.[3] The crusades have inspired more research regarding images of impurity in Muslim anti-Christian polemic; however, these observations have been embedded in larger studies of Muslims, the crusades, and propaganda and have not focused on the specific theme.[4] By contrast, work on Western Christian polemic against Muslims abounds.[5] The preponderance of studies on gender issues in medieval Islam has centered on the status and activities of women, images of women in literature, and sexuality.[6] With a few important exceptions, little has been done on concepts of the body per se, or on the ways in which gender was used metaphorically.[7] Examinations of disease, animals, or food are relatively few, and these have focused on specific ailments or problems in conceptualizing medical processes.[8] Despite the centrality of purity in Islamic legal thought, relatively little has been written on it for the medieval period.[9] I hope that this book and studies such as Carole Hillenbrand's *The Crusades: Islamic Perspectives* will prompt further research in these areas.

The issue of pollution as a tool in Jewish anti-Christian polemic has been avoided in the past by scholars because of historiographic, modern political, and social forces.[10] Anna Sapir Abulafia, in her comparison of the language of the Hebrew Crusade Chronicles and the *Toledot Yesu* stories showed that nineteenth-century scholars and translators of the Hebrew chronicles were reluctant to deal with the anti-Christian epithets they contained out of embarrassment and fear of provoking modern anti-Semitism.[11] Since that time a handful of scholars have begun to investigate more visceral aspects of medieval Jewish anti-Christian polemic and the Christian response.[12] A number of researchers, from Joshua Trachtenberg to Willis Johnson, have commented on the existence of Christian anti-Jewish polemic that described Jews as physically deformed or diseased.[13] Despite increased research into aggressive, negative imagery in both Christian and Jewish writings, scholars focusing on Jewish texts encounter the same quandaries as their nineteenth-century predecessors. For example, David Berger refrained from translating the invective *hari'a* as "shit" for Mary in the main body of *Niẓẓaḥon ha-yashan,* a late-thirteenth- early-fourteenth-century anti-Christian polemic.[14] In an article dealing with kabbalistic views of non-Jews, Elliot Wolfson felt obliged to disassociate himself from certain modern, in this case, Jewish, authors who used negative and even demonic imagery drawn from medieval Kabbalah to depict Islam and Christianity.[15] The most dramatic example of how volatile the issue of even unwittingly portraying medieval Jews in a way that a modern audience finds disturbing is the reaction Israel Yuval's article, "Vengeance and Damnation, Blood and Defamation: From Jewish Martyrdom to Blood Libel Accusations," elicited from Ezra Fleischer and Mordechai Breuer.[16]

show, clear evidence exists for such exchanges among members of all three faiths and linguistic traditions. Thus, Marcus's observations on northern France and Germany resonate for much of the rest of medieval Europe and the Muslim Mediterranean.[25]

The potential effect of a religious majority's accusations that one or more religious minorities or foreign enemies were diseased or impure was very different from that of the same accusation by a member of a minority against the majority. Whether or not medieval Christian authors specifically intended their works to spark physical violence against Jews, suggestions that Jews suffered from peculiar diseases and required a Christian child's blood or the host to cure them, or that they defiled Christian holy objects out of spite, often resulted in Jesus' death or injury.[26] Western Christians and Muslims during the crusades used such imagery in sermons specifically to spur listeners to join in holy war against the other. In this case, metaphors of pollution were explicitly designed to provoke violent action.[27] In contrast, a Jew who called Christians leprous and accused them of being worshipers of a putrid corpse endangered not only himself or herself but the entire local Jewish community as well.[28] Similar dangers faced Jews and Christians who openly criticized Islam while living under Muslim rule. Some have suggested that this fear may have accounted for Jews' relative silence regarding Muslims, yet as others have pointed out, Christians were not always so cautious.[29] The level of animosity expressed may have been the same on all sides, but only the minorities were ever in danger.

What then does it mean to have two or more religious communities employing similar polemical tropes when the potential response was so different in each? What was the function of the polemic in each group, and why did the Jews in Europe indulge in such language at risk to themselves?

The human body served as a cornerstone for late antique and medieval attempts to mark the persons and practices of their religious opponents as unacceptable. Preoccupation with bodily functions in premodern religious debates makes sense in the context of Mary Douglas's contention that beliefs and rules concerning the body's products reflect the social structures and tensions in a given culture. All beliefs about the body form a symbolic basis for describing the society that professes them. According to Douglas, rules about consumption and excreta are particularly indicative of a community's concerns about societal boundaries.[30] In later essays Douglas maintained that accusations of disease and contagion are frequently moralized and then used as tools to control individuals or groups perceived as threatening.[31] Seen in this light, references to impure corpses, blood, excreta, and disease in late antique and medieval polemic were expressions of anxiety about maintaining the hierarchy and the divisions between rival religious communities. In turn, the somatic images contained in the polemic were part of a medieval language of symbols based on the body.

In *The Anatomy of Disgust* W. I. Miller maintains that disgust is an important tool in "confirm[ing] others as belonging to a lower status and thus in [the] zero-sum game of rank necessarily defining oneself as higher."[32] In his brief treatment of the Middle Ages, Miller states, "Intense disgust in this period is not focused on vile substances like excrement but on people who inspire horror, fear and loathing: the leper, the Jew, the heretic, and for the monks and priest and hence much of the official discourse, women."[33]

My research and indeed the examples Miller provides to substantiate his remark suggest that excrement, menstrual blood, and other body fluids did elicit intense disgust during the period in question. Polemicists attacked their opponents by intimately associating them with these fluids and thus rendered them objects of profound contempt and horror. A Valentinian in late antiquity or a Muslim or Jew in the Middle Ages might repudiate the "orthodox" Christian doctrine of the incarnation on the following grounds: "You err in saying that something holy entered into a woman in that stinking place—for there is nothing in the world as disgusting as a woman's stomach, which is full of feces and urine, which emits discharge and menstrual blood and serves as a receptacle for a man's semen—you will surely be consumed by a "fire not blown" (Job 20:26) and descend into the deepest hell."[34] In such a case the author was not merely arguing that divinity and the human body are incompatible. In this and similar texts, the graphic enumeration of bodily fluids serves to provoke revulsion in the reader. This visceral emotion stands between the reader (or hearer) and any thought of accepting the idea of God's embodiment and birth. The language in this passage also indirectly marks Christians as disgusting because they adhere to such a belief. Jewish invectives that stated that Jesus and eventually all Christians had intercourse with or were products of menstruating women, Christian tales of Jews abusing the host wafer in order to cure themselves of anal bleeding, or Christian and Muslim suggestions that the other was bestial and smelly functioned in a similar fashion. The abhorrence that these accusations were designed to evoke was more personalized, however. Rather than a hypothetical event being disgusting and therefore worthy of rejection, real people could be categorized in the same way.

Thus examining the rhetoric of disgust that developed among Pagans, Jews, Christians, and Muslims in late antiquity and the Middle Ages reveals strategies for establishing boundaries between communities. A number of methods coexisted: listing the differences in points of doctrine and decrying the stubbornness and blindness of the opposing group for not grasping the "truth"; creating laws against certain types of social interaction between members of differing faiths; and forcing members of minority religions to wear distinctive dress. Yet the first of these methods, arguing over doctrine, appeals to an intellectual, though admittedly emotionally charged, distinction between the majority and minority faiths. The latter two are legal approaches, which often seem to have been observed more in the breech than in the adherence.[35] Describing one's opponent and his or her religion as disgusting and polluted differs in nature from these other tactics by evoking a gut-wrenching emotional antipathy that is closely linked to a variety of other feelings: fear, contempt, hatred.[36] The polemic of filth was more effective than subtle theological argumentation because it created simplified categories of good and evil by translating condemnation based on abstract theological and metaphysical reasoning into images of physically disgusting people or behavior. According to Robert Scribner in his studies of Catholic-Protestant conflict, this type of literature was popular propaganda, composed for internal consumption and designed to incite the believers who read it. Furthermore, he argued, reducing one's enemy to filth was a form of popular attack that was easily grasped by any who read, heard, or saw it.[37]

In short, insinuating that the other was both morally and physically filthy served two functions. First, it fostered a sense of community solidarity based on hatred. Second, it set up barriers against interfaith intimacy on any level. When medieval Christians, Jews, or Muslims directed epithets of physical dirt at the very bodies of "unbelievers," the polemic became deeply personalized, making each member of the opposing community a producer or product of vile substances and thus undesirable as an associate. Hence on a number of levels somatic polemic served the same functions in both majority and minority communities. Within the Christian, Pagan, or Muslim community, however, hatred-based solidarity and social barriers created by repugnance often served as an incitement to violence either against a religious minority—often the Jews—or against a military enemy, as in the case of later medieval Christian-Muslim polemic.

For Jews (and Christians and Muslims, when they found themselves in the position of being a religious minority), invectives, calls for vengeance, stories that portrayed the majority group in a negative fashion, and rituals and customs designed to emphasize the separation between minority and majority communities or to ridicule the belief systems of the majority all need to be seen as part of what James Scott has dubbed the "hidden transcript," the "critique of power spoken behind the back of the dominant."[38] According to Scott, these hidden critiques of power need to be spoken in places free of surveillance and control by the dominant.[39] In such locations anger at humiliations inflicted by those in power may be safely vented and, more important, subverted.[40]

Rabbinic study circles, private Jewish homes, and synagogues were just such safe spaces. Expressions of rage, desire for vengeance, and mocking or crassly derogatory language referring to Christians and their rituals that appear in Hebrew literature need to be seen as part of medieval Jews' verbal resistance to Christian oppression, serving much the same functions for medieval Jews as certain forms of rap music do for the contemporary African American youth community.[41] Because Hebrew liturgical poems, or *piyyuṭim,* were sung in the synagogue, a place in which the entire community gathered, and could be changed at every service according to need or circumstance, they were ideal vehicles for voicing Jewish rejection of Christianity.[42] According to Jewish tradition, *piyyuṭim* were created in response to religious persecution.[43] That medieval Jewish texts were written in an alphabet and language that most Christians could not understand served in part to hide anti-Christian invectives and stories from official scrutiny, a venue not available to most Christians under Muslim rule. Extreme obfuscation through the use of difficult vocabulary or heavy metaphorization also aided in this process, as did the degree to which a single phrase could trigger a complex set of associations that might not be recognized by an outsider.[44] Thus it is not surprising that calls for vengeance and invectives similar to those in the Hebrew First Crusade Chronicles and the *Toledot Yesu* tradition are commonly found in these poems, especially those produced by the Ashkenazi communities that bore the brunt of European Christian anti-Jewish violence during the twelfth and thirteenth centuries and needed to resort to covert expressions of resistance to the pressures and dangers that the Christians inflicted on them. The anti-Christian invectives in the *piyyuṭim* and in other genres of Jewish literature, arguments, and stories designed to make the persons or doctrines of Pagans and Christians repugnant or silly and easily dismissed, and the rituals and customs that emphasized Jews' separation from and rejection of the religion of their overlords were all hidden acts of rebellion.

In the early centuries of the Jewish-Christian conflict there was no need for dissembling because neither group was in the majority. Once Christianity gained political power, Jews had to be more careful about voicing their critiques of Christians. Despite the need for caution, mounting evidence indicates that Jews continued to express their rejection of Christianity's claims via poetry and ritual, especially during Purim and Passover. Christians sometimes were aware of or suspected such activity but initially did little.[45] The translation projects of the twelfth and thirteenth centuries led to new kinds of polemic and greater awareness of one another's arguments.[46] The decisive shift came at the Paris Talmud Trial of 1240 when a Jewish convert to Christianity, Nicolas Donin, denounced the Talmud as containing blasphemous slurs against Jesus and Mary.[47] As William Chester Jordan has shown, such accusations were not new, but the public forum and the consequences of Donin's charge were.[48] Copies of the Talmud were burned or censured, and a novel form of Christian missionizing began; Christians studied the Talmud and other forms of extrabiblical Jewish literature in order either to attack and delete offensive passages or to find evidence to prove the truth of Christianity to Jews. Jews, like Muslims, were forced to listen to sermons and to endure the presence of Christian preachers in their places of worship.[49] The "hidden transcript" was no longer a secret, and the status of the synagogues as safe havens of free expression and ritual was severely threatened.[50] The twelfth and thirteenth centuries were only the beginning of a more open but vastly more vicious and deadly exchange of invectives between Jews and Christians involving bodily fluids, animal metaphors, disease, and gender during the late Middle Ages.

While Muslims in the eastern Mediterranean and Western Christians did not need to disguise their words from one another, as European Jews did from Christians, extreme frustration, fear, and anger likewise fueled visceral polemic against the other. Muslims and Christians were frustrated by the other's victories during the crusades and horrified at the other's occupation of what they considered "their" holy places. Hillenbrand has argued that during the crusades Muslim writers drew on old stereotypes of northern Christians.[51] While this is true, especially regarding Westerners' complexion and savagery, somatic anti-Christian polemic increased during this time, and metaphors of impurity seem to have multiplied and gained an intensity not extant during the early Middle Ages. This intensity, like the linguistic virulence of Jewish anti-Christian invectives, reflects the level of crisis that the Christian invasions posed.

Christian anti-Jewish narratives were vehicles for encouraging oppression and expressions of resistance against Jews, who were increasingly viewed as physically as well as theologically threatening, and against church policies that insisted on Jews' protected status. Jeremy Cohen has traced the long tradition that holds Jews killed Christ and has shown that during the twelfth and especially the thirteenth centuries Christian thinkers allotted a greater level of responsibility, knowledge, and malice to Jews in their role in the crucifixion than in previous centuries.[52] Building on Cohen's observations, Robert Chazan has noted indications from the tenth to the twelfth centuries that northern European Christians saw Jews not only as challengers to the Christian faith, and as descendants of those who killed Jesus, but also as a malevolent presence ready to do harm to Christians whenever the opportunity arose.[53] Chazan has gone on to argue that from the mid-twelfth century Christian perceptions of Jewish enmity intensified in all levels of society. Even Bernard of Clairvaux, who sought to prevent anti-Jewish violence, confirmed the widespread perception of Jewish antagonism to Christians and their faith.[54] That Christian depictions of Jews as dirty and violent were defensive responses to belief in Jewish malice does not diminish their function as oppressive narratives. What these texts were "resisting" was the challenge, whether theological or physical, to Christian superiority and domination of the Jews based on that "superiority." Jews saw themselves as spiritually superior to their violent Christian neighbors; however, the Christians were in fact dominant, both in sheer numbers and in political power.

However threatening European Christians saw Jews during the early Middle Ages, this impression increased during the twelfth and thirteenth centuries and was nurtured by accusations and imaginative stories of child murder and of the deliberate profanation of Christian holy objects.[55] Christians likewise invented grotesque rituals by which Muslims supposedly desecrated Christian holy spaces or objects, the better to prompt their fellow Christians to war and to create a barrier of aversion against conversion to Islam.[56] Christian tales of Jewish humiliation and divine defeat were thus often used as an attempt to reassure coreligionists that God was willing and able to thwart supposed Jewish malice. Muslims reassured their fellows in a slightly different way, by comparing Christians to despised, impure animals in contrast to the lionlike Muslims. Christian avowals that Jews merited death, even if Church law forbade executing them, may be seen as resistance to official Church policy, in word and, occasionally, in deed.[57] By frequently evoking the dichtomy between purity and pollution, authors of all three faiths attempted to create and defend communal hierarchies using the most visceral, easily understood imagery available. Therefore, the urgency of the rhetoric on all three sides may be attributed to the deepened sense of danger. Ironically, part of that "threat" was voluntary conversion, religious sharing, and otherwise amiable relations that sometimes created bonds of solidarity that defied the pressures of violence and calls to religious loyalty.[58] If late antiquity is interesting because attitudes toward the body, gender, and religious deviance first coalesce to form a particular form of polemic shared by all groups, then the twelfth and thirteenth centuries are pivotal, because during that period the polemic on all three sides finally collides.

Organization of This Book

Part 1, "Beginnings: From Divine Incorporation to Bodily Insult in Late Antiquity and the Early Middle Ages," consists of two chapters dealing with evidence from antiquity to the early Middle Ages. Chapter 1 focuses on Pagan, Jewish, and Christian attitudes toward the physical body in relation to the world of the divine. I demonstrate that all three groups had similar views of the body and that menstruation, foul smell, excrement, and skin disease formed a network of somatic associations centered on the woman's body. These, along with metaphors based on impure or undesirable foods, were a shared language of symbols on which much of the religious polemic of the period drew.

Chapter 2 explores how this network of beliefs about the physical world in relation to the divine functioned in early polemic. I begin by showing that Jews evoked excrement and ritual impurity of various kinds to mark non-Jews and "deviant" Jews, as well as Christians, as repugnant. Late antique Pagans, Christians, and Manichaeans did not have such a well-developed system of categorizing impurity, so they used graphic descriptions of human organs and bodily functions to denigrate one another. Much of the argumentation centered on disagreements regarding the doctrine of the incarnation, which Pagans, Manichaeans, and many Christians found deeply disturbing. By the fifth century onward in Eastern Christian polemic regarding the incarnation, the language became less graphic; however, early medieval Christians in the West continued to concern themselves with the problem of placing God-as-Jesus in a "filthy" womb. The eighth and ninth centuries marked an important shift as Eastern Christians focused their virulence against the new "heresy," Islam, and its founder, Muhammad. Muslims likewise translated and adopted earlier polemical imagery regarding the incarnation in their writings against Christianity, which entered into Jewish polemic with the composition of the *Qiṣṣat Mujādalat al-ʿUsquf,* a Judeo-Arabic anti-Christian tract. The Jewish compiler of this text combined earlier impurity-based arguments with graphic descriptions of the stench and filth of human existence that had been common to late antique Pagan, Manichaean, and Christian polemic. This new approach, along with midrashic, talmudic, and poetic texts using metaphors of impurity to attack Christianity, became part of the medieval Jewish repertoire in the twelfth century when the *Qiṣṣat* was translated from Arabic into Hebrew.

Part 2, "The Twelfth and Thirteenth Centuries: Intensification and Collision of Jewish-Christian-Muslim Polemic," focuses on the use of impurity in Jewish, Christian, and Muslim invective from twelfth-, thirteenth-, and early-fourteenth-century Europe. Chapter 3 provides background in the shifting attitudes toward women, the human body, and disease; the rise of Marian and eucharistic piety among Christians; the new developments in Christian and Jewish Scholasticism, in terms of both methodology and the impact of the many translating projects; and the changing nature of Jewish-Christian-Muslim relations during these centuries. All these factors coalesced to pave the way for a visceral polemic that relied on graphic accusations of impurity, filth, and disease to denigrate religious opponents.

In chapter 4 I maintain that despite the increased emphasis on and piety surrounding Christ's humanity, attitudes toward the human body during the twelfth and thirteenth centuries made the mixture of divinity and human corporeality an uncomfortable one for many people. Jews, who shared many of the views of the body with Christians and yet had no obligation to accept the doctrine of the incarnation, played on the paradox of pure divinity contained within a filthy human body, whether in Mary's body in the form of a fetus or in Christians' bodies in the form of the Eucharist. Like those of their late antique Pagan, Manichaean, and Christian predecessors, Jewish critiques of the incarnation centered on the dirt of Mary's body rather than Jesus'. Incarnation arguments in Jewish anti-Christian polemic during this period drew from or elaborated on ideas expressed in the *Qiṣṣat*; however, the *Qiṣṣat* would not have been translated and used so widely in the twelfth century had not the arguments been particularly relevant. Christians, for their part, became aware of Jewish argumentation against the incarnation and repeated the graphic descriptions of Mary's and Jesus' uncleanness only to turn them into a demonstration of Jews' carnality and filth.

Muslims did not develop new or more graphic argumentation against Jesus' incarnation in the womb. Rather they focused on the Holy Sepulcher as a vile place because it represented Christian belief in Jesus' death, a doctrine they rejected and could safely criticize in the strongest language possible without denigrating Jesus or Mary, whom they respected as prophets. Christians, drawing from earlier traditions, set up Muhammad as a false "incarnation" or "god," disgusting in life and, most of all, in the manner of his death. Both Muslims and Christians focused on the other as polluting violators of sacred space whose entry into the Holy Land, especially Jerusalem, was akin to rape, each viewing the other as "men gone wrong." Both Muslims and Jews repeated abbreviated invectives such as *'ahl al-rijs* (the people of filth) or *ben niddah* (son of a menstruating woman) in chronicles, polemic, and poetry; for Muslims, they expressed profound scorn for Christians, and, in the case of Jews they were a language of resistance. These terms were derogatory in their own right and overturned Christian claims to purity and sexual continence. They, like accusations of disease or comparisons with impure animals, emphasized the filth and pollution of Christians and the Christian faith. However, in the case of Jewish invectives, they also reminded their Jewish audience of more elaborate midrashic traditions or oral traditions from the *Toledot Yesu* that provided the highly negative contexts for them. *Piyyuṭim,* perhaps more than any other genre of Jewish literature functioned as the prime venue for epithets of anger at Christian abuse. The synagogues in which these poems were sung served as safe havens in which Jews could voice their absolute repudiation of Christianity. However, increased Christian awareness and surveillance of Jewish polemic and behavior coupled with an upsurge of persecutions caused Jewish resentment to rise and at the same time severely curtailed safe avenues for its expression.

Chapter 5 begins with an overview of the long-standing association of sin with sickness and the impact of the "medical revolution" of the twelfth and thirteenth centuries. I then turn to Christian accusations that Jews suffered from certain diseases as a result of either punishment by God or diet. Christians also contended that Jews had peculiar physical characteristics such as swarthy skin or red hair, all of which were negatively valued. Christians portrayed Muslims as dark depending on the relative "evil" of the given persons or their refusal or willingness to consider conversion. Muslims likewise alluded to northerners' (Christians') inherent stupidity and lust for blood to make them repugnant in their coreligionists' eyes. Jews rebutted Christian slurs by maintaining that Christians were more susceptible to leprosy or were "pale and fair" because they had intercourse with their menstruating wives. In their choice of diseases and physical traits, Muslims, Christians, and Jews played on a network of medical theories and theological associations to mark their opponents grossly carnal, gluttonous, and lustful. Often these physical failings were closely tied to the female body and its products, especially menstrual blood, enabling Jews and Christians to use the female/matter versus male/spirit dichotomy, which had been in existence since antiquity, to label their opponents as spiritually flawed.

Chapter 6 explores how Jews, Christians, and Muslims used iconographic, fable, bestiary, and other animal traditions to represent one another as (1) too stupid and irrational to qualify as proper men; (2) impure and savage, making them bestial rather than "manly"; and (3) feminized and dirty. Muslims, Christians, and especially Jews used animal imagery as a way to subvert one another's claim to righteousness and power. Specific beasts were associated with particular traditions and characteristics, making them ideal vehicles for visual polemic in the Jewish and Christian contexts. An animal depicted in an illuminated manuscript or on a cathedral could be interpreted in different ways depending on the audience (this is especially important when considering the debate about who created the illuminations on Jewish manuscripts) and convey a wide range of polemical meanings in a succinct form. Furthermore, the "enemy" would not necessarily recognize and understand the polemic behind an artistic depiction of an animal or that the image was polemical.[59] Such subterfuge was more important for the Jewish than for the Christian or Muslim communities since the latter had no need to hide their rhetoric. Unlike written forms, sculptures and illuminations of animals required familiarity with the interpretive traditions surrounding them but did not require the ability to read and thus could reach a wider audience than more complex and learned written polemical genres. While even in manuscripts Muslims do not seem to have engaged in visual polemic using animals, Muslim anti-Christian animal similes were common in oral epics, and thus, like the cathedral sculptures in the Western Christian world, would have reached a wide audience.

If the beginning of our story lies in late antiquity it certainly does not end in the thirteenth or even fourteenth century.[60] Early modern polemic against Jews or between Catholics and Protestants also used crassly corporeal images of menstruating, eating, excreting, and vomiting to render their religious opponents abhorrent and their theology unworthy.[61] However, somatic polemic involving pollution and dirt seems to have become an integral part of

Europeans' religious language during the twelfth through fourteenth centuries; thus I have elected to focus on these middle years. I have chosen the mid-fourteenth century as the terminus ad quem for this book. The onslaught of the plague beginning in 1345, its horrendous effects on the body, and the concomitant accusations against Jews in Europe open new issues regarding the body and disease both in the Near East and in Europe. While studying the impact of changing views and roles of the body, disease, and gender in polemic between Jews, Christians, and Muslims in the late medieval and early modern period would undoubtedly be fruitful, I leave this task to others.

Methodology

I wish to show that Jews, Christians, and Muslims drew from a common set of symbols in their disputes with one another but gave the symbols different valences. For a Jew to call a Christian a pig, for example, did not have an identical meaning to the Jew as it did to the Christian, who also likened Jews to swine, but the understandings each community assigned to this and other epithets were based on medical and biological theories and cultural realities that either transcended religious boundaries or were at least known to both sides. I hope that future scholars studying specific instances of interfaith conflict will be increasingly inclined to examine how each side manipulated polemical tropes to its own needs. Showing the profound extent to which Muslim, Christian, and Jewish discourses about the other were intertwined is the first step in this process.

Which is not to say that scholars have made no effort in this direction. David Nirenberg notes the relationship between Jewish anti-Christian Purim rituals and the ritual violence that marked Christian Easter week celebrations. He further noted the participation of Muslims in ritualized Christian anti-Jewish violence.[62] The recent collection of articles on Passover and Easter published at Notre Dame continues in the same comparative vein.[63] Both Ivan Marcus's *Rituals of Childhood* and Daniel Boyarin's study of Christian and Jewish concepts of martyrdom examine specific areas of common cultural understandings in Jewish and Christian communities.[64] Israel Yuval's work focuses on the interplay between Jewish and Christian polemic.[65] The intersection of Muslim and Jewish and, to a lesser extent, Christian polemic regarding interfaith relations and gender has also attracted the attention of some scholars.[66] Most studies of interfaith disputes examine the polemical and political positions of both or all three sides, even if the scholar in question is interested in the writings of one group more than the other.[67] However, this approach is different from arguing that the underlying symbols used in the rhetoric of both groups are the same, or at least very closely linked, which is what I attempt to show in this book.

Methodologically, the most problematic chapters to write were the first two. Boyarin in his *Carnal Israel* outlines the difficulties of attempting to write a history of late antique Jewish attitudes toward the body. Unlike Christian and even Pagan texts from the same period, the dating of Jewish sources is often uncertain. Rabbinic sources are chronologically complicated texts as the sayings in a particular text are often attributed to rabbis long dead by the time the Talmud or a particular midrash was compiled. This problem has led some scholars to attempt to "re-create" earlier attitudes based on the genealogies of the rabbis to which a particular set of sayings is attributed, while other scholars have insisted that a particular rabbinic text reflects only the period in which it was written down. Boyarin adopts a middle ground, namely that these texts may contain earlier material but are also products of the period in which they were composed so that it is nearly impossible to pinpoint precisely in which chronological layer a particular text belongs.[68] The obstacles indicated by Boyarin are compounded when trying to compare Jewish views to those of Pagans and Christians. One is faced with attempting to fit chronologically amorphous Jewish texts within a comparatively precise time line of the development of Pagan and Christian attitudes toward the body.[69] The same kinds of problems are present when attempting to compare polemical texts from Pagan, Jewish, Christian, Manichaean, and even Muslim communities, though with the arrival of Islam, Jewish texts begin to be slightly less difficult to date. In chapter 1 I examine texts from roughly the first century B.C.E. to the sixth century C.E. However, some of the philosophical and medical texts may be earlier, and some of the midrashic texts may have been written later. This choice may be frustrating for scholars who expect a precise chain of development and change in texts within a particular tradition or across several religious and cultural traditions. Yet without a broad view such as the one I have taken in chapter 1, a comparison of Jewish discussions of corporeality in relation to the divine to those of other religious traditions in antiquity would be extremely difficult. Shifts most certainly occurred, and I have tried to take them into account when possible, yet the focus of this book is not to provide a history of attitudes toward the human body, food, smell, and the divinity but rather to examine how these views functioned in religious polemic. Chapter 2 does this for late antiquity and the early Middle Ages.

The analysis of gendered, somatic polemic in multiple cultural-religious traditions has required reading sources in many languages. Some of my argumentation is based on examinations of the vocabulary that late antique and medieval authors chose in their metaphors for and insults directed toward the religious other or in their depictions of the body in general. Where my analysis focuses on such linguistic questions, or there is some debate as to how a passage should be translated, or the text is difficult to obtain or translate, I have provided the passages in their original language in the notes. For the sake of economy I have not provided the original language when the texts are readily available and their linguistic complexities have no direct bearing on the book.

Throughout this book I attempt to balance my discussions of religious traditions. If at times one group is allotted more attention than another, I do not wish to imply that one is more important, interesting, or blameworthy than another; rather the issue being discussed is more relevant to one group than to another. Although my portrayal of Jewish-Christian-Muslim relations is disturbing, that Muslims, Christians, and Jews, in the midst of opposing one another in the most visceral, bitter language possible, held similar assumptions about the body, sinfulness, and religious purity points to a high degree of sharing among them. Thus this book suggests that late antique and medieval Jews and Christians were not separate communities that interacted only grudgingly but rather that they were members of two faiths in a single culture, holding common values and assumptions. One finds greater differences between Muslims of the eastern Mediterranean and European Christians and Jews. Nevertheless, the commonality of metaphors, fears, and values present in the polemic from both sides of the Mediterranean adds to the growing scholarship suggesting that the Near East and Europe were inextricably intertwined.[70]

PART I

From Divine Incorporation to Bodily Insult in Late Antiquity and the Early Middle Ages

CHAPTER ONE

The Stench of Humanity

Corporeality and the Divine in Late Antique Religious Thought

"Pagans and Christians (though not all Pagans or all Christians) vied with each other in heaping abuse on the body; it was 'clay and gore,' a 'filthy bag of excrement and urine'; man is plunged in it as in a bath of dirty water."[1] The vivid equation of the human body with a bag of feces that E. R. Dodds quotes comes from the Christian diatribe against Pagan gods, written around 300 C.E. by Arnobius of Sicca.[2] Slightly later in the same century, another Christian, Gregory of Nyssa, maintained that the dove was a common symbol for the spirit "either because it has no intestines or because this bird detests fetid odors."[3] Anyone who wished to approach the beauty and light of the divine had to "distance himself from every bitterness and bad, fleshly odor" and elevate himself "above every base and terrestrial thing."[4] Pagan Roman literature, which clearly influenced Christian attitudes, is filled with graphic descriptions of diseased or decaying bodies.[5] Pagans also saw the human body as a barrier to interaction with the divine. The Platonist Apuleius maintained that though demons might interact with men, gods could not because they would be polluted by human contact.[6] Saint Augustine of Hippo (354–430 C.E.) ridiculed Apuleius's theory because it made the gods inferior to demons: the latter were beyond pollution, whereas the gods were not. Augustine asked how gods might be contaminated by humans, examining each of the human senses. Under smell, Augustine singled out stinking human bodily fluids, suggesting that the odor of human effluvia was a particular issue for those Pagans who maintained that gods and humans needed to remain separate.[7]

Dodds's observation may be applied to Jews (though not all Jews) of antiquity as well. For example, in the Mishnaic tractate *Pirke Avot* potential sinners are reminded of their origins as "a putrid drop" and their ultimate end as "dust, worm, and maggot."[8] Later Hekhalot literature expands on the *Avot* passage; angels challenge the mystic's right to ascend into the heavens or call angels to earth because of his smelly, impure nature.[9] Odor and an earthy constitution as well as impurity define the essence of being human (as opposed to divine or angelic) in these texts, much as in Gregory of Nyssa's treatise, where the soul, like the dove, had to be divested of all that was malodorous and earthly in order to ascend to God.[10] In the midrashic tradition, humans who enjoy prolonged contact with the divine presence cease to suffer from or require those bodily functions so inappropriate to the heavenly realms. Version A of *Pirke Avot de Rabbi Nahan* (ca. third century C.E.) elaborates on this theme:

> R. Nathan said: "Why was Moses made to wait all these six days before the Word came to rest upon him? So that he might be purged of all food and drink in his bowels, before he was sanctified and became like the ministering angels.[11]

This emphasis on consumption and elimination supports Michael Swartz's hypothesis that more than mere ritual purity was necessary for the divine-human encounter and indicates that his observations extend beyond the Hekhalot tradition.[12] Whether man, or his soul, in the case of Christian and Pagan literature, ascended to see the face of God and the angels or the heavenly denizens descended, humans had to be purged of food, flux, and decay.

In Jewish, Pagan, and Christian writings about the nature of God, a primary concern was to separate divinity from the biological functioning of the human body. Distancing heavenly beings from the individual human was one aspect of this separation. Eschewing any suggestion that God's body operated in ways similar to our own was another, even in the face of long-standing (though very different) anthropomorphic traditions. Howard Eilberg-Schwartz has argued that passages in the Jewish Scriptures that ascribe human characteristics to God avoid attributing "lower" functions such as hunger, thirst, and sex to him.[13] Later Jewish traditions elaborated on this theme. According to *Genesis Rabbah* (ca. 500), God granted humans four attributes from the higher beings (angels) and four from the lower (animals). Like animals, humans eat and drink, procreate, excrete, and die.[14] Alon Goshen-Gottstein has argued that even in passages from Jewish literature that exult in the beauty of God's body/form, or in the fact that man was made in God's image, we must distinguish between form and function.[15] The most explicit expression of this differentiation comes from the *Pseudo-Clementine Homilies*, a set of Christian "adventure stories" or romances written sometime in the third century by a group that retained strong theological affiliations with Judaism. In these texts God has a body, but it is a body of light whose limbs and organs have no function except an aesthetic one.[16] Thus even in the most anthropomorphic Jewish and Christian traditions writers were careful to separate God from any semblance of the oozing impure fetidness that, in their view, marked the human bodily condition.

Schlomo Pines has shown that this passage from the *Pseudo-Clementine Homilies* drew heavily on Pagan philosophical debates, particularly those of the Stoics and Epicureans, about the existence and nature of gods' bodies.[17] This concern to attribute limbs and organs to gods for beauty's sake parallels the remarks of Vellius the Epicurean in Cicero's *De Natura deorum* (written ca. 44 B.C.E.). There Vellius maintained that the gods must have at least the appearance of human form. He felt obliged to qualify his position by explaining that the gods have the shape of a body, but it is not really a body; they have something analogous to blood, but it is not actually blood.[18] Thus if the gods are to have bodies these bodies must be divested of their materiality, much as the luminous god in the *Pseudo-Clementine* was divested of his. For Cotta, the Academician in Cicero's imaginary conference, even the semblance of a body could not be tolerated:

> When you consider the uses and aptitudes of the limbs in a man, are you not forced to conclude that the gods have no need of them? What is the use of feet to a being who does not walk? Or of hands to a being who does not handle? . . . And the organs of reproduction which nature has added to our bodies will be useless to a god. As with the external organs so with the internal, also the heart, the lungs, the liver, and the rest. Take away their use and what beauty is in them? And yet you want your god to have such human parts for beauty's sake![19] For you assume that reason can exist only in a human body. Then another may assume that it can exist only in an earthly body: in a body which is born and grows up; in a body which learns; in a body which is composed of mind and matter, which is frail and transient: in short only in a mortal body. But if you would resist such influences, why are you concerned with shape alone?[20]

Any comparison of the functions or activities of Pagan gods and those of humans had become unthinkable. Cicero seems to have taken for granted that his readers agreed that gods neither walked nor had sex.[21] That gods should have an earthly body, composed of matter and subject to normal human life cycles, was unacceptable.[22]

The conjunction of the human soul and body disturbed some Pagan thinkers for much the same reasons that anthropomorphism did: it involved mingling divinity and corporeality. In such systems the soul was an alien, heavenly being trapped in an "odious tunic."[23] Philosophers such as Plotinus (204–70 C.E.) attempted to distance the soul from the passions and physical accidents of the body.[24] The Christian Tertullian (d. 220 C.E.) struggled between Plato's image of the body as a prison for the soul (*Phaedo* 62 c. 6) and Paul's view that the body was the temple of God's spirit (1 Cor. 6:19; 2 Cor. 6:16–7:1). Though he accepted the words of the apostle, Tertullian nevertheless maintained that the body's enclosure "obstructs" the soul and "pollutes [it] by the concretation of the flesh." The soul was "purified" of the flesh by death.[25] Other Christians objected to an anthropomorphized pantheon and the doctrine of the divine soul on the same grounds as did the Pagans. Regarding gods' possession of human organs, limbs, and genitalia, Arnobius reproached his Pagan readers:

> Do the gods, then, have sexes, and do they carry about them the filths of genital organs, to mention which by their names is disgraceful for modest mouths? What, then, remains for us except to believe that after the manner of unclean quadrupeds they are transported into madness of passions, either with raging desires into mutual embraces and in the end, their bodies broken and dissipated, become feeble through the disintegrations of lust?
>
> And since there are functions peculiar to the female sex, we must then believe that goddesses, too, fulfill the conditions that bind them when the months roll around, conceive and remain pregnant with nausea, suffer miscarriages, and in premature delivery sometimes give birth to seven-month infants.[26]

Likewise human souls could not be the children of the Supreme Being because leaving the perfection and unfettered state of heaven was inconceivable:

> [To] seek these earthly parts only to pass their lives enveloped by gloomy bodies amid phlegm and blood—these dung-sacks and filthy urinals! . . . But perhaps the King of the Universe—and for human lips to say this is consummate rashness—for this reason (to benefit the world) sent hither the souls begotten from Himself, that they who had been divine with Him, not having any share in contact of body or the bonds of time, should be sunk into human seeds, spring forth from the wombs of women and keep up the most insipid wailings, suck and drain breasts, smear and spot themselves with their own filth, then in their fright be hushed by the rocking of the nurse and by the sound of rattles.[27]

To be human, for Arnobius, was to be encased in filth. Internal organs and the liquids they produced were representative of this filth. Equally characteristic of the bodily state was the absence of physical control; sexual activity caused the body to become "broken" and "feeble," and infancy was marked by incontinence, wailing, and dependence on nurses.[28] Like Cicero's character Cotta, Arnobius found the suggestion that the gods might have a body of any kind untenable, but he permitted no hint that these useless "divine" limbs and organs might possess any beauty. In contrast to Plotinus, no amount of distance between a "heavenly" soul and the excrement-filled human body could be sufficient; souls were simply not born of God.

While there were differences between Pagan, Jewish, and Christian views about the relationship of humans to the divine, particularly when one delves into the individual purity systems of each group, nevertheless the commonalities sufficiently outweighed the variations to create a shared base of assumptions and values about both human nature and the divine. Even in the case of the soul/body dichotomy, which, according to Daniel Boyarin and others, was not accepted by rabbinic Jews, Nissan Rubin has provided evidence that from the fifth generation of early talmudic, or tannaic, rabbis (135–170) onward, the soul gained an increasingly more elevated status than its physical counterpart.[29] The soul was seen as a heavenly gift to an earthly, impure body.[30] Abhorrence for the leaking human body constituted a shared language through which Pagans, Jews, and Christians "heaped abuse" not only on the human form in general but also on the bodies and moral status of their religious adversaries.[31] Without a common set of symbols among Jews, Pagans, and Christians, polemic used by one group against another would have been powerless to insult or counterattack. However, before turning to corporeal metaphors as polemical weapons in late antique religious literature, it is necessary to examine more closely the nature and meanings of this imagery.

While Arnobius of Sicca's diatribe may be a spectacular example, foul smell, unspecified dirt, blood, human waste, and sundry other types of effluvia, and impurity occur to varying degrees in all the Pagan, Jewish, and Christian texts discussed so far. Biologically and symbolically, these formed a network of associations culminating in the rotting corpse, the horror of which, according to Peter Brown and Carolyn Walker Bynum, was a prime source for late antique Pagan and Christian rejection of the body.[32] Not only was death a constant and deeply disturbing aspect of human life during this period, the corpse was also at the apex of most late antique ritual impurity systems.[33] Decay, however, was but the most extreme example of the flux and corruption to which the human body was subject. The intake of food and the excretion of feces and urine as well as all bodily fluids and their accompanying odors served as tangible, despised reminders of this process that was so incompatible with a pure, unmoved, and uncorrupted deity or deities.[34]

Women and Bodily Pollution

While both men and women ate, digested, excreted, and eventually decayed, women's more than men's bodies were associated with dirt, waste, and rot, thus paving the way for "female" as a negative ontological category in relation to the spiritual world. Christian authors frequently compared the process of resurrection to a seed that must first rot in the ground and then produce a plant from decay and disintegration, or to the worms and other insects that "spontaneously" generate from rotting flesh. Thus decay was an intimate part of generation, even spiritual generation.[35] In the Jewish mystical texts the human suppliant is frequently addressed as "yalud 'ishah"—born of a woman—and is reminded in graphic terms of the dirty, polluted nature of such origins in contrast to the purity of the angelic realm.[36]

Temporarily leaving aside the important issue of women's ritual purity and impurity, both Galenic and Aristotelian medical schemes designated women's menstrual blood as the primary contributor of matter to the fetus, in contrast to the man's semen, which provided spirit and form.[37] In a culture in which spirit was placed in opposition to the physical body, Aristotle's schema automatically distanced women from the divine. Likewise, women produced more "residue" (in the form of menstruation) than did men because they were too cold and wet in nature to fully "concoct" nutriments.[38] Aristotle placed semen and menstrual blood in the same category as excrement and urine; however, semen is the purest or most concocted of the residues whereas the production of menstrual blood is likened to that of diarrhea.[39] Aristotle frequently connected putrescence, moisture, and (spontaneous) generation. One passage from *Generation of Animals* is particularly telling for there Aristotle uses a cognate of the word *residue* (περισσος / περιττος—the word in the texts is περιττωμάτων) and parallels it with "putrescent soil" (γης σηπομένης), both of which generate certain kinds of insects and crustacea. Thus the lines between semen, menstrual blood, and excrement—all of which Aristotle categorized as "residues"—and rot were very fine. Moisture added another tie between women's bodies and the decaying process, since it was women's nature, cooler and moister than that of men, that was the source of her generative powers, and moisture was also an essential component of decay.[40] The Roman writer Pliny, while less systematic than Aristotle, seems to have viewed hemorrhoids, diarrhea, nose- and mouth bleeds, and menstruation as closely related phenomena.[41] Already in the Hippocratic corpus women and their wombs were associated with excrement and other foul-smelling substances because these were prescribed as the primary contents of drinks, pills, fumigations, and suppositories intended to cure women's diseases. Medical writers saw such measures as loathsome, however, and not intended for men.[42]

Von Staden has pointed out that Greek philosophers equated dung with putrefaction, and the Greek vocabulary dealing with pollution, especially corpse pollution, is derived from the word κόπρος, dung.[43] This connection between feces and the womb's fluids strengthen Bynum and Brown's arguments that the womb especially was associated with decay in later Christian and Pagan texts. Amy Richlin has shown that in Roman literary texts genitalia in general were regarded as ugly, soiled, and disgusting but women's genitalia most of all. The poetic vocabulary describing the vagina emphasized its filth and foul odor and sometimes drew explicit parallels between the woman's genitals and excrement, the anus, and/or decay.[44] In one poem the "swarming worms" of a woman's vagina recall the worms that devour the corpse in the grave: "For although I might seem to be well enough prepared / I would need ten handfuls of [aphrodisiac] colewort / for me to rub the ditches of your groin, and beat the swarming worms of your cunt."[45]

Owsei Temkin has demonstrated that Christians in late antiquity accepted Pagan medical theory and allowed it to exist alongside tales of miraculous healings through prayer.[46] Indeed, classical medical theories provided the basis of much "gnostic" and Christian argumentation and symbolism of the period.[47] In many of the theogynies included in the Nag Hammadi library, a collection of "gnostic," mostly Christian writings, and related texts, a female aeon, usually Sophia, attempts to generate without her male consort. The result is a deformed creature, or as Irenaeus expressed it, "an amorphous substance, such as her female nature was able to produce," who then becomes the ignorant "god" of this world.[48] The view that women could generate without intercourse with a man but that the product would be deformed and soulless was commonly held by medical thinkers.[49] In the Nag Hammadi texts medical theory about the imperfect nature of the woman's seed and the association of the female with matter and passion in contrast to male rationality and spirituality is adopted and transformed into an explanation of cosmological evil.[50] In *De Carne Christi* Tertullian used gynecological theory to refute those who maintained that Christ was born *through* a virgin and was *in* her womb but not *of* her womb, that is, was not created from her flesh:

> Furthermore when he mentions the breasts of his mother—which without doubt he sucked—midwives, doctors and naturalists should respond if normally breasts give milk at any other time if the womb has not suffered through the birthing process when the veins carry that filthy bilge (*sentinam*) of internal blood from it [the womb] and by this transfer distill [it] into more pleasant substance, milk. Whence it is that during lactation menstruation stops. So if the Verb made himself flesh without receiving anything from the womb, if the womb produced nothing, did nothing, suffered nothing, how did its flow transfer into the breasts which do not change [anything] unless they have [something on which to work]. But it could not have had this flow to make into milk without the causes of this blood, namely the severance of its flesh [through the birthing process].[51]

For Tertullian, the hypotheses of Galen and other medical thinkers about the relationship of menstruation and breast milk are fundamental to demonstrating that Jesus had a material body.[52] Tertullian's choice of the word *sentinam*, which normally refers to the filthy water that collects at the bottom of ships, or to the dregs of society, indicates that he also accepted medical writers' designation of menstrual blood as dirty, even in the midst of trying to convince his opponents that God-as-Jesus drew his substance from the womb. That Tertullian had to present the argument at all suggests that various Christian groups were unwilling to accept a full conjunction of divinity and women's genital blood.

There are indications throughout the Talmud and midrashim that Jews of late antiquity were also familiar with and adapted Pagan astrological, climatological, and humoral medical theories.[53] By the time *Sefer Asaph*, the first Hebrew medical treatise, was compiled (ca. sixth century), Hippocrates, Galen, and Discorides were accepted as familiar authorities by Jewish medical practitioners.[54] Discussions of gynecology and gestation were no exception to this trend.[55] In *Midrash Tanḥuma'* the fetus feeds from the mother's blood, and the blood is converted to milk once the infant is born, precisely the explanation favored by most Pagan medical thinkers.[56] While Jewish authors of this period did not elaborate on their medical views to the same degree as did Aristotle or Galen, that a Jewish author would include this detail suggests that he shared the common humoral theory behind the process—that women's bodies were wet and cold. A number of Jewish writers, like their Pagan and Christian counterparts, also connected women with filth, foul smell, and decay. The contents of the womb were not only seen as impure, but also as dirty (*milukhlakh*).[57] In a long moralizing passage against women, we find:

> "And why must a woman use perfume, while a man does not need perfume?" "Adam was created from earth," he answered, "and earth never putrefies but Eve was created from a bone. For example: if you leave meat three days unsalted, it immediately goes putrid."[58]

These remarks expand on the biblical text, which would have made no sense in a Pagan context. However, the topoi are very similar. The woman's body is dirty in ways men's are not. It smells bad (hence the need for perfume) and is in imminent danger of decay, much as the old women of Roman satirical poetry were living vessels of rot, filth, and stench.

Perhaps more disturbing to men of late antiquity than the matter/spirit dichotomy, decay, or waste embodied in the genital fluids of women was the fear that that blood inspired. According to Aristotle, if a menstruating woman looked at a mirror it became red.[59] For Roman authors, menstrual blood had the power both to harm and to help, but in either case it was primarily associated with poison:

> But nothing could easily be found that is more monstrous than the monthly flux of a woman. Contact with it turns new wine sour, crops touched by it become barren, grafts die, seeds in gardens are dried up, the fruit of trees falls off, the bright surface of mirrors in which it is merely reflected is dimmed, the edge of steel and the gleam of ivory are dulled, hives of bees die, even bronze and iron are at once seized by rust, and a horrible smell fills the air: to taste it drives dogs mad and infects their bites with an incurable poison.[60]

A woman's toxic qualities could be harnessed as an insecticide and a weather check.[61] Menstrual blood was a prime ingredient for cures for gout, tumors, abscesses, scrofula, certain fevers, and the bite of mad dogs, diseases that spring mainly from external or internal poisons.[62] Most of the dangerous properties listed by Pliny involve agriculture, tools, or animals. Yet men were personally imperiled as well: "if this female power (menstruous discharge) should issue when the moon or sun is in eclipse, it will cause irremediable harm; no less harm if there is no moon; at such seasons sexual intercourse brings disease and death upon the man."[63] The threat only existed under specific conditions, and Pliny did not specify the type of disease that the man could contract.

In Jewish, Christian, and, eventually, Muslim texts, leprosy and other skin ailments were commonly linked to intercourse with a menstruating woman, though a variety of other diseases such as lameness and epilepsy also could result from the encounter.[64] Jewish and Christian texts that espoused a direct causal relationship between "leprosy" and coitus with the menstruant usually placed it in the context of divine punishment for violating the prohibitions in Leviticus 15:19–24, 18:19, and 20:18.[65] For Christians, the days of menstruation were counted among several periods during which sex was forbidden. Religious festivals were also to be characterized by abstinence and brought dire consequences for the resulting child if the parents acted otherwise:

> When one should especially abstain from [one's] wife. What many punishments are given to those who conduct themselves otherwise! Are some beasts more incontinent? Before all for however many days of the Lord or other festivals come, no one should know his wife. And as long as women endure a flux of blood it ought to be observed similarly: because of that which the prophet said, 'you shall not approach a menstruating woman' (Ez. 18:6). For whoever knows his

> wife during menstruation or does not wish to contain himself on the day of the Lord or on any other solemn day which comes, those who are conceived then are born either lepers or epileptics, or even demoniacs. And then, whoever are leprous are not born from wise men who in other days and festivals remained chaste but mostly from rustics who do not know how to contain themselves.[66]

Some Jewish texts also attributed disease and deformity to other types of sexual misconduct on the part of parents, but most focus on coitus during menstruation.[67] Certain Jewish texts, such as *Leviticus Rabbah* (fifth century C.E.), incorporated scientific analogies in their religious exegeses:

> "If a woman produce offspring, bearing a male child, she shall be unclean seven days" (Lev. 12:2). What is written after this? "When a man shall have a rising, etc." (Lev. 12:3). What has one subject to do with another [that they should be juxtaposed]? Said R. Tanḥum b. Ḥanilai: This may be compared to a she-ass which was sick and was cauterized, and her fetus emerged with a cauterization mark. What caused it to come out with a cauterization mark? The fact that its mother was cauterized. Likewise, who caused a newborn child to be leprous? Its mother, who did not observe the days of her *niddah.* R. Abin said: This may be compared to a vegetable garden into which a well empties; as long as the well empties into it, it will grow lichen. Likewise, if a man comes in to his menstruating wife, he produces leprous children. R. Abin applied this to the verse: "The fathers have eaten sour grapes and the children's teeth are set on edge" (Jer. 31:29) and these the children apply to the parents the following verse: "Our fathers have sinned and are not; and we have born their sins" (Lam. 5:7).[68]

Leprosy is still the punishment children must suffer for the misdeeds of their parents; disease is still the result of sin. The tale, however, does not end there. Whatever one may think of the passage's "science," the author(s) clearly attempted to create parallels between the production of leprous children by coitus during *niddah* (menstruation) and other natural phenomena, whether it be the growth of lichen or the presence of a birthmark on a foal similar to the cauterization scar on its mother. Such parallels suggest that in the writer's (and readers') minds, the fluids of menstrual intercourse were in some way to blame instead of, or along with, God's displeasure.

The most extensive warnings about the danger posed by the menstruant are contained in the *Baraita de Niddah,* a Jewish text from the sixth or seventh century C.E. that purports to outline the laws of interaction with and purification for the menstruating woman, but that in fact is far more stringent than any requirements in the Bible or the Talmud:

> [T]he sages taught and said that she who has intercourse with her husband and she is *niddah* causes her children not to receive Torah, and not only that but she causes them even to the twentieth generation to be destroyed, her children are afflicted with leprosy.[69]

Later in the text the husband is urged to exhort his wife to be careful of *niddah*, "lest you bring defects on our children."[70] Defects caused by *niddah* include boils, leprosy, and one-armedness. Apart from hindering the children from receiving Torah, these ailments are similar to those enumerated as punishment for marital intercourse during menstruation by Caesarius of Arles (502–543 C.E.) quoted above and by Pseudo-Jerome who states that such children will be deprived of limbs or will be lame, blind, or leprous.[71] Yet the most curious passage consists of a debate in the *Baraita de Niddah* over the various sexual misdeeds that might cause the blood to "change" and enter the body of the child during birth. In this passage the blood of menstruation and childbirth become the toxic instrument of God's punishment of sinners and their children, manifesting itself as leprosy, much as in Christian literature children are born leprous or lame for a variety of parental sins during intercourse.[72] No longer is *niddah* a mere metaphor for iniquity; the blood becomes quite literally the cause of disease and thus the medium through which God's wrath is inflicted.

According to Anne Carson, it was a woman's "wet, leaky nature" that made her epitomize pollution, uncontrolled emotions, and physicality.[73] Thus stench, excrement, generative fluids (especially menstruation), matter, poison, disfiguring disease, lack of emotional control, and decay were all intertwined in late antique scientific and religious literature and closely connected to the woman's body. In addition, between the first and sixth centuries and in the Middle Ages, Jewish symbolism and legal restrictions surrounding the *niddah* were becoming increasingly harsh.[74] Already in the biblical corpus, the term *niddah* can refer to menstrual impurity, the menstruant herself, impurity deriving from any female genital flow, or impurity in general.[75] Rachel Biale, David Biale, and Tirẓah Meacham have shown that in the prophets and Lamentations *niddah* was closely linked to all sorts of sinful behavior.[76] The most graphic expression of this metaphor may be found in Lamentations 1:8–9:

> Jerusalem sinned grieviously therefore she became filthy (*niddah*); all who honored her despise her, for they have seen her nakedness; yea, she herself groans, and turns her face away. Her uncleanness (*ṭuma'tah*) was in her skirts; she took no thought of her doom, therefore her fall is terrible.[77]

Sin results in *niddah* impurity. Yet the imagery in the text also roots *niddah* in the context of the menstruating female body by presenting an anthropomorphized, feminine Jerusalem whose uncleanness has stained her skirts, much as a real woman might inadvertently bleed on her clothing. Thus, in at least some biblical writings, the sinner(s) is equated with the menstruating woman.[78] Jonathan Klawans is reluctant to accept impurity as a metaphor in the Bible, arguing instead that there are two kinds of impurity: ritual and moral. *Niddah* falls into a peculiar category since the substance causes ritual impurity; however, the *act* of having intercourse with a menstruant falls into the category of sexual sin.[79] Yet I would argue that in this passage the state itself, that is, the process of bleeding, not sexual misbehavior, is intended. The description is too graphic to understand it otherwise, and, I would suggest, it was intended to create both repugnance in its audience and recall the status of impurity, ritual or moral, or perhaps both. Like the bible, the Qumran texts attribute a variety of meanings to the term *niddah*, including menstrual impurity but also general sinfulness or pollution.[80]

Both the length of time during which a menstruating woman was considered impure and the prohibitions she had to follow were extended. Already in the Torah the *zavah* (a woman with an abnormal genital flux) was closely associated with the *niddah*.[81] Of the two, the *zav* (a man with an abnormal genital flux) or *zavah* suffers the greatest impurity, requiring a seven-day hiatus between the cease of the flow and the reestablishment of purity and a sacrifice, in addition to the bathing and laundering required of a *niddah*.[82] The parallels between the *niddah* and the *zavah* set forth in Scripture laid the groundwork for their near-fusion in qumranic and rabbinic texts.[83] Meacham has demonstrated that in the Talmud eventually all menstruating women took on the status of a *zavah* and counted seven days from when their bleeding ceased.[84]

As the duration of time in which a woman was considered polluted doubled, so too did Jewish male anxieties about what an impure woman should be allowed to do. Two issues stood at the center: the extent to which the *niddah* should participate in prayer, touch holy objects, or enter synagogues; and the extent to which the *niddah* should perform household tasks and serve her husband. Related to the second question is whether a menstruating woman should adorn herself in any way or wear attractive clothing.[85] In both the Jerusalem and Babylonian Talmuds the *zav, zavah, niddah,* and parturient are allowed to read Torah.[86] Regarding what the *niddah* may do for her husband, there was already some disagreement expressed in the Babylonian Talmud, but the general tendency in the Talmud itself was toward leniency.[87] In contrast to the Talmud, the legal and moralizing literature that followed tended to forbid the menstruant from serving her husband and children, eating and praying with them, and wearing jewelry or makeup. The menstruant's family, as well as the woman herself, were barred from the synagogue.[88] Thus, among rabbinic Jews, like the Jews of the Qumran before them, there was an increasing tendency to view impurity, especially that produced by a woman's body, as antithetical to holiness. As a result, "uncontaminated" members of the community were encouraged to shun the menstruant. Rules that extended the period in which the menstruant was regarded as unclean and limited the physical contact between the woman and her husband, children, and God may be interpreted as defensive barriers to literally "distance" men and holy things from female pollution.

That women's bodies and blood were the focus of Jewish men's worries, rather than impure emissions in general, becomes clear when contrasting the development of restrictions stemming from seminal impurity to those from menstrual impurity. Shaye Cohen and Sharon Koren have emphasized the relative parity between the two kinds of impurity in biblical and early rabbinic writing; indeed, of the two, initially seminal impurity imposed the greater number of restrictions to one so polluted, for laws banning the ejaculant from the sancta are older and more deeply rooted in Jewish law.[89] Koren argues that Hekhalot mystics were first concerned with avoiding seminal impurity in part because of their belief that sexual activity was inimical to ascent to the divine. *Niddah* could also disrupt this process but was a relatively secondary concern. However, because of the strong influence of the *Baraita de Niddah* and traditions related to it, menstrual impurity surpassed that of the ejaculant, both as a barrier to mystical pursuits and as a source of danger for those who came into contact with it.[90] Klawans, in attempting to explain why menstrual impurity received relatively more attention by post–Second Temple sources, suggested that it was because of *niddah*'s dual status as both a form of ritual and moral impurity, and as the latter, would have continued to be relevant for the married Jewish couple.[91] This hypothesis is plausible, but I suspect that the impulse to expand the laws in Judaism that restricted contact with the *niddah* was also tied to the widespread fear among Pagans, Jews, and Christians that the menstruant was physically dangerous. As Jews became more familiar with and appropriated Pagan medical theories about menstruation, these in turn added impetus to legal reforms that distanced and "protected" Jewish men and children from their bleeding wives and mothers.[92] Apart from certain shifts in Zoroastrianism, the development of even stricter purity regulations for the menstruant, parturient, and gonorrheaic have no parallel in Pagan and Christian thought.[93] Being associated with the bleeding, female body was an insult and profoundly incompatible to divinity in any of the religious systems of late antiquity, though the nuances of that incompatibility varied depending on the religion and culture in question. The metaphors and laws that the *niddah* inspired in Judaism added a further, negative dimension to the already extant network of associations tying the woman's body, her womb, and its blood to decay, excrement, foul smell, and disease in Pagan and Christian as well as Jewish thought.

Excrement and Smell

Foul smell and excrement possessed their own set of negative meanings that would have increased the harshness of invectives coupling them with the female body. In Jewish, Christian, Manichaean, and Greco-Roman thought, pleasant or foul smell could stand alone as markers of good and evil, or their presence could serve to define the moral value of other substances or people. Sweet fragrance and immunity to decay were powerful indications of holiness and desirability. Marcel Detienne emphasizes that in Greek literature sweet smell was a particular feature of gods and anything associated with them.[94] In the fourth century the Christian poet Ephrem the Syrian celebrated Jesus' transformation of myrrh along with the transformation of humankind using a smell analogy: "By You the sweet spices smelled sweet in the oil with which Mary anointed You. / Blessed is Your scent that made us smell sweet."[95] Thus, much like the Greek gods, Jesus' holiness is manifested both by his own pleasant scent and by his ability to imbue his believers and substances that touched him with a lovely odor. In Manichaean texts demons and the archons of darkness were commonly called "stinking and foul," whereas the sons of light were characterized by their sweet fragrance. Light and fragrance battled darkness and stench, making these categories the markers of absolute good and evil.[96]

Nor was smell an indicator of sanctity or evil among heavenly beings alone. The bodies of saints could also be identified by their scent or lack thereof. The holiness of the Christian Saint Stephen's body was manifested by the wonderful perfume that emanated from the coffin and healed those who smelled it.[97] BT Bava Meẓia 83b–85a contains a curious "hagiography" of R. El'azar b. Shimon, in which R. El'azar has fat removed from his stomach and placed in the July sun. Because the fat neither stinks nor rots, his actions are proven righteous. Later his corpse is kept in the attic by his wife for many years and does not rot.[98] R. El'azar b. Shimon's proof of sanctity lies in his dead flesh's lack of scent, whereas Saint Stephen's lies in his corpse's actively pleasant odor. The sentiment behind each story is the same. What is expected of a corpse or severed flesh is that it will rot, and with rot will come the reek of decay. The bodies of Saint Stephen and R. El'azar defied that expectation and thereby were shown to partake of the heavenly realms.

Stench versus fragrance often symbolized the demonic versus the divine, but it also marked the division between the human and the divine. In Jewish mystical and magical texts, as Michael Swartz has shown, the scent of humans was repugnant to angels. Many of the food restrictions placed on the would-be visionary were not based on an extraordinarily stringent set of purity laws as previously thought but instead were intended to prevent the mystic from reeking of pungent food and flatulence.[99] To become sufficiently holy to converse with heavenly beings, one had to be divested of smell. To impute stench or fragrance to a person was to consign him or her symbolically to the world of materiality, and, potentially, evil, or to the divine realms.

The digestive processes and organs were antithetical to God because they resulted in the production of waste material. Plato and Galen following him argued that the intestines were coiled so that humans need not eat and eliminate constantly and thus engage in activities that were inimical to philosophy.[100] They also maintained that the human body was constructed in such a way as to divide the souls and thus protect the divine from pollution as much as possible. In this system the least of souls, that which dealt with the bodily appetites, had its seat in the midriff or lower portion of the body, thus creating a hierarchy of the lower body, which controlled the processes of digestion, generation, and elimination of waste, and the upper body, which contained the divine, rational soul, respiration, and perception.[101]

This dichotomy between digestion and contemplation of the divine, between the lower and the upper body, finds parallel expressions in Jewish and Christian literature as well. According to one midrash, Moses' upper half is as God, but his lower half is man.[102] In this text the part of the human body that is allowed to participate in the divine as opposed to the part that is utterly human and earthly mirrors the division established by Plato and Galen. In version A of *Pirke Avot de Rabbi Nathan* Hillel is quoted as saying, "The more one eats, the more he eliminates. The more flesh, the more worms and maggots. But the more good works, (the more) one brings peace to himself."[103] Clement of Alexandria (150–215) had an equally dim view of excessive eating:

> "Desire not," says Scripture, "rich men's dainties" (Prov. 23:3) for they belong to a false and base life. They partake of luxurious dishes, which a little after go to the dunghill. But we who seek the heavenly bread must rule the belly, which is beneath heaven, much more the things which are agreeable to it, which "God shall destroy" (1 Cor. 6:13).
>
> But totally irrational, futile and not human is it for those who are of the earth, fattening themselves like cattle, to feed themselves up for death.[104]

In both *Pirke Avot de Rabbi Nathan* and Clement of Alexandria's *Paedagogus* eating merely results in excrement and more flesh for the grave. Excrement and rot are contrasted to the path of God, much like the opposition Pagan thinkers established between the needs of the lower body and philosophy. Clement specifically creates a spatial hierarchy with the belly below heaven and doomed to destruction by God, much like the internal bodily hierarchy described by Pagan medical and philosophical thinkers. The comparison of those who take pleasure in eating to irrational cattle is precisely the parallel drawn by the Roman philosopher Seneca.[105] For both Clement and Seneca, taking excessive pleasure in food was favoring man's animalistic nature over his divine or philosophical one. Furthermore, not only did such indulgences cause individuals to fall short of the ideal rationality that distinguished humans from other animals, they marked a disintegration of the masculine ideal in particular, since men, more than women, were associated with rationality and philosophy.

In excess, feces and intestines marked their possessor not only as animal but also as evil. For example, in Proverbs and the prophetic writings clothing covered in excrement is a metaphor for iniquity. To have such clothing removed or cleansed signifies the erasure of transgression.[106] Already then, in the Hebrew biblical context, human solid waste was a powerful image of the sinfulness of Israel as a whole or of certain individuals.[107] From at least the first century C.E. onward, ulcerated, rotting, uncontrollable bowels became a symbol of profound wickedness for Pagan, Jewish, and Christian writers, just as bowels that were impervious to decay demonstrated a person's holiness. For Plutarch (ca. 46–120), the emperor Sulla's many vices literally devoured him from within:

> By this mode of life he aggravated a disease that was insignificant in its beginnings, so that for a long time he knew not that his bowels were ulcerated. This disease corrupted his whole flesh also, and converted it into worms, so that although many were employed day and night in removing them, what they took away was as nothing compared with the increase upon him, but all his clothing, baths, hand-basins, and food were infected with that flux of corruption, so violent was its discharge. Therefore he immersed himself many times a day in water to cleanse and scour his person. But it was of no use; the change gained upon him rapidly, and the swarm of vermin defied all purification.[108]

Like Sulla, the wicked king Herod suffered from ulcerated intestines and genitals that putrefied to the extent of spawning worms. This disease, according to the Jewish historian Josephus (ca. 37–100 C.E.), was God's punishment for Herod's sins.[109] Arius faired no better in the writings of those Christians who deemed him a heretic. Arius may have suffered from excessive diarrhea as opposed to ulcerated bowels, but the bodily and symbolic locus of his "evil," like that of Sulla and Herod, was his intestines.[110] Plutarch, Josephus, and Rufinus, Arius's detractor, used intestinal stench, rot, and excrement as a way of underlining the profundity of these figures' wickedness and of creating revulsion in their readers. The desired effect and symbolism is the same in all three. Hence unpolluted, good divinity found its nemesis in the organs of excrement, regardless of a given author's religion.[111]

Ritual impurity added a further dimension to Jewish views of the abdomen, for nearly all polluting substances had their origin there.[112] Excrement (*ẓo'ah, ẓo'i, ẓe'ah,* or *ḥari / ḥari'*) and urine (*sheten* or *shein*) are not included in the list of levitical impurities. Its production or contact with it required no purification ritual, as did other impure bodily substances. Nevertheless, there are indications elsewhere in the biblical corpus that excrement was viewed as impure in that it drove away God's presence and could not be tolerated in any place consecrated to God.[113] Based on evidence from the Dead Sea Scrolls and Josephus's *Wars of the Jews*, Hannah Harrington has argued that the Jews of the Qumran regarded defecation as ritually unclean.[114] The Mishnah and the Talmud are less clear. On the one hand, there are a number of passages in the Mishnah that explicitly state that feces were ritually clean.[115] However, there are also ample passages demonstrating that the divine world was not to come into contact with human waste. BT Berakhot contains many of these in its explication of proper privy etiquette. For example: "On entering a privy one should say: 'Be honored, ye honored and holy ones that minister to the Most High. Give honor to the God of Israel. Wait for me till I enter and do my needs and return to you.'"[116] The holy ones or angels who normally accompany a person cannot be expected to enter a place of defecation, for the excreting human cannot remain in the presence of holiness. Human excrement was not a "legal" form of impurity in that it is not among the impure substances designated in Leviticus. Nevertheless, it was more disturbing than simple "dirt" because there was a long tradition in Judaism, beginning with certain biblical texts and continuing in the qumranic and rabbinic literature, in which human waste was incompatible with divine or angelic presence. Jewish post-biblical aversion to excrement may have been heightened by similar sentiments in the surrounding cultures. Regardless of the origin, the implied impurity and the biblical association of fecal matter with sin are important to recall when reading references to excrement in Jewish polemic, for they would have increased the degree of aversion sparked in Jewish readers or hearers. However, even without the added legal understanding of such insults, Pagans and Christians shared enough excremental symbolism with their Jewish neighbors to have grasped the sharpness of this type of invective when encountered.

Skin Disease

Skin disease was also morally marked. Determining the clinical nature of many of the diseases mentioned by Greek, Roman, and Jewish writers is difficult at best. However, Mirko Grmek argues that leprosy began to intrude on the awareness of Greek and Roman physicians as early as the fifth or fourth century B.C.E., though it was labeled a foreign disease, originating among the Phoenicians or Egyptians. By the time Pliny was writing in the first century, it was a new, terrible disease that had spread throughout Italy and most of Europe.[117] Whether the biblical term *ẓara'at*, usually translated as "leprosy," in fact referred to a strain of leprosy is debated.[118] In contrast to the attitudes in various forms of Christianity and Paganism, in Jewish law *ẓara'at* was considered a severe ritual impurity requiring social ostracism, priestly examination, and sacrifice if cured.[119] All saw skin ailments as potential signs of divine wrath. Pliny queried whether the new diseases might be punishments from the gods.[120] He, along with the rabbis, also associated pigs, "the most brutish of beasts," with scrofula and scaly skin disease.[121] In Pagan polemic against the Jews, the Jews are expelled from Egypt because they have leprosy and scabs and are an impious people, detested by the gods.[122] The alleged impiety and skin ailments of the Jews are inextricably linked in these texts. The ancient Israelites, like many other peoples of the ancient Near East, thought that skin disease was a punishment from God.[123] The people of Israel are frequently threatened with the specter of *ẓara'at* or other skin ailments if they disobey God's law.[124] A number of biblical characters are chastised by God by being stricken with leprosy.[125] Following the precedent established in the biblical corpus, dermatological afflictions were closely linked to sin and divine punishment in later Jewish literature. The writers of the Dead Sea Scrolls were primarily interesed in *ẓara'at* as a literal affliction, yet they connected it with transgression. In some of the liturgic poetry in the Qumran purification is accompanied by thanks for forgiveness of sin and the lifting of disease.[126] In the Talmud and midrash *ẓara'at* and its relatives, such as boils and scabs, are used metaphorically to connote transgression and are also the punishment for iniquity. On the whole in rabbinic literature skin diseases are tied to specific sins: sexual immorality, especially having intercourse during menstruation, spreading evil rumors, pride, and blasphemy.[127] According to Philo (20 B.C.E.–50 C.E.), "impiety and lawless iniquity" result in

> diseases of the body which separately afflict and devour each limb and each part, and which also rack and torture it all over with fevers, and chills, and wasting consumptions, and terrible rashes, and scrofulous diseases, and spasmodic convulsions of the eyes, and putrefying sores and abscesses, and cutaneous disorders extending over the whole of the skin, and disorders of the bowels and inward parts, and

> convulsions of the stomach, and obstructions in the passages of the lungs preventing the patient from breathing easily, and paralysis of the tongue, and deafness of the ears, and imperfections of the eyes, and general dimness and confusion of all the other senses.[128]

The wages of sin are disease of any kind, yet skin problems have pride of place in Philo's list. In *On the Unchangeableness of God* Philo transformed the levitical law of *ẓara'at* into an allegory for conscience, transgression, and religious knowledge in which leprosy is equated with "voluntary depravity," namely, the soul's willful rejection of what it knows to be right, which in turn pollutes the soul.[129]

In both works by Philo skin disease is a sign of iniquity. The first text is much more literal, listing real sicknesses that result from unlawful behavior. In the second "leprosy" is detached from any actual bodily complaint, becoming instead a metaphor for man's polluting sinfulness. Early Christian literature used leprosy in ways similar to the Jews. For example, in Tertullian's *Contra Marcion*, Elisha's healing of Naaman the Syrian "was significant throughout the nations of the world of their own cleansing in Christ their light, steeped as they were in the stains of the seven deadly sins: idolatry, blasphemy, murder, adultery, fornication, false-witness, and fraud."[130] Much later, Isidore of Seville likened the scabby eruptions discussed in Leviticus to heretics who infiltrate the Church.[131] Augustine compared pride to the pernicious humors that caused scabies and boils.[132]

As in Philo's text, skin disease in these Christian texts signals the sinfulness of man. For Tertullian, the literal healing of leprosy is the outward indication of spiritual cleansing. Also, the sins for which skin disease is a metaphor—blasphemy, adultery, fornication, false-witness, pride—are similar to those for which transgressors are struck with leprosy in rabbinic literature. This similarity provides further proof that to Jews, Christians, and, perhaps to a lesser extent, Pagans, leprosy and associated diseases were common symbols of iniquity and divine retribution.

Their long history of being a divine affliction for sins, especially sexual sins and sins of the tongue, plus the severity of the ritual pollution that *ẓara'at* entailed in the Jewish tradition made leprosy and other skin ailments an ideal polemical tool in interfaith conflict. Any person or group compared to a "leper" would be automatically associated with impurity, sin, and a deforming disease, making the person or group unfit for inclusion in the community. Heresy or faith in another religion fit neatly into these sets of associations. Because *ẓara'at* was a disease, polemicists could extend the metaphor to argue that incorrect belief and its adherents were contagious and destructive, much as was "leprosy." Pagans, Jews, and Christians all leveled accusations of "leprosy" against undesirable outsiders, though the exact nuances of this invective varied with the religious and chronological context.

Thus skin disease, digestion and excrement, and foul smell could stand as either individual symbols or part of a web connected by their associations with women's genital blood and decay. In either instance, they marked the corruptible, animal side of the human being or the individual as a sinner in opposition to incorruptible divinity. That menstrual blood, a profoundly negative substance in its own right, could be linked to all these symbols made it the most powerful weapon in a shared language of signs.

Food and Animals

Not all forms of impurity or despised bodily emissions related to menstrual blood or the female body. Most food had no special link to the female body and is in a separate category from anything discussed so far. True, certain kinds of food were designated unclean, much like a leper or menstruant, and what a person eats provokes digestion and elimination. Food is that which is taken into the body, whereas odor, menstrual blood, excrement, and even disease emanate from the body. Diet affected the status of a mortal being in relation to the divine, even as the body's discharges did. Sometimes the moral value of food was closely related to the waste it produced. Detienne has shown that the Phoenix was admired by the Romans because according to mythology it ate nothing at all or subsisted on rays of the sun. Its excretions, if any, were the worms thought responsible for the production of cinnamon—a highly prized spice.[133] In a text attributed to the Christian Lactantius (260–320), the Phoenix also eats no earthly food.[134] Although certain foods were forbidden or at least discouraged by individual groups such as the Pythagoreans, in general there was no system of prohibited foods among the Greeks or apparently the Romans.[135] Some animals, while allowed as food, had a morally negative value, such as the dog. The dog along with goats and pigs were sometimes despised as dung-eaters.[136] In addition to being associated with leprosy, swine were viewed as filthy and so earthy that their souls served as "salt" to keep them from rotting.[137] Also, creatures (including humans) who were poisonous or who ate poisonous substances were reviled.[138] Women in particular were associated with such animals or behaviors. Medieval medical thinkers, drawing from classical views, frequently (and incorrectly) compared the anatomy of the human womb to that of the pig.[139] In Greek and Roman medical literature noxious substances, such as sweat, and excrement were more likely to appear in prescriptions for ailing women, and women were closely associated with rot and poison, both through the production of menstruation (a kind of poisonous substance) and in their supposed immunity to many poisons.[140] Thus, while lacking the elaborate ritual purity laws that governed eating in Zoroastrianism and Judaism, certain food animals were morally marked in Greek and Roman culture. A creature or person could be positively or negatively valued through what he or she ate, and excreted, or embodied.

For Zoroastrians and Jews, acceptability before God depended very much on avoiding certain foodstuffs.[141] Food laws served as a wellspring of potential symbols from which the ancient Israelites and later generations of Jews could draw to outline relationships both with other Jews and with non-Jews. Howard Eilberg-Schwartz, in his anthropological analysis of ancient Israelite religion, has observed that unclean, predatory animals frequently functioned as metaphors for Israel's enemies, whereas Israel itself is equated with pastoral animals, whose cloven hooves and cud-chewing place them in the realm of the ritually permissible. Thus the inedible versus the edible in the ancient Jewish legal code served as an indicator of the broader social divisions within Israel's universe.[142] Following Lévi-Strauss and others, Eilberg-Schwartz argues that food and other animal regulations need to be seen as potential metaphors for sexual mores. In this schema the restriction against yoking an ass and an ox together (Deut. 22:10) is a warning against marriage with foreigners, for as Eilberg-Schwartz has shown, the ass and the ox were frequently metaphors for resident foreigners and Israelites respectively.[143] These observations about ancient Judaism prove extremely useful for analyzing animal impurity metaphors in late antique Jewish texts as well. Pagans, Christians, and "bad" Jews were often equated with unclean animals.[144] Romans were frequently compared to pigs or other sorts of unclean beasts.[145] Sometimes specific individuals were targeted, as in *Genesis Rabbah* 63:8 where the emperor Diocletian is said to have been mocked and beaten by Jewish children while he was herding swine as a boy. While Romans did not regard the pig as ritually impure and thus inedible, any Roman would have been insulted by such an analogy given that pigs were linked with leprosy, dung, and rot in Roman (and Jewish) culture and medical lore.[146] However, Jews were not the only ones who used animal metaphors or even their system of food impurities.

Tacitus, the Roman historian, drew on the tradition of the pig as a brutish creature only one step from putrefaction and combined it with his knowledge of Jewish dietary laws to polemicize against the Jews. He maintained that because Jews in Egypt were afflicted with the scabious plague for which the pig is known, Jews refrain from eating pork. This disease did not occur through natural contagion but rather was the result of the Jews' behavior that was hateful to the gods.[147] In Tacitus's and similar schemas, Jews are simultaneously equated with a loathsome, dirty, diseased beast and condemned for being antisocial because they do not eat this animal like other nations do.[148] The choice to equate pigs and Jews is much like the midrashic authors' use of unclean animals to symbolize non-Jews and undesirable Jews. That Romans and Jews focused on pigs as a way of denigrating one another suggests that for at least some impure animals Roman and Jewish invective relied on the same matrix of associations.[149] Not only did Romans and postbiblical Jews draw from a common set of beliefs about the pig, but, as with the biblical Jewish texts analyzed by Eilberg-Schwartz, food codes indicated broad social and religious divisions between two groups. Both Jews and Romans symbolized outsiders and potential undesirables, namely, one another, by allusions to unsavory animals.

As Christianity began as a sect of Judaism and both faiths shared much Scripture in common, it is not surprising that the two religions drew on a common symbolic background. However, one of the characteristics that distinguished Christianity from most forms of Judaism was its eventual rejection of the purity laws, including those dealing with food. Nevertheless, unclean or undesirable food figures prominently in Christian writing as a marker for moral and religious outsiders. Already in Matthew 7:6, 15–17, good is distinguished from evil through metaphors of food and despised animals such as dogs, swine, and wolves.[150] As in the Jewish Scriptures, threatening individuals are portrayed as carnivorous and unclean beasts, whereas believers are represented by pastoral animals: sheep. Evil deeds are "bad fruit," and the goodness of God is described in terms of food.[151]

In the *Clementine Recognitions* the dogs and swine of Matthew 7:6 become those who argue against Christian preachers with excessive circumlocutions.[152] Both the author of the *Epistle of Barnabas* (ca. 100 C.E.) and Novitian (fl. 210–280 C.E.) in his treatise *On Jewish Meats* transform the unclean animals of the Torah into those who are religious and moral undesirables. Animals who have neither cloven hooves nor chew their cud represent those who fail to walk firmly in virtue and digest the divine precepts, namely, heretics and Jews.[153] The prohibition against eating hyenas in reality refers to the law against adultery, just as the prohibition against eating the hare warns against men having intercourse with other men and boys.[154] Pork is forbidden as a reproof against "a life filthy and dirty, and delighting in garbage of vice, placing its supreme good not in generosity of the mind, but in the flesh alone."[155] This description of the swine is similar to the Roman contention that pigs were especially brutish, earthly, and far from philosophy. These traditions of the pig as both literally filthy and symbolically representative of people polluted with sin and false belief became part of the medieval Latin Christian tradition with the writings of Isidore of Seville (ca. 560–636) and Rabanus Maurus (780–856). For Rabanus Maurus, Jews are among those who are filled with "unclean things" (*immunditiis*), a condition they pass on to their children, based on the curse in Matthew 27:25, "His [Jesus'] blood be on us and our children," that the Jews called down upon themselves.[156]

Within this emerging Pagan, Jewish, and Christian iconography of animals, sexual malpractice and religious difference and undesirability are placed side by side, especially in the Christian tradition. Animals that do not fall into neat categories but possess the characteristics of more than one category, such as the hare who chews cud but does not have cloven hooves, represent both religious indecision or failure and, in the writers' minds, perverted sexuality or perverted masculinity in particular. This "perversion" could come in the form of the choice of sexual partners in the case of those symbolized by the hare, or those who preferred flesh over mind and spirituality—something directly contrary to Christian and Pagan ideals of masculinity—as in the case of those represented by the pig—a comparison that also had feminizing associations.[157] These links between "bad" religion and masculinity and feminization are only implied by the parallels in classical and late antique literature, but they will become quite explicit in the Middle Ages. Jews likewise used impure animals or animals that rendered others unclean to portray "bad Jews" and, eventually, Christians as devouring and violent toward "good" Jews. Very often those devouring animals were strongly and negatively masculinized; their own pollution is demonstrated by their unwillingness to accept the restrictions relating to the woman's body, and they contaminate others by acting as carnivores and tearing the flesh, making it—namely, the women or other Jews who are the focus of their attentions—forbidden for consumption by members of the Jewish community.[158]

The frequency with which sexual impropriety appears in *Barnabas* and *On Jewish Meats* supports Eilberg-Schwartz's theory that food laws can symbolize sexual prohibitions. The use of unclean animals as metaphors in Jewish and Pagan interfaith polemic may be interpreted as expressions of anxieties about sexual liaisons between members of different religions. While I do not deny the validity of this hypothesis, this choice of comparison, religious undesirable = unconsumable food, reflects Jewish, Christian, and Pagan fears not only about intermarriage but also about religious incorporation. Likening one's enemy to an inedible, forbidden animal served symbolically to mark him or them as unsuitable for absorption by the body of believers. Sexuality and religious integration shared metaphors of food perhaps because intermarriages were invariably a locus of changing or compromising religious affiliations. Greek and Roman use of unclean animals to denigrate their enemies may have functioned in a way similar to that in Jewish literature. Perhaps Jews became the target of this imagery because of Roman resentment at their refusal to assimilate fully into Roman society, even in the face of Roman policy to encourage former outsiders to adopt Roman religion and customs.

Thus substances that entered the human body as well as those that were excreted from it were important signifiers of an individual or group's religious and moral status among Pagans, Jews, and Christians. These markers could be used to evaluate individuals within a single religious community, or they could be used as polemical tools to malign religious outsiders. Essential to this process was that Pagans, Jews, and Christians shared basic understandings about how the body worked and the symbolic value assigned to it and its functions. While differences existed between the major groups, the body, its fluids, smells, skin diseases, and food were seen by all as barriers to holy status or contact with the divine. Connecting nearly all these threads of potential bodily disgust was the body and blood of women, which helped to create a naturalized, binary opposition between the corporeal and the divine. By gendering categories of unclean versus clean, material versus spiritual, which could then be applied to individuals or religious communities, authors could call on a range of symbols to imply a spiritual hierarchy with themselves at the top.[159]

CHAPTER TWO

The Seeds of Rotten Fruit

Corporeal Disgust and Impurity as Late Antique and Early Medieval Religious Polemic

Pagans, Jews, and various Christians evoked impurity and bodily dirt as a way to create theological and emotional obstacles between themselves and those with whom they disagreed. Jews directed accusations of many types of impurity at other Jews whom they deemed unacceptable, at Pagans, at Pagan idols and temples, and at Christians.[1] Even in the midst of legal arguments, the primary intent was polemical, to create barriers of religious and physical revulsion between "good Jews" and undesirables. Whereas Jews emphasized impurity in general, Pagans and Christians specifically emphasized the filthy nature of bodily effluvia. In all cases, however, the basic function of the polemic was the same. Because Jews had a more extensive system of purity laws than did most Pagans and Christians, equating an undesirable with a certain kind of uncleanness was deemed sufficient to repulse any who would be tempted to cross a religious divide. Pagan philosophers and many Christians who were loath to allow contact between the human body and anything from the divine realm found the Christian doctrine of the incarnation especially distasteful. This distaste prompted Pagans and various Christian groups to attack the doctrine by underlining the absurdity of divinity being "trapped" in the filthy womb of a woman and subject to human weakness. The older, classical associations of women with the world of matter, the medical and religious convictions that menstrual and parturient blood was poisonous, and the increased severity with which the impurity of menstrual blood was regarded all contributed to making the womb a focus for the incarnation debates. While this type of argumentation was presaged in late antique Jewish anti-Christian invective, it did not become a central part of Jews' rejection of Christianity until around the ninth century, when Jews and Muslims both adopted the bodily weaknesses and filth of Mary's womb as themes in their attacks against Christianity.[2]

In the rhetoric of late antiquity concerns about social boundaries were not passively reflected by purity laws regarding the human body.[3] Rather, purity laws, along with philosophical and medical ideas about the body, were tools with which writers actively sought to shape hierarchy and dividing lines. While William Miller has shown that disgust has been a formidable weapon in interpersonal and social struggles throughout Western culture, invective that inflamed repugnance of human effluvia was particularly effective given late antique views of the body.[4] For members of a majority religion, accusations of pollution or graphic descriptions designed to make the religious other disgusting were a way to confirm the inferior, indeed, repugnant status of their opponents, whereas for minorities, especially the Jews, this polemic was one of the few types of resistance available.[5] Words could be shaped into a type of religious violence.[6] A discussion about "renaming" foreign gods in BT 'Avodah Zarah in response to the commands in Deuteronomy to destroy idols explicitly outlines the method of "attack."[7] From the passage "and [you shall] destroy their name out of that place" (Deut.12:3), R. Jose b. R. Judah argues that all trace of the idol must be destroyed.[8] The rabbis further explained this phrase by maintaining that the idol must be renamed: "If [the heathens] called it Beth Galya [the house of revelation], call it Beth Karya [house of concealment], if they called it 'En Kol [the all-seeing eye], call it 'En Qoẓ [the eye of the thorn]."[9] That which non-Jews regarded as praiseworthy was not only to be destroyed literally, but also through verbal inversion. In a world in which Jews were a religious minority, "destruction" through words was a comparatively safe, nonmilitary form of defiance.[10] The hostility and the course of action advocated in this passage outline the tactics of resistance against non-Jewish religions taken by the rabbis. While not all attacks were based on such a close homonymic parody, many were grounded in name-calling, verbal play, and scriptural manipulation and were centered on types of impurity. These epithets functioned as part of what James Scott has called the hidden transcript—the "discourse which takes place 'offstage,' beyond direct observation by powerholders," and which "consists of those offstage speeches, gestures, and practices that confirm, contradict, or inflect what appears in the public transcript."[11] Such insulting wordplay was both riskiest and most effective when the dominant society became aware of its existence. It was risky because of the retaliation that might result but effective because it made a point without directly challenging authority through disobedience or violence.[12] Often the content and tactics of late antique invective did not have to remain disguised because they involved groups of equal power (or powerlessness).[13]

Jewish Impurity Polemic

Scholars of the Dead Sea Scrolls and rabbinic literature have argued that both sects polemicized against other Jews of whom they disapproved by accusing them of impurity.[14] Slanders involving uncleanness were applied not only to Jews but also to the persons, holy places, and gods of the gentiles and Christians, or *minim,* as they were often called.[15] Most antigentile polemic in the Talmud is a mixture of legal dispute and invective that involves many different sorts of ritual pollution. For example, the Mishnah of 'Avodah Zarah (3.7) contains a discussion about what someone who lives next to an idolatrous temple should do if the building collapses, especially if one of the walls were shared by the temple and his house:

> [If the wall] belonged both to him and the shrine it is judged as being half and half. Its stones, timber and rubbish defile like a creeping thing (*sherez̦*) as it is said, "Thou shalt utterly detest it (*shaqez̦ tishaqz̦enu*)" (Deut. 7:26). R. Akiba says [it defiles] like a niddah, as it is said, "Thou shalt cast them away as an unclean thing (*davah*), thou shalt say to it get thee hence" (Is. 30:22). As a niddah defiles [an object] by carrying it, so also an idolatrous object defiles by its being carried.[16]

Sherez̦ (vermin) and *sheqez̦* (abomination—verb *shiqez̦,* "to abhor") are closely connected in the biblical corpus.[17] Touching *sherez̦* rendered a person unclean until evening.[18] The first half of the Mishnaic passage plays on the close association between the two terms to justify attributing the impurity status of *sherez̦* to the wood and stones of a Pagan temple. The second argument is likewise based on a game of biblical word association. Since in Isaiah 30:22 idols are called "*davah*" (sickness), a term usually referring to a woman suffering from her menstrual cycle, the polluting power of anything linked to an idol is the same as a *niddah.* Weaving together a chain of biblical associations, the exchange in the Mishnah of 'Avodah Zarah successfully attached two types of opprobrium to the idol and its temple—the defilement of *shereẓ* and *sheqeẓ* and of *niddah.* They are presented in ascending degrees of uncleanness, suggesting that one of the discussion's goals was to find a satisfyingly negative analogy for the idol and its accouterments. Disagreement is implied by the juxtaposition of two opinions, yet there is no clear statement of contradiction, raising the possibility that both terms apply.[19]

The pollution of impure animals, *niddah, zav,* corpses, leprosy, and excrement were all ammunition for the establishment of the religious outsider, whether "bad" Jew, Pagan, or Christian. These categories of uncleanness figured prominently in Jewish invective because they were intimately associated with the human body and as such had great power to disturb and disgust. Even unspecified impurity was deemed sufficient to create a divide between the "righteous" and the undesirable. BT Shabbat 145b–146a explains that idolaters are ontologically polluted, in contrast to Jews:

> Because they did not stand at Mount Sinai. For when the serpent came upon Eve he injected his filth/pollution (*zuhama'*) into her [as for] the Israelites who stood at Mount Sinai, their filth/pollution (*zuhamatan*) departed; the idolaters, who did not stand at Mount Sinai, their filth/pollution (*zuhamatan*) did not depart.[20]

No legal issues are attached to the story; it provides mythological origins for an already accepted belief, namely, that gentiles are impure. In the process, the tale denigrates Pagans for their essential filth while placing Jews on a higher plane due to their freedom from pollution. This strategy can be understood within the theories of Douglas, Miller, and Scott. That the rabbis focused their remarks on the relative purity or impurity of Jewish and Pagan bodies points to the tension, at least among Jews, over the boundaries between the two societies. The hierarchy of unpolluted Jews and "filthy" gentiles encouraged not only avoidance of non-Jews but also disgust and contempt for them. These negative feelings strengthened the divisions between the two communities and effectively undermined any Roman claim to superiority.[21] The nature of the pollution attributed to gentiles was unimportant as long as the language and imagery evoked were vivid enough to provoke revulsion in the audience.[22]

Choosing specific kinds of impurity allowed Jewish polemicists to highlight certain undesirable qualities that they believed, or wished their audience to believe, the targeted group possessed. Linking idols, their worshipers, and the land outside Israel to the impurity of corpses attributed the greatest possible degree of pollution in the Jewish system; anyone so contaminated profoundly defiled objects and other people he or she touched.[23] According to Tosefta Ḥullin, meat in the hands of *minim* is forbidden: "this is as the flesh of sacrifices to the dead." The text even rates meat in the hands of the *minim* as more prohibited than that in the hands of gentiles.[24] Gentiles and Christians, along with their gods and their land or food, were powerfully corrupting forces that infected the Jew who came into direct contact with them and in turn polluted those around him or her. Since a corpse was unclean in Pagan religious systems, any non-Jew who heard an intimation of such an association would have been deeply affronted. For Jew, Pagan, and Christian to compare a god or its image to a corpse was to announce its earthy, finite nature, a nature that doomed it to fleshly disintegration—the very opposite of divinity.

Comparing a person or object to "creeping things" or "vermin," as the term *shereẓ* may be translated, would have been unflattering even leaving aside impurity or the commonly held view that such creatures were born of earth or waste. Adding these two factors merely increased the discomfort associated with such a comparison. By likening the holy objects, places, and people of other religions or types of Judaism to *shereẓ,* the rabbis verbally rendered them small and despicable and therefore unworthy of respect.

Impure animals were also a metaphor for forbidden sexual relations. The relationship between unclean animals and unsanctioned sexual unions is made in a lengthy passage dealing with marriage between a *ḥaver* (scholar) or his daughter and an *'am ha-'areẓ.* Scholars are discouraged from marrying the daughters of the *'ammei ha-'areẓ* because they are "an abomination *(sheqeẓ),* their wives vermin *(shereẓ)* and about their daughters it is said 'cursed is he who lies with any beast (Deut. 27.21).'"[25] Thus to have sex with the women of the *'ammei ha-'areẓ* is equivalent to having intimate relations with animals, an act clearly forbidden in the Torah, bringing God's curse, and, in Leviticus 18.23, defilement, upon the human participant. However, the wives and daughters of the *'ammei ha-'areẓ* are not merely reduced to the category of animals; they are unclean, small, despicable animals, unworthy of respect, and polluting to any who touch them, much like Pagan temples and utensils. The daughters of the sages as well as the rabbis themselves were at risk from this "bestial contamination" if they married an *'am ha-'areẓ* because the latter treated their wives as a lion does his prey.[26] Again the *'ammei ha-'areẓ,* in this case the men, are equated with a type of animal. The male *'am ha-'areẓ* is violent like the lion, for he strikes (his wife). The lion is not associated with impurity in the same way that *sheqeẓ* and *shereẓ* are, though according to biblical law the lion's prey constitutes defiling food precisely because the lion tears the animals it catches.[27] By extension, any daughter of the sages married to such a man would be tainted because she had been "torn" by a lion (her *'am ha-'areẓ* husband).[28] The text as a whole serves to insinuate that the *'ammei ha-'areẓ* are impure by associating them with certain animals and portraying them as bestial, violent, and sexually uncontrolled. Women who are or have been made part of the familial circle of the *'ammei ha-'areẓ* are "inedible." Such a condemnation would have provided strong inducement to avoid not only marital liaisons but general socializing and religious interchange as well.[29]

The violence or impurity of certain animals also appears in Jewish polemic against non-Jewish nations, especially Pagan and, later, Christian Rome.[30] In one section of *Leviticus Rabbah* 13:5, containing a series of meditations on the identity and nature of the four nations in Daniel 7, Babylon, Media, Greece, and Edom are likened respectively to a lion, a wolf, a leopard, and an unnamed but doubly destructive beast. The authors of the midrash are more interested in indicating the violence of the other nations than their pollution or sexual misbehavior.[31] A little later, however, another set of animal analogies is presented that compares the same nations to the various unclean animals listed in Leviticus 11:1–8.[32] Finally Persia/Edom (Rome) is equated to a swine "[b]ecause it [i.e., the swine] is on a par with the three others put together. R. Simon b. Laqish said: It is even more than that."[33]

Of the violent animals to which the non-Jewish peoples are compared, Edom is the most destructive; its animal, the pig, is singled out as more impure than all the others. The placement of Edom at the apex of peoples categorized as dangerous or polluted suggests that by the time *Leviticus Rabbah* was written, in fifth- or sixth-century Palestine, Christianity was the most pernicious of all Israel's enemies past and present, at least in the eyes of the text's author(s).[34] This imagery also appears in Hebrew liturgical poetry, or *piyyuṭim,* from the same period. For example, in the poems of Yanni, who was writing in sixth-century Palestine, Edom is regularly associated with the pig, while the nations such as Babylon and Persia, which had oppressed Jews in the past, are likened to lions, bears, and leopards.[35] Here, as in the midrashim, these comparisons serve to mark Edom, meaning the Byzantine Empire, as violent, subhuman, and impure.[36] In one *piyyuṭ* the author expressed the wish that Edom should creep on the ground like a snake or other crawling animals and eat the dust of their (the people of Israel's) feet.[37] This last simile places the Christian empire in the category of *shereẓ,* vermin, but it also recalls God's curse against the serpent in Genesis 3:14–15 in which the serpent is doomed to crawl on its belly and be trampled by the woman's offspring. In the context of the biblical citation, along with being polluted, Edom is a cursed, lowly creature whose enmity toward Israel was preordained, as is its eventual humiliation at the feet of Israel. Such associations conveyed scorn and disgust for Christian oppressors, and they expressed the poet's hope for divine vengeance while at the same time enacting Israel's defeat of Edom verbally when physical retaliation was unsafe.[38]

Leprosy worked to label heretics and other outsiders as polluted and dangerous. Leprosy was frequently associated with Christianity and heresy (*minut*).[39] In *Midrash Rabbah Leviticus* 15:9 Babylon, Media, and Greece are compared to a series of skin diseases, all of which had the potential for being declared *ẓara'at,* "leprous," and thus unclean.[40] No doubt is left about Edom, however, which is called a "plague of leprosy (*neg'a ẓara'at*)."[41] Perhaps even a more curious link between Christianity and leprosy in early Jewish literature comes in the form of an analogy between Gehazi, the greedy servant of the prophet Elisha (2 Kings 5), and the founder of Christianity, Jesus himself.

In these tales, Elisha states that Gehazi's leprosy is his "reward" *(sakhar)* for studying the eight unclean things (*shmonah shereẓim*). Likewise, Jesus is rejected by his own teacher, R. Joshua b. Perahiah, for remarking on the appearance of a female innkeeper.[42] The structure of the narratives parallels Gehazi's sin to Jesus', perhaps indicating that studying *shereẓim* and assessing the beauty of strange women were supposed to be analogous. This interpretation is strengthened since leprosy was often seen as the punishment for sexual sin. By closely juxtaposing the details of these two tales, the rabbis implied that Jesus studied that which was impure, vile, and sexually charged, effectively discrediting him as a teacher worthy of being followed. While Gehazi and his descendants alone are described as leprous, the close mirroring of events in each of the stories sets the expectation that Jesus and his "descendants" would also be leprous, even as both led Israel astray and rejected the overtures of their teachers to repent.

The comparisons to impure animals allowed the writers and compilers to polemicize against gentiles from two angles. Not only could non-Jews be marked as unclean, but they were also marked as bestial, much like the *'ammei ha-'areẓ* in BT Pesaḥim 49a–b. Placing gentiles, Christians, and their teachings in the category of polluting, "inedible" animals made their incorporation into the community and beliefs of the "faithful" repellent. The accusation of leprosy and other skin diseases also served to repel Jews from adopting the beliefs and practices of outsiders. However, the tenor of this revulsion differed from that occasioned by impure animals. Rather than evoke images of vermin, violent predators, and unconsumable meat, midrashic and talmudic texts linked Christianity in particular with a hideously deforming and incurable disease that was traditionally a sign of God's wrath for profound sinfulness and one of the highest forms of ritual impurity.[43]

Much of late antique Jewish excremental polemic is couched in trickster tales and was part of what James Scott has called "backstage talk."[44] In both talmudic and midrashic anecdotes the "tricks" the rabbis play on their opponents are verbal ones in which the rabbis deftly avoid being trapped by difficult questions and in turn manipulate their adversaries into degrading their own people or religion. In *Pesiqta' Rabbati,* Emperor Hadrian asks R. Joshu'a b. Hanna' why God's name is involved in the five commandments given to Israel, so that Israel is punished when it sins while the other nations are not punished since God's name is not involved in their commandments.[45] Rather than respond directly, the rabbi takes Hadrian for a stroll and points out a series of statues of him. When they arrive at a privy, R. Joshu'a claims that the emperor has no authority in this place because no statue of him is there. Hadrian exclaims: "And you are a Sage among the Jews! Would such be the honor due to a king that a statue of him be set up in a place that is loathsome, in a place that is repulsive, in a place that is filthy?"

> R. Joshu'a replied: "Do not your ears hear what your mouth is saying? Would it redound to the glory of the Holy One, blessed be He, to have His name mentioned with murderers, with adulterers, with thieves?" The emperor dismissed R. Joshu'a, who went hence.[46]

The emperor who questioned R. Joshu'a's wisdom and sought to exalt his own people over the Jews is instead proven a fool, tricked into likening non-Jews to a filthy outhouse and meekly assenting to their being called murderers, adulterers, and thieves. Jews reading the tale would have been vicariously avenged against the established hierarchy of power by the wit of R. Joshu'a.[47] At the center of Hadrian's (and by extension, all gentiles') humiliation is an outhouse, the disgusting qualities of which are emphasized by Hadrian himself.[48]

The Talmud occasionally encouraged active denigration of Pagan holy places. The Gemarah, which follows the aforementioned Mishnah 'Avodah Zarah 3.7, urges a Jew to make a privy out of what was once holy to non-Jews, thus desecrating the place through the regular deposit of an impure substance.[49] Just as the Bible metaphorically covered sinners in excrement, here the sinful shrine or god is literally buried in human waste. A similar sentiment is behind the uncensored versions of a passage in BT Gittin 57a in which Jesus is consigned to boiling excrement (*ẓo'ah rotaḥat*) as are "all those who mock the words of the wise."[50] Through the symbolic values attributed to excrement, Jesus, "god" of the Christians, is marked as a sinner and tied to a lower bodily substance universally understood as abhorrent to divinity. In all these texts excrement is a tool to express contempt and elicit disgust for outsiders and their gods and to create a barrier against sympathy for or conversion to their ways and religion(s). Miller has argued that disgust works to maintain hierarchy but that at the same time claims of superiority are vulnerable to "the defiling powers of the low"; or to quote his colorful analogy, "[a] teaspoon of sewage will spoil a barrel of wine, but a teaspoon of wine will do nothing for a barrel of sewage."[51] The Jewish authors of these texts quite literally added a "teaspoon of sewage" to the claims of often more powerful non-Jews in an effort to supplant the established hierarchy with their own assertions of moral and religious superiority. Instances in which rabbis outsmarted their opponents added drama, humor, and perhaps a sense of satisfaction for the Jewish audience that their wise men were intellectually more powerful than the rulers of this world. The humiliation of Jews' potential adversaries would have strengthened the bonds of communal unity for the Jewish readers over and against any curiosity or interest in Pagans or Christians. If any Jew acted on the advice given in BT 'Avodah Zarah 47b, he would have merely brought verbal invective to physical fruition in a small act of war against those whom he saw as the oppressors of his people.

Menstrual pollution was one of the prime accusations leveled against Jews who did not adhere to "correct" religious ideology.[52] For example, in BT Niddah Samaritans are targeted:

> The daughters of the Samaritans are regarded as menstruants from their cradle and the Samaritans impart uncleanness to a couch underneath as to a cover above since they cohabit with menstruants because

> [their wives] continue [unclean for seven days] on account of a discharge of any blood, on account of their [uncleanness).[53]

Slightly later in tractate Niddah the daughters of the Sadducees are compared to the Samaritan women as long as they follow in the ways of their fathers.[54]

Along with the Samaritans and the Sadducees, proselytes and the *'amei ha-'areẓ,* "people of the land," were regarded as suspicious.[55] In BT 'Avodah Zarah 36b daughters of idolaters are *niddah* from their cradle, the same tactic used against Samaritan women in BT Niddah. Later in the 'Avodah Zarah passage, R. Dimi repeats a Hasmonean decree that any who have sexual relations with Pagan women are guilty of having intercourse with a menstruant, a slave, a non-Jew, and a married woman. There is great concern to prevent intermarriage (or nonmarital intimate relations) with any kind of non-Jew, a point the rabbis make explicit.[56] By equating non-Jews to a variety of people who if Jewish would be impure and forbidden, the lawmakers sought to make gentiles repugnant as potential partners. The Hasmonean decree does this by applying as many unsavory categories as possible. The rabbinic statement that gentile and Samaritan women are *niddah* from their cradle draws on the growing fear about menstrual impurity to create a strong barrier between the non-Jewish and "bad" Jewish woman and any "upright" Jewish man who might seek her as a mate. Yet sexual avoidance of religious undesirables was only a small part of the equation. Fear of becoming polluted through close physical proximity (within spitting range) would have inhibited sociability and discussion between opposing religious groups.[57] Depending on the date of a given text, *niddah* in particular would have elicited images of sinfulness, physical deformity, disease, and isolation from holy space and people. Nor did the accusation have to be limited to women or even people.[58] Drawing from Leviticus 18, *Midrash Tanḥuma'* states that all idolaters are *benei niddot* (sons of menstruating women) and *sheqeẓ* (abomination) because they do not keep away from their menstruating wives.[59]

Ben niddah became one of the standard derogatory names for Jesus in the *Toledot Yesu,* Hebrew anti-Gospels, and other medieval Jewish texts.[60] According to the *Toledot,* Miriam, Jesus' mother, is tricked by an evil neighbor into thinking that the man is her husband and is forced to have intercourse with him while menstruating, making her son, Jesus, a *ben niddah.*[61] The ignominy of Jesus' origins is uncovered, so the story goes, by his brazen and disrespectful nature and is confirmed by further inquiries about his parentage.[62] The connection between the bad behavior of Jesus and his being conceived in nonhalachic circumstances strongly resembles the *Baraita de Niddah*, which tied moral deformity (inability to study and obey Torah) to intercourse with a menstruant.[63]

In depicting Jesus as the son of a menstruating woman, the writers of the *Toledot* were not only associating him with an egregious impurity, they were painting him as one whose nature was morally flawed. That he attempted to lead the people of Israel astray and practiced magic was not surprising, considering that he was conceived by adultery while his mother was menstruating. Anyone who would follow such a person was sadly deceived at best. At worst, they were idolatrous worshipers of an impure sorcerer. By making the founder and "god" of Christianity a *ben niddah,* by extension the entire religion was impure and iniquitous even as the sinful, biblical Israel of Lamentations was "filthy" (*niddah*). These negative epithets served as a "renaming" much like the renaming of Pagan temples described in 'Avodah Zarah. An exact parallel to this process exists in the second example of a *Toledot Yesu* text that the editor Samuel Krauss provides. Throughout that text Jesus is called "the bastard."[64] In the talmudic tradition the biblical characters Balaam and Gehazi are euphemisms or prototypes for Jesus.[65] Neither of these figures has a positive connotation in the Bible; Balaam was a Moabite prophet who attempted to curse Israel, and Gehazi was the servant of the prophet Elisha who cursed Gehazi with leprosy for his greed and disobedience.[66] By establishing a set of alternate, derogatory names for Jesus, all of which had extended defamatory stories attached to them, the Jewish polemicists created a chain of associations about Christianity and its founder that prevented either of the two from being viewed neutrally by a Jewish audience.[67] Only a few key words would have been needed to remind listeners and readers of the lengthy and damning context from which they sprang and why Christianity, Paganism, or other types of Judaism were to be avoided. The obscurity of some of the epithets had the added benefit of being able to hide insults to outsiders while allowing the Jew to express his contempt even when it might be politically dangerous to do so.[68]

The impurities that functioned as polemical tools in these Jewish texts are the same substances and processes that Pagans, Jews, and Christians found disturbing and undesirable about the human body and antithetical to divinity. Jews were drawing from a preexistent impurity system that already designated these substances as polluting. However, the broad, non-Jewish, cultural discomfort with which these substances and processes were regarded may well have combined with Jews' sense of the importance of ritual purity to push Jewish invective against undesirables to emphasize certain bodily functions and food. This possibility is strengthened by the evidence for similar attitudes toward bodily corruption and effluvia among many Jews, even rabbinic Jews, Pagans, and Christians. In the Jewish polemic no one form of pollution was favored over another, though the choice of a certain kind of uncleanness evoked a very specific set of associations. Also, Jews sometimes played with the degrees of severity of individual sorts of pollution to augment the insult, as in the case of Mishnah 'Avodah Zarah 3.7 or *Midrash Rabbah Leviticus* 13:5 and 15:9.

Pagan, Christian, and Manichaean Polemic: The Filth of the Incarnation

Pagans, Christians, and Manichaeans used impurity and bodily effluvia to attack their opponents, but their tone differs from that of Jews. They frequently took pains not only to label their adversaries as impure but also to describe their filth in detail. Furthermore, much of this polemic centered on the problems of incarnation:

> And with the spittle and clay he (Christ) fashioned the missing member and bestowed it on the blind man, as upon Adam, by the command of his Godhead and the spittle of his humanity—and once again by the clay. For all things were in him in their fullness; suffering in his flesh, impassibility in his Godhead, until he arose from the dead, never again to suffer, to "die no more."[69]

Such was Epiphanius's retort to those who attempted to alter or separate the human Jesus from the divine Christ. The impulse to do so was widespread, common to nearly all the early theological schisms and debates within both Christian and Pagan circles, for as Jaroslav Pelikan has indicated, Christians inherited the Pagan philosophical notion that God was impassible, meaning that God desired nothing, needed nothing physically or emotionally, and suffered neither change nor pain. Thus many of the doctrinal disagreements within the Church revolved around differing views of how to reconcile the biblical story of God's suffering in the person of Christ and the firmly held belief that God was above suffering.[70] By using spittle to symbolize the humanity of Christ,

Epiphanius struck at the crux of what late antique writers found disturbing about the doctrine of the incarnation: human effluvia and bodily needs. These imperfections, it was felt, were unworthy of divinity.

Especially unworthy were the impure fluids in and around the womb. For Pagans, Manichaeans, and many Christian groups of late antiquity, the most offensive aspect of the Christian doctrine of the incarnation was the contact between divinity and the virgin Mary's womb, pushing various groups to argue that any kind of body, even a physical body, would have been a more acceptable receptacle for God than one derived from the blood of a woman's uterus. That God associated with the substances of female reproduction and human elimination was horrendous to imagine. Arnobius, for example, evoked the "unclean outpouring" of the animal birthing process that the gods, if really born, must have undergone, identified coition not simply as an activity of animals, but of "unclean" animals (*quadrapedum inmundorum*), and then spelled out the consequences of female gods possessing reproductive organs.[71] This latter tactic must have been especially shocking to both Pagan and Christian readers because of the ritual impurity of menstruating and postpartum women.[72] Thus to say that the gods themselves were subject to these bodily functions was to make the very source of holiness polluted. Arnobius's argument against Jupiter's adulterous liaisons is based on disgust for the physical, human body, particularly those "lower functions" that Plato and Galen had designated as inimical to philosophy.

> This abuse you give him [Jupiter] could perhaps be borne with were you to couple him with persons of equal rank and if you made out that he had committed adultery with the immortal goddesses. But I ask, what beauty was there, what charm in human bodies which could arouse, which could captivate the eyes of Jupiter? Skin, flesh, phlegm, and all the filth encased in the intestines—at which not only Lynceus of the piercing gaze could shudder, but the very thought of which any other might try to shun.[73]

While several traits of the physical body are mentioned as reasons Jupiter would be repelled by intercourse with a human woman, the intestines are singled out for opprobrium. The language of Arnobius's text, in which the abdominal organs are filthy and sex is the occupation of unclean creatures, was designed to provoke revulsion and contempt for the bodies of the gods, much as Jewish writers' efforts to link idols, Pagans, and "bad" Jews to impure animals, menstruation, and excrement were intended to belittle the beliefs of opponents. Associating gods with the transient, limited body of a human being was insufficient as a polemical stance. Arnobius divorced the Roman gods from any semblance of divinity in the most effective, radical manner possible by suggesting they were subject to or mingled with the digestive and generative processes. The power of his polemic to horrify and repel depended on the web of associations that linked the womb and the intestines to decay and the lower, animal aspects of the human body in contrast to the upper, "divine" functions.

The very arguments that Arnobius and his colleague Minucius Felix (third century C.E.) directed against Pagan theology were turned against Jesus by the Pagans. That divinity should descend into a human body was, for Celsus (fl. ca. 180 C.E.), to go from goodness to evil, from beauty to ugliness.[74] However, Celsus's statement did not refer to the soul's descent from God or to adulterous liaisons of Greek and Roman gods with humans but rather to the incarnation of God in the person of Jesus. He viewed evil as inherent in matter ('υλη) and argued that Jesus could not have resurrected bodily because "God could not have taken back his spirit once it had been polluted by the nature of the body."[75] Occupying the womb of a woman was especially objectionable to Celsus and other Pagans hostile to Christianity, even when they were willing to overlook other polluting smells and effluvia and imagine that God might occupy a body of some sort.[76] Porphyry (225–305) argued that it made more sense to believe that gods dwelled in images than in a woman's womb:

> If, however, a Greek were so stupid to think that the gods dwelt in images, still his reasoning would have been clearer than that of one who believes that the divine essence came into the body of the virgin Mary, became an embryo, was born and wrapped in swaddling clothes and was made filthy by the blood of the choron and bile and even worse things.[77]

Suggestions that God would have done better to avoid the embryonic stage in favor of assuming an adult human or angelic body or the form of a statue are related conceptually to the attempt in Cicero to give the gods a body or form that was essentially different from that of human beings.[78] Again the human body is seen as undesirable and incompatible with divine status. Yet Porphyry's detailed description of how the womb's filthy contents would soil the god-child indicates that a woman's innards were a particularly potent source of the human pollution and dirt from which Pagan authors were eager to distance their gods.[79] For the same reasons that Arnobius's graphic descriptions of gods becoming pregnant or being born would have been shocking, so too was the Christian doctrine of the incarnation. Both cases involved bringing divinity into close contact with a substance that was not only poisonous and impure but also epitomized matter and decay, the very opposite of divinity.

Christians had to tread warily in acknowledging the humanity of Christ. Origen criticized the Epicureans and the Stoics because they maintained that the gods had bodily form, thus making God subject to corruptibility.[80] When speaking of the Christian doctrine of the incarnation, Origen was careful to distance the divine Logos from the experiences of the human body and soul of Jesus.[81] Although Origen was unwilling to allow Jesus anything less than a completely human body, born of a woman, he had no qualms suggesting that Jesus' body was a worthier vessel for God's Logos than any other body, because it was created from a virgin rather than in the normal fashion.[82] By insisting on the special status of Mary's body, Origen attempted to mitigate Celsus's objections to the womb as an unworthy dwelling place for divinity. God became flesh but only up to a point. Athanasius, like Origen, attempted to distance Jesus from any pollution derived from Mary's womb, or physical suffering.[83]

Other writers or groups, both Christian and non-Christian, reacted much more radically than did Athanasius or Origen. Each had its peculiar way of dealing with the common cultural unease surrounding mingling the divine with the human. Even a limited survey of the numerous apologetic works available from this period provides ample evidence that horror of the dirty, impure, human body, which the human womb was often seen as epitomizing, was a major factor in the various doctrinal disputes.

Excommunicated for his teachings in 144, Marcion caused considerable turmoil within the Church by denying that the creator God presented in the Old Testament was good. Christ represented a new revelation from the good, divine force. Marriage and reproduction were especially heinous in Marcion's view.[84] Unlike many other Gnostic Christian groups, Marcion maintained that a divine Christ took a real, human body, suffered, was crucified, and rose again. Christ's human body did not, however, come from a woman's womb. Tertullian (160–220), in his *Adversus Marcionem,* asked Marcion how being in the womb and being born was less dignified for Christ than his horrible sufferings and execution.

> Clearly you have rejected the lie of birth: but the flesh itself you have made known as real. Evidently the real birth of God is the worst of depravities. . . . So speak at length about that most blessed and revered work of nature; to inveigh against everything that you are; destroy the origin of the flesh and soul; call filth the uterus, the workshop for the production of such an animal as man; and persecute the impure and shameful torments of birthing and on that following it: dirty, anguishing, ludicrous results. However, when you have destroyed all of that [which] you confirm as unworthy of God, will birth be more unworthy than death, infancy than crucifixion, nature than punishment, flesh than damnation?. . . If Christ truly endured these things, to have been born was less [than these things]. If he endured duplicitously, as a phantom, he could have been born duplicitously. . . . If he was truth, he was flesh; if he was flesh, he was born.[85]

In another work dedicated solely to disputing heretical views of the incarnation we find a parallel passage in which the author describes at length the unpleasant substances and undignified activities associated with birth and infancy.[86] The focus of Marcion's reformulation indicates that the cultural aversion against associating divinity with the human womb had disturbed certain Christians sufficiently to provoke a radical change in doctrine to accommodate the objections. Marcion's willingness to grant God-as-Jesus a physical body capable of suffering shows that of all the aspects of human existence, being in a womb and infancy were the most hideous to him. Like the Pagan and then Jewish polemicists, Marcion's rebellion against associating divinity with the womb was based on the sentiment that the womb was both filthy and impure.[87] Marcion, like Celsus and Porphyry, felt that the Christian God would have been better off creating or taking a body from some other substance than the human flesh that develops in a woman's womb. In the *Adversus Marcionem,* Tertullian insisted that the flesh of angels could not be equated with the flesh of man and that with angelic flesh Jesus could not have died. By granting Jesus a superior, less human body, Marcion sought to make the incarnation more palatable, even as Celsus was to suggest later in the century. Furthermore, for Marcion and others, life in the womb was even worse due to the proximity to human waste. In the *Adversus Marcionen* Tertullian asked, "If he [Christ] despised it [the flesh] as terrestrial and, as you say, stuffed with excrement, why was he not therefore ashamed of his simulacrum?"[88]

As portrayed by Tertullian, Marcion may not have been quite as graphic as Arnobius, but his sentiments were similar. Evocations of excrement and blood from the womb in connection with God-as-Jesus served to remind the audience that to accept what became the orthodox Christian view of the incarnation meant to bathe God in those substances that were least worthy of divinity. Jews underlined the degrees of ritual impurity of their opponents and their opponents' gods, and Jews, Christians, and Pagans alike used parturient and menstrual blood and excrement to denigrate the beliefs of those with whom they disagreed. Christians, and Pagans, lacking the stratified purity system of the Jews, relied on the power of graphic description to create a barrier of disgust in their audiences, even as Tertullian, in his attempt to counter Marcion, attempted to turn that same vivid picture of human waste into a testimony of the humility and love for humanity of God-as-Jesus.

For Valentinius and other Gnostics, there was no question of any part of the divinity being embodied in human flesh; matter was generally believed to have been created by the evil demiurge. According to Epiphanius, the Valentinians maintained that "he (Christ) has brought his body down from above and passed through the Virgin Mary like water through a pipe. He has taken nothing from the virgin womb, but he has taken his body from above."[89] Evidently Valentinius and his disciples felt that if Jesus was not conceived by the usual sexual act, it was not possible for Mary to have had a normal, human infant.[90] Valentinius argued either that Christ passed through Mary or that he only temporarily came into contact with matter and the weaknesses and sufferings having a physical body entailed.[91] The contents of the womb, the source of flesh and its dreaded weaknesses, had to remain untouched.

Mani (ca. 216–276), a native of Parthian Mesopotamia, founded Manichaeism, which, though based in part on Christianity, was a distinct religion. He and many of his followers were part of the same culture as the various Pagans, Christians, and eventually Jews who punctuated their religious debates with images of dirty wombs, excrement, and polluting smells that drove away the gods.[92]

Two Christs may be distinguished in the Manichaean system. The first, the "savior" Christ who descended to teach men how they might free the spark of divinity from the prison of matter, did not take a body. The second, the "suffering" Christ or Jesus, is a more ambiguous figure who is the divine spark in the world who suffers as a result of its imprisonment.[93] Usually the "historical" Jesus was associated with the first Christ, who only appeared to struggle and die on the cross.[94] However, in the crucifixion, occasionally the two seem to be intermingled, and Christ's death on the cross was described as having a salvific effect even as it did in Christian texts.[95] Yet even when Faustus, Augustine of Hippo's Manichaean nemesis, came close to suggesting that a bodily and divine Jesus might have been combined, he was careful to avoid incarnation in the womb. He argued that it was "an injurious misrepresentation on your [Augustine's] part to speak of this writer [the Gospel writer Matthew] as making the Son of God the inmate of a womb."[96] Faustus sought in this passage to distance divinity from the womb. By reinterpreting the Gospel story, Faustus strengthened his case against the incarnation by demonstrating that even according to Christian Scripture God did not occupy a womb. Christians who thought otherwise committed a horrible slander against God.

In truth, Faustus desired to bypass the human body altogether, much as Marcion and Celsus did before him. Augustine cited Faustus as saying, "The Holy Spirit by his influence and spiritual infusion, makes the earth conceive and bring forth a mortal Jesus, who, as hanging from every tree is the life and salvation of men."[97] Seemingly any material substance was preferable to that gained from a woman's womb. How strongly Manichaeans felt about the womb is apparent from a letter by Mani to the Christian bishop, Marcelius: "And would that . . . they did not say that the Only-begotten, the Christ who has descended from the bosom of the Father, was the son of a woman, Mary, born of blood and flesh and women's ill-smelling effluent!"[98]

This theme is repeated in a variety of Manichaean psalms.[99] In all the passages the womb is a place of pollution or dirt. Mani's letter is the most explicit, as it specifically designates the fluids in the womb as a source of his rejection of the incarnation and describes them as "ill-smelling." Given the symbolism assigned to odor in Manichaean texts, calling women's effluvia "ill-smelling" was not simply an expression of disgust but also a designation of evil. Human effluvia of any kind was the constant reminder of the body's irrevocable defilement. Thus, in accusing Christians of conceiving of God/Light-as-Jesus as an inhabitant of a womb, dwelling amid its fluids, which were by definition impure and foul smelling, Mani and his followers reproached Christians for associating the Son of Light with the essence of evil. Reminding Christians of the practical consequences of the doctrine of the incarnation was intended to disgust and repulse them from continuing in their faith, much as Arnobius sought to repel Pagans and Christians by his vivid enumeration of the Pagan gods' bodily functions.

Mani, Arnobius, and others' polemic based on the woman's body derived its power from the shared cultural view of the womb and its blood as unclean and closely related to matter (as opposed to spirituality) and waste. However, menstrual and parturient blood was not the only weapon in late antique rhetoric of disgust. Speaking against the Elchasaite practice of washing food in order to purify it, Mani said:

> [T]his body is defiled and molded from a mold of defilement. You can see how, whenever someone cleanses his food and partakes of that (food) which has just been washed, it seems to us that from it still comes blood and bile and flatulence and excrements of shame and the defilement of the body.[100]

Likewise, people's need to pass waste proved that ritual baptisms failed to purify.[101] For Mani—as for the Pagan philosophers, Christian writers, and rabbis discussed in chapter 1—the often-smelly liquids and gases produced by the body marked it as antithetical to spirit and light. Here, however, the digestive system and the womb, as prime vessel of bodily fluids generally recognized as dirty and often polluting, has become a tool for Manichaean anti-Christian polemic. Christians not only believed something unworthy of God, but they also actively "cast" the son of God into a "filthy womb."[102]

What better way to battle filth than with more filth? Epiphanius and Augustine ingeniously turned the Manichaean preference for aspects of the natural world, because they were supposedly more pure than animal (including human) flesh, into an occasion for depicting Mani and his followers as eaters of dirt. At the hands of Epiphanius the water Mani posited as more pure than the defecating humans who washed in it became the very effluvia Mani despised as defiling. Mani, known for his ascetic eating habits, becomes a glutton, so driven by the despised body that he drinks a dirty fluid, sweat.[103] Augustine, in his turn, argued that fruit must be unclean because it is fertilized by manure. In an attack on Manichaean vegetarianism, Augustine posed the following riddle: "Flesh is nourished by the productions of the earth, not by its excrements; while the earth is nourished by the excrements of the flesh, not by its productions. Let them say which is cleaner."[104] In this scheme, eating the products of the earth rather than flesh brought the diner one step closer to excrement. Using the same reasoning, the Manichaean Jesus could be attacked as most foully impure, since he was a product of the earth and was contained in its fruits. This "fruit" was nourished by manure and waste from the cities, which in Augustine's estimation was filthier than anything in a virgin's womb.[105] The pure earth is transformed into a *cloacam,* and the divine Jesus comes into close contact with, or worse, is the product of human waste. In avoiding the womb to seek a purer substance for the divine body, Mani/Faustus suggested an alternative that, in the able hands of Augustine, was made to seem infinitely more dirty.

Thus "orthodox" Christians, Manichaeans, gnostic Christians, and Pagans evoked detailed, visceral descriptions of excrement and female genitalia in debates about the incarnation of God-as-Jesus in the Christian doctrine, or of the Pagan gods in their bodily forms assigned to them by mythological traditions. Some polemicists such as Origen and Athanasius did so merely to present arguments distancing God-as-Jesus from the womb's pollution. Others defending the doctrine of the incarnation, such as Augustine of Hippo or Tertullian, often attempted to turn this rhetoric against those seeking to dispute it. Augustine depicted the Manichaean understanding of divinity as miring God ín more "dirt" even than the Christian system. For Tertullian, that God was willing to endure such indignities was a testimony of his Love. However, Tertullian also reminded Marcion that Marcion himself had his origins in the "filth" of the womb, thus subtly distancing him from holiness.[106] The authors of active imputations of association with bodily filth, either on the part of the divinity in question or on the part of the believers themselves, all sought to create a barrier of revulsion between contesting belief systems based on shared beliefs about foul smell, excrement, and women's genital blood. While Pagan, Christian, and Manichaean polemic focused primarily on the issue of the *polluting* role of the womb and intestines in the incarnation, it called on the same emotions and values as Jewish accusations of menstrual or bestial impurity or juxtapositions of Pagan holy places to privies.

Later Polemic

Internal Christian Debates

Conjoining divinity to humanity, with its sufferings, corruptibility, and weaknesses, continued to be a major point of contention between Christian groups. By the fifth century, however, the rhetoric began to change. Attacks using lengthy evocations of human filth ceased against any theology perceived as involving a true melding of man and God. This change is noticeable not only in Nestorian, Monophysite, Monothelite, and Orthodox polemic but also in later polemic addressing Manichaeans, and groups perceived to be like them, which had been associated or targeted with visceral imagery of the womb.[107] Evocations of impurity and filth in contexts other than debates over the incarnation occur, however, in early medieval refutations of Paulicians and Bogomils, commonly identified as "Manichaeans" by Eastern Christian authors.[108]

Like earlier authors, Peter of Sicily (ninth century) accused his adversaries of general impurity and extreme sexual misconduct, including intercourse with menstruating women.[109] Christian authors from the fifth to the tenth centuries frequently labeled those whom they deemed heretical as "impure" or "filthy," yet such epithets became a standard refrain, without the detail common to previous texts.[110] Similar evocations of impurity, vomiting, or stench occur in eleventh-century antiheretical texts from the Latin West.[111] Occasionally authors indulged in more colorful analogies involving corruption or undesirable animals. Cosmas the Priest, writing near the end of the tenth century, compared the Bogomils in Bulgaria to pigs:

> As for us, let us leave them to go their own way to perdition; you can correct an animal more quickly than a heretic. The pig turns from the pearl to gather excrement; similarly heretics stuff themselves with their filth and distance themselves from divine teaching.[112]

In another tenth-century text attacking the Bogomils, Theophylact Lecapenus (933–56) likened impenitent heretics to gangrenous limbs, and in Euthymius of the Periblepton (ca. 1045), a certain Peter is proven a heretic rather than a saint because his body, instead of exuding a sweet smell at death as a saint's body should, had become that of a wolf.[113] These accusations, whether passing assignations of impurity or detailed analogies of heretics and dirty animals or diseases, were intended to mark religious dissidents and their belief systems as repugnant, even as they did in early Pagan, Jewish, Christian, and Manichaean polemic. Much of the somatic symbolism is the same. Pigs continued to be linked with excrement and wrong belief. Freedom from rot, whether as decay in the grave or as a gangrenous disease, still served as a determinant of holiness. Smell is implicit or explicit in all these images, for excrement-eating pigs, decomposition, and gangrene all evoke stench and its concomitant associations with evil.

Heretics, and even occasionally Jews, were depicted as attacking orthodox Christians in a similar manner. A number of chronicles and tracts describe Bogomils treating Christian baptism as a form of pollution.[114] Tales of heretics or Jews defecating or urinating in churches or on holy objects served to outrage the Christian readership by underlining their profound contempt and animosity for those things that Christians held to be the most clean and holy. These stories also marked heretics and Jews as sources of filth. Cases in which heretics or Jews converted reaffirmed Christian belief in the divine protective power of Christian symbols.[115] If "Manichaeans" or Jews in fact treated Christian rituals or objects as impure or actively desecrated Christian places of worship, then these acts would have been expressions of resistance against the dominant faith.[116] By actively polluting or attacking Christian sacred places or objects, or treating Christian ritual as defiling, religious minorities created a barrier of miasma and scorn between themselves and conversion to the Christian faith. These acts also would have vented feelings of anger at Christian persecution.

While much of the symbolism in these later texts and in the pre–fifth century sources is the same, the woman's womb and human viscera no longer occupy a central place in the polemic of impurity and filth. This change suggests that horror of human organs and feminine effluvia was no longer a key strategy for denigrating religious opponents or refuting Christological beliefs, at least in these intra-Christian debates. Regarding the Christological debates, authors of all theological dispositions were inclined to deny that divinity had suffered any of the indignities and impurities concomitant with incarnation, including those associated with birth and infancy.[117] When refuting Pagans who were clearly disturbed by Christ's birth and infancy, Nestorius described the problem but did not revel in vivid verbal depictions of human effluvia:

> When, therefore, O Pagan, you hear of the infant, placed in a manger, wrapped in swaddling clothes, do not take offense at the flesh which is seen, but ponder the dignity of that infant. Ponder the mother begetting by the divinity which bore itself, one formed by the humanity in her, and that which she by divine action formed one wrapped in swaddling clothes according to the flesh, but containing all things by the providence of the divinity, suckling according to the nature of the body, but by the divinity furnishing richly to all who are born the nourishment of milk.[118]

Humanity and divinity are carefully separated here and throughout Nestorius's work. Indeed, Nestorius's primary objections to Cyril and all those who advocated using the title "Theotokos" was that they attributed suffering to God.[119] Cyril himself took pains to argue that the Word really took on flesh, paradoxically mixing humanity and divinity, but that the immutable nature of the divinity was not thereby diminished.[120] Although he mentions the weaknesses of the body, he attributes no graphic language to his opponents, nor does he use any in his refutations, even when describing the role of the Virgin's body in the incarnation process.[121]

Occasionally the profound purity of Mary's virginal flesh is emphasized as a way to demonstrate her worthiness as a vessel for the Christ against those who impugned her special status.[122] Severus of Antioch (465–538) felt compelled to argue against those who maintained that Christ in fact drew his body from his mother's blood, as did other human children according to contemporary medical theory.[123] The need of Severus and other authors such as Leontius of Byzantium (ca. 485–543) to defend the special purity of Mary's flesh suggests that some individuals in Severus's own time were troubled by contact between and even mixture of divinity with a womb's blood. In contrast to authors before the fourth century, however, these writers refrained from reminding their readers of the womb's proximity to the intestines and their contents, or of the impure blood contained within the womb. Peter of Sicily, who had been quite willing to evoke impurity against heretics in a general way, did not resort to lengthy descriptions of the uncleanness of human organs either in reference to "Manichaeans" (Paulicians') critiques of Christianity or as a method of refuting the Manichaeans, despite the importance of the joining of Jesus' humanity and divinity in these debates.[124] Thus from the fifth century onward, although Christians in Greece and the Middle East regarded an absolute mingling of divinity with the body's passions, suffering, and corruptibility as unacceptable, the polluting qualities of the human body in general or of Mary's womb in particular no longer had a central role in polemicists' rhetoric against other Christians.

There are a number of possible explanations for this shift. Not all Christian polemicists writing before the fifth century engaged in somatic-based polemic designed to repulse their readers. For example, Novatian's (210–280) *Treatise on the Trinity* uses very mild language, although Novatian was very much concerned to defend both Christ's humanity and his divinity.[125] Ephrem the Syrian (ca. 306–373) wrote against Manichaeans and "gnostíc" Christians without detailing their revulsion for human organs.[126] Perhaps later polemicists simply preferred to continue in this milder tradition of disputation rather than the more vituperative, corporeal strain.

Further, the shift may lie in changing attitudes to the body. Averil Cameron has posited that after the fourth century Byzantine Christians, in contrast to Christians in the Latin West, "were more interested in defining the subtleties of heresy than in discussing female sexual organs and reproduction as such."[127] The onus of Western preoccupation with the physical details of sexuality and their negative evaluation, according to Cameron, lies with Augustine and the medieval scholastics who drew from him.[128] Certainly the lack of evocations of effluvia and bodily organs in later, Eastern Christian polemical writings supports Cameron's assertions. Contemporary Latin writers, unlike their Greek- and Syriac-speaking counterparts, continued to use the body and filth in their theological discussions. Hildefonsis of Toledo (d. 667) argued against those who maintained that God was soiled by the generation process in terms reminiscent of Augustine:

> [Those] who think this [that God was soiled by the generation process] ought to consider therefore, the rays of the sun which they certainly do not praise as a creation of God but adore as God, diffused everywhere through the stench of sewers and everything else horrible, and to work on these according to its nature, yet is not therefore sullied by any contamination, although visible light is by nature more conjoined with visible filth. How much less therefore could the incorporeal, invisible word of God be polluted by the chaste, most pure and singularly glorious female body . . . ?[129]

Like Tertullian, Augustine, and Epiphanius, Hildefonsis graphically describes the filth with which his opponents' own "god" (the sun) may associate. If the sun's rays are not polluted by sewage and other earthly dirt, then neither can God's Word be rendered unclean by a woman's womb. Despite Hildefonsis's protestations about the purity of Mary's body, the passage creates a parallel not only between God's word and the rays of the sun but also between the womb and sewers, indicating that the late antique vision of the womb as a place of filth had been incorporated into early medieval, Western thought.[130]

According to Leo Scheffczyk, Hildefonsis along with other fifth- to ninth-century European theologians drew attention to Mary's humanity and, by association, Jesus' as a way to counter the Priscillian and Arian heresies, among others.[131] Both Paschasius Radbertus (d. ca. 865) and Ratramnus of Corbie (d. after 868) described the bodily functions of the pregnant Mary in considerable detail, as did many of the later authors whose sermons came to be attributed to Hildefonsis.[132] Ratramnus did so in order to refute those who maintained that it was "unseemly that the son of God proceeded through the womb."[133] Radbertus, on the other hand, was eager to demonstrate that God-as-Jesus was in no way contaminated by dwelling in a woman's womb. Sin through sexual passion was one form of pollution (from which Mary was completely free, according to Radbertus); however, Radbertus also addressed the possibility of physical uncleanness.[134] Both borrowed from *Contra Helvidius* by Jerome (340–420), who drew from Tertullian and Origen.[135] Thus Ratramnus and Radbertus were familiar with some late antique somatic-oriented polemic and found its images applicable to their own theological battles in ways that fifth- to ninth-century Christian writers in Greece, Syria, and Asia Minor did not. Hildefonsis, Radbertus, and Ratramnus defended the Virgin's womb as a place of divine habitation, yet the need to do so indicates that a noticeable number of Christians in the Latin West were uncomfortable with this aspect of Christian doctrine, much as Manichaeans and various Christian groups in late antiquity had been. That Mary's potentially unclean viscera were central to the defense by Ratramnus, Radbertus, and Hildefonsis of Jesus' human birth supports Cameron's contention that early medieval Latins retained the patristic abhorrence of the body, especially the female body, whereas Byzantine Christians did not.

A bifurcation of Eastern and Western attitudes to the female body would go a long way toward explaining the shifting tone of Christian internal polemic from the fifth century onward. Eastern Christians, less interested in or repelled by human physicality, ceased to focus on bodily fluids as a problem in the doctrine of the incarnation. Rather, they emphasized suffering and ignorance as logical contradictions to an all-powerful, all-knowing divinity. By contrast, Latin-speaking Christians continued to be disturbed by or to defend the juxtaposition of pure divinity with filthy humanity. As a result, graphic evocations of Mary's blood and excrement persisted in early medieval Latin texts. Early evidence of Western Christian preoccupation with the corruption or purity of Mary's womb also sets the stage for later medieval polemic between Jews and Christians in which the contents of Mary's womb become a contentious issue. The number of manuscripts from the twelfth and thirteenth centuries that contain the works of Hildefonsis and Pseudo-Hildefonsis (including those of Radbertus) on Mary indicates that these authors' visions of the relationship between the human body and divinity in the person of the Virgin continued to influence Christians precisely at the period in which the humanity of Jesus and devotion to Mary was being reformulated and given a central place not only in Christian piety but also in Jewish-Christian debates.[136] However, other factors need to be considered when explaining the shift in Eastern Christian polemic about the incarnation.

Christians from the fifth century onward agreed on such basic premises as the impassibility of God; they merely had to decide *how* humanity and divinity mingled in the person of Jesus without subjecting divinity to the weaknesses of human existence. The fundamental assumptions and their implications no longer needed explanation, so that when one theologian referred to Jesus being in the womb of Mary, being an infant, or suffering, any other theologian would have known and accepted that the womb or intestines' filth or corporeal disintegration were part of the "problem."

The respective audience and position of Christianity before and after the fifth century also may have contributed to the intensity of somatic polemic in early Christianity and its relative decline starting in the fifth century. Between the first and the third centuries, Christianity was not an established, accepted religion, nor did it have a well-developed hierarchy of leaders with the power to decide and enforce orthodoxy. Constantine's conversion to Christianity in 312 C.E. was a turning point in Christian history. However, with the political and theological struggles between the orthodox and Arian churches and the brief return to Paganism under Julian, the fourth century was an unstable period for the Church. Because Christianity was struggling both to define itself and to survive in the face of outside pressures, authors wrote polemic that not only set forth the doctrinal issues but also was intended to evoke strong negative emotional reactions, thus appealing to their readers or hearers on theological and emotional levels. Graphic bodily imagery satisfied the second of these two. However, by the fifth century Christianity had been confirmed as the official religion of the empire, Paganism was on the defensive, and the Church had had time to consolidate its structure of authority. As pressures on the Church lessened, so too did the vituperative tone of polemic; Christian leaders had other institutional means with which to pressure Pagans and "heretical" coreligionists into conformity rather than having to rely exclusively on written or verbal arguments.

The tone of Christian anti-Paulician and anti-Bogomil polemic can be explained in part by the level of perceived threat. Paulicians were from Armenia primarily, a land that alternated between self-rule and Byzantine, Persian, and, later, Muslim domination. Even when functioning as an independent state, Armenia was constantly having to strike a balance between Persian and Byzantine influences and political ties. Often persecuted as heretics by the Byzantines, the Paulicians aroused further animosity because they occasionally allied with Byzantium's enemies, such as the Muslims. The Paulicians were also on the wrong side of the iconoclastic controversy. Partially tolerated by Emperor Leo III (717–741), who like the Paulicians strongly opposed the veneration of icons, the Paulicians were persecuted again once the iconophiles regained power.[137] That this heretical group was foreign and thus often beyond the control of the Byzantine church, was a potential ally of the church's enemies, and was evidently successful in its missionizing attempts combined to make it seem especially threatening. Thus the language used against it was harsher than that found in the debates between Nestorians, Monophysites, and Monothelites.

Bogomilism arose in Bulgaria during a period in which Christianity was just beginning to be reestablished after an influx of mostly Pagan Slavs and Bulgars.[138] Thus when Cosmas the Priest was writing in Bulgaria in the tenth century, the level of competition between orthodox Christianity, Bogomilism, and Paganism was similar to that which existed between the various interpretations of Christianity, Manichaeanism, and Paganism in late antiquity. Political strife in Bulgaria and Byzantium's eventual annexation of Bulgaria allowed Bogomils to spread unchecked so that in the eleventh century, when Euthymius of the Periblepton encountered them in Constantinople, their numbers and their appeal must have seemed threatening indeed.[139] To answer this threat, polemicists writing against the Bogomils, like those writing against the Paulicians, resorted to the language that would provoke disgust in their audience.

Thus the changed tone of eastern Mediterranean Christian internal polemic during the fifth to the ninth century may be attributed to a number of causes: the increasing disinterest in bodily imagery relative to theological and philosophical issues; the lessening of governmental pressures on Christians and the stronger Church hierarchies that provided other avenues by which to encourage dissenting Christian groups to convey; and finally the widespread familiarity among Christian writers of the problems of the incarnation, which made detailing the bodily functions involved unnecessary.

Jewish and Muslim Polemic against Christianity and the Christian Response

With the arríval of Islam in the seventh century, Christians were faced with a new and powerful religious and political opponent. Jews and non-Orthodox Christian groups had reason to welcome the Muslim conquest since it relieved them of persecution from the Orthodox majority. Under Islamic rule, Jews and non-Orthodox Christian groups were *dhimmi,* tolerated but subordinate religious minorities subject to a variety of special taxes and dress and worship codes; nevertheless, many regarded this state of affairs as an improvement over Byzantine rule. For Orthodox Christians in Muslim territory the conquest was more traumatic: they were suddenly subject to religious restrictions and strong pressures to convert.[140] This unaccustomed state of affairs was disturbing also because it violated one of their prime "proofs" of religious superiority, namely, that military and political dominance was a sign of God's favor.[141] Muslims, eager to gain converts, cultivated the philosophical dialectic of their Christian subjects and drew from iconoclastic and anti-Manichaean polemic and trinitarian debates between Nestorians, Jacobites, and Orthodox Christians.[142] 'Abbasid rulers actively encouraged the study and translation of classical learning into Arabic and sponsored religious debates.[143] Muslim interest in converting Christians using Christians' own style of disputation, the defensive position in which Orthodox Christians found themselves, and the freedom of expression open to the formerly suppressed minorities such as the Jews and non-Orthodox Christians in many ways paralleled the religious and political milieu in which late antique corporeal polemic flourished. Given the themes that Muslim anti-Christian polemicists chose, Muslim investigation of classical learning and interest in religious disputation seem to have included older styles of invective in which the womb and the need to eat and excrete were central modes of attack. Jews may have transmitted these views to Muslims as well. That Islam's own laws of purity marked menstrual blood as impure and a barrier to holiness may have made such polemic especially compelling to Muslim writers.[144]

The degree to which Muslims seem to have been influenced by both Christian and Jewish polemic is apparant in some of the internal invective linking "bad Muslims" to the bodily sins of their parents. As Etan Kohlberg has shown, Shi'i traditions frequently labeled their Sunni enemies as bastards and sons of menstruating women. Individuals of such parentage were predestined to hate and fight against the "family of the Prophet," namely,

'Ali and his descendants. In one tale when the son of a Shi'i general heard of this tradition, he bragged that it could not be true because he hated 'Ali and was neither of these. Abu Dulaf al-Qasim, the boy's father, then revealed that his son was the product of the rape of his brother's menstruating concubine, thus making the youth both a bastard and the son of a menstruating woman according to Islamic law.[145] The use of these epithets, the idea that such status would damage the moral and religious inclinations of the child, and, in particular, the topos of the circumstances of a "bad" individual's conception being hidden and then later revealed as the root of their ill nature all strongly resemble the *Kallah Rabbati* and slightly later Jewish traditions about Jesus. In this instance, Muslims seem to have borrowed a theme from Jewish anti-Christian polemic and adapted it to their own needs. Similar restrictions and discomfort about menstruation and illigitimacy among Muslims, Jews, and, to a lesser extent, Christians made this mode of polemic especially appealing and powerful to Muslims, not only for Shi'i-Sunni disputes but also for Muslim anti-Christian polemic regarding the incarnation.

Christians in Byzantium and the Middle East had to defend the doctrine of the incarnation against Muslim and Jewish evocations of Mary's impure womb, the undignified squalor of infancy, the need for food and sleep, and Jesus' death.[146] Already in Sura 5:75 one of the proofs against Jesus' divinity is that he, like his mother, ate.[147] In the eighth century, John of Damascus, in his *Disputation of a Saracen and a Christian,* was the first to indicate that contact with a woman's body was particularly distasteful to Muslims, "[H]e [the Muslim] tells you, 'How did God descend into the womb of a woman?'"[148] The word *koilian* in this passage, which Sahas translates as "womb," means "belly" or "bowels" and thus alludes to intestinal imagery as well to the womb.[149] Other, slightly later polemical works written by Muslims themselves or containing Muslim critiques of the Christian doctrine of the incarnation are even more explicit. In the tenth-century *Letter to the Emir of Damascus*, which purports to be a certain Arethas's response on behalf of the Byzantine emperor to the queries of the Muslim ruler of Damascus, the author records the following objection and suggested response:

> If you [the Muslim] say, "How could the most holy God descend into the bowels of a virgin, there where there are blood and excrement?" For myself, I say to you, "How could God condescend, when he created Adam and Eve, to put his hand, to make them, on the genital organs of the man and woman?"[150]

Other texts from this period question the appropriateness of God entering a womb without enumerating the reasons for regarding it problematic.[151] Some Muslim authors also listed the needs, attributes, and failings of Jesus' own body as reason to reject the Christian doctrine of the incarnation.[152] Christians, on the other hand, sought to demonstrate that Muḥammad and his followers sought only physical, in contrast to spiritual, rewards. They insisted that Muḥammad's heaven was a licentious, obscene place, even as Muḥammad himself had been given to excessive sexual indulgence as witnessed by his multiple wives and his marriage to Zaynab, the wife of his friend.[153] The nineth-century Eulogius of Cordoba even went so far as to assert that Muḥammad intended to have sexual intercourse with the Virgin Mary once in paradise, an accusation that gave license to a string of invectives against the Prophet, all involving impurity and dirt: "impure dog," "habitation of a spirit of impurities," "filth of dirt."[154] Such tales would have been deeply repulsive to Christians for whom the highest levels of sanctity were tied to virginity, even as such name-calling would have left no doubt in their minds as to how Eulogius expected his readers to feel about Islam and its founder.

Christians, and seemingly Jews, attacked the Muslim conception of the afterlife, stating that since according to the Muslim view of paradise people ate and drank there, then Muslims' heaven was full of excrement.[155] Since the dichotomy between sweet and foul smell had cultural and religious associations in Islam similar to those in Pagan classical, Manicheaean, Christian, and Jewish circles, such an accusation belittled Muslims' paradise and also denied it any association with the divine by Muslim as well as *dhimmi* standards.[156] The Muslims retorted that rather than produce normal human waste, the believers would secrete musk-smelling sweat, the pleasant fragrance thus negating any evil or earthly connotation of heavenly digestion.[157]

The Prophet Muḥammad or Muslims themselves were often equated with pigs, or the Prophet was portrayed as rotting after his death and devoured by swine, dogs, or, in one case, vultures.[158] Since the pig and, to a lesser extent, the dog were impure or despised animals according to Islamic law, these comparisons were a profound insult to Muslims.[159] Pigs and vultures would have been associated with decay and garbage and thus repulsive, no matter their status in ritual law. To the Christians making the accusations, these details linked Muḥammad and his followers to long-standing traditions in which the worst heretics were either swine themselves or food for swine: filthy food for a filthy, decaying animal. As John Tolan has pointed out, the

Christian "antibiographies" of the Prophet Muḥammad were designed to portray him as the mirror opposite of Jesus.[160] The pong of Muḥammad's cadaver affirmed the permanence of the "pseudo"-prophet's death in contrast to Jesus' escape from decay through resurrection, even as this dichotomy between the smelly corpse (Muḥammad) and the scentless heaven-bound body (Jesus) reiterated to Christian readers the earthly, even demonic origins of Islam in contrast to their own religion.

The most graphic and lengthiest example of using corporeal disgust as polemic comes from a Jewish text written no later than the mid-tenth century. The *Qiṣṣat Mujādalat al-'Usquf,* composed in Judeo-Arabic, is the earliest systematic refutation of Christian dogma that we have by a Jewish author.[161] Its approach and arguments, though drawing on earlier Jewish anti-Christian polemic, marks a significant change. That its sole purpose was to refute Christianity is unusual enough, but it also incorporates discussions of Christian Scripture and, more important for the study at hand, filth and excrement in ways reminiscent of late antique Pagan, Christian, and Manichaean polemic. Like the Muslims, the writer objected to the view that God-as-Jesus came into contact with the contents of a woman's womb, that he was subject to emotional and physical weaknesses common to humans, and that others were able to impose their will on him. Like the Muslim texts or Christian records of Muslim objections to the incarnation, the womb's filth is emphasized: "You say: I have a God, who dwelt in the innards [of a woman], in the filth of menstrual blood and in the dark confinement of the womb [literally, "the abdomen (אלבטן)]."[162]

The word translated as "innards" (احشاء /אחשא) also means "bowels" or "intestines," thus evoking an association with excrement in the reader's mind. Menstrual blood is not characterized by its impurity but rather by its filth, *wasakh* (وسخ /וסך). More frequent is the Arabic *danas* (دنس /דנס), which seems to imply both filth in the physical sense and ritual uncleanness.[163] Sometimes this uncleanness is linked directly with menstruation, as in the passage: "you worship a god who dwelt in the womb, in the filth of menstrual blood (*dams al-ḥidah*)," where *danas* is the first term of an *'iḍāfah*; that is, it is in a construct state with *al-ḥiddah* (the menstruation).[164] Elsewhere filth is something separate from menstruation: "she [Mary] carried him [Jesus] in the confinement of the womb, in darkness, filth and menstrual blood for nine months."[165] In this second example, the author may have been expressing a general sentiment that the abdomen and the womb are dirty places, or perhaps *danas* is an allusion to human waste. The wording of the *Qiṣṣat* and the Muslim and Christian tractates that contain similar discussions indicate that the womb continued to be antithetical to divinity not only because of its ritually impure status (at least according to Muslim and Jewish law) but also because of its long-standing association with human waste and dirt.

The Jewish author of the *Qiṣṣat* delighted in reminding the reader of the human Jesus' need to eat and thus defecate and urinate. Usually this was done in the context of Jesus' infancy. However, in one instance the writer produces an argument very similar to the Christian critique of Muslims' concept of paradise:

> You claim that he has a divine and a human nature and that he ascended into heaven in both divine and human nature, the two natures being [like] perfect twins, and that he thus reclined on the throne with the Father. If this is the case, then also fear and terror, anxiety and trembling, sadness, hunger, thirst and defecation reclined on the throne since the human nature cannot be sustained without food, drink and defecation. Tell me: was he [really] in heaven, if he was partaking in food and defecating?! Woe to you because of this terrible blasphemy![166]

In the *Qiṣṣat* the pollution is twofold. Not only are the heavenly realms sullied by human waste, as in the Christian invective against Islam, but the god of the Christians is himself the source of filth. While a variety of needs and emotions are enumerated in this passage, the writer dwells on eating and excreting in the last two sentences, suggesting that of the various human frailties, these were especially objectionable.

Food was also a powerful tool of religious denigration; the choice of certain foods marked Jesus and his followers as gluttonous, foul smelling, and impure.[167] They deserved to be put to death because they did not observe the laws of the Torah: "[H]e [Jesus] caused all of you to be uncircumcised, forever impure with no possibility of cleansing yourselves of impurity. . . . He also ordered you to eat pork and to make sacrifice of bread and wine which becomes smelly dung inside your bodies."[168] Because of their failure to observe the laws of the Torah, Christians are irredeemably impure, an accusation that had been common in earlier forms of Jewish polemic against other Jews, Pagans, and heretics. That impurity derives in part from the consumption of pork, which the Jewish writer is careful to single out, recalling Jewish midrashic equations of Romans and Christians with the pig in particular.[169]

Stench points to the profound lack of holiness of Jesus, his believers, and the rituals in which they engaged, a symbol that both Christian and Jew would have understood.[170] The final sentence, "He ordered you . . . to make sacrifice of bread and wine, which becomes smelly dung inside your bodies," plays on the long-standing dichotomy between decay and stench and sanctity and fragrance. The word *muntin* (منتن/מנתן), translated as "smelly," also means "putrescent" or "rotting." Thus the Eucharist—the bread of life, the body and blood of Jesus, and, by extension, Jesus himself—becomes a decaying, dead thing, excrement and foul smelling, the very opposite of divinity. Furthermore, the Christians themselves are filled with stench and waste because of their consumption of that which they regard as holy.[171] Baptismal waters, according to the author of the *Qiṣṣat,* worked in a similar fashion. That Jesus consented to be baptized demonstrated that he was unclean and in need of purification. Indeed, baptismal waters are so foul that their odor makes birds ill and render all who submit to them impure.[172]

Like Manichaeans, Pagans, and Christians centuries before them, Muslims and Jews reminded Christians of the messy, impure, or dirty aspects of human conception and bodily existence in order to repel and thus dissuade them from their belief in the incarnation and to deter coreligionists from joining them. Jews went further by targeting cherished Christian rituals, Christian believers, and even Jesus as impure and dirty. The *Qiṣṣat* combined the polemic of ritual pollution and excrement that had been common to the rabbis and Jews of the Second Temple with the graphic descriptions of effluvia and stench that characterized Pagan, Christian, and Manichaean invective in late antiquity.[173] Christians used a similar approach in their attacks against Muslim descriptions of paradise and Muslim believers. Thus the web of negatively valued bodily states, foul smell, unspecified dirt, blood, human waste, decay, and impurity that colored religious polemic in late antiquity reemerged with the coming of Islam.

A comparison of Muslim and Christian use of somatic polemic from this period with those voiced by the author of the *Qiṣṣat* reveals a difference in degree.[174] For example, the *Qiṣṣat* targets the womb as a reason for rejecting the Christian doctrine of the incarnation at least five times in contrast to the once or twice common to Muslim and Christian texts.[175] Even given the composite nature of the document, the repetition of accusations was presumably a conscious choice on the part of the compiler and cumulatively appears harsher than any of the other polemical texts examined so far.[176] The degree of vehemence in the *Qiṣṣat* probably reflects the level of heretofore unexpressed

Jewish anger toward Christians. After the Islamic conquest Jews would have been able to express negative feelings about Christianity in ways not possible under Christian domination; the language of resistance could now be freely vented.[177]

Andalusian Muslim and Christian discussions of the incarnation follow patterns similar to those in early polemical works written elsewhere in the Muslim world. For example, Ibn Ḥazm (d. 1064) asks who took on flesh in the placenta *(mashimah)* of Mary and unified with the nature of the Messiah, the Father, or the Son. When the Christians respond the Son, Ibn Ḥazm notes that it is to avoid saying this of the Father. He continues:

> Then it is said in one of his gospels that the Word is God and became flesh. Then [that] it [the Word] was God and the Word took flesh in the placenta of Mary, so the supreme God himself took on flesh in the placenta of Mary. So on this, thus the Father, the Son, and the Word, all of them took on flesh in the placenta of Mary. And in their faith: that the Son is the one who took flesh in the placenta of Mary.[178]

Ibn Ḥazm suggests that all members of the Trinity, including the Father, the most supreme God, took on flesh from Mary and, he uses *mashimah* to shock his Muslim readers. This, however, is the full extent of his evocation of unclean bodily substances in relation to the divinity.[179] Ibn Ḥazm and other Iberian authors addressed the issue of God's becoming polluted as a result of being in Mary's womb, but their language is not nearly so graphic or extensive as that of the *Qiṣṣat.*[180] Thus the *Qiṣṣat,* like many other polemical works transported from the eastern Mediterranean dealing with Christian belief, fit neatly into debates about the incarnation in medieval Iberia while at the same time being sharper in tone and degree than Muslim-Christian dialogues.

Visceral anti-Christian polemic appears in Europe in the ninth century, making it approximately contemporaneous with the *Qiṣṣat.* Like the *Qiṣṣat*, it was written in Muslim lands, although this time by a Christian convert to Judaism who fled his native France to Spain. Bodo-Eleazar's language was so offensive to his former coreligionists that his words have been destroyed; our knowledge of his arguments comes from his Christian disputant, Paul Alvarus of Cordoba, whose polemical use of dirt and pollution easily match that of any late antique author. The filth and impurity of the woman's body (as well as the uncleanness of Eleazar's blasphemies, according to Alvarus) seem to have been very much part of Eleazar's objections to Christianity.[181] After berating Eleazar for presuming that purity can be conquered by pollution, any more than the sun's rays can absorb impure filth, Alvarus reminds Eleazar that he himself came from an unclean womb.[182] For questioning the purity and appropriateness of the virgin body as a receptacle for the Messiah, Alvarus reviles his former coreligionist in the strongest terms: "Listen scoundrel, and full of every execration and abomination, impure and horrible spirit, and for you, you have dared to blaspheme the living God."[183] This remark is typical of the tone of Alvarus's invective against Eleazar and the Jews.[184] Alvarus also turned the specter of filth to his advantage when attacking the Jewish ruler, or "Messiah." He depicts the Messiah as imprisoned and thrown in a latrine brimming with filth and worms. Then he urges, "Cry to him in a loud voice, for perhaps your messiah purges his stomach, or he relieves his bladder with an effusion of urine, or silently expels the stench of shit from his anus, or forces out a noisy inflation of the stomach and thus does not hear your lengthy lamentation."[185]

In his letters to Eleazar, Alvarus fights dirt with dirt, reveling in evocations of human waste, dirt, and bad smell. Any Jewish imputations against Mary's and Jesus' bodily natures are answered by attempting to make Eleazar, other Jews, and the Jewish Messiah vastly more foul than Eleazar's depiction of Mary. In this endeavor Alvarus was assisted by his knowledge of Jerome, for much of Alvarus's imagery in his letters to Eleazar and in other epistles find strong parallels in Jerome's letters and biblical commentaries.[186] Eleazar, a former Christian cleric, would have been familiar with the same Christian patristic sources as Alvarus and would have drawn on Jewish anti-Christian polemic as well, though the exact nature of sources cannot be known without a copy of his side of the disputation. Certainly the bodily pollution of Mary was one of the points of contention, which led Mendoz to suggest the possibility that Eleazar borrowed from the *Toledot Yesu*.[187] It is also possible that some version of the *Qiṣṣat,* or Muslim polemic containing similar argumentation, had already reached Muslim Spain where Eleazar settled after his conversion and that it is from these sources that he drew his invective against Mary's body.

The exchange between Eleazar and Alvarus is the most graphic of the early medieval texts from Latin Europe, but a number of other texts testify to similar kinds of polemic. According to Amulo, another ninth-century French

Christian, Jews rejected the view that divinity could die and referred to Jesus as a rotting corpse, cursed Jesus, and stated that he was born of an adulterous union between Mary and Pandera.[188] Many of Amulo's remarks are more closely connected to the *Toledot Yesu* tradition than to the *Qiṣṣat*.[189] Nevertheless, some of the Jewish argumentation recorded by Amulo, Alvarus, and Gregory of Tours parallels the *Qiṣṣat*, as do Jewish critiques contained in Byzantine and Syrian Christian polemic. These shared themes point to the possibility of a tradition of oral anti-Christian invectives that circulated among Jews throughout the Mediterranean, whether in Latin, Byzantine, or Muslim lands.[190] Instances in early Hebrew *piyyuṭim*, part of an oral, albeit learned, Jewish tradition, in which Christians are depicted as worshiping a dead man, linked to impurity, and indulging in or originating from sexual promiscuity tends to confirm this impression.[191] It was, however, the translation of the *Qiṣṣat* from Judeo-Arabic into Hebrew in the twelfth century and the adoption and expansion of its methods—extensive summary, citation, and distortion of the New Testament coupled with accusations of dirt and impurity—that had the greatest impact on medieval European Jewish anti-Christian polemic.[192] Objections to or attempts to defend the filthy womb and bowels of Mary, or the bodily weaknesses of Jesus, continued to be popular in Byzantine and Near Eastern Jewish, Muslim, and Christian polemic into the thirteenth century. The duration of these invectives testifies to their power to disturb.[193] Yet these tactics became a central component of twelfth- and thirteenth-century Jewish and Christian confrontation in the Latin West in a new way.

The Hebrew translation of the *Qiṣṣat* was but one of several texts or trends in religious thought that traveled westward and were imbued with new meaning in the twelfth and thirteenth centuries. Further complicating and challenging attitudes toward divinity and physicality among twelfth- and thirteenth-century Latin Christians especially was the spread of Bogomil belief from the Balkans into western Europe, forming the communities that came to be known as the Cathars.[194] Eastern Christian traditions about the murderous intentions of Jews toward Christians or of their desire to desecrate Christian holy objects and places became part of Latin lore at a very early period. However, they attained new, sinister meaning in the thirteenth century.[195] Palestinian *piyyuṭim* written under Byzantine rule demanding vengeance for Christian wrongs and containing negative depictions of Christianity became the basis for later Ashkenazi liturgical poetry.[196] Choice of diet, smell, and the symbolic value of the pig became increasingly important in the twelfth and thirteenth centuries and were often assigned gendered meanings that they lacked during late antiquity and the early Middle Ages. This transfer of stories and beliefs along with the influx of Arab and Greek medical and philosophical traditions, while not solely responsible for the shifting nature of Jewish-Christian relations or of views of the body in twelfth- and thirteenth-century Europe, were important factors.

PART II

Twelfth–Fourteenth Centuries

Intensification and Collision of Jewish-Christian-Muslim Polemic

CHAPTER THREE

Twelfth- and Thirteenth-Century Contexts

During the twelfth and thirteenth centuries, the influx of learning from the Greek and Muslim world and the study of religious texts from other traditions combined with the shifting and conflicting traditions about physicality and the bodies of Mary and Jesus to lay the groundwork for a powerful corporeal religious polemic. The symbols of this polemic were known and used by Jewish and Christian communities in twelfth- and thirteenth-century Europe. In many ways this somatic polemic was very similar to that of late antiquity and the early Middle Ages, both in content and in function. In the later Middle Ages, as in the earlier periods, polemic based on impurity, filth, and disease was used to repel its hearers. It was a form of resistance or incitement to the audience. Muslims continued old argumentation about the inappropriateness of associating God in the form of Jesus, according to Christian belief, with the interstices of a woman's abdomen, though this later polemic, like its early medieval counterpart, used far less graphic language than did similar discussions in Jewish and Christian compositions from the Latin West. Latin Christian anti-Muslim polemic, both visual and written, increased. Often anti-Muslim sentiments were expressed in the form of negative biographies of the Prophet Muḥammad. However, among both Muslims and Christians the crusades provided new impetus for polemicizing as each attempted to incite their coreligionists to war. As in late antiquity and the early Middle Ages, in this later period discomfort with the conjunction of divinity and human corporeality, especially female corporeality, was at the center of the debate.

There were, however, many differences. Jewish purity laws had become more harsh in regard to women; Christians and Jews tended to emphasize rational and medical explanations; attitudes and theories of disease had shifted toward an almost essentialist view of the difference between types of humans; and attitudes toward certain animals, such as the pig or the hyena, had taken on new, more negative connotations. Most important, the consequences of filth polemic in twelfth- and thirteenth-century Europe were different from those in late antiquity and the early Middle Ages. Certainly Pagans and Christians persecuted Jews under Roman and Byzantine rule. Sometimes this violence was sparked by suspicions similar to those in medieval Europe that there had been Jewish desecration of the host or cross. Yet such outbreaks in the early eastern Mediterranean or even in the early Latin West never attained the level of persistence and violence that similar beliefs later incited in Europe during the twelfth, thirteenth, and, especially, fourteenth centuries when the blood libel reached its height. Despite the rise in Christian anti-Jewish and, to a lesser extent, anti-Muslim sentiment and violence, Jews, Christians, and Muslims increasingly borrowed from one another, sometimes explicitly as in the case of Christian clerics receiving tutoring in Hebrew and Jewish exegesis or Arabic and the Qur'an from rabbis or Muslims. At other times cultural and social exchanges were less obvious, or the evidence for them is embedded in texts whose purpose was to decry or discourage such interaction, as the Hebrew martyrological poems or crusade chronicles, or texts such as *Sefer Ḥasidim* in which Jews are discouraged from too much interaction with Christians or contact with their books and objects, yet whose stories and genre point to a high degree of social and literary exchange at all levels of Jewish and Christian society.

The purpose of this chapter is to discuss the essential developments in Europe during the twelfth and thirteenth centuries that allowed visceral images based on the filth of bodily effluvia to become a central theme in polemic between Jews and Christians and an incitement to anger and verbal or physical violence during this period, even more than in earlier eras. Before turning to a detailed discussion of the two key pieces of this puzzle of the translation of certain medical and polemical texts from Greek or Arabic into Latin and Hebrew, and the shifts in attitudes toward the body, particularly the bodies of Jesus and Mary, an overview of scholarship concerning twelfth- and thirteenth-century majority-minority relations is in order.

Historiography

That the twelfth and thirteenth centuries were a period of change in Europe and that these changes contributed to the degradation of the status of women, lepers, Jews, and other minorities has been demonstrated countless times. Explanations of the relationship between the new developments in twelfth-century Europe and the rise in persecution of the minorities have varied, however. Some, most notably R. I. Moore, in *Formation of a Persecuting Society*, have attempted to study the phenomenon as a whole, arguing that the impulse to persecute lepers, Jews, heretics, and others during this period derived from the same set of forces. Moore maintained that the simultaneous development of restrictions against Jews, lepers, and heretics, as well as homosexuals and prostitutes, beginning in the eleventh century and reaching its height in the twelfth and thirteenth, was not pure coincidence but derived from the Church's increasing efforts to reorganize and create categories.[1] John Boswell focused on the treatment of male homosexuals, though he too saw the increasingly harsh treatment of this minority as symptomatic of a general trend that affected all who were dubbed "undesirables." He also attributed this trend to twelfth- and thirteenth-century Christian efforts to categorize and regulate the surrounding world.[2] James Brundage's work on the history of Church law regarding sexual practice demonstrated that the renaissance in legal studies during the twelfth century resulted in strictures that were often detrimental to women's status and image.[3] Monastic women, in France at least, suffered a noticeable decline in freedom of movement, wealth, and power. Penelope Johnson attributed this shift to several causes, among which was the polarization of men's and women's place in Christian society; women were to remain pure, inside the home or cloister, whereas men occupied public spaces. Johnson likewise saw a connection between the persecution of minorities such as Muslims, Jews, and heretics and the decreasing power of monastic women. All these groups were victims of "hardening attitudes" and rejection of dissent.[4] According to Moore, developing broad classifications that denied individual difference generated stereotypes and myths whose strength was augmented by their basis in realities. For example, he suggested that according to the textual evidence (though not the archaeological), it is quite plausible that there was an epidemic of leprosy during this period. Jews, stereotyped as moneylenders, were in fact pushed into this occupation. Thus lepers and Jewish moneylenders were in evidence, yet the rhetoric that described lepers as filthy, sexually perverted sinners, or the Jews as stinking, carnal lovers of material wealth, went far beyond the reality to create a horrific, generalized, and threatening image of both groups.[5]

Following Lester Little, Moore noted the importance of Christian insecurity in the face of the drastic changes during the twelfth and thirteenth centuries, especially the shift from a barter to a money-based economy.[6] He also briefly acknowledged the applicability of Mary Douglas's theories regarding the role of pollutative language in indicating anxiety about social boundaries.[7] According to Moore, however, the real power and impetus behind these persecutions—whether of heretics, prostitutes, or other groups—lay with the secular and ecclesiastical authorities. Most "successful" instances of persecution were a direct result of some authority's active pursuit of the trial and punishment of the accused.[8]

Other scholars have noted the similarities between anti-Jewish rhetoric and the visual and verbal invective directed against one or two other groups. Ruth Mellinkoff has shown that Jews and peasants were often depicted as coarse, swarthy, and diseased in paintings of Jesus' betrayal and passion.[9] Rafael Ocasio has explored similar color codification in the visual representations of unconvertable Muslims in Alfonso the Wise's *Cantigas de Santa Maria.*[10] Bénédicte Bauchau noted that while Jews were not depicted as specifically leprous, in the late Middle Ages they were accused of being carriers of the disease and of having some of the same physical symptoms, such as bad breath or sexual voraciousness, a trait Jews were sometimes also said to share with women.[11] Sara Lipton, while focusing on Jews, examined the parallels between representations of Jews, heretics, philosophers, and moneylenders in the *Bible Moralisée*. She suggested that while Christian audiences distinguished between members of these groups, Jews were a convenient, readily understood symbol for the evildoer.[12]

Scholars dealing solely with the deterioration of Jewish status during the twelfth and thirteenth centuries have refined and elaborated on the contention that economic specialization and increased dependency on the government for the enforcement of payment sparked deep resentment in all segments of the Christian population, especially as churches, monasteries, and lords found themselves hopelessly indebted to Jews, often as a result of borrowing for the crusades.[13] A number of authors, most notably Robert Chazan, Jeremy Cohen, and Peter Brown, have emphasized the importance of the new missionizing efforts on the part of Christians. Already in the twelfth century increasing numbers of Christians began to seek out Jews willing to teach them Hebrew, ostensibly better to interpret the Scriptures. By the thirteenth century Christians began to study systematically not only the Hebrew Bible but also extrabiblical writings such as the Talmud and the midrash and incorporate what they learned from these texts in their preaching and writing to and against the Jews. Similar efforts were directed toward the conquered

Muslim communities in Iberia. These efforts placed devastating pressures on Jewish communities, and Christian attitudes toward Jews substantially worsened as Christians became aware of negative remarks against Jesus and Mary in the Talmud and the midrash.[14] Christians who learned Muslim doctrine well generally condemned Muslims as heretics but regarded them more favorably than the Jews because they at least accepted Mary's virginal conception and birth and Jesus' messianic status.[15]

Anna Sapir Abulafia and Gavin Langmuir have emphasized the role of rationality versus irrationality. Langmuir delved into the realm of religious phenomenology, attempting to catalog the nature of religious thought and intolerance as a whole, and then applied his observations to the medieval Jewish-Christian conflict.[16] Both Langmuir and Sapir Abulafia, however, pointed to the shifts in medieval intellectual culture during the twelfth and thirteenth centuries caused by the influx of new philosophical paradigms, courtesy of the many translations of classical and Muslim authors from Greek and Arabic into Latin.

Reason became a serious gauge by which to measure the validity of religious belief. Jews and Muslims presented rational challenges to Christian belief above and beyond those intrinsic to the new Christian scholastic thought. Sapir Abulafia argued quite convincingly that the Christian scholastic response was to label Jews and Muslims as irrational. Since the ability to reason was thought the characteristic that distinguished humans from animals, to impugn Jews' capacity to reason was tantamount to equating them with beasts. From the supposition that Jews were subhuman, belief that Jews were child murderers and even cannibals was but a small step.[17]

In the twelfth and thirteenth centuries Jewish society and attitudes toward outsiders and women were changing just as they were in the Christian world. Jews in Germany and northern France were developing new methods of studying the Bible and the Talmud, which, according to some scholars, strongly resembled aspects of the new Christian scholasticism.[18] During the course of the Spanish reconquest, Arabic-speaking Jews translated medical and philosophical works from Arabic or Judeo-Arabic into Hebrew, so that not only were these works preserved for later generations of Iberian Jews, but they were made available to their northern coreligionists. The influx of this "new" material sometimes caused conflict, much as it did in the Christian community.[19] Paralleling developments in Christian anti-Jewish polemic, for Jewish thinkers rationality became a criteria for assessing religious beliefs, both Jewish and other, and Jews studied and incorporated Christian Scripture into their anti-Christian polemic.[20] Like the Christians, Jews sometimes used a common rhetoric to denigrate a variety of outsiders or religiously "dangerous" people. For example, Elliot Wolfson has shown that in certain kabbalistic texts, Islam, Christianity, the demonic, and feminine aspects of God became closely associated.[21]

The legal restrictions on women became harsher, and the literary portrayals of women in Jewish literature, especially literature from Spain, frequently followed the misogynistic tendencies present in certain forms of Christian literature.[22] Susan Einbinder has recently argued that Jewish female martyrs were increasingly portrayed as polluted by Christian assaults and as passive, rather than active, resisters to Christian violence and conversion attempts, a phenomenon she relates to the deteriorating status of Jewish women.[23] This image of women vulnerable to contamination from religious outsiders parallels the observations of Miri Rubin regarding the role of women in Christian host miracle stories. In these tales women were responsible for giving or selling the host to the Jewish enemies of Christ. Thus women in both communities were seen as potential "weak links," more likely than their male counterparts to succumb to the predations of the religious "enemy."[24]

Scholars working on interfaith relations without focusing specifically on issues of religious polemic emphasize the high degree of sociability among Jews, Christians, and Muslims. Not only did Muslims regularly form business partnerships with Jews or Christians and vice versa, but members of two or more of the three religious groups frequently joined together in religious festivals and veneration of holy individuals, despite the protests of religious authorities.[25] Judaicists have increasingly objected to portraying Jewish history as primarily a history of persecution, condemning this approach as "lachrymose" and inadequate. Mark Cohen, for example, has insisted that the dichotomous model of tolerance toward Jews and other minorities in medieval Muslim lands and persecution of Jews by medieval European Christians is an inaccurate overgeneralization.[26] William Chester Jordan and Katherine Ryerson note the frequent and often amiable social and economic relations between Jews and Christians in northern and southern France, even in the face of increasing governmental and institutional pressures on the Jews.[27] Chazan, in his studies of the Hebrew Crusade Chronicles, has been careful to note that Christian behavior toward the Jews and Jewish expectations of their Christian neighbors were far from uniform and that Jews both expected and received help from the burghers and Christian authorities.[28] More important for the current study, various scholars such as

Ivan Marcus, Marc Epstein, and Susan Einbinder have begun delving into the ways in which Jews, especially from northern Europe, borrowed from and transformed Christian symbols, rituals, and literary genres for their own means.[29] Familiarity with and use of Christian symbols suggests a profound degree of cultural sharing between Christians and Jews in all regions of Europe and sets the social foundation for the network of common symbolic meanings that are at the heart of Jewish, Christian, and even Muslim polemic evoking bodily impurities, dirt, disease, and animals.[30]

Muslim contact with Christians and Jews of Latin Europe, and vice versa, was relatively less intimate than Jewish-Christian contact, except in Iberia, Sicily, and the crusader kingdoms. Yet Muslims likewise shared many of the same fundamental assumptions about the meaning of the body in relation to the divine and like their Jewish and Christian counterparts were quite willing to use the body, food, and animals as polemical tools for expressing their disagreements or anger at Christians in particular. Scholars of medieval Muslim-Christian relations are increasingly insisting on the profound influence of Muslim scientific, polemical, and fable literature and oral traditions on European Christians (and Jews) during the twelfth and thirteenth centuries, even in parts of northern Europe where there was no consistent, noticeable Muslim population.[31]

While one may argue with the particulars of each scholar's hypothesis, certain elements are consistently evoked to explain both the tensions and the commonalities between marginalized groups and the Christian (or Muslim), usually male, majority. The crusading and missionizing efforts of Christians and the concomitant discovery and translation of Muslim, Jewish, and classical texts by Christians and Jews led to greater knowledge of outside faiths, science, and philosophy.[32] This knowledge could be and was used as a polemical tool. Anxiety among both Christians and Jews, whether financial, religious, or stemming from general discomfort with the many social and institutional changes taking place, also fueled hostility between the two religious communities. Christian devotion focusing on the humanity of Jesus and Mary has also been cited as a prominent cause of antagonism between Christians and Jews.[33] The various explanations offered by these scholars sketch out a range of contextual forces and new developments that affected Jewish-Christian invective in the twelfth and thirteenth centuries. I would suggest, however, that the impact of translations of new medical tracts into Hebrew and Latin on concepts of the human and animal body, God, and the nature of the "other" need deeper investigation. Further, the importance of attitudes toward the body, especially the female body, in shaping the rhetoric of religious polemic in the twelfth and thirteenth centuries needs to be heeded. The shifting definition of what it meant to be both human and female in turn influenced Christian theology about Mary, her body, and its relationship to Jesus' own humanity, as well as Jewish approaches to the Christian doctrine of the incarnation in particular and the religious outsider in general.

Transmitting Ideas: Texts, Orality, and Images

One of the first methodological problems that arises with any argument that medieval European Jews and Christians knew of and played on one another's polemics, religious doubts, beliefs, practices, and medical theories is communication. The same issue arises when arguing for exchanges among Byzantines, those in the Muslim world, and Europeans, since a reading or speaking knowledge of Greek or Arabic in the West or Latin in the East required a very high or specialized level of education. In his autobiography, Usamah ibn Munqidh portrays himself and other Muslims as having frequent conversations with Latin Christians, though he states elsewhere that he does not speak Frankish.[34] If he had such conversations, the Franks themselves probably learned Arabic, though a few Muslims learned Latin or European vernacular languages during the crusades.[35] Few Christians knew Hebrew, though the number began to rise in the twelfth century.[36] Though Jews certainly spoke the European vernacular of the area in which they dwelled, it ill equipped them to study learned Christian texts, even if they had access to them. This problem is underscored in the introductory exchange between a Christian and a Jew in an Old French anti-Jewish dialogue:

> <christianus> "Omnis credencium // letetur populus: Nostra redempcio, // natus est parvulus. /I Carnem induitur // in alvo virginis // Et carne tegitur // maiestas numinis." //
> <judaeus> Ne t'entent pas, por ce c'oscurement paroles. Parole a moi francois et espon tes paroles! . . . Ce que diz en latin en francois me glose![37]

Here the Christian begins to sing of Jesus' incarnation in Latin, and the Jew has to stop him and request that he continue in French because he cannot understand Latin. Rendering the dialogue into Old French was probably as much for the benefit of a less learned Christian audience that also did not understand Latin well as a reflection of linguistic barriers between Christians and Jews. Nevertheless, the thirteenth-century Christian author clearly understood that a realistic portrayal of a Jewish-Christian dialogue needed to be in the vernacular rather than Latin. Anecdotal evidence from Muslim, Christian, and Jewish sources strongly suggests that such interfaith discussions took place and were an important source of knowledge of the religious other.[38] Furthermore, Jewish study and translation Latin texts were becoming more common than is often acknowledged, paralleling Christian study of Jewish polemical, philosophical, and medical texts. Both Christians and Jews were reading and translating Arabic texts, and many Western Christians were doing the same with Greek theological and medical sources.[39] Muslims had long been in the habit of translating or otherwise familiarizing themselves with the exegetical and scientific literature of non-Muslims.[40] These activities along with oral exchanges and Jewish knowledge of Christian visual symbols changed the nature of Jewish-Christian relations and polemic in twelfth- and thirteenth-century Europe.

Translations: Polemical Texts

Spain was the meeting ground of polemical traditions both from the Latin West and from the Islamic Near East, including polemic about the incarnation. Ḥafṣ ibn Albar al-Qūṭī, son of Paul Alvarus, the ninth-century Christian opponent of the convert Bodo/Eleazar, composed the first anti-Muslim polemic by a Western Christian in Arabic.[41] Thomas Burman has shown that one Christian anti-Muslim text, *Tathlith al-waḥdānīyah*, used ideas from Abelard and Hugh of St. Victor in combination with Muslim and Eastern Christian theological and polemical arguments.[42] Iberian Christians were willing to overlook their doctrinal differences with Nestorian and Jacobite Christians in order to make use of such authors as the Nestorian ʿAmmar al-Baṣri (d. 825).[43]

Mozarabs (Arabic-speaking Christians of Spain), Jews, and Muslims, like their Near Eastern coreligionists, read one another's writings and then used what they found to their advantage in polemic against one another. This tactic included scriptural and extrascriptural texts, such as *ḥadith*.[44] According to Burman, Ramond Marti, the thirteenth-century Dominican missionary famous for the inclusion of Islamic and Jewish traditions in his religious polemic, borrowed this technique from Christian polemical works he had read in Arabic. Thus the "innovative argumentation" used by thirteenth-century missionizing friars derives at least in part from Latin Christians' discovery of polemical tactics long extant in the Muslim world.[45] This process was aided not only by translations of texts such as the Qur'an into Latin but also by the translation of polemical tracts such as the *Liber denudationis*, also known as *Contrarietas alfolica*, a Christian anti-Muslim polemic written in Arabic sometime after 1085 (that version is now lost) and the *Apology of al-Kindi*, composed between 750 and 1050 and translated in the 1140s.[46]

David Berger, in the introduction to his edition and translation of the *Niẓẓaḥon Yashan*, noted that just as many Christian polemicists from the twelfth and thirteenth centuries were incorporating extrabiblical Jewish texts into their polemic, Jews from the same period were making extensive use of the New Testament in their anti-Christian polemic. The first European Jewish polemicist to do this, according to Berger, was Jacob b. Reuben, working in southern France and Spain, in his *Milḥamot ha-Shem* (1170).[47] Yet, as Stroumsa and Lasker have pointed out, Jacob b. Reuben cites Nestor ha-Komer, the reputed author of the Hebrew translation of the *Qiṣṣat Mujadalat al-'Usquf*, in chapter 11 of his disputation.[48] The Hebrew text of the *Qiṣṣat*, like the Arabic versions, makes extensive use of the New Testament. Thus, as with Latin Christian polemic, the inclination to make use of texts holy to one's religious opponents came to European Jews via the discovery and translation of Arabic, in this case Jewish, religious polemic. Once having received the inspiration, however, European Jews and Christians developed this technique according to their own needs.[49]

Since Jacob b. Reuben already knew of and quoted *Sefer Nestor ha-Komer* in 1170, Lasker and Stroumsa argued that the *Qiṣṣat*, along with Bahya ibn Paquda's *Duties of the Heart*, must have been one of the first Jewish Arabic compositions to have been translated into Hebrew as Jews from Muslim Spain moved into Christian lands. From Iberia and Provence *Sefer Nestor ha-Komer* traveled to northern France and Germany. The Hebrew version was altered in a number of significant ways: the Arabic glosses were exchanged for Latin ones; Arabic summaries of the Scriptures were replaced with direct quotations from the Hebrew; rabbinic citations were added; and relatively neutral terminology for Christian holy objects, rituals, and figures in the Arabic were replaced with highly negative equivalents.[50]

Jacob b. Reuben was remarkable not only because he was one of the first European Jews to quote and translate Latin Scripture, and the first to show knowledge of *Nestor ha-Komer*, but also because he translated and incorporated substantial portions of Gilbert Crispin's *Disputatio Iudei et Christiani* (ca. 1093) into his *Milḥamot ha-Shem*.[51] No one who has studied European Jewish anti-Christian disputations would maintain that medieval Jews' *primary* method for learning Christian doctrine and anti-Jewish argumentation was through reading Latin disputational texts. That at least one Jew could and did, however, needs to be noted.[52] Later Jewish polemicists expanded their knowledge of Christian doctrine and Scripture, though much of that knowledge probably came through oral communication between Christians and Jews rather than through the study and translation of written texts.[53]

Italy's proximity to and mercantile connections with Byzantium promoted translations of Greek as well as Arabic texts into Latin. While medical and philosophical texts have received the most attention, patristic and Byzantine theological works were of great interest to Latin thinkers. Pope Eugene III (1145–53) commissioned Burgundio of Pisa to translate, among other patristic writings, John of Damascus's *De Fide Orthodoxa*, a text that had already been partially translated by the Hungarian Cerbanus. *De Fide Orthodoxa* had a substantial impact on Western theologians' thought regarding the nature of the incarnation, for in this text John addressed the process by which God became incarnate in the womb and the effect of death on God-as-Jesus.[54]

Individuals from the circle of Gilbert of Poitiers (1070–1154) such as Hugh of Honau seem to have been especially interested in Eastern Christians' discussion of the nature of the incarnation. Hugh obtained a compilation of translated extracts from Greek theologians, *De differentia naturae et personae* and *De sancto et immortali Deo* from Hugo Etherianus, a Pisan living in Constantinople. Hugh hoped that these texts would assuage "these dangerous doubts of the Latins." Hugo also translated a Greek Christian enumeration of the theological errors of Latin Christians.[55] Thus European Christians and Jews were actively seeking out new information about the theological positions of outsiders as part of an effort not merely to understand the nature of the incarnation more precisely but also to obtain new tools for refuting their opponents. The translation of theological and polemical texts from multiple languages, whether from Latin and Arabic into Hebrew or Greek and Arabic into Latin, was at the center of this endeavor. The translations shaped or directed much of the discourse between Jews and Christians in the twelfth and thirteenth centuries, although Europeans molded the methods and ideas they obtained to suit their own needs.

Translations: Medical and Philosophical Texts

Though the majority of medical and philosophical translations may have been from Greek and Arabic to Latin or Hebrew, textual transmission could and did go in any direction, including from Latin to Hebrew. If the boast of one anonymous twelfth-century Jew is to be believed, most of the basic medical texts from Salerno being used in Christian universities, a collection known as the *Ars medicinae*, had been translated from Latin into Hebrew by the twelfth century. Given that many of the texts listed by the author have been in fact discovered, his claims seem to be legitimate.[56] Joseph Shatzmiller argued that while early in the twelfth and even into the fourteenth century Jews had access to medical material in Arabic that was inaccessible to Christian doctors, Jews felt increasingly obliged to turn to Latin medical and even, in one instance, theological and philosophical texts. This inclination was based in part on the need for Jewish doctors to become licensed through the same processes as Christian doctors and, on rare occasion, to attend university.[57]

The degree to which Jews and Christians worked together to translate relevant scientific texts and that a number of Jews were turning to Latin texts to obtain their information is significant on several levels. First, it means that medieval Christian and Jewish medical knowledge and theory was identical except for a few changes idiosyncratic to each religion.[58] Also, references to medical theories would have been understood by Christian and Jew alike. Presumably certain Jews elected to translate medical texts from Latin into Hebrew because most of their coreligionists were unable to read them in Latin any more than they were in Arabic. Finally, Jewish knowledge of Latin and thus, potentially, the intricacies of Christian intellectual culture and texts, at least in southern France, seems to have been more prevalent in the thirteenth and early fourteenth century than imagined. The partial translation of Gilbert Crispin's *Disputatio* by Jacob b. Reuben, who was also working in southern France and Spain, demonstrates that some Jews did not confine their curiosity or linguistic skills to medical texts.

Courtesy of these many translations, whatever their language of origin, most of the texts about male and female biology and nature that had informed the classical and late antique views about the body were available again by the twelfth and thirteenth centuries and subject to new scrutiny. But the context, and sometimes even the content, of these texts had changed. Pliny's natural history, with its emphasis on the woman's blood as both an antidote to and a powerful source of poison, had been available throughout the Middle Ages and enjoyed considerable popularity.[59] These attitudes were emphasized by the early medieval encyclopedic works of Isidore of Seville and Rabanus Maurus, which were also very popular.[60] The ideas of Galen and Aristotle on generation and heredity were initially made available in the West through or in conjunction with the writings of Ibn Sina (Avicenna) and were combined with views based on Pliny and other early Latin writers.

Basim Musallam has argued that Ibn Sina's *al-Ḥayawān*, the biological section of his *al-Shifa'*, was a conscious defense of Aristotelian views over those of Galen. In Ibn Sina's discussion of theories of generation in *al-Shifa'*, however, he deviated from his Aristotelian focus in order to accommodate the discovery and implications of ovaries, thus embracing the Hippocratic and Galenic hypothesis that women produced seed. Nevertheless, Ibn Sina posited a close relationship between menstrual blood and women's seed and ultimately assigned the same passive, material function to women's seed as that given by Aristotle to menstrual blood.[61] Albertus Magnus in *De Animalibus* drew heavily from the Latin translation of *al-Ḥayawān* and from the Arabic-Latin translation of Aristotle's *De generatione animalium*.[62]

This balancing of Hippocratic, Aristotelian, and Galenic theories of generation was common both in the literature inherited by European Christians and Jews and in the biological writings they themselves produced. For example, Maimonides criticized some of Galen's views in his *Medical Aphorisms*, yet he also compiled a book of excerpts from Galen's medical writings and based the first chapter of his *Regimen of Health* on Galen and Hippocrates.[63] Even in his philosophical work, *Guide for the Perplexed*, which is generally recognized as an example of medieval Aristotelianism, Maimonides cited Galen's discussion of life from sperm and menstrual blood from *De usu partium* in support of part of his explanation of evil.[64] Constantinus Africanus, whom Joan Cadden characterized as primarily Galenic in his outlook, nevertheless presented theories of generation with a distinctly Aristotelian slant while still including Hippocratic and Galenic ideas.[65] Writers of medieval medical compendia and commentaries, such as Nathan b. Yo'el Falaquera (late thirteenth century), Yehudah ha-Kohen ibn Mattqa, Albertus Magnus (ca. 1193–1280), and Taddeo Alderotti (d. 1295), all presented a mixture of Hippocratic, Aristotelian, Galenic, and, of course, Soranean views of the male and female body and genital fluids, though some tended more strongly toward one theoretical model than another.[66]

Musallam argued that in Islam "the theory of equal contribution of male and female [in generation] removed, perhaps completely, the possibility of rationalizing the unequal treatment of women by reference to a supposed biological inferiority of females."[67] The same was not true in western Europe, despite the acceptance by many of the Galenic two-seed theory.[68] Rather the association of women and their blood with rot and poison was enhanced by similar remarks in Aristotle and others, which were then quoted by medieval authors.[69] Jewish and Christian thinkers alike debated whether actual menstrual blood or some other kind of blood formed or nourished the fetus. Whichever solution they chose, menstrual blood was invariably harmful to the fetus, due to the blood's filthy nature.[70] Drawing from the Latin translation of Ibn Sina's *al-Ḥayawān* (*De animalibus*), one commentator on *De Secretis mulierum*, a medical tract falsely attributed to Albertus Magnus, suggested that even the air around the menstruating woman could cause illness in a man.[71] The classical view that a menstruant's gaze could harm a mirror was expanded so that she could also render a child grievously ill by merely looking at it.[72] Old women, especially those who ate coarse foods, were seen as especially dangerous because they could not menstruate and thus stored up "extra" poison that could then harm any young children on whom they gazed. The poor-quality food added to the residues and bad humors in their bodies, which in turn combined with the menstrual waste trapped in the womb after menopause.[73] Because of their cold humidity women did not contract leprosy (described as "putrid" and "corrupt" matter) during coitus but passed it on to their male partners.[74] Thus their very biological natures made women the carriers of poisonous rot, regardless of whether they themselves were capable of being infected by it.

That which made women potentially poisonous was also their source of fertility. According to the *De secretis mulierum*, Ibn Sina argued that the hairs of a menstruating woman placed in manure will generate serpents. The text and commentaries published by Lemay draw clear connections among the fertility of rotting earth, the woman's blood, and the relative venomousness of the animals generated.[75] In the *Salernitan Questions*, an early and highly influential collection of medical questions and answers, fruit is more likely to rot during a waxing moon because the moon causes an abundance of cold, wet humors that are the source of rot.[76] The moon had long been tied to women's menstrual cycle, and this text emphasizes this link by attributing to the moon precisely those humoral characteristics normally associated with menstruating women.[77]

Finally, Sharon Koren has demonstrated that in the *Zohar*, one of the major Jewish mystical works of thirteenth-century Spain, the biological theories connecting fertility, menstrual waste, and poisonous evil attained new cosmological significance. In the *Zohar* red waste descending from the left, female side of the Godhead is responsible for creating demons, the *Sitra Achra* (the "Other Side"), the demonic parallel to the divine, "other gods" (perhaps a reference to Christianity), and the souls of the gentile nations, the enemies of the Jews.[78]

Such a biological worldview depicted women as profoundly alien: inhuman in their immunity to disease in comparison to men and children, yet dangerous to all around them. Furthermore, continuing to associate women with decay, disease, bad smell, and even worms not only made women physically disgusting but also placed them on the "wrong side" of the spiritual hierarchy. As in late antiquity hell and evildoers were marked by foul smell and devouring worms, much as women were in some medical, philosophical, and mystical literature.[79] The proliferation of discussions of the woman's body as a vector of disease and of potentially dangerous fertility underscores the profound fear many medieval Christian and Jewish men had of women's bodies and sexuality.[80]

The introduction of a large body of "new" medical material from the Arabic- and Greek-speaking worlds sparked debate about the woman's body, along with other medical and philosophical questions. It also provided fuel for greater focus on the human body in general and the female body in particular, much of which was far from positive. Long-held beliefs about the nature of menstruation and the woman's body inherited from Pliny and Isidore of Seville combined with equally damning Aristotelian and Arab discussions of the woman's ability to poison with a glance and contaminate the fetus or man who came into contact with her womb or genitals. As Cadden and Jacquart and Thomasset rightly have pointed out, no monolithic theory of generation or of the woman's body existed.[81] Yet of the theories circulating in twelfth- and thirteenth-century Europe, few if any did not have some negative implications about the female body.

Translated medical material informed and expanded on Western understanding of leprosy and related diseases. Texts such as the *Baraita de Niddah* and the sermons of Caesarius of Arles that connected intercourse with a menstruating woman and the contraction of leprosy by either the man or subsequent child were well known and influential in twelfth- and thirteenth-century Europe.[82] They were reinforced by discussions of leprosy and its causes in translated Greek and Arabic medical texts, many of which provided clinically accurate descriptions of skin diseases.[83]

The extent of clinical leprosy's spread both chronologically and geographically in Europe is still debated, but most scholars have presented evidence that lepromatous leprosy afflicted medieval Europeans, especially during the twelfth and thirteenth centuries.[84] More important to the present study than whether the diseases described in medieval texts were in fact what modern doctors would diagnose as leprosy is the mechanics of "leprosy" according to medieval authors and the diseases that medieval medical writers related to leprosy. These diseases included cancer, tumors, hemorrhoids and diarrhea, nosebleeds, bad breath, scrofula (a manifestation of tuberculosis), pustules, measles, chickenpox, acne, and melancholy. All these ailments had as their ultimate source an excess of extremely corrupt blood, that is, black bile, which to varying degrees caused the body to rot from within.[85] While these sicknesses all had the same root cause, leprosy, followed by cancer, were seen as the worst, as impossible or nearly impossible to cure.[86] Though cold and dry, in contrast to the woman's normally cold and wet nature, the melancholic, like the woman, purged his body of gross, waste blood. Medieval medical writers explicitly compared this hemorrhoidal or nasal bleeding to menstruation.[87]

Similar to children conceived of a menstruating mother, individuals who carried an overabundance of impure, melancholic blood in their bodies, frequently bore its mark on their bodies and characters. Laurence Wright has demonstrated through his analysis of the Old French vocabulary of leprosy that burning, red, or even black skin was commonly associated with leprosy.[88] Medieval medical texts also linked melancholy, which was strongly tied to the planet Saturn, with a dark or ruddy complexion (or contrarily, a pale one) and a series of undesirable moral characteristics, such as greed, treachery, anger, cruelty, stubbornness, and profound fearfulness.[89] According to the Latin text of Alcabitius, Saturn presided over the Sabbath (Saturday) and "servants and vulgar men" (*servos et viles homines*), who included tillers of the land, gravediggers, tanners, bath attendants, leather and metal workers, and Jews, individuals whose station in life was denigrated by the majority of the Christian population.[90]

The special association of skin disease and sin, especially sexual transgression or heresy, continued from the early Middle Ages into the twelfth and thirteenth centuries.[91] Jean-Louis Flandrin has argued, however, that during the thirteenth century explanations of leprosy were medicalized rather than moralized.[92] Instead of interpreting leprosy contracted by a child as a result of divine punishment for intercourse during menstruation, medical writers argued that the disease resulted from the exceedingly corrupt blood by which the child was nourished.[93] In truth, medical writers tended to create "scientific" explanations for any phenomenon they encountered or imagined to be true. For example, the various versions of the prose *Salernitan Questions* explore biological explanations of many of the bestiary tales, such as why a unicorn will approach a virgin and no one else, or how the Phoenix can be resurrected from the ashes.[94] The presence of such "scientific" explanations did not negate the moralized versions, or even the moral lessons implicit in the bestiary tale but unspecified in the medical texts. Nor should one suppose that medicalized discussions of leprosy and related ailments were necessarily morally neutral either. Quite the contrary, as I discuss in chapter 5.

Transmission: *Baraita de Niddah* and Laws of the Menstruant

The trend toward stringency in Jewish laws and expectations regarding the menstruant that began in late antiquity continued into the Middle Ages. Traditions from the *Baraita de Niddah* warning against contact with anything a menstruant touched, let alone intercourse with a menstruant, and prohibiting menstruating women from entering a synagogue or a room full of religious books, touching books, or answering "amen" to prayers became integral to medieval Ashkenazi and Sephardi practice and attitudes.[95] The *Zohar,* like the *Baraita de Niddah,* warned of the dangers of a menstruant's nail and hair clippings.[96] While legal writers recognized that these were traditions rather than proscriptions of law, nevertheless rabbis praised women for their piety in following these practices and discouraged any who would dissuade them.[97] Even those *responsa* (letters from rabbis answering specific legal questions) that attempted to mitigate the severity of the menstruant's isolation from daily activities and contact with her spouse and children point to the degree to which the menstruating woman was shunned in Jewish communities. For example, R. Meir of Rothenberg had to insist:

> Those who throw keys or money into the hands of their wives during their menstruation period should be sharply rebuked. Throughout this period until her immersion in a ritual bath, the wife should put down such articles for the husband to pick up, and the husband should put them down for the wife to pick up but throwing articles to each other at this period is prohibited.[98]

Both the popular practice of spouses throwing objects to one another while the wife was *niddah* and the alternate practice advocated by R. Meir ensured that the husband and wife came into no physical contact with one another while she was considered impure. Koren has demonstrated that mystical communities such as the Ḥasidei Ashkenaz in Germany and the kabbalistic circles in southern France and Spain adopted and expanded on the severe strictures advocated in the *Baraita de Niddah* above and beyond those in the Talmud. These warnings and rules derived from the *Baraita de Niddah* applied both to the individual male mystic and to the female aspect of the Godhead.[99]

Scholars have suggested a number of possible motivations for these shifting attitudes toward women in medieval Judaism. Judith Baskin has argued that the Ḥasidei Ashkenaz were influenced by Christian views of the woman as inherently carnal and responsible for the fall from Paradise and that these attitudes plus the desire to emulate Christian sexual asceticism led this community of men to minimize their contact with women, even their wives, as much as possible. Lengthening the separation period between the *niddah* and her husband and expanding the restrictions regarding contact between husband and wife during that period would have been part of this endeavor. Koren agrees but also argues for motivations based on long-standing purity requirements for divine visions derived from the Hekhalot texts and from the *Baraita de Niddah*.[100] Yedidyah Dinari and Israel Ta-Shma both emphasized fear of the menstruant as dangerous as the motivation for practices separating her from people, holy objects, and space.[101]

Certainly there was a continued fear of divine or demonic punishment for those who violated the customs of *niddah*.[102] As with the initial stages of this shift in Jewish attitudes toward the menstruating woman, however, discomfort with or fear of women in this state derived in large part from the mixture of theology and current medical lore. Gynecological theory had pride of place in religious medieval texts even more than in rabbinic ones. Eleazar of Worms incorporated the argument that menstrual blood served to nourish an infant both while still a fetus and after birth (in the form of milk) in his commentary to the prayer *Nishmat Kol Ḥai*.[103] Nachmanides' commentary on Leviticus is rife with references to biological theories. For example, integral to his commentary on Leviticus 12:2 is a discussion of the two-seed theory and an explanation of Aristotle's ("Greek philosophers") view that all matter is taken from the woman. In his commentary on Leviticus 18:19 Nachmanides disputed those who suggested that menstrual blood nourished the fetus since this blood was lethal poison. Any mixture of menstrual blood with the "good" blood of the womb would result in the child having boils or leprosy.[104] Fundamental to kabbalistic theogyny was the definition of female blood as potentially poisonous and as the matter from which the world, especially the demonic world, was created.[105] Abraham Abulafia (thirteenth century) likewise saw menstrual blood as primordial matter—echoing Aristotelian beliefs—and connected to evil.[106]

Thus Jewish attitudes toward the menstruant, like those of Christians, were colored by gynecological theories. Unlike the Christians, however, medieval Jews also inherited and expanded on a set of religious practices and fears derived largely from the *Baraita de Niddah* that marked the menstruant as religiously as well as physically threatening in the extreme.

Textual and Visual Communities

In his exploration of orality and the transmission of ideas among Christians and heretics in eleventh- and twelfth-century Europe, Brian Stock has argued, "Literacy is not textuality. One can be literate without the overt use of texts, and one can use texts extensively without evidencing genuine literacy. In fact, the assumptions shared by those who can read and write often render the actual presence of a text superfluous."[107] Shared acceptance of a text or set of texts and interpretations by a group of individuals formed what Stock termed a "textual community," regardless of the ability of the entire community actually to read the texts. Textual knowledge and modes of allegorization could be and were transmitted orally. Indeed, for Stock, one of the surest signs of a community's having passed into true "textuality" was the point at which the "organizing text" no longer needed to be "spelt out, interpreted, or reiterated. . . . [I]nteraction by word of mouth could take place as a superstructure of an agreed meaning, the textual foundation of behaviour having been entirely internalized."[108]

James Scott was not interested in oral culture per se, but his insistence on the importance of euphemisms and trickster tales as vehicles for resistance fits neatly into Stock's concept of the medieval textual community. Derogatory epithets, stories, or pictorial representations frequently functioned as abbreviations for more complex sets of polemical associations.[109] Such agreed upon associations within a group may be said to be the foundation of a "textual community of polemic" in which the full narrative and its meaning no longer needs to be spelled out. In subsequent chapters I demonstrate that the polemical "texts" overlapped into the Jewish, Christian, and even Muslim communities so that, like Stock's heretics and Christians, ultimately they were using a symbolic language comprehensible to all sides, though each presented its own interpretations.

Stock applied his theory to the transmission and transformation of interpretations of the Bible and other religious texts and rituals among medieval, primarily heretical, Christians. His hypothesis applies equally well, however, to textual knowledge and transmission between highly learned and less learned members of the Jewish community and also between Jews and Christians. To argue for a textual community between Muslims and the other two monotheistic faiths is more difficult since the Muslims had used the Qur'an, not any part of the Bible, as their religious foundation.[110] Nevertheless, I argue, there were enough commonalities among the religious texts, shared symbols and assumptions about certain animals, correct behavior, the body, and gender that at least a partial textual community could exist. Furthermore, Stock's model need not be confined to the realm of religion.

During the twelfth and thirteenth centuries, even earlier in the Muslim world, medical theory was becoming part of a common well-known language that was structurally fundamental in a wide array of discourses not immediately related to medicine.[111] Most important for our purposes, medical theory was becoming an integral part of religious metaphor, familiar to the learned and, eventually, to peasants in Europe. Monica Green in her studies of the *Trotula* texts and other gynecological works has repeatedly emphasized the importance of orality in the transmission of basic medical knowledge.[112] Since this kind of knowledge had become part of Jewish and Muslim popular literature, some of which was oral, suggests that not just the learned classes of these communities knew and appreciated medical theory as well.[113] That medical theory found its way into vernacular sermons in Europe from the thirteenth century onward shows the degree to which medicine was becoming integrated into all levels of religious thought; medical theory and knowledge was not simply the province of medical practitioners of varying levels of education or of university-educated theologians.[114] Given the level of shared knowledge and the reciprocal translation of medical texts among the Muslim, Jewish, and Christian communities in the twelfth through fourteenth centuries, it is not surprising that Jews, Christians, and Muslims were able to use medical ideas as a basic language of "proof" in their polemic against one another. Furthermore, oral exchanges were an important form of communication among Muslims, Christians, and Jews, even when the subjects discussed were extremely sensitive.

In addition to the tales of conversations between Franks and Muslims in Usamah ibn Munqidh's autobiography, a number of brief indications in chronicles suggest that oral information was important for Christian-Muslim understandings of one another during the crusades. The Muslim pilgrim Ibn Jubayr noted that the Franks publicized in their own languages their intention to take the holy city of Medina, a behavior that added to Muslims' shock at the venture.[115] Oderic Vitalis reported an incident in which Muslim women sang songs of vengeance and encouragement in Turkish to the Muslim soldiers. The Christians obtained interpreters to translate the songs and based their choice of action on them.[116] Muslims were even aware of the visual polemic that Europeans created of them, for one al-'Umari describes the Franks drawing a picture of an Arab beating Jesus and saying this is the Prophet of the Arabs beating the Messiah.[117] We know from Christian sources that Christians believed Muslims abused Christian holy objects and images.[118] Thus Muslims and Christians made an effort to familiarize themselves with what each was *saying* about the other, suggesting that the polemic that each created was dynamic, potentially responding to or seeking to reverse the propaganda of the other. This kind of oral exchange along with shared scientific knowledge, views of the body, and textual influences may account for some of the similar themes in Muslim and Christian polemic during this period.

David Berger has argued that repeated accounts, complaints, and warnings in both Christian and Jewish sources of conversations and even disputations between Jewish and Christian neighbors and associates need to be taken seriously. Interreligious debate did not occur exclusively under the official, staged auspices of Christian rulers, as was the case in the "Talmud Trial" of Paris and the Barcelona debate.[119] Efforts on the part of some Christians actively to seek out Jews to learn Hebrew and Jewish exegetical traditions not only resulted in greater Christian understanding of Jewish texts and contemporary Judaism; the Jews in their turn gained a considerable grasp of Christian exegesis and belief.[120] Vernacular sermons, songs, both religious and secular, and other public displays of faith would have allowed Jews knowledge of and access to Christian interpretations and symbolism.[121] The obverse is true of Christians learning of Judaism, insofar as medieval Jews performed rituals where Christians might have seen them, or sang, told stories, preached, and wrote in a language and alphabet their Christian neighbors would have understood and in a place where Christians would have heard them.[122]

Words, written or spoken, were joined by visual depictions in books, on windows, and on walls to convey stories and religious concepts. Most scholarly studies on church art have focused on art in cathedrals, but murals were prevalent in small, local churches and, according to Ellen Ross, these were extremely important for the transmission of shifting theologies about Jesus and Mary.[123] Sculptural or painted images were sometimes more than illustrations of written texts. Debra Hassig has cautioned that images and their signification could convey very different meanings, theological and otherwise, from those expressed in the texts they accompanied.[124] Many of the same principles of communication and meaning apply equally well to Jewish manuscript illumination. Indeed, the iconographic signification of many of the images were deeply intertwined in Judaism and Christianity.[125] Thus the visual was an equally vital pathway of communication among members of differing faiths during the Middle Ages. Sculpture and painting with their interpretations were an integral part of the interlocking medieval Jewish and Christian textual, polemical communities.

Mary and the Humanity of Christ

Historians of the Christian West have long noted that starting in the twelfth century and certainly by the thirteenth, the humanity of Jesus became increasingly important as a focal point for Christian devotion. Jesus' ministry and sufferings were literally imitated, even to the point that some of his most devoted followers were pierced with the wounds of his crucifixion.[126] The emphasis on the gruesome aspects of Jesus' pain and death has led Ross to refer to this understanding of Christ as the "gospel of gore."[127] In medieval Christian eyes, the real humanity of the Son of God could be seen in his birth and normal child-mother relations, his sorrow, physical pain, death, and reincarnation in the blessed bread and wine of the Eucharist.[128] Yet however vital and awe-inspiring Christians found Christ's humanity, belief in his divinity was never diminished. As in late antiquity and the early Middle Ages, this juxtaposition of divinity and humanity caused consternation in some circles, all the more as the mundane and potentially polluting realities of Jesus' human existence came to the fore.

Christians of late antiquity attempted to resolve their discomfort that God-as-Jesus was subjected to corporeal indignities by formulating theories that distanced Jesus' divinity from his body, especially from his mother's abdomen. European Christians of the twelfth and thirteenth centuries, on the other hand, focused their attention on creating a theology of Mary's body that set her flesh above the corruptible impurity characterizing most human existence. This approach was not new, it had been the basis for Radbertus's arguments in the ninth century.[129] Yet for Radbertus, Mary's special purity stemmed from her freedom from sexual passion in the conception of Jesus.[130]

Twelfth-, thirteenth-, and fourteenth-century Christians approached the problem of Mary's status in a number of new ways. Drawing from Augustine and pseudo-Augustinian texts, some argued that the process of conceiving Jesus through the Holy Spirit purified Mary of sin and fundamentally altered her body and the birthing process.[131] Others—Anselm (1091–1153), Peter Lombard (ca. 1100–1164), Bernard of Clairvaux (1091–1153), and Aquinas (ca. 1125–1274)—were primarily concerned with distancing God-as-Jesus from the original sin that all human children inherited from their parents. Nevertheless, that the Holy Spirit had also cleansed Mary's *flesh* was at least implicit in much of their writings.[132] Peter Lombard quoted John of Damascus's *De fide orthodoxa*:

> After the consent of the sainted Virgin, the Holy Spirit came into her according to the word which the angel of God had said, purifying (*purgans*) her, preparing [her] for the reception of the power of the divine Word, and at the same time for generation. And then it overshadowed her by the most high God, existing by itself, Wisdom and Virtue, this is the Son of God, *homousios* with the Father, which is consubstantial, as divine seed, and joined to itself animated flesh out of the most holy and most pure blood of the Virgin.[133]

Albertus Magnus likewise quoted part of this passage from John of Damascus and affirmed in good Aristotelian form that Jesus, like other human children, took his body from his mother's blood; Albertus refuted those who suggested that another substance, such as earth, would have been more suitable.[134] He further posited that Mary's womb needed to be specially prepared to house divinity.[135]

Having Mary purified at the point of conceiving Jesus or even some time after her own conception was insufficient for other theologians, such as the author of the *Mariale*, attributed to Albertus Magnus, and Duns Scotus (ca. 1265–1308). Rather, Mary had to be completely free from any taint from the moment of her inception.[136]

Whether Christian writers maintained that Mary was purified from the moment of her conception or at some later date, these doctrines served to distance her from the rest of humanity. Such a step was necessary because according to Aristotelian and even Galenic theories of generation, which had become a standard part of the scholastic writers' arsenal, Jesus' body, the essence of his humanity, was derived entirely from Mary's blood. If "woman [was] his humanity," then the body of the woman from whom it derived had to be cleansed and set above the rest of human, physical nature and the spiritual failings that such materiality implied. Thus the impetus for the doctrine of the immaculate conception and similar twelfth- and thirteenth-century arguments about Mary's cleansing was the same impulse that motivated trinitarian or anti-incarnation polemic among Pagans, Christians, and Manichaeans from the second to the fourth centuries and early medieval arguments against Mary's need for purification after childbirth.[137]

Some years ago Charles Wood explored medieval medical and theological views of menstruation in conjunction with the doctrine of Mary's immaculate conception. He noted that "the specifics of Marian theology would seem to deny the very possibility of a regular menstrual cycle."[138] According to Wood, biological theories making lactation—which everyone agreed Mary experienced—dependent on generation and the presence of blood in the womb pushed Christian thinkers to accept that Mary also menstruated, despite the profound purity attributed to her in the doctrine of the immaculate conception.[139] Wood rightly saw a contradiction between the states of impurity, disease, and sinfulness with which menstruation was associated and a doctrine that removed Mary from any of these attributes. But the cause and effect he posited need to be reversed. Beliefs in the Virgin's supernatural purification, whether during Jesus' conception or Mary's, developed *because* Mary menstruated rather than from biological theory dictating that Mary must have bled, despite the theological mandates of the immaculate conception. The "new" medical theory, circulating courtesy of recent translations of Greek and Arabic texts, inspired thinkers to reexamine the world, including the human body and religious issues surrounding it, in light of these theories. As Aristotelian and Galenic explanations of generation were applied to the most sacred birth of all, in Christian eyes, a theology was created to purify Jesus' humanity enfleshed in Mary from the filth and sin normally associated with the womb's blood.

Mary's definition as Jesus' flesh did not end with his birth and physical separation from her body. Dramatic tales of her death and funeral, accompanied by miracles punishing malicious Jews who attempted to harm the body, were imported from the eastern Mediterranean. Some of these stories also told of Mary's physical assumption into heaven.[140] Whereas early Latin writers indicated that as the pure container of divinity it was only appropriate that Mary escape corruption, twelfth-century authors such as Guibert of Nogent and the writer of the Pseudo-Augustinian treatise on the assumption insisted that putrefaction was unworthy of Mary, who was the flesh of Christ:

> [T]he soul of Mary rejoices by the radiance of Christ, and by his glorious regard. . . . And by what more excellent and special prerogative is she honored by the Son? Possessing in Christ her own body which she generated, radiant on the right hand of the Father[,] . . . Throne of God, inner chamber of the heaven of the Lord, room, rather tabernacle of Christ, [she] deserves to be where she is. Such a precious treasure is more worthy to serve heaven than earth; so much chastity justly incorruptible, any end results in no decay. That most sacred body, from which Christ took on flesh, and united divine and human nature[,] . . . consigned [to be] the food of worms. . . . I greatly fear to speak of the common lot of decay, the future of worm-infested dust. From which if I should experience nothing higher except my own, I should say nothing except [about] the manner of my own [death]. That without any ambiguity, ending in death, after death is a future of rot, after rot, worms, after the worm, as is appropriate, the most abject dust. Which does not seem acceptable to believe of Mary: because the duty of incomparable grace greatly propels reverence.[141]

Because Mary's body was, quite literally according to medieval medical theory, Christ's body, Christian authors felt compelled to argue that Mary experienced no decay in death. Otherwise, as Warner indicated, Mary would have been less than the saints whose sanctity was proven by their incorruptible flesh, and she would have been associated with the sinfulness of which decay was a sign.[142] More important, the very flesh of God would have succumbed to the putrescent fate of fallen man.[143]

The dichotomy between Mary's purity and the final end of the rest of humanity finds simplified expression in the pervasive comparisons of Mary and flowers, delicious food (honey), and perfume in Christian sermons, scholastic literature, and poetry.[144] Some of the floral symbolism derives from the application of Isaiah 11:1–3 ("And there shall come forth branch from the root of Jesse and a flower shall rise from the root. And the Spirit of the lord shall rest on him, of wisdom and intelligence, a spirit of counsel and strength, a spirit of knowledge and devotion. And the spirit of the fear of the Lord will fill him") to Mary and her son.[145] Technically, Christian allegorizations of this passage equated the Virgin with the branch and Christ with the flower. Iconographically, however, Mary was frequently shown bearing some kind of flower, generally a lily or rose, along with the infant Jesus, so that she herself became linked with the flower.[146] For the eleventh-century Fulbert of Chartres, Mary was a "lily among thorns," demonstrating that she had been preserved from all impurity of flesh and spirit.[147]

But evocations of flowers and fragrant spices served not merely to emphasize Mary's sanctity and purity; they also served as an extreme contrast of Mary to the diseased bodies of the supplicants whom, if repentant and sufficiently devoted to her, she habitually rescued.[148] Mary was a veritable warrior against rot. This topos is perhaps best illustrated in a lengthy, complicated section from Gautier of Coincy's *Miracles de Nostre Dame*, in which those suffering from a rotting soul, stinking leprosy, ulcers, and vomiting due to gluttony are encouraged to turn to the Virgin.[149] Yet Mary's power over decay was not merely in healing. Terrible disease characterized by foul smell was also her weapon. Gautier's depiction of a murderer struck with leprosy is extremely graphic: his stench fills the air so that all must hold their noses, his heart putrefies within his body, and his flesh is so eaten by disease that he hardly seems human. Repentance brings Mary's forgiveness and healing.[150] Later in the text the audience is exhorted to avoid sin and overeating, and women are called on to embrace chastity and virginity so that they may be pure and sweet smelling, like lilies who become violets in the Virgin's garden of paradise.[151]

Tales of Mary's healing or interceding on behalf of an individual or humankind also served to distance her from the rest of humankind by making her a powerful, heavenly being.[152] Paradoxically, her intercessory power derived from her very physical, human maternal connection with nursing Jesus: "You (Mary) have command over him (Jesus), because him, high maiden, you nourished from your breast."[153] Her milk was also a source of spiritual and physical healing and revelation.[154]

Making Mary's breast and the act of nursing Jesus the medium through which she could could compel divine action served to balance divinity and humanity not only in Jesus but also in Mary herself. Ross has argued that from the twelfth to the fifteenth century even the goriest depictions of Jesus' humanity were coupled with representations of his divinity.[155] The converse may also be true and applicable to Mary as well as to her son. Nevertheless, like arguments favoring her assumption into heaven without bodily decay, or the profound purity of her womb's blood, Mary as *mediatrix* set her apart from humanity without entirely depriving her of it. Through her, Jesus' own purity, a necessary corollary to his divinity, could be preserved even in the midst of an increased emphasis on Jesus' and Mary's humanity. Thus in twelfth- and thirteenth-century Europe the focus of defensive theology shifted from Jesus to Mary. Mary's body was the center of concern in late antiquity and the Middle Ages because in both periods the female blood from which the child was supposedly formed was linked to disease, decay, and uncleanness, both ritual and otherwise. These states of beings were seen as anathema in God. Various late antique Christian groups attempted to solve the problem of combined divinity and filthy humanity inherent in the doctrine of the incarnation by proposing various theogynies that removed God-as-Jesus from any contact with the womb or even the human body as a whole. Once a single doctrine of Christ's nature was established, however, manipulating the mixture of divinity and humanity in Jesus' own body was no longer an option, so Christians turned their attention to Mary's body and nature instead.

Mary was not the only medium in Western Christian theology through which God-as-Jesus took on corporeal existence and interacted with humanity. The other was the Eucharist. Divine embodiment in bread and wine, which was then consumed by regular human beings, posed many of the same troublesome quandaries as did the doctrine of the incarnation. Already in the ninth century the bread had to be especially consecrated, like Mary's body, according to Paschasius Radbertus. Ever concerned with the dignity of God, he likewise maintained that "it is not proper that Christ be eaten by the teeth."[156] A century later Berengar of Tours (999–1088) began a debate about the nature of the Eucharist that would continue well into the late Middle Ages. Berengar, drawing from Ratramnus and from Aristotelian and Platonic reasoning in Boethius, argued against separating substance or essence from accidents in the Eucharist. In other words, the external characteristics of an object (accidents), in this case the bread and wine, should coincide with the actual nature of the object (bread and wine), or if the bread and wine were really physically changed into the body and blood of Christ, then they should have the appropriate external characteristics, such as the smell and taste of flesh and blood. Since the Eucharist, to all appearances, remained bread and wine, no substantive change had taken place. Like Ratramnus, Berengar argued that a spiritual but not a substantive or material transformation occurred. Lanfranc and later Christian theologians who grappled with these issues disagreed with Berengar, but they did so using the same philosophical vocabulary and rules.[157]

By arguing that the bread was not literally the body of Christ, Berengar avoided any suggestion that God-as-Jesus suffered again, crushed by the teeth of the faithful, or was digested and excreted by Christians, or worse, by unbelievers or mice. Having proclaimed Berengar a heretic, twelfth- and thirteenth-century theologians did not have this luxury. Certain individuals such as Peter Lombard attempted to distance divinity from these indignities by insisting that only the "accidents" were chewed and digested, not the actual body of God.[158] Reason and faith were also key elements to ingesting the host; since animals and unbelievers lacked these qualities, the Eucharist could not be truly received by mice or unbelievers, even if they did manage to eat it.[159] Nevertheless, Christians continued to fret and to rebel. Alan of Lille argued against allowing the Eucharist to a criminal three days prior to his hanging because it was counter to the dignity of God, who would be understood as still being in the dead man's stomach.[160] While many saintly women lived on the eucharist, rejecting all other food, Roland Bandinelli (Master Roland of Bologna, twelfth century) told of a man who attempted to live exclusively from the host in order to prove that his body's excretions must include the eucharistic bread. On the fifteenth day the man died. Bandinelli explained that the sinful man was consuming his own body from within, not the body of Christ.[161]

The reality of the bread's transformation into the person of Christ was confirmed by *exempla* in which doubtful Christians and Jews saw the bread become flesh or a child able to speak, bleed, or even flee those who wished to harm him.[162] The profound holiness of the Eucharist was manifested by the sweet smell or honeyed taste of the bread.[163] These tales along with Christian scholastic discussions insisting on the real, physical transformation and presence of Jesus in the bread can be seen as part of the increased emphasis on the humanity of Christ, for they simultaneously confirmed his childhood, in the case of certain eucharistic miracles, and his suffering and death.

Yet the need to write many *exempla* proving the literal embodiment of God in the Eucharist, plus learned arguments that carefully separated the fate of the bread passing through the digestive system from God, also demonstrates that not all Christians were comfortable with this mingling of divinity with the messy aspects of corporeal existence. Such discomfort and the solutions proposed to mitigate it find a strong parallel in the simultaneous development of theories of Mary/Christ's body that shielded God-as-Jesus from the strongest human pollutions: menstruation, decay, and sin. The performance of healing via the host, plus the fragrance and unexpected delicious taste of the bread, emphasized the wafer-Christ's divine power and purity in much the same way that Marian tales confirmed the heavenly potency and purity of the Virgin. Thus the emerging twelfth- and thirteenth-century views of the Eucharist need to be studied conjointly with those of Mary, for together they form a theology that reveled in the humanity of God at the same time that it distanced divinity from bodily filth and pollution.[164]

Conclusion: Concepts of Divinity and the Human Body

As in late antiquity, the Christian doctrine of the incarnation forced a collision of attitudes about pure divinity and unclean humanity. Twelfth- and thirteenth-century Europe differed from the late antique and early medieval Mediterranean in a number of ways. Questions about the nature of Mary and the Eucharist opened by Radbertus and Ratramnus and then ignored in the Carolingian period became central in the twelfth and thirteenth centuries. Whereas in late antiquity attempts to assuage discomfort over divinity taking on human flesh and dwelling in the womb of a woman had focused on Jesus himself, in the twelfth and thirteenth centuries these efforts centered on Mary and on the Eucharist.

With the translation of Greek and Arabic polemics and medical material, curiosity and speculation about women's bodily functions magnified among both Jews and Christians, who shared essentially the same medical traditions and texts. As a rule this scrutiny resulted in an intensification and elaboration of preexisting beliefs that women's blood, indeed sometimes their whole bodies, was a corrupt, filthy source of disease. The choice of associations (smell, leprosy, decay) served to further women's connection with matter and sinfulness. Increasingly stringent laws separating the menstruant from her family because of her "harmful" impurity probably combined with medical attitudes to make a woman's blood particularly horrific in Jewish thought. These negative biological theories fed into Christian theology and were in part responsible for Christian efforts to distance Mary (and thus Jesus) from any human impurity, especially her own. They also, as we shall see, profoundly colored Jewish anti-Christian polemic against the incarnation and the Christian response. To a much lesser degree they also filtered into Muslim and Christian polemic regarding one another's occupation of holy sites in and around Jerusalem.

CHAPTER FOUR

Filthy Womb and Foul Believers

The Incarnation and Holy Spaces in the Jewish-Christian-Muslim Debate

Much of Jewish and Christian polemic that invoked dirt and impurity during the twelfth and thirteenth centuries attacked or defended the doctrine of the incarnation. At the center of this exchange was Mary. Jewish arguments against the incarnation focused on the abdomen of Mary as a place rendered unclean by menstrual blood, excrement, urine, and semen. Christians, having learned of Jewish objections either orally or later in the thirteenth century by reading Jewish texts, attempted both to defend the purity of Mary and God and to create a counterattack. In their counterattack Christians punctuated their "dialogues" with crass bodily epithets to suggest that Jews were far dirtier than Mary and Jesus could ever be according to Jewish interpretations of the incarnation. Similarly, coarse Jewish polemic against the bodies, holy objects, spaces, and rituals of Christians intimated that the Christian human body or church was a profoundly unsuitable habitation for God. Muslims and Christians likewise developed epithets of impurity in which either the holy spaces of the other were depicted as unclean or the presence of the other in "legitimate" holy spaces polluted mosques or churches. Muslims, though continuing to reproach Christians for suggesting that God-as-Jesus could have entered the dirty, limiting space of a womb as they had in the early Middle Ages, reserved their most graphic evocations of impurity for the Church of the Holy Sepulchre and the bodies and habits of the crusaders. Since the Muslims utterly rejected the Christian belief that Jesus had died, polemicizing against Jesus' supposed grave site circumvented negative remarks about Mary—a revered figure in Islam—yet gave full vent to their abhorrence of the Christian doctrine of the incarnation by focusing on Jesus' supposed death and the implication of decay. Thus, while evocations of stench, cadavers, unclean effluvia, and general impurity may seem to target Jewish, Christian, and Muslim believers without reference to the incarnation, often they were attempts to inveigh against or reaffirm the doctrine of the incarnation, directly through the bodies of Mary and Jesus or indirectly through the bodies and sacred buildings of believers.

Christian argumentation regarding Mary's role in the incarnation can be characterized as reactive rather than proactive; it defended Christian doctrine in response to specific, known Jewish objections. Christian eucharistic polemic against the Jews, on the other hand, was more offensive, perpetrating tales of Jewish desecrations of the host or of Jews murdering Christian children, which the Jews then had to counter, often by appealing to the authorities.[1] When such appeals failed, filthy words became violent action, resulting in the death of the accused Jews.[2]

In Jewish anti-incarnation polemic focusing on Mary or the Eucharist, Jews frequently demonstrated a sound knowledge of Christian theological debates in relation to current medical theories. Jewish polemicists were thus able to exploit the theological and biological beliefs that linked excrement, stench, rot, hell, and women in contrast to fragrance, holiness, and the exceptional bodies of Mary and Jesus. These polemicists also played on Jewish purity customs that targeted women's reproductive fluids as highly polluting to Jewish sensibilities and thus antithetical to divinity.[3] Graphic descriptions of Mary's abdomen served to establish a barrier of disgust between the Jewish audience and the central tenets of Christianity; increased male fear of and discomfort with women's bodies added to the aversion. Based on the hierarchy of spirit/male versus matter/female, Jesus' origins from a woman's body marked Christian belief as material rather than holy. This dichotomy was heightened by graphic descriptions in Jewish polemic in which Christian negative stereotypes of Jews were aimed against the Christians themselves.

Muslim-Christian polemic was likewise gendered. Rather than feminize one another, Christians and Muslims created a rhetoric of hypermasculinity and violence. In crusade chronicles and related texts Muslims are depicted as excessively cruel and bloodthirsty, like animals. They actively seek to desecrate Christian holy places using excrement, animals, and blood. Christians had long maintained that the Prophet Muḥammad and his male followers indulged excessively in sex, as evidenced by the four wives allowed to Muslim men and the larger number of wives taken by the Prophet himself. During the twelfth and thirteenth centuries, Christians emphasized and elaborated on this strain of polemic.[4] During the crusades, Muslims depicted the Franks as excessively warlike, promiscuous, incapable of understanding or enforcing appropriate female behavior, and potential violators of Muslim women's bodies and Muslim sacred space. In Muslim chronicles, European Christian women alternate between libidinous or indistinguishable in behavior and dress from European men; Muslim writers regarded both extremes as reprehensible. The danger posed by Christian men to Muslim women became a metaphor for Christian invasion of mosques, particularly al-Aqsa and the Dome of the Rock in Jerusalem, and these places, like women, became impure as a result.[5] In the case of Muslim-Christian polemic, therefore, the Aristotelian dichotomy male/female, or spiritual or rational/material or irrational, does not apply. Rather excessive masculinity became a negative category with which to make the enemy disgusting and inspire one's fellows to join in holy war. In these texts Christians and Muslims were irrational in one another's eyes because of their bestial, sexual violence rather than their association with the female body.

As with the generalized Christian anti-Jewish invective contained in discussions of the incarnation, Christian polemic contained in *exempla* reveled in scatological associations. Christians—like Jews—sought to create barriers against social interaction of the two groups by marking their opponents and their beliefs as abhorrent. This language of dirt and irrationality may also be seen as an attempt to reassert Christians' spirituality and metaphorical masculinity in the face of Jewish invective. The angst caused by Jewish arguments against the incarnation created in the vessel of Mary and in the host derived in part from the need to defend Christian doctrine not only against Jews but also against Cathars and doubting Christians. For example, in their anti-Jewish disputations both Odo of Cambrai (fl. 1140) and Guibert of Nogent (ca. 1055–1125) referred to Christians who agreed with Jewish objections, and Alan of Lille (d. 1202) refuted "heretics" who rejected Jesus' (and Mary's) corporeal incarnation and the physical presence of Jesus in the Eucharist.[6]

Mary's Body, God's Dirt

Virginal Conception and Birth

Jewish and Christian disputes over Mary's virginal conception and birthing of Jesus centered on purity, ritual or physical. In all the polemic it is Mary's purity or impurity that is key; Jesus is a secondary consideration. While Christians also may have been addressing doubts and disputes internal to the Christian community, an examination of the rhetoric from both Jewish and Christian polemicists shows clearly that each side was familiar with the other's arguments and that the Jews were cognizant of the theological problems engendered by the Catholic doctrine of the incarnation. Christians and Jews alike used the language of physical dirt; in their defense of Mary, however, Christians mingled corporeal pollution with metaphors of physical filth to symbolize spiritual corruption. Thus Jews were "dirty" because of their spiritual blindness. Furthermore, Christians attempted to create "scientific" parallels between the natural world and Mary to prove both the possibility and the resulting purity of Jesus' virginal birth, a tactic that became grounds for ridicule by their Jewish counterparts.

Jews capitalized on Christian doctrinal idealizations of Mary as devoid of sexual desire. In *Sefer Yosef ha-Meqane'*, a Jewish anti-Christian text from the mid-thirteenth century, Jesus is the "offspring of whoredom" (*'ul ha-zimah*).[7] Similarly, in Ashkenazi *piyyuṭim* and in the Hebrew Crusade Chronicles, Jesus is a *ben niddah* (son of menstruation), *ben zonah* (son of whoredom or lust), or *mamzer* (bastard).[8] Such terms, derived from the *Toledot Yesu* tradition, denigrated Jesus by impugning the sexual behavior of Mary.[9] In the face of Christian idealizations of Mary as one who not only had never had intercourse but also had never experienced lust, such accusations were especially repugnant to Christians.[10]

Jewish suggestions that Jesus was simply the offspring of Joseph and Mary were nearly as disturbing to Christians as accusations of adultery for precisely the same reasons.[11] For Mary to have had sex with Joseph at any point meant that she might have felt passion, which, according to Christians, was the root of impurity and original sin. The Pseudo-William of Champeaux (1123–48) created a Jewish verbal adversary who argued that Christ was ineffectual against original sin, since being born of a woman caused Jesus himself to be stained by sin. If Jesus could not keep himself pure, how could he purify anyone else? Pseudo-William retorted:

> When you say that Christ is subject to original sin, you lie utterly. He did not have original [sin] because he was not conceived in iniquity. . . . On the other hand he was conceived of a stainless *(immaculata)* virgin, and born without being generated from male seed and therefore was not a participant in original guilt. That was the nature in which the first

> man was placed, after which it was corrupted by sin. Because if he had not sinned and likewise experienced corrupt and sordid delight in generating, indeed he would have remained in the quiet, placid nature in which he was made. Why was he (Adam) conceived without sin? Because he experienced no ardent desire. But because he sinned, carrying that sin in himself, he corrupted the pristine goodness of his nature. . . . And then, since Christ in his conception was free of all sensuality, he carried no stain *(maculam)* of sin, on the contrary with the cooperation of the Holy Spirit he had a placid and pure conception. . . . [H]e was not from the corruption of the flesh nor was he in the least ill from original sin, rather he was able to and did heal us from our sickness because his mother remained a virgin after giving birth.[12]

Pseudo-William was not alone; this was a common Christian interpretation that "concupiscence is sin," as Guibert of Nogent also argued. In Vision 6 of the *Scivias* Hildegard of Bingen (1098–1179) saw the "unchaste" in the following way:

> Some are hairy of body and seem dirty in soul, because they are pervaded with unclean human pollution; for they are evil and *unchaste* in flesh, shamelessly polluting themselves with the ordure of vice, and contaminating their souls with the stains of filthy human sin as a swine rolls its body in mud.[13]

Christian authors used the language of physical dirt to discuss both terrestrial and spiritual uncleanness, switching easily from one category to the other.[14] For Christians, true dirt came only from sin, and the worst sin, the one that infected all of humankind, was the first one, sexual desire. If Jesus were the product of such passion, even in marriage, then not only was Mary deeply polluted, but God-as-Jesus himself was as contaminated as any other human being, a scenario that undermined Christian theologians' and popular writers' strenuous efforts to distance Mary, and thus Jesus, from the impurities of human existence.[15]

The natural mechanics of the virgin birth became fodder for lively invective on both sides. The authors of *Sefer Joseph ha-Meqane', Sefer Niẓẓaḥon Yashan* (late thirteenth, early fourteenth century), and *Vikuaḥ ha-Radaq* (thirteenth century) had their Christian disputants contest that Mary conceived and gave birth through some part of her head. Scholars have questioned whether these arguments derived from Cathar anti-Catholic polemic.[16] By having Jesus born from Mary's head, God-as-Jesus was distanced from any hint of impurity connected with the womb, an idea very much in accord with Cathar anticorporeal doctrines.[17] Yet as David Berger rightly insists, Mary's conception through her ear, courtesy of her hearing and obediently agreeing to God's word, was common in Catholic poetry and art,[18] especially in bestiary traditions connected with Mary. The weasel, par excellence, typified Mary and the conception of Jesus because it was believed to conceive through the ear and give birth through mouth.[19] Vultures were evoked because they conceived without sex, and bees, mice, and flies, which generated spontaneously from such low matter as excrement and corpses, were cited as examples of asexual reproduction in the natural world.

Guibert of Nogent, Martin of Leon (d. 1203), William of Bourges (1150–1209), and Jacob b. Reuben's Christian spokesman (ca. 1170) all employed these traditions to counter Jewish objections that Jesus' conception without male seed was impossible.[20] Sapir Abulafia emphasizes the use of rational, scientific argument in these texts as the basis for the "truth" of Christianity. Jews' inability to grasp these natural parallels to the incarnation demonstrated their faulty reasoning ability and thus called into question their humanity, or in the case of Jacob b. Reuben's Christian, the stupidity of his reasoning pointed to the Christian's base, animalistic intellect.[21] Yet rationality is only part of these "scientific" arguments. Purity from sexual passion was at the core of Christian analogies of Mary's virginal conception of Jesus with the asexual reproduction of certain animals. Just as Jewish accusations that Mary had sexual relations attacked her purity in Christian eyes, comparing her to animals that did not engage in coitus defended it.

This Christian defensive strategy backfired. Given the negative associations normally attached to excrement and rotting matter from which many of these animals were said to spring, or feed, in the case of vultures, likening the most pure of women to these creatures was disastrous polemically, however sound the biological theory behind it. Jacob b. Reuben rather mischievously countered Christians' animal analogies by citing Isaiah 41:14, "Fear not you worm of Jacob," and Job 25:6, "how much less a man who is a maggot, and a son of man who is a worm." According to Jacob, since the first text clearly refers to all Jews, following the Christians' logic, all Jews must be born without sexual intercourse. Jacob b. Reuben states about the passage from Job: "we do not say this thing except in language of contempt."[22] Thus he implies that Christians call their God a worm. Worse, the analogy lent support to the association of Mary with human excreta in Jewish polemical texts.

Defending Mary's continual virginity posed serious problems for Christian polemicists. In the passage cited from Pseudo-William of Champeaux, Jesus' stainlessness is dependent in part on Mary remaining a virgin *after having given birth,* a physiological impossibility. Jews challenged this process in their anti-Christian polemic and in Christians' descriptions of Jewish arguments in anti-Jewish dialogues.[23] Christians defended the feasibility of postpartum virginity by comparing Jesus to light passing through glass without breaking it, or to the fire that burned the bush but did not consume (Exod. 3:2).[24]

Like arguments about the virginal conception of Jesus, ultimately these analogies were intended as proof of Mary's purity. If Jesus passed through Mary like light through glass, then Mary experienced neither pain nor bleeding either from the breaking of her hymen (which would have destroyed her virginity) or from the tearing and afterbirth that normally accompany labor.[25] Freedom from pain and bleeding pointed to Mary's exemption from Eve's curse ("I will greatly multiply your pain in childbearing; in pain you shall bring forth children"), further affirming her purity from original sin, and it meant she was pure in the Levitical sense, namely, she did not bleed after birth and thus required no purification under Jewish law.[26] Both the author of *Vikuaḥei Radaq* and of *Niẓẓaḥon Yashan* understood the theological principle underlying this Christian doctrine and sought to counter it:

> You may argue that he was not defiled in her womb since Mary had ceased to menstruate and it was the spirit that entered her; subsequently, he came out unaccompanied by pain or the defilement of blood. The answer is that you yourselves admit that she brought the sacrifice of a childbearing woman. Now it is clear that this sacrifice is brought as the consequence of impurity from the fact that the same sacrifice of two turtle doves or two pigeons is brought by a leper, a woman who has had impure issue, and one who has given birth. Indeed to this day they call the day that she came to the Temple and brought her sacrifice "Light" [Lichtmess], and fast for forty days in commemoration of the forty days she remained impure from Christmas until "Light" as it is written, "If a woman be delivered and bear a manchild, then she shall be unclean seven days" (Lev. 12:2). The additional "three and thirty days" (Lev. 12:4) make forty.[27]

The author of the *Niẓẓaḥon* used the Christians' own festival celebrating Mary's purification as proof that Mary must have been rendered as physically impure as any other woman and by extension must have in fact experienced pain, proving that she fell under the curse of Eve.[28]

In all these arguments, whether dealing with Jesus' conception or his birth, the primary issue is the purity of Mary's body. Christians chided Jews for being "literal minded" and not grasping that sin was the true pollution.[29] Nevertheless, the Christians' more "abstract" form of purity or impurity was dependent on physical manifestations of Mary's body: whether she experienced passion, intercourse, or pain.[30] Encoded in these experiences were the human effluvia that Leviticus and subsequent Jewish law and traditions designated as ritually impure, namely, semen, menstrual blood, and postpartum blood.[31] When associated with divinity these substances were abhorrent to Jews and, for all the protestations to the contrary, disturbing to Christians.

The Foul Bowels of a Woman

Of all the stages of the incarnation in which Mary played a role, the one about which Jews and Christians became most exercised were the nine months of Jesus' fetal formation and nourishment in Mary's womb. God-as-Jesus' derivation from menstrual blood and proximity to Mary's unexcreted waste challenged Christian and Jewish ideals of holiness as pure, fragrant, and clean. Instead the Catholic doctrine of the incarnation firmly associated God-as-Jesus with a profoundly impure and, following the biological theories of the day, poisonous substance. That Jews saw Jesus' dwelling in Mary's womb in this light infuriated Christians because this critique came precisely at the time in which Mary's humanity and special purity was becoming the focal point of their devotion. Christians' verbal retaliation targeted Jews as weak-minded and soiled. The vehemence of their polemic underscores the degree to which Jews had succeeded in pinpointing the most vulnerable area of twelfth- and thirteenth-century Christian sensibilities. Although this issue was inherently sensitive, it was the existence of Christians, such as Cathars, who *agreed* with the Jews that intensified the pitch and importance of the Jewish-Christian debate on this subject within the Christian world.

That Jews and some Christians found God's indwelling in Mary's womb distasteful becomes clear when comparing the arguments of Jewish polemicists to those of "heretics" captured by the Inquisition. Joseph Qimḥi (ca. 1160–1235) protested:

> Now that he (Jesus) has come and appeared to the world, you believe that he is the living God and the King of the world. I am astonished and cannot believe this thing. That the great and fearful God Whom no eye has seen, Who has neither form nor image, Who said, may His Name be exalted, "For man may not see me and live" (Exod. 33:20)—how shall I believe that this great, inaccessible, hidden God needlessly entered the belly of a woman, the filthy *(miṭunafim)* foul *(musraḥim)* bowels [or "intestines"] of a female, compelling the living God to be born of a woman?[32]

In the early fourteenth century, a young, ostensibly Christian woman, also from the south of France, expressed qualms about the incarnation similar to Qimḥi's:

> And having heard this [that a woman had been forced to give birth on the road], she was reminded of the filth *(turpitudo)* which women emit at birth, and when she saw Christ's body elevated at the altar, she was reminded of that filth which would have affected the Lord's body. And because of that thought she fell into an error of faith, that is that the body of the Lord Jesus Christ was not there.[33]

Both Qimḥi and the young woman, Aude, were deeply disturbed by the implications of the Christian doctrine of the incarnation, namely, that God would be subjected to the contents of a woman's womb. For Jews, the abdomen of a woman was an objectionable dwelling for God for two reasons: the contents of the womb were dirty and ritually impure, and the intestines (bowels) were filthy. These characteristics combined to make the womb an unacceptable habitation for God.[34] Depicting Mary's belly as soiled played on shared Christian and Jewish distaste for women's genital fluids and human excrement to create disgust for the doctrine of God-as-Jesus dwelling in a woman, a reaction some Christians had, regardless of Jewish rhetoric.[35]

Whatever proofs or counterarguments Christians and Jews attempted to marshal regarding the special nature of Mary's blood, both were aware that standard gynecological theory dictated Jesus derived his bodily existence from Mary's blood.[36] For example, Gilbert Crispin stated, "Who created the first man without male seed, out of nothing, without the male seed of any other, is he who could create the man, Christ, from the flesh of his mother."[37] The acceptance of this biological theory made the nature of Mary's flesh, here equated with her blood, central to the Jewish-Christian debate.

An anonymous thirteenth-century Jewish polemicist, erroneously identified with David Qimḥi, abbreviated as Radak, son of Joseph Qimḥi, best exemplifies this melding of medical theory, theology, and polemic. After dispensing with any suggestion that Jesus entered or exited Mary via any orifice other than the vagina, the author insists that like any other thirteen-year-old, Mary menstruated. While she was pregnant she ceased menstruating since the menstrual blood was needed to nourish the fetus, and she continued to be free of monthly bleeding while nursing because the menstrual blood was transformed into milk for the fetus. At this point the author did not elaborate on the theological consequences of such an observation in the context of the incarnation; however, the implication would have been clear to anyone familiar with medical thought and Christian theology. Jesus had been created and nourished by menstrual blood not only as a fetus but also throughout his infancy. Pseudo-Radak continued:

> Know that menstrual blood is practically mortal poison. If a man were to drink a single cup of it he would die in a few days or become leprous, for that blood is absolutely filthy and dirty. It is a miracle that the fetus is nourished from that same blood for nine months without harm, only weakness. And when it leaves the womb of its mother, it does not have the power to walk on its feet because it fed from that blood all those months. It is not so with animals which immediately leave the mother's womb and walk. Why? Because livestock and animals do not have menstrual blood and their fetus is nourished from pure blood from the heart which is good blood, healthy and clean. Thus when it leaves the mother it walks immediately. So, Jesus, whose mother conceived him from the Holy Spirit and who was not nourished from that filthy blood in the bowels of his mother, should have walked the first day of his birth, and spoken with the intelligence he would have attained when thirty years old.[38]

The question of why human infants were unable to walk immediately after birth, in contrast to animals, which were supposedly inferior to humans, was a point of discussion among both Christian scientists and theologians at the time.[39] Pseudo-Radak chose the most physiological of the circulating explanations, which placed the onus firmly on the nature of the menstrual blood that fed the embryo.[40] With a stroke of singular originality he then applied it, along with other harsh characterizations of menstrual blood, to

Jesus. According to Pseudo-Radak's formulation, for Jesus to have been truly created by the Holy Spirit he would need to have been free of menstrual contamination. Because Jesus was like any other infant and was not able immediately to walk and speak at birth, clearly his creation and growth followed the path of human development, making him completely dependent on this profoundly poisonous substance, menstrual blood.[41]

For any Jew reading this text, such an irrevocable association of Jesus with menstrual blood would have been extremely damning given the degree to which *niddah* was reviled as a dangerous force intolerable to God in twelfth- and thirteenth-century Jewish culture. Nor would hearing or reading these arguments have been comfortable for any Christian.[42] Basing the objections on scientific grounds added weight beyond that of Christian and Jewish religious proofs and visceral emotions, as both sides accepted the biological premises of the polemic. The true barb of Pseudo-Radak's polemic, however, lay in his combining these elements with a detailed explication of the deleterious properties of menstrual blood and their implied effect on the Christian God. Mary, a healer and the purest of women in Christian thought, had been transformed into a vile container of poison. Her son, the supposed embodiment of divinity, was a helpless product of this poison and therefore human.

While biology crept into other polemical texts, few were quite so "scientifically" driven as the text attributed to David Qimḥi. Rather Jewish and Christian writers centered their attacks on analogies of impurity and dirt. The author of *Niẓẓaḥon Yashan,* along with Joseph ha-Meqanne' (Official), from whom he was drawing, compared the Christian doctrine of the incarnation to the sin of the golden calf in Exodus 32:1–6. The Israelites' sin was understandable, they argued, since the people probably reasoned: "There is nothing in the world more pure and clean than gold. Perhaps the spirit of God has entered it, and it possesses the Holy Spirit."[43] Joseph Official had R. Nathan demand of the bishop, "[How] will I be able to say that he (God or the Holy Spirit) entered a woman, and he warned us 'do not touch a woman for three days' (Exod. 19:15) for the sake of one time that he wanted to speak to us?"[44]

Jewish arguments that Adam was superior to Jesus because he was drawn from clean earth rather than subjected to the womb's impurities are related to the analogy of the golden calf and paralleled Christian debates about whether angelic or earthly flesh might have been better than human.[45] In the discussion of both Adam and the golden calf, Jews attempted to demonstrate that any kind of body would have been preferable to one that had taken shape amid the fluids of a woman's womb. Christians disputing such theories about God, whether raised by Jews or by members from their own ranks, maintained either that angels were also corruptible and thus as unsuitable as humans or, in the case of Odo of Cambrai, that the foulness of human viscera and effluvia was an illusion of the senses. Reason dictated that the human body was "cleaner than the moon, more precious than the sun."[46] In the first case suggesting that angels were, in comparison to God, impure and despicable, insinuated that Jews had a corrupted vision of purity and divinity. Odo's counterargument, while more subtle, had the same implications, with the added insult that Jews, like peasants, were dependent on their coarse senses and lacked rationality.[47]

Joseph Official and the writer of the *Nizzaḥon Yashan* were equally sharp, for in the analogy of the golden calf they trapped their supposed Christian interlocutors just as Odo had "outwitted" his Jewish one. In the Jewish texts both sides accepted that worshiping the golden calf was a sin, yet because of the purity of gold relative to a woman's body, this sin was less grievous than the Christians' belief that God entered a woman's womb. The author of the *Nizzaḥon Yashan* even had the Christians enthusiastically agree with his explanation of the Israelites' mistake, thus making them seem even more foolish and sinful when he detailed the implications of having God enter Mary's womb:

> Accursed are you blind men who have eyes but do not see how you will be judged and entrapped in hell. Why an a fortiori argument applies here: They erred in worshiping a clean thing like gold, and yet their iniquity was marked before God who said "When I make an accounting, I will bring them to account for their sins" (Exod. 32:34) and refused to grant them complete forgiveness. Certainly, then, you who err in saying that something holy entered into a woman in that stinking place for there is nothing in the world as disgusting as a woman's stomach, which is full of feces and urine, which emits discharge *(zivot)* and menstrual blood, and serves as the receptacle for man's semen—you will certainly be consumed by 'a fire not blown' (Job 20:26) and descend to deepest hell."[48]

Joseph Official did not list the impurities of women. Nevertheless, his citation of Exodus 19:15 as a counter to the incarnation clearly suggested that contact with a woman's body made encounter with the presence of God impossible.[49] By extension, Jesus could not have embodied the presence of

God while a fetus in Mary's womb, though Joseph leaves this conclusion for the reader to draw. In the passage from *Niẓẓaḥon Yashan* not only are the impurities normally associated with a woman's womb, menstrual blood and *zavah,* listed, but semen is listed as well.[50] Thus the woman, specifically Mary, becomes the container of all human pollution, female and male.[51] Bathed in these impurities was the Christian "god" Jesus.

Nearly all the Jewish polemical tracts from the twelfth and thirteenth centuries evoke Mary's unclean womb and blood as an objection to God's embodiment as a fetus.[52] Constant references to Jesus as a *ben niddah* or *yiḥus zimah* (one of impure descent) in Hebrew polemical dialogues, poetry, and chronicles reinforced the *Toledot Yesu* story of Mary's seduction or rape while menstruating and emphasized the profound pollution Jesus received through Mary's body.[53] Christian polemicists from the period likewise described their Jewish counterparts as finding Jesus' confinement in Mary's womb horrific in terms very similar to those voiced in Jewish texts:

> In one thing especially we laugh at you and think that you are crazy. You say that God was conceived within his mother's womb, surrounded by vile fluid, and suffered enclosure within this foul prison for nine months, when finally, in the tenth month, he emerged from her private parts (who is not embarrassed by such a scene!). Thus you attribute to God what is most unbecoming, which we would not do without great embarrassment.[54]

What becomes clear in examining both the Jewish argumentation and Christian accounts of it is that proximity to levitically impure fluids in the womb was not the only objection to the fetal status of God-as-Jesus. In the passage above Leo, the Jew whom Odo of Cambrai either actually debated or created for the purposes of the disputation, used the word *fetidus* to describe the womb, which indicates specifically "foul smell." The author of the *Niẓẓaḥon Yashan* forthrightly called the womb "that stinking place" *('oto maqom ha-saruaḥ),* and Joseph Qimḥi called her intestines foul or stinking *(musraḥim).* Such vocabulary was common.[55] Menstrual blood itself was in part the cause of this "stench," for as Koren has shown, in the *Zohar* the fragrant sacrifices of Rosh Hodesh were needed to mask the smell of the Shekhinah during her "menstruation."[56]

A more obvious source of bad smell than Mary's blood, however, is the feces and urine to which Joseph Qimḥi and Odo of Cambrai alluded and which the author of *Nizzaḥon Yashan* specified. While Jesus' own production of excrement is evoked in Jewish polemical texts, especially in the context of his infancy, the content of Mary's intestines and their repugnant nature colored the descriptions of a number of Jewish polemicists.[57] The Virgin Mary's name was frequently replaced by the word *hari'a,* another term for excrement in Jewish polemical texts.[58] Lengthy, graphic argumentation designed to invalidate the Christian doctrine of the incarnation by pointing out that God-as-Jesus would have come into contact with human waste in Mary's body has been reduced to a single word—*shit.* Playing on this renaming of Mary, Joseph Official unified biological, menstrual, and scatological polemic in a single sentence: "Is he [Jesus] not the one who is born from a clod of dust, from *hari'a?*"[59] Claims to special status for Jesus and Mary were not merely disproved by their normal, human bodily processes; Mary had become the very excreta and blood that so disgusted Jewish and Christian readers, and through her, so had Jesus.

Christians vehemently denied that God-as-Jesus could be polluted by Mary's viscera. Returning to the metaphor of Jesus as a ray of light, Christians insisted that just as sunlight could not be sullied by any filth through which it passed, neither could God be soiled by dwelling in a womb.[60] Guibert of Nogent and Odo of Cambrai both denied that the physical world could contaminate God.[61] However, whereas Odo simply decried the Jew Leo's stupidity, Guibert of Nogent counterattacked. He responded to Jewish horror of God-as-Jesus in a virgin's womb with repeated allusions to Jews' own filth due to their sinful behavior and misconceptions:

> If you want to detest through natural paths, oh how many times have you vomited yesterday's meat and the previous day's wine with your most fetid mouth? . . . But to God authors of that ilk dedicate nothing more than known sin.[62]

The Jews who had rejected Mary as impure had themselves become spewing vessels of filth. In using such language, Guibert of Nogent expressed fury and sought verbal revenge against the Jews, whom he believed had blasphemed Mary and Jesus. Jews likewise vented their anger at their Christian oppressors and their distaste for the Christian doctrine of the incarnation by targeting she whom the Christians held most dear. Mary became pivotal in the Jewish-Christian debate during the twelfth and thirteenth centuries because newly explored, often negative gynecological theories, shifting purity practices within

Judaism regarding *niddah*, and the exhalted place being developed for Mary in Christian theology had conjoined to make her a profoundly problematic figure to Jews and some Christians.

Infancy, Death, and the Corruption of God

Childhood and mortality exemplified humanity at its most vulnerable and its most physically fluctuating (not a state suitable for God). Infancy was characterized by constant feeding, uncontrolled excreting, and rapid growth; death represented the ultimate disintegration of bodily integrity.[63] Both periods were marked by stench. Even when discussing some other stage of Jesus' life, his embodied capacity to excrete and thereby stink is cited by Jewish polemicists. As with scatological references to Mary and her womb, identifying Jesus as the producer of foul odors and effluvia was designed to instill repugnance toward Christianity and its founder and to characterize Christianity's concept of God as grossly carnal:

> Infancy in particular occasioned expressions of disgust and disbelief: Do you not remember that when the Messiah was a child, he used to do childish things, and you cannot deny what I am saying to you. If things are as I say they are, then look and see what your belief is according to your own words! A child defecates in his clothes and urinates in his bed and laughs with children and sometimes cries. Is it really correct to make him into a God, when he did all which I have mentioned above?[64]

For Joseph Qimḥi, who made a similar complaint against Christianity, however, Jesus' dependence on his mother for milk and comfort seems to have been a particular source of outrage:

> Indeed if she (Mary) had not suckled him, he would have died of hunger like other people. If not, why should she have suckled him? He should have lived miraculously! Why should she have suckled him for nothing that he should engage in all foul and miserable human practices?[65]

As in their discussions of the virginal conception and birth, Jewish authors were careful to insist that claims that Jesus was truly human once out of the womb had physical consequences. To deny these consequences was to deny Jesus' humanity. Not only did eating imply weakness, but the consumption of food and drink led to human waste, which seems to be what Qimḥi meant by "foul and miserable human practices."[66] Eating was also a precursor to rot.[67] Given that milk was believed to be concocted menstrual blood, necessary for the child's nourishment because of the child's origin from it, that God nursed and was dependent on a woman for all other physical needs must have seemed especially degrading to Qimḥi. The implied uncleanness of this physical exchange went hand-in-hand with arguments that God-as-Jesus was profoundly polluted by contact with Mary's body.[68] Indeed, when Christians responded at all to this objection to the incarnation, their replies were part of their defense of human (female) flesh as a worthy receptacle for God.[69] Reproaching Christians for the "normal" mother-child relations between Mary and Jesus would have been especially disturbing to Christians given that these relations were becoming a focal point of piety.[70]

In a passage from *Sefer Nestor ha-Komer* the author teasingly demands of the Christian what food Jesus brought with him to heaven and reminds his interlocuter that where food is digested, excrement and flatulence follow.[71] In general, the production of such effluvia and their concomitant smell marked an individual as lacking in holiness, or indeed as being of demonic origins.[72] Evoking God-as-Jesus' messy, mewling infancy or heavenly farts generated unseemly humor and diminished the dignity of the Christians' god.[73] On a more sinister level, the uncontrolled urination and defecation of the infant Jesus not only indicated the degree to which Christians had abased God but also were symbolic of the uncontrollable threat Christian religious pollution posed to Jewish society.[74]

Language of corruption and threat among Christians, Jews, and Muslims was most developed when attacking one another's bodies or rituals or in the polemic surrounding Jesus' crucifixion or Muḥammad's death. Depicting Jesus as a corpse contradicted a fundamental tenet of Christianity: Jesus' resurrection and his promise of eternal life to his believers. Portraying Muḥammad as subject to death did not contradict basic Islamic doctrine, but the ways in which Christians, and sometimes Jews, described Muḥammad's demise were designed to disgust their Christian and Jewish audiences and would have been repulsive to Muslims as well. Jewish authors of polemical dialogues were fairly restrained in their discussion of Jesus' death. Many noted that God is not supposed to be able to suffer and argued against any attempt to distinguish between the human aspect of Jesus capable of suffering and the godly aspect that was not. Others insisted on the contradiction between praying that he be spared the "cup" of death if it were God's will that Jesus die and Jesus and God being one and the same indivisible substance.[75] Occasionally Jewish authors merely emphasized that the indignity and helplessness of Jesus' death was unbefitting for God.[76]

While Jewish polemicists dealt only sparingly with Jesus' death and Christian polemicists even less, it was a common theme in *piyyuṭim* and Hebrew chronicles, resulting in part from their use of the *Toledot Yesu* tradition.[77] Constant recollections of Jesus' death, whether by calling him the "hanged one," a "corpse," or describing the crusaders as visiting Jesus' grave, reminded the Jewish audience of Jesus' status as a dead man with all the impurity that that state entailed.[78] Yet authors of *piyyuṭim* and chronicles rarely ended by announcing that Christians worshiped a cadaver. Like many of his coreligionists, R. Abraham, in his poem "'adabrah bezar ruḥi" (I Will Speak in the Sorrow of My Soul), referred to Jesus as a "trampled corpse" *(peger muvas)* as a way of indicating his humiliation, defeat, and worthlessness:

> We flee to eternal life in the shadow of your wings for we are left abandoned and sighing. / They bow without partaking of the hanged one, a trampled corpse [who] shames all who trust in him.[79]

Those who recorded Christian persecutions often characterized their own dead as having been trampled and otherwise desecrated after death.[80] By depicting Jesus' body as abused in a similar manner, Jews showed the "god" of the Christians as helpless and defeated, thus negating Christian claims of Jesus' power. Furthermore, Jews could be vicariously avenged for the humiliation inflicted on their loved ones by affirming that although the Christians had left slaughtered Jews naked and trampled in the dust, the very god of the Christians had been stepped on and sullied.

Jewish authors also emphasized Jesus' death and resulting uncleanness by describing him as a putrid or stinking corpse.[81] The author of the *Niẓẓaḥon Yashan* also alluded to this disturbing aspect of God-as-Jesus' end:

> "I am a worm and no man" (Ps. 22:7). Thus he admits that worms will cover his flesh, and if he were God he should not have said something that is not so, even out of modesty.[82]

This embellishment underscored decay, the physical aftermath of death, and undermined the Christian image of Jesus, risen after three days, his new, heavenly, altered body untouched by the rot that awaited other living beings at death. Given that the failure to decay and the lack of smell or fragrance were marks of holiness at least in the Christian world, attributing stench and putrescence to Jesus distanced him in the profoundest way possible from pure, incorruptible divinity.[83] Aware of this potential criticism, Christians were careful to insist that Jesus' body was not subject to decay after death.[84]

In drawing from the long-established antibiography tradition surrounding the Prophet Muḥammad, few Christian authors from the twelfth- through early fourteenth century surpassed the venom of the early medieval author Eulogius or even al-Kindi.[85] Like the Jewish polemic regarding Jesus' death, Christian tales of Muḥammad's death, the fate of his body, and the failure to resurrect drew on the dichotomy of fragrance/holiness versus stench/heresy.[86] The Jewish author of *Nizzaḥon Yashan* played with these Christian legends of the Prophet Muḥammad to create a parallel between Jesus and Muḥammad and make each repulsive to his readers. Under threat of death by the Khazar king unless they converted to one of the other three religions, both Christian and Muslim opt for Judaism, each proclaiming respectively of the other's "god":

> Muḥammad, their god, got drunk from wine and was thrown into the garbage and when pigs came and passed through the dump, they found him, dragged him, surrounded him, killed him, and ate him" whereas "belief in Jesus is evil, wanton and worthless. The Torah of his believers . . . is a shame and a disgrace, a lie and a betrayal, for he was crucified, and hanged and was unable to save himself.[87]

By evoking not only Christian tales of Muḥammad's death but also Christian depictions of him as the Muslims' god, the author was able to make the parallel even stronger; both were "false gods," and both died shameful, and especially in Muḥammad's case, smelly, impure deaths, as marked by Muḥammad's bed of garbage and devouring pigs as his executioners. For Jews and Muslims, such a death marked Muḥammad doubly unclean, for he came into close contact with unclean animals, swine, and was torn and eaten by predators, a fact that made "food"—here read religion—inedible according to Islamic as well as Jewish law.[88]

In Christian crusade chronicles, *chansons de geste,* and other literary depictions of Islam, Muḥammad's followers or his idols often suffer a similarly ignominious end, torn by animals or crusaders and trampled in the mud.[89]

As Tolan indicates, the agents of this degradation were either the Franks or the Muslim followers, who, feeling betrayed by their lack of victory, turn on their own gods to befoul them.[90] By making their own warriors desecrate and destroy the idols, Christians portrayed themselves as victors over their enemies but also as participants in the deserved humiliation of Islam and its founder, using the "idols" as a kind of proxy for the Prophet. The level of violence and shame-inducing imagery in these texts points to Christians' anger at, and perhaps fear of, Muslims. Because after the first crusade Christians were largely losing to the Muslims (and even the victories of the first crusade were bought at great cost, with many losses) at least in the Levant, these tales of the violent degradation of Muḥammad, his symbols (real or imagined), and his followers would have served to strengthen Christian resolve to continue the crusades, to provide a sense of victory even when there was none, and to imbue hearers with disgust for the Islamic faith, thus discouraging conversion and fueling passion for war. Those authors who chose Muslims as the perpetrators of the degradation of their own "idols" could both show Islam/Muḥammad stripped of all dignity and make the Muslims themselves faithless to their "gods" and disgusting because of their participation in filthy—albeit deserved in Christian eyes—acts.

Later Christian authors embellishing earlier polemic about Muḥammad's actual death make his demise even more lengthy and undignified than those from the early Middle Ages. In Alexandre du Pont's (fl. 1258) *Roman de Mahomet,* Muḥammad languishes in pain for a week. He and his followers are linked with a variety of vices: pride, avarice, mortal anger, and gluttony.[91] Others sought to link his death by pigs with the Jews. Gerald of Wales accused Muḥammad of "judaizing" because he forbade eating pork, thus "since he preached impurity and filth he was devoured by pigs which he had repudiated as impure animals."[92] Pedro Pascual, writing in the beginning of the fourteenth century, and those who borrowed from him portrayed Muḥammad's death and consumption by pigs as the result of a Jewish woman's trick; she misled his followers into venerating the Prophet's foot, the one piece of his body that she did not throw to the pigs. As Tolan points out in his analysis of this text, Muḥammad's death is made that much more disgraceful because it is at the hands of another despised minority, a Jew and a woman.[93] By associating Muslims with Jews, either explicitly, as in these texts, or in passing, as in describing the destruction of synagogues alongside that of mosques and "heathen shrines," Christian authors linked Muslims with the negative associations attached to Jews.[94] That Muḥammad, and thus Islam, was carnal and focused on earthly pleasures was part of the parallel Christian authors drew. Roger Bacon made the link between the two faiths and their "terrestrial" focus explicit.[95] Fidentius of Padua (ca. 1266–91) did not draw a direct analogy between Muḥammad, Islam, and Judaism; however, he emphasized that Muslims indulged in "luxuria" and were avaricious, violent, and stank—invectives that echo many of those being leveled against Jews and that would have inspired similar repugnance among Christians.[96]

Repeated insistence on the part of many Christians that Muḥammad was venerated by Muslims not merely as a prophet but also as a god established the Prophet as Jesus' competitor in divinity as well as humanity. While Muslims would have vehemently repudiated any suggestion that Muḥammad was divine, even as they repudiated similar Christian claims for Jesus, in this Christian schema, to attack Muḥammad's conduct, body, and manner of death explicitly or implicitly evoked those of Jesus by way of contrast. The focus on Muḥammad's death in particular targeted a nonexistent "incarnation" in which the "false god" Muḥammad was discredited through stench, a humiliating death, disposal by impure animals and failed prophecy. The purity of the Christians' own incarnate god showed in stark contrast, except in the *Niẓẓaḥon Yashan* where Jewish polemic against Jesus is combined with Christian invectives against Muḥammad to mark both figures as disgraced in the manner of their deaths and far from the purity and power incumbent on divinity.

Even after death Jesus was subject to the polemic of stench and excreta. Though self-censorship and Christian authorities may have succeeded in removing any direct reference to Jesus from BT Gittin 57a, in most copies of the Talmud that survived into modern times, this passage was very much in the minds and vocabulary of twelfth- and thirteenth-century Jews. For example, they were well aware of the unexpurgated version that described Jesus and those who disrespected the sages in a hell of boiling excrement. A number of Jewish texts from the period evoke this talmudic passage in a polemical context. In the *Chronicle of Solomon bar Simson* the doomed David b. R. Nathaniel taunts the crusaders and burghers, "In hell you (the Christians) shall be judged along with your deity and in boiling excrement, for he is the son of a harlot."[97] As in the talmudic passage, by placing Jesus and his followers in a smelly substance with links to evil and the material (as opposed to the spiritual) world, the chronicler drew on the powerful cultural associations surrounding human waste to obliterate any claim for Jesus' purity and divinity. During the Paris Talmud Trial, the convert to Christianity,

Nicholas Donin, is depicted as raising the specter of Jesus boiling in excrement as one of the many unsavory depictions of Christians in Jewish postbiblical writings. Donin mockingly explains that Jewish texts place Jesus and his followers in boiling excrement "to make us [Christians] stink."[98]

From his origins in a female abdomen full of menstrual waste and feces to his end in an excremental hell, Jesus had come full circle in Jewish anti-Christian polemic. While Mary became equated with "shit" with the eponym *hari'a,* Jesus was eternally doomed to be surrounded by or a producer of it as an expression of Jews' contempt for Christianity, their rejection of the incarnation, and their fear of contamination. Furthermore, this insult had been extended to include all Christian believers, so that they embodied the stench and polluting qualities of the God they so wished to emulate.

In the Hebrew account of the Paris Talmud Trial, Rabbi Yeḥiel did his utmost to convince the Christian audience that the Jesus in question was not the same as the one the Christians revered.[99] Ultimately, however, an especially insulting aspect of Jewish anti-Christian polemic had been revealed to the wrong audience. The hidden transcript was no longer hidden or even in doubt. Shortly after the Paris Talmud Trial Pope Gregory IX (r. 1227–41) recorded and distributed Jewish invectives about Jesus boiling in excrement, the stench of baptism, the adultery and impurity of Mary, and comparisons of churches and latrines.[100]

Yet the reason this invective and its revelation was so devastating was not simply because of its essential crassness. Augmenting the insult were the symbolic meanings attached to bodily waste and smell, meanings deeply grounded and shared by both religious communities. Christians understood quite well that in saying Jesus was condemned to an excremental hell and that Christians smelled bad, Jews not only repudiated Christian claims to purity and holiness but also placed the majority religion at the lowest rung of the spiritual hierarchy. When Christians retaliated, they retaliated in kind.

Polluted Temples and Stinking Rituals

God taking on human form and existence in the person of Jesus was the most literal "incarnation" in Christian theology, yet it was not the only one. God-as-Jesus' embodiment in the bread and wine of the Eucharist was another. This bread was further "enfleshed" when consumed by the human recipient. More abstractly, God also dwelled in the physical spaces of churches, mosques, and synagogues and in the bodies of the faithful. These were not literal incarnations in the same way as Jesus' human embodiment or the Eucharist, but they were closely related. As a result all these were targets for scatological and polluting rhetoric; in showing that the bodies and venerated spaces and objects of the religious other were unclean, Muslims, Christians, and Jews demonstrated that these "houses of God" were unworthy, even ridiculous. Therefore, either God did not dwell in them or the religious other's concept of God was faulty. Because Christians could not attack an embodied Jewish god, they slandered the bodies of Jews themselves. Jews did both. This polemic was one of vengeance and defensiveness on the part of both groups. During the crusades, Muslims and Christians used very similar insults. For them, however, usually the presence and behavior of the other in their holy spaces, especially those in Jerusalem, served as the source of pollution; the buildings themselves were not inherently foul. While anger and vengeance may have partially motivated this kind of polemic on both sides, the primary intention seems to have been as a spur to war.[101] That Christians, Muslims, and Jews resorted to graphic invectives invoking one another's filth indicates the degree to which all felt threatened, a feeling reinforced by growing Christian awareness of Jewish invectives and early familiarity on the part of both Christians and Muslims of one another's tactics.

Jews contrasted churches to the Temple in which the true presence of God literally dwelled (1 Kings 8; 2 Chron. 5:13–7:3). By making such a comparison, medieval Jews assigned to Christians the belief that a church was an embodying space for God and thus equivalent to a kind of "incarnation." Though not precisely correct, there was much in Christian rhetoric about churches that lent itself to this interpretation. Jacobus de Voragine, in his discussion of the dedication of churches, made clear parallels between the church and the Temple: the church, like the Temple, was a refuge for those pursued by the law, the place all could come and be assured their prayers were heard by God, and the site of sacrifice to God, this time not with the blood of animals but with songs of praise and—more significantly—with the host.[102] That the church altar was the place in which God's embodiment in the bread took place further linked the church building to a kind of incarnation by proxy.[103] Finally, Jacobus insisted on the need to consecrate churches and thus drive out demons who might attempt to dwell there; presumably God's spirit was to inhabit the sanctified space instead. According to Jacobus, the church building and its consecrating rituals directly paralleled or recalled both the embodied life of God-as-Jesus and the spirit-filled Christian;

both were the Spritual Temple of which the First and Second Temples of the Jews were mere shadows.[104]

Just as the purity of Mary's and Jesus' bodies had become a point of contention between Jews and Christians, so too did the supposedly unsullied nature of religious buildings and the persons of Jewish and Christian believers because all represented a place where divinity and the material world could connect. Similarly in Kabbalah, the Shekhinah, the normally feminine, divine presence on earth, was vulnerable to being polluted by the actions of the unworthy and was herself sometimes the source of uncleanness and gentile and demonic power.[105] Thus for both Jews and Christians, a person or object's claim to a liminal status between the divine and human worlds made both threatening and easily subject to impurity.[106] By proving that the person or object was indeed impure, the potentially divine aspect or "indwelling," along with its threat, was negated. In short, someone or something covered with excrement could not or should not be a vessel of God. Nor could the person or religious space embody a tempting religious alternative at the outskirts of the community of "true believers."

Houses of Rot: The Ridicule of Christian Holy Spaces as Dwellings of God

Much of Jewish polemic against Christian churches focused on their dual functions as houses of God and tombs of the holy dead, including Jesus himself. One of the many derogatory terms for a church was *beit ha-mishuqaẓ,* "house of abomination" or house of "uncleanness," and Jesus is occasionally called *ha-mishuqaẓ* "the abomination" or "the unclean one."[107] Such language tied the nature of a church building to Jesus' own identity. *Sheqeẓ* and the words derived from it have the added connotation of impure vermin because of the term's close association with *shereẓ,* creeping animals, which were usually forbidden as food under biblical law. Thus, in using cognates of *sheqeẓ,* Jewish poets and historians could simultaneously insinuate that their religious enemies were loathsome reptiles or insects and their churches were filled with such creatures while indicating Jesus' and churches' general state of impurity. Jewish authors were also drawing on the frequent association in the Talmud of *shereẓ, sheqeẓ,* idolaters, and undesirable Jews. By association, therefore, Jesus and his followers became idolaters and heretical Jews, and churches were houses of idolatry.

Christians had developed their own symbolic associations for creeping animals that were to some extent shared by or at least known to Jews. By the twelfth and thirteenth centuries in Christian texts and sculpture, vermin, especially snakes, toads, flies, and worms, had come to signify the sinfully excessive attachment to material goods and the rot and consumption all had to endure after death. Perhaps the best example of the public display of the link between toads, snakes, and wealth in Western Christian iconography is the sculpture of the "rich young man" at the main entrance of the Strasbourg cathedral that depicts serpents and toads crawling up the leg and backside of a seemingly healthy, smiling young man who is eating an apple. (See figs. 1 and 2.) Jews also referred to the devouring worms of the grave, and they would have been familiar with this Christian topos both by seeing it as part of external decoration on churches and, perhaps, by hearing *exempla* and fables from their Christian neighbors and wandering preachers. Thus calling Jesus *ha-mishuqaẓ* and a church *beit ha-mishuqaẓ* reminded the Jewish audience

Figure 1. Reproduction of "The Tempter" holding an apple. Toads, lizards, and serpents crawl beneath his robe. West façade, south portal, Cathédral de Strasbourg.

Figure 2.
Original statue of the Tempter, Musée de la Cathédral de Strasbourg. Close-up toads, lizards, and serpents.

that Jesus was mortal and subject to decay, in contrast to Christianity's assertion of a resurrected deity who was embodied yet impervious to rot and the attacks of vermin. In this light the church itself became a tomb filled with worms, unclean because of the creatures that inhabited it but also unclean because of corpse pollution (Jesus'), the most severe of all impurities in the Jewish system. Furthermore, by linking the church with the grave, Jews suggested that rather than a place of divine indwelling, it was the habitation of impure spirits and demons.[108]

The relationship between Christian holy space and Jesus' status as a corpse becomes even clearer in Jewish references to the Holy Sepulchre.

R. Eliezer b. Nathan described a crusader who "went to seek impurity *(ṭum'ah)* on a distant road, the crucified, buried one, placed in a deep pit."[109] In this example impurity seems to indicate Jesus, or perhaps the Holy Sepulcher where the Christian seems to be going. R. Eliezer wrote as if Jesus were still buried there—a clear negation of the resurrection and an implication that the Holy Sepulcher was nothing but an impure tomb. In a passage from the short prose chronicle of the first crusade, the author suggested that the Holy Sepulcher contained not one but many impurities. According to him, the Christian princes urged one another, "[L]et us also go with them, for every man who will go on this path, and will turn onto a path to ascend to the grave of the pollutions *(ṭuma'ot)* of the crucified one will be proper and ready for hell."[110] The reference to the manner of Jesus' death, to the Holy Sepulcher as a grave, and to the many pollutions of its occupant—again the implication is that Jesus is still there—all served to deny Jesus' status as the incarnate God and the Holy Sepulcher as the ultimate sacred space.

The one Christian building that Muslims targeted as being despicable in its own right was the Church of the Holy Sepulcher. Rather than evoke decay, Muslim writers referred to the church as *al-qumamah,* meaning "refuse" or "garbage."[111] In so doing they characterized the Church of the Holy Sepulcher and, presumably, the Christian belief in the death and resurrection of Jesus that the church particularly honored as dirty and worthy of utter rejection. They characterized Christian believers similarly by providing uncomplimentary "substitute" titles such as *'ahl al-rijs* (the people of filth), *'ahl al-ḍalāl* (the people of error) and *'ahl al-ghadr* (the people of treachery).[112] Much like the terms *haria'* for Mary and *ben niddah* for Jesus in medieval Jewish writing, a single word or term could encapsulate all of Muslim poets' and chroniclers' disgust and rejection of this set of beliefs. Some authors were more expansive, however. Imād al-Dīn al-Iṣfahānī (1125–1201) alludes to what kind of "garbage" this church contained in his choice of what follows after the epithet. According to him, the Christians proclaim that this is the place of crucifixion and sacrifice, a place of ornamentation—specifically, pictures and sculptures forbidden in Islam—and of food and drink. He plays with words so that the Christians proclaim, "We are generous with our souls, [but] miserly about the place (or barrenness?) of the spirit. This is our garbage (meaning the Church of the Holy Sepulcher), in it is our meeting (place), from it our resurrection is established."[113] This passage implies that all the Christian rituals, objects, and concomitant beliefs in this building are to be equated with garbage. Furthermore, it subtly denies these crusaders a part in the resurrection by having them state that it is established from this "garbage." I would suggest that al-Iṣfahānī further denies the church any semblance of holiness by playing with the word *maḥall,* a normal and expected word for "place" or "location," and *maḥl*, meaning "barrenness," "drought," or "deceit." Yet without a *shadda* indicating a double consonant or any other vowels, the reader of the text is left with a choice between the two readings.[114]

Al-Harawi (d. 1215) explains the term differently. He acknowledges that it is a play on what the Chrstians call "*al-Qiyamah*" (the Resurrection) but states that in reality it was a place of bad odor where people threw their "impurities" and criminals were crucified or had their hands removed.[115] By emphasizing this aspect of the place's history, he links it with death, offal, and evil action, all of them highly inappropriate associations for an esteemed prophet such as Jesus. Al-Harawi's description also would have reminded his readers of the Christian belief in Jesus' very human, shameful, dirty death, a death that Muslims did not attribute to the human prophet Jesus, let alone consider in relationship to God. Thus the onus of that dirt and shame fell on the Christians who invented the belief rather than on Jesus himself.

Lesser saints also contaminated the church in Jewish eyes. In the long prose chronicle of the first crusade, a group of Jews "did not wish to enter the shrine of idolatry and to smell the odors of the skins of idolatry/abomination."[116] In this text the author seems to be insinuating that Christian occupants themselves stank, or perhaps the "odors of the skins of idolatry" is a reference to the bodies of Christian saints kept in the church. In either case, the church is not only a house of idolatry but also one of foul odors. The ability of Christians, whether dead or living, to make the church stink recalls its status as a tomb and should be seen as an extension of the characterization of Jesus as a polluting corpse. The church's evil nature—indicated by its foul smell—and uncleanness made it a highly unsuitable dwelling for God, as well as an architectural monument to Jesus as a dead man rather than a living God and to Christianity's "worship" of the dead.

By insinuating that churches were dirty tombs, Jews undermined Christians' claim that these buildings were sanctified houses of God in another way. Jewish tradition from biblical times onward associated demonic habitation with outhouses and other places of filth, ruins, graves, and Pagan temples.[117] By labeling Christian places of worship filthy sepulchers and houses of idolatry, Jews suggested that churches were the dwellings of demons rather than God. Such an accusation struck at the core of the theology of those like Jacobus de Voragine who saw churches as the one place too holy to be sullied by demonic presence.

Jews were quick to point out the extent to which even cathedrals failed any comparison to the Temple. Depicting cathedrals as filthy attributed to them a level of pollution and indignity that had been intolerable to God's presence in either of the biblical Temples and thus should have been intolerable in cathedrals if they were true houses of God. According to the author of *Niẓẓaḥon Yashan,* R. Kalonymous, on being asked by King Henry to compare the cathedral of Speyer to the Temple of Solomon, replied that while the Temple of Solomon had been so filled with the glory of God not even the priests could bear to remain, "[i]n this case, however, if one were to load a donkey with vomit and shit and lead him through the church, he would remain unharmed."[118] Here the holy space of Christians rather than the Christian God is shown to be profane and ridiculous because human excreta can be brought into the church without divine repercussions. In the same tradition as R. Joshua b. Hanina versus the Emperor Hadrian in *Pesiqta' Rabbati* 21:2 or R. Gamliel versus the Pagan philosopher Proclos in Mishnah 'Avodah Zarah 3.5, R. Kalonymous has tricked King Henry into allowing him to insult his opponent's faith. Because at the beginning of their discussion the king had sworn not to harm R. Kalonymous for his remarks, he is forced to content himself with remarking, "If not for my oath, I would have you decapitated."[119] As in the earlier tales, the vehicle for the humiliation of non-Jewish religious belief and rabbinical wit is excrement.[120]

Jewish authors literally heaped impurity on impurity when writing about the God, holy spaces, and members of the majority who had so profoundly injured and insulted them. Much of this rhetoric reflects the anger and sorrow sparked by Christian persecutions of Jews in northern Europe both during and after the first crusade. It also reflects fear: "Impure ones *(ṭime'im)* and swine lie in wait for their (the Jews') blood, / cruel ones encircle them, pure ones, to destroy them, a flame of fire which passed among the condemned."[121] In this poem by R. Abraham b. Meir, Christians themselves are described as doubly unclean—both "impure ones" and "swine"—in contrast to Jews (the "pure ones")—and as mortally dangerous. In such an atmosphere removing any temptation to enter the sacred space of Christians or to believe in the divine presence dwelling in the church or Jesus and Mary was vital.[122] Human waste and decay was the most powerful vehicle for making the Christian God, in all his incarnations, despicable in Jewish eyes. Stories of victory and even humor at the expense of the Christian majority, such as that provided in the contest between R. Kalonymous and King Henry, were essential to maintain morale within the Jewish community.

Both Christians and Muslims contended that the presence of the other contaminated the holy city and buildings of Jerusalem. In various versions or summaries of Pope Urban's speech urging Christians to wrest Jerusalem from Muslim possession, the pope accuses Muslims of intentionally desecrating holy places. For example, in Robert of Rheim's *Historia Heirosolimitana*, the pope claims, "They subvert its altars through filthy iniquities, they circumcise Christians and the blood of circumcision they either pour over the altars or plunge in the vessels of the baptistery."[123] Paired with Christian assertions that Muslims felt the only way to "purify" al-Aqsa and Jerusalem was with Frankish blood, Muslims are made to appear obsessed with Christian blood and grotesque in their ritual misuse of it.[124] According to Sivan, some Muslim authors in fact used such imagery, presumably to emphasize the gravity of the Christians' pollution of Jerusalem and its sanctuaries.[125] Frequently Christian authors asserted that Muslims stabled animals in the Church of the Holy Sepulcher.[126]

When Muslim authors specified the nature of the Christians' pollution of the Dome of the Rock, it was not through real animals but paintings and carvings of impure animals, in particular pigs, and Christian holy figures.[127] Ibn Jubayr is rather more literal in his description of Acre under Christian occupation: "It stinks and is filthy, being full of refuse and excrement."[128] Harking back to early Byzantine-Muslim conflicts, Hillenbrand underscores a tale from *The One Thousand and One Nights* in which Byzantine Christians used the excrement of the Patriarch as incense in their churches.[129] In both the Christian and the Muslim writings, therefore, authors attempted to denigrate one another's rituals and (holy) spaces through their association with the bodily functions of animals and humans and the resulting stench. This technique most resembles the verbal play of R. Kalonymous, in which he imagines a donkey capable of strolling through the cathedral burdened with all manner of unpleasant excreta. Yet here these Muslim and Christians do not posit a hypothetical but level direct accusations against one another. Unlike much of the Jewish-Christian polemic surrounding holy space, the focus of disgust-based polemic between Muslims and Christians is on the bodies, animals, and rituals of living individuals rather than the dead (in Jewish eyes) Jesus and saints. Neverthelesss, the focus remains on the dirt of the body. Usually, however, Muslim and Christian authors simply indulged in labeling their foes with a series of nouns or adjectives demarcating their extreme dirt, foul smell, and polluting nature, without specifying its source. It was the duty of Ṣalaḥ al-Dīn or the Christian crusade leaders—depending on the texts—to rid the holy city and its environs of this uncleanness.[130] To emphasize the saintliness of Ṣalaḥ al-Dīn and his army and the renewed purity of Jerusalem and its sanctuaries, a number of Muslim authors linked all these metaphorically and literally with perfume and other sweet smells.[131]

Debra Strickland has argued that images of Muslim executioners of female Christian saints should be interpreted as an expression of Christians' fear of Muslim violation of Christian women and "contamination" through willing sexual interaction.[132] These fears were strong on the part of Muslims as well as Christians, as Hillenbrand has indicated.[133] In the literature of both, chroniclers and poets lament the capture and rape of women or insinuate that women are in imminent danger from the men of the other side.[134] Depictions of one another as violent toward women and children was part of each side's attempt to demonstrate the bestial cruelty of the other.[135] For Christians, Muslims raping women or taking many wives and female (Christian) slaves were extensions of the excessive sexuality of Islam's founder, Muḥammad. Fidentius of Padua first describes Muḥammad as "most fetid in the sin of luxury" for having fifteen freeborn wives and two handmaidens.[136] Possession of multiple wives is placed side by side with Fidentius's description of Muḥammad as a spiller of human blood. Slightly later in his tractate, Fidentius describes all Muslims in much the same language, pairing "fetid luxury," lust, and cruelty.[137] Roger Bacon likewise emphasized Muḥammad's polygamy, asserting that he forcibly took all beautiful women from among his followers, proof that Islam allowed many sins.[138] The emphasis of these texts and other "biographies" on the violent sexuality of the Prophet Muḥammad and his followers served to hypermasculinize them in such a way as to link masculinity with cruelty and lust rather than rationality. Muslim triumph was a violation of proper Christian masculinity. Fidentius makes this emasculation fairly explicit when he presents the Christian settlers of the Holy Land as effeminate and insufficiently virile in the face of Muslim opposition.[139] In the passage cited and discussed earlier in which Muslims were portrayed as using the blood of circumcision from forced Christian converts, the blood and the act are intimately and particularly male, so that Muslim men ravage the very source of Christian masculinity the better to violate, in a different way, Christian sacred space and objects. The suggestion that Muslims would use Christian blood to purify their sacred spaces functioned in a similar albeit more general way, as most of the blood presumably would have come from male crusaders.[140]

While Muslims did not have a tradition like that of the Christian "antibiography" of Muḥammad on which to draw, images of violence and the threat or reality of rape also created an image of bestial hypermaleness for the crusaders. In one poem seemingly from the time of the initial crusades, though quoted by a later author, Ibn Taghribirdi (ca. 1411–70), pillage, rape, and the Christian invasion are equated by playing on the similarity between the verb *salaba* "to plunder," "steal," "gather booty," and the word for "cross," *ṣalīb* (the words or their roots differ only in the kind of *s* they use):

> The sword is cutting and blood is spilt / How many Muslim men have become booty (*salīb*) / And how many Muslim women's inviolability has been plundered (*salīb*)? / How many a mosque have they made into a church! / The cross (*ṣalīb*) has been set up in the *miḥrāb*. / The blood of the pig is suitable for it. / Qur'ans have been burned under the guise of incense."[141]

As in certain of the Christian descriptions of the Muslims, the crusaders' violence dominates the poem. Through the juxtaposition of events—raping women, making mosques into churches—and internal rhyme, all the crusaders' activities become a form of rape, whether of Muslim women or of Muslim sacred space. Given the continued and quite common practice of same-sex love between men in the medieval Muslim world, it is possible that even the reference to Muslim men as *salīb* may have been meant to imply a forced, violating sexual encounter.[142] The result is impurity signified by pig's blood and the destruction and misuse of holy objects, namely, the Qur'an. In a striking passage, Ibn Khallikan also depicted the Holy Land as a woman raped by the crusaders: "The holy, pure land has been made healthy, and it was the menstruating one (*al-ṭāmith*) [before]."[143] Hillenbrand quite rightly points out that *al-ṭāmith* does not merely mean polluted, as the original translator of the passage in the *Recueil des historiens des croisades* had interpreted it, but also refers to menstruation.[144] However, the verb *ṭamatha* also has the meaning "to deflower a girl." In choosing this word, therefore, Ibn Khallikan conveys two images of the crusaders and their effects on the land. First, they had rendered the (female) land sick and impure and as a result prohibited to her husband (the Muslims) until her purification.[145] Second, the crusaders had raped her (the land) or taken away her virginity and therefore her purity. Thus sexual violence and impurities resulting from the male crusaders' acts become combined in this passage.

Attributions of rape to the crusaders should be seen in the context of a long-standing Muslim tradition that Ifrangi, or Franks, lacked any notion of propriety in relations between men and women. While anecdotes to this effect sometimes functioned to make the Europeans seem humorously uncivilized, they also denigrated Europeans in Muslim eyes.[146] Muslims, like their Christian counterparts, were eager to show their opponents as excessively preoccupied with sex. According to one chronicle, not only did the crusaders target Muslim women, but European prostitutes came to alleviate the Christian warriors' frustration as a kind of religious sacrifice. That the author, Imād al-Dīn, intended to dismay and disgust his Muslim audience by this tale may be seen in his denunciation of the sinfulness of this behavior and in his choice of similes; the Europeans' love play is described in terms of birds, lizards, and dungeons, even implying that lizards ascended the vaginas of the prostitutes.[147] Nor did he stop there. Imād al-Dīn marveled at the European women who took up arms, commanded men, and made themselves indistinguishable from the men until their armor was removed in defeat.[148] While his account very likely reflects actual practice among some crusader women and Muslims had their own positive tradition of women warriors, in the broader context of his work, that European women should dress as men and go to battle further demonstrated the crusaders' lack of sexual propriety and emphasized their violent masculinity; so preoccupied were they with war and the concomitant conquest/violation of the Holy Land that even their women became men.[149]

Christian-Muslim polemic regarding sacred space tended to be more violent in the actions described if not in the vileness of the chosen invectives than was Christian-Jewish polemic. This tendency derives not only from the simple fact that Christians and Muslims were at war but also from the fact that the two seemed evenly matched in the early years of the Crusades. This focus on violence and male violation of actual women or holy spaces on the part of both Christian and Muslim writers indicates the threat that each perceived in the other and perhaps the level of violence needed to overcome that threat. Impurity and filth served to encourage revenge in war and to underscore the "untouchability" of the land contaminated by the presence of the other's dominance and religious rites. By extension, the religion of the other would be equally abhorrent. In all three traditions stench and fragrance are important indicators of evil and holiness respectively and the capability of a "sacred" space to house the presence of God. In most of these texts stench and impurity derive from human effluvia or the decaying body, suggesting that the late antique and early medieval traditions about the body, smell, and holiness continued to hold considerable sway in all three traditions and to influence one another in the twelfth through fourteenth centuries.

"This Is My Body": From Host to Divine Children in the Polemic of Incarnation

Jewish antieucharistic polemic targeted Christianity and the doctrine of the incarnation at all levels, verbally befouling Christian ritual, believers, and Jesus himself. Perhaps the most forceful piece of polemic in this regard comes from *Sefer Nestor ha-Komer:*

> [B]ut he [Jesus] commanded you to be baptized in the stinking waters *(bemai ha-zaḥanah),* to buy a rotten tree and make from it an image from which there is no benefit, to eat the flesh of swine and every creeping thing *(sherez̩)*, to sacrifice bread, wine, *communio* in Latin, bringing it into your body and making from it excrement and stench *(bi'ush).*[150]

Here the baptismal waters are but one of many sources of bad odor. The suggestion that the wood from which crucifixes were made is rotten (*'ez̩ riqbon,* literally "tree of rot"), or, alternatively, that they were a place where humans themselves decayed, and that communion, the ingestion of the body and blood of God-as-Jesus, is transformed into excrement both explicitly or implicitly evoke stench. Not only are Christian believers polluted because they eat pigs and creeping things, in the process of receiving communion they literally turn their God into excrement.

The power of this passage is its portrayal of Christians as impure and repugnant in every conceivable way: what they ate, what they excreted, contact with objects they worshiped, and the rituals they endured. By making the Christian believer's body as dirty as possible, the so-called incarnate God, Jesus-in-the-Eucharist, was also subjected to this multiplicity of filths, even as God-as-Jesus had been subjected to the uncleanness of Mary's abdomen while a fetus. Like Mary, then, the Christian faithful became dirty, unsuitable dwellings for God, and thus by extension the very divinity of Jesus and of the embodying eucharistic bread was called into question.

Jews frequently mixed invectives of eating impure foods with those against the Eucharist. The bread of the host is rendered repulsive by describing it as "blood-stained, abhorrent and nauseating."[151] Jewish polemicists especially delighted in citing Isaiah 65:1–4 as applying to Christians:

> I was ready to be sought by those who did not ask for me; I was ready to be found by those who did not seek me. I said, "Here am I, here am I," to a nation that did not call on my name. I spread out my hands all the day to a rebellious people, who walk in a way that is not good, following their own devices; a people who provoke me to my face continually sacrificing in gardens and burning incense upon bricks; who sit in tombs, and spend the night in secret places; who eat swine's flesh and broth of abominable things is in their vessels.

The broth of abominable things may refer, in the medieval Jewish application of this verse, to the Eucharist, or simply to the nonkosher foods Christians habitually ate, or to both. Jewish polemicists pointed out that of all the people in the world, namely, Jews, Christians, and Muslims, only Christians ate pigs' flesh, which demonstrated the falseness and impurity of Christianity or, specifically, of the Christians themselves, who were full of uncleanness.[152] This uncleanness was both literal and figurative: literal because of the Christian diet; figurative because of the error of Christian beliefs. More shocking was the implication that Christians, in the eating process, rendered their God filthy, both because of what they ate when not consuming the host and because of the biological functions the host had to undergo in the digestive system.[153]

Christians attempted to respond to known Jewish objections and to retaliate in kind, as they had done with Jewish polemic against Mary. Indeed, contact between God-as-the-host and the human digestive system were of intense concern to Christians both in the context of the Jewish-Christian debate and among their own believers.[154] Jewish objections that transubstantiation mired God-as-Jesus, the host, in excrement were disturbing precisely because they echoed Christians' own doubts. In his sermon "in natale Domini" against the Jews, Martin of Leon addressed the problem of whether the host was digested and became part of intestinal filth.[155] William of Bourges, familiar with Jewish texts because he was a convert from Judaism to Christianity, solved the problem neatly by drawing a parallel between the bread of the host and the manna by which God fed the Israelites in the desert (Exod. 16). Just as according to Jewish tradition the people of Israel did not excrete the heavenly manna, neither is the host excreted.[156]

Christian authors went on the offensive when developing *exempla* to combat objections to the Eucharist and related phenomena. Latin Christians initially imported from the Byzantine world tales of the Eucharist, crucifixes, and images of Mary or Christ bleeding in protest of Jews' or heretics' abuse of them. Originally these tales were part of the iconoclastic debate; that the host and image bled, or performed some other comparable miracle, demonstrated that they contained the real presence of Jesus, Mary, or a saint.[157] With the rise of a eucharistic theology in the West that insisted on the real presence of Christ in the host, these Eastern tales were embellished and became popular *exempla* through which preachers could demonstrate the true presence in the bread and wine. Western theologians did not develop a theology of presence in images and other holy objects.[158] Nonetheless, these holy objects, like the host, bled in Western retellings, so that they too need to be seen as part of Christian polemicizing about the incarnation and Jewish malevolence toward the persons of Mary and Jesus.[159] The presumed malice of the Jews is clearly directed at the person whom the object represents, and the true power and humanity of Mary or Jesus are demonstrated by bleeding. This same representative power existed in the young boys Jews were accused of killing, for they were substitutes for Jesus or the Christ child seen in the host.

The primary thrust of Christian anti-Jewish polemic regarding the host followed the pattern of accusations for a variety of holy objects—the production of stories depicting Jews actively seeking to desecrate the objects. The same tactic was used against unbelieving Christians, albeit with a lethal difference.[160] Tales of Jews desecrating the host, or worse, killing little boys in place of the Christ child, often depicted and provoked popular anti-Jewish violence, whereas Christians who "tested" the host usually converted or were dealt with by the official channels of the Inquisition.[161] The imagery in these anti-Jewish tales, however, followed an insulting topos common to both Jews and Christians, linguistically to envelope their opponents, their holy places, and even their God in human waste in an attempt to reestablish threatened hierarchies by placing the "enemy" firmly in filth.

Christians reveled in tales of Jews' showing their contempt for Christianity by casting holy objects or the bodies of martyred Christian victims into latrines. In *The Life of William of Norwich,* the Jews initially want to throw the body into "an impure place" *(immundo loco)* "so as to augment the shame and disgrace" *(tanquam in obprobrii et dedocoris augmentum)* of the boy's (and by extension, Christ's) death. Only the fear of eventual discovery prevents the Jews from hiding the body in the local cesspool.[162] In certain versions of the ritual murder of little Sir Hugh, Jews cut the form of a cross on the child's stomach, remove the insides, and cast them and the body into a privy *(cloacam).*[163] Here the Jews are depicted as denigrating not only a Christian child in the profoundest and most disgusting manner possible but also the holy symbol of Christianity itself. Having Jews carve a cross on little Sir Hugh made the child's status as a surrogate for Jesus very clear.[164] Christian authors demonstrated that Jewish efforts to befoul these child Christ surrogates are ultimately thwarted by God by attributing a sweet smell to the boys' bodies, thus playing on the symbolic parallels between fragrance and holiness in Christian and Jewish thought.[165] Furthermore, it served to counteract Jewish accusations that Christians or Jesus himself stank.

Jews were also suspected of using human waste to express their scorn for Christian holy objects. Ricord, in his *Gesta Philippi Augusti,* was repelled at the thought of Jews employing Christian sacred objects for everyday household use, but he was especially horrified that Jews, according to him, placed jeweled crosses and church vessels "into a deep pit where one was accustomed to void (one's) stomach" *(in foveam pro fundam ubi ventrem purgare solebat).*[166] Matthew Paris recounted that a certain Jew bought an image of Mary and the infant Jesus with the express purpose of defecating on it.[167] Gautier de Coincy tells a similar story, of an image of Mary being cast into a privy. As in the stories of child martyrs, Mary's purity is emphasized, thereby negating any pollution the Jews attempted to inflict on her, and her power is manifested in the miracles she performs after the attack and in the promise of vengeance against the Jews.[168]

Frequently in *exempla* Jews (and doubting Christians) are depicted as committing similarly befouling acts of disdain against the host: Jews attempted to feed the host to dirty or despised animals such as swine and dogs, or to put it in a shoe and walk on it, presumably in a symbolic act of domination and humiliation (or simply the better to hide it).[169] In Rudolf von Schlettstadt's *Historiae Memorabiles* a Jewish woman spits on the host.[170] Yet Christian authors depicted Jews as not merely soiling the host but also as actively hurting it, much as they are described as doing in blood libel accounts in which the victims were local children rather than the Christ child incarnated in a piece of bread.[171] Thus Jewish violence against the innocent and helpless was an integral part of medieval Christian propaganda.

In these Christian texts, by attempting to cast Christian objects and children into the latrine, Jews reveal their own attachment to excrement. Their lack of success shows their powerlessness in face of true holiness, and their method of attempted denigration points to their own depravity. However, elaborate literary devices designed to undermine or deny that Jews were capable of befouling and humiliating Christians and their sacred objects and through these objects Mary and Jesus suggest that Christians were fearful of Jews' power and desire to pollute Christianity and felt the need to demonstrate God's power to defend against such attacks.[172] That Jews frequently deposited Christian holy objects, children, and the Eucharist in filth and in places abounding in excreta, such as latrines and pigsties, points to the magnitude and uncontrolled nature of this potential pollution in Christian eyes. This trope is comparable to Jews' depiction of Jesus as a constantly excreting baby, or as a ghost in an ocean of human waste, as a way to indicate the uncontrolled, threatening Christian uncleanness.

Beginning in the twelfth and thirteenth centuries Jews and Christians became trapped in a circle of aggressive, polluting speech against one another whose tragic culmination was Jews' deaths at Christian hands or their own under extreme Christian pressure. As Chazan has argued, Christian *belief* that Jews regularly committed acts of violence against them, especially against innocent Christian children and Jesus and Mary, becomes vital in understanding medieval Christian attitudes toward the Jews.[173] Christians felt physically and spiritually besieged by Jews. Many Christians chafed at the church's restrictions against violence to the Jews. Thus their tales of fragrant victory against the smelly malevolence of the Jews were Christians' own transcript of resistance both against the Jews themselves and against the church authority that protected Jews and the Christian scholars who consorted with them.[174]

In the case of Muslim-Christian polemic the physical threat was real. Both sides accused each other of excessive violence in a general way and of sexual violence against women and against Jerusalem and its sanctuaries. In this sense each saw the other as "men gone wrong." Muslim writers in particular used the image of the violated, impure, female body in their polemic, but the onus of causing this pollution was on the Christians, not the "woman" herself.

The Jews, however, were a primary target of Christian violence, both verbal and physical.[175] As Jews' own transcript of resistance became known to Christians, Christians' sense of Jewish "oppression" grew more intense. Christians' belief in a Jewish "threat" resulted in a discourse of Jewish dirt and violent depravity and in the physical persecution of Jews. In turn, persecutions and accusations of filth intensified Jewish fear, anger, and motivation to slander Christians, giving Christians more opportunity and cause to underscore Jewish malevolence toward Christianity.

At the very core of this spiral of verbal violence was the incarnation debate and the problem of Mary's and Jesus' purity. Jews targeted the Eucharist, the body of Jesus, and thus the body of Mary because Christian doctrine on each disturbed their sense of purity and divinity and because these doctrines disturbed many Christians' sense of purity and divinity even as they were becoming the focal point of Christian piety. Muslims, instead of focusing on the body of Mary—though that type of anti-Christian polemic continued—targeted the Church of the Holy Sepulcher for much of their somatic polemic, for it embodied the Christian belief in Jesus' death, something Muslims were unwilling to accept for the Prophet Jesus, much less for God-as-Jesus. Jewish somatic polemic against Christian sacred space and the bodies of Christian believers was based on their perceived status as extensions of the incarnate God. Christians, on the other hand, could only attack the bodies of the Jews, which they did, with words and with weapons. They took much the same approach with Muslims. However, the life and smelly death of the Prophet Muḥammad, according to the Christian antibiographies, stood as a kind of anti-incarnation against which they could contrast that of Jesus, despite Muslim beliefs to the contrary.

While the bodies of Jesus and members of the opposing religion, whether Jewish or Christian, were an important part of the incarnation polemic, for Jews and Christians, Mary and her blood were at its center. Large portions or sometimes entire Christian anti-Jewish tracts were dedicated to defending her purity against Jewish objections. Most Jewish anti-Christian tracts from the central Middle Ages at least mentioned the impurities of Mary's womb as a reason to reject Christianity, and many of the longer ones returned repeatedly to this subject. Even Jesus' weakness in infancy and his dependency on Mary's milk became linked to the potent uncleanness inherent in all women's wombs.

The vehemence of the Christian response corresponds to Jewish "success" in finding the issues in twelfth-, thirteenth-, and fourteenth-century Christian theology that were simultaneously the most precious and the most difficult to defend. Clerics and theologians continually sought to legitimate the true presence of Jesus in the Eucharist.[176] Christians compared the Eucharist to honey; Jews called it stinking and nauseating.[177] While Jewish polemicists insisted on

Mary's milk and nursing of Jesus as proof of her and her son's impurity, Christians were writing poetry and miracle tales extolling the purity of Mary's milk and its resultant healing power and Mary's ability to command Christ because she had nursed him as a baby.[178] Christians were carefully developing doctrines like the immaculate conception and the assumption to distance Mary and thus Jesus from all moral or physical impurity derived from their humanity while Jews were developing arguments insisting on Mary's and Jesus' moral turpitude and their link to the most despised human bodily fluids and functions. Jesus' very physicality through Mary was becoming a cause of celebration among Christians.[179] Jews graphically countered these devotional strains by describing Mary's menstrual blood and feces as a grotesque reminder of what such female physicality meant when applied to divinity. Thus the preoccupation with Mary's body in Jewish-Christian polemical discourse derived from the combination of new medical explorations of the woman's body among both Jews and Christians, the application of these theories to theology among Christians, the ever harsher attitudes toward the menstruant in Jewish thought, and the exaltation of Mary's and Jesus' humanity in Christianity.

Attributions of grotesque carnality via belief in or the production of excrement or menstrual blood was a way to distance one's opponent in the most extreme way possible from holiness. Paul Freedman has suggested that exaggerated physicality, irrationality, and involvement with waste in the characterization of peasants resembled medieval stereotypes of women; however, male peasants were marked by excrement rather than blood.[180] Yet at times in the religious polemic excrement, woman, and blood became one, as in the retort by Joseph Official about Jesus' origins. Jews and Christians alike used the same vocabulary of dirt and stench to characterize the "filth" of a woman's (Mary's) womb and that of latrines. Thus the dividing line between these two was very fine. In the Jewish mystical tradition non-Jews were quite literally the product of supernal menstrual blood and the denizens of the left, female side of God.[181] In the invectives of Hebrew poetry and chronicles not only was Jesus a *ben niddah* but so also were all who followed him. Thus Christians were feminized because of their association with menstrual blood. Neither Christian nor Jew, in the eyes of the other, was a suitable habitation for God, precisely because of his association with the lower, often female bodily functions.

CHAPTER FIVE

Impure, Sickly Bodies

The diseases and physiological traits used by Christians and Jews to denigrate one another all derived from an excess of dirty, poisonous humors or contact with such fluids, menstrual blood in particular. The ailments—leprosy, diarrhea, and other anal fluxes—as well as the secondary results—pale, dark, or red skin, foul breath or general stench—sprang from the body's attempt to rid itself of internal corruption, much as women naturally rid themselves of "waste" blood each month.

Sometimes the parallel between the sickly, oozing religious other and menstruating women was made explicit. At other times it was not, yet gender was a continual thread in this thirteenth-century polemical theme. Unlike the late Middle Ages and early modern period in which Jewish women as well as men were thought to kill Christian children in order to cure themselves of excessive menstruation, thirteenth-century Christian tales of special Jewish ailments, menstrual or otherwise, were directed specifically at Jewish men. Jewish assertions that Christians suffered from leprosy more frequently than did Jews were based on accusations that Christians had intercourse with their menstruating wives. In defensive interpretations of Isaiah 53, the so-called chapter of the suffering servant, some Jewish exegetes were, curiously enough, even led to feminize their own Jewish people.[1]

From the twelfth to the thirteenth century in western Europe the rhetoric of disease began to shift from the realm of legend and curse to that of "scientific" discourse.[2] Yet behind the careful scientific arguments based on theories of diet and humoral imbalance was a long tradition of religious polemic based on scatology, impurity, blood lust, and expectations of divine vengeance. These threads of "science" and polemic intertwined so that old ways of thinking about the religious other as spiritually and physically sick were reaffirmed and augmented according to the new standards of scholastic knowledge and inquiry emerging in the twelfth and thirteenth centuries. Thus even when a text did not directly invoke religious exegetical traditions of the other as struck by God, these views were still current enough that readers would have invariably recalled tales of cursed Jews or impure Gentiles as they read or heard medical explanations of why their religious enemies were more sickly than they. The cumulative effect of the merging of religious polemic and medical theory was doubly to "damn" the targeted group. Jews or Christians (depending on the faith of the writer) were not only repugnant to God and all true believers, but their very bodies were by nature disgusting and in some cases dangerously contagious.

Muslims also based some of their polemic against Christians and Jews on scientific beliefs, as they had been doing for several centuries. Their rhetoric drew primarily from astrological and climatological theories that were expansions of Hippocrates, Ptolemy, Aristotle, and other ancient thinkers who had been translated during the early Middle Ages.[3] Muslim writers used this body of knowledge to emphasize northern Christians' inherent physiological and, by extension, intellectual inferiority; only on rare occasions did they seek to make Christians or Jews repulsive by suggesting that they were suffering from contagious diseases.[4] Like other kinds of philosophical and scientific knowledge, climatological and astrological models from the ancient, Arab, and Byzantine worlds were entering the West during the twelfth and thirteenth centuries through the translation projects. Latin Christians shaped these theories to fit their own theological and polemical ends, as Jews did and had been doing in both the Near East and Europe.[5] All three groups applied these theories to create or counter arguments that the religious other was disgusting and/or feminine that worked alongside disease-oriented polemic.

Polemicists' choice of diseases, mostly skin ailments and anal discharges, was aimed to mark the religious other not only as disgusting but also as dangerous and contagious. Miller describes horror, which he equates with "fear-imbued disgust," as unlike simple fear because it denies flight as a true option:

> Because the threatening thing is so disgusting one does not want to strike it, touch it, grapple with it. Because it is frequently something that has already gotten inside of you or takes you over and possesses you, there is often no distinct other to fight anyway. Thus the nightmarish quality of no way out, no exit, no way to save oneself except by destroying oneself in the process.[6]

Miller was speaking generally, but his words apply to the fear of disease, particularly to the horror of deforming sicknesses with poor prognoses. Though medieval people did not have a theory of contagion that included bacteria and viruses, they perceived disease as transferable from one individual to another by a variety of means: corrupt air, which could emanate from the infected person or from some other source; eyesight, whereby the sick person could "transfer" illness by the rays they sent forth from their eyes or the healthy person could grow ill by the same method by looking at a sick person; poison; and sexual intercourse.[7] Thus more than any other type of polemic the characterization of the religious other as filled with poisonous humors that erupted into disease or "deforming" physiological features marked the other as someone to be feared, despised, and repulsed. The dread that close contact might make the religiously righteous, healthy individual sick was at the heart of medieval fears. On the one hand, such accusations recognized the religious other as dangerous and powerful; on the other, they deprived him or her of power by making outcasts of the person or group to which he or she belonged. Fear and distaste were intended to result in avoidance, which neutralized the danger of contamination or murderous cures.[8] Physical anti-Jewish violence on the part of Christians was the most extreme form of "neutralizing" the perceived threat of Jews and their diseases.

Douglas, in her comparison of patterns of witchcraft and leprosy accusations, has argued that charges of "insidious harm" served as tools to maintain barriers and hierarchies between disparate classes or groups and also as a means to challenge such hierarchies.[9] Disease is less likely to render someone a pariah in a society in which hierarchy is relatively unimportant.[10] In the context of medical polemic between thirteenth-century Christians and Jews, Christian presentations of Jews as sickly may be seen as an expression of feeling threatened and resorting to extreme measures to reassert the "correct" societal and religious order. That Jewish men in particular were targeted and assigned diseases that often likened them to women was a further effort to naturalize their subordinate position in relation to Christian men and to nullify any higher status or honor Jews gained through wealth, political patronage, or protection.[11] Ultimately such rhetoric was equally damaging to women, whatever their faith, for as Miller points out, in "feminizing Jews," Christians also "judaized" women and so augmented the negative stereotypes of both by association with one another.[12]

If in the incarnation debate Christians frequently found themselves on the defensive against Jewish objections, then in medical polemic it was Jews who were forced to counter a barrage of Christian invectives. Although Jewish suggestions that Christians were more prone to leprosy because Christian men did not refrain from intercourse with menstruating women may be seen as an "aggressive" polemic, for the most part Jews were reduced to defensively refuting suggestions that they were dark, murderous, and prone to disease.[13] Indeed, charges that Christians were leprous may be seen as part of this defensive strategy. More often Jews inverted Christian rhetoric, turning Jewish "faults" into physical and spiritual virtues. In so doing, Jews created a resistance narrative that undermined the hierarchy Christians were attempting to assert. Christians were either "feminized" because of their association with menstruation and leprosy or the feminine characteristics of Jews became positive spiritual attributes for which Jews ultimately would be rewarded.

Muslim and Christian strategies using climatological arguments were different since the negative physiological and intellectual characteristics that Muslims and, to a lesser extent, Christians attributed to one another as a result of climate were not contagious. The lack of contagion made the other seem simultaneously less threatening and possibly less horrific than tales of leprosy and anal bleeding.[14] Nevertheless, Christians especially turned climate against Muslims and astrology against Jews the better to feminize both.

Methodology and Sources

A few words need to be said about the state of the available sources. In comparison to the number of medieval Christian medical treatises and encyclopedias, relatively few of the comparable Jewish sources have been published. A careful search of medieval Hebrew compendia, now in manuscript, might reveal more anti-Christian medical polemic than I have been able to find so far. Even many of the twelfth- and thirteenth-century Christian sources (and Latin translations of Arabic sources) are available only in early modern editions, making manifest the possibility that the allusions to Jewish illnesses are later accretions. Even when modern editions exist, many are from the nineteenth or early twentieth century. Sometimes the early editors used later medieval copies of thirteenth-century texts, risking the possibility of later additions, especially since accusations of Jewish disease proliferated in the late Middle Ages and the early modern and even modern periods.[15] This state of affairs has led Willis Johnson to suggest that the account of Jewish men bleeding on Good Friday in the tale of the clerk and the Jew's daughter was not originally part of Caesarius of Heisterbach's story.[16] Clearly a thorough examination of the manuscripts of each of the documents that inform this chapter would be a desideratum. Though scholars are right to be concerned about the possibility of later accretions, the sheer number of indications from thirteenth-century texts that attribute some variety of illnesses to Jews suggests that Christians did indeed begin to associate Jews with certain ailments during this period. Furthermore, such testimonies find parallels in thirteenth- and early-fourteenth-century texts for which we do have modern critical editions. These parallel texts strongly indicate that similar remarks in less well edited texts should be assumed to be genuine without compelling reasons to believe otherwise.

From Divine Curse to Medical Discourse: Christian Invectives of Jewish Diseases

Curses of Disease

Medieval Christian accusations that Jews were in some way diseased derive from a variety of legendary and exegetical traditions, all of which link Jewish suffering with punishment for their shedding of Jesus' blood. Many of these eventually came to be linked with certain forms of the blood libel, the belief that Jews required Christian blood to cure ailments incurred by their role in Jesus' death.[17] Four major strains converge in twelfth- and thirteenth-century Europe: the tale of the bleeding cross or image in Beirut; theological traditions about blackness and the physiognomy of Christ's tormentors and executioners; exegesis regarding Jesus' passion, especially from Matthew 27:25, in which the Jews supposedly absolve Pilate from responsibility for Jesus' death, crying, "May his blood be on us and our children" (Et respondens universus populus dixit: Sanguis eius super nos, et super filios nostros); and finally the life and death of Judas Iscariot. Other traditions, such as the belief that Jews stank, at least metaphorically, until they were baptized also came into play.

In Byzantium, Armenia, Ethiopia, and among Christians living under Muslim rule a variety of early medieval Christian stories circulated about Jews being miraculously healed by Christian saints and objects. A large number of these relate to the so-called cross of Beirut, in which Jews are said to have found a cross or image of Jesus in a recently purchased house.

They proceeded to desecrate and recrucify the image. As a result, blood and water flowed from the statue's side, which the Jews collected and used to cure all the sick of their synagogue. They told the bishop of this miracle, converted, and the vials of holy blood and water continued to be revered and used to cure the sick.[18] This story was brought to the Latin West by Sigebertus Gemblacensis (b. ca. 1030) and was elaborated and widely distributed in collections of *exempla.*[19]

Several characteristics of these tales should be noted. First, in all versions the authors make it very clear that Jews abused the crucifix or image as a way of reenacting the crucifixion and expressing their anger at and rejection of Christianity. Second, there is no indication in any of the versions I have read that the Christian authors believed that Jews regularly "recrucified" Jesus as part of a ritual or that the illnesses from which the Jews suffered and were healed were congenital as a result of their ancestors' involvement with Jesus' execution. In the Armenian version, however, the Jews are made ill as a punishment for the tortures they inflict on the image. The diseases are so horrible and deforming that they can barely move. The bishop pities them, saying, "I know you acted unconsciously as your fathers did; if then you believe in Christ with all of your heart, you will find healing for your souls and your bodies. For God is compassionate and merciful toward sinners."[20]

The attitude expressed by the bishop stands in stark contrast to a similar story recounted by Caesarius of Heisterbach (ca. 1180–1240). According to Caesarius, when the inhabitants of Damietta learned that the Muslims had defeated the Christians, they joyfully dragged a crucifix through the streets with much cheering and mockery to spite the crusaders. In punishment, God afflicted them all with throat ulcers, rendering them unable to swallow, and then aided the Christians to take Damietta. At the end of the tale Caesarius remarks:

> Be sure of this at least, that even to this day Christ is crucified in His members, sometimes by Jews, sometimes by Saracens, and sometimes by false Christians. . . . I have even heard that in our times, Christians have been crucified by Jews; but I have never yet heard that anyone had been literally crucified by Christians; but I understand that some have been lately crucified by Saracens.[21]

Here Caesarius makes no connection between permanent physical illness and abuse of Jesus, as he does in other *exempla.*[22] Nevertheless, in this story, as in the Armenian one, dire physical affliction is the natural punishment for attacking Jesus, even by symbolic proxy. Unlike the Armenian text, the perpetrators neither repent nor are forgiven and cured; rather Caesarius used the tale to spread rumors of Jewish and Muslim murderous reenactments of the crucifixion on the bodies of contemporary Christians.

This same pattern of grave illness or deformity attributed to the "tormentors of Christ" was an integral part of Western Christian iconography of the passion, as Ruth Mellinkoff and William Jordan have demonstrated. Open sores, bulbous noses, protruding or crossed eyes, and grotesquely malformed limbs were common characteristics of the Jewish tormentors of Jesus.[23] Jordan, focusing on Stephanos, the man said to have offered a sponge soaked in vinegar to Jesus when Jesus proclaimed he was thirsty (John 19:28–30; Matt. 27:46–50), shows that this character was consistently portrayed not only as diseased but also as unrepentently malicious.[24] Thus in this visual and textual interpretive tradition clearly visible physical deformity and disease signified profound malice toward the Christian God and truth; Jews whose vindictiveness was particularly infamous in Christian eyes were made as outwardly repulsive as possible, the better to reflect their spiritual depravity.[25]

Scholars focusing on the rise of the blood libel in the medieval West have puzzled why or how the accusation could arise seemingly simultaneously across Europe.[26] This is not the place to resolve those disputes, yet the step from suggesting that Jews used Jesus' blood and water, which miraculously sprang from an abused crucifix to cure their sick, or that Jews who actively persecuted Jesus were malformed to portraying Jews as perpetually diseased because they were the descendants of Jesus' willful killers is a small one.[27]

Among the many "deformities" of the tormentors of Jesus were dark skin and red hair. Both physical characteristics became markers of the sinful, treacherous, violent Jew. To understand the meanings of these attributes as they relate to Jews, however, other associations outside of their connection with Judaism need to be examined.

Dark skin, whether innate or obtained by long exposure to the sun or dirt, was frequently a marker of evil and sinfulness in Mediterranean and European Christian sources. The Ethiopian's black skin was used as an allegory of humans' sinful state before conversion, and in many cases the individual became white once baptized.[28] Patristic literature is full of tales of saints' visions of devils in the guise of Ethiopians sent to tempt the ascetic. Not surprisingly these demons take on the other trappings of religious evil such as foul smell.[29] In *Dulcitius,* a tenth-century play by Hrotsvitha of Gandersheim, the title character's villainous nature is humorously emphasized when he becomes covered in kitchen soot and is mistaken for a demon. In this instance blackness is not merely a sign of the individual's bad spiritual or moral state; it is a source of ridicule and debasement.[30]

The same kinds of patterns continued into the late Middle Ages. However, negative associations were interspersed with positive or neutral depictions of dark skin.[31] Hahn has shown that in many of the vernacular romances, or *chansons de geste,* of the high Middle Ages individuals, particularly Muslims, were not only portrayed as dark but also as ugly and misshapen.[32] Peasants similarly were depicted as dark, malformed, and occasionally religiously misguided, but these characteristics derived as much from peasants' dirtiness from toiling in the earth as from being burned by the sun or marked as sinful.[33] Stereotyping peasants as dark resulted from overlapping late antique and medieval exegetical traditions in Judaism, Christianity, and Islam that dubbed Ham as the progenitor of Africans, monstrous races, *and* peasants.[34] Yet as Paul Freedman has shown, the supposed dirtiness of the soil-bound peasant was a source of ridicule, much like Dulcitius's sooty face in Hroswitha's play.[35]

Baptism was frequently the "cure" for Muslims' "deformities," pigmentational or otherwise.[36] Dark skin functioned like disease. It was an external signifier of internal moral corruption, much as leprosy, the sicknesses of Jews, or the ulcers inflicted on citizens of Damietta were described in other medieval texts. Also, black skin could be inherited from sinful (white) parents, much as leprosy could develop in a child not merely because his parents had intercourse while the mother was menstruating but also because they had intercourse during religious holidays.[37] Like these other ailments, blackness and any physical "deformities" that accompanied it could be remedied by spiritual conversion and transformation.[38]

Like leprosy, blackness served as a positive symbol of abjectivity. Just as Christ was depicted as a leper in medieval Christian *exempla*, so too was he a black man, since he carried the stigma of humankind's sin. He and his followers could cry with the Beloved in the *Song of Songs* 1:4, "I am black but I am beautiful" *(Nigra sum sed formosa),* for in this context black skin demonstrated physical, outward suffering and humility for the sake of spiritual internal beauty and purity.[39] Thus even when European Christians designated black skin as an admirable spiritual and physical quality, often its praiseworthiness was rooted in its perceived ugliness.

Black or dark skin and its negative companions—misshapen limbs, sinfulness, and physical and spiritual disease—were attributed to the Jews and sometimes Muslims by northern European Christian writers and artists.[40] The relationship between disease, dark skin, and Judaism is evident in the interplay of text and image in the French *Bible moralisée* on Genesis 47:29:

> The sickness of old Jacob signifies the sickness of the old Jews. That Joseph comes before Jacob and Jacob urges him to do good signifies Jesus Christ who comes before the Jews and urges them to do good.[41]

The accompanying image is of hunched gray- or black-skinned Jews going before a straight-limbed, strikingly pale figure of Jesus holding up his hand in blessing or instruction.[42] The only clear indicator of the illness that made the Jews' state parallel to that of Jacob is their dark skin.[43]

In European Christian iconography dark-skinned men were frequently depicted as executioners of the saintly. Realistic portrayals of Africans in this sinister role figure in thirteenth-century carvings and other forms of visual decoration along with depictions of dark individuals with distorted features.[44] Despite the clear representation of Africans in some instances, the point was not that executioners of Jesus and other saints were African, although such a designation would have perhaps reminded the viewers of the Muslims who were perceived as enemies of Christendom in their own right. Rather artists were using blackness to couple cruelty with the series of highly negative symbols discussed above.

In a twelfth-century *Evangelistary* and the Chichester Psalter (ca. 1250), distinctive hats mark the swarthy tormentors of a pale Jesus as Jewish, not African.[45] Their features are grossly distorted to emphasize their ugliness and depraved joy in Jesus' sufferings. Many of the Jews of the Chichester Psalter also have red hair. According to Devisse, the color red vied with black as a symbol of evil.[46] In portraying Jews with both red hair and dark skin the illuminator of the Chichester Psalter doubly emphasized them as violent evildoers. Red hair or skin frequently distinguished Judas from the other apostles, so that in portraying other Jews with red hair, Christians were making an implicit parallel between Judas and all Jews, although the negative symbolism of red hair predates Christianity.[47]

Artistic depictions of Jews as red-haired or red-skinned further linked them with the Red Jews of Gog and Magog, locked away by Alexander the Great and destined to fill the armies of the Antichrist in his final attack on Christendom. In the Christian tradition the Jews of Gog and Magog were extremely sinful to the point of cannibalism and were violent, impure, and poisonous.[48] For example, in the *Gottweiger Trojankrieg,* written at the end of the thirteenth century, the Red Jews of Gog and Magog are portrayed as follows:

> This was the land of the red Jewry / which is still spoken of today. / They were a poisonous lot indeed. / . . . / Virtue and modesty / were perverted in all of them / in general they were huge and horrible, / and so thoroughly unclean / that anyone who looked at them closely / experienced a physical reaction of fright.[49]

Not only are these Jews immoral and frighteningly disfigured, but they are threatening because of their poisonous nature and impurity. All these characteristics were designed to inspire fear-imbued disgust. Their physical features and uncleanness inspired regular disgust, while references to their noxiousness insinuated the possibility of contagion, making these Red Jews not merely disturbing but dangerous. The recollection that this horrific people were destined to overrun and massacre most of Christendom before the last triumphant battle of Christianity made that danger more palpable if distant.

The early-thirteenth-century author and crusader Jacques de Vitry combined Judaism with disease even more than did the author of the *Gottweiger Trojankrieg.* In his *Historia Orientalis* Jacques de Vitry included several chapters on the diverse peoples living in the Middle East. One of these chapters focused on various types of Jews living in the East, most of whom are "those who live in the parts of the East where it is said Alexander enclosed them in the Caspian Mountains from which they will go out during the time of the Antichrist and return to the Holy Land."[50]

> The others [are] Jews whose fathers cried, as the Gospel says, "The blood of Jesus Christ be on us and on our children," who are scattered throughout the world, serfs and vassals, and so it is as the prophet says, "Their strength has turned to ash" And so they do not make use of arms and also like women every month they suffer, and for this it is written "The Lord struck them in [their] posteriors and gave them eternal opprobrium"—which is to say God struck them in [their] shameful parts and gave them a perpetual reproach—, because since they killed their brother, the true Abel, Jesus Christ, they are made vagabond and broken throughout the lands like the cursed Cain, they

> have a trembling head, which is to say a fearful heart, shaking night and day, and they do not believe at all in their own lives.[51]

In linking Matthew 27:25 ("May his blood be on us and our children") with Cain and the Jews' exile and political servitude, Jacques de Vitry was drawing from exegetical traditions that were well established in late antiquity and the early Middle Ages. In that homiletical strain Jews were murderous, cruel, and ignored by God because "[their] hands are full of blood" (Isa. 1:15).[52] Jerome had already hinted that in Matthew 27:25 Jews had permanently cursed themselves; however, he did not specify that they were diseased.[53] Accusations that the curse included physical ailments seems to have been an innovation of the twelfth and thirteenth centuries.[54]

In descriptions by Jacques de Vitry and other chroniclers, exegetes, and preachers of the "cursed" Jews, anal ailments and feminizing language take pride of place.[55] In the passage cited above, Jacques de Vitry explicitly linked these condemned Jews to women in two ways: the Jews did not bear arms, and they "suffer every month." The word for "month" in this passage is *lunison,* implying a close connection to the moon. Such a connection further cemented the association between women's monthly sufferings—and thus those of the "cursed" Jews—and menstruation, since according to many ancient and medieval medical thinkers, the moon regulated women's menstrual cycles. This "feminization" of the willfully rebellious and violent Jews and their descendants may be seen as an extension of the long-standing Christian tendency to see heretics and religious deviants as spiritual "women," even as pious women were masculinized.

Conversely, the parallel that Jacques de Vitry established between Jews and women insinuates that women as a general category, like these Jews, are "struck" in their "shameful parts" or "posteriors." While making no explicit reference to the so-called curse of Eve, menstruation along with military subordination or weakness became a punishment equal to that merited by the "killers of Christ." Women's profound culpability and deservedly weak and degraded state are taken for granted by de Vitry, for their physical and, by implication, spiritual state is the measure against which the descendants of the most depraved Jews in Christian eyes are evaluated.[56]

Writing almost a century earlier, between 1112 and 1117, Rupert of Deutz likewise feminized Jews in his highly allegorical biblical commentary, *De Sancta Trinitate et Operibus Eius.* By interweaving a variety of biblical passages, Rupert of Deutz depicted Jews and heretics not only as spiritually feminized but also as diseased and deformed; all these conditions reflected Jews' and heretics' violent and inferior spiritual state.

In his commentary on Leviticus 12:2, Rupert contends that women's blood surpassed men's semen in polluting qualities because men were polluted by Satan's lies through women rather than the other way around.[57] That women's ability to conceive derived from an overabundance of flux was also part of women's punishment for having listened to Satan in the Garden of Eden.[58] Thus Rupert established women as cursed in their own right with physical symptoms, specifically, bleeding.

The Israelites, like women, had imperfect souls.[59] Synagoga was compared to a series of deceptive and sinful women, such as Delilah, the treacherous Philistine wife of Samson (Judges 16), and Jezebel, the murderous wife of Ahab (1 Kings 21).[60] In Rupert's allegory of 1 Kings, which he connects to Luke 4:23–26, Ahab is the *frater patris,* the Jewish people who persecuted and killed the son of God, unable to recognize a prophet in their midst. "Jezebel, which is interpreted 'a flux of blood,' is the synagogue about whom it is said therefore: 'His blood be on us and our children,' from now on does not cease to flow with blood."[61] Here Rupert blurred the line between menstrual or uterine blood, implied by the term *fluxus sanguinis*, and the blood of violence, that shed by the executed Jesus. He also attributed a distinctly feminine affliction to Synagoga, thus adding to the already female identification inherent in the feminine noun *synagoga,* which was then further emphasized by his equation of Synagoga to biblical women.[62] The passages regarding women in general and Synagoga in particular create a cumulative picture of *Synagoga,* and by extension the Jews, as the quintessential "bad" woman who not only leads the righteous—Adam, Samson, Ahab—astray but plots to murder the righteous as well.

Rupert linked blood, violence, illness, and deformity as attributes of the heretic and the Jew. These were frequently tied to menstrual blood, but this was not always the case. For example, Rupert explained Esau's or Edom's redness and hairiness by attributing cruelty and murderous intent and actions to him. In the womb Esau desired to murder his brother Jacob. Symbolically Esau represents the Jews who cruelly called out, "May his blood be on us and our children." Both are red with the blood of their fratricidal desires.[63] As in the passages that suggested Synagoga/Jezebel suffered a flux of blood as a result of Matthew 27:25, Rupert insinuates in his allegory of Esau that the Jews are burdened with some kind of negative physical marker because of the curse they called upon themselves. In the case of Esau, however, there is no attempt to feminize the Jews.

Fluxes of semen and blood mentioned in Leviticus symbolically represent blasphemous muttered words in Rupert's system.[64] Leprosy, caused by intercourse with a menstruating woman, is an ailment Rupert usually reserved for heretics.[65] The levitical laws of this disease were, for Rupert, the map that demonstrated how parts of the pure church could be transformed into a body abhorred by God.[66] Yet in Exodus:

> "Put," he (God) said, "your hand in (your) bosom. Which when he (Moses) put it in (his) bosom, he pulled (it) out leprous, white as snow" [Exod. 4:6]. Certainly the hand pulled out leprous from the bosom is the synagogue cast from the grace of God. Out of the side of his salvation which the lance ruptured, this hand is retracted from his bosom, covered with the shining leprosy of its sin. . . . Behold we see this people segregated from the fortress of God, and without doubt by the judgment of the high priest, Christ, condemned to leprosy, having torn clothing, a naked head, mouth covered by cloth, crying,—it is not worthwhile to deny—contaminated and filthy.[67]

Jews, as much as heretics, were metaphorical lepers because of their rejection of the true understanding of Jesus. In this passage, however, Rupert carefully emphasized the horrific and humiliating nature of the disease. Calling those who suffered from it "contaminated and filthy" *(contaminatum ac sorditum)* directed readers' attention to the disgusting traits of the "leper" and may be seen as an attempt to make Jews and Judaism repugnant to his Christian audience. His description of the segregated life of the leper—exiled from God's fortress, naked, and ragged—recalls the language of conquest and political powerlessness, the very state of the Jews that demonstrated their rejection by God in favor of the Christians, at least in Christian minds. Lepers, whether heretics or Jews, are not directly feminized as in the allegory of Jezebel. Yet by reminding his readers of biological and symbolic connections between leprosy and menstrual blood, Rupert connects "wrong belief" to the woman's body. Even in the case of the red, hairy Esau, Christians familiar with basic medieval biological theory would have associated his condition, and thus the Jews', with conception during menstruation.[68]

While Rupert of Deutz is far more elaborate in his creation of analogies, both he and Jacques de Vitry linked the shedding of blood, especially Jews' willful slaying of Jesus as depicted in Matthew 27:25, with menstrual blood, the diseases associated with that blood, and political subordination.

The underlying parallel assumed by both men is that just as women were beneath men in authority and power, spirituality, and physical perfection, so were Jews beneath Christians. This hierarchical analogy took on more sinister meaning for Jews and women, as Jacques de Vitry and Rupert of Deutz linked the woman's, and therefore the Jews', body with shameful or disfiguring disease, which in turn was retribution for their role in the often violent death of holy men.

After Jacques de Vitry, thirteenth-century authors of *exempla* and chronicles continued to attribute violence, disease, and womanlike bleeding to Jews. Like Jacques de Vitry, they were both more literal and more straightforward than Rupert of Deutz, suggesting that actual Jews suffered from real ailments instead of creating elaborate metaphors of Synagoga afflicted with figurative diseases, as did Rupert. *Exempla* writers differed from Jacques de Vitry in that while he singled out a specific group within the larger Jewish population, they broadened their attacks to include all Jewish men.[69] Later authors also changed the nature of Jews' association with violence and disease. Jews were afflicted because of their ancestors' self-curse, and their search for healing drove them to draw blood either from the host or a Christian child.

The differences in details and choice of stories indicate that Thomas of Cantimpré (ca.1263) and Caesarius of Heisterbach did not derive their accounts of Jews from a shared written source. Given that one of the stories clearly describes the same event or plot and both indicate Jews bleed annually, however, it seems likely that the two authors were drawing from common or similar oral reports.[70]

Both authors depict Jews in a highly negative light. But Caesarius seems to have been interested primarily in depicting Jews as ridiculous and deservedly humiliated, whereas Thomas of Cantimpré's Jews are far more sinister. For example, Caesarius recounts how a Jewess seduced by a cleric convinces her parents and neighbors that she is carrying the Messiah, only to give birth to a daughter.[71] In two tales of Jewesses' conversions, Jews and their faith are made unappealing, in the first because they literally smell bad before baptism, and in the second because of the filthy reconversion rituals they invite the young woman to undergo.[72] In many of Thomas of Cantimpré's tales the Jews are not merely repugnant but homicidal. He includes two stories of Jews killing Christian children and then explains why Jews bleed:[73]

> In the cross it seems to intimate that out of the malediction of their parents there still runs a vein of villainy in the sons, by the stain of

> blood: so that through this importunous flow the impious offspring is incurably tormented [lit., "crucified"] until he recognizes he is being punished for the blood of Christ and is healed. Furthermore I have heard certain of the most learned Jews of our time converted to the faith [i.e., Christianity], have said how a certain prophet of theirs at the end of life prophesied to the Jews, saying: Most certainly, he said, know that you can in no way be healed from that by which you have been punished through the most shameful torture, except by the blood of a Christian. Which word the forever blind, impious, violent Jews bring up every year in every province for shedding the blood of a Christian in order that they be healed of such blood.[74]

Like his teacher Jacques de Vitry and like Rupert of Deutz, Thomas specifies that Jews are cursed with a flow of blood because of Matthew 27:25. Whether only certain Jews or all Jews suffer from this ailment is not clear, but the locus of such Jews has now shifted from the Holy Land to Europe. That Thomas intended to include all Jews rather than just the direct descendants of those who had cried "Let his blood" seems the most likely of the two options. As in the other works, this flow of blood is linked directly to the willful violence Jews supposedly inflicted on Jesus and is very shameful. Thomas did not attempt to argue that the flow of blood feminized the Jews in any way or that it came from their posteriors; to do so would have interfered with the parallel he was establishing between Jesus' death on the cross and the Jews' sufferings through the application of the verb *crucio* and its derivatives to the Jews. Yet his admiration and emulation of Jacques de Vitry makes his familiarity with these traditions probable. Thus the suggestion that the Jews' illness caused them shame may have been a veiled reference to either their "feminization" or the anal nature of their ailment.[75]

For all the similarities or dissimilarities in the works of Thomas and his predecessors, something had changed irrevocably. The narrative cited above follows an account of the Jews' murder of a little girl and is itself presented as an explanation of why Jews murder a Christian each year. Disease was no longer merely the punishment for violence against the son of God; it was also the motivation for the regular brutal killing of Christians, in particular, children. Thomas did not specify that Jews needed to kill children as opposed to adults, but his other narratives of the murder of children by Jews implied that children were Jews' special victims. The unsympathetic and often cruel treatment Jews meted out or intended for their offspring who converted to Christianity, according to Thomas, underlined Jews' lack of strong parental love and thus their lack of sympathy for the children of their enemies.[76] Thomas of Cantimpré's narrative already depicted the Jews as disgusting because of their so-called shameful illness. Portraying Jews as merciless abusers and killers of children would have added Christian rage to that disgust.

The line between suggesting that Jews were diseased as a punishment for their ancestor's self-curse and that Jews killed Christians to obtain healing was one many Christian writers were not willing to cross. In his tale of Damietta, Caesarius of Heisterbach reminded his audience of rumors that Jews, Muslims, and heretics crucified Christians at the same time that he admitted that he knew of no such actual case. In his account of the amorous liaison between a Jewish girl and a cleric, the young woman merely says:

> I am much loved by my father who watches over me so much that neither I can come to you, nor you to me except on the sixth night of the festival which precedes your Passover. Then Jews are said to labor under a certain infirmity, which is called a flux of blood, that occupies them around that time they can think of little else.[77]

In Odo of Cheriton's (or Pseudo-Odo's) version of the same story the woman does not specify with what the Jews are afflicted:

> If you desire to accomplish what you propose, come to me in secret on the night of preparation for Passover, because my father and many other of our people are exhausted and tormented by diverse fears and infirmities on that day, thus on that night no one among us would presume to suspect any evil.[78]

Odo's attribution of both disease and fear to Jews recalls Jacques de Vitry's description of cursed, sick Jews quaking with terror. With the phrase "my father and many other of our people" *(pater meus et plures alij de gente nostra),* Odo seems to intimate that some but not all the Jews suffer from these afflictions.[79] Caesarius of Heisterbach, on the other hand, includes all Jewish men and clearly indicates that they suffer from a "flux of blood." This phrase in itself would have evoked images of menstruating or gonorrheic women of the Bible.[80]

Neither author accused Jews of seeking or needing Christian blood for their cure; nor do they explain why Jews bleed or suffer sickness on this day. Thus the connection between the Jews' ailment(s) and Matthew 27:25 was either lost in these two texts or had become so ubiquitous that neither author felt obliged to elaborate on what was a minor element of the plot. In these stories, however, that the Jews suffered on or around Good Friday connected their illness to the death of Jesus and the role they were believed to have had in his execution. The Dominican Joannes Balbus (d. 1298) likewise stated that Jews were shamed by anal bleeding every year on the day of the crucifixion, thus insinuating that their humiliation and disease resulted from their assent to Jesus' death.[81]

A number of thirteenth-century chronicles suggest that Jews required Christian blood for medicinal purposes, though without indicating the symptoms Jews exhibited. According to the *Annales Marbacenses,* in 1236 "near the monastery of Fulda Jews killed certain Christian boys in a certain mill house in order to elicit blood from them (the boys) for their (the Jews') healing; for this the citizens of that town killed many of the Jews."[82] The chronicler goes on to state that there was an investigation of whether Jews required Christian blood for Passover.[83] Another chronicle, written during the years 1242–90, says that in 1287 Jews kill the Christian Werher: "as if in a press with much violence they squeezed blood from him, by which they are said to be healed."[84]

By about 1300, when Rudolf von Schlettstadt wrote his *Historiae Memorabiles* in the aftermath of the Rindfleisch massacres of 1298, the view that disease, a punishment for the crucifixion, prompted Jews to seek Christian blood was a well-established paradigm in northern Europe.[85] On two occasions in his narrative Rudolf identified Jewish infirmity as punishment for Jews' abuse of Jesus.[86] In the second of these a Jewess who has converted to Christianity because of the miracles she has seen reports the following to her Christian benefactress:

> I heard from the Jews that certain of the Jews, namely who during the passion of Christ cried out before Pilate, "his blood be on us and on our children," that all Jews who are descended from them bleed every month and often suffer from dysentery so that they frequently die of it. They are healed, however, by the blood of a Christian man, who has been baptized in the name of Christ.[87]

The Jewess goes on to describe how the Jews obtained a host through the agency of a Christian serving girl and then stabbed the host, which oozed blood and water from its wounds and then transformed into a beautiful child who ran away. Witnessing this miracle prompted the woman to convert and flee her coreligionist who sought to kill her for her choice.[88]

Much like Thomas of Cantimpré, Rudolf depicts the Jews as homicidal, even toward their own. Only certain Jews, those who were direct descendants of those who had cried, "Let his blood be on us and our children," are debilitated by disease. Here the "Christian blood" needed to effect a cure comes from the host, not a Christian neighbor. The two were evidently interchangeable, as the converted Jewess specifies that the blood of a baptized Christian was necessary while in the body of the story the Jews sought their healing from the Eucharist.

The nature of the Jews' illness is curious; they are afflicted both with monthly bleeding and lethal diarrhea. Specifying that the bleeding occurred on a monthly cycle associated the affliction with menstruation. Attributing both bleeding and diarrhea to the Jews effectively combined two tropes in medieval polemic: feminization and scatology. In part these may be seen as extensions of the metaphors of filth that were so favored in the incarnation debates and that appear in polemical uses of animal analogies. However, the "feminization" in these Christian texts takes a very different turn. In the *exempla* it is always Jewish men who suffer from punitive disease. Without specifying that Jewish women never suffer from this, Caesarius of Heisterbach, Odo of Cheriton, and Rudolf von Schlettstadt strongly imply that they do not; the Jewish women in their stories are healthy enough to move about freely and have social and sexual intercourse and, in the case of Rudolf's protagonist, are somewhat surprised by their menfolk's sufferings.

Jacques de Vitry clearly targets Jewish men in his polemic. He enumerates the "manly" activities, such as bearing arms or taking political control, that Jews fear or are incapable of doing. Their inability as well as their disease make them "women." This rhetoric would make little sense if it were intended to include women also. Even Thomas of Cantimpré's venom seems directed primarily at Jewish men, as the Jewish women he depicts frequently are converts to Christianity who must be defended against the murderous predations of the male members of their families. This tendency to depict Jewish women as converts is a characteristic Thomas shared with other *exempla* writers, even going back to the tale of the Jewish boy who is cast into the oven by his father but whose mother raises the alarm and is eventually converted with her son while the unrepentant father is executed.[89]

This feminization process underscores the degree to which Christian men felt that Jewish men were a threat to the social, political, religious, and sexual hierarchy that was supposed to exist among religious groups. Thwarted militarily during the crusades—albeit by Muslims, not Jews—in debt to Jews and others, also because of the crusades, and prevented by both church and state from wreaking vengeance on the Jews for Jesus' death or the mockery to which Jews were suspected of subjecting Christianity, Christian men vented their feelings of impotence on the only other men lower on the socioreligious ladder. They did so by combining a long-standing exegetical trope of Jewish violence toward Jesus with fantasies of contemporary violence. These fantasies "admitted" that Jewish men had the power to harm Christians. Yet this very potency was rooted in need deriving from a profoundly degrading ailment that marked Jewish men both as the target of divine violence (violence that Christians were, at least in theory, forbidden to enact) and as womanlike. Thus God inflicted the violence Christian men could not, and Jewish men were made demonstrably inferior, spiritually and physically, to Christian men by being made women. Christian hierarchy had been restored, at least on parchment.

Willis Johnson quite rightly traces Jewish anal bleeding to the tale of Judas's death.[90] The Christian tendency to equate all Jews with Judas, whose bowels burst or poured out from his anus, added a sinister quality to Christian scatological polemic. Not only did such an equation link Jews with human waste, it drew on a long-standing trope in which only those who were heretics and evil died in such a fashion.[91] For the Christian polemicist William of Bourges, Judas's ignominious end fulfilled the prophecy "Cursed be he who takes a bribe to slay the innocent" (Deut. 27:25), a curse that applied equally well to "orphans of the traitor," namely, Jews.[92] This analogy between Judas and Jews created a complex of meanings: it denigrated Jews by associating them with uncontrollable diarrhea and a death even more shameful than that of Jesus; it marked Jews as dangerous traitors; and it promised eventual revenge for Jews' treachery and spiritual stubbornness. As in other polemical genres, the scatological element of Christian accusations of Jewish disease served to create a barrier of disgust between Jews and Christians. Even Christian authors' choice of feminine characteristics to attribute to Jews centered on a substance that was associated with waste, stench, and disease-producing poison, menstrual blood. Thus feminization and scatology blended into a single category, and both served symbolically to reestablish Christian dominance over Jews and to create a wall of miasmic revulsion between the two faiths.

Christian Medical Discourses

Existing simultaneously with Christian *exempla,* chronicles, and biblical commentaries that depicted Jews as diseased and bleeding were Christian scientific tracts that expounded on the astrological or biological basis for Jewish peculiarities. This reshaping of a theological curse into biological "truth" is part of the general trend during the thirteenth century to create "scientific" explanations for phenomena authors assumed to be true.[93] Indeed, sometimes the medical and the theological were mixed in a single document. In the *Problemata Varia Anatomica,* when addressing why Jews suffered from an anal flux, the anonymous author first proffered the theological response before turning to the medical ones: "because during the time of Christ's passion they cried 'His blood be on us and our children!' Likewise it is said in the psalm: 'He struck them in the posterior.'"[94] Even in medical texts, the exegetical tradition of the divinely cursed, diseased Jews remained an ever-present assumption. And even in those texts that did not refer directly to that tradition, references to sickly Jews would have reminded readers of stories of the cursed Jews.

Both Johnson and Irven Resnick, who have examined the medieval medical sources and addressed whether anal bleeding constituted a feminization of Jews in the Middle Ages, agree that hemorrhoids and menstruation "were functionally interchangeable" in medieval medical theory.[95] Analogous though they may have been, Johnson has argued that any attempt to see discussions of cyclical anal bleeding by Jewish men as a type of feminization is an imposition of modern sensibilities on medieval texts. Yet as Resnick has pointed out, these discussions of Jewish hemorrhoids are often embedded in discussions of menstruation, as in Albertus Magnus's description of hemorrhoids as a sort of unnatural menstruation from which Jews regularly suffered.[96] Such juxtapositions suggest that medieval writers saw a direct connection between hemorrhoids in Jewish men and menstruation. Other Christian texts explicitly compared or equated Jewish male bleeding to menstruation, as in the case of Bernard Gordon's *Lilium Medicinae,* or *Problemata Varia Anatomica.*[97]

Furthermore, this ailment is inextricably linked to arguments that Jews were melancholic, which automatically attributed to Jews a series of characteristics such as pallor and timidity. These, according to Resnick, were traits associated with women.[98] Given this evidence, there seems little reason to doubt that from the thirteenth century onward Christian medical discourse, like theological discourse, feminized Jewish men. I want to examine the reasons and implications behind the *method* by which Jews were feminized in medieval medical texts. Using a different vocabulary but ultimately metaphors similar to those of Christian chroniclers and *exempla* writers, authors of scientific texts combined color symbolism, scatology, and menstruation with disease to create an image of Jewish men as downtrodden and stricken by their self-inflicted, internal poisons.

According to Christian medical literature, Jews' bodies were either intrinsically prone to the diseases associated with corrupt blood or suffered from them because of diet and social habits. In describing Jewish bodies as naturally in need of the purging of corrupt blood, this literature made Jewish men biologically comparable to women; in attributing Jewish melancholy and disease to the eating and social habits of the Jews, it insinuated that the blame for Jewish suffering lay with the cultural and religious differences that Christians imagined distinguished Jews from proper (i.e., Christian) society. By means of these dietary accusations, Christians also linked Jewish male bodies to old women's bodies.

Albertus Magnus seems to suggest that two types of people suffered from hemorrhoids, Jews and those who ate coarse foods:

> [H]emorrhoids are caused from a superfluity of coarse blood, because when such blood abounds in the body, it descends to the lower part, where there is a plurality of veins, namely in the womb, and thus a vein or two is frequently ruptured, and thus blood flows through the opening at any time. Thus this mostly happens to those living from coarse and salty food, just as to the Jews, by nature, and because that blood is coarse and of an earthy nature, therefore over this flux of blood the moon does not dominate, rather over menstruation.[99]

Though hemorrhoids differ in a number of respects from menstruation in this text—hemorrhoids can occur at any time, are not governed by the moon, and are normally a temporary condition caused by diet—the reason that medical thinkers equated menstruation and hemorrhoids is clear. Both were caused by an excess of corrupt blood. Elsewhere, Albertus narrowed the gap between the two conditions: in his *De Animalibus* he called hemorrhoids unnatural "menstruation" and admitted that usually hemorrhoidal bleeding occurred during the middle or end of the month due to the moon's influence.[100] What is significant about this and other texts is not merely that Jews undergo a bodily function similar to women, making them comparable or equivalent to women, but also that Jews' bodies, like women's, are natural producers of a poisonous, dirty substance. That Jews' blood spilled from their anus only emphasized the filthiness of their bodies. Unpurged melancholic or putrid blood would result in leprosy, ulcers, or cancer.[101] Thus the method by which Jews were feminized was one that transformed them into living containers of rot. Such a depiction could only have made them loathsome in Christian eyes.

Medieval medical thinkers believed that because women naturally carried the poisonous blood in their bodies, they were largely immune to leprosy. Although protected from leprosy, women transmitted the disease to men through sexual intercourse.[102] Thus women's very freedom from the corrupting sickness more closely linked them to it and made them dangerous carriers. Jewish insusceptibility to leprosy, on the other hand, was due to Jews' avoidance of intercourse with menstruating women.[103] Yet suppositions of Jewish good health was hardly a compliment; Malcom Barber speculates that Christian belief that Jews were immune to leprosy eventually led to accusations that Jews joined with the lepers in the plot to poison the wells in 1321.[104] Thus like women, especially prostitutes, who had intercourse with infected men and then passed the disease on to men, Jews became the vessels of poison because of their willingness to associate with lepers. The method of transmission was less intimate than that of prostitutes, but the principle was the same. Again freedom from the disease simply led to a closer connection with it, with the accompanying presumption that Jews were responsible for spreading the disease or sicknesses deriving from it.

Curiously, the rabbit and the pig, animals with which Jews were identified in Christian iconography, yet forbidden to eat according to levitical law, were listed among the foods likely to increase hemorrhoids and melancholy.[105] As with comparisons to menstruating women, such linkages served to strengthen Christian impressions of Jews as sickly in especially unpleasant and shameful ways. Metaphorically likening Jews to two animals that were impure according to the "old law" and that could render the Christian eater sick pointed to the danger of attempting to incorporate—literally "eat"—Jews in Christian society. Furthermore, any comparison between Jews and ritually unclean animals would have been especially insulting to the Jews themselves.

Whether Albertus Magnus intended to suggest that Jews suffered hemorrhoids because they ate coarse food or that they naturally had this flux regardless of their diet is not clear.[106] Other medical writers clearly attributed the Jews' sufferings to their consumption of roasted, salty, or coarse ("gross") foods. In the quodlibet studied by Peter Biller, the author, Henry, argued:

> But he who is melancholic has a lot of melancholic blood, and manifestly must have a flux of blood, and Jews are of this sort. I prove this because they use roast foods and not boiled or cooked, and these are difficult to digest, as is said in the fourth book of the *Meteora.* Item, they have roast fat, such as oil, etc., and these are difficult to digest. Another cause is that digestion with wine [lacuna] therefore those who do not drink wine have many superfluous and undigested humors. They are of this sort, therefore, etc.[107]

The writer of *Problemata Varia Anatomica* specified that it was Jewish *law* that forced Jews to follow an unhealthy diet:

> One should reply otherwise (than according to the theological reason), and more naturally, because Jews eat phlegmatic, cold foods, because many good meats are prohibited in their law.[108]

These arguments suggest either that Jews' own gourmandise resulted in their illness—that is, by choice they ate tasty but unhealthy food—or that the very process of following their faith, as opposed to the freer, healthier Christianity, forced them into a state of perpetual sickness.[109]

In the first instance, eating roasted meat created a parallel between Jews and the Christian nobility; roasted meat had long been listed as the food of kings and also as the cause of their ailments.[110] Medical writers of the thirteenth century continued to warn their royal advisees against consuming too much roasted meat lest they suffer hemorrhoids, tumors, or melancholy as a result.[111] By implication Jews indulged in the food of the wealthy and suffered the consequences. This gastronomic connection between Jews and the Christian nobility served perhaps as a subtle critique of Jews' role as moneylenders and their relative—real or perceived—wealth to the detriment of their Christian neighbors with the help of royal sponsorship or protection.[112] Jews were literally sickened by overconsumption.

In the second instance—Jewish dietary law forced Jews to eat badly—the entirety of Judaism is thrown into question. In *Problemata Varia Anatomica* Christianity's freedom from the old law allows its adherents to eat what they need in order to be healthy. The law of God as interpreted by the Jews, however, forces Jews into a state of disease. The Jews are thereby cursed to sickness by their faith just as surely as in evocations of Matthew 27:25.

Another element is added when we compare the two passages cited above to Pseudo-Albertus Magnus's discussion of old women in *De Secretis Mulierum:*

> What happens in women who do not menstruate is that the retention of the menses results in an abundance of evil humors, and old women no longer have enough natural heat to digest such matter. This is especially true of poor women who are nourished by coarse food, which contributes to the poisonous matter.[113]

There is no question in any of the manuscripts of Jews becoming more poisonous because they *fail* to bleed or of having a menstruous or menopausal eye as do the old women described in *De Secretis Mulierum.* What medical discussions of bleeding Jews and this description of old women have in common is diet. Both Jews and old women suffered from an excess of "evil humors" because of the indigestible nature of the food they ate. In each case a critique of lifestyle is implicit, though in the case of the Jews this critique was based on eating rich food or being prohibited from eating healthily because of religious law, whereas in the case of old women their bad diet resulted from their poverty. In either instance, these eating habits placed old women and Jews outside the bounds of "correct" or admirable society and made their bodies houses of unclean humors.

Worse, these internal poisons made both Jews and old women a danger to children. Old women inadvertently or maliciously killed young children because so much bad blood infected their glance.[114] While the medical texts do not discuss the cure for Jewish illness, chronicles and *exempla* from the thirteenth and fourteenth centuries depict Jews as killers of young children, this time not via infection as in the case of old women, but because Jews sought a cure for their affliction in the tender bodies of Christian children. In both cases Jews and old women were malignant outsiders because of the poisonous, filthy nature of their blood.[115] Thus their bodies became not only objects of disgust but also objects of fear and danger.

Bad diet was not the only cause of melancholy. Many of the Christian medical texts describe fearfulness as either a cause or a symptom of melancholy:

> But this (bleeding) abounds greatly among Jews because they are for the most part melancholic. Because the melancholic shuns dwelling and assembling with others and likes secret or solitary places, and Jews naturally withdraw themselves from society and from being connected with others, as is patent, therefore they are melancholics. Item, they are pallid, therefore they are of melancholic complexion. Item, they are naturally timid, and these three are the contingent properties of melancholics.[116]

In this quodlibet love of solitude, pallor, and timidity all seem to be symptoms of melancholy. In other texts Jews are melancholic *because* they are fearful:

> The second natural reason is because Aristotle said in the book *De Caelo et mundo* because motion makes heat, motion is the cause of health, and heat causes digestion, as is demonstrated by Aristotle in the fourth [book] of *Meteorologica* and the second [book] of *De Anima.* But because Jews neither labor nor are in motion nor are in conversation with men, and so because they are in great fear because we avenge ourselves for the passion of Christ our redemptor all these produce coldness and impede digestion. Therefore much melancholic blood is generated in them which is expelled or purged during the time of menstruation.[117]

In the first passage, from an early-fourteenth-century quodlibet, Jews' antisocial behavior and fear are results of their illness or natural disposition, thus in part removing the blame for this behavior from the Jews themselves. They were merely sick.[118] The author of the second text, *Problemata Varia Anatomica,* insinuates that Jews are lazy—a frequent complaint among Christians as Jews became more involved with moneylending—and that they are terrified, not initially because of some humoral imbalance but quite rightly because the Christians were prepared to avenge the death of Jesus. Implicit in the second reason is that Jews were responsible for Jesus' death and thus deserved the violence Christians might inflict on them. Again, the Jews' illness springs from choices they have made or actions they or their ancestors have taken, and so in this Christian medical treatise, Jews have become their own worst enemies: they have made themselves sick. Furthermore, Jews have made themselves undesirables on two levels: because of their antisocial and unproductive habits and because they are diseased.

Fearfulness was also a sign of subjugation. The *Problemata Varia Anatomica* in particular suggests an image of terrified Jews awaiting the righteous vengeance of the Christians who are in power. This and the other texts describing Jewish timidity should be compared to Jacques de Vitry's depiction of the shivering, fearful, womanlike Jews, cursed by bleeding and political disenfranchisement in retribution for their role in Jesus' death. Indeed Resnick notes that the symptoms Jacques de Vitry attributed to the Jews match exactly those regularly assigned to melancholics.[119]

Yet this fear was but one of the characteristics of melancholics that indicated their lowly status. Al-Qabīṣī (d. 967), or Alcabatius as he was known in the West, not only attributed worry or fear to those governed by Saturn—and who were therefore melancholic—but also stated that fullers, farmers, and other "vile" professionals such as bath masseurs, sailors, and servers of drink were likewise associated with Saturn. Evil smell, Jews, and dark-skinned people were under that planet's rule.[120] Elsewhere in the text tilling the land, sailing, and "lowly laborious things" are also assigned to Saturn.[121] Placing Jews in such company emphasized their lowly and despised status in Christian society. In *De Secretis Mulierum* an individual governed by Saturn is said to be "evil, greatly distrusting, malicious, irate, sad, and of wicked life. He likes foul smelling things, and is always dressed in dirty clothes."[122] A similar sentiment is expressed by Al-Qabīṣī when he describes those governed by Saturn as being involved with dead substances and working as tanners; both professions evoked stench and dirt.[123] Evil temperament manifested itself through a love of foul things. Such imagery may be seen as yet another type of scatological polemic designed to make Jews seem disgusting in the eyes of their Christian neighbors.

By the thirteenth century black hair had become so ubiquitously associated with the Jews that the author of the *Mariale,* a work falsely attributed to Albertus Magnus, used humoral theory to argue that Jesus must have had black hair, since that was the coloring of most Jews.[124] Red was a close second contender, but the author eventually rejected it in favor of black because "to red is attested mobility and infidelity but to black firmness and stability."[125] The author of *De Secretis Mulierum* was less complimentary; for him, darkness was an outward manifestation of the unsavory qualities of those born under Saturn's influence: "Saturn . . . causes the child who is born under its domination to be dark in color with flat black hair, a tormented face, a thick beard, a small chest, clefts in his heel."[126] Associating Jews with such coloration and qualities would have played into long-standing negative theological or exegetical attitudes toward dark skin and hair or red skin and hair. That such depictions of the character and color of Jews were couched in astrological and physiological terms added "scientific" weight to the theological "truths" Christians had already accepted.

Whether framed as science or as divine curse, color and disease had become part of the standard Christian vocabulary of exclusion and disgust in the thirteenth and early fourteenth century. While many of the motifs in Christian literature about the meaning of certain diseases and coloring existed well before the thirteenth century, pigmentation and sickness became pervasive in anti-Jewish literature during the thirteenth and the first decade of the fourteenth century in new ways. This shift may be attributed in part to the blossoming of translation and the study of new medical literature from the eastern Mediterranean; however, Christians in the Latin West transformed the information they received for their own polemical purposes. Much of the Christian polemic about Jewish disease reveals how deeply threatened and helpless Christians felt in the face of the child murders Christians imagined were perpetrated by the Jews and in the face of ecclesiastical and royal prohibitions against avenging these deaths and the death of Jesus.[127] Depictions of trembling, bleeding Jews served as a kind of substitute violence in which Jewish blood was shed by God even when Christians were prevented from doing it themselves, and at the same time Christians could be satisfied with the thought that Jews lived in such terror of Christian vengeance that they made themselves ill. That the Jews' sicknesses made them like women or servants symbolically rectified the hierarchy that Christians perceived was violated by Jewish economic power and royal and ecclesiastical protection. Associations with dirt, foul smell, and repugnant diseases were designed to repel Christian sympathy for and sociability with Jews while at the same time furthering the feminization process by calling on the cultural and biological associations between the woman's body and the production of filth.

From Bad Air to Repugnant Character: Climate and Astrology in Muslim-Christian Polemic

Whiteness, or being "undercooked" in the womb, was negatively valued in Persia and the Muslim Mediterranean no less than blackness or being "overcooked" was throughout Europe and the Middle East.[128] Sa'id al-Andalusi (b. 1029) placed northern Europe in the category of those nations showing no interest in science:

> The rest of this *tabaqat* (category [of nations]) which shows no interest in science resembles animals more than human beings. Those among them who live in the extreme North, between the last of the seven regions and the end of the populated world to the north, suffered from being too far from the sun; their air is cold and their skies are cloudy. As a result, their temperament is cool and their behavior is rude. Consequently, their bodies became enormous, their color turned white, and their hair drooped down. They have lost keenness of understanding and sharpness of perception. They were overcome by ignorance and laziness, and infested by fatigue and stupidity.[129]

Thus northerners were innately big, ugly, and stupid—barely above animals. Increasingly, love of war and hunting and poor hygiene were added to this list of traits, so that while Muslims noted Europeans' courage in battle, that courage was their only virtue.[130] Extreme pallor was sometimes compared with leprosy and its concomitant stench.[131] Comparing Franks to lepers would have been one more way to underscore the crusaders' pollution, although the association of leprosy, impurity, and sin was not as strong in the Islamic tradition as it was in the Christian.[132] Emphasis on the infrequency with which northern Europeans bathed along with comparing them to lepers and animals would have made them seem more disgusting to the Muslim audience.

These climatological theories established a naturalized hierarchy from which Muslims could draw. This "biological" hierarchy reinforced the already extant religious one, which, in Muslims' minds, the crusaders had breached. Astrological beliefs about the dominance of specific planets over certain peoples also created a kind of naturalized hierarchy. Muslim texts suggesting that Jews, because of their observation of the Saturday Sabbath, were allied with Saturn and all its undesirable attributes, such as dirt and subservience, functioned in a similar fashion: they "put Jews in their place" physiologically as well as religiously.[133] In his memoirs, 'Abd Allah b. Buluggin, who ruled Granada in 1073–90, cited the arguments of astrologers who maintained that the character of Saturn reflected that of the Jews whom it ruled, namely, that they were dirty, miserly, cunning, and deceitful, just as the Sun, which ruled the Christians, accounted for Christians' blond hair and red or white skin. Christians obtained their inclination toward celibacy from the Sun's barrenness.[134] Of Muslims, on the other hand, the astrologers said, "Aren't they the people of Venus? Venus is indicative of faith, cleanliness, virtue, ablution, freedom from impurity, and the lawfulness of marriage, concubinage, perfume and jewlry."[135]

This association of Muslims and Venus served two possible purposes. First, it linked Muslims with purity, cleanliness, and beautiful, sweet-smelling things, all characteristics that were diametrically opposed to the stench, dirt, and impurity with which both Jews and Christians were linked in Muslim climatological and astrological literature. Second, Venus may have countered long-standing Christian polemic suggesting that the veneration of the Ka'ba in Mecca was a continuation of pre-Islamic worship of Aphrodite or her Roman equivalent, Venus. For the Christians, the supposed link between the goddess of love and the Ka'ba was one more indication of Muslims' sexual promiscuity.[136] The passage in the *Tibyan* counteracts these allegations by emphasizing that Venus represented various kinds of lawful sexual activity and sexual purity, *turh.* Christian chastity, by contrast, reflected not sexual virtue but infertility, *'aqm.*

These scientific explanations of human difference addressed ethnic or geographic divisions rather than religious ones. Nevertheless, because certain planets and regions and its peoples had become so closely associated with a specific religion as well as physiological and cultural traits, astrological and geographic theory was easily manipulated into a kind of religious polemic, or at least worked alongside it. The interweaving of climatological and religious polemic was especially pertinent during the reconquest and the crusades when Muslims were forced to confront Western Christian culture and religious beliefs on a regular and intimate basis.

Climatological theory had been developed by people living near the Mediterranean or in Persia, so it is not surprising that these areas were and continued to be portrayed as ideal for intellectual and physiological achievement.[137] Northern Christians, who inherited these theories, had to rework them to establish themselves as superior to those against whom they were battling. They did so by addressing and reversing the positive attributes of those in the East. According to Guibert of Nogent, Easterners were too smart for their own good:

> The faith of the Easterners . . . has never been stable. . . . Apparently, these men, because of the purity of the air and the sky in which they are born, as a result of which their bodies are lighter and their intellect more agile, customarily abuse the brilliance of their intelligence with many useless commentaries. . . . Out of this came heresies and ominous kinds of different plagues. Such a baneful and inextricable labyrinth of these illnesses existed that the most desolate land anywhere could not offer worse vipers and nettles.[138]

In this passage Guibert is referring to the Byzantines, but capitalizing on the tradition that Muhammad learned from a heretical Christian monk, Guibert ultimately establishes this aerial tendency toward heresy as the cause of Islam and its spread.[139] Acknowledging the tradition that the eastern Mediterranean climate imbued its inhabitants with great intelligence and health, Guibert transformed this virtue not only into a vice but also into multiple illnesses of the worst kind. Its physical assets result in spiritual devastation, so that the land itself becomes metaphorically "desolate" and full of vermin and nettles.

William of Malmsbury tackled the issue of courage. He quotes a sermon that described in detail Turkish deviance, avoidance of hand-to-hand combat, and quickness to flight and European willingness to do battle. All these were due to climate:

> Europe is in the third climate of the world; how small a part of that do we Christians live in! For all those barbarous peoples who live in far distant islands frequent the icebound ocean, living as they do like beasts—who could call them Christian? . . . It is a fact well known that every nation born in Eastern clime is dried up by the great heat of the sun; they may have more good sense, but they have less blood in their veins and that is why they flee from battle at close quarters; they know they have no blood to spare. A people, on the other hand, whose origin is in the northern frosts and who are far removed from the sun's heat, are less rational but fight most readily, in proud reliance on a generous and exuberant supply of blood. You are of a race originating in the more temperate regions of the world, men whose readiness to

> shed blood leads to a contempt for death and wounds, though you are not without forethought, for you observe moderation in camp, and in the heat of battle you find room for reason.[140]

As Strickland has noted, William of Malmesbury (or the author of the sermon) has taken the characteristics of those living in far southern climes normally reserved for the Sudan or India and applied them to the Muslims of the Near East.[141] Furthermore, he directly addresses the view that Northerners are uncouth, prone to fighting, and irrational, agrees with it and yet carefully removes the worst of these traits to the far north (Iceland?) and suggests that the French, English, Scandinavian, and German audiences belong to a more temperate area whose inhabitants can lay claim to plenty of blood, courage in battle, and reason. The potential crusaders possess the best of both worlds, rationality and courage in war, whereas the "superior" Saracens may possess cleverness but are without bravery. By shifting the definition of climatic zones slightly, William reversed the environmental hierarchy established by ancient scientists and adopted and elaborated by those living in the Muslim world so that his own people were on top.

Christian anti-Islamic astrological polemic was mixed up with polemic regarding the Muslims' so-called idolatry in Mecca. Petrus Alfonsi explained that the Meccan pilgrimage derived from the cult surrounding the two idols, one black in honor of Saturn and another white in honor of Mars, established by the sons of Lot, Ammon and Moab. Alfonsi worked to make the remnant Muslim rituals surrounding these idols degrading and disgusting, saying that Muslims pointed their bare bottoms at the statues as they threw stones at them.[142] According to him, the Muslims' many ablutions were in honor of Venus, and Muslims painted their mouths and eyes in the manner of women *(ad modum feminae)* as part of the star's cult.[143]

Usually, however, Christians suggested that the hot temperatures of the region of their origin or astrology (the influence of Venus) made Muslims lascivious.[144] Though he did not link his remarks to climate or the planets, Alfonsi also followed this more traditional critique, describing Muḥammad as both libidinous and violent.[145] These depictions of the Muslims as excessively sexual, violent, fearful in battle, or womanlike in their worship either feminized them or marked them as faulty men. Muslims' fear of hand-to-hand combat resembled Jews' timorousness, though it was not as drastic. Repeated assertions of Muslim mens' excessive sexuality demonstrated their attachment to gross, bodily pleasures rather than spiritual ones. They also served as the foundation for Christian fears, whether real or imagined, of Muslim sexual violence toward Christian women during battle. All of these characterizations demonstrated that Muslims fell short of the masculine ideal of rationality, spirituality, restraint, and prowess in battle.

Leprous Gentiles and Discolored Jews: Physiognomy and Disease in Jewish Polemic

Jews were well aware of Muslim and Christian use of astrology, color, and disease to denigrate Judaism. They were also aware of the potentially positive meanings of physical abjectivity in Christian thought. Jewish polemicists applied these meanings to themselves in a defensive effort to reverse Christian anti-Jewish medical discourse. Jews also used astrology, humoral physiology, color symbolism, and the association of leprosy and menstruation to good effect to create an offensive strategy of their own.

Associating Jews with Saturn in a negative way began as early as Tacitus (275–76).[146] Yet as Moshe Idel has demonstrated, medieval Jews themselves began to claim affiliation with Saturn. As in Muslim and Christian discussions, Saturn ruled over the Jews because of its connection with Saturday, the Sabbath.[147] In contrast to Muslim and Christian discussions of Jews and Saturn, Jews emphasized the positive aspects of Saturn such as its dominance over others and its affiliation with intelligence. The thirteenth-century mystic Abraham Abulafia maintained:

> Among the stars, the power of *Sabbatai* (= Saturn) corresponds to it (the land of Israel) because it *(Sabbatai)* is the highest among its companions, and behold, the supernal is appropriate to the supernal, and the nation of Israel is superior to all nations.[148]

Here Saturn is used to demonstrate Jews' superiority to non-Jews. Such an assertion contradicted the subservient status ascribed to Jews by Muslim and Christian astrological texts. Abulafia's portrayal of Saturn's superiority was not, however, entirely out of line with non-Jewish characterizations. Roger Bacon, who used Saturn as a venue for critiquing Judaism, nevertheless noted:

> [I]f Jupiter is in conjunction with Saturn, he signifies the sacred books and of the sects that of the Jews, because it [the sect of the Jews] is

> more ancient than the others and prior to them, just as Saturn is the father of the planets and more remote and prior in the egress of the planets and in their order in existence. All faiths acknowledge it, and it acknowledges no other, just as all planets are in conjunction with Saturn and he with no one of them because of the slowness of his motion.[149]

Although Bacon eventually managed to turn this description against Jews, it clearly suggests Saturn's supremacy in age, position, and attitude in relation to the other planets and connects its status to Judaism. I would argue that Abulafia and others like him took advantage of such lore that even the Christians of the period accepted about Saturn to claim supremacy for Jews.

Another thirteenth-century Jewish Kabbalist, R. Joseph b. Shalom Ashkenazi, addressed directly some of Saturn's negative attributes and shaped them into positive ones. According to him, God placed the power of the *sefirah,* Ḥokhmah (wisdom), in Saturn.[150] This statement alone played on non-Jewish astrological writings that linked Saturn with intelligence and countered suggestions in some of these texts that the intelligence of Jews and others ruled by Saturn took the less complimentary form of cunning and deceit. Joseph b. Shalom did not stop there, however. He acknowledged Saturn as a destructive force, governing darkness and black bile, but explained that this was because it was completely unconcerned with corporeal life, focusing only on the spiritual.[151] Jews and their planet have thus been transformed from the materialistic to the supernal and intellectual.[152]

Jewish response to Christian depictions of them as dark, ugly, or deformed centered on Jewish interpretations of Isaiah 53, the so-called suffering servant chapter.[153] Jews had a long tradition of a stricken, suffering, even leprous Messiah who was connected to this chapter of Isaiah that worked together with an equally long tradition of associating Jews with the darkened maiden in Song of Songs who was nevertheless God's chosen.[154] Rashi (= R. Shelomoh b. Yiẓḥaq, d. 1105) maintained that chapters 52 and 53 of Isaiah referred to the entire people of Israel, not to a single messianic individual, who in turn suffered for all the sins of the *other nations,* not Israel's. The more profound Israel's debasement, the greater the nations' eventual astonishment and recognition of their own sins.[155] Rashi's commentary becomes an occasion to enumerate the sins of non-Jews—Christians would have been foremost in his mind—in contrast to the virtue of the Jews, who do not engage in such behavior yet endure humiliation and violence at the hands of gentiles. Rashi thus sought to reassure his audience that eventually the proper spiritual or moral hierarchy would be reestablished. Two aspects of Rashi's commentary are striking: his willingness to embrace ugliness, illness, and subjection as characteristic of all Jews and one of the forms this "ugliness" took:

> "When many people were appalled" (Isa. 52:14), when many were astonished about you in seeing your (plural) humiliation and they said to one another behold, "his appearance is marred among men" (Isa. 52:14), see how their form is darker than that of other men, as we see with our own eyes. . . . [F]rom their great shame and humiliation they were as those who hide [their] faces from us, their faces bandaged in hiding in order that we may not see them, like a man stricken *(minuga')* who hides his face and fears revelation.[156]

While the the root *(naga')* of the word *stricken (minuga')* can simply mean "to touch," it was often used in reference to disease or impurity, leading Neubauer and Driver to assume that the text's description implies leprosy.[157] If it were, leprosy would have emphasized sin as the root cause of the servant's suffering. It also would have underscored Israel's involuntary exile from the rest of society; the leper's status as an outcast mirrors Jews' degraded position as relative outsiders in the midst of Christian society. Indeed, the humiliation and fear described in the passage, coupled with the bandaged face, mirror Rupert of Deutz's exegesis of Exodus, in which the leprous Synagoga is ragged and humilated, her mouth wrapped with cloth, "unclean and filthy." For Rupert, this state pointed to Jews' theological error, their rightful rejection by God, and their powerlessness. In the exegesis of Rashi, however, the meaning of these signs is directly reversed so that sickness and political subjugation have become indications of Israel's special spiritual role in the world. Among the physical marks of Jews' chosen status are darkness and disfigurement. Thus Rashi claimed for the Jewish people the very characteristics attributed by the Christian world to Jesus as symbols of his humility: leprosy, blackness, and deformity.[158] By playing on the dual meanings of these physical states in the Christian world, Rashi co-opted their positive connotation and deftly negated their negative symbolism in relation to the Jews.

Other medieval Jewish biblical commentators continued to assign a positive, even redemptive meaning to Israel's sufferings. They also continued to remark on Israel's "sickliness." Joseph Qara commented on the phrase in Isaiah 53:3, "Despised and rejected of men," saying, "for you do not have any people in the world who is touched (or "struck" [הגיע]) by pains like its (Israel's) pains and sickness like its sickness."[159] Abraham ibn Ezra (1092–1167) alluded specifically to Muslim and Christian suggestions that Jews were misshapen: "how many nations are there in the world who think that the features of the Jew are disfigured unlike those of other men, and ask whether a Jew has a mouth or an eye in the land of Ishmael and in Edom!"[160] David Qimḥi repeated Ibn Ezra's observation but went in a direction none of the others had before him:

> The simile of the lamb [Isa. 53:7] is intended to express his bodily torment and his harmlessness: and the simile of the sheep *(raḥel)* to express the monetary pressure he suffered which is compared to fleecing, the prophet likens Israel to a *raḥel* [ewe] and not to a *keves* [generic name for a sheep] for with every species the female is weaker than the male, thus Israel in exile is very weak.[161]

Not only does David Qimḥi adopt his predecessors' characterization of Jews as being perceived as so marred that non-Jews wonder if they possess normal facial features, he embraces the female gender as symbolically appropriate for Jews' existence in exile. The "femaleness" of Jews in this text seems to be tied to financial helplessness, since the "sheep *(raḥel)* before the shearers" is equated with extortion. I suspect the monetary pressure referred to in the text would have been that which was being increasingly levied by Christian rulers, both in the form of loans for themselves and in the periodic resetting of the terms of loans between Jews and Christians in ways that were detrimental to the former.[162] Ultimately, then, the ewe was a metaphor for Jews' political and financial powerlessness in a Christian world, much as Jacques de Vitry's or Rupert of Deutz's feminization of the Jew was intended to indicate the hierarchical parallel of man over woman and Christian over Jew. Unlike Jacques de Vitry and Rupert of Deutz, for David Qimḥi this hierarchical parallel was neither right nor eternal; God would rectify, indeed reverse it at the end-time.

For Qimḥi and for Ibn Ezra, Qara, and Rashi, disease and disfigurement typified Jewish existence as it did for numerous Christian writers between the twelfth and early fourteenth century.[163] For both Jewish and Christian authors, Jewish ugliness and illness indicated profound sinfulness and violence, with one radical difference. For Jewish exegetes and polemicists, these ailments were signs of *Christian* sin and *Christian* violence, not Jewish. The greater

Israel's affliction and rejection by Christians and even by God, the greater Christians' own sin, since it was for the evildoing of the Gentile nations that Jews were atoning. Thus Christians' accusations against the Jews became the instrument of their own condemnation.

Clearly repeated Christian accusations that Jews were ugly nettled Jews, as we see in the polemical manuscript *Sefer Vikuaḥ Teshuvah li-Minim.* The author of this text was confronted by a Gentile who contrasted Jews' ugliness to his own people's handsomeness. The Jew retorted that Jews were once beautiful but had ceased to be so after the destruction of the Temple. "But," the author defiantly adds, "the Holy One Blessed be He is to return beauty to us, as it is said in Jeremiah, 'Again I will build you, and you shall be built, O virgin Israel! Again you shall adorn yourself with timbrels and shall go forth in the dance of the merrymakers.'"[164] This text is very much part of the same strain as the Jewish biblical commentaries; the Jewish author accepted without question the premise that Jews lacked beauty but insisted that they would eventually be redeemed. Jews' eventual return to physical normality, even to surpassing good looks, receives special emphasis, however, suggesting that real or perceived physical differences between Jews and Christians were becoming increasingly problematic for Jews.

Joseph Official and the author of the *Niẓẓaḥon ha-Yashan* faced a similar accusation but took a more biological, indeed botanical approach:

> "And so I make you despised and abased before all the peoples" [Mal. 2:9]. One of the apostates said to R. Natan, "You (plural) are more ugly than any man who is on the face of the earth and the sons of our people are very beautiful." He answered him, "Just like *Schwetschken* which are called *prunels* which grow among thorns, what kind of flower do they have?" He said to him, "White." "And the flower of the apple?" He said to him, "Red." He said to him, "So we are from clean white seed, thus our faces are black, but you are from seed which is red, from menstrual blood, therefore you develop them (children?) gold and red. But the meaning is: while we are in exile, as it says in the Song of Songs, "Do not gaze at me because I am swarthy, because the sun has scorched me, my mother's sons were angry with me, they made me keeper of the vineyards; but my own vineyard I have not kept!" But when I kept my vineyard I was very beautiful, as it is written: "And your name went before you among the nations because of your beauty" [Ezek. 16:14].[165]

Joseph Official combined medical theory and religious metaphor in this text. The passage in *Nizzaḥon Yashan* is similar, except that its author maintained that the actual *fruit* starts out as dark or white and then changes as it develops, and he was even more explicit about menstrual blood as the cause of Christians' coloration:

> This then is the testimony that Jews are pure of menstrual blood so that there is no initial redness. Gentiles, however, are not careful about menstruant women and have sexual relations during menstruation; thus, there is redness at the outset, and so the fruit that comes out, i.e. the children, are light.[166]

Drawing a parallel between human and botanical development, including coloration, was relatively common in medical circles.[167] The human physiological theory underlying these two texts draws from the view that children who had been born of or exposed to too much menstrual blood while developing in the womb would be reddish in color and prone to a variety of illnesses such as measles. Eventually they would become paler as the corrupt blood dissipated from their bodies.[168] Thus to accuse the Christians of having red or dark babies was tantamount to accusing them of intercourse with menstruating women, a connection both authors take pains to emphasize. Having made such an argument, the Jewish authors de facto established that Christians were impure and sexually immoral according to both Jewish law and their own canon law and were contaminated and sickened by an overabundance of putrid blood.[169] The latter of these two connections may be seen as a direct answer to Christian depictions of Jews as melancholic and thus dark and in need of womanlike purging. If Jews, for reasons of diet or divine curse against their ancestors, suffered a severe humoral imbalance, Christians were afflicted with sickness because of the present generation's bad actions. The greater onus of intent, choice, and blatant sin—intercourse with a menstruating woman was a biblical interdiction; eating roasted meat was not—fell on Christians. Furthermore, while Jews' bodies and blood may have resembled women's, Christians were contaminated by the very source of poison and disease itself, menstrual blood.

Joseph Official attempted to further distance Jews from the stigma of darkness and bad blood by citing the passage in Song of Songs. In the passage the woman, taken to represent Israel, is darkened by the sun, not by any inherent biological quality.[170] The evocation of the bride's beauty while she attended her own vineyard, in contrast to her darkened state once she was forced to tend the vineyards of others, plants Joseph's counterargument firmly in the exegetical tradition of Rashi, Ibn Ezra, and others, for it alludes to the belief that Israel's appearance changed only after exile. Because of the anger of others she (i.e. the Jews) has been made swarthy and forced out of her home to do the work of others. Finally, the choice of apples as representative of Christians served as an additional barb in Official's polemic. Since the apple had come to be designated as the "forbidden fruit" of the tree of knowledge, comparing the Christians to that fruit recalled Eve's original sin and its biological consequence, menstruation. Hence Official combined theological metaphor with biological theory to insist that Christians, not Jews, should be ashamed of their complexions since they were derived from corrupt blood.

Suggesting that Christians were unclean from birth because they were conceived during menstruation marked them as abhorrent in Jewish eyes in two ways. First, conception during menstruation made Christians ritually unclean. Gentiles were ritually unclean anyway according to talmudic law, but now they were doubly so. Second, it depicted Christians as not merely sick but also filled with putrescent blood on the verge of erupting into some of the most culturally despised diseases in the Middle Ages, leprosy and its dermatological relatives (at least according to medieval medical theory). Such an image of Christians would have made them profoundly disgusting to their Jewish neighbors, indeed to Christians themselves.

Christians were not merely on the verge of disease; they were in fact sick, even as adults. By the fourteenth century the association of non-Jews with leprosy as a result of having had intercourse with the their menstruous wives was well established among Jewish polemicists. Isaac Polgar stated in his *'Ezer ha-Dat:*

> [A]ll who look into our Torah [will find] upright practices and righteous and pure laws, for example: our distancing from the woman all the days of her menstrual sickness, for it (the distancing) is the cause of cleanness and purity and is preparation for the seed to generate and also is cause of our freedom (literally, "rescue") from the sickness of the body which is the leprosy existing among many of the nations around us.[171]

Isaac's contention that Jews do not suffer from leprosy because they refrain from intercourse during their wives' *niddah* capitalized on the widely circulating belief among Jews and Christians that Jews were immune to leprosy for precisely that reason. The inverse of Jews' being free of leprosy because of their healthful or righteous sexual practices was that Gentiles frequently were afflicted with the disease. In the context of disputing Christians' veneration of saints, the author of the *Niẓẓaḥon Yashan* insinuated precisely this: "[W]e thank God for saving us from being afflicted with impure issue *(zav),* leprosy, and skin disease *(sarufei 'esh)* as they (the Christians) are, for the Lord is the one who cures us."[172] All these ailments were associated with an excess of gross, poorly concocted humors, according to medieval medical theory.[173] Thus in Jewish estimation Christians became the very vessels of oozing, foul humors that Jews were accused of being.

Complexion also entered into Christians' so-called leprous status. On numerous occasions the author of *Niẓẓaḥon Yashan* insists that Christians be equated with Esau or Edom, not Jacob.[174] Included in that designation was Edom's redness, a characterization that derived in part from the old play on words in Hebrew between the proper name and the color red. In the Middle Ages such a designation had taken on new connotations of disease and treachery that Christians, such as Rupert of Deutz or the artist of the Chichester Psalter, were regularly applying to the Jews. By insisting on Christians' identification with the red Esau, Jews threw Christian accusations of menstrual contamination, violence, and treachery back onto Christians. Like Rupert of Deutz, the author of the *Niẓẓaḥon Yashan* targeted Edom as red and violent:

> The truth of the matter is that Esau was called Edom, i.e., ruddy, because of the evil that would befall him. . . . "The voice is the voice of Jacob, but the hands are the hands of Esau" (Gen. 27:22). Consequently when it thunders they make the sign of the cross with their hands, as a sign that Esau's hands were always committing murder.[175]

The *Zohar* specifically linked Esau's redness to leprosy and his derivation from menstruation. While expounding on the levitical chapters dealing with leprosy and explaining the relationship between leprosy and red or white skin, the author cites Genesis 25:25 ("The first came forth red, all his body like a hairy mantle; so they called his name Esau") and states that "Esau's redness came from the dross (or "filth" [*zohema'*]) of gold."[176] The choice of *zohema'* and the biblical context indicate that Esau and the Christian nation he symbolized were ontological lepers. In the *Zohar* "dross" of gold or fire was part of the dark red or black waste that descended from the female side of God: the divine equivalent of menstruation. This feminine waste matter not only was associated with Esau and violence but also was responsible for creating "other gods." Thus, in effect, all of Christianity (and in theory, Islam) derived from supernal menstrual blood, without benefit of divine masculine seed.[177] Since Christians (Edom) were "conceived" of menstruation they were red and leprous, much as they were in the less metaphorical texts *Sefer ha-Meqanne'* and *Niẓẓaḥon Yashan.*

The Gentile nations were thus like the Aristotelian mole, a clotted bit of blood aborted because it had no spirit, or like the serpents of Pseudo-Albertus Magnus that spontaneously generated from menstrual blood in the ground.[178] By making non-Jews solely the product of the female side, Jewish mystics feminized non-Jews in a peculiar way. They did not suggest that Christians and other Gentiles were biologically similar to women, as Christian polemicists attempted with regard to Jews. Rather Moshe de Leon and Joseph Hamadan equated their religious enemies with the poisonous or sickly by-products of women's blood.[179] This insult was perhaps the worst of all, for while women in themselves might have some redeeming qualities, their blood was the quintessential source of disease, uncleanness, and, therefore, separation from the divine, in medieval Jewish and Christian eyes. Such a characterization might have made Gentiles despicable in Jewish eyes, yet linking non-Jews with physical poison and the demonic aspects of the supernatural world also emphasized the profound danger they represented.

Arguments that Christians were leprous or otherwise sickly and discolored because of their contact with menstrual blood in the womb similarly linked them to women's blood and to Jewish tales of Christianity's founder, Jesus, who was also a *ben niddah.* However, in these less complicated polemical texts the emphasis is on disease and complexion. Jews countered Christian accusations that Jews were ill either by retorting that Christians were even sicker or by co-opting sickness and disfigurement and transforming them into positive qualities. By identifying leprosy as the primary disease of Christians, Jews drew on a long-standing series of associations between leprosy and the woman's body but also between leprosy, heresy, and sin. Thus with a single invective Jews could simultaneously insinuate that Christians suffered from a horribly disfiguring disease, that they had deviated from religious truth, and that they were immoral. Apart from making Christians repugnant to a Jewish audience, this invective was an attempt to counter parallel Christian claims against the Jews. Jewish polemic about color operated in a similar fashion. Associating Christians with redness linked them with all the violence, treachery, and menstrual-based disease by which Christians often characterized the Jews.

Jewish adoption of negative traits, such as disease and blackness, for themselves requires some explanation. Ruth Mellinkoff, in her exploration of what she calls anti-Semitic iconography in Jewish manuscripts, suggests that Jews had so internalized negative, anti-Jewish stereotypes that they did not notice when Christian artists inserted them in their illumination of Jewish manuscripts.[180] I would agree with Marc Epstein that Jews were well aware of the meaning of these signs and attempted to subvert them.[181] This process is much easier to see in text than in image. Jewish exegetes and polemicists took Christian suggestions that Jews were diseased, black, and feminized and attributed to themselves the positive theological qualities these traits were beginning to acquire in the Christian world.[182] As if this powerful sleight-of-hand were not enough, Jewish exegetes successfully turned the negative aspects of such accusations against the Christians by making humble Jewish suffering the direct reflection of Christian sin.

Such defensive measures were necessary because of the power and persistence of Christian polemic to the contrary and the increasingly dire consequences when such polemic was believed. Jews may have chosen to redefine disfigurement and femaleness in order to reverse the negative hierarchy Christians were attempting to impose symbolically on them, but they also used these traits as active accusations against the Christians as a way of signaling Christians' dangerous and undesirable nature. Christians, in turn, were becoming dangerous in a literal sense precisely because they found Jews so threatening. Christians adopted the strongest rhetorical measures available to emphasize the "correct" spiritual and social hierarchy and to warn their coreligionists of Jews' "bloodthirsty" nature. In the end, the Christian rhetoric of Jewish illness and femininity fostered the very myth that made Jews so frightening: Jewish men killed Christian children to "cure" themselves of their cyclical womanlike bleeding.

Christian attempts to portray Muslims as inherently fearful in battle, lustful, and womanlike in their devotional practices resemble Christian polemic associating Saturn, Jews, and women. Muslim anti-Christian polemic using climate, humors, and astrology seem to be somewhat less gendered, although by implication Christians lacked the true qualifications of manhood because of their lack of rationality and their bestial habits. What is strikingly different in Muslim-Christian and Jewish-Christian biological polemic is that in the twelfth to mid-fourteenth century, Christians did not focus as strongly on frailties or illnesses that would make individual Muslims disgusting or threatening. Both Christians and Muslims sought to make the other seem disgusting and ridiculous in the eyes of their fellows, but the extreme evocations of oozing sores and nether regions are absent. I suggest that this difference reflects the relatively greater threat that European Jews and Christians felt the other posed because they lived in such close proximity and shared resources, culture, and language on a daily basis, thus increasing the potential for assimilation on either side. Muslims and Christians found one another threatening, and their polemic reflects this, but distance and relatively greater difference made loss of identity to the other side *seem* like a less imminent, widespread threat. As a result metaphors of contagion or imagery to evoke extreme disgust are less frequent.

CHAPTER SIX

Signs of the Beast

Animal Metaphors as Maledictions of Resistance and Oppression

Fables in both the Western and Eastern traditions have had a long history of being the language by which slaves and conquered peoples, including the Jews, satirized their oppressors without the latter's knowledge.[1] In medieval Europe individual animals embodied rich iconographic and interpretive associations. The image of an animal, either alone or in conjunction with a written text, was often used to remind viewers of moral tales and relatively complex theological ideas.[2] Muslims likewise attributed specific characteristics and values to certain animals.[3] Thus, animals became vehicles par excellence through which Jews, Christians, and Muslims could mock and vent their fears and aggressive dislike of the religious other. Like arguments regarding the incarnation or medical polemic, much of this material has its roots in late antique or early medieval rhetoric. Changing circumstances and attitudes prompted medieval authors to shift the emphasis of or to create new meanings for old symbols.[4] Marc Epstein and others have shown that Jews were well aware of Christian bestiary traditions and their polemical connotations. According to Epstein, Jews co-opted and reformulated Christian animal symbolism, even those with strong anti-Jewish content, into a fierce anti-Christian polemic.[5]

For Jews, animals, even more than epithets such as *ben zonah* or *haria,* which recalled or reinforced anti-Christian stories and doctrines without having to spell them out, could vividly indicate Jewish suffering, purity, and ultimate triumph, in contrast to Christian violence, uncleanness, and defeat, while safely obscuring the anti-Christian rhetoric.[6] Whereas the efficacy of *piyyuṭim* in disseminating anti-Christian feelings to the entire community may have been compromised by the difficulty of the poetic language, animals posed no such problems, as their symbolic value was part of the Jewish "visual community" and accessible even to those with poor Hebrew or those who were illiterate.

Animal imagery functioned in a similar way in medieval Christian and Muslim circles, except that Christians and Muslims, unlike Jews, had no reason to hide their hostility to religious outsiders. Like the other forms of propaganda, bestial symbols directed against Jews and Muslims had the potential to incite their Christian audience to violence, especially since fables and representations of animals figured prominently in sermons and church art and thus circulated to a wide public. Muslims' use of animal symbolism differed in that while a rich tradition of illumination existed, including for fable texts such as *Kalīlah wa-Dimnah*, Muslim artists do not seem to have used images of animals to create subversive commentaries and polemic to the same degree that Christians and Jews did.[7] Nor did sculpture and images of animals figure as prominently as decoration certainly of holy buildings or even of secular ones in the Islamic Mediterranean as they did in the Western Christian tradition.[8] Instead, Muslim use of animals as a way of denigrating others was primarily textual, whereas Christians and Jews combined both textual and visual methods.

Thirteenth- and fourteenth-century Christian use of animal metaphors against Jews, and to a lesser extent Muslims, underscored more than many other forms of polemic Christian fear of both groups as a physical as well as a spiritual threat. Muslim, Christian, and Jewish animal polemic marked the religious other as irrational, filthy and polluting, or violent.[9] Even when the primary objective was to characterize the other as stupid or unclean, violence remained a strong undercurrent.

The links between rationality as an especially masculine attribute, at least in its fullest form, and rationality as the distinguishing marker between humans and beasts added another, gendered element to this polemic. Ruth Karris has shown that by the late fourteenth and fifteenth century freshmen at medieval universities were subjected to hazing rituals that included covering them with filth and dressing them with fangs, horns, and tails, then stripping them of their "bestiality" by removing these accouterments. According to her, this ritual was not marking a transformation from animal to human but from an uneducated, irrational male to a "proper" man devoted to the life of the mind in the supremely male world of the university.[10] Such late medieval rituals merely expressed in concrete terms a dichotomy between rational masculinity and irrational bestiality that was already well in place by the twelfth century, not only in the Christian world, but also in the Jewish and Muslim ones, since all three had inherited and expanded it from the Greek and Roman philosophical traditions.[11] What such traditions suggest is that there was a "right" way and a "wrong" way to be a man in the Middle Ages. Often tying one's opponent to a filthy animal served to feminize him because of women's strong association with dirt and impurity. Accusing someone of being irrational like an animal, or of being a violent animal, did not merely suggest that the person was inhuman but also that he was the wrong kind of man and despicable for that reason.

All these uses of animals, to mark the other as irrational, unclean, violent, feminine, or masculine but in an undesirable way, point to profound anxiety on the part of each of the communities regarding clear boundary definitions; confusion about the boundaries between human and animal, male and female, or good and bad masculinity all serve as metaphors to express concerns about the violation of religious borders.

Dumb Animals

Starting in the twelfth century, Christians appealed to reason as proof of Christianity's validity over Judaism.[12] This trend was part of a broad philosophical movement in which Christian thinkers attempted to apply logic to their discussions of God.[13] A recurring theme in this type of anti-Jewish polemic was the comparison of Jews to animals; their inability to perceive the perfect rationality of Christianity demonstrated that they, like animals, lacked the capacity to reason. Petrus Alfonsi's *Dialogi contra Iudaeos* (composed ca. 1108–10) lies at the root of such arguments, yet as Tolan has rightly emphasized, Alfonsi's exchange with his Jewish alterego, Moses, is generally polite in tone, and both parties espouse the ideal of rationality.[14] Alfonsi came close to insinuating that Moses and other Jews were irrational, like beasts, in a discussion of Isaiah 11:6–7. After upbraiding Moses for his interpretation of the verse, Alfonsi remarked:

> Indeed by those beasts which live by flesh and prey we understand impious men and robbers. For the rest [we understand] tame and simple cattle, about whom the prophecy said that Christ commanded that they dwell together and have peace. But what he wanted to be understood about the men, the prophecy implies in the following when it annexes

> "because the earth is filled with the knowledge of the Lord" (Isa. 11:9). And not even on this account did he say cattle which when they have no rational soul, neither can they have understanding of the Lord, which is the recognition of God.[15]

In the continuation Alfonsi argued that the Jewish doctors misunderstood this verse and the nature of the Messiah. Following the parallels created in this passage, if having a rational soul is necessary for comprehending God and Jews do not grasp God's message or nature, by implication Jews, like beasts, lack reason and cannot understand God. Alfonsi never made this connection explicit, although he frequently railed against certain talmudic beliefs as irrational and therefore unworthy of God.[16] Asserting that all Jews were in fact like animals and incapable of reason would have been peculiar indeed, as Alfonsi's own conversion to the "rationality" of Christianity belied such a position.

Other Christian and Jewish polemicists were less restrained.[17] Peter the Venerable (ca. 1092–1156) reveled in likening Jews to beasts based on Jewish refusal to accept Christianity and on their belief in the Talmud. In the first chapter of his *Adversus Iudeorum inveteratam Duritiem,* Peter suggested that Jews had the sense of an ass because they compared God's generation of Jesus to human generation.[18] Indeed, when Peter was not making general remarks about Jews' "bestial" intellects, he favored analogies between Jews and asses, cows, and horses, because these creatures, in his view, were especially stupid.[19] Peter took the same approach with Islam. After a lengthy paragraph discussing the difference between animal and human intelligence, Peter announced that he would be more stupid than an ass or cow were he to believe in Muḥammad's status as a prophet.[20] The author of *Niẓẓaḥon Yashan* shared Peter's taste for barnyard animals as a method of ridicule. He suggests that the people who believed in the golden calf were the worst kind of idiots, having exchanged the glory of God "for a similitude of an ox that eats grass" (Ps. 106:2). Yet those who would worship a human being as God, according to the *Niẓẓaḥon* writer, show even less sense. Here Christians, as well as the rebellious Jews, are stupid because they worship an animal, or a statue of one.[21] Playing on the word *peṭer* (פטר), meaning "firstborn," Peter the Apostle was dubbed "Peter the ass" or "the firstborn of an ass," a term that demeaned the apostle's solemn position in the Church and linked him with a creature universally understood as foolish and stubborn.[22]

Modern scholars who have examined Christian polemicists have argued that in comparing Jews to irrational beasts, Christians called into question the very humanity of the Jews.[23] While less studied, the same interpretation could be applied in reverse to parallel allegations from Jewish polemicists against Christians.[24] Nor was this tactic confined to a single group. Heretics, Muslims, peasants, bad Christians, and demons were also depicted as or compared to animals.[25] Thus in the Middle Ages slander based on animal imagery was a common way to deride undesirables, whatever their social, religious, or ontological status. Yet while this type of invective was designed to throw doubt on the humanity of its target, the meaning of bestial polemic varied depending on the kinds of animals evoked and the adjectives and contexts that qualified them. The bestial imagery examined so far served to denigrate the intelligence of the religious other. Peter the Venerable's choice of cows and other farm animals emphasized the deservedly (in his mind) servile status of the Jews and, perhaps in a moment of wishful thinking, of the Muslims. In the hierarchy of creation, not only were Jews and captured Muslims below humans but they were also equivalent to stupid animals forced to toil for peasants, the lowest members of human society. The ultimate fate of cattle was to be slaughtered for food when they had outlived their plowing or milk-providing abilities.[26] The Church had long held that Jews were to "serve" Christians in both a theological and a literal sense; however, by ranking them as bovines, Peter underlined the contemptibility of the Jews and Muslims and their beliefs in both the human and animal worlds.[27] Similar imagery in the *Niẓẓaḥon Yashan* likewise reflected Christians' low status in a Jewish worldview, but the servitude or defeat of the Christians was a desirable future event, not a present social reality.[28] In both cases placing the religious opponent at the bottom of both the human and animal chains of being was a defensive measure. If members of the religious other and their beliefs were ridiculous and on a par with the lowliest of beasts very much under the control of man, then they should not be seen as threatening.

These formal "disputation" texts were not the only genre of Christian expression in which this tactic was employed. Gautier de Coincy's treatment of Jews was very similar in tone to that of Peter the Venerable; however, Gautier's vehicle of expression was a lengthy collection of miracles of the Virgin, which he began in 1218 and ended in 1236, the year of his death.[29] For Gautier, as for Abelard and Peter the Venerable, Jews' inability or unwillingness to accept Christianity demonstrated their animalistic stupidity.

Like Peter the Venerable, Gautier sought to place Jews at the bottom of even the hierarchy of animals:

> More bestial than mute beasts / Are all Jews, there is no doubt. Blind they are, they see not a speck, / Because neither miracles nor prophesy / nor reason, nothing speaks to them / their hearts cannot be softened.[30]

A little later in the same tale, one of the characters urges, "God, you ought to kick them (the Jews) like an old dog, and say "shame!"[31] By calling Jews more animalistic even than other beasts and likening them to a dog at the mercy of its master's boot, Gautier sought to make Jews despicable in the eyes of his Christian readers and reassure Christians of their superior status by placing Jews firmly below humankind and most animals.

Animals were also used in the Latin and Old French infancy gospels to highlight Jews' stubborn disbelief and mendacity. According to the texts, wild animals come and do homage to the child Jesus and docilely follow him home, much to the shock and dismay of the Jews who had assured Joseph and Mary that their son had been attacked by lions. Jesus upbraids the Jews, calling them his enemies, and states that the mute beasts are wiser than they are.[32] The gospel writers are playing on Isaiah 1:3, "The ox knows its owner and the ass its master's crib; but Israel does not know, my people does not understand," which Peter the Venerable cited against the Jews.[33] In the Gospels, however, the oxen and asses have been exchanged for predatory animals, presumably as a better example of Jesus' power over even dangerous nature. Yet the parallel between the Jews and wild carnivores suggests not only that Jews lack even animal wisdom but also that they, not the savage beasts, pose the true peril to Christ and his followers. Here the message of stupidity and threat are combined.

In the bestiary tradition, all people, including Jesus, were compared to animals. The difference lay in the ignominious or noble symbolism assigned to them. In this genre, the intelligence of Jews was ridiculed and found wanting in comparison to one of the smallest animals. For example, much in the same spirit as Peter the Venerable and Gautier de Coincy, Philippe de Thaun in his Old French bestiary juxtaposes the irrational, foolish ass (representing Jews) to the lion, which symbolizes Christ.[34] Most bestiaries from the *Physiologus* onward contain an entry for the ant, explaining that the ant wisely splits her grain of wheat in half, so that when the rains come the grain will not germinate and thus deprive the ant of food. The need for splitting the grain is likened to the need to observe the division between the Old and New Testaments. Since the Jews fail to do this, they starve spiritually.[35] Guillaume le Clerc, writing between 1210 and 1211, elaborates more fully in his bestiary:

> This must thou not forget / the Jews who do not wish to find / meaning or symbol in the letter / Are deceived most foully / they do not see deeply / The corn they keep entirely whole until it rots in their corner. / Much greater sense has the ant.[36]

Not only is his description of Jewish "blindness" fuller than that of many other bestiaries, Guillaume deftly managed to compare Jews not merely to the symbolic ant, representing the good Christian, but also to the industrious insect who possessed greater intelligence.[37] Like his Christian contemporaries, Guillaume contrasted the reasoning capacities and religious insights of the Jews unfavorably to that of beasts even within the category "animal." Each of these authors maximized the level of denigration of the Jews in the eyes of their audiences. That this motif appeared in texts other than Christian tracts in Latin dedicated exclusively to disrupting Jewish beliefs suggests that these views were promulgated to a diverse audience. While bestiaries were often commissioned by monastic or noble patrons, they, along with collections of miracles of the Virgin and *exempla,* served as reservoirs for anecdotes for sermons preached to lay masses.[38] Thus the message that Jews, because of their beliefs and rejection of Christianity, were the lowest of beasts spread to all segments of medieval Christian society. Some authors, such as Gautier of Coincy, even suggested that Jews should be treated like the dogs they were.

Christians occasionally compared Muslims to servile animals, as Peter the Venerable's remarks indicate, but these comparisons were rare relative to similar Christian rhetoric regarding the Jews. In the face of losses during the crusades, Christians would have had difficulty asserting a typically servile status for Muslims.[39] Some Christians feared that Muslims would impose this status on them. Oderic Vitalis's version of Pope Urban's speech at Clermont contains the following statement:

> They (the Muslims) have destroyed churches and slaughtered Christians like sheep. The infidels have made stables for their beasts in

> the churches. . . . They have carried off many prisoners into exile in distant lands, and binding them with thongs have forced them to submit to the yoke and to cultivate the fields laboriously, dragging the ploughs like oxen, and to undergo other cruel labors more fitting for beasts than for men.[40]

Here Christian holy places have been reduced to barns and Christians to beasts of labor, serving the Muslims. There is no question of likening Muslims to a subhuman, bovine state; rather the Christians themselves have lost their humanity, dominance, and thus manhood. That the call to war was also a call to regain that manhood may be seen in Oderic's subsequent emphasis that the crusade was a man's endeavor. Women long to go but cannot.[41] The "sons of Jerusalem" are exhorted to be "manly" *(viriliter)* in freeing their "holy mother," Jerusalem.[42] Jerusalem has become the damsel in distress whom the knights must rescue and thereby rescue their own status as men.

Jewish fabulists likewise toyed with hierarchies of animal species in order to critique Christian and, to a lesser extent, Muslim society. Epstein has argued that though Berechiah ha-Naqdan never mentioned Christians explicitly in his fables, he drew on common anti-Jewish themes from Christian bestiary and fable traditions and subtly altered them into a critique of Christianity.[43] This theory is equally true of the fables contained in the *maqamat* (rhymed prose frame narrative) *Meshal ha-Qadmoni* of Isaac ibn Sahula, written in Castile during Alfonso X's reign. Like Berachiah, Ibn Sahula's prologue implies that the fables contain secrets and that their wisdom is directed against "Edom," the Christians, and "Yemen," perhaps a reference to the Muslim world generally.[44] Ibn Sahula, even more than Berachiah, was concerned with rationality as a defining feature of the human being, and much of his lengthy work may be understood as an assertion of Jews' superior rationality and thus spirituality in contrast to that of the Christians and Muslims.[45] Both authors turned the Christian polemic associating Jews and the stupidity of barnyard animals against the Christians themselves. One example from each of the authors suffices to demonstrate their approach.

In the first gate, or chapter, of *Meshal ha-Qadmoni* Ibn Sahula spins a tale based very loosely on the conflict in the Arabic fable collection *Kalīlah wa-Dimnah,* which ends with Dimnah's execution.[46] In Ibn Sahula's story the animal kingdom is ravaged by the appetites of the lion who rules it. Fearful, the animals gather to seek counsel. The ox and the ass lead the animals to a lovely, peaceful land flowing with milk and honey.[47] The lion, desperate for food, is lured by his adviser, the fox, into putting his other advisers on trial regarding the worth of their lineage with the aim of trapping the stag, whose family is humble. The stag sees through the plot and brags of his father's love of knowledge and authorship of a book on logic. At the lion's urging the stag lectures about logic, mathematics, astronomy, natural science, metaphysics, political science, and the nature of the soul. The lion is overwhelmed by this display of learning and grants the stag his life and many honors.[48]

This tale undermines Christian allusions to Jews' supposed bovine stupidity and subservience in several ways. By making the ass and the ox the wise leaders of the other animals, Ibn Sahula attributed wisdom and spiritual insight to animals associated with Jews and their profound stubbornness and inability to grasp spiritual truths. So great is their spirituality that the ox and the ass are able to lead the other animals to a land whose description references the promised land of the messianic age, a land that the lion, when offered, rejected initially.[49] These creatures are not only wise; they outsmart the powerful lion, who is at best an ambiguous figure.

Epstein suggesets that the lions in Berachiah ha-Naqdan's fables and in Jewish art should be identified with the lion of Judah.[50] Among Christian writers the lion was seen as a symbol for God or Christ because it breathed life into its stillborn young three days after their birth, thus mirroring the death and resurrection of Christ, a tradition with which some medieval Jews were familiar.[51] Here, I believe, Ibn Sahula played on the dual symbolic value of the lion for his Jewish audience—as a metaphor both for the true messiah and for the "false" messiah of the Christians—along with Christian and Muslim associations of the lion with rulership to imply that the most noble of the Christians was misguided, foolish, and brutal. The lion could signify Jesus or, more likely in this case, King Alfonso, or perhaps both. The "Jewish" oxen and asses come out well because of their wisdom, and the "Christian" lion is made more stupid, and thus despicable, than some of the most lowly of the animal kingdom.

As Epstein has shown, in Hebrew manuscripts the stag or deer, along with rabbits and unicorns, often symbolized the Jews.[52] Lest there be any doubt, Ibn Sahula states explicitly that the stag *(ha-ẓevi)* is Israel.[53] Thus the Jew, in the form of the stag, a creature of lowly birth and a frequent target of predatory (Christian) animals, establishes himself as the most intellectual and rational of all the creatures. Furthermore, the stag, in his discussion of the states of the soul and sinfulness, indirectly links the lion with impurity, materiality, and sin. Adopting the Platonic tripartite division of the soul, the stag explains of the two lower souls: "The first type is the vegetative soul, linked to earth. The second is the animal soul that desires, sick every day."[54] By contrast, the rational soul is characterized by wisdom and restraint of appetites and desire. The sinful soul, the stag explains, is

> drowning in bodily greed, cut off from all wisdom and intelligence, [she] holds cheap glorifying her creator for her desire, and not having her desire she has become the whore. And she has become impure with impurity of [many] degrees and the lust of men a mistress. . . . [A] wild ravening beast she is efficient.[55]

Such a soul is forced to dwell in hell, the abode of idol worshipers, sorcerers, and deniers of the Messiah's coming, a place of pain and boiling excrement.[56] The lion, though repentant by the end of the story, fits the stag's description of one who has allowed the lower souls to rule and become mired in sin. The lion was so driven by his physical appetites that he devoured the inhabitants of his kingdom and was prepared to do the same to members of his court, showing he is governed by his base appetites, not wisdom and restraint. The lion scoffed at the suggestion that the messianic age had come in which wolf and lamb should live together in peace, saying that their ancestors had waited long to no effect.[57] By reacting this way, the lion came close to denying the messianic age, making him a candidate for hell. The lion further links himself with sorcerers, for he attempts to compare his father, who was "deeply read in spells and incantations," to that of the stag.[58] Thus the lion's family and "wisdom" consist of forbidden knowledge that would earn him a place in hell, in contrast to the extensive, proper wisdom of the stag and his ancestors. Behavior, desires, and knowledge like that of the lion render the person/soul impure and sick, dooming it to an eternity of boiling excrement—a term closely associated with Jesus in the Talmud and the Hebrew Crusade Chronicles. Even the word Ibn Sahula chose for the animal soul's "sickness" *(davah)*, implies ritual uncleanness, for it is used specifically in relation to the menstruating woman in the Bible. The lion, by following the animal soul, feminizes himself in a profoundly negative fashion. All these characteristics of the sinful or animal soul, greed, lack of spirituality and rationality, and even menstruation, were applied by Christians to Jews. In this tale, however, the stereotypes are reversed, for the unreasoning, "menstrual" uncleanness of such a soul stood in marked contrast to the rational purity and thus true "masculinity" of the Jewish stag and the barnyard animals.

The most devastating yet artful Jewish attempt to render Christians contemptuous because of their barnyard foolishness is Berechiah ha-Naqdan's fable of the ass in the lion's skin. In this tale an ass finds the hide of a lion and decides to clothe himself in it, thus making himself king. So disguised the ass terrorizes the sheep and shepherds in the area. The ass's master eventually finds his lost animal and curses its presumption.[59] Though simple at first glance, the tale may serve as an allegory in which the ass is Christ presuming to take on the mantle of Judah, only to be shown as a fool and humiliated for his arrogance by God (the master).

Berachiah's story about the donkey and the lion was merely a subtler and more entertaining effort to overturn the same Christian tradition. The ass was an appropriate representative of Christians or Christ, since the Christians took Zechariah 9:9 ("Behold, your king comes to you triumphant and victorious is he, humble and riding on an ass, on the colt, the foal of an ass") as a prophecy of Jesus' entry into Jerusalem.[60] Furthermore, using the ass as a symbol of Christians played on Christian and Jewish views of the animal as foolish, irrational, and thus an obvious symbol of religious blindness and obstinacy.

The biblical citations with which Berechiah peppered his fable are also suggestive of anti-Christian intent. In his speech against the donkey, the master incorporates part of Obadiah 3: "The pride of your heart has deceived you."[61] The entire book of Obadiah consists of a diatribe against Edom for its evil treatment of Israel. Medieval Jews saw this text as a prophecy of Roman and Christian abuse of Israel and of God's final judgment against the non-Jewish, especially Christian, world.[62] Thus any citation from Obadiah in a medieval Jewish text was likely to be interpreted in the context of Christian anti-Jewish hostility. In Berechiah's fable the citation from Obadiah served as a condemnation of Jesus for having pretended to be the king Messiah. The master's speech begins with a partial citation from Ezekiel 28:2: "Because your heart was high (proud)."[63] The entirety of the verse reads as follows:

> Son of man, say to the Prince of Tyre, thus says the Lord God, "Because your heart is proud and you have said I am a god, I sit in the seat of the gods in the heart of the seas, yet you are but a man and no god, though you consider yourself wise as a god."

No more appropriate text could be chosen for an allegory about one who claimed to be both God and the Messiah.[64] The ass, like the king of Tyre, is stripped of all adornment, cast to the ground, exposed, and shamed before all.[65]

Any number of Berechiah's fables may be seen as tales about some aspect of Jewish-Christian relations. However, in this instance Jesus or Christianity is ridiculed for his or its foolishness and presumption while being portrayed as a threat to others. Just as Peter the Venerable and the authors of the infancy gospels invoked Isaiah 1:3 against the Jews, Berechiah invoked this verse against Jesus and, by extension, Christians. However, in Berechiah's version, it is the ass who does not know his master's crib.[66] In the fable's moral the donkey is said to represent the son of a vile and nameless man *(ben naval u-bli shem)* who has no spirit of wisdom. He is also the son of mockery *(ben buz)* dressed in fine linen.[67] The very image of a donkey wrapped in a lion's skin provokes a sense of the ridiculous, especially when compared to a real lion: precisely the sentiment about the Christian Messiah Berechiah hoped to spark in those readers able to penetrate his allegory. In this fable Jesus becomes a foolish, servile animal, even as Jews were depicted in the writings of many of their Christian contemporaries. Any claim to Christian majesty or authority is thus rendered ludicrous.

An important difference exists, however, between Berechiah's portrayal of the ass and most of the Christian depictions of bestial Jews examined so far. Berechiah's donkey is also a threatening character. Dressed as a lion, he tears his prey, men and sheep, until shepherds and farmers abandon their fields and livestock.[68] In the end the ass is condemned for shedding innocent blood, and the moral depicts a man who lures others into serving him while treating them as slaves.[69] This image of bloodshed and religious seduction is consistent with other, more straightforward depictions of Christianity in Jewish polemics from this period and is indicative of the potential danger Christians were seen as posing (or which Jesus had posed) to the Jewish community.[70] Despite the harm inflicted by the erring donkey, Berechiah's tale is ultimately one of victory and vengeance. Just as Christians portrayed Jews as beasts well within the control of humankind, namely, rational Christians, so too did Berechiah end his tale with the humiliation and punishment of the ass by its human master. Such was the fate of Jesus and his followers anticipated by Berechiah and many of his coreligionists.[71] The human, masculine rationality and dominance about which the Christians bragged was an illusion. Creating an image of Christianity or Jesus as ridiculous, temporary, and soundly defeated granted Jewish readers a vicarious victory and superiority over their religious opponents and reaffirmed their loyalties to their faith through laughter and recollection of the ultimate judgment awaiting Christians.

Dangerous Beasts

The verb *liṭrof* (לטרוף) that Berechiah used in connection with the ass-lion's hunting activities means "to prey upon," "to tear to pieces," or "to declare ritually unfit for eating," since meat, according to Jewish (and Muslim) law, that has been torn by a carnivore is *ṭaref,* impure. This link among bestiality, violence, and impurity is common in medieval Jewish, Christian, and Muslim texts. The efforts of Berachiah ha-Naqdan and Christian authors such as Peter the Venerable to render their religious opponents nonthreatening by likening them to lowly, foolish beasts was a desperately needed defensive measure precisely because Christians and Jews saw one another as profoundly dangerous. The attributes of both uncleanness and predatory behavior served to convey this sense of peril, not only in Christian and Jewish texts but also Muslim and Christian writings about one another. Invectives of bestial filth also established a hierarchical dichotomy between members of the pure, "true" faith and the repulsive, misguided other. Metaphors of carnivores or poisonous creatures were often employed to indicate physical threat, whereas impurity pointed to the danger of spiritual pollution. Eating or being edible was an integral part of this animal-based polemic designed to mark the enemy as either impure or the creator of impurity and therefore off-limits to the believer. Wild animals, such as the bear or boar, also became symbols of the triumphant violence Pagan or Christian leaders inflicted on Jews. In Christian, Jewish, and Muslim artistic and literary traditions, the threatening religious other was frequently represented as hunters and their dogs, tearing their hapless prey, the religious "innocents."[72]

The *Bible moralisée* is filled with animal symbolism polemicizing against a wide variety of individuals, only some of whom were Jews or seen as related to Jews.[73] Serpents, worms, frogs, pigs, and ravens functioned to mark Jews as both polluted and harmful to Christians. Often the author(s) of the *Bible moralisée* codex 2554 associated these creatures with usury or usurers.[74] That they were usurers did not automatically make the people whom these animals represented Jews; however, even when the author did not explicitly connect usury with Judaism, he often closely paralleled the two. For example, after explaining that God curses those who are "wormy" *(tigne)*, the author remarks:

> Here the sons of Israel come and take wormy and mangy lambs who have their members broken, and they make an offering to God and God refuses it. That the sons of Israel made offerings of their wormy and mangy lambs and God refused them signifies those who make offerings of worms of usury, and of covetousness and of simony and God refuses these offerings and turns away from them.[75]

The primary opprobrium is focused on Christians who engage in usury and other inappropriate practices or attitudes regarding money. Nevertheless, by discussing the offerings of the people of Israel in conjunction with those of usurers, the author created a parallel between the "wormy" offerings of Jews and those of usurers. Accompanying this parallel is an illustration that seems to show a woman in the process of pawning her child to a Jew, an ominous pictorial allusion to the harm Christians imagined moneylending Jews could inflict.[76] In her analysis of another manuscript of the *Bible moralisée,* Sara Lipton notes that a man afflicted with worms is equated with a "great usurer" and is depicted in Jewish dress.[77] In the same manuscript, the artist and scribe construct a visual equation between the raven, which is said to signify the usurer, and the Jew, who is represented in the frame immediately after the raven in his role as moneylender.[78] Text and image also work together in codex 2554 to link both the raven and the pig with usurious Jews.[79]

All these animals were impure according to levitical law.[80] Because insects and worms were believed to generate spontaneously from corpses, menstrual blood, and other decaying matter, they were doubly unclean. Usurers and Jews were devoured internally by these creatures, making them profoundly rotten and poisonous, living containers of decay (see also figs. 1 and 2 in chapter 4).[81] Ravens and the other "cursed" birds discussed in the *Bible Moralisée* were carnivores and often scavengers. That they fed off rotting flesh augmented their polluted status.[82] The authors of *Bibles moralisées* were drawing from a tradition established since the second and third centuries C.E. in which the impure beasts of Leviticus were allegorized to represent religious undesirables.[83] As I argued in chapter 1, the equation of the religious undesirable with unconsumable, polluted food reflected anxiety about religious incorporation; just as the unclean animal was unsuitable for absorption into the physical body, so too were Jews, usurers, heretics, or gluttonous or lustful individuals unsuitable for absorption into the body of believers. By the thirteenth century, however, Jews were invariably linked with not one but many impure beasts, indicating that while they were not the only group to cause Christian anxiety, they were a central source. This vision of Jews as polluted animals, linked with decay, worked hand in hand with the growing association of Jews with filth due to their moneylending activities. Because the Church considered money and the desire for it dirty, Jews, who were becoming synonymous with moneylending during this period, were the dirtiest of all those involved in mercantile activities.[84] The automatic association of Jews with pollution and the resulting abhorrence would have been difficult for Christian audiences to avoid because the rhetoric of filth came from so many directions.

Not only did Christians feel apprehensive about Jews' presence and assimilation into Christian society, they feared Jews' perceived ability or desire to "devour" or in some other way destroy Christians. That the usurer, Jewish or otherwise, was threatening may be seen in a French *Bible moralisée*'s rendition of the creation story in Genesis. The author explains, "The large fish signify the rich usurers who eat the small who are poor people."[85] The rod of Moses that becomes a venomous, stinging serpent "signifies the Jews and miscreants who keep the Old Law and are stung and poisoned by the serpent."[86] The venom in this analogy is not simply internal poison, harmful only to the misguided. In the previous illustration the serpent bites the foot of Christ, while in the accompanying frame, men in pointed hats (usually an indication of Jewish identity) carrying a dead lamb are struck down by Christ and God as Christ steps on the heel of one of the men.[87] The serpent biting Christ's heel and then Jesus stepping on one of his adversaries is a clear allusion to Genesis 3:15: "I (God) will put enmity between you (the serpent) and the woman, and between your seed and her seed; he shall bruise your head, and you shall bruise his heel." The pictorial parallel between the Jews and the serpent who actively seeks to harm Jesus would have suggested to viewers that Jews were the malicious adversaries of Jesus, linked to the primeval serpent. The dead lamb served to trigger a number of associations. First, it reinforced the malevolence of Jews by subtly connecting the serpent's attack in the previous frame with Jews' involvement with the crucifixion; they were the killers of Christ, the "lamb of God."[88] Second, the lamb served to remind Christian viewers not only of the violence of Jewish sacrifice but also of its filth. Lipton has demonstrated that in Christian discussions of Old Testament sacrificial practices and in the sacrificial iconography of the *Bible moralisée* itself, the bloody animal sacrifices of the Jews palpably disgusted Christian authors and artists and were contrasted with the clean, pure sacrifice of the Christian Eucharist.[89]

Depicting the Jews as struck down violently and, in the text, poisoned by the serpent's venom would have prompted Christians to consider the ultimate, just vengeance to which the Jews were condemned. Just as the predatory ass in Berechiah ha-Naqdan's fable was humiliated and punished, providing Jewish readers with reassurance and vicarious triumph over Jesus or the Christians, so too did the image and text of the *Bible moralisée* confirm the superiority and final victory of the Christian faith.

Muslim and Jewish uses of spontaneously generated vermin were not as elaborate as the set of associations in the *Bible moralisée* tradition, but they were present nevertheless. The illuminator of the Rylands *haggadah*, a mid-fourteenth-century manuscript from Catalonia, went farther than the biblical text when illustrating the plague that should have corresponded to the plague of locusts. The Egyptians are attacked by serpents, lizards, and a wild boar rather than flies, gnats, or locusts as one might expect were the *haggadah* following the biblical account more closely (see fig. 3).[90] These creatures, except for the boar, fall into the category of *shereẓ* ([impure] creeping things). The image is especially subversive because precisely the same disgusting animals with whom the Christians linked the Jews overwhelm the powerful gentiles.

Figure 3. *Rylands Haggadah* 16b. Reproduced by courtesy of the University Librarian and Director, The John Rylands University Library, University of Manchester.

Thus, on the one hand, the Jews' enemies are made impure by association with these creatures, and, on the other, they are vanquished by these serpents/ Jews.[91]

While suggesting that Jews would have willingly accepted an impure creature as a symbol for themselves or as an agent for desired outcomes may seem odd, doing so was in fact part of Jewish subversions of Christian anti-Jewish animal symbolism. Epstein has already demonstrated that the Jews accepted the hare—also impure according to levitical law and a negative Christian symbol for the Jews—as a representation of themselves.[92] I would argue that the same is true of snails and owls, creatures that figure in the marginal illumination of both the Rylands and Barcelona *haggadot*.[93] Sometimes the snail is depicted naturalistically, but in one instance it has the head of a bearded man, possibly representing a Jew (fig. 4).[94] Lillian Randall, in his article on snails in marginal decoration in Christian manuscripts from the thirteenth and fourteenth centuries, has shown that snails were often a symbol of cowardice and were associated with the moon and with usury, becoming linked with Lombards who were regarded as "unchivalrous" and cowardly and despised for their role as pawnbrokers and usurers.[95] These stereotypes closely mirror those of the Jews in Christian society, and by the mid- to late-fourteenth century Jews, Sarracens, and Lombards were being placed in the same category of undesirable merchant-strangers.[96] Randall notes that the snail was often paired with the hare and that in Christian manuscripts fear of the snail (or hare) was part of the "world turned upside down" motif. By placing snails in the marginal decoration of their own manuscripts as representations of themselves, Jews accepted their current, weak, besieged status in the Christian world while simultaneously alluding to a time when the Christian world would be turned upside down, with the Jews on top.[97]

Christian and Jewish use of vermin is similar at least in the sense that both groups understood them to be threatening in their capacity to render one impure by contact if not through more drastic measures such as biting. The Muslim approach was somewhat different. In a poem dedicated to Ṣalāḥ al-Dīn, Imād al-Dīn al-Iṣfahānī stated, "Your enemies are like buzzing flies."[98] By contrast, Ṣalāḥ al-Dīn and his forces are compared to the nobler and more dangerous lion.[99] In this text the simile served to suggest that Christians were despicable and dirty, for Muslims also accepted the Aristotelian theory of spontaneous generation.[100] It also mocked Christian military efforts as annoying at best and incapable of posing a true threat in the face of the powerful lion (Ṣalāḥ al-Dīn) who would devour them. Such descriptions differ sharply

Figure 4. *Rylands Haggadah* 29b. Reproduced by courtesy of the University Librarian and Director, The John Rylands University Library, University of Manchester.

from the Christian imagery where vermin were either unclean or threatening. Instead the "swarming" Christian flies are portrayed as terrified of Muslims even before their birth.[101] Attributing this fear to the crusaders added to the scorn with which Muslims would have viewed Christians and made them appear unworthy, "unmanly" opponents in war.

Christians or "bad" Muslims as despised animals in contrast to noble predators symbolizing Muslim warriors was a fairly common motif in the Arabic oral epics composed or becoming increasingly popular during the crusades.[102] Dogs, swine, and sometimes hyenas are the most common representations in these texts for Christians or sometimes Zoroastrians, whereas the good Muslims are lions.[103] Chroniclers also indulged in such invective. Ibn Jubayr, for example, referred to the Christian king of Acre as a pig and his mother as a sow.[104] Pigs, of course, are impure in Islamic law. Dogs have a more ambiguous status. In the ḥadith, the Prophet praises those who give a thirsty dog water; on the other hand, dogs, along with scorpions, can be killed in the *ḥaram*, and keeping dogs that have no practical use diminishes the believer's portion in paradise.[105] In *Sīrat al-Ẓāhir Baybars*, eating dog flesh can restore health but subject the eater to uncontrollable lusts and personality changes.[106] Calling someone a dog, therefore, was degrading in medieval Muslim society, for it suggested that the person was lustful, uncontrolled, and categorized among the vermin unworthy to enter holy space.[107] Equating someone with a hyena suggested that he was a carrion eater and therefore impure and, unlike the lion, disinclined or unable to hunt for himself. Yet labeling the Christians as any of these animals did not merely serve to mark them as contemptible, as in the case of the Christian "flies" in Imād al-Dīn's poem. These creatures could and did attack and even defeat Muslims.[108] Such allowances in the epic traditions recognized that Christians, whether Byzantine or Western, possessed a modicum of power. The choice of animals and the infrequency or ephemeral nature of such defeats, however, suggested that Christians' loathsome nature ultimately doomed them to failure, reassuring audiences.

Dogs were servants of humankind and thus as an invective could point to the lowly status of Jews, as Gautier de Coincy did when he had one of his characters advocate that Jews be kicked like an old dog. Dogs could turn on their masters, however, and a rabid dog was uncontrollable and life-threatening. Yet the rabid, ferocious, or despicable dog was a common metaphor for the religious other among Muslims and Jews as well as Christians. Dogs along with various predators signified extreme violence, violence that, in the eyes of the writers, had gone beyond the bounds of human behavior. I have suggested that portraying enemies' aggression as excessive attributed a kind of negative hypermasculinity to the religious other, as seen in the language of rape that accompanied these portrayals. Likening a group or an individual's cruelty and love of bloodshed to that of predators was connected to this idea, for such imagery tended to be applied to men and male activities, not women. Sometimes comparisons with predators could be positive, but for the most part they stripped their targets of rationality, humanity, "good" masculinity, and any claim to sympathy or respect on the part of the audience.

Hillenbrand has noted that comparisons by Muslims between crusaders and animals were especially common. More specifically, this bestiality was connected to their preoccupation with war. Usamah ibn Munqidh, as Hillenbrand points out, praised the Franks for their bravery in battle but implies that they do nothing else well. Indeed, Usamah managed to simultaneously compare the Franks to pack animals and allude to their obsession with war.[109] The geographer al-Dimashqī (d. 1327) described the Franks as follows: "Their coloring is in the nature of an egg (i.e., white) and they are like predatory beasts; they are concerned for nothing except war, and killing, and hunting, they do not know (of) our learning and they do not fear our proof (i.e., they do not accept our religious law)."[110] Here the choice of vocabulary suggests more menacing creatures than beasts of burden. Predatory, warlike behavior is linked directly to lack of education and culture, implying that the Franks are capable only of animalistic violence, not these rational pursuits.[111] Abū Shama remarked that the Franks conducted themselves like demons, wolves, and evil jinn.[112] While the language is not as strong as that found in Christian anti-Jewish and anti-Muslim polemic, the message of these writers is the same: because of their savagery and lack of intelligence, Western Christians are beasts, not men.

Using a combination of convoluted wordplay and exegesis, Peter the Venerable turned the Jews at Jesus' execution into rabid, bloodthirsty, impure, barking dogs. Like other assignations of bestial nature in *Adverus Iudeorum Inveteratam Durietiem,* Peter's simile was intended to point to the irrationality of the Jews, but in this case Jews were not merely stubborn and stupid but also murderous.[113] Elsewhere, Peter was less specific regarding the Muslims, contenting himself with referring to their "bestial cruelty" and "bestial love of human blood."[114] Other authors compared the Muslims, like the Jews, to a rabid or enraged dog.[115] Gautier de Coincy was fond of calling Jews dogs both as a form of denigration and as a sign of their viciousness. The Jew as "stinking dog" *(puant chien)* stands in stark contrast to the Virgin Mary, who is compared to flowers or honey and lauded for her sweet smell and purity.[116] The anonymous author of *De expurgatione sanctae terrae* did not explicitly state that Muslim "dogs" stank, but he linked them with corpses and thus the stench of rot since they run to battle like rabid dogs to a cadaver.[117] Gautier emphasized the malicious aspect of Jews' canine incarnation by calling them "treacherous dogs" *(felon chien, felon viautre, fauz gaingnon).*[118] In the story of the Jewish glassmaker's son whose father casts him into a furnace for having taken communion with Christian schoolmates, the villainous father is "l'enragié chien" (the enraged dog).[119] Gautier's choice of adjective is similar to Peter the Venerable's comparing the Jews who crucified Jesus to rabid dogs and other authors' comparison of Muslims to rabid dogs and predators. Both terms suggest malicious, unreasonable violence. Thus the revulsion and contempt that the terms "dog," "impure," and "stinking" were designed to provoke in Christian audiences were immediately mixed with a warning against the danger of Jews' malice. The plots of the miracle tales themselves underscored Jewish ill will toward and active abuse of Mary, Jesus, objects related to Mary and Jesus, and Christians. These small but frequent verbal reminders in the tales reinforced the broad message of Jewish malevolence that is central to the plots.

In Alfonso X's version of the glassmaker's son in *Cantigas de Santa Maria,* the refrain does the work of Gautier's and Peter the Venerable's polemical adjectives. The poem begins with: "To the Mother of he who delivered Daniel from the lions / She protected a boy of Israel from the fire."[120] By evoking the story of Daniel and the lion's den, Alfonso implied a parallel between the father who attempted to kill the boy and the lions who were to devour the biblical Daniel.[121] Because these lines constitute the refrain, the association of lions and the murderous Jewish father would have been reinforced throughout the song for the audience. The more obvious parallel from Daniel 3 in which King Nebuchadnezzar casts Daniel's three companions, Shadrach, Meshach, and Abednego, into the furnace, much as the Jewish boy is cast into the burning oven by his father, is not evoked directly until stanza 9, though Alfonso alludes to it in stanza 7 when he refers to the "fiery furnace" *(forn' arder).*[122] In stanza 7, the father is characterized as a cruel traitor *(traedor cruel)*, and his action is treachery *(felonia)*; this language is similar to that in Gautier's *Miracles.*[123] Those who recalled the biblical story of Daniel and his companions well would have seen another link between Jews and bestiality in the reference to Nebuchadnezzar, a king deprived of his reason and forced to dwell among animals because of his haughtiness.[124] The glassmaker of Alfonso's tale also suffered from madness *(folia)*, but his end, unlike that of Nebuchadnezzar, was not a happy one.[125]

Scholars have noted that Gautier adopted language and added details to his tales that cast Jews in a worse light than other authors writing in the twelfth and thirteenth centuries.[126] Yet Alfonso "el Sabio," in his rendition of the tale of the glassmaker's son, while not as blunt in his vilification of the Jewish father as was Gautier de Coincy, nevertheless characterized the father as bestial, cruel, and insane, precisely the traits Gautier de Coincy assigned to the father in his version.[127] The harsh language or visual signs that drew parallels between Jews and aggressive, violent, and often dirty or impure animals are indicative of the deep anxiety and concomitant hostility Jews inspired in many Christians. Christian artists and writers always expressed their fear and anger in the framework of eventual victory, thus reassuring their audiences of the superiority of Christianity and the power of God and Mary to protect, or at least avenge, the Christian victims of "rabid" Jews.

The tale of the Jewish glassmaker's son is one of many stories that originated in the Christian East and depicted Jews as murderers of young children or as violent desecrators of the host.[128] The language of animalistic violence was equally present in blood libel accusations, which were based on events that occurred in the twelfth and thirteenth centuries. In *The Life of William of Norwich,* one of the first accusations of Jewish ritual murder in Europe, the author, Thomas of Monmouth, compared the Jews and their emissary to a cruel wolf ready to "rend" and "devour" *(diripiat et devoret)* the young lamb (William).[129] The savagery with which the boy was murdered immediately led some to suspect that the perpetrators were Jews.[130] Thus the image and expectation that Jews were comparable to vicious animals had very real consequences. Yet in this early text, based on "real" events, the same pattern of redemption and vengeance is present as in the later, literary representations of Jewish animalistic hostility. Jews in *The Life of William of Norwich* do not stink; however, William's holiness is manifested by his body's fragrant odor and imperviousness to decay or the ravages of wild animals.[131] By contrast, one of the Jews responsible for murdering the child is killed and left in the woods and devoured by the very ravens and dogs that were unable to touch the corpse of William.[132] Thomas of Monmouth was careful to note that all the Jews who had participated in the attack were later exiled, died suddenly, or killed by Christians. William's murder is avenged by God, and the child himself becomes a powerful saint able not only to heal but also to wreak revenge on any who show him disrespect.[133] The death and desecration of the Jewish murderers and the Christian child's power after death serve to ensure that Christianity retained its place of superior holiness and power in Thomas of Monmouth's narrative.

Predatory, animalistic violence was a common characteristic that Jewish chroniclers and poets assigned to their Christian persecutors. Images of hunters and dogs (representing Christians) attacking rabbits and deer (representing Jews) are ubiquitous in both Sephardi and Ashkenazi illuminated manuscripts (figs. 4, 5, and 6).[134] Any anticipated victory or vengeance, however, was usually expected during the end-times; it was not the immediate, "happy" conclusion of Jewish-Christian conflicts. In the marginal illuminations of the *Barcelona Haggadah,* a pig and a dog (usually metaphors for Christians) serve a hare (representing Jews) and sometimes the hare chases the hunting dog.[135] These illuminations, according to Epstein, depict the anticipated reversal of power between Jews and Christians during the messianic era.[136] That the hare was associated with the reversal of the world order in Christian manuscripts would have made it an even more appropriate and powerful symbol for the eventual overturn of Christianity.[137]

Under the guise of fable in Berechiah ha-Naqdan's *Mishlei,* oppressed "animals" show superior wisdom or gain vengeance against those who seek to expel or enslave them.[138] In some instances no promise of redemption exists. In the tale of the wolf and the lamb, the lamb is devoured despite its innocence. In this fable Berechiah was simply following the ending as it was detailed in many Christian nonpolemical *isopets,* or fable collections. Yet the wolf's accusation that the sheep has caused him shame and that the lamb's distant ancestor sinned against the wolf is reminiscent of Christian allegations of Jews' collective, permanent guilt for Jesus' crucifixion.[139] The image of non-Jews as predators and the people of Israel as sheep or cattle is one that Eilberg-Schwartz asserts is present even in Jewish biblical texts. In creating contrasts between predators and docile creatures of the field, Berachiah and other Jewish authors were drawing from anti-Roman and anti-Christian polemical traditions in *Leviticus Rabbah* and *Genesis Rabbah.*[140]

Hebrew poetic or historical accounts of actual violent encounters between Jews and Christians constantly employ verbs of devouring and slaughter. Christians are likened to wolves, bears, lions, leopards, and pigs as a way of pointing to their extreme violence.[141] The crusaders are depicted as ready to devour the Jews with greedy mouths, drawing from Isaiah 9:11, or they are likened to the "wolves of the steppes" mentioned in Jeremiah 5:6 and Zephaniah 3:3.[142] Jews are the pure sheep to be slaughtered in a ritually correct fashion. Though the primary imagery is that of ritual sacrifice, nevertheless,

Figure 5. *Barcelona Haggadah* fol. 17v. Add. 14761. By permission of the British Library.

according to the chroniclers, some of the martyrs also invoked the laws of kosher slaughter and the prayers over meals before killing themselves.[143] Such language suggests that being subject to gentile violence entailed impurity for the victims. Indeed, by depicting themselves as "torn" *(ṭaraf)* by carnivores, Jewish poets and chroniclers implied that they were polluted by the crusaders; they had become *ṭref* meat. The descriptions of the fate of Jewish

Figure 6. *Barcelona Haggadah* fol. 18r. Add. 14761. By permission of the British Library.

corpses frequently emphasize dishonor and uncleanness. Crusaders drag the bodies naked through the mud and leave them unburied to become food for wild animals and birds.[144] Literally dirty as well as shamed, the martyrs are reduced to carrion. The chroniclers drew from II Kings 8:12—"[Y]ou will slay their (Israel's) young men with swords . . . you will rip up their women with child"—to portray the fate of the martyrs or their corpses once they fell into the hands of the Christians.[145] R. David b. R. Meshullam elaborated on this theme in gruesome detail:

Behold the deed of the trusting daughters
In the heat of the day stretched out naked before the sun
Beautiful among women, their belly split and plowed, bringing forth a placenta from between their legs, a fetus.[146]

As Einbinder has argued for this and other poems using similar imagery, the women's defilement is twofold: their bodies remain unburied, and the blood of birth streaming from their wombs is impure by Jewish law.[147] The language of this passage also dehumanizes the victims by using vocabulary applicable to animals. The verb *mifulaḥot* (מפלחות) in line 3, which I have translated as "plowed," in its active form also refers to nonhuman birthing. In the final line, *valad* (ולד), or fetus, is the word for the young of animals. Had David b. Meshullam wished to avoid such connotations, he could have chosen *'ubar* (עבר), the term commonly used for a human embryo.

Though images of bestial eating, birthing, or corpse desecration carried connotations of impurity for the Jews who fell prey to the crusaders, I do not believe that the poets and chroniclers intended to cast the martyrs in a negative light. The constant affirmation of Jewish purity in contrast to the uncleanness of the Christian attackers stands firmly against such an interpretation. Rather, the *payṭanim* (writers of *piyyuṭim*) and chroniclers underscored the defilement that, in their minds, resulted from being "incorporated" or otherwise touched by Christians.

Much of the animal imagery in Jewish writing regarding the crusades and other persecutions has parallels in both metaphor and function to animal imagery in Christian writing. In R. Ephraim of Bonn's *Sefer Zekhirah,* an account of Jewish sufferings during the second crusade, the monk Radulf, who preached violence against the Jews, is dubbed the "barker" *(noveaḥ)* because he "barks" (preaches) the call to crusade. Furthermore, "Wherever he went he spoke evil of the Jews of the land and incited the snake and the dogs against us."[148] As in the writings of the thirteenth-century Christian author Gautier de Coincy and others, the dog imagery serves both to express contempt and to indicate danger for those against whom the "dog" or "dogs" turn. Similar to the *Bible moralisée,* likening the Christians whom Radulf incites to the snake, suggests primeval malice, threat, and contamination from poison. The comparison also suggests impurity as snakes belong to the category of creeping things *(shereẓ).*

Abraham b. R. Yom Tov, as recorded in the first crusade chronicle traditionally attributed to Solomon bar Simson, lamented, "Woe, O Lord God!

Why have you abandoned your people Israel to calumny, plunder and shame, destroying us through the hands of a people as impure as the pig, who eat us?"[149] By referring to Christians as pigs, Jews could simultaneously mark them as violent predators and as profoundly impure. In a modern context, one might not think of pigs as predators. Yet in medieval Christian peasant households, pigs were a danger to infants and young children. Semiwild pigs allowed to roam in the forest until the time came to gather them and distribute their young to the lord and other pig owners imperiled the swineherds as well as stray children.[150] *Payṭanim* often referred to the Christians as pigs *(hazirim),* and in this, as in the comparisons to wolves, leopards, and other more traditional predators, they followed the example of earlier midrashic authors who compared Edom and the other nations to various kinds of undesirable beasts.[151] *Payṭanim* sometimes specified that these were "pigs of the forest" who "frightened us, devoured and ate us."[152] This phrase also appeared in *Midrash Rabbah Leviticus*, but to its medieval audience it would have recalled contemporary livestock management practices, with all the dangers these entailed.

Calling one's religious opponents pigs added a dimension of insult absent from other animal metaphors: pigs were impure. Indeed, in *Midrash Rabbah Leviticus* 13:5 pigs are called the most impure of all creatures, which, according to the author, is the reason Edom especially should be equated with them. From a practical standpoint, comparing Christians to pigs must have seemed especially apt to medieval Jews precisely because swine were such an integral aspect of the Christian diet and a source of many cheap household goods, which must have been especially repugnant to Jews.[153] Furthermore, pigs had long been associated with dirt, disease, and heresy. In calling Christians swine, Jews marked them as spiritually diseased, turning an old Christian anti-Jewish invective against the Christians themselves.[154]

Two fables from Berechiah ha-Naqdan demonstrate how profoundly filthy, as well as ritually unclean, medieval Jews regarded pigs. In one tale a boar makes his home near the court of the king lion. The lion is upset, demanding that the boar leave because its presence and habits make the lion's habitation unclean. The boar agrees in word but "makes his heart hard and his neck stiff" and continues to surround his lair with dung, until the enraged lion has him killed.[155] In another fable a sow who has been wallowing in mud in the forest is invited to a wedding feast of two deer at which every delicacy is provided in abundance. "A deer looked upon the sow, her gaping mouth befouled with filth for she had rooted in the dung heap, had eaten to her full, and showed the remains."[156] No amount of persuasion will entice the sow from the food of her birth. Berechiah's moral establishes the sow as a symbol for those who never abandon their sins, thus making the sinner's soul "awful and filthy" (מוראה ונגאל). That Berechiah aimed his remarks in both of these stories at Christians as opposed to transgressors in general is suggested by the term *nokhriah 'avodato* (נכריה עבודתו), which Hadas translates variously as "he is a strange work" and "one whose comportment is repulsive."[157] The word *'avodah* can mean "work," but it can also mean worship; the customary term for idol worship is *'avodah zarah,* literally translated as "strange worship." *Nekhar* and its cognates have a number of definitions. However, in the context of worship, or habits, "strange" or "foreign" seems the best translation. A "strange god" is *'el nekhar,* and in *Sefer Ḥasidim, nekhar* commonly designates Christians.[158] Thus *nokhriah 'avodato* is best translated as "strange (or foreign) is his worship" and should be understood as a reference to the "foreign" worship of the Christians.[159] The reference to the "stiff neck" of the boar in the first fable turns the Christian accusation that Jews were stiff-necked in their refusal of Jesus into an indictment of Christians' own stubborn adherence to a false and foul religion. The warning at the end of the parable not to envy the "uncircumcised" likewise suggests that Christians were targets of the tale of the boar and the lion, as this term was a common anti-Christian invective.[160]

From the outset, using swine to symbolize Christians in these two fables labels Christians as impure, as it did in *piyyuṭim* and Jewish chronicles. Likewise, the same imagery turned against Jews in Christian texts marked them as sinful, greedy, and unclean. Unlike the other Jewish texts examined, the author of the *Mishlei Shu'alim* emphasized the dirtiness as opposed to the violence of the swine. The primary vehicle for this message was the pigs' delight in and production of excrement, which is equated with their "foreign worship." The ultimate implication is that Christians, who are swine, adore human waste. This image worked to inspire profound disgust and avoidance in a Jewish audience and to reinforce Jewish belief in their own religious purity.

The same imagery and forces in Berechiah's book were at work in the Christian bestiary tradition, which is unsurprising, given that Berechiah was drawing from both Christian bestiary and fable literature.[161] Early medieval compilations that attached moral significance to animals, such as the *Physiologus,* the *Etymologiae* of Isidore of Seville, and Rabanus Maurus's *De rerum naturis,* already associated swine with filth, gluttony, luxury, and Jews. The texts' popularity led to wide dissemination of these views in the late Middle

Ages.[162] As in Berechiah, pigs' devotion to dirt inspired a thirteenth-century Christian author to link them with unbelievers:

> The pig *(porcus)* is a filthy beast *(spurcus);* it sucks up filth, wallows in mud, and smears itself with slime. Horace calls the sow "the lover of mud." Sows signify sinners, the unclean and heretics: it is prescribed in Jewish law that the flesh of beasts with cloven hooves which do not chew the cud shall not be eaten by the faithful. The Old and New Testaments, the Law and the Gospels, support this: because heretics do not chew the cud of spiritual food, they are unclean.[163]

Here sinners are unclean because they, like the pig, "eat" polluted food. This same author applied a variety of biblical passages to the pig, each pointing to the filth and sinfulness of the animal and those whom it symbolized. Drawing from a peculiar reading of Psalm 16:14 by Rabanus Maurus and Isaiah 65:3–4 ("A people . . . who eat swine flesh, and broth of abominable things is in their vessels"), the author equates sinful behavior and disbelief with eating impure swine's flesh.[164] In both instances in which eating is described, heretics, sinners, and Jews are impure because they consume impure things, whether they share the sow's diet or actually eat the pig itself.

Muslims are not mentioned in the bestiary texts, although Christian hearers and readers could have substituted "Muslim" for "heretic" and made an indirect association with certain animals in that way. Such elaborate metaphors were perhaps deemed unnecessary, as Muḥammad was so closely tied to the dogs or pigs that, in Christian lore and iconography, devoured his dead or drunken body.[165] In these tales the Prophet Muḥammad became the very dirt that these creatures ate, making him doubly filthy—unclean because these creatures ate unclean things, and impure because the animals themselves were contaminating. In Christian texts, like Jewish ones, evoking the filthy, polluted pig established a powerful barrier of disgust between religious communities, for this association marked the religious other as a devourer of food of dirt; such a person was literally stuffed with filth.

Portraying the other as a consumer of impurity was a common theme in Muslim polemic as well. Bad Muslims and non-Muslims were defined by their willingness to eat all manner of unclean, forbidden food such as pigs, cats, dogs, and people.[166] This diet was defined by excess, much like Muslim characterizations of the Frankish thirst for war. For example, in *Sīrat al-Amīra Dhāt al-Himma,* the queen of the Christian kingdom of Georgia eats an entire pig every day for breakfast.[167] These practices not only defined the non-Muslims as impure and inhuman, or at least uncivilized, they were also viewed as threatening. According to one epic, the Christian king of Rhodes maintained that Muslim flesh was lawful food but that Christian flesh was not, and so the Muslims risked becoming their enemy's unholy meal.[168]

What Muslims seem to have especially feared was to be forced to eat or associate with pigs. In the epics converts or captives had to eat pork or become swineherds.[169] Being required to eat pork not only polluted Muslims; it signified a profound loss of status: Muslims were placed in a position servile to Christians, and Muslims themselves became associated with the most vile creatures. This sentiment is close to Oderic Vitalis's version of Pope Urban's exhortation, in which Christians were reduced to pack animals. Indeed, later in his narrative, Oderic insinuates that Muslims were to blame for Christians' consumption of unclean food and cannibalism.[170] That the believer should be reduced to eating polluted flesh was a horrifying and humiliating vision; however, the onus of the disgusting behavior in both the Muslim and Christian texts ultimately fell on the group that demanded it or created the circumstances that allowed it to happen.

The pig was but one of a variety of unclean animals that became symbolic of Jews in Western Christian texts.[171] The *niticorax,* or owl (literally "nightcrow"), and hyena were also tied to Jews in various Christian bestiaries. Like the pig, they were unclean according to levitical law and according to their eating habits and stench as well. Commonly, the *niticorax* was associated with Jews because it prefers darkness to light, even as the Jews preferred the darkness of their unbelief over the light of Christ.[172] A number of bestiaries or aviaries, elaborating on certain versions of the *Physiologus,* explain that the *niticorax* or *fresaie* (screech owl) is "foul and stinking," roosts in its own droppings, resides in graves or caves, and is "like sinners who delight in their sin, which is the stench of human flesh." Throughout this unsavory list of characteristics, Christian authors clearly link the owl with the Jews.[173]

Like the *niticorax* and pig, the hyena was profoundly filthy: not only did it dwell in tombs but it also devoured the bodies of the dead. Its supposed capacity to change from male to female was seen as a metaphor for Jews' shifting between the worship of the one true God and the worship of idols in the Old Testament.[174]

Christian artists made the connection between the consumption of dirt, especially excrement, and false (Jewish) belief even more pointed than

Figure 7. Portal of Notre-Dame-la-Ronde in Metz, the "bestiary."

those confined to the written word. Michael Camille has demonstrated that medieval artists and scribes frequently indulged in satirical commentaries on texts by drawing animals, both real and imaginary, in the margins of manuscripts. These animals could either stand alone or engage in a variety of silly or grotesque activities designed to parody the texts. Similar motifs appear in the "marginal" sculpture of cathedrals and monasteries.[175] For example, a lintel on the exterior of the Strasbourg Cathedral displays several motifs common to bestiaries: the lion breathing on its dead cubs to resurrect them three days after their birth; the pelican wounding its breasts in order to feed its young; the self-immolation of the Phoenix. Occasionally they constituted part of the central decoration of a church entry, as in the case of the western portal of the Magdeburg cathedral, which features a lion breathing on its cubs and a pelican ripping open its breasts for its young. The portal of Notre-Dame-la-Ronde in Metz (figs. 7 and 8), which focuses entirely on animals and human-animal hybrids, is a spectacular example. Marginal art drew from *exempla,* fables, bestiaries, and miracles of the Virgin, all of which were closely related genres and served as material for the preaching

Figure 8. Portal of Notre-Dame-la-Ronde in Metz, the "bestiary."

programs of friars.[176] Stained-glass windows also contained images that followed the iconographic and exegetical themes of the *Bible moralisée* and related literature.[177]

It is in this context that sculptures of sows or of Jews embracing swine on cathedrals in Germany and what is now northern France need to be understood. In their examination of the rise of this motif, Isaiah Shachar and G. C. Druce noted the importance of the bestiary tradition for comprehending images linking Jews and pigs.[178] What Shachar and Druce did not realize is that carvings associating Jews and swine were often part of a much broader decorative scheme using certain animals or other iconography loaded with anti-Jewish symbolism. Taking Metz as an example, the sow nursing Jews that Shachar identified is part of the interior carving in the smaller of the two thirteenth-century churches, Notre-Dame-la-Ronde.[179] A number of animals amid the grotesques and other figures that are part of the "bestiary" decorating the portal of that church had strong anti-Jewish associations: the owl (top center, fig. 7), the boar (lower center, plate 3), a hybrid rabbit (bottom, far right, fig. 8) and, more vaguely, cows or oxen (far left, plate 3; top center,

Figure 9. Portal of Notre-Dame la-Ronde in Metz, Life of St. Steven and St. Helen's Discovery of the True Cross.

plate 4). The life and martyrdom of Saint Steven and Saint Helen's discovery of the true cross and its rescue from the Jews who were hiding it (fig. 9) occupy the other side of the portal. Neither of these stories portrayed Jews in a favorable light.[180] Because of their spatial relationship to one another, the bestiary and these sculpted narratives of saints and biblical figures create parallel morals or messages; the panels of each side are to be read with its opposite pair. Coupled with these, the sow and the nursing Jews form part of a visual anti-Jewish message that was an integral element of the church's decorative scheme.[181] A similar though less obvious parallel exists in the friezes of the south and north facades of the Strasbourg cathedral in which the sculpture of a naked Jew being dragged and shat upon by demons on the south fadade may be positionally paired with an image on the north facade of a boar being attacked by hunters and dogs. These and other external and interior carvings make anti-Judaism a persistent polemic throughout the cathedral, externally and internally.[182]

Shachar notes that twelfth-century representations of the sow and her young appear as part of a visual narrative of vices, the pig symbolizing luxury or greed. Thus he does not see any direct link between these images and the Jews, either in Germany or in England.[183] Furthermore, in his discussion of the two English bestiaries that drew from Rabanus Maurus, he notes that the authors replaced Rabanus's "Jews" with a generic "this" *(hoc)* and attributed the impure qualities of the pig to sinners and heretics in general. The authors' decision may have been driven by a desire to make the moral more applicable to a wide variety of Christian readers. Regardless of the reason, according to Shachar, the removal of the word *Jews* deprived artists (and readers) of one aspect of the symbolic iconography surrounding the sow, namely, the equation of sows and Jews.[184] Though Shachar's suggestion that the writers of the bestiaries were attempting to broaden the interpretive scope of the sow to make it directly applicable to Christian sinners is reasonable, that the pig also represented the Jews remained implicit in the text, paintings, and carvings of the sow. Jews, because of their ties with usury, were closely associated with the sins of luxury and greed and the "pollution" Christians linked to involvement with money.[185] The citation of Matthew 27:25 ("Let his blood be on us and our children") was so strongly associated with Jews that the readers of the bestiaries would have understood that the morals listed by the authors also applied to Jews.[186] Paintings and carvings of owls, rabbits, and other animals that were frequently used to symbolize Jews also would have conjured both the vices for which the given animal was known and its association with Jews.

The tendency either to depict Jews with other "undesirables" or to use Jews as signifiers of heretics or sinners was becoming increasingly common in this period. According to Lipton, this blurring of boundaries between Jews and "bad" Christians did not mean that no distinction was recognized; rather Jews were a convenient "inversion" of the good. Heretics and Jews posed similar kinds of threats to the Christian community and thus were often linked. Finally, there was considerable fluidity between categories of Christian and Jew so that in the eyes of artists and writers, Christians might become Jews either literally or figuratively, just as Jews might convert to Christianity.[187] Thus a pig might be used equally as a metaphor for the wealthy, heretics, or Jews, depending on the exegetical need of the moralizer. Similarly, a rabbit recalled sexual excess, indecisiveness, homosexuality, and Judaism simultaneously.

Whomever the sow and nursing piglets were intended to represent, the image is one of inherited pollution through consumption. The female pig is filthy, and her young drink her dirt or sin and thus absorb the unclean nature of their mother.[188] Lest the viewer miss this lesson, by the thirteenth century the friezes and capitols of various churches in Germany were decorated with Jews (identifiable by their pointed hats and beards) nursing or milking sows.[189] Elsewhere a Jew embraces or kisses a pig or seems to reach for its hindquarters.[190] Similarly, in the *Bibles moralisées,* Jews and other individuals worship and kiss the anuses of goats, whereas heretics embrace cats or kiss their anuses.[191] In the *Legenda Aurea* Saint Dominic reveals the god of the heretics to some repentant women:

> At once they saw a hideous cat leap out from their midst: he was as big as a large dog, had huge flaming eyes, a long wide, bloody tongue that reached to his naval, and a short tail that stood up and exposed the filth of his hind parts whichever way he turned, and emitted an intolerable stench. After the beast had stalked to and fro around the women for some time, he climbed up the bell rope and disappeared into the belfry, leaving foul traces behind him.[192]

Here, as in the images in the *Bible moralisée* and certain sculptures on German cathedrals, the animal's rectum and stench indicate the evil and disgusting nature of false belief and, by association, the repulsive quality of people who adopted the condemned faith or practices, whether they be heretics or Jews.

Owls likewise embodied stench because of their love of graves and corpses, and refusal to clean their nests of excrement. Representations of owls often relied on viewers' memories of these associations, unlike the explicit carvings of pigs. However, in the bestiary portal of Metz, to one side of the owl is a naked person holding his buttocks, perhaps in preparation to defecate (fig. 7). This motif is repeated in the other panel (fig. 8). The presence of a pig in the sculpture affirmed the link with filth. Thus here the owl is but a part of a larger evocation of sin, excremental dirt, and Judaism. The story of Saints Steven and Helen (pl. 9) added an element of Jewish violence and deceit to the polemic. Text, tradition, and visual imagery also worked together in the Norwich cathedral to create a potent anti-Jewish polemic based on the owl. Mariko Miyazaki has shown that owls were favored as a motif in the Norwich cathedral in the wake of William of Norwich's supposed martyrdom at the hands of the Jews. The owls are attacked by other birds, following a common theme of many bestiaries and misericords of owls in England.[193] This choice, I would argue, consciously drew on the abundant description of the Jews' filth and bad smell in Thomas of Monmouth's *Life* and their final, dirty end—devoured by ravens and other animals. The misericords and other carvings served both as an expression and a reminder of

Jews' pollution and violence, much like the combined portal carvings and the sow in Notre-Dame-la-Ronde in Metz.

As with rabbits and snails, Jewish artists sought to subvert these associations, though they did so through manuscript illumination, not carvings. Owls figure in the marginal illumination of the Rylands *haggadah* and the Barcelona *haggadahs* and in one northern manuscript as well (see figs. 4, 5, and 6).[194] Sometimes the owl merely rests, perched in the margins. At other times, like the hare, the owl is the target of the hunter, a victim of undeserved violence (pl. 4). I suggest that Jewish adoption of unclean animals assigned to them by Christian rhetoric is related both to Jewish images of themselves in *piyyuṭim* as polluted by Christian attacks and to Jewish adoptions of Saturn, dark skin, or other deformities also attributed to them by Christians and Muslims. Following the explicitly stated logic in Jewish biblical commentaries in which Jews are dark, all of these characteristics, on the one hand, marked Jewish existence in exile and, on the other, proved the Jews' chosen status in contrast to Muslims or Christians. Outward appearances were deceiving; ultimately the Jews would be the pure ones. In the meantime, the responsibility for the suffering and pollution the Jews experienced lay with the other nations, much like Muslims and Christians blamed one another for having to eat impure foods. Any associated impurity or filth returned to the agent, in this case, the Jews.

Linking religious undesirables with foul-smelling animals, animals which fed on corpses, or these creatures' excrement, was profoundly degrading, disgusting, and was a powerfully negative gesture in its own right. The existence of countersymbols, such as the panther and the coot, whose goodness was marked by their fragrance and refusal to touch filth, emphasized how greatly religious outsiders deviated from the ideals of purity, righteousness, or even basic humanity, placing them at the noxious end of two extreme poles.[195] As embodiments of a network of characteristics and associations, all of which were morally weighted, individual animals were excellent forms of both visual and verbal shorthand and thus convenient vehicles for communicating social and religious condemnation or praise. *Payṭanim* and Jewish historians could convey their views of crusader violence and impurity with a few brief references to certain animals. This literary device would have been especially useful to the *payṭanim,* who were working under the poetic constraints of rhyme, meter, and rhythm. Much the same kind of economy of symbolism was at work in the oral epics that became so popular among Muslims during the crusades. Both the *piyyuṭim* and *sīrat* literatures were powerful means of conveying intense emotions and messages to a broad, listening public.

The writers and artists of *Bibles moralisées* faced similar problems of conveying complex stories and exegesis in a small space, so again animals served as convenient metaphors for some of the morals they were trying to transmit. Likewise, on cathedrals or other religious architecture, artists could communicate a series of ideas with a single image: Jews were carnal, impure, consumers of filth, deeply involved with money and worldly pleasures, and hostile to Christianity, like Christians who indulged in "Jewlike" activities. Christian viewers would have known the meanings of these various images because these animals figured as characters in sermon tales. Just as sermons provided the stories that contextualized or explained depictions of animals in stone or painted on windows, these same animals continually reminded Christian viewers of the lessons these animals were supposed to teach, just as the *piyyuṭim* sung in the synagogues or the public recitals of epics kept alive the memory of Jewish and Muslim bravery and purity in the face of Christian aggression and pollution. In all three traditions the excessive, animal-like violence marked the religious other as having gone beyond or never having attained the restrained, reasoning status of men. That they, in their inherent filth, were capable of polluting the "pure" or "clean" believer was part of their threat.

Feminizing Beasts

I have argued that Muslims, Jews, and Christians used certain animals to suggest that their opponents were inhuman, unmanly, or the wrong kind of men. In Christian anti-Jewish polemic, animals sometimes also signified feminization. In *Disciplina Clericalis,* a collection of entertaining stories by Petrus Alfonsi, students flee the melodious voice of a young woman, fearing bewitchment and death. One of the students recounts a similar experience with an owl, whose voice likewise transfixed the audience with its song, despite its ugly voice. The owl's singing portended death, like that of the woman.[196]

There is no mention of Jews in this tale, or of the owl's legendary filth, in part perhaps because Alfonsi was writing from a background in Judeo-Muslim traditions rather than from the perspective of Western Latin bestiaries. Hassig demonstrates, however, that owls and hoopoes were drawn so as to strongly resemble one another, thus creating a series of iconographic links among owls, Jews, hoopoes, and women. These birds and the Jews and women associated with them were unified by their filth.[197] In bestiaries "bad" women, like Jews, are often linked with filth-producing animals, though not always the same animals. In one English bestiary, the author quotes Proverbs 11:22, "As a jewel of gold in a swine's snout, so is a fair woman who is without discretion," in his discussion of sows.[198] The citation is a passing one, without exegetical elaboration of the connection between women and swine, yet in reminding the readers of this biblical passage, the link between the two is clearly established. Prostitutes and old women were said to use ointment made from the dung of crocodiles in order to make them seem young and beautiful.[199] This assertion established that these women were deceitful and hypocritical, like the crocodile and, by association, insinuated that they were dangerous and demonic devourers of men. They, like the Jews or the animals that symbolized them, were covered in excrement. Here filth is a deterrent to condemned sexual liaisons rather than to religious conversion; however, the disgust and fear of contamination and incorporation are very similar to that implied by the Christian animal iconography of the Jews.

The people against whom the crocodile imagery is directed are not merely women; they are the elderly. Richard de Fornival, in his *Bestiaire d'amour,* promised his lady love that once she was old, filthy, and incapable of caring for herself, like an aged hoopoe or screech owl, he would still love her.[200] The hoopoe, unlike the owl, was generally depicted positively because of its devotion to its aging parents. Nevertheless, it was also known for collecting human dung, feeding on foul-smelling excrement, and dwelling in tombs, as was the owl.[201] In the *Bestiaire d'amour,* like the bestiaries in which old women and prostitutes smear themselves in crocodile dung, an aged woman is assumed to be covered in feces and to smell bad. The method of conveying this expectation is through animal imagery, much like that used to compare Jews to filthy creatures. As in medical texts, the bodies of old women and Jews were similarly contaminated and repugnant, thereby placing them outside the realm of holiness and at the unwanted and dreaded margins of human (Christian) society.[202]

In using the hyena, most well known for its supposed ability to change gender, as a symbol for Jews, Christian authors introduced an element of gender ambiguity into their vision of religious difference. According to most composers of bestiaries, the instability of the hyena's gender served as a metaphor for Jews' wavering between adoring God and pursuing riches, easy living, and even idol worship. The mutability of the hyena's gender, like Jewish indecisiveness, was singled out as the characteristic that made it unclean, though the hyena engaged in a number of unsavory activities, such as digging up corpses, that could also have accounted for its impure status in the Bible.[203] This focus on the hyena's ambiguous gender as the primary reason for its uncleanness and monstrosity underscores Christian anxiety about blurred boundaries and violated hierarchies. The Jews occupied a liminal place in Christian society: they were not Christians—indeed, they were the killers of Christ—yet the Church protected them; they were supposed to be subservient to Christians, yet they had financial power over peasants, lords, and the Church itself. Just as the hyena transgressed the "natural" order of male over female by being both and neither, the Jews constantly threatened or violated the "natural," spiritual hierarchy of Christian over unbeliever. Gender, or the confusion thereof, was simply the metaphor by which Christians expressed their anxiety regarding the ambiguous religious position of Jews in Europe, even as the gendered categories pure and impure, spiritual and material, were tools by which both Christians and Jews attempted to delineate the divisions between their communities.[204]

Certain authors were quite straightforward in their use of gender to demarcate spiritual hierarchy. When describing the hyena, although Philippe de Thaün does not mention the Jews, he states clearly that the hyena signifies a man whose covetousness and greed has made him like a woman.[205] Guillaume le Clerc does refer to the Jews:

> This beast (the hyena)—doubt it not—denotes the Children of Israel, who at first firmly believed in the true father omnipotent and held to him loyally, but afterwards became as females when they partook of delicate foods and gave themselves up to pleasures, to the flesh and luxury.[206]

Like late antique authors, both Philippe de Thaün and Guillaume le Clerc saw an individual's gender as mutable, at least metaphorically, depending on his or her adherence to or rejection of spiritual and philosophical ideals and behavior. Just as late antique and early medieval women could become like men through their bravery in the face of martyrdom, dedication to Christianity, and feats of asceticism, so too could the masculinity of heretical men devolve into the female state.[207] In the thirteenth-century text of Guillaume le Clerc, Jews, like bad Christians, had become feminized men, marked by their love of fleshly things. Guillaume's description of the hyena and those whom it symbolized reinforced long-standing associations of women, rot, filth, and carnality. However, here the religious other is not merely polluted by feminine effluvia or other kinds of dirt, he *is* a woman spiritually, with the physical and moral pollution and lack of rationality and spirituality that such a designation could imply.[208] Marking Jews as "women" reinforced and "naturalized" the hierarchical dichotomy between Christian and Jew. This simile also suggested that women were like Jews. In a period in which Jews were increasingly seen as threatening, polluted, diseased, and bestial, such a comparison can only have been devastating for medieval Christian views of women.

Added to the hyena's transgression of clearly defined gender was an element of illicit, forced sexuality. Hassig has noted that certain Christian illuminators depicted the hyena with exaggerated genitalia or clearly indicate that the hyena's chosen corpse was female (fig. 10). She connects this iconographic strain to Christian fears (as manifested in Christian law of the period) of Jewish intercourse with and thus defilement of Christian women.[209] Similar to the Jewish women naked and bleeding from their genitals, torn by Christian "wolves," in these illuminations predatory defilement has a sexual aspect. The vulnerable boundaries of Christian society, as with

Figure 10. MS Harley 4751, fol. 10r, the hyena. By permission of the British Library.

Jewish society, are women. Christians (and Jews) disapproved of miscegenation in any form. Yet if "male" symbolized dominance and righteousness and "female" symbolized subordination, depicting Jewish male rape of a Christian woman, even metaphorically, was to describe the ultimate reversal of Christian power and the "invasion" of Christian domestic and religious space. The hyena both combines feminization with violent male nature gone wrong and ties these to the Jews.

> Wouldn't it be dreadful if some day, in our own world, at home, men started going wild inside, like the animals here, and still looked like men, so that you'd never know which were which?[210]

Each of the interlocking categories of polemical animal metaphors served to evoke disdain and disgust for the religious other, to profoundly marginalize them, and, most of all, to vent deep anxieties about the slippery boundaries between communities and to reassure each community's members of their holiness and ultimate victory. The violence or accusations of homicidal malice that permeated all three types of animal imagery indicate the degree to which all three communities saw the other as a source of physical as well as spiritual danger. For Jews, this danger was real; for Christians, it was imagined, but this fact did not make the Christians feel less threatened.[211] As a result some Christian authors resisted the Church's protection laws and used animal imagery to urge their audience toward violence against Jews, either openly or by implication. Muslims and Christians understood the other to be a threat, although of the two, the Muslims evoked more animal imagery and used it to suggest that their foe was not only disgusting but unworthy. Descriptions of one another's extreme predatory behavior in the writings or art of all three groups also aided in dehumanizing their opponents by making them repugnant, subhuman killers of the innocent.

As "foolish asses," Jews and Christians became objects of ridicule for one another and therefore unworthy of being taken seriously. Comparisons to these and other "low" animals emasculated and dehumanized the religious other by denying his rationality, the definitive characteristic of masculine humanness. Such similes, along with the Christian association of Jews with animals iconographically related to women, also emphasized the religious other's appropriately low or servile status in contrast to that of the "true believers," either in this world or the next.

This imagery existed in Christian and Muslim polemic against one another, but because they were more or less equal in power this belittling rhetoric was less credible to its intended audience. Muslims, who were gaining the upper hand in the Levant, engaged in such comparisons, both to provide encouragement in war and to restore verbally the "proper" hierarchy.

Dirt and impurity in relation to animals worked on a number of levels. Certainly, as Eilberg-Schwartz has hypothesized for biblical laws regarding beasts, animal metaphors manifested fears of sexual relations with members outside the community.[212] Sexualized images of the hyena-Jew devouring a Christian woman make this relationship of miscegenation and animal metaphor fairly explicit. As I have argued, however, likening one's enemy to impure food in the form of a prohibited animal marked the outsider as unsuitable for absorption into the body of believers or for social interaction. Symbolic predators that "devoured" the faithful, thereby rendering them polluted, at least in the Jewish schema, expressed fears of forced religious incorporation, violence, and concomitant pollution. On a more basic level, graphic images of bestial filth rendered the religious other physically abhorrent, thus discouraging social interaction and conversion.

Starkly dividing the world into humans and "beasts" sharpened the delineation between Christian, Jew, and Muslim. That people needed these metaphors and parables suggests that they feared that the boundaries and hierarchies between communities were too fluid. This anxiety is exemplified not only in the constantly shifting hyena but also in the commonality of dog and pig metaphors. Both the dog and the pig were integral to medieval human society, occupying a liminal space between the animal and human world. They were useful to humans when controlled but could savagely turn on the people with whom they lived. Likewise, the religious other looked "human" and dwelled alongside believers, yet they could turn on their neighbors in a moment; Jews (in the Christian imagination) lured children into their homes for harm; and Jews and Christians (in reality or the imagination) converted or fraternized with the "enemy" to do their former coreligionists injury. So too did Muslims fear that the native Christian population, or renagade Muslims, would turn against them.[213] Depicting the religious other as a dog or a pig simultaneously marked the other's liminal status as (male) human beings and members of society, but of the wrong faith, and emphasized the outsider's profound difference as a source of violence and pollution that needed to be controlled and dominated.

Conclusion

Anthropologists following in Mary Douglas's footsteps have quite rightly pointed to the need to take into consideration the peculiarities of each culture and the way in which substances and functions like menstruation are interpreted in that specific cultural context.[1] This perspective is one that historians and literary scholars can appreciate. This book explores bodily functions—excreting, bleeding, eating, and being eaten—in a specific historical milieu, namely, how members of different faiths in late antiquity and the Middle Ages used these organic processes to insult one another. Ultimately, I return to Douglas's original contention that bodily effluvia, or the body as a whole, are signifiers of control or the lack thereof. Rules and, I would add, symbolic traditions about them point to tensions in a given society or societies. Accusations of disease function to ostracize feared or unwanted members of society. Julia Kristeva argued similarly, "It is thus not the lack of cleanliness or health that causes abjection [read here "horror, disgust"] but what disturbs identity, system, order."[2] The obvious tension in late antiquity and the Middle Ages to which these discussions of excreta point center on issues of intercommunal and interfaith relations. Metaphors of animals devouring the faithful, especially women, expressed fears of assimilation and miscegenation. Lengthy discussions of excrement and women's bodily functions attributed to both women and men suggest worries about violated borders and hierarchies of communities, as Douglas suggested for the ancient Israelite culture that produced Leviticus. Many of these accusations also created a rhetoric of disease that was intended to establish religious hierarchy on "scientific" foundations and, in the case of contagious diseases or those requiring treatment through the death of others, fueled fear of and disgust for specific groups. Yet these evocations of blood and excrement also indicate anxiety about the violation of gender boundaries between men and women and also between men and men. Douglas's early arguments resonate so well in medieval Jewish, Christian, and Muslim texts because her starting point was in many ways Leviticus. Directly or indirectly, in the case of Islam, this and related biblical or Qur'anic texts, along with Greek and Roman philosophical notions about the body and divinity, are at the root of many of the meanings and uses late antique and medieval authors assigned to the body, both human and animal.

The word *uses* is important here, for what should now be abundantly clear is that the bodies and genders of humans and animals were the means by which late antique and medieval cultures chose to talk about religion, social standing, and communal affiliation. The body was the template from which a symbolic language was created. Purity laws and biological theories became tools by which to generate and grant validity to arguments of religious and physiological inferiority or superiority. As late antique Jews, Pagans, and Christians increasingly adopted and adapted one another's values and scientific lore, the somatic language of each group became increasingly similar and thus comprehensible to members of the other faiths. Pagans, Christians, and Jews capitalized on these shared meanings in their polemics, creating invectives that not only warned members of their own communities but that also would have made sense and been deeply insulting to those against whom they were polemicizing.

Medieval Christians, Jews, and Muslims continued to build on this inheritance of intertwined associations regarding the body, divinity, and animals and the methods by which they were used. In the Middle Ages three factors account for the strong similarities in the symbols and methods of polemic between Jews, Christians, and Muslims: continued sharing of the same daily cultures among Jews and Christians in Europe and among Muslims, Jews, and Christians in the Near East, North Africa, and Iberia; an intensification of interaction between the Muslim- and Christian-dominated worlds beginning in the twelfth century with the translation projects, the reconquest, and the crusades; and the common intellectual and cultural inheritance from late antiquity that came in the form of shared texts but also in the form of certain deep mutual assumptions in the Near East, Byzantium, and western Europe about bodily excreta, smell, animals, and the divine. The threads connecting these shared assumptions were strengthened beginning around the twelfth century not only by increased familiarity with one another's written texts but also by personal contact through missionizing, war, and pilgrimage and the resulting familiarity with one another through *oral* exchanges. Despite the difference in languages, I argue that oral and sometimes visual exchange between Western Christians and Muslims and between Christians and Jews in western Europe was a real and powerful force.[3] Commonalities were less strong between Muslim symbols and notions and those of European Christians and Jews because Muslims of the Near East and Europeans lacked the same degree of shared daily culture. Nevertheless, those of the eastern and western Mediterranean lands and northern Europe possessed a mutually meaningful language of symbols regarding the gendered human and animal bodies.

In much of antique and medieval polemic bodily functions were applied directly and clearly to discussions of the religious other. The meanings had been vastly expanded from the philosophical, biblical, or qur'anic texts, and when evoking these somatic symbols in relation to their theological opponents, late antique and medieval authors were extraordinarily graphic. Detailed descriptions of the impurities, diarrhea, oozing sores, blackened or leprously pale skin, uterine blood, and the stench of decomposition were designed to create a barrier of disgust between members of differing religious groups. Such images were a form of verbal or visual violence that was destructive in its own right as well as an impetus to physical violence among Muslims and Christians. The intensity of the sentiment sought serves as a gauge of the levels of anxiety and anger between communities. Thus, for example, beginning in the fifth century Eastern Christian groups moved away from this type of polemic when other forms of institutional control over "heretics" and Jews were available. During the conflicts among Orthodox Christians, Paulists, Bogomils, and Muslims, however, this kind of imagery reasserted itself. Graphic somatic polemic never entirely disappeared in western Europe, which in part may reflect a greater preoccupation with the body than existed in the East. It intensified and grew in quantity, however, between Muslims and Christians as a result and tool of jiḥad and the crusades, and between Catholics, "heretics," and Jews as the result and tool of a number of growing pressures and insecurities, including Christian crusading violence against Jews (and "heretics"); increasing rapprochement between Jews and Christians on a daily basis; shifting economic and institutional realities between Jews and Christians broadly and between Jews in relation to changes in royal, monastic, mendicant, and papal goals and expectations and piety and economic difficulties of Christian laymen and laywomen in cities and rural areas; and relations between men and women.

What is fascinating and, I would argue, especially significant about this polemic is its demonstration of the simultaneous juxtaposition of extreme anger and fear and cultural sharing and understanding between religious communities. The volatile emotions expressed in these texts make it easy to assume that the only story they tell is one of violence and oppression, whether verbal or physical or both. Yet I would assert that such high emotions and evocations of violated bodily borders point precisely to intense cultural and religious integration of communities, for it is when the other becomes so close as to be nearly indistinguishable from oneself that he/she/they become the most threatening to those who wish to maintain the boundaries of separate communal or religious identities. This phenomenon manifests itself both in other expressions of medieval policing of interfaith boundaries and in nonmedieval literary and historical contexts.[4] Equally important is that many individuals in the Middle Ages remained undisturbed or only moderately so by the increasingly close relationships they had with members of other faiths and cultures. Had not a large body of people who felt this way existed, there would have been no need for such strong rhetoric to the contrary. Perhaps the most concrete example of the varied attitudes of members of different faiths toward one another is the reactions of the Jews and Christian burghers when faced with the threat of anti-Jewish violence and demands of the crusaders in the Rhineland. Ultimately these confrontations ended disastrously, but the fact remains that many Jews sought their Christian neighbors' aid in the struggle against the crusaders. A century or so later, warnings in texts such as *Sefer Ḥasidim* against extensive socializing between Jews and Christians, or cautionary tales about Christians (and to a lesser extent, Jews) infiltrating Muslim ranks and society in Arabic chronicles, oral epics, and polemical texts, point to the continuation, indeed augmentation, of such intermixing during the Middle Ages.

I began this conclusion with a reminder about the importance of specific cultural contexts. My examination of gender, impurity, and disgust as a form of interfaith polemic has been comparative in its approach and has covered a substantial chronological span, though always within the limits of historically related groups who continued to interact with one another. Yet the broad tendencies sketched in this book—the use of the human body and its functions or of animals as sources of symbolic meanings; gender as a metaphor of hierarchy; disgust and/or scientific theories as tools for maintaining religious and communal boundaries; and the intimate relationship between the female body and disgust—not only deepen our awareness of how Jews, Christians, and Muslims related to one another during late antiquity and the Middle Ages but also have applications in other times and other sets of relationships. In the introduction I discussed Robert Scribner's research on scatological polemic between Catholics and Protestants in early modern Europe. Kristeva has explored the intersection of disgust, gender, the female body, and the religious other in the context of Greek and post-Freudian literature, even as Joan Scott noted the use of feminization as a way of establishing a hierarchy between the British and the Indians during the colonial period.[5] All these examples remain within a Western cultural tradition, yet the bleeding female and excreta have served to mark or otherwise combat the religious or cultural other in non-Western or mixed contexts as well. During the Boxer Rebellion in China (1900), young male Boxers attributed their initial failure to take the Beijing cathedral to the women inside who exposed themselves and "waved dirty things." The Boxers responded by creating a brigade of women who would be unaffected by the pollution and bad magic of the Christian women.[6] In the modern Nigerian novel *Songs of Enchantment,* animals, menstrual blood, fat, and lust all serve to make the character Madame Koto, and by extension the accommodation with Westernization that she represents, both horrific and powerful.[7]

Thus in these nonmedieval and non-Western traditions, gender, especially the female gender, uncleanness, and conflict with the other intersect. If I am correct that at least in the medieval period such language represented the worst that one group could conjure against another, then one must wonder if the same is true of other times and contexts and ask why this set of associations is so powerful and common in multiple cultures. What do our bodies and our effluvia really mean to us that we should impose abstract connotations on them signifying both great power and great danger? What effect did or does such negative imagery, often having the female body at its center, have on real women? Or when birds or other creatures are at the center of such rhetoric, on animals? How is it that peoples may live side by side, be friends on a daily basis, work together, read and admire one another's books and art, and yet at the same time produce vituperative, debasing, and violent polemic that can quickly disintegrate into physical persecution? Such questions do not apply merely to the Middle Ages but to propaganda and the nature of violence and violent language in a large variety of periods and regions, past and present. I have attempted to answer these questions, at least in part, for late antique and medieval Pagans, Jews, Christians, and Muslims. Exploring them in more ancient or more modern contexts must remain the task of others.

Notes

Introduction

1. Note that I am restricting this study to written, spoken, and "artistic" polemic from this period. Other kinds of polemic included bringing animals into a space considered holy by another, hanging or burying others with despised animals, or disinterring and mutilating the body, all of which constitued a kind of public denigration of the religious other. Even private, unobserved desecrations could be viewed as a type of polemic for it served as an individual's affirmation of his or her allegiance in counterdistinction to the now-"defiled" other, and he or she could brag about the act to his or her community. For a brief discussion of such behavior, see Ivan G. Marcus, "A Jewish-Christian Symbiosis: The Culture of Early Ashkenaz."

2. E.g., *Christian Arabic Apologetics during the Abbasid Period, 750–1258,* ed. Salil Khamir Salil and Jorgen Nielsen; A. Abel, "Le chapitre sur le christianisme dans le 'Tamhîd' d'al-Bâqillâni," 1:1–11; Sa'd ibn Mansur ibn Kammunah, *Ibn Kammuna's Examination of the Three Faiths;* Thomas E. Burman, *Religious Polemic and the Intellectual History of the Mozarabs, c. 1050–1200.*

3. Abel, "Chapitre sur le christianisme"; idem, "La letter polémique 'd'Aréthas' à l'émir de Damas"; Abū 'Īsā al-Warrāq, *Abū 'Īsa al-Warrāq Yahyā ibn 'Adī: De l'incarnation,* 46–47; *The Polemic of Nestor the Priest,* ed. and trans. Daniel J. Lasker and Sarah Stroumsa. Lasker and Stroumsa's introduction to the latter contains very useful bibliography on Muslim polemic dealing with similar themes, such as the incarnation as found in the Judeo-Arabic *Qiṣṣat.*

4. Carole Hillenbrand, *The Crusades,* 257–327; Emmanuel Sivan, *L'Islam et la Croisade.*

5. E.g., see Penny J. Cole, "'God the Heathen have come into your Inheritance' (Ps. 78:1)"; Norman Daniel, *Islam and the West;* Benjamin Liu, "'Affined to the Love of the Moor'"; Debra Higgs Strickland, *Saracens, Demons, and Jews*; John Tolan, *Saracens;* idem, "Un cadavre mutilé: Le déchirement polémique de Mahomet"; idem, "Anti-Hagiography"; idem, "Peter the Venerable on the 'Diabolical Heresy of the Saracens.'"

6. Fedwa Malti-Douglas, "Tribadism/Lesbianism and the Sexualized Body in Medieval Arabo-Islamic Narratives"; Sahar Amer, "Lesbian Sex and the Military from the

Medieval Arabic Tradition to French Literature"; Stephen O'Murray and Will Roscoe, *Islamic Homosexualities; Women in the Medieval Islamic World: Power, Patronage and Piety,* ed. G. Hambly; D. A. Spellberg, *Politics, Gender, and the Islamic Past;* Barbara Freyer Stowasser, *Women in the Qur'an, Traditions, and Interpretation; Women in Middle Eastern History,* ed. Nikkie Keddie and Beth Baron; B. F. Musallam, *Sex and Society in Islam;* Abdelwahab Bouhdiba, *La sexualité en Islam.*

7. Fedwa Malti-Douglass, *Women's Body, Women's Word;* Annemarie Schimmel, *My Soul Is a Woman;* Musallam deals with this topic somewhat: *Sex and Society in Islam.*

8. Musallam, *Sex and Society in Islam;* Michael W. Dols, "The Leper in Medieval Islamic Society"; idem, "Leprosy in Medieval Arabic Medicine"; *Contagion,* ed. Lawrence I. Conrad and Dominik Wujastyk. However, see the excellent study of Geert Jan van Gelder, *God's Banquet.*

9. See, however, Marion Holmes Katz, *Body of the Text;* A. Kevin Reinhart, "Impurity/No Danger"; Hava Lazarus-Yafeh, "Some Differences between Judaism and Islam as Two Religions of Law."

10. The topic has barely been addressed for Jewish-Muslim polemic. But see Elliot R. Wolfson, "Ontology, Alterity, and Ethics in Kabbalistic Anthropology"; Tolan, *Saracens,* 16–18.

11. Anna Sapir Abulafia, "Invectives against Christianity in the Hebrew Chronicles of the First Crusade." Also see the historiographic discussion of Purim by Elimelch Horowitz: "'Ve-nahafokh hu' yehudim mol sona'eihem be-hagigot ha-purim."

12. Sapir Abulafia, "Invectives"; idem, "Jewish-Christian Disputations and the Twelfth-Century Renaissance"; idem, "Christian Imagery of the Jews in the Twelfth Century"; idem, "Bodies in the Jewish-Christian Debate"; idem, *Christians and Jews in the Twelfth-Century Renaissance*; *[Sefer nizzahon yashan] The Jewish-Christian Debate in the High Middle Ages,* ed. and trans. David Berger; William Chester Jordan, "Marian Devotion and the Talmud Trial of 1240"; *Polemic of Nestor the Priest;* Israel Yuval, "Ha-Nakam ve-ha-k'lilah ha-dam ve-ha-'alilah me-'alilot kedushim le-'alilot dam."

13. Joshua Trachtenberg, *The Devil and the Jews,* 44–52, 147–52; Willis Johnson, "The Myth of Jewish Male Menses"; idem, "Before the Blood Libel." Also see S. W. Baron, *A Social and Religious History of the Jews,* 11:129; Benedicte Bauchau, "Science et racisme," 21–35; Peter Biller, "Views of Jews from Paris around 1300"; idem, "A 'Scientific' View of Jews from Paris around 1300"; Christian Delacampagne, *L'Invention du racisme,* 123–24, 127, 331; Johannes Grabmayer, "Rudolf von Schlettstadt and das aschkenasische Judentum um 1300"; Harriet Goldberg, "Two Parallel Medieval Commonplaces"; Andrew Colin Gow, *The Red Jews;* R. Po-chia Hsia, *The Myth of Ritual Murder,* 130, 138; idem, *Trent 1475,* 107–8; Israel Levi, "Le Juif de la légende"; Lester K. Little, *Religious Poverty and the Profit Economy in Medieval Europe,* 49–53; Isidore Loeb, "Le Juif de l'histoire et le Juif de la légende"; Ruth Mellinkoff, *Outcasts,* 1:111–208; Hyam Maccoby, *Judas Iscariot and the Myth of Jewish Evil* (Maccoby's book should be used with caution); David Nirenberg, *Communities of Violence,* 62–63; Léon Poliakov, *Histoire de l'antisémitisme,* 1:160–61.

14. *Jewish-Christian Debate,* 302, note to line 1 of p. 152. I thank William Chester Jordan for reminding me of Berger's reticence to translate this phrase.

15. Wolfson, "Ontology, Alterity, and Ethics," esp. 133–34.

16. Ezra Fleischer, "Yahasei Notsrim-Yehudim be-yamei ha-benaim be ra'i 'akom"; Mordechai Breuer, "Dimiono shel ha-historion ve-ha-'emet ha-historit."

17. Israel Yuval, "Nakam Adonai hi' nikamat hekhal': Historia lelo' Haro ve-lelo' maso' panim."

18. Jeremy Cohen, "The Jews as Killers of Christ in the Latin Tradition, from Augustine to the Friars"; Robert Chazan, *Medieval Stereotypes and Modern Antisemitism,* 41–73. Note that Chazan and Marcus disagree with Yuval's hypotheses. See Chazan, *Medieval Stereotypes,* 74–94; Marcus, "A Jewish-Christian Symbiosis."

19. Marcus, "A Jewish-Christian Symbiosis."

20. Ibid.; and idem, *Rituals of Childhood;* Haym Soloveitchik, "Three Themes in the *Sefer Hasidim*"; Susan L. Einbinder, "Signs of Romance"; idem, "Pucellina of Blois"; William Chester Jordan, "Jews on Top."

21. Jacob Katz, *Exclusiveness and Tolerance.* Also see Marcus's and Mark Cohen's discussion of these issues: Marcus, "A Jewish-Christian Symbiosis"; Mark R. Cohen, *Under Crescent and Cross.*

22. Cohen, *Under Crescent and Cross*; Nirenberg, *Communities of Violence;* Ross Brann, *Power in the Portrayal.*

23. Italy, while pivotal for many other kinds of exchanges between the West and the Byzantine and Muslim worlds, does not seem to have been a center for somatic, pollution-oriented polemic.

24. B. Z. Kedar, *Crusade and Mission;* Burman, *Religious Polemic;* idem, "Tafsīr and Translation"; Marie Thérèse d'Alverny, "Translations and Translators"; Jeremy Cohen, "Scholarship and Intolerance in the Medieval Academy"; idem, *The Friars and the Jews;* Robert Chazan, *Daggers of Faith;* Beryl Smalley, *The Study of the Bible in the Middle Ages; Polemic of Nestor,* 1:27–32; Joseph Shatzmiller, *Jews, Medicine, and Medieval Society,* 38–55; John Tolan, *Petrus Alfonsi and His Medieval Readers,* 42–131; Sapir Abulafia, *Christians and Jews in the Twelfth-Century Renaissance,* 94–106; David Berger, "Gilbert Crispin, Allan of Lille, and Jacob ben Reuben"; idem, "Christian Heresy and Jewish Polemic in the Twelfth and Thirteenth Centuries"; idem, "Mission to the Jews and Jewish-Christian Contacts in the Polemical Literature of the High Middle Ages"; Bernhard Blumenkranz, *Juifs et Chrétiens,* 17:47–51; Frank Talmage, "A Hebrew Polemical Treatise"; Yosef Hayim Yerushalmi, "The Inquisition and the Jews in the Time of Bernard Gui."

25. Marcus briefly compared the use of impurity in Christian anti-Muslim polemics and sermons to that which appears in Christian and Jewish writings from the time. Marcus, "A Jewish-Christian Symbiosis."

26. For examples of the devastating violence such accusations caused, see Miri Rubin, *Gentile Tales;* Ephraim of Bonn, in *Sefer Gezerot Ashkenaz ve-Tsarfat,* by Abraham Meir Habermann, 124–32, summarized in Chazan, *Medieval Stereotypes,* 54–57.

27. Sivan, *Islam et la Croisade,* esp. 67, 106, 199; Cole, " Religious Pollution."

28. Chazan, *Medieval Stereotypes,* 47–51, 60–63; William Chester Jordan, *The French Monarchy and the Jews,* 78, 137–41; idem, "Marian Devotion"; Solomon Grayzel, *The Church and the Jews in the XIIIth Century,* 275–79, 308–11; Yerushalmi, "Inquisition"; Marcus, "A Jewish-Christian Symbiosis."

29. Brann, *Power in the Portrayal,* 71–90; Cohen, *Under Crescent and Cross,* 145–61; Sarah Stroumsa, "Jewish Polemics against Islam and Christianity in Light of Judeo-Arabic texts"; Kenneth Baxter Wolf, *Christian Martyrs in Muslim Spain.*

30. Mary Douglas, *Purity and Danger,* 3–6, 114–39; idem, *Natural Symbols,* 70–71; idem, *Implicit Meanings,* 53–56, 60–72.

31. Mary Douglas, *Risk and Blame,* 34–36, 83–101.

32. William Ian Miller, *The Anatomy of Disgust,* x.

33. Ibid., 154.

34. *Jewish-Christian Debate,* Heb. p. 27, Eng. p. 68.

35. The literature on legal restrictions imposed on medieval European Jews is vast. For a good overview, see Cohen, *Under Crescent and Cross,* 30–51.

36. Miller, *Anatomy,* 2, 24–37, and the psychological studies he cites there.

37. Robert W. Scribner, *Popular Culture and Popular Movements in Reformation Germany,* 54–69, 295–99; idem, *For the Sake of Simple Folk.*

38. James C. Scott, *Domination and the Arts of Resistance,* xii; also see xi, 3–5. According to Scott, both those in power and subordinated groups have hidden transcripts that are in contrast to the "public transcript," which is the self-portrayal put forth by those in power (see 13–18). Most of the evidence for a Muslim "hidden transcript" appears during the inquisition against the Moriscos in Iberia and thus falls outside the chronological boundaries of this book.

39. Ibid., 18, 120–24.

40. Ibid., 36–41, 109–18.

41. Tricia Rose, *Black Noise,* esp. chap. 4, 99–211. Also compare with earlier curses and songs against the white community cited by Scott, *Domination,* 5, 38–44. Daniel Boyarin has also applied Scott's theories to Jewish texts directed against Pagans and Christians; see his *Dying for God.*

42. Ismar Elbogen, *Jewish Liturgy; Masoret ha-piyyuṭ,* ed. Binyamin Bar Tikva and Efraim Hazan; Jakob Josef Petuchowski, *Theology and Poetry;* Jefim Schirmann, "Hebrew Liturgical Poetry and Christian Hymnology."

43. See Wout J. C. van Bekkum, "Anti-Christian Polemics in Hebrew Liturgical Poetry (*piyyuṭ*) of the Sixth and Seventh Centuries," esp. 300. Originally, according to Pirkoy b. Baboy (late 8th century) and R. Yehudah bar Barzilay (12th century in *Sefer ha-'Itim,* ed. Jacob Schor, 252), the *piyyuṭim* were to teach about the laws and festivals when the government forbade such teachings in the synagogue but allowed singing.

44. The allegorization in the fables of Berachiah ha-Naqdan is so profound that it was only recently that a modern scholar realized that the text had any polemical content. See Marc Michael Epstein, "'The Ways of Truth Are Curtailed and Hidden.'" Ashkenazi *piyyuṭim* are infamous for the difficulty of their language, which probably accounts for their relative neglect by scholars of history and literature. (*Piyyuṭim* have been studied in some depth for their linguistic and poetic peculiarities.) Happily they

have begun to receive more attention. See Susan L. Einbinder, *Beautiful Death;* idem, "Jewish Women Martyrs"; idem, "The Troyes Laments"; idem, "The Jewish Martyrs of Blois"; Jordan, *French Monarchy,* 19–22, 72, 140–41, 216, 219, 234–35; Elisabeth Hollender, *Synagogale Hymnen;* idem, "Zwei hebräische Klagedichtungen aus der Zeit nach dem Zweiten Kreuzzug"; Rubin, *Gentile Tales,* 93–103, 196–98; Yosef Hayim Yerushalmi, *Zakhor,* 42–52; Yuval, "Ha-Nakam ve-ha-k'lilah."

45. Saint Agobard, *De Insolentia Judaeorum, PL* 116, cols. 71–73; idem, *De Judaicis Superstitionibus, PL* 116, col. 85; Amulo, *Liber contra Judaeos, PL* 116, cols. 146–47; James Parkes, *The Conflict of the Church and the Synagogue,* 234–39, 251–55, 291–97; Rubin, *Gentile Tales,* 48–69.

46. d'Alverny, "Translations and Translators"; Cohen, *Friars and Jews; Polemic of Nestor,* 1:27–32; Shatzmiller, *Jews, Medicine, and Medieval Society,* 38–55; Smalley, *Study of the Bible;* Tolan, *Petrus Alfonsi,* 42–131.

47. Sapir Abulafia, *Christians and Jews,* 94–106; Berger, "Gilbert Crispin, Allan of Lille, and Jacob ben Reuben"; idem, "Christian Heresy and Jewish Polemic"; idem, "Mission to the Jews"; Blumenkranz, "Nicolas de Lyre et Jacob ben Ruben"; Chazan, *Daggers of Faith;* Jeremy Cohen, "Scholarship and Intolerance"; Talmage, "A Hebrew Polemical Treatise"; Yerushalmi, "Inquisition," 317–76.

48. Jordan, "Marian Devotion"; idem, *French Monarchy,* 137–39.

49. Jordan, "Marian Devotion."

50. Peter Browe, *Die Judenmission im Mittelalter und die Päpste;* Robert Chazan, "From Friar Paul to Friar Raymond"; idem, "Maestro Alfonso of Vallodolid and the New Missionizing"; idem, *Daggers of Faith;* Jeremy Cohen, "The Christian Adversary of Solomon ben Adret"; idem, *Friars and Jews;* Jordan, *French Monarchy,* 137–41, 150; Kedar, *Crusade and Mission;* Ch. Merchavia, *ha-Talmud,* 227–34, 237–60.

51. Hillenbrand, *Crusades,* 321–22.

52. Cohen, "Jews as the Killers of Christ."

53. Chazan, *Medieval Stereotypes,* 1–18.

54. Ibid., 41–73; for Bernard of Clairvaux, see 44–46.

55. Ibid., 58–73.

56. Cole, "Religious Pollution"; Hillenbrand, *Crusades,* 308.

57. See Scott, *Domination,* 13–18. One might see the Christian miracle tales and calls to violence as part of the dominant group's hidden transcript and official Church policy as the public transcript. However, these Christian texts were not hidden from minority groups or from "official" representatives of the Church. Rather, they were extremely public, often widely accessible, and usually composed by clerics or friars.

58. Robert Chazan, *European Jewry and the First Crusade,* 85–108; Rubin, *Gentile Tales,* 104–16; Hillenbrand, *Crusades,* 311–12, 375–78.

59. Marc Michael Epstein, *Dreams of Subversion in Medieval Jewish Art and Literature.*

60. Nirenberg, *Communities*; Rubin, *Gentile Tales*; Scribner, *Popular Culture* and *For the Sake of Simple Folk*; Klaus Hödl, *Die Pathologisierung des jüdischen Körpers.*

61. Scribner, *Popular Culture* and *For the Sake of Simple Folk;* Isaiah Shachar, *The Judensau,* 33–64; Hsia, *Trent 1475,* 107–8.

62. Nirenberg, *Communities,* 220 n. 73.

63. *Passover and Easter,* ed. Paul F. Bradshaw and Lawrence A. Hoffman.

64. Marcus, *Rituals of Childhood;* Boyarin, *Dying for God.*

65. Yuval, "ha-Naqam ve-ha-q'lilah"; idem, "ha-poshim 'al shtei hasa'ifim," 528; idem, "Easter and Passover as Early Jewish-Christian Dialogue," in *Passover and Easter*; idem, "Passover in the Middle Ages," in *Passover and Easter.*

66. Brann, *Power in the Portrayal;* Burman, *Religious Polemic;* Tova Rosen, *Unveiling Eve.*

67. See, e.g., Chazan, *Daggers of Faith;* and Anna Sapir Abulafia and G. R. Evans, Introduction to Gilbert Crispin, *The Works of Gilbert Crispin, Abbot of Westminster;* Brann, *Power in the Portrayal.*

68. Daniel Boyarin, *Carnal Israel,* 24–25; also idem, *Intertextuality and the Reading of Midrash.*

69. See, e.g., Peter Brown, *The Body and Society.*

70. See, e.g., Sahar Amer, "Lesbian Sex and the Military"; idem, *Ésope au féminin;* Maria Rosa Menocal, *The Arabic Role in Medieval Literary History;* Josef Meri, *The Cult of Saints among Muslims and Jews in Medieval Syria;* Dorothee Metlitzki, *The Matter of Araby in Medieval England.*

Chapter 1. **The Stench of Humanity**

1. E. R. Dodds, *Pagan and Christian in an Age of Anxiety,* 29.

2. Arnobius, *Adversus Nations* 2.37 (English translation: *The Case against the Pagans*).

3. Gregory of Nyssa, *Traité de la virginité,* 11.4. The idea that the dove had no intestines and was therefore more pure and less corporeal also appears in Tertullian, *De baptismo,* 8.3. See Gregory, *Traité,* p. 388 n. 3.

4. Gregory, *Traité*, 11.4. Cf. 12.3.20ff.

5. Amy Richlin, *The Garden of Priapus,* 114, 123; Dodds, *Pagan and Christian,* 28–29; Martial, *Sixty Poems of Martial, in Translation,* 5.60. The philosopher-emperor Marcus Aurelius emphasized the pointlessness of valuing the body by outlining the ignominious deaths of various philosophers. Marcus Aurelius, *The Communings with Himself of Marcus Aurelis Antonius, Emperor of Rome, Together with His Last Speeches and Sayings,* 3.3 and 2.12, in which he exclaims that the dead are despicable and unclean (ευκαταφρόνητα και 'ρθπαρα).

6. Apuleius, *De deo Socratis*, 4. On the nature of the invisible gods and the barrier between them and humans, see *De deo Socratis*, 2–4; on the nature and role of demons, see 6–16. On this subject generally, see Dodds, *Pagan and Christian,* 37–38.

7. Augustine, *De civitate Dei*, 9.16. Seemingly any foul smell was potentially polluting given the parallel that Augustine drew between the stench of sacrifice and the smell of living humans.

8. *Pirke Avot* 3:1: "Know from where you came and to where you are going and before whom you are to give account. From where you came: a putrid drop. And to

where you are going: a place of dust, worm and maggot. And before whom you will give account: the king of kings of kings, the Holy One, Blessed be He." דע מאין באת ולאן אתה הולך ולפני מי עתיד ליתן דין וחשבון מאין באת מטפה סרוחה ולאן הולך למקום עפר רמה ותועלה ולפני מי אתה עתיד ליתן דין וחשבון לפני מלך מלכי המלכים הקדוש ברוך הוא

In the poetic texts of the Qumran scrolls, the filthy impure origin of humanity is a frequent theme; see 1QH V 19–21, XX 24–25, XXII. English: *DSST,* 320, 356, 358 respectively; Hebrew: Emile Puech, "Un hymne essénien en partie retrouvé et les béatitudes"; Hebrew: Eleazar L. Sukenik, *The Dead Sea Scrolls of the Hebrew University,* respectively; 4Q Festival Prayers (4Q507) frag. 1. Hebrew: *Discoveries in the Judean Desert*, 7:176; English: *DSST*, 411.

9. *The Book of Enoch by Rabbi Ishmael the High Priest*, 6, trans. P. Alexander, 1:261; and the appendix to 3 Enoch 48:6–8, p. 1:315; *Pesikta' de Rav Kahana',* ed. Bernard Mandelbaum, 20.3, 85a; *Ma'seh Merkavah,* paras. 79, 313, 317, 565, 40, and 22 in *Synopse zur Hekhalot Literatur*, ed. Peter Schäfer, 38–39, 64–65, 139–40, 216–17. On angelic revulsion of humans in the heavenly realm, see Michael D. Swartz, *Scholastic Magic,* 69, 76, 160–62, 166–69; and idem, "'Like the Ministering Angels.'" Cf. [*Talmud Minor tractates*] *Abot de Rabbi Nathan* = *Masekhot Avot de Rabbi Natan*, version A, chap. 19, ed. Solomon Schechter, 69–70 (English: *The Fathers according to Rabbi Nathan,* trans. Judah Goldin, 93). On the dating of these texts, see Swartz, *Scholastic Magic,* 212–14; P. Alexander's introduction to 3 Enoch, 225–29; H. L. Strack and G. Stemberger, *Introduction to the Talmud and Midrash*, 321–22, 246–47.

10. Thus I would agree with Daniel Boyarin's statement that "for rabbinic Jews, the human being was defined as a body" (Boyarin, *Carnal Israel,* 5), though perhaps not quite in the way Boyarin intended the remark. He distinguishes between Hellenistic/Greek-speaking Jews' formulation in which the human being was "a soul housed in a body" and the rabbinic, in which the human being was a body, though "animated" by a soul. Overall he maintains that rabbinic Judaism was more positive toward the body and sexuality (with a few exceptions) than Hellenistic Judaism, Christianity, or Paganism. I argue throughout this chapter that while there were differences between Greek- and Roman-oriented views and rabbinic Jewish attitudes toward the human body, ultimately the spirit vs. matter/body, masculine vs. feminine dichotomy holds for both. Note that Boyarin sees the Qumran texts as belonging to a Hellenistic, anticorporeal strain of Judaism (77–78 n. 1). Whether Hekhalot texts were part of mainstream rabbinic Judaism has long been a matter of debate. For an overview of the relevant theories and literature, see Elliot R. Wolfson, *Through a Speculum that Shines,* 74–81.

11. *Avot de Rabbi Nathan*, chap. 1. Hebrew: Schechter p. 1; English: Goldin p. 11. A little later in this first chapter the righteous are said to refrain from eating, drinking, and trafficking on the Sabbath and they are nourished by the Shekhinah. Compare the text above with Philo, *Life of Moses* in *Works*, vol. 6, II, 14, 68–70, esp. 69, in which Moses is said to purify himself from everything that is of a mortal nature, namely sex, food, and drink; *Pirke de Rabbi Eliezer,* chap. 41 (56Bi) (ca. 8th–9th century), in which those who heard God's voice on Mount Sinai, like angels, were immune to insects, pollution, or the worms of the grave. Hebrew: *Pirke de Rabi El'iezer,* ed. Chaim Meir Horowitz, 160. English: *Pirke de Rabbi Eliezer (The Chapters of Rabbi Eliezer*

the Great) according to the Text of the Manuscript Belonging to Abraham Epstein of Vienna, trans. Gerald Friedlander, 327; *Midrash Rabbah bimidbar (Numbers)* 7.1; *Midrash Devarim rabah,* ed. Saul Lieberman [*Midrash Rabbah Deuteronomy*] 11.4 (450–800 C.E.); and *Midrash Tanḥuma'* [in *Ginze Midrash,* ed. Zvi Meir Rabinowitz] meẓor'a 18, in which the women do not menstruate in the desert while the Shekhinah is with the people of Israel; Arthur Marmonstein, *The Old Rabbinic Doctrine of God,* 2:92–93. The relevant section of *Midrash Rabbah Deuteronomy* is quite late coming from the school of Mosheh ha-Darshan (11th-century Narbonne). Strack and Stemberger, *Introduction,* 333–35.

12. This hypothesis is a central argument in his *Scholastic Magic* and his article "Like Ministering Angels."

13. Howard Eilberg-Schwartz, *The Savage in Judaism,* 138–39, 194, 217; idem, "The Problem of the Body for the People of the Body." Eilberg-Schwartz focuses on sexuality and genitalia in particular in his *God's Phallus and Other Problems for Men and Monotheism,* 59–133.

14. *Bereshit Rabba*, ed. J. Theodor and C. Alberg [*Midrash Rabbah Genesis*], 8.11. A parallel passage may be found in *Avot de Rabbi Nathan*, chap. 37. Also see *Bereshit Midrash Rabbah* 8.10 in which God distinguishes Adam from a divine being by making him sleep. These texts are part of a series of polemical passages (8.8–8.11) probably aimed at Christians. Jacob Neusner suggests "Gnostics" were the primary target. Jacob Neusner, "Genesis Rabbah as Polemic: An Introductory Account." On the problem of identifying anti-Gnostic polemic in rabbinic writings, see Ithmar Gruenwald, "The Problem of Anti-Gnostic Polemic in Rabbinic Literature."

15. Alon Goshen-Gottstein, "The Body as Image of God in Rabbinic Literature." Also see Wolfson, *Through a Speculum,* 13–124, esp. 68. On a few occasions Gershom Scholem implied that God was depicted as having organs ("*Shi'ur Komah:* The Mystical Shape of the Godhead," esp. 33, 44). However, in the examples he uses (Justin Martyr, *Dialogue with Tryphon,* chap. 114 [*Dialogue avec Tryphon,* ed. and trans. Georges Archambault]; *Sefer ha-Bahir,* para. 172 [*The Bahir*, ed. and trans. Aryeh Kaplan, Hebrew p. 227, English p. 66]), only God's limbs and genitalia are discussed, not his internal organs. On God's genitalia, see Wolfson, *Through a Speculum;* idem, "Erasing the Erasure/Gender and the Writing of God's Body in Kabbalistic Symbolism"; idem, "Images of God's Feet."

16. *Clementine Homilies* (*Die Pseudoklementinen*) XVII, 7, 2–4; English: *Ante-Nicene Fathers,* ed. Alexander Roberts and James Donaldson, 8:319–20. See discussion by Goshen-Gottstein, "Body as Image of God," esp. 172–73; and Shlomo Pines, "Points of Similarity between the Exposition of the Doctrine of the Sefirot in the *Sefer Yezira* and a Test of the *Pseudo-Clementine Homilies*."

17. Pines, "Points of Similarity," esp. 73–76, 99, 104–5.

18. Cicero, *Nat. D.* 1.44–49. See also 1.74–75 (English: *The Nature of the Gods,* trans. Horace C. P. McGregor).

19. Cicero, *Nat. D.* 1.92.

20. Cicero, *Nat. D.* 1.98.

21. Gerard Mussies ("Identification and Self-Identification of Gods in Classical and Hellenistic Times," esp. 2) notes that one of the ways by which Pagan gods were recognized by their devotees was the gods' manner of movement: they glided through the air rather than separating their feet to walk.

22. Myths that anthropomorphized the gods and detailed their fits of passion, wars, sexual exploits, and births were an embarrassment to be dismissed out of hand or allegorized. See Cicero, *Nat. D.* 139–43. Pagan philosophical attacks go back to pre-Socratic thinkers. For example, see Gerson's discussion of Xenophanes' theology in L. P. Gerson, *God and Greek Philosophy,* 17–20. For the difference between Stoic and other, current philosophical concepts of God, see 145–46, 154, 170.

23. Or as Festugière translated it: "Such is the enemy you have put on like a tunic" (τοιουτός 'εστιν 'ον 'ενεδύσω 'εχθρὸν χιτωνα). *Corpus Hermeticum,* ed. A. D. Nock, 7.3. Cf. *Hermetica: The Greek Corpus Hermeticum and the Latin Asclepius in a New English Translation,* trans. Brian Copenhaver, *Corpus Hermeticum* 7.24; 10.30–36; 12.43–48; Nock's version, 81–84, 113–36, 174–92 respectively. For the historical and intellectual background and influence of the *Hermetica* literature, see Garth Fowden, *The Egyptian Hermes.* Plotinus compared the soul's descent into the material body to a man immersed in mud and filth (πηλός and βορβορος): Plotinus, *Enneads* 1.65. Cicero in *The Dream of Scipio*, 3, 8–9, also treated the body as a limiting prison, the death of which should be no sorrow and which needed to be governed in its passions by the soul, much as gods govern the earth. Cicero, *Laelius on Friendship [Laelius de amicitia] and The Dream of Scipio [Somnium Scipionis]*. For further sources, see Dodds, *Pagan and Christian,* 23–33, 78–79.

24. The first section of the first Ennead is dedicated to distancing the soul from the passions and changes of the body, much as the gods of Cicero/Cotta had to be disassociated from human emotions. See especially *Enneads* 1.1.4–5, 9–10, 4.3–4.8.

25. Tertullian, *Quinti Septimi Florentis Tertulliani de anima* 53.5–6; English: *Ante-Nicene Fathers,* 3:230.

26. Arnobius, *Adv. Nat.* 3.10 [*The Case against the Pagans,* p. 199]. Also cf. Arnobius, *Adv. Nat.* 3.13–14; Marcus Minucius Felix (3d century C.E.), *Oct.* 23.5; Tatian (fl. ca. 172 C.E.), *Oration ad Graecos and Fragments,* 21; Athenagoras (fl. ca. 177 C.E.), [*Apologia pro Christianis*] *Plea for the Christians,* 19–22, 30, in *Supplique au sujet des chrétiens,* 130–39, 186–91. For a general discussion of Pagan and Christian objections to anthropomorphism, see Jaroslav Jan Pelikan, *The Christian Tradition,* 1:28–32. The same sorts of issues (subjection to bodily functions and passions) were a problem for late antique Christians trying to grasp the nature of the spiritual resurrected body. Carolyn Walker Bynum, *The Resurrection of the Body in Western Christianity, 200–1336,* 59–114.

27. Arnobius, *Adv. Nat.* 2.37, 39. Cf. 4.21, which uses a similar argument against the birth of Jupiter.

28. Cf. Aristotle, *Eth. Nic.* 3.1.111a–2.111b.10; and Seneca, *Lucil,* vol. 3, Epistle 124, 8–17. On Roman distaste for the unmolded, uncontrolled infant body, see Florence Dupont, *Daily Life in Ancient Rome,* 219–22. For the continuation of these attitudes

in later (Western) Christian literature, see Shulamith Shahar, *Childhood in the Middle Ages*, 14–20.

29. Boyarin, *Carnal Israel,* 5–10, 38–42; Goshen-Gottstein, "Body as Image of God"; Nissan Rubin, "Body and Soul in Talmudic and Mishnaic Sources."

30. BT Sanhedrin 91a–b; *Mekhilta de Rabi Yishma'el,* tractate Shirata, chap. 2, 2:21–22; *Leviticus Rabbah* (redacted ca. 400–500 C.E.), 5:5; Rubin, "Body and Soul."

31. This attitude is especially significant in the context of Mary Douglas's contention that beliefs about the body form the symbolic basis for describing the society that professes them. Douglas makes this argument in many of her works, but see especially *Natural Symbols.* For a provocative application of her theories to late antiquity, see John G. Gager, "Body-Symbols and Social Reality."

32. Brown, *Body and Society,* 5–8, 26–28, 85–86, 92–102, 293–303; idem, "Bodies and Minds"; Bynum, *Resurrection,* pt. 1.

33. On corpse pollution in Greek thought, see Robert Parker, *Miasma,* 32–48; Louis Moulinier, *Le pur et l'impur dans la pensée des Grecs d'Homère à Aristote,* 76–116, 176–98, 205–12, 400–407. For the Zoroastrians also, the corpses of humans and certain types of animals are chief in the hierarchy of ritual pollution. Dietrich Brandenburg, *Priesterärzte und Heilkunst im alten Persien,* 22, 25–30; Mary Boyce, *Zoroastrians,* 44–45, 52–53, 59; Jamsheed K. Choksy, *Purity and Pollution in Zoroastrianism,* 16–19, 24–50, 69, 105–10; A. V. Williams, "Zoroastrian and Judaic Purity Laws"; [*Avesta*] Fargard 3.2–4, Fargard 5–10, 12, in *The Zend Avesta*, pt. 1, *The Vendidad.* Unfortunately, relatively little research has been done on Roman concepts of purity. For corpse pollution (human and animal) in the biblical code, see Hannah K. Harrington, *The Impurity Systems of the Qumran and the Rabbis,* 69, 143; Julius Preuss, *Biblical and Talmudic Medicine,* 508; Num. 19:11–20, 22; 31:19–20; Deut. 21:22–23. The sacrifice of the red cow posed curious contradictions to some of the purity laws. See Harrington, *Impurity Systems,* 165–69; Jacob Milgrom, "The Paradox of the Red Cow (Numbers XIX)"; idem, "Two Kinds of Haṭṭa't"; idem, "Sin Offering or Purification Offering." During the Second Temple period and after, various Jewish groups expanded on these biblical regulations in their own way. For example, according to the Dead Sea sect, a woman carrying a dead fetus pollutes as if she were a corpse herself (11QT19 50:10–19, *Megillat ha-miqdash* = *The Temple Scroll,* ed. Yigael Yadin; English: *DSST*, 169–70). In the rabbinic system the woman only becomes impure after the fetus leaves her body (Harrington, *Impurity Systems,* 75). On rabbinic law regarding corpse pollution, see BT Shabbat 81a; Mishnah Ohalot 1:1–3, 6:1 (*The Mishnah Treatise Ohaloth/Maskhet Mishnah Ohalot,* ed. Abraham Goldberg); Harrington, *Impurity Systems*, 37–40, 72–75, 141–79. Most interesting for our purposes is that the rabbis created a special category of impurity that applied only to the corpse. Rather than simply being one of the *'avot ha-ṭum'ot,* i.e., one of the sources of impurity (literally "fathers of impurity"), the corpse was *'avi 'avot ha-ṭum'ah*, "the father of the fathers of impurity," indicating that the human cadaver was the greatest source of uncleanness. For a clear, basic explanation of these terms, see *The Talmud,* ed. Adin Steinsaltz, 157. On Christian debates about corpse impurity, see Bynum's discussion of Jerome and Vigilantius, *Resurrection,* 92–94, and her discussion of Tatian and Aristides, 31. Christians tended to reject purity regula-

tions. See, e.g., *Didascalia Apostolorum,* chap. 26; Bynum, *Resurrection,* 47; Brown, *Body and Society*, 89, 433–44. While the author of the *Didascalia* and other Christians ultimately may have rejected ritual purity laws, that they discussed them indicates they were familiar with the laws of the peoples around them.

34. In *Resurrection,* Bynum also notes the link between eating and decay, at least in Christian thought.

35. Pope Clement I, [*Epistola ad Corinthos*] *Épître aux Corinthiens,* chaps. 23–25, pp. 140–45; Justin Martyr, *Apologies, I Apology*, chap. 19, English: *Ante-Nicene Fathers,* 1:169; Cyril of Jerusalem, *Catechetical Lectures,* in *Catéchèses mystagogiques,* lecture 18, paras. 5–21, in *PG* 33 and *The Works of Saint Cyril of Jerusalem*, trans. Leo P. McCauley and Anthony A. Stephenson; Bynum, *Resurrection,* 24–26, 29–32, 76–79, 112–13. On p. 221 Bynum explains the importance of ceasing to eat or decay in twelfth- and thirteenth-century miracles about female saints by arguing that this was in response to medical and theological associations of the fertile, female body with decay. The female body was literally food because it produced milk and, before that, nourishment in the womb, and putrefaction because it expelled more waste products than did men, in the form of menstrual blood. Also see Brown, "Bodies and Minds," 484. For Pagan and Jewish examples, see Marcus Aurelius, *Communings* 9.3; and *Pirke Avot* discussed above.

36. *Synopse zur Hekhalot-Literatur*, paras. 79, 181, 791, 149, 313, 317, 565, on pp. 38–39, 80, 64–65 or 139–40, 216–17 respectively; Swartz, *Scholastic Magic*, 166–70; Joseph Schulz, "Angelic Opposition to the Ascension of Moses and the Revelation of the Law." On angelic purity, see Glenn Peers, *Subtle Bodies*.

37. Aristotle was more extreme than Galen in his formulation, arguing that male seed contributed only form and no matter, whereas Galen maintained that both parents contributed matter to the child. Drawing from Plato and the Hippocratic writers, Galen thought that the male seed provided the material for the veins, arteries, and nerves. Galen, *On Semen* 2.1–6; idem, *On the Usefulness of Parts (De usu partium)* 14.2.302–7, 320–21; idem, *On the Natural Faculties* 2.3.83. At 2.3.85–86 Galen asks, "And what is semen? Clearly the active principle of the animal, the material principle being the menstrual blood." Later in the passage he explains that semen draws the blood to it and feeds on it. However, in his *De usu partium* 14.2.289, Galen states that "menstrual blood is not the principal or suitable material for the generation of the animal." Aristotle, *Gen. an.* 1.19–21; 2.1, 4–5. Also see: Anthony Preus, "Galen's Criticism of Aristotle's Conception Theory"; Lesley Dean-Jones, *Women's Bodies in Classical Greek Science,* 149–93. Roman authors also adopted this view. Pliny, *HN* 7.15.

38. Aristotle, *Gen. an.* 1.19–20; 2.1, 4; Galen, *Usefulness of Parts* 14.2.296–303. This view also appears in some of the Hippocratic writings. For an overview and analysis, see Dean-Jones, *Women's Bodies,* 55–61. Cf. Soranus, *Gyn.* 1.22. For Greek text and French trans., see Soranus of Ephasus, *Maladies des femmes*.

39. For semen and menstrual blood as residue like urine and excrement, see Aristotle, *Gen. an.* 1.18.724b–19, esp. 1.18.725a–b. For the comparison between menstrual blood and diarrhea see *Gen. an.* 1.20.728a.

40. Aristotle, *Gen. an.* 1.1.715a.20–715b.25 and 1.16.721a.5–15; 3.11.762a.10–15; and idem, *Mete.* 4.1.379a–379b.5 (the passage in *Meteorologica* is talking about the

relationship of decay to temperature and humidity, not generation). Also see Anne Carson, "Putting Her in Her Place," 135–69; Ann Ellis Hanson, "The Medical Writer's Woman"; idem, "Conception, Gestation, and the Origins of Female Nature in the *Corpus Hippocraticum.*" For other Greek and Roman sources on spontaneous generation and its impact on Jewish thought, see Pieter W. van de Horst, "Two Notes on Hellenistic Lore in Early Rabbinic Literature," esp. 252–55.

41. Pliny, *HN* 11.90.233; 26.82.131. In the first of these citations ("In the human race alone a flux of blood occurs in the males, in some cases at one of the nostrils, in others at both, with some people through the lower organs, with many through the mouth; it may occur at a fixed period" [profluvium eius uni fit in naribus homini aliis nare alterutra, vel utraque, quibusdam per inferna, multis, per ora, stato tempore]), singling out the human male suggests that fluxes in females were not unusual. When he speaks of cyclical bleeding in some men it is hard not to see the parallel between that and women's monthly bleeding. The second passage links bleeding from the nose, mouth, bowels, and uterus by proposing a common treatment for all of these complaints, implying that to Pliny they were equivalent nosologically. Cf. Hippocrates, *Airs, Waters and Places,* 3, in *Hippocrates,* vol. 1 (New York, 1962–67), in which women living in districts subjected to warm southeast and southwest winds suffer frequently from vaginal discharges whereas men from the same region are afflicted with diarrhea, dysentery, hemorrhoids, and fevers. Also see Hanson, "Medical Writers' Woman."

42. Heinrich Von Staden, "Women and Dirt." Galen, some generations later, protested the use of menstrual blood, along with sweat, urine, excrement, and earwax, as medicinal substances—all of which were equally disgusting in his eyes (Galen, *On the Temperaments and Powers of Simple Drugs,* 10.1, in Galen, *Opera omnia,* 12.245–53; and Von Staden, "Women and Dirt," 9). The Roman naturalist Pliny the Elder decries some of these medicines as "shameless beyond belief" (excedit fidem inpudens; Pliny, *HN* 28.13.52–53); however, he frequently recommended them. To cite but a few examples, see 28.7–8 for medicinal uses of human saliva and earwax; in 28.13, before calling the use of semen, baby feces, and scrapings from gymnasium walls "shameful," Pliny wrote of the healing properties of sweat taken from bodies at the gymnasium and baths. Richlin implies that the gendered application of such "cures" were also adopted by the Romans. See her "Pliny's Brassiere," esp. 211. However, while dung and similar distasteful substances are frequent ingredients in medicine for women's illnesses, they are not used exclusively on women. See, e.g., Pliny, *HN* 28.58.209; 28.72; 28.74, though in this same section he also recommends that fresh excrement or its ashes be used for fluxes in the uterus.

43. Von Staden, "Women and Dirt," esp. 9 and the references there.

44. Richlin, *Garden,* 25–30, 56, 69, 82, 108, 113–15, 169–70. To give some examples, in poem 97 Catulus attacks Aemilius, saying: "I thought it made a difference / whether I smell Aemilius' mouth or his ass. / Neither was more pure or impure than the other" (Non [ita me di ament] quicquam referre putavi, / utrumne os an culum olfacerem Aemilio. / nilo munius hoc, niloque immundius, illud) (*Cattullus Tibullus ad Pervigilium Veneris,* 168–69. My translation differs slightly from the one given there). The implication in these lines is that Aemilius engaged in oral sex (either cunnilingus or

fellatio, though of the two cunnilingus would have been the more abhorrent and insulting because of the intensely negative view of women's genitals), and thus his mouth is nasty smelling and impure. On Roman attitudes toward oral sex, see Richlin, *Garden,* 25–28, 69, 108–9; for her discussion of this poem, see 27–28. The genitalia of old women were particularly detested and associated not only with dirt but decay as well. In the priapic poem 57 dealing with the prospect of having intercourse with a wealthy, older female partner, the male writer called her: "Crow and decay, old tomb / made putrid by the crowd of centuries" (Cornix et caries vetusque bustum / turba putrida facta). Cited and translated in Richlin, *Garden,* 113–14.

45. "Nam quamvis videar satis paratus / erucarum opus est decem maniplis / fossas inguinis ut teram dolemque / cunni vermiculos scaturrientes." Priapic poem 46, ll. 7–10, as cited and translated in Richlin, *Garden,* 123.

46. Oswei Temkin, *Hippocrates in a World of Pagans and Christians*. This is not to say that Christians never criticized doctors or asserted the superiority of spiritual healing over medicine. See 168–70.

47. For a critique of the category of Gnosticism or gnostic Christianity, see Michael A. Williams, *Rethinking "Gnosticism."* Overall, I agree with Williams's arguments, but the terms "gnosticism" and "gnostic" are so widely used they are difficult to escape. What I mean by the term in this instance is what Williams calls "biblical demiurgical" texts, namely, texts that create a mythology based on a distinction between a transcendent divine being and a hierarchy of beings responsible for creating and managing the material world, which are below the transcendent divinity. On terminology, see Williams, *Rethinking "Gnosticism,"* 265–66.

48. Irenaeus, *Adversus Haereses* 1.2.2. *Apocryphon of John,* trans Frederick Wisse; *The Hypostases of the Archons,* trans. Bentley Layton; *On the Origin of the World*, trans. Hans Gebhard Bethge and Orval S. Wintermute; *Eugnostos the Blessed and the Sophia of Jesus Christ,* trans. Bouglas Parrott; *A Valentinian Exposition,* trans. John Turner; *The Paraphrase of Shem,* trans. Frederick Wisse, all in *Naghammadi Library in English*, ed. James Robinson (San Francisco, 1981), 103–7, 157–60, 162–67, 220–21, 438–40, and 309–25 respectively. *Paraphrase of Shem* is rather different from the others in that the world comes about through the interaction and struggle between Mind and Womb. Also see Williams's discussion in *Rethinking "Gnosticism,"* 127–32.

49. Galen, *De usu partium* 14.7; Aristotle, *Gen. an.* 3.1.749a34–749b7; 4.1.764a6–11; Aristotle, *Hist. an.* 6.2.559b20–560a17.

50. Another example of mixing biology and theology is Athenagoras's explanation of the final resurrection and of the impossibility of cannibalism that he founded on classical theories of digestion. Athenagoras, *The Resurrection of the Dead,* 4–9, in Athénagoras, *Supplique*, 227–49; Temkin, *Hippocrates*, 128–30; Bynum, *Resurrection*, 31–33.

51. Ceterum cum et ubera matris suae nominat,—sine dubio quae hausit—respondeant obstetrices et medici et physici de uberum natura, an aliter manare soleant, sine uuluae genitali passione suspendentibus exinde venis sentinam illam interni sanguinis et ipsa translatione decoquentibus in materiam lactis laetiorem. Inde adeo fit, ut uberum tempore menses sanguinis vacent. Quodsi verbum caro ex se factum est, non

ex uuluae communione, nihil operata uulua, nihil functa, nihil passa quomodo fontem suum transfudit in ubera quem nisi habendo non mutat? Habere autem fontem non potuit lacti subministrando, si non haberet et causas sanguinis ipsius, auulsionem scilicet suae carnis. Tertullian, [*De carne Christi*] *La chair du Christ*, 20.6 (pp. 292–95), and in *Ante-Nicene Fathers,* 3:539.

52. Galen, *De usu partium* 14.8; Dean-Jones, *Women's Bodies,* 211–22. Soranus implies a connection between milk and menstrual blood in *Gyn.* bk. 2.19 when he warns that the wet nurse ought not to have sex while nursing because intercourse will stimulate the menses and thus cause the milk to be of inferiority quality.

53. Stephen Newmyer, "Talmudic Medicine and Greek Sources"; Samuel J. Kottek, "Concepts of Disease in the Talmud." (Kottek does not address the relationship of the talmudic views of diseases and their causes, but anyone familiar with the Hippocratic corpus cannot help but be struck by the similarities between it and many of the ideas Kottek describes.) Also see Horst, "Two Notes." Both Newmyer and Kottek point to evidence from the Talmud and Galen of Jewish medical practitioners. Also see Temkin, *Hippocrates,* 86–93. This is not to say that no medical lore peculiar to Jewish traditions existed. See, e.g., K. Codell Carter, "An Illustration of the Religious Foundations of Talmudic Medicine: Tractate Megillah fol. 27b–28a."

54. Newmyer, "Talmudic Medicine"; Süssmann Munter, *Mavo' le-sefer Asaf ha-rofe'*; "Asaph ha-Rofe," in *Encyclopaedia Judaica.* The dating of the work is rather tenuous.

55. Abraham Wasserstein," Normal and Abnormal Gestation Periods in Humans: A Survey of Ancient Opinion (Greek, Roman, and Rabbinic)"; Preuss, *Biblical and Talmudic Medicine,* 381–431. This is not to say that there were no differences. For example, rabbinic Jews believed that women had a seed and that in order to have a boy the woman needed to "ejaculate" first. See Wasserstein for references.

56. *Midrash Tanḥuma'*, tazri'a 2, 5.

57. Ibid., tazri'a 1; [*Midrash Rabbah Leviticus*] *Midrash Vayikra rabbah,* (Emor) 27:7.

58. מפני מה האשה צריכה להתבשם והאיש אינו צריך להתבשם? אמר להם אדם נברא מאדמה והאדמה אינה מסרחת לעולם אבל חוה נבראת מעצם משל אם תניח בשר ג» ימים בלא מלח מסריח מיד הוא (*Midrash Rabbah Genesis* 17:8). Cf. *Pirke Avot* and Hekhalot literature cited above.

59. Aristotle, *Aristotle on Sleep and Dreams,* 2.459b25–460a20.

60. Pliny, *HN* 7.15.64. Rackam translates *monstrificum* as "remarkable." However, that does not convey the negative tone implied by the word, so I have substituted its English cognate. The word can also mean simply "strange." The passage continues to enumerate odd, often poisonous properties of menstrual blood. Compare *HN* 28.23.77–82; Richlin, "Pliny's Brassiere." Menstruants were not the only ones with such powers. According to Pliny, those who have magical powers or the evil eye or have been licked or bitten by a poisonous animal affect the world around them in ways similar to the menstruant.

61. Pliny, *HN*, 28.23.77–78. Richlin, "Pliny's Brassiere." In BT Shabbat 110a, the menstuant can repel serpents by throwing some of her hair and nails at the snake and saying "I am menstruous." תשקול ממזיה ומטופרה ותשדי ביה ותימא דישתנא אנא

62. Pliny, *HN* 28.23.82–85. At 28.10.44 Pliny remarks that "it is held that snake bites and scorpion stings are relieved by intercourse, but that the act does harm to the woman" [quin et a serpente, a scorpione percussos coitu levari produnt, verum feminas venere ea laedi]. This passage does not specify that the woman was menstruating, but it nevertheless suggests that the woman's body, in particular her genital region, has power over poison. Urine from a man or a woman has similar curative properties (28.18.66–67). Women's milk always has beneficial properties (28.21). These views reflect the division between the upper and the lower body: both are powerful healers, but the lower is also harmful. Richlin, "Pliny's Brassiere," esp. 205. Richlin argues that the ailments that can be aided by menstrual blood are characterized by loss of bodily control. I concur with this observation, but poison, whether from an outside source or from internal corruption, strikes me as the more pervasive motif. On skin diseases' derivation from corrupt, excessive humors, see Mirko D. Grmek, *Diseases in the Ancient Greek World,* 165–66.

63. Pliny, *HN* 28.23.77.

64. For the connection between leprosy and menstruation in Arabic medicine, see Horst Müller-Bütow, *Lepra.*

65. *Kallah Rabbati* 2, 52a, 16, 17, in *Massekhot kalah*, ed. M. Higger (New York, 1936), 186–87; also in *Maskhet Kalah Rabbati*, ed. Hayim M. Mendel; trans. in *The Minor Tractates of the Talmud*, ed. Abraham Cohen, vol. 2; *Midrash Tanḥuma', meẓor'a* 22b, 3. Other texts indicate that the menstruant is dangerous to men but do not specify the disease or cause of death. See BT Pesaḥim 111a; *Avot de Rabbi Nathan*, chap. 2, Schechter pp. 8–9, Goldin pp. 16–17; *Tanna de be Eliyahu,* in *Sefer Tanna de be Eliyahu,* ed. Shmu'el mi Shinoui; *Tanna de be Eliyahu = The Lore of the School of Elijah,* trans. W. G. Braude and Israel Kapstein (Philadelphia, 1981), *ER* 75–76, pp. 208–11. This text attained its final form in the tenth or eleventh century, but its core dates to the third century. A version is contained in BT Shabbat 13a–b. On *Tanna de be Eliyahu,* see Tirzeh Meacham, "Mishnat masekhet Nidah 'im mavo ma hadurah bekortit 'im he'arot be-nusaḥ, be farshant ure'arikah u-ferakim be-toldot he-halakhhah uve-re'alyah," 157–58; Strack and Stemberger, *Introduction,* 369–71. On the dangers of menstruants in the Jewish tradition generally, Shaye Cohen, "Menstruants and the Sacred in Judaism and Christianity"; idem, "Purity and Piety"; Preuss, *Biblical and Talmudic Medicine*, 123. Christians expanded the levitical prohibition (and resulting penalty) to having intercourse during festivals and Sundays. See Caesarius of Arles, sermon 44.7, in *Sancti Caesarii Arelatensis Sermones*, 103:199; idem, sermon 292.7 (*PL*, 39, col. 2300); Jerome, *Commentary on Zachariah* 3:13:1 (*PL*, 25, col. 1591); idem, *On Isaiah* 64:6, in *S. Hieronymi presbyteri opera*, pts. 1, 2 A, pp. 736–37, or *PL* 24, cols. 617–18; *Biblia Latina cum glossa ordinaria;* Gregory of Tours, *De virtutibus sancti Martini*, 2, chap. 24 in *PL* 71, cols. 951–52; Jean-Louis Flandrin, *Le sexe et l'Occident,* 162–63; James A. Brundage, *Law, Sex and Christian Society in Medieval Europe,* 91–92, 155–56.

66. "Quando praesertim ab uxore abstinendum. Quas plerumque poenas dent qui aliter se gerunt. Nonnulli bestiis incontinentiores. Ante omnia ut quoties dies dominicus aut aliae festivitates veniunt, uxorem suam nullus agnoscat. Et quoties fluxum sanguinis mulieres patiuntur, similiter observandum est: propter illud quod ait propheta, 'Ad mulierem menstruatam non accesseris' (Ezech. 18:6). Nam qui uxorem suam in profluviis

positam agnoverit, aut in die dominico, aut in alia qualibet solemnitate adveniente se continere noluerit; qui tunc concepti fuerint, aut leprosi, aut epileptici, aut etiam forte daemoniaci nascentur. Denique quicumque leprosi sunt, non de sapientibus hominibus, qui et in alliis diebus et in festivitatibus castitatem custodiunt, sed de rusticis maxime, qui se continere non sapiunt, nasci solent" (Caesarius of Arles, sermon 292.7, in *PL* 39, col. 2300, attributed to Saint Augustine). The idea that *rustici* were more likely to have intercourse with their menstruant wives is similar to views expressed in the Talmud that *'amei ha- 'areẓ*, people of the land, forced their wives to have intercourse at inappropriate times. See BT Pesaḥim 49a–b.

67. *Kallah Rabbati*, chap. 2, 52a, 16, 17, Higger, p. 187; *Baraita de Niddah* in *Tosefata 'atikata*, pt. 5, ed. Haim Meir Horowitz (Frankfurt, 1890) chap. 1, halachah 1, pp. 2–3. In these texts it is not clear whether the deformities are the result of moral impropriety on the part of the parents or magical or medical reasons.

68. אשה כי תזריע וילדה זכר מה כתיב בתריה? אדם כי יהיה בעור בשרו וכי מה ענין זה לזה? אמר רבי תנחום ברבי חנילאי משל לחמורה שרעת ונכוות ויצא בנה כווי מי גרם לולד שיצא כווי? שרעת אמו וניכוות כך מי גרם לולד שיצא מצורע? אמו שלא שמרה את נדתה. אמ' ר' אבין לגינת ירק שמהעיין לתוכה. כ"ז שהמעיין לתוכה היא עושה ביצין כך כל מי שהולך אצל אשתו נידה סוף שמעמדת בנים מצורעים. ר' אבין קרא עליה אבות יאכלו בוסר ושיני בנים תקהינה והן קוראין על אבותיהם אבותינו חטאו ואינם ואנחנו עוונותיהם סבלנו (*Vayikra' Rabbah* 15:5). English translation slightly revised from *Midrash Rabbah Leviticus,* in *Midrash Rabbah,* ed. H. Freedman and Maurice Simon, trans. J. Israelstam and Judah Slotki. On this passage see the brief comments of Preuss, *Biblical and Talmudic Medicine*, 123. Concerning the belief that the young child could inherit the acquired defects of the parents, see Hippocrates, *The Seed*, 11, in *Hippocrates.*

69. שנו חכמים ואמרו המשמשת את בעלה והיא נדה גורמת לבניה שלא נחלו תורה ולא עוד אלא שהיא גורמת להן אפילו לעשרים דור לסיף בניה לוקין בתצרעת (*Baraita de Niddah,* chap. 1, halakhah 2, p. 3). On *Baraita de Niddah* generally and its place among early discussions of the nature and legal status of the menstruant, see Cohen, "Menstruants"; idem, "Purity and Piety."

70. והחכם באנשי בשעה שהוא יושב על מטתו אומר לאשתו בתי הזהרי בנדותיך שלא תגרמי לבנינו את המומין (*Baraita de Niddah*, chap. 1, halakhah 5, p. 7). According to the *Baraita de Niddah,* even the nail clippings of the menstruant are dangerous, for anyone who steps on them is stricken with boils (chap. 2, halakhah 4, p. 16).

71. Jerome, *On Isaiah* 64:6, in *S. Hieronymi* pts. 1, 2 A, pp. 736–37, or *PL* 24, cols. 617–18; Flandrin, *Sexe et l'Occident*, 163.

72. *Baraita de Niddah*, chap. 2, halakhah 7, p. 20. Having intercourse with one's menstruating wife is but one of the sexual activities mentioned. The final deed for which R. 'Eli'ezar gives the explanation of "changing blood" during birth is laughter and frivolity during sex. For blood as the cause of leprosy, also see *Leviticus Rabbah* 15.2. There a person's health depends on the balance of water and blood in the body. Too much blood causes leprosy. On this text, see Kottek, "Concepts of Disease," esp. 17–18. This passage does not link "leprosy" to menstrual blood in particular, but it is strikingly reminiscent of Hippocratic explanations of the causes of skin diseases. (See Grmek, *Diseases*, 165.) Hemorrhoids were a guarantee against leprosy, and as we have seen, anal bleeding was closely related to menstruation in Greek and Roman medical

theory. Thus it would seem that for Jews, like Pagan medical thinkers, leprosy resulted from an excess of bad blood/humors. Menstruation was simply the worst possible type of blood. In early Christian examples, however, the punishment for intercourse with a menstruant and sundry other sexual sins may have been the same, but none of the texts indicate that the woman's blood was the cause for all of them.

73. Carson, "Putting Her in Her Place."

74. Rachel Biale, *Women and Jewish Law,* 147–74; Yedidya Dinari, "Ḥilul ha-qodesh 'al-yadei niddah ve-takanat 'Ezra'"; idem, "Minhagei ṭum'at ha-niddah-me-koram ve-hishtalshelutam"; Cohen, "Purity and Piety" and "Menstruants"; Meacham, "Mishnat maskhet Niddah 'im mavo," 158–63, 170–87; idem, "An Abbreviated History of the Development of the Jewish Menstrual Laws"; Israel Ta-Shma, "haraḥaqot niddah be-Ashkenz ha-qodem."

75. In Lev. 15:19, 20, 24, 33, and 18:19, the word refers to "the distancing which comes as a result of the impurity of regular monthly menstruation of the woman." In Lev. 15:25–26, the regulations of *niddah* are applied to those having an irregular flow of blood; and in Lev. 12:2, 5, to those having recently given birth. The act of taking one's brother's wife is also called *niddah* (Lev. 20:21). In this case *niddah* seems to indicate sexual sin. However, the authors of Ezech. 22:10 and 36:17 and Lam. 1:8, 17 use *niddah* to refer to the menstruating woman herself rather than her ritual state. In Ezra 9:11 *niddah* is applied to the lands and activities of non-Israelites. Finally in Num. 19:9, 13, 20, 21, and 31:23 one finds the term *maï-niddah,* "waters of *niddah,*" which were composed of the ashes of the red heifer offering plus water. In Num. 19:9 this water is simply for "sin," though later in the chapter the mixture is sprinkled on someone who has been contaminated by a corpse. Thus in Numbers *niddah* is used to designate a substance that removed impurity. Later rabbis interpreted *maï-niddah* as meaning the water in which the menstruant bathed. On the etymology and meaning of נדה see Meacham, "Mishnat maskhet niddah 'im mavo," 150–52; and Moshe Greenberg, "The Etymology of *niddah* 'Menstrual Impurity.'" Greenberg notes that *niddah* may be related to the Syriac verb meaning "to abhor, loathe," thus giving it a stronger sense than "to distance, avoid."

76. Biale, *Women and Jewish Law,* 154; David Biale, *Eros and the Jews,* 30; Meacham, "Mishnat Maskhet Nidah 'im mavo," 152.

77. חטא חטאה ירושלים על-כן לנידה היתה כל-מכבדיה הזילות כי-ראו ערותה גם היא נאנחה ותשב אחור טמאתה בשוליה לא זכרה אחריתה ותרד פלאים

78. This is not to say that nowhere is *niddah* presented as impurity resulting from sin without any explicit link to women. See Zach. 13:1 and Ezra 9:11.

79. Jonathan Klawans, *Impurity and Sin in Ancient Judaism,* 26–31, 32–36, 38–42.

80. For an example of *niddah* in the sense of "menstruation," see 4Q274 [4Q Tohorot A] frag. 1, col. 1, ll. 7–8, in *The Dead Sea Scrolls Uncovered,* ed. Robert Eisenman and Michael Wise, Hebrew p. 207, English p. 209 and also in *DSST*, 88. Text and discussion in Joseph Baumgarten, "Zab Impurity in the Qumran and Rabbinic Law; and see articles by Joseph Baumgarten and Jacob Milgrom in *Time to Prepare the Way in the Wilderness,* 1–8 and 58–68 respectively. For extended meanings of *niddah,* see *The Manual of Discipline/Rule of the Community* (1QS), col. IV, l.5, which describes the

spirit that "detests all unclean idols," literally "idols of *niddah*" (מתעב כול גלולי נדה) and later in the same text, 1QS col. IV, ll. 9–10, in *Dead Sea Scrolls of St. Mark's Monastery,* ed. Millar Burrows, vol. 2. English: *DSST*, 6, 7. Also see col. V, ll. 19–20, *DSST*, 8. The extension of meaning in the *Manual of Discipline* parallels the use of the term in Ezra 9:11 wherein *niddah* was applied to the impurity of non-Jewish peoples. Also see Klawan, *Impurity and Sin,* 75–79.

81. See Lev. 15:19–24. This passage is embedded in a discussion of the laws concerning the *zav* and *zavah,* and in verse 19 the verb *zavah* is also used to describe the woman's state. In Lev. 15:25 the *zavah* is defined as one who has a discharge of blood for many days when it is not time for menstruation or one whose bleeding lasts beyond the normal cycle. In this passage her impurity is likened to that of *niddah.*

82. Lev. 15:13–15, 19, 28–30; Harrington, *Impurity Systems*, 221–22.

83. For the close association of *zavah* and *niddah* in the Dead Sea scrolls, see *Damascus Covenant* 5:6–7 (Hebrew text may be found in Philip R. Davies, *The Damascus Covenant;* and in S. Schechter, *Documents of Jewish Sectaries,* 114). English: *Dead Sea Scrolls in English,* ed. and trans. Geza Vermes, 101, or *DSST*, 36; 4Q Tohorot a/ 4Q 274 ll. 4–8, *Time to Prepare the Way*, 1–8, 58–68; Baumgarten, "Zab Impurity"; *DSST*, 88; *Dead Sea Scrolls Uncovered*, 205–10; Harrington, *Impurity Systems*, 85–89. There is no indication one way or the other that the "equivalency" between the *niddah* and someone afflicted with gonorrhea indicated in 4Q274 meant that the menstruant was expected to lengthen her purification period to equal that of a *zavah*, as eventually occurred in rabbinic thought. Nevertheless, this equation of *niddah* and *zav/zavah* parallels a similar melding of the two terms and status in rabbinic literature. Baumgarten draws attention to the fact that the Samaritans regarded *niddah* as more polluting than *zav*, since seven days of purification were required for the former and only one for the latter. The severity attached to *niddah* by the Samaritans corresponds to the general tendency of late antique Jews to regard menstrual impurity as one of the greatest impurities. See Baumgarten, "The laws about fluxes in 4Q Tohora a (4Q 274)," in *Time to Prepare the Way*, 1–8.

84. Meacham, "Mishnat masekhet nidah 'im mavo," 174–87.

85. Biale, *Women in Jewish Law,* 158–74; Cohen, "Menstruants"; Dinari, "Hilul ha-Kodesh"; idem, "Minhagei tuma'at ha-niddah."

86. JT Berakhot 3.4; BT Berakhot 22a. Dinari, "Hilul ha-kodesh."

87. BT Ketuvot 61a. Also see Biale, *Women and Jewish Law,* 158–63; and BT Shabbat 64b, in which R. 'Akiva overturns the ruling of previous sages prohibiting the menstruating wife from adorning herself for her husband. According to him, such behavior might cause the husband to divorce his wife. Concern that the husband might be tempted to defy the laws of *niddah* was insufficient to dictate law in this case.

88. *Avot de R. Natan,* chap. 2, version A, Hebrew, Schecter pp. 8–9, English, Goldin pp. 16–17; Mordecai Margulies, *Ha-Ḥiluqim she-bein 'anshe Mizraḥ u-vene 'Ereẓ Yi'sra'el,* difference 11, p. 79; *Baraita de Niddah,* chap. 1, halakha 2, p. 3, chap. 1, halakhah 4, p. 6, chap. 2, halakhah 5, pp. 16–17, chap. 2, halakhah 4, p. 16, chap. 3, halakhah 4, pp. 30–33; Dinari, "Minhagei ṭum'at ha-niddah"; idem, "Ḥilul ha-qodesh"; Cohen, "Purity and Piety"; idem, "Menstruants." Of these the *Baraita de Niddah* was perhaps the most influential. Early gaonic protests against stringent separation of the menstruant

indicate that not all were in favor of such practices, yet the gaonim would not have had to object so vehemently had these customs not been deeply ingrained in the populace. On inconsistency in early responsa, see Dinari, "Ḥilul ha-qodesh"; Cohen, "Menstruants."

89. Cohen, "Menstruants" and "Purity and Piety"; Koren, "Woman from Whom God Wanders," 21–23. Also see Harrington, *Impurity Systems,* 91–94, 247–48; Jacob Milgrom, "Studies in the Temple Scroll." On semen in the Greek tradition, see indirectly Parker, *Miasma,* 74–79. In Roman: Richlin, *Garden*; in Zoroastrian: Choksy, *Purity and Pollution,* 88–94.

90. Koren, "Woman from Whom God Wanders," 23–26, 55–61, 64, 68–74, 76–81, 85–89, 116–18. She also argues that in some circles the menstruant was viewed as demonically possessed and was strongly associated with the severest impurity—corpse pollution, which added to her status as a source of danger and obstacle to holiness. See 55–61.

91. Klawans, *Impurity and Sin,* 107–8.

92. Note, however, that the trend in Christianity was to make menstrual laws *less restrictive* than in post–Second Temple Judaism. See Meacham, "Mishnat masekhat Niddah 'im mavo," 159. This tendency is consistent with Christianity's rejection or spiritualization of Jewish purity and dietary laws in general. However, that many Christians continued to observe or worry about menstrual laws at all is testimony to the power of menstrual regulations.

93. Parker notes that Greeks did not prohibit intercourse with the menstruant, and while in the medical texts menstruation is a "cleansing," and thus one might assume it should be avoided precisely because it contains bodily impurities, there is no evidence that Greeks (and Romans) viewed menstrual blood as impure in a religious sense. The status of the parturient was less certain. See Parker, *Miasma*, 32–73 (here he is mostly concerned with the pollution of the dead), 100–101; Moulinier, *Pur et impur,* 63–71. On the other hand menstruation was considered polluting by the Zoroastrians. See Boyce, *Zoroastrians,* 45; Choksy, *Purity and Pollution,* 60, 90–92, 94–99. Boyce notes that the rules concerning the menstruant became increasingly strict over time. Choksy confirms this and indicates that women were often seen as "polluted allies of the Evil Spirit" and were thought capable of polluting with their gaze (96–97). These developments in Zoroastrian thought are important for they may have influenced the Jews of Bablyonia. Indeed, Shaye Cohen has noted that in BT Shabbat 110a, the word used for "menstruous" is the Persian term *distana* ("Menstruants," 294 n. 25). This is one of the few talmudic texts in which the body of the menstruant is designated as physically dangerous. Christian views of the menstruant and what she should be allowed to do varied. Some maintained that she was not impure at all, whereas others prohibited intercourse with her and denied her access to the eucharist. There was no systematic effort in Christian communities to exclude her from sacred spaces or objects or from household chores. See Cohen, "Menstruants," esp. 287–90.

94. Marcel Detienne, *The Gardens of Adonis,* esp. 48–49. For images of decay and foul-smelling effluvia, whether excrement, genital fluid, or other types, as negative signifiers in Roman literature, see Richlin, *Garden,* esp. 26–30, 69, 114–23.

95. Ephrem the Syrian, *Hymns,* trans. Kathleen E. McVey, hymn 22, stanza 28, p. 184.

96. On the bad smell of demons, see *A Manichaean Psalm-book,* pt. II, ed. and trans. C. R. C. Allberry; "Psalms of Thomas": "Concerning the Coming of the Soul," ll. 21 and 30, p. 209. On sweet odor of Light versus the stink of the enemy, see "Psalms of Thomas": "Concerning the Coming of the Soul," ll. 17–18, 23, p. 205; ll. 24–30, p. 206; "Psalms of Thomas," ll. 3, 8–9, 30, p. 214; ll. 1–3, p. 215.

97. *Epistula Luciani,* 2, *PL,* 41, epistle 8, col. 815. Also see Peter Brown's discussion in his *The Cult of the Saints,* 91–93.

98. On this text, see Daniel Boyarin, "The Great Fat Massacre"; idem, *Carnel Israel,* 200–212, 219–25.

99. Swartz, *Scholastic Magic*, 167–68. Purity was still an issue. See the rest of his chapter on this. Also compare with the passage from *City of God* cited earlier in this chapter in which Augustine criticizes Apuleius's belief that the gods cannot abide the smell of humans.

100. Plato, *Timaeus,* 72e–73a. (English translation from Plato, *Collected Dialogues,* ed. Edith Hamilton and Huntington Cairns). Galen, *De usu partium* 4.18.19. These views of eating and excreting came to be shared by the Romans as well. Cf. Seneca, *Epistulae Morales*, epistles 15.2–4, 92.7–11, 110.12–13. On the culture of eating in Roman society, see Dupont, *Daily Life,* 269–86; Anthony Corbeill, "Dining Deviants in Roman Political Invective." On excremental imagery in Latin poetry, see Richlin, *Garden,* 26–28, 63, 108, 128–29, 168–70, 206.

101. Plato, *Timaeus,* 69d–70a. Galen is not so blunt in his valuation of the various segments of the human body, but he clearly followed Plato in this matter. See Galen, *De usu partium* 4.13, 6.18.

102. *Midrash Rabbah Deuteronomy* 9.4.

103. *Avot de Rabbi Nathan*, version A, chap. 28, Schechter p. 86, Goldin p. 117. Also see *Avot de Rabbi Nathan*, version A, chap. 1, Schechter p. 5, Goldin p. 12. Compare this text with Seneca, *Epistulae Morales,* vol. 3, epistle 110.3.

104. Clement of Alexandria, *Paedagogus*, bk. 2, chap. 1.4:1, 7:4, in Clément d'Alexandrie, *Le pédagogue*, bk. II, 16–17, 22–23. English translation from *Ante-Nicene Fathers,* 2:238, 239. Tertullian also tied the ingestion of food to death and decay in his *De Ieiunio adversus psychicos* (ed. A. Reifferscheid and G. Wissowa, chaps. 3 and 17, in *Opera*, pt. 2, CCSL, 1259–60, 1276–77), arguing that Adam's sin (and therefore the root of human mortality) was gluttony. Also see Bynum, *Resurrection*, 40–43.

105. Seneca, *Epistulae Morales*, vol. 2, epistle 92, 6–9. On Roman attitudes toward and practices of excessive eating, both literal and metaphorical, see also Carlin Barton, *Sorrows of the Ancient Romans,* 51–53, 71–72, 90, 110–12. She points out that Romans also saw asceticism as a form of excess. See 52, 75–76, 79.

106. Prov. 30:12; Isa. 3:4; Zech. 3:3–5. In Isa. 28:8 the bad behavior and the errors of the prophets are represented by the abundance of vomit and excrement. Cf. 1 Kings 14:10, Job 20:7, Zeph. 1:17, where the wicked perish quickly and completely like dung *galal.* Defecating in the camp where God's presence dwelled is included amid a list of deuteronomic sins (Deut. 23:12–14). In Ezekiel chaps. 4–6 the requirement to eat food cooked over human dung serves as a warning to the Israelites that they will have to eat impure food during their exile.

107. Urine, on the other hand, had no such associations in Hebrew Scriptures.

108. Plutarch, *Sulla* 36, in *Plutarch's Lives*, vol. 4 (1959); and Dupont's discussion in *Daily Life*, 242–43. Also see *Sulla* 37.

109. Flavius Josephus, *Jewish Antiquities,* bk. XVII, chap. 6.5. Cf. *Midrash Rabbah Numbers* 7:4 on the punishment of the Israelites in the desert.

110. Rufinus, *Historiae Ecclesiasticae,* vol. 2, pt. 2, 979; and Willis Johnson's discussion of this and related Christian texts in his "Myth." The death of Judas in Acts 1:18–19 ought to be considered in light of the cultural associations with burst intestines.

111. Boyarin argues that the requirement to bless God after urinating and/or defecating "shows clearly two things: first the acceptance of fleshliness in its most material and lower-body forms as the embodiment of God's wisdom, and second the definition of the human as his or her body" (*Carnal Israel*, 34). While I do not necessarily disagree with this statement, I do not think that the prayer suggests as strong an ideological divide between the rabbis and the more Hellenized Jews such as Philo and Paul as Boyarin seems to suggest. Having a physical body created by God was integral to being human in rabbinic Judaism, but for rabbinic Jews, as for many Pagans and Christians, the lower bodily functions created a divide between God and humans, and in the most ideal or holy state, humans were exempt from all or part of these processes. The more closely someone was associated with excreta, the farther he or she was from God.

112. The big exception is the food prohibitions.

113. Ezek. 4:12–14; Deut. 23:12–14[15]; Harrington, *Impurity Systems,* 100.

114. Harrington, *Impurity Systems,* 100–103. She is drawing from Flavius Josephus, *Wars of the Jews* 2.8.9; 1QM 7.6–7 (Hebrew text in Sukenick, *The Dead Sea Scrolls*, 1–19, pls. 16–34, 47; English: *DSST*, 100); 11QT 46:13–16 (Hebrew text in *Megillat ha-miqdash: The Temple Scroll;* English: *DSST*, 168). Albert I. Baumgarten, in "The Temple Scroll, Toilet Practices, and the Essenes," opposes equating the Essenes of Josephus and their toilet practices with the members of the Dead Sea group.

115. See, e.g., BT Makhshirin 6:7; JT Pesahim 7:11. Urine on the other hand can transfer uncleanness because it is wet. BT Tovel Yom 2:1; BT Kelim 1:3. For further references to similar citations in the Sifra and tosefta, see Harrington, *Impurity Systems*, 101 and n. 48. Also see Preuss, *Biblical and Talmudic Medicine,* 356.

116. הנכהס לבית הכסא אומר התכבדו מכובדים קדושים משרתי עליון תנו כבוד לאלהי ישראל הרפו ממני עד שאכנס ואעשה רצוני ואבא עליכם (BT Berakhot 60b). Epstein notes that "the honored and holy ones" are angels who guard the sage. See n. 5, loc. cit. The human need to defecate is contrasted to angelic nature when R. Abaye has the person explain to the person's heavenly escort, "for this is the way of human beings" (שכן דרכן של בני אדם). For a general discussion of excrement and privies, see Preuss, *Biblical and Talmudic Medicine,* 546–52. Later in Berakhot 61b–62a the rabbis stipulated that one should not relieve oneself while in sight of or aligned along the same axis as the Temple. Nor, according to R. Papa and R. Hisda, may a person recite the *Shema'* if he has excrement in his anus or on his flesh or has hands still in the privy (BT Yom'a 30a). Also see Harrington, *Impurity Systems,* 101; Koren, "Woman from Whom God Wanders," 49. Cf. discussions in BT Berakot 62a and *Avot de Rabbi Nathan,* chap. 40 (Schechter p. 168; Goldin p. 168); and in passing, Baumgarten, "The Temple Scroll."

117. Grmek, *Diseases,* 165–71; Pliny, *HN* bk. 26.1–6.

118. Grmek, *Diseases*, 154–64; Preuss, *Biblical and Talmudic Medicine,* 323–37.

119. Lev. 13–14. Both the Dead Sea Scrolls and the Mishnah required lepers to live outside the walls of the city and call out their status. Within the ideal practices of the Jews of the Qumran, the *meẓor'a*'s isolation paralleled that of the menstruant and the person with gonorrhea (in contrast to the rabbinic system in which the leper was the only one exiled from the town boundaries), though the three were not supposed to touch or associate with one another. The rabbis also closely associated the leper with the corpse. Harrington, *Impurity Systems*, 78–84, 181–213, and the literature cited there; Milgrom, "4Q Tohora a"; Baumgarten, "Laws about Fluxes"; idem, "Zab Impurity"; Hyam Maccoby, "Corpse and the Leper"; Mishnah Neg. 5:1; tosephta neg. 7:6; BT San. 47 a–b; BT Hul. 7b; BT Ned. 64b; BT Avodah Zar'a 5a; Kel. 1:7; BT Zeb. 117a; BT Pesah,im 66b–67a; 11 QT 48:14–15, 4Q tohrot a (4Q 274) 1:1–3; English: *DSST,* 169, 88 respectively.

120. Pliny, *HN* 26.6.9. The people of Delos were punished with a skin disease for burying a corpse on the island—something they were forbidden to do because of the island's sacred status. See Parker, *Miasma*, 218; Grmek, *Diseases,* 168. By contrast, in the *Zend-Avesta* "leprosy" is one of the "brands" that the evil god Angra Mainyu inflicted on mortals, but there does not seem to be any implication that the sufferer is to blame. See *Avesta. Vendidad,* Fargard, II.ii.29, 37; Brandenburg, *Priesterärtzte und Heilkunst*, 16, 33–36.

121. Pliny, *HN* 8.77.207; BT Kiddushin 49b; Preuss, *Biblical and Talmudic Medicine,* 345; Peter Schäfer, *Judeophobia,* 69, 74–75; Claudine Fabre-Vassas, *The Singular Beast,* 22–25, 49–51. Fabre-Vassas is dealing with much later sources.

122. Diodores Siculus, *Bibliotheca Historica,* 34/35, 1, 1f, in *Greek and Latin Authors on Jews and Judaism,* ed. Menahem Stern, vol. 1, no. 63; Justin, *Historia Philippicae,* bk. 36, epitoma 2,1ff, in ibid., vol. 1, no. 137; Lysimachus in ibid., vol. 1, no. 158; Apion in ibid., vol. 1, no. 164; Chaeremon, *Aegyptiaca Historiae* in ibid, vol. 1, no. 178; Tacitus, *Historia,* bk. 5, 3; Schäfer, *Judeophobia*, 15–33.

123. *Leviticus 1–16,* ed. and trans. Jacob Milgrom, chaps. 13 and 14; Harrington, *Impurity Systems*, 190–92.

124. Deut. 24:8, 28:27, Isa. 3:17. In Lam. 4:15 a sinful Israel is shunned and called "unclean, unclean"—phrasing that echoes the *meẓor'at's* stipulated warning to any who approach. In Lev. 14:34 God clearly takes credit for the existence of *ẓar'at* in the promised land—indeed, he actively put it there! On this, see Harrington, *Impurity Systems*, 191.

125. Num. 12; 2 Kings 15:1–5; 2 Chron. 26:19–23. Job's plague boils (*shiḥin*) came from Satan, but indirectly they were of divine agency. Job's friends certainly interpreted his afflictions as a punishment from God, though in the end God corrects them (Job 2:7). *Ẓara'at* could also be sent as a curse, as in the case of Gehazi, the servant of the prophet Elisha, and Joab and his descendants, 2 Kings 5 and 2 Sam. 3:29 respectively. Also see Preuss, *Biblical and Talmudic Medicine*, 335–39.

126. To give one example, the author of fragment 34, col. V of 4Q512 mentions the "impure disease" (מנגע הנדה) and asks for "mercy for all my hidden fault" (תחנן על כול נסתר[ו]ת אשמ[ה) (*Qumran Cave* 4, 3: 262–68). English text in *DSST*, 441. But see all

of 4Q512, pp. 441–42; and Joseph Baumgarten, "The Purification Rituals in *DJD* 7"; idem, "Zab Impurity"; Harrington, *Impurity Systems,* 81–83. Cf. 4Q512 with 1QH XIX. 18–22, XII. 3–6 (*DSST,* 353–54).

127. *Midrash Rabbah Leviticus,* meẓor'a 16:1, meẓor'a 17:3; *Midrash Tanḥuma',* tazir'a 16, meẓor'a 1–2; *Midrash Rabbah Numbers* 7:5, 16:4–5; *Midrash Rabbah Deuteronomy* 6:8–14 (composed between 450 and 800 C.E.; see Strack, 335); *Avot de Rabbi Natan,* chap. 9, version A, Hebrew, Schechter pp. 39–42, English, Goldin pp. 54–57; *Pesikta' Rabbati* 7:7, 14:9, 17:6; *Pirke de Rabbi Eliezer,* 53, 76Bi; BT Sanhedrin 97a. More texts are listed in Preuss, *Biblical and Talmudic Medicine,* 335–39, 342–45. Sometimes the fault is unspecified, as in *Midrash Tanḥuma',* meẓor'a 24b, 9. Cf. *Midrash Rabbah Genesis* 20:4 in which the serpent who tempted Adam and Eve is also punished with leprosy and scales. Also see Klawans, *Ritual Impurity and Sin,* 98–104.

128. Philo, *On Rewards and Punishments,* 25.143. English translation in *The Works of Philo*, updated ed., trans. C. D. Younge, 678. For Greek and an alternate translation, see Philo, *Works,* vol. 8, Loeb Classical Library.

129. Philo, *On the Unchangeableness of God,* XXVI.123–XXVIII.135.

130. Tertullian, *Adversus Marcionem* 4.9.6, in *Opera*, pt. 1, pp. 559–60. Also see *Contre Marcion,* ed. and trans. René Braun.

131. Isidore of Seville, *Quaestiones in Vet. Testamentum—in Leviticum,* chap. 16.5, in *PL* 83, col. 335. My thanks to Adam Knobler of The College of New Jersey for this reference.

132. Augustine of Hippo, *In Evangelium Joannis* 25.16 (on John 6:15–40) in *PL* 35, col. 1604. Translation in *Tractates on the Gospels of John 11–27,* trans. John W. Rettig.

133. Detienne, *Gardens*, 33.

134. Lactantius, [*De Ave Phoenice*] *The Phoenix,* in *Ante-Nicene Fathers*, 7:325.

135. Parker, *Miasma*, 296–307, 457–65.

136. Ibid., 357–58, 360.

137. Cicero, *Nat. D.,* 2:160; Pliny, *HN* 8.77.207.

138. Pliny, *HN* 28.6.31–33; Detienne, *Gardens,* 13–14.

139. Danielle Jacquart and Claude Thomasset, *Sexuality and Medicine in the Middle Ages,* 26–31, 35.

140. See discussion pp. 26–32 and notes above.

141. Zoroastrians occupied an intermediate ground between Jews and Pagans of the Roman Empire. Zoroastrians forbade certain vermin (*xrafstra*) and animals that were labeled "daevic," belonging to the evil side, avoided carrion, and had a variety of laws about the preparation of food, mostly designed to protect the holy fire from the pollution of the dead. Brandenburg, *Priesterärzte und Heilkunde,* 22, 69; Choksy, *Purity and Pollution,* 13, 103–4, 106. Regulations about animals that were permissible or forbidden to eat are far more elaborate even in early Judaism, and the Talmud elaborated on these rules. See Lev. 11: 3–21, 23–29, 31, 39–44; 22:5, 8; Deut. 14:9–29; and BT Menaḥot 101a–b as an example of later elaboration of one of these laws.

142. Eilberg-Schwartz, *Savage*, 122–26.

143. Ibid., 120–28. Klawans disagrees with the approaches of Douglas and Eilberg-Schwartz, protesting that they and others who seek a symbolic or metaphorical system

in the Bible do not define what they mean by "metaphor" and sometimes mistake "moral impurity" as metaphor (*Impurity and Sin,* 31–38). In some instances he makes good points. The idea that there is a deep underlying symbolic system on which impurity laws of any kind are based need not contradict the reality of impurity, whether metaphorical, moral, ritual, or a combination thereof.

144. Examples of this tactic are numerous. See especially BT Pesaḥim 49b, which I discuss in detail in chapter 2.

145. "Edom" or "Esau" substitute for any unequivocal reference to Rome, and other previous enemies of Israel are also denigrated as impure animals. See *Midrash Rabbah Genesis* 63:8, 12; *Midrash Tanḥuma',* toledot 65b 9; *Midrash Rabbah Leviticus* 13:5. Depending on the date of composition, when the midrashic texts use "Edom" or "Esau" it is difficult to ascertain whether the target was Pagan Rome or Christians, since eventually these terms came to refer to the Christian world.

146. Pliny, *HN* 8.77.207; BT Kiddushin 49b; Preuss, *Biblical and Talmudic Medicine*, 345; and my discussion of leprosy earlier in this chapter.

147. Tacitus, *Historiae* 5.3.1; 5.4.1–4, in *Tacitus in Five Volumes*. Schäfer, *Judeophobia*, 74–75. However, as Schäfer points out, most Pagan writers were fairly sympathetic to Jews' abhorrence of pork (66–81).

148. Compare with Fabre-Vassas's observations on this phenomenon for a later period in her *Singular Beast.*

149. For examples of Jews associating Romans with pigs, see *Midrash Rabbah Genesis* 63:8; *Midrash Rabbah Leviticus* 13:5. The remark in *Midrash Rabbah Leviticus* that swine are the worst of all impure animals is a reflection of the extent of Jewish antipathy to "Rome" but is also perhaps a retaliation against Pagan uses of the same type of slander against the Jews.

150. Also see Luke 6:43–45.

151. Matt. 6:9–11.

152. *Die Pseudoklementinen*, ed. Bernhard Rehm, 2d and improved edition, ed. Georg Strecker (Berlin, 1992), *II Rekognitionen in Rufins Übersetzung*, 3:1 (95–96). English translation in *Ante-Nicene Fathers*, 8:117.

153. Novitianus, in *Opera quae supersunt,* ed. G. F. Kiercks (Turnholt, 1972), *On the Jewish Meats*, 3, English translation in *Ante-Nicene Fathers*, 5:647; *Epître de Barnabé,* ed. Robert A. Kraft, trans. Pierre Prigent, 10.1–3c, 11a–11e (pp. 148–51, 156–59), English translation in *Ante-Nicene Fathers,* 1:143–44.

154. Noviatianus, *On the Jewish Meats*, 3, in *Ante-Nicene Fathers,* 5:647; *Epître de Barnabé*, 10:6a–7c.

155. Novitianus, 3.

156. Rabanus Maurus, *De rerum naturis*, bk. VII, chap. VIII, "De pecoribus et iumentis," in *PL*, cols. 206–7; Isaiah Shachar, *Judensau,* 4–8.

157. On Christian views of homosexual behavior, see Bernadette J. Brooten, *Same-Sex Love between Women,* although she is concerned with women rather than men. On Jewish views, see Michael L. Satlow, *Tasting the Dish.* Sexual relations between men in Roman society were widely practiced and tolerated, but it was not without highly negative connotations, especially for adult men who were passive partners. See Richlin, *Garden.*

158. Lev. 17:15. For this kind of imagery in the Jewish tradition, see chaps. 2 and 6.

159. On gender as a prime way for signifying power relationships, see Joan Wallach Scott, "Gender," esp. 44–50. See also Ross Shepard Kraemer, "The Other as Woman."

Chapter 2. **The Seeds of Rotten Fruit**

1. Accusations of impurity against other Jews, Pagans, and Christians or heretics have caused considerable confusion to scholars who have assumed that talmudic discussions of gentiles' uncleanness related only to their legal status. Adolf Büchler, "The Levitical Impurity of the Gentile in Palestine before the Year 70"; Gedalya Alon, "The Levitical Uncleanness of Gentiles." Cf. Moshe Halbertal, "Coexisting with the Enemy"; and Michael L. Satlow, *Tasting the Dish,* 83–118, 146–53, 203–22. Though not interested in impurity, Halbertal recognizes that more than simply legal issues are involved in the Mishnah's discussion of Pagans. Satlow shows that much of the sexual misbehavior and resulting impurity of which Jews accused Pagans was part of the anti-Pagan rhetoric of both the rabbis and the Hellenistic Jewish authors.

2. See *Polemic of Nestor,* 1:15–19, 30–35.

3. On rules about consumption and excreta as reflections of the social structures, tensions, and fears about disintegration of social boundaries, see Douglas, *Purity and Danger,* 11–16, 137–53; idem, *Natural Symbols,* 70–71; idem, *Implicit Meanings,* 53–56, 60–72.

4. Miller, *Anatomy,* 2, 24–37, and the psychological studies he cites there.

5. See the comments of Miller, *Anatomy,* x.

6. On language as violence, see Judith Butler, *Excitable Speech,* 1–52.

7. The relevant passages are Deut. 7:5, 25–26, and 12:1–3.

8. BT ʻAvodah Zara 45b.

9. כיצד היו קורין אותה בית גליא קורין אותה בית כריא עין כל עין קוץ (BT ʻAvodah Zara 46a). כריא literally means heap, pile, digging, ditch, or well.

10. Rebellion and physical warfare were another option that Jews occasionally chose. However, this course of action was dangerous and did not satisfy the daily need to assert the worth and even superiority (in the eyes of the Jews who were polemicizing) of the Jewish faith and culture over that of the Roman overlords.

11. Scott, *Domination,* 4–5. The public transcript is the official code of behavior and views established by those in power.

12. Ibid., 156. According to Scott, the knowledge must be enough to imbue a sense of dread among members of the dominant culture without being so specific as to cause reprisals.

13. As in the case of two differing Christian sects, or when the dominant group was not strong enough to pose much danger, as sometimes occurred in the early stages of Jewish-Christian relations.

14. Joseph Baumgarten, "Halakhic Polemics in New Fragments from Qumran Cave 4"; Jacob Neusner, *A History of the Mishnaic Law of Purities,* pt. 15, p. 10. For his discussion of Samaritans and Sadducees, see 63–67.

15. Identifying Christians in rabbinic literature is difficult because they were often called *minim* (heretics), a term that could also refer to various types of Jews whose beliefs the rabbis found objectionable. Much of the typology that was assigned originally to the Romans came to refer to the Christians, especially as Christianity became the dominant religion in the empire. Thus in the polemical literature Christians fall into both categories of Jew and non-Jew. On the identity of *minim* in rabbinic literature, see R. Travers Herford, *Christianity in Talmud and Midrash;* Alan Segal, *Two Powers in Heaven;* Lawrence H. Schiffman, *Who Was a Jew?* 51–78; M. Simon, *Verus Israel,* 179–201; Gruenwald, "The Problem of the Anti-Gnostic Polemic"; William Horbury, "The Benediction of the *minim* and Early Jewish-Christian Controversy"; Stuart S. Miller, "The *minim* of Sepphoris Reconsidered"; Simon C. Mimouni, "La *'Birkat ha-min'*"; Naomi Janowitz, "Rabbis and Their Opponents." This is but a small selection of the literature dealing with the issue.

16. שלו ושל עבודת כוכבים נידון מחצה על מחצה אבניו עציו ועפרו מטמאין כשרץ שנאמר שקץ תשקצנו ר"ע אומר כנדה שנאמר תזרם כמו דוה צא תאמר לו מה נדה מטמאה במשא אף עבודת כוכבים מטמאה במשא (BT 'Avodah Zara 47a–b).

17. The word *sheqeẓ* in the Bible is used to describe animals, usually small animals or insects, that are forbidden to be eaten (see Lev. 7:21; 11:10–13, 20, 23, 41–42; Isa. 66:17; Ezek. 8:10). *Shereẓ* is used in close connection with *sheqeẓ* in Lev. 11 and refers to both small sea creatures and insects. Most animals in this category are also impure. The noun *shereẓ* comes from the verb *sharaẓ,* normally translated as "to swarm or teem." See Lev. 11:10, 20, 23, 29, 31, 41–44. In verse 21 God indicates which *shereẓ* the people of Israel *may* eat. In this instance *shereẓ* means "insect." In Lev. 22:5 a person may be made unclean by touching a *shereẓ.* Also see Deut. 14:19.

18. Lev. 22:5–7.

19. Cf. BT Shabbat 82a–83b. See the discussion of this text and issue in Klawans, *Impurity and Sin,* 113–14; Christine Hayes, *Gentile Impurities and Jewish Identities,* 131–38. Both take this passage strictly as a discussion of ritual or moral impurity. Certainly it could, and some rabbis did understand the passage thus, but I would argue that the evocation of multiple types of impurity here had a polemical purpose as well.

20. שלא עמדו על הר סיני שבשעה שבא נחש על חוה הטיל בה זוהמא ישראל שעמדו על הר סיני פסקה זוהמתן עובדי כוכבים שלא עמדו על הר סיני לא פסקה זוהמתן (BT Shabbat 145b–146a). My translation differs slightly from Epstein's. He translates *mizuham* and *zuhamah* as "lustful" and "lustfulness," but the word means "dirty, filthy, polluted, contaminated," with a slight implication of bad smell. Cf. BT Shabbat 127b and Jubilees 4Q219 col. II, ll. 23–25 (4Q Jubilees d). Hebrew text in J. C. van der Kam and J. T. Milik, "A Preliminary Publication of a Jubilees Manuscript from Qumran Cave 4: 4QJub d (4Q219)," esp. 72. This text parallels Jubilees 9:21–22, in *Old Testament Pseudepigrapha,* 2:96. Unfortunately Hayes does not address this passage, for it has applicability to her idea of "genealogical impurity" (for an explanation of this term, see Hayes, *Gentile Impurities,* 7, 58–59). I do not, however, maintain that this passage is trying to establish the legal purity status of gentiles.

21. Cf. the comments of Andalusian laborers against their overlords noted by Scott, *Domination,* 130.

22. The authors of the Dead Sea Scrolls dealt with heretic (from their perspective) and rebellious Jews in much the same fashion as the rabbis treated Pagans in the passage above. See 1QS col. II, l. 25–col. III, ll. 1–6. Hebrew text: *Dead Sea Scrolls of St. Mark's Monastery,* ed. Millar Burrows, vol. 2, fasicule 2; English: *DSST,* 5; 1QM XIII, ll. 4–5 (*The War Scroll*). Hebrew text in Sukenik, *The Dead Sea Scrolls;* English: *DSST,* 107. That this and similar passages from Qumran documents were intended to insult outsiders and incite readers to shun them may be seen in the invectives that do not address purity. Calling one's religious opponents "sons" or "spirits" of *beli'al* was an insult and clearly marked these individuals as undesirable and antithetical to holiness, although the term has nothing to do with impurity. Speaking of their "filthy uncleanness" is an extension of the same insult. For an example of this common invective, see 1QS (*Rule of the Community/Manual of Discipline*) col. II, ll. 18–25 to col. III, ll. 1–26; and CD col. IV, ll. 13–17 (*Damascus Covenant*). Hebrew text: Schechter, *Documents,* 115; English: *DSST,* 35. On this issue, see Jörg Frey, "Different Patterns of Dualistic Thought in the Qumran Library."

23. The association of Pagans with corpse impurity is based on Ps. 106:28: "then they attached themselves to Ba'al of Pe'or and ate sacrifices offered to the dead." ויצמדו לבעל פעור ויאכלו זבחי מתים See BT 'Avodah Zarah 32b, 48b, 50a. However, in BT 'Erubin 30b the land of the gentiles is compared to a graveyard and its respective pollution. Cf. BT 'Avodah Zarah 75b; BT Pesaḥim 92a; Klawans, *Impurity and Sin,* 95–96, 134–35; Hayes, *Gentile Impurities,* 114–16, 199–204. These observations are part of very serious legal discussions about correct behavior around idols and their temples, the utensils of non-Jews, foreign lands, and the purification requirements for proselytes. Yet the law is also part of a polemical discourse. For a purely polemical text, see the spirited exchange in Mishnah 'Avodah Zarah 4.7 and its subsequent gemara BT 'Avodah Zarah 54b–55a.

24. בשר שנמצא ביד גוי מותר בהנאה ביד המין אסור בהנאה היוצא מבית ע"ז הרי זה בשר זבחי מתים (Tosefta Ḥullin 2.20–21). On this text, see Herford, *Christianity,* 177–78; Schiffman, *Who was a Jew?* 64–67.

25. שהן שקץ ונשותיהן שרץ ועל בנותיהן הוא אומר ארור שוכב עם כן בהמה (BT Pesaḥim 49b). My translation differs slightly from Epstein's.

26. Ibid.

27. Lev. 22:8.

28. Another type of pollution may be alluded to in the phrase "cohabits and has no shame." The authors of the text may have been hinting that the *'ammei ha-'areẓ* failed to observe the laws of *niddah.* Or they may have meant that the *'ammei ha-'areẓ* forced their wives into sexual positions that were frowned on in some rabbinic circles. On sexual acts, see BT Nedarim 20a–b; BT Pesaḥim 112b; BT Gittin 70a; BT Niddah 17a; BT Eruvin 100b; Biale's discussion of these texts in *Eros and the Jews,* 50–53.

29. For other instances of the rabbis attempting to create a rift between those whom they categorized as *'ammei ha-'areẓ* and themselves, see Mishnah Demai 2:2–3; BT Shabbat 63a; BT 'Avodah Zarah 39a.

30. Hayes notes that the concerns surrounding the *'ammei ha-'areẓ* are the same as or similar to those concerning interaction with gentiles (*Gentile Impurities,* 138–42).

I would not go so far as to say that rabbinic rules and comments about the potential impurity of either *facilitated* interactions between these two groups and rabbinic Jews. See *Gentile Impurities,* 142.

31. The view that the non-Jewish nations are violent is a common trope in midrashic texts.

32. Babylon is equated with the camel (*gamal*) based on a play on words in Ps. 137:8 between the words *gamal* and *gamul* (recompense). The rock badger alludes to Media and the hare to Greece. Cf. *Genesis Rabbah* 63:12 and *Midrash Tanḥuma',* toledot 65b 9.

33. ששקולה כנגד שלשתן רשב"ל אמר יתירה (*Midrash Rabbah Leviticus* 13:5). The text begins with Persia (פרס), playing on the similarity between the country's name and the verb "to have cloven hooves" (הפריס) and the noun "hoof" (פרסה) in Lev. 11:7. For the rest of the text it is Edom, not Persia, that is compared to a pig. Edom is also associated with sorcery and blasphemy in this text, both of which were linked to Jesus in the Jewish tradition. While not conclusive proof, the association of Edom, sorcery, and blasphemy supports the identification of Edom as a euphemism for the Chrisian empire in this instance. Cf. *Genesis Rabbah* 63:8.

34. See Jacob Neusner, "Midrash and Leviticus," 60–67. Making Edom the worst of the nations derives in part from the eschatological impetus in the author's choice to structure his comments around Daniel 7: the last must be the worst before ushering in the new age. Similar expectations were voiced in *Pesiqta' Rabbati.* See Joshua Schwartz, "Gallus, Julian and Anti-Christian Polemic in *Pesiqta Rabbati.*"

35. Yannai, *Maḥazor piyuṭe Rabi Yanai la-Torah vela-mo'adim.* Edom compared to pigs: vol. 1, poem 23 (Gen. 25:19), l. 34, p. 163; vol. 1, poem 30 (Gen. 32:4), l. 89, p. 199; vol. 2, poems for the holidays: Yom Kippur, ll. 131, 145–46, pp. 220, 121. Other nations as predatory animals: vol. 2, poems for the holidays: Yom Kippur, ll. 125–30, p. 219. Also see vol. 2, poem 135 (Deut. 2:2), l. 48, p. 127.

36. Depictions of Edom or Esau as violent abound in Yannai's poems. One particularly striking remark is הוא אהב דם לכן שמו אדום \ והוא עשו והוא אדום (He loved blood [*dam*] therefore his name is Edom / and he is Esau and he is Edom), *Yannai,* vol. 1, poem 30 (Gen. 32:4), l. 77, p. 198.

37. Edom eating dust like a snake: ibid., vol. 2, poem 121 (Num. 23:10), ll. 27–32, p. 100. The word for Edom here is דומה (*dumah*), meaning "suspect woman" or "prostitute" (the word can also mean "silence" or "grave" or refer to the angel of the dead). On the use of this word for Christians, see vol. 1, pp. 45–46.

38. Rabinovitz notes that the Samaritans *did* rebel and were brutally repressed, prompting Yannai to actively discourage his fellow Jews from such a course of action. *Yannai*, vol. 1, p. 50. Pleas to God to avenge the Jews for the wrongs inflicted by other nations, especially Edom, were quite common: *Yannai,* vol. 1, poem 30 (Gen. 32:4), pp. 191–201; vol. 2, poem 119 (Num. 20:14), pp. 81–89; vol. 2, poem 135 (Deut. 2:2), pp. 123–29; vol. 2, "Qedushta li-parshat zakhor," pp. 247–50. On the prevalence of requests for divine vengeance in *piyyuṭim,* see Yuval, "Ha-Naqam ve ha-qlilah," esp. 37–38.

39. BT Sanhedrin 97a: Morris Goldstein, *Jesus in the Jewish Tradition,* 133–34; Herford, *Christianity*, 207–10.

40. The diseases are *se'et* (שאת), *ṣapaḥat* (ספחת), *baheret* (בהרת). See Lev. 13, esp. 13:2.

41. Cf. *Midrash Rabbah Numbers* 14.10 in which the kings of Edom are rejected by God and afflicted with leprosy; and *Pesiqta'Rabbah* 17:8. On anti-Christian polemic in *Leviticus Rabbah,* see Burton L. Visotzky, "Anti-Christian Polemic in *Leviticus Rabbah.*" Visotzky did not discuss the passage in question, probably because it has no reference to Christian doctrinal disputes, as do most of the sections he examines. Also see chapters 8, "Midrash and Genesis," and 9, "Midrash and Leviticus," of Neusner, *What Is Midrash?* 52–67.

42. BT Sotah 47a and Sanhedrin 107b. The portion dealing with Jesus, disciple of R. Joshua b. Perahiah, has often been deleted. See Epstein's notes on both of these passages. Also see Herford, *Christianity,* 50–54, 97–103. Richard Kalman has demonstrated that in Babylonian sources Jesus was frequently portrayed as a rabbi or rabbinical student, in contrast to Palestinian texts: Kalmin, "Christians and Heretics in Rabbinic Literature of Late Antiquity."

43. See discussion and qualifications by Klawans, *Impurity and Sin,* 98–104.

44. Scott, *Domination,* 17–28, 36–44. Also see Kalman, "Christians and Heretics," and Janowitz, "Rabbis and Their Opponents," for the meanings and strategies behind debates between rabbis and *minim.*

45. The implication here is that the non-Jewish nations are more privileged than the Jews because they can sin without consequence whereas the Israelites cannot.

46. *Pesiqta'Rabbati,* 21:2, trans. Braude.

47. For examples of this kind of tactic in other cultures, see Scott, *Domination,* 36–44.

48. On the vulnerability of the "higher orders" to disgust and its role in the maintenance of hieararchy, see Miller, *Anatomy,* x, 8–9; on the relationship between disgust and contempt, see also 31–33. For similar tactics in rabbinic literature, see *Midrash Rabbah Genesis* 63:8 and Mishnah 'Avodah Zara 3.5. In the latter passage the focus is on Jewish use of Pagan baths. On this subject, see Liliane Vana, "Les rélations sociales entre juifs et païens à l'époque de la Mishna," esp. 160–67.

49. BT 'Avodah Zarah 47b.

50. כל המלעיג על דברי חכמים נידון בצואה רותחת The context of these remarks is that 'Onqelos bar Qaloniqos, the son of Titus's sister, wishes to convert to Judaism and calls a series of people up from the dead. Jesus, or "the sinners of Israel" (פושעי ישראל), is the last of these. Bala'am is another. His punishment is similar to that of Jesus: he dwells in boiling semen (זרע רותחת). The text begins in BT Gittin 56b and continues into BT Gittin 57a. See Epstein's notes to the passage and Herford, *Christianity,* 67–71.

51. Miller, *Anatomy,* 8–9. Miller himself takes the comment about sewage and wine barrels from Paul Rozin and April Fallon, "A Perspective on Disgust."

52. The following discussion focuses on rabbinic literature. For nonrabbinic examples, see CD col. V, ll. 6–15 (*Damascus Covenant*). Hebrew text in Schechter, *Documents of Jewish Sectaries,* 114, English: *DSST,* 36; *Psalms of Solomon,* 8:12, 20–22, in *The Old Testament Pseudepigrapha,* 2:659; Joseph L. Trafton, *The Syriac Version of the*

Psalms of Solomon, English trans. 88–89. According to his version, the relevant lines are 13, 23–26. Greek pp. 31, 33, Syriac pp. 30, 32.

53. בנות כותים נדות מעריסתן והכותים מטמאים משכב תחתון כעליון מפני שהן בועלי נדות והן יושבות על כל דם ודם (BT Niddah 31b). Cf. Tohoroth 5:8, in which Samaritan women are equated with non-Jews or someone so mentally impared she is incapable of adhering to impurity laws. Also cf. BT 'Avodah Zarah 46a, in which a rabbi is polluted because the spittle of a Pagan noblewoman flies upon him while they are talking.

54. BT Niddah 33b. The same passage contains a tale of a Sadducee who accidently spat on a high priest while conversing with him. The priest rushed home to his wife, who assured him that Sadducean women also showed their blood to the sages. The implied fear in this passage is that Sadduceans did not follow the same regulations regarding *niddah* as did the rabbis, so the Sadducean man would have transferred menstrual impurity to the high priest through his saliva because the Sadducean would have had intercourse with his wife who had not purified herself according to rabbinic standards. On this and related passages, see Satlow, *Tasting the Dish*, 96–99.

55. BT Bava Qama 38b; BT Niddah 33b; BT Shabbath 13a, 15b; BT Berakot 47b; BT Hagigah 18b, 24b–25a; BT Ḥullin 35a–b; and possibly Demai 2:3 and BT 'Avodah Zarah 69a, 75b. On the identity of the '*ammei ha-'areẓ* and the changing meaning of the term, see Peter Haas, "The *Am Ha'Arets* as Literary Character."

56. "Geneba said in the name of Rab: With all the things against which they decreed the purpose was to safeguard against idolatry" (וגניבא משמיה דרב אמר כולן משום עבודת כוכבים גזרו בהן). Here the text is referring not only to the prohibition against the daughter but also to various food prohibitions contained in the "eighteen decrees." On these, see the section on gentile impurity. Later the text focuses entirely on the potential of intimate relations with non-Jews to lead astray and quotes Deut. 7:4. For a discussion of these and parallel passages, see Satlow, *Tasting the Dish,* 92–118, esp. 100. Hayes disagrees, saying that rabbinic prohibitions regarding intermarriage were only partial and many of the more extreme comments may be later interpolations: *Gentile Impurities,* 145–63. I would argue, partial or not, the rabbinic sentiment is largely negative, something with which she herself seems to agree.

57. This is not to say that there was no social interaction among gentiles, Samaritans, and rabbis. That the rabbis made the effort to discourage it suggests that its occurrence was sufficiently frequent to disturb them. Also, the very stories that discourage interaction are told in the context of discussions, meals, and so on, among members of differing groups. For social interaction between Jews and Pagans in particular, see Vana, "Rélations sociales."

58. See the discussion in Mishnah 'Avodah Zarah 3.7 and BT Shabbat 82a–83a above. Also see "Letter of Jeremiah," verse 29 (cf. verses 10–11, 40–44, 68), which dates anywhere from ca. 317 B.C.E. to the Maccabean period (164–63 B.C.E.) and the historical introduction to the Letter of Jeremiah in *The New Oxford Annotated Bible with the Apocrypha,* ed. Herbert G. May and Bruce Metzger. The tactic of this author is to maintain that idols cannot be gods because Pagans do not treat them with respect. As part of his demonstration of the invalidity of idols, in verse 29 the writer points out that Pagan sacrifices may be touched by menstruants and parturients.

59. *Midrash Tanḥuma'*, meẓor'a 13. Also see *Midrash Rabbah Genesis* 63:8, which explains the verse in Gen. 25:25 "and the first (Esau) came forth red" (ויצא הראשון אדמוני) by explaining that Esau (here a euphemism for the Romans or Christians) issued first "So that he might issue and his stench (*siriuto*) with him. R. Abbahu said: Like the bath attendant who first scours the bath house and then washes the king's son; so also did Esau issue first so that he might come out and his stench come out with him" (למה יצא עשו תחלה כדי שיצא הוא ותצא סריותו עמו א"ר אבהו כהדין פרביטא שהוא משטף את בית המרחץ ואח"כ מרחץ בנו של מלך. כך למה יצא עשו תחלה ותצא סריותו עמו). The term *siriut* probably refers to the impure matter of the birthing woman's womb (which is closely related to *niddah*) since the explanation that follows speaks of a "house" that should be cleaned first. Had Esau not passed through this *siriut,* Jacob would have. However, given the literal meaning of the term, it is possible that the authors intended to suggest that Esau had a filth peculiar to him. *Genesis Rabbah,* in *Midrash Rabbah,* vols. 1–2, 63:8.

60. Versions of the *Toledot Yesu* stories exist as far back as the ninth century and continue to appear in a variety of forms as late as the nineteenth. The traditions contained in it may have existed in oral or written form prior to the ninth century. Certain aspects of the "anti-Gospel" such as Jesus' illegitimate birth, being the son of Pantera, and a magician who derived his powers from having engraved the divine name on his skin and led Israel astray appear in earlier literature. See BT 100b; Origen, *Contra Celsum* 1.28, 32–33; *Gospel of Nicodemus, Acts of Pilate* I.1, in *New Testament Apocrypha,* 1:451. On the history of the *Toledot* tradition, see Samuel Krauss, *The Jewish-Christian Controversy from the Earliest Times to 1789,* 1:12–15, esp. 12 n. 31; [*Toledot Jesu*] *Das Leben Jesu nach jüdischen Quellen,* 28–32; William Horbury, "The Trial of Jesus in the Jewish Tradition." On the talmudic and midrashic reports of Jesus' illegitimacy, status as a magician, and so on, see Herford, *Christianity,* 35–50, 304–6, 348–60; Dalman, *Jesus Christ,* 20–27.

61. The circumstances of Jesus' birth in these stories make him a *mamzer* (bastard) according to Jewish law. Indeed, *mamzer* is another common epithet for Jesus in the *Toledot* tradition and was known to Christian writers as well (see above).

62. *Das Leben Jesu,* Hebrew pp. 38–40, German trans. pp. 50–52, Hebrew 64–68, German trans. 83–88, Hebrew 118–19, German trans. 122–23. This portion of the *Toledot* was drawn from a third-century text, the *Kallah Rabbati. Kallah Rabbati,* chap. 2, sections 1 and 2. Hebrew edition: *Masekhet Kallah,* 190–92; English translation in *Minor Tractates.* On the dating of the text, see Strack, *Introduction to the Talmud and Midrash,* 249–50. On the text's relationship with the *Toledot Yesu,* see Herford, *Christianity,* 48–50. The similarity to the later *Toledot* stories is striking, although there is no indication that Jesus was meant specifically in the *Kallah Rabbati* passage. Herford and Goldstein argue that the *Kallah Rabbati* passage has nothing to do with Jesus. Goldstein, *Jesus,* 72.

63. Assuming that the tentative dating assigned to both texts is correct, the *Baraita de Niddah* was written after *Kallah Rabbati,* so one is not the source of the other. However, the precepts expressed in each derive from a similar worldview. For another example of the "inherited" tendency toward evil actions because of the defiling actions of the parents, this time in internal Jewish polemic, see *Psalms of Solomon,* 8:20–22. The

Psalms of Solomon are a set of poems originally written in Hebrew but that have come down to us in Greek and Syriac. For the dating and intended target of these poems, see Wright's introduction to the *Psalms,* 640–41. The link between the failings of the parents and those of the children is reinforced in *Kallah Rabbati* 1:16, which lists ten categories of people who are like *mamzerim* but are not classified as such legally. One of these categories is a *ben niddah.*

64. *Leben Jesu,* Hebrew 64–88, German trans. 88ff. For a list and discussion of the derogatory names assigned to Jesus in the *Toledot* tradition and in the medieval Hebrew Chronicles of the First Crusade, see Sapir Abulafia, "Invectives against Christianity," 66–72.

65. BT Sanhedrin 106a–b; BT Sanhedrin 107b; BT Soṭah 47a; BT Gittin 56b–57a. On this, see Herford, *Christianity,* 47–48, 50–54, 63–78, 97–103. Herford raises the possibility that Gehazi refers to Paul as opposed to Jesus in BT Soṭah (97–103). However, given that the tale of Gehazi is immediately followed by a parallel story in which the Gehazi-like character is explicitly listed as Jesus in uncensored manuscripts and editions of the Talmud, Gehazi probably refers to Jesus rather than Paul. See notes 3 and 11 in Epstein's translation of BT Soṭah 47a.

66. The biblical story of Balaam is contained in Num. 22–24. The tale of Gehazi may be found in 2 Kings 5. The image of these two became worse in later Jewish literature. For references, see n. 65 above.

67. *Pesiqta' Rabbati* 21:6 refers to a "whore's son" (ברא דזניתא) who argues that there are two gods (תרין אלהים). In his translation of the text Braude states in a footnote that "whore's son" refers to a heathen or renegade Israelite (*Pesiqta Rabbati: Discourses for Feasts, Fasts and Special Sabbaths,* 422 n. 24). However, I think it is equally or more likely that a Christian was meant here. In either case, this is another example of derogatory "renaming." Jesus was not the only one to whom this tactic was applied. The use of "Esau" and "Edom" for Rome and/or Christianity is an example of the same ploy. In BT Sanhedrin 43a the disciples of Jesus are given names that allow the rabbis to connect them to a verse of the Bible condemning each to death. Also see Kalmin, "Christians and Heretics in Rabbinic Literature of Late Antiquity," especially his concluding remarks.

68. Scott, *Domination,* 115–16, 152–54, 160–66.

69. Epiphanius, *Panarion,* 7.57.18, 12. The Greek for this portion of the *Panarion* has remained unavailable to me. The incident to which this passage is referring comes from the Gospel of John 9:1–8, in which Jesus cures a man born blind by spitting on the ground and rubbing the resulting clay on the man's eyes.

70. Pelikan, *Christian Tradition,* 1:52–55, 73–105, 174–206, 228–36, 244–77, 2:37–90; John Meyendorff, *Byzantine Theology,* 32–41, 151–59.

71. Arnobius of Sicca, *Adv. Nat.* 4.20; 3.10. The identification of intercourse as a bestial activity, a view that was not present in *De Natura deorum*, was common to a number of Christian writers, though many Pagan philosophical schools scorned excessive sex as a mark of lack of self-control. For sex as an animalistic behavior, see Brown's discussion of Tatian and the Encratics: *Body and Society,* 92–99. For a summary of

Greek and Roman philosophical views of sex, see Brundage, *Law, Sex, and Christian Society,* 12–21.

72. Parker (*Miasma,* 100–103) indicates that the Greeks do not seem to have viewed the menstruant as impure (the evidence is unclear), though purity from menstrual contamination was a requirement for entering a temple in late, non-Greek cults. No systematic study of Roman purity laws has been done, but see H. Wagenvoort, *Roman Dynamism,* 170–75. My thanks to Carlin Barton of the University of Massachusetts for this reference. Within the Christian world menstruating women were expected to abstain from the Eucharist up until the sixth century, when Gregory the Great overturned this custom. See Brown, *Body and Society*, 146, 433–34. Greek religious texts indicate that women and dogs who had recently given birth rendered those within the household impure. See Parker, *Miasma,* 48–50. Pregnant women were not impure themselves but at greater risk of contracting impurity, according to Parker (48). Cf. Wagenvoort, *Dynamism*, 196–98. Brundage has found evidence that pregnant and parturient women were impure according to the Christian tradition, but the sources he provides come from the early European Middle Ages, a little late for our purposes. See Brundage, *Law, Sex and Society,* 156–57.

73. Arnobius, *Adv. nat.* 4.23.

74. Origen, *Contra Celsum* and *Contre Celse* 4.14. My translation is based on Borret's French translation and his Greek edition.

75. οὐκ 'άν γὰρ 'απειλήφει 'ό δεδωκε πνέυμα 'ό θεὸς καταμεμολυσένον τῇ τοῦ σώματος πύσει (Origen, *Contra Celsum* 6.72). For matter as evil, see 4.65. It should be noted that Celsus expressly states that he is oversimplifying somewhat and that evil is difficult to explain.

76. Origen, *Contra Celsum* 6.73. Cf. Athanasius, *De Incarnatione* 44.1–5, and the anonymous fourth-century Latin disputation, *Consultationes Zacchie Christiani et Apolloni philosophi,* 9.1–2.

77. Eἰ δὲ καὶ τις των 'Ελληνων κουφο τὴν γνώμην 'ω'εν τοὶ 'αγαλμασιν 'ενδον οἰκειν νομίζειν του θεου πολλω καθαρώτερον εἰχε τὴν 'έννοιαν του πιστεύοντος 'ότι εἰς τὴν γαστέρα Μαριας της παρθένου εἰσεδυ τὸ θειον 'έμβρυόν τε 'εγένετο καὶ τεχθὲν 'εσπαργανώθη, μεστὸν αἵματος χορίου καὶ χολης καὶ των 'έτι πολλων τούτων 'ατοπωτερων (Porphyry, *Porphyrius "Gegen die Christen," 15 Bücher,* ed. Adolf von Harnack, 4.22 frag. 77. English translation in Joel Rembaum, "The New Testament," 41). Rembaum noticed the similarities between the passage from *Contra Celsum* cited above, this passage from Porphyry, and the *Nestor ha-Komer* text. For a new translation of all the Porphyry fragments, see *Porphyry's Against the Christians,* ed. and trans. R. Joseph Hoffman. For the passage cited above, see 86–87; however, Hoffman's rendering does not mention the chorion so I have preferred Rembaum over Hoffman. For further mention of Porphyry's aversion to the idea of Jesus' birth from a woman, see Augustine, *De civitate Dei* 10.28. Cf. *Consultationes Zacheri*, 10; the emperor Julian's remarks to Photius in *The Works of the Emperor Julian,* 3:188 (Latin), 189 (English); and to Origen, *Contra Celsum* 3.42.

78. Cicero, *Nat. D.* 1.44–49.

79. When speaking of God becoming "polluted" from incarnation and/or occupying the womb, both Celsus and Origin used various forms of the verb μυλύνω, "to sully, stain, defile, corrupt." Athanasius used the same vocabulary when he stated, "Therefore, neither when the Virgin gave birth did he suffer himself, nor when he was in the body was he polluted, but rather he sanctified the body" ('όθεν οὐδὲ της παρθένου τικτούσης 'έπασχεν αὐτός οὐδὲ 'εν σώματι 'ών 'εμολύνετο 'αλλα μαλλον καὶ τὸ σωμα 'ηγιαζεν). Athanasius, *De incarnatione*, 17.26. The noun most often used to designate the woman's (Mary's) belly in *Contra Celsum* is μιασμα, which, according to Parker, "is like dangerous dirtiness that individuals rub off on one another like a physical taint." He links the word to a variety of other Greek words, the primary meaning of which is "dirt" but which also imply religious danger (Parker, *Miasma,* 4–9, quotation on 8). Thus it would seem that from the outset the Greek vocabulary combined the concepts of impurity and dirtiness.

80. Origen, *Contra Celsum* 1.21 and 4.14.

81. Ibid., 4.15. Elsewhere in his disputation Origen vehemently denied that Jesus' visible body was in any sense God (2.9). However, Origen did state that the Son of God and Jesus formed a single entity after the incarnation, consisting of the Logos plus the body and soul of Jesus. On Origen, see Pelikan, *Christian Tradition,* 1:48–49.

82. Origen, *Contra Celsum* 1.69.

83. Athanasius, *Contra gentes; and De incarnatione,* 17.26–37. Cf. 43.28–34 and 54.14–15.

84. Robin Lane Fox, *Pagans and Christians,* 332; Henry Chadwick, *The Early Church,* 38–40; Pelikan, *Christian Tradition,* 1:73.

85. Plane nativitatis mendacium recusasti: ipsam enim carnem veram edidisti. Turpissimum scilicet Dei etiam vera nativitas. 7. Age iam, perora in illa sanctissima et reverenda opera naturae; inuehere in totum quod es; carnis atque animae originem destrue; cloacam voca uterum, tanti animalis, id est hominis, producendi officinam; persequere et partus immunda et pudenda tormenta et ipsius exinde puerperii spurcos anxios ludicros exitus: tamen, cum omnia ista destruxeris, ut Deo indigna confirmes, non erit indignior morte nativitas et cruce infantia et natura poena et caro damnatione. 8. Si vere ista passus est Christus, minus fuit nasci, si mendacio passus est, ut phantasma, potuit et mendacio nasci . . . . 9. Si veritas fuit, caro fuit, si caro fuit, natus est. (Tertullian, *Adversus Marcionem*, 3.11.6–9). Also see 1.8–9; 2.27.1–3, 3:8–9; Origen, [*Homeliae in Ezechelien*] *Homélies sur Ezéchiel,* 1.4. Cf. Tertullian's description of the beliefs of Apelles and Philomenes in *De Carne Christi,* in *Tertulliani Opera, pars II, Opera Montanistica,* 7–9; Pelikan's discussion of Tertullian and Irenaeus's reaction to Marcion and his followers' views of the incarnation in *Christian Tradition,* 1:75–81; Hippolytus, *Refutatio omnium haeresium,* 7.38; and Epiphanius, *Panarion*, 3.44.

86. Tertullian, *De Carne Christi*, 4.1.

87. This is evident in the passage from *Adversus Marcionem* cited above, where Marcion was portrayed as calling the uterus "cloacam" (literally, "sewer drain"). Birthing and that which follows was, among other things, *spurcos*, an adjective that can mean "dirty" or "impure." In *De Carne Christi,* the substantive of *spurcos* was used to designate the genitals, and the contents of the uterus were *foeda,* "filthy, foul, ugly and unseemly." *Foedus* can also mean "shameful" or "dishonorable." See definition II under

foedus in E. A. Andrews, *A Latin Dictionary*. Perhaps this is the definition Tertullian/ Marcion intended. However, given the various words for dirt in both passages and the fact that the text is describing the fluids of the uterus, not the genitals or the sexual act that might have some moral connotation, "filth" seems the more logical meaning in context. Both *Adversus Marcionem* and *De Carne Christi* used *immundus* or its substantive, *immunditia*: "impure, unclean, filthy."

88. Si aspernatus est illam ut terrenam et, ut dicitis, stercoribus infersam, cur non et simulacrum eius proinde despexit? (Tertullian, *Adversus Marcionem,* ed. Braun, 3.10.1). On Marion's belief that Jesus' body was but an appearance, also see Hippolytus, *Refutatio,* 10.19.

89. Epiphanius, *Panarion,* 2.31.7, 4 (Greek edition in *Opera,* ed. Karl Holl and Jurgen Dummer). Cf. similar remarks about the Valentinians by Tertullian, *De Carne Christi,* 19.5.

90. Tertullian insisted that to deny the carnal act did not necessarily entail denying the flesh entirely (*De Carne Christi,* 19.3–4). The descriptions of Valentinian views of the incarnation are partially confirmed in the *Gospel of Philip,* which has a strong Valentinian character. *The Gospel of Phillip,* trans. Wesley W. Isenberg, in *The Nag Hammadi Library*, 134.

91. Valentinian created two Christs, one spiritual and one psychic. The latter, who occupied a middle ground between the spiritual and material worlds, suffered, whereas the spiritual Christ remained untouched. On this, see Tertullian, *Adversus Valentinianos,* 27.2 (*Contre les valentiniens,* ed. Jean-Claude Fredouille). For the entire dual Christology, see 27.1–3.

92. Lane Fox, *Pagans and Christians,* 562–71.

93. Eugene Rose, *Die manichäische Christologie,* 57–60, 89–109.

94. Sometimes someone else dies on the cross, such as Simon of Cyrene or the son of Mary, who was different from the Christ. See Rose, *Die manichäische Christologie,* 125–26.

95. Ibid., 123–28. Also Jews are "murderers of God." See *Manichaean Psalmbook*, pt. II, Psalm 241, ll. 19–20, p. 43.

96. Augustine, *Contra Faustum,* 23.2, in *PL* 39, col. 467 (English translation by Richard Stothert, corrected digital edition, 1996).

97. Augustine, *Contra Faustum,* 20.11, *PL* 39, col. 376. For the importance of trees, especially fruit trees, in Manichaeism, see the end of this section in 20.11 col. 378, and also book 6.8, cols. 233–34. Likewise see Rose, *Die manichäische Christologie,* 93–94; and Jorunn Jacobsen Buckley, " Tools and Tasks," esp. 406.

98. Epiphanius, *Panarion,* sec. V.6, 9. The Greek text for this portion of Epiphanius has remained unavailable to me. However, Epiphanius is quoting from Hegemonius's *Acta Archelai,* ed. Charles Henry Beeson, 5.7. I have included both the Greek and Latin version below:

> καὶ μὴ μονογενῆ τὸν 'εκ τῶν κόλπων τοῦ πατρὸς καταβάντα Χριστόν, Μαρίας τινὸς γυναικὸς 'έλεγον εἶναι υιόν 'εξ αἵματος καὶ σαρκὸς καὶ τῆς 'άλλης δυσωδίας τῶν γυναικῶν γεγεννῆσθαι

et non unigenitum, qui de patris sinibus descendit Christum, Mariae cuiusdam mulieris esse dicerent filium, ex sanguine et carne a reliquis mulierum spurcitiis generatum.

99. *Manichaean Psalm-book,* φαλμοὶ Σαρακωτων, l. 16, p. 175; "A Psalm to Jesus," ll. 19–20, 25–26, p. 120; ll. 23–33, pp. 121, 245; ll. 22–27, p. 52.

100. Buckley, "Tools and Tasks," 400. He is quoting from the *Cologne Mani Codex* (*The Cologne Mani Codex,* trans. Ron Cameron and Arthur Dewey, and *Der Kölner Mani-Kodex,* ed. Ludwig Kuenen and Cornelia Römer), 80.23–81.13. The Elchasaites were a Jewish-Christian baptist group.

101. Buckley, "Tools and Tasks," 401.

102. "A Psalm to Jesus" (*Manichaean Psalm-book*, 120–23), part of which is cited above, is a difficult piece to interpret. Parts of it seem to imply that some power, an unidentified "they," in fact imprisoned the son of God in a womb (ll. 25–26, p. 120; ll. 19–25, p. 122). However, lines 31–32, p. 121—"Thy holy womb is the Luminaries that conceive thee / The trees and fruits in them is thy holy body"—bely such a literal interpretation. I would argue that this and similar psalms refer to the Christians who believed that the son of God entered Mary's womb courtesy of the Holy Spirit.

103. Epiphanius, *Panarion,* 5.33.3. For the Manichaean view that baptism was a sin against the water, see Buckley, "Tools and Tasks," 401–2.

104. Caro non purgamentis terrae, sed fetibus pascitur: terra vero purgamentis carnis, non fetibus fecundatur. Eligant quid sit mundius (Augustine, *Contra Faustum*, 6.8).

105. Augustine, *Contra Faustum*, 20.11, *PL* 39, cols. 376–77.

106. Terullian, *De Carne Christi,* 4:1–2.

107. Nestorius objected to the title "Bearer of God" (Theotokos) popularly assigned to Mary, mother of Jesus. He argued for the title "Bearer of Christ" (Christokos) instead and attempted to solve the problem of conjoining divinity and humanity in Christ by maintaining that the divine nature remained separate from Jesus' human one. Thus while the human nature of Jesus may have been ignorant, sorrowful, hungry, and so on, the divine aspect of Jesus remained untouched. Cyril of Alexandria objected vehemently to the title Christokos and insisted that the humanity of divinity within the person of Jesus formed a *single* hypostasis, thus making the Virgin Mary the bearer of God. The Church spent much of its energies in subsequent years attempting to devise a theology that compromised between these two positions. Monotheletism (the doctrine of one divine will in Christ) was one of the many failed compromises. On these conflicts, see Chadwick, *Early Church,* 194–212; Judith Herrin, *The Formation of Christendom,* 107–10, 206–11; Pelikan, *Christian Tradition,* 2:37–90. The iconoclastic debate also touched on issues of combining suffering humanity and divinity in Christ; however, I do not deal with this conflict. On iconoclasm, see Myendorff, *Byzantine Theology,* 42–53, esp. 49; Pelikan, *Christian Tradition*, 2:91–133. On later dualist heresies in the Byzantine empire, namely, the Paulicians and Bogomils, see *Christian Dualist Heresies in the Byzantine World c. 650–c. 1450,* ed. and trans. Janet Hamilton and Bernard Hamilton with Yuri Stoyanov.

108. On the Paulicians and Bogomils, see *Christian Dualist Heresies*, 1–55.

109. Petrus Siculus, *Historia Manicaeorum, PG* 104, cols. 1251/1252, 1267–70, 1291/1292, 1293/1294. Also see the translated passages in *Christian Dualist Heresies,* 81–84, 86.

110. Cyril of Alexandria, *Sur l'incarnation* 683c, in *Deux dialogues christologiques,* ed. and trans. G. M. de Durand, 202/203; Shahdost (fl. 751), the Nestorian bishop of what is now modern Teheran, compared the Monophysites to "swine" who corrupted the "vineyards of the divine scriptures": *A Nestorian Collection of Christological Texts,* 2: 6; Maximus, Confessor, *Opuscules théologiques et polémiques,* trans. Emmanuel Ponsoye, XV, p. 211, also in *PG* 91, cols. 179/180; Leontius Byzantinus, *Against the Nestorians and the Eutychians, PG* 86, cols. 1319/1320; Petrus Siculus, *History, PG* 104, cols. 1239/1240, 1241/1242, 1251/1252, 1267/1268–1269/1270, 1291/1292, 1293/1294, 1299/1300, 1303/1304, partially translated in *Christian Dualist Heresies,* 66–67, 71, 81, 89, 90; Theophanes, *Chronographia,* ed. C. de Boor, 1:501, trans. in *Christian Dualist Heresies,* 60 (Theophanes lived ca. 760–817); tenth-century abjuration formula: *Christian Dualist Heresies,*104–5; Euthymius, Zigabenus, *Panoplia,* in *Opera omnia, PG* 130, Titulus 27, cols. 1289/1290–1291/1292, 1301–2; trans. in *Christian Dualist Heresies,* 181, 188.

111. See, e.g., *Cartulaire de l'abbaye de Saint-Père de Chartres,* ed. M. Guérard, 1:111–12, translation in *Heresies of the High Middle Ages,* trans. Walter L. Wakefield and P. Evans, 78–79.

112. *Christian Dualist Heresies,* 117. Also see p. 127, where Cosmas states that the Gospel suffers at the hands of heretics "like 'a gold ring in a swine's snout' (Prov. 11:22); so sweet food becomes deadly." Cf. the remark of the Nestorian bishop Shahdost cited in n. 110 above.

113. Theophylact Lecapenus, *Letter to Tsar Peter of Bulgaria on the Bogomils* ("L'epistola sui Bogomili del patriarca constantinopolitano Teofilatto," in *Mélanges Eugène Tisserant,* 2:88–91); and Euthymius of the Periblepton, *Letter,* trans. in *Christian Dualist Heresies,* 99, 157 respectively. On belief in werewolves in this region, see John V. A. Fine, *The Early Medieval Balkans,* 163.

114. See the tenth-century abjuration for repentent Paulicians, Cosmas's discourse against the Bogomils, and the letter of Euthymius of the Periblepton in *Christian Dualist Heresies,* 106, 129, 149 respectively. For Euthymius, see G. Ficker, *Die Phundagiagiten.* Abjuration texts in "Les sources grecques pour l'histoire des Pauliciens d'Asie Mineur. IV. Les formules d'abjurations."

115. Agapius, *Kitāb al-'Unwan,* ed. and trans. Alexandre Vasiliev, pt. II, fasc. 2 (pp. 439–40); Euthymius of the Periblepton in *Christian Dualist Heresies,* 149. Both texts are rather late: Agapius was writing in the tenth century and Euthymius in the eleventh. On Agapius, see Parkes, *Conflict,* 293. More common than degradation through human waste were violent deeds against holy objects. Jews are portrayed as reenacting the crucifixion. See Pseudo-Athanasius, *Sermon on the Miracle of Beirut,* in *PG* 28, cols. 797/798–805/806; *Le synaxaire Arménien de Ter Israel,* ed. and trans. G. Bayan, 104–6; Pseudo-Cyril, *Sermon sur la Pénitence attribué à Saint Cyrille d'Alexandrie,* ed. and trans. P. M. Chaine, 6: 492–528. In this last text a Manichaean woman also stabs the host. The story of Jews attacking a holy image only to have water and blood

pour out from it came to be known in the Latin West through Sigebert Gemblacensis (ca. 1030–1112), *Chronica,* ed. Ludwig C. Bethmann, 333. On these texts, see Parkes, *Conflict,* 291–97. In these stories the heretics or Jews usually convert as a result of the miraculous bleeding and healing power of the holy object. Parkes argues that these tales were part of pro-icon propaganda in the Eastern Christian world, the logic being that if unbelievers were affected and converted by the power of icons or the host, then their power must be true.

116. Without confirmation from sources originating from the various groups so accused, we cannot ascertain for certain whether these reports are in any way true. Clearly the Christian writers of these reports presented their interpretations of these activities to suit their beliefs and agendas, and they may have invented them entirely. However, before completely dismissing these tales as the fancies of Christian polemical imagination, one needs to consider that given the cultural meaning assigned to impurity in general and to excrement in late antiquity and the early Middle Ages, urinating in a church or on an icon or washing the "pollution" of baptism from a child would have been a symbolically consistent and effective way to express rejection of the majority faith. Also the suggestion in BT 'Avodah Zarah 47b to create a privy out of an idol's abandoned temple indicates that such behavior occurred to some minority groups.

117. See, e.g., Nestorius, *The Sermons of Nestorius,* sermon 9, p. 39.

118. Ibid., sermon 20, p. 100.

119. Ibid., sermon 8, pp. 23–25; sermon 9, pp. 27–29, 36–38; sermon 10, pp. 42–53; sermon 27, pp. 114–19; Nestorius, *The Bazaar of Heracleides,* I.i.11–39–42, II.ii, pp. 29–33, 91–95. His adherents followed suit. See *Nestorian Collection,* 4–6, 25–31, 46–47, 57–61, 86, 92, 98–99, 114.

120. Cyril of Alexandria, *Sur l'incarnation,* 679e, 682d–684e, 692a–697a, 698a–e, 700d–701d, 712d–713a, pp. 194/196, 202–9, 232–47, 250–53, 258–61, 296/297; *Le Christ est Un,* 716d–717c, 719e, 721c–722b, pp. 310–13, 320/321, 326/327. Both treatises are in *Deux dialogues christologiques.*

121. *Christ est Un,* 717b, pp. 312/313. Cf. the polemic of the Monophysíte bishop of Antioch, Severus (465–538) against Julian Harlicarnassus (d. after 518). The problem of divinity suffering thirst, hunger, the need for sleep, or pain is at the center of the discussion, but the uncleanness of the human body is not. Severus Sozopolitanus, *La polémique anti-julianiste,* 2A:10–12, 17, 29, 36–37, 63–64, 82–84; 2B:172–73, 268; 3:10–11, 23–25, 64. On Severus and Julian, see Chadwick, *Early Church,* 206–7.

122. See, e.g., John of Damascus, *Against the Heresy of the Nestorians and the Eutychians, PG* 95, cols. 189/190, 221–24; Leontius Byzantinus, *Aganst Nestorians and Eutychians, PG* 86, cols. 1325–30, 1335/1336; Petrus Siculus, *Sermon II against the Manicheans, PG* 104, cols. 1337–40. Also see John Myendorff's discussion in *Byzantine Theology,* 146–47.

123. Severus, *La polémique anti julianiste,* 2A:130–36, 2B:266–67, 126.

124. Petrus Siculus, *History,* in *PG* 104, cols. 1249–52, 1283/1284; idem, *Sermons, PG* 104, cols. 1305–14, 1317/1318, 1323/1324, 1331–46. Peter's *History* is also partially translated in *Christian Dualist Heresies,* 69, 72. Also see John of Damascus, *Dispute of an Orthodox with a Nestorian, PG* 96, cols. 1319–36; Peter the Higoumenos's

abridgment of Peter of Sicily in *Christian Dualist Heresies,* 94; a tenth-century abjuration ceremony for "Manichaeans" in *Christian Dualist Heresies,* 103, which anathematizes anyone who "says that the Lord brought his body from above and made use of the womb of the mother of God like a bag"; Euthymius Zigabenus's *Panoply, PG* 130, Titulus 24, cols. 1215/1216–1219/1220, partially translated in *Christian Dualist Heresies,*173, 186. On these texts, see *Christian Dualist Heresies,* 1–55; Pelikan, *Christian Tradition,* 2:216–27. For passing mention of Manichaeans, see Pseudo-Leontius Byzantinus, *On the Sects, PG* 86, cols. 1213/1214; Théodore de Mopsueste, *Les homélies catéchétiques,* homélie 5:8, p. 111; Nestorius, *Bazaar of Heracleides,* I.1, p. 8; Severus of Antioche, *La polémique anti julianiste,* 2B:173.

125. Novatianus, *De Trinitate,* in *Opera,* ed. G. F. Diercks, 11–78; trans. in *Ante-Nicene Fathers,* 5:611–44.

126. Ephraem the Syrian, *S. Ephraim's Prose Refutations of Mani, Marcion and Bardaisan.* However, Ephraem is aware that these groups find aspects of physical existance "foul." See, e.g., "First Discourse to Hepatius," 1:xxi–xxiii (English translation).

127. Averil Cameron, "Sacred and Profane Love," 17.

128. Ibid., 16–17. While Augustine may have a lot to answer for, the writings of Jerome were also key in transmitting the late antique view of impurity, filth, and the sexual female body as interconnected concepts. The ninth-century western European writers Radbertus, Ratramnus, and Paul Alvarus all drew on Jerome.

129. Debent igitur intueri, qui hoc putant, solis hujus radios, quem certe non tanquam creaturam Dei laudant, sed tanquam Deum adorant, per cloacarum fetores et quaeque horribilia usquequaque diffundi, et in his operari secundum naturam suam, nec tamen inde aliqua contaminatione sordescere, cum visibilis lux visibilibus sordibus sit natura conjunctior; quanto minus igitur poterat pollui verbum Dei non corporeum neque visibile de femineo corpore casto utique, et mundissimo, atque singulariter glorioso ubi humanam carnem suscepit . . . ? (Hildefonsis of Toledo, *De virginitate perpetua SS. Mariae adversus tres infideles,* chap. 44, *PL* 96, col. 131). Cf. col. 97, in which Hildefonsis equates his human condition to earth, corruption, putrefaction, and worms.

130. Of course, the Greek- and Syriac-speaking world always had access to the foundations of such associations since they continued to study the Greek medical texts and had greater access to them than did their coreligionists in the West, who were limited to Latin. See Temkin, *Hippocrates,* 228–40; and articles in *Symposium on Byzantine Medicine,* ed. John Scarborough; Monica Green, "The Transmission of Ancient Theories of Female Physiology and Disease through the Early Middle Ages." Refuting the polluting qualities of the womb for God by the analogy of sunlight shining through excrement was extremely common both in late antiquity and in the late Middle Ages. See *Porphyry's against the Christians,* 87 n. 67; Jacob b. Reuben, *Milhamot ha-shem,* 15; *Jewish-Christian Debate,* 350–54.

131. Leo Scheffczyk, *Das Mariengeheimnis in Frömmigkeit und Lehre der Karolingerzeit,* 58–98; on Hildefonsis, see 60–61. Priscillian, from Spain, was denounced as a "Manichee" because of his dualistic theology in 380 (Chadwick, *Early Church,* 169–70). Authors from this period usually emphasized the earthly natures of Mary and Jesus by glorifying the daily, human relations of the mother and child. Scheffcyzk,

Mariengeheimnis, 122–36, 150. Scheffczyk indicates that Carolingian authors normally depicted Mary as a heavenly personage (123).

132. Ratramnus, *Liber de Nativitate Christi, PL* 121, cols. 81–102, esp. cols. 86, 90–93, 98, 101–2; Paschasius Radbertus, *De partu virginis,* 50–54, 58–61, 66, 72–76. Also in *PL* 96, cols. 210–12, 215–17, 220, 224–28 [Pseudo-Hildefonsis (Fulbert of Chartres) *Sermones, PL,* 96, *Sermo VIII,* col. 270; [Pseudo-Hildefonsis] (identity unknown) *Sermo X,* cols. 273–74, *Sermo XI,* col. 273, *Sermo X111,* col. 282. On the attribution of the sermons, see the manuscript contents in Ann Matter's introduction to Radbertus, 25. Paschasius Radbertus, *PL* 120, cols. 1372, 1385. In the past, many of Radbertus's works have been attributed to Hildefonsis of Toledo. See Scheffcyzk, *Das Mariengeheimnis,* 39, 46–47, 53–56; Matter, introduction, 16–39; R. Maloy, "The Sermonary of St. Ildephonsus of Toledo." Cf. Ambrosius Autpertus (d. 784), who also discussed the corporeality of Mary: *In Purificatione Sanctae Mariae,* 3, in Ambrosius Autpertus, *Opera,* part 3, 986–87; and Scheffcyzk, *Das Mariengeheimnis,* 127–37.

133. [T]urpe fuisse Dei Filio per vulvam processisse (Ratramnus, *De nativitate domini,* chap. 3, *PL* 121, col. 85). Also see chap. 1, col. 83. In cols. 83–84 he scolds his readers for assuming that Christ could have been born in any way other than the usual human one. He cites the myth that serpents' young chew their way through their mothers' sides, or that weasels conceive through the mouth and give birth through the ear—are these more appropriate for the Redemptor?

134. Radbertus, *De partu virginis,* 47–49, 54, 56, 58–62, 66, 72–74, 75–79 (or *PL* 96, cols. 207, 209, 212, 213, 215–17, 220, 224–25, 227–29); idem, *PL* 96, *Sermo III,* col. 257. For other authors who did not believe that Mary required ritual purification after childbirth, see Scheffcyzk, *Das Mariengeheimnis,* 143. Many of the examples he cites belong to the Byzantine milieu.

135. Scheffczyk, *Das Mariengeheimnis*, 145; Ratramnus, *De nativitate christi*, cols. 97–98; Radbertus, *De partu virginis*, 47, 66 (*PL* 96, cols. 207, 220); Eusebius of Caesaria, *Adversus Helvidium de Mariae Virginitate Perpetua*, in *PL* 23, cols. 193–216, esp. cols. 212, 214. Radbertus was also familiar with the dispute between Cyril of Alexandria and Nestorius; see 50–51, 83 (*PL* 96, cols. 210, 232).

136. For a selected listing of manuscript contents and the manuscript history of Radbertus's *De partu virginis,* see Matter's introduction, 16–36.

137. *Christian Dualist Heresies,* 10–24; George Ostrogorsky, *History of the Byzantine State,* 160–61, 221–22, 237.

138. *Christian Dualist Heresies,* 25–29; Fine, *Early Medieval Balkans,* 171–72.

139. *Christian Dualist Heresies,* 26–36; Ostrogorsky, *History,* 256–69, 360.

140. John C. Lamoreaux, "Early Eastern Christian Responses to Islam"; Cohen, *Under Crescent and Cross,* 52–74.

141. Lamoreaux, "Early Eastern Christian Responses." On the importance of political dominance in Byzantine Christian self-understanding, see David M. Olster, *Roman Defeat, Christian Response and the Literary Construction of the Jew.*

142. A. Abel, "La polémique damascénienne et son influence sur les origines de la théologie musulmane." Of course, there is the problem of language. Some Christians chose to write in Arabic, and Abel suggests that Muslim familiarity with philosophical

argumentation and Christian Scripture came from Christian converts to Islam. On conversion to Islam in the early period, see Richard Bulliet, *Conversion to Islam in the Medieval Period.*

143. David Thomas, in Warraq, *Anti-Christian Polemic in Early Islam,* 3. 'Abbasid rule begins with the accession of al-Saffah in 750 C.E.

144. Muslim purity laws are very similar to Jewish ones. However, they differ in a number of important respects, for example, leprosy and corpses are not unclean according to Islamic law. Menstruation is, though the mode of transmitting this impurity is not identical to that in Jewish law. See Hava Lazarus-Yafeh, "Some Differences between Judaism and Islam as Two Religions of Law"; A. Kevin Reinhart, "Impurity/No Dagger." I suspect that Reinhart's conclusion that Muslims did/do not find ritual impurity troubling or problematic but rather a barrier to performing ritual duties that can be overcome simply by the requisite ablutions is true but might be profitably nuanced by examining impurity in nonlegal texts. The same conclusions may be reached regarding early Jewish laws on genital fluids, but the most colorful discussions of these fluids are often not in legal texts. Menstruation, according to Muslim tradition, prevented women from attaining the highest spiritual levels, such as prophecy. The exceptions to this, Mary, mother of Jesus, and Fatima, are sometimes portrayed as not menstruating. Jane Smith and Yvonne Haddad, "The Virgin Mary in Islamic Tradition and Commentary"; Barbara Freyer Stowasser, *Women in the Qur'an,* 59–60, 77–80; Denise L. Soufi, "The Image of Fatima in Classical Muslim Thought," 152, 157–58, 165, 169–70.

145. Etan Kohlberg, "The Position of the *walad zina* in Imami Shi'ism." On this type of polemic, also see Soufi, "Image of Fatima," 113–14.

146. Muslims do not believe that Jesus in fact died. *Qur'an*, Sura 4:157. However, medieval Muslims were quite willing to use the fact that the Christians did believe Jesus was crucified and laid in a tomb to argue that Jesus endured things inappropriate for God. See, e.g., Abu Bakr Muḥammad ibn aṭ-Ṭayyib al-Baqillānī, *Kitāb at-Tamhīd,* 97–98. Al-Baqillānī died in 1013. On this text, see A. Abel, "Le chapitre sur le christianisme dans le 'Tamhīd' d' al-Bâqillānī."

147. و امله صديقة كانا يا كلن الطعام انظر كيف نبين لهم الايت ثم انظر انى يؤفكون ("And his mother was a woman of truth. They both ate food. Behold how We show men clear signs and behold how they wander astray"). I am using Aḥmed Ali's translation of the *Qur'an* 5:75. Ali alters the line slightly: "They both ate the (same) food (as men)." However, this interpolation is unnecessary and obscures the meaning slightly: the proof is not that Mary and Jesus ate the same kind of food as everyone else and thus are mortal, not divine, but rather that they ate at all.

148. Καὶ 'εάν σοι είπη, Πῶς κατῆλθεν 'ο Θεὸς εἰς κοιλίαν γυναικός (John of Damascus, *Disputatio Saraceni et Christiani,* in Daniel Sahas, *John of Damascus on Islam,* 150/151). John of Damascus has altered Sura 3:42 to make it support Christian doctrine more than it does. The text does say that God purified and chose Mary over the women of the nation, but it does not say that the Spirit of God and the Word descended into her. It should be noted, however, that the authorship of the *Disputatio* has been questioned. Sahas does not commit himself absolutely to the text's authenticity, but the evidence he presents strongly supports it. See Sahas, 99–102. Adel Théodore

Khoury, *Les théologiens byzantins et l'Islam,* 68–82. Cf. the *Disputatio* with a ninth-century Christian author, Ammār al-Baṣrī, *Kitāb al-burhān,* 57, 174–75. This Nestorian Christian was one of the first to set his arguments for Christianity into Arabic. See Hayek's introduction, 33–41.

149. In the seventh and eighth centuries, two different Christian authors of disputations with a Jew felt compelled to defend their belief that Jesus took corporeal form, was born of a woman, and ate, drank, and slept. Sargis Istunaya de-Gusit, *The Disputation of Sergius the Stylite against a Jew,* 7.1, pp. 16–17. Gregentius, *Disputatio cum Herbano Judaeo, PG,* 86, cols. 657/658. This author was also very eager to defend the purity of Mary's body and genital blood; see cols. 671/672, 709/710, 763/764. On this text, see Olster, *Roman Defeat,* 138–57. Cf. both texts with the remarks by Priscus the Jew in Gregory of Tours, *The History of the Franks,* 6.5, p. 330.

150. A. Abel, "La lettre polémique 'd'Aréthas' à. l'émir de Damas," translation of this passage on p. 359. On this text, also see Khoury, *Théologiens,* 219–34. Similar objections are raised in Arthur Jeffery, "Ghevond's Text of the Correspondence between 'Umar II and Leo III," relevant passages on 278, 318–20; Leo VI, the Wise, *Ad Omarum Saracenorum Regem de fidei Christianae veritate et mysteriis et de variis Saracenorum haeresibus et blasphemiis,* in *PG* 107, cols. 319, 321; on this text, see Stephen Gero, *Byzantine Iconoclasm during the Reign of Leo III,* 44–47; Dominique Sourdel, "Un pamphlet musulman anonyme d'époque 'abbaside contre les chrétiens," relevant passages on pp. 13–14 (French trans.), 27 (Arabic); al-Jāḥiẓ, *Al-Mukhtār fī-al-radd 'ala al-Naṣārā,* 33 (sec. 7, "ĝumūḍ qaulhum fī al-masīḥ"); al-Baqillānī, *Kitāb at-Tamhīd,* 95–97.

151. Abū 'Isā al-Warrāq, Yaḥyā ibn 'Adī, *De l'Incarnation,* Arabic: vol. 1, pp. 17, 46–47, 67; French trans.: vol. 2, pp. 13–14, 39, 57; Nicetas Byzantinus, *Refutation of the False Book which Muhammad the Arab Wrote, PG* 105, cols. 739/740; Theodore Abu Qurra, *Opuscula, PG* 97, cols. 1513/1514, 1537/1538, 1539/1540. See also *Schriften zum Islam: Johannes Damaskenus and Theodor Abu Qurra.* The tone of all of these authors' discussions, whether they are Muslim or Christian, is very much like that of the internal Christian polemic about the incarnation examined earlier in this chapter. Abū 'Isā Muḥammad b. Harun b. Muḥammad al-Warrāq (fl. 9th century) probably derived much of his knowledge from having carefully studied the polemic and theology of the different Christian denominations. On Muslim knowledge of and dependence on Christian argumentation, especially that which came out of Damascus, see Abel, "Polémique damascénienne." On Nicetas of Byzantius and Theodore Abu Qurra, see Khoury, *Théologiens,* 110–62 and 83–109 respectively.

152. One writer protested that "He (Jesus) was nursed for two years, comported himself and grew year by year like any child, crying, sleeping, eating, drinking, knowing hunger and thirst all his life" (Sourdel, "Pamphlet musulman," 13 [French trans.], 27 [Arabic]). Cf. *Disputatio Saraceni et Christiani,* attributed to John of Damascus, in Sahas, *John of Damascus on Islam,* 152/153, and Abū 'Isā al-Warrāq, who challenged Christians because they "asserted it (the word) was a small confined body in flesh, bone, nerve, and vein in the flowing of blood and passage of food and drink and the organs which contain them" (*De l'incarnation,* Arabic, p. 84). My translation

differs slightly from Petti's. His translation is as follows: "ils affirment (du Verbe) qu'il est un corps infime, contenu et habitant dans la chair, les os, les nerfs, et les veins, dans les vaisseaux sanguins et les voies d'alimentation et de boisson et là où ils se déposent" (p. 71).

153. John of Damascus, "Heresy of the Ishmaelites," 136–37; *Risalat al-Kindi,* trans. Tartar, 148–53; Theophanes, *Chronicle,* trans. Turtledove, 35; Eulogius, *Memoriale Sanctorum,* in *CSM,* 2:376, 398–99; Tolan, *Saracens,* 54, 61–62, 86, 93, 238.

154. "canis impurus," "habitaculum spirituum immundorum," "sordium cloaca." Eulogius, *Memoriale Sanctorum,* 376; Tolan, *Saracens,* 93.

155. Abel, "Lettre polémique," 368–69; Georgius Hamartolos, *Chronicon breve,* bk. IV, chap. 235, in *PG* 110, cols. 867/868. On Hamartolos, see Khoury, *Théologiens,* 180–86. Cf. the later remarks of Ramon Lull, *Libre del gentil e los tres savis,* trans. Bonner, *Doctor Illuminatus,* bk. 4, p. 160; Tolan, *Saracens,* 266–67. On Jewish suggestions that Muslim's paradise was filled with excrement and the meaning of paradisiacal food to Muslims, see Muslim, *Ṣaḥiḥ Muslim bi-sharh al-Nawawi,* "Jana" 51 no. 18; Geert Jan van Gelder, *God's Banquet,* 22–23. Obviously this accusation on the part of Jews was not to defend the doctrine of the incarnation.

156. For example, as with Jews and Christians, that a corpse have no smell, or smell pleasant and/or fail to decompose was a sign of divine favor or "sainthood." Josef Meri, *The Cult of Saints among Muslims and Jews in Medieval Syria,* 25–26, 159. Most of Meri's sources date from a later period; however, these attitudes seem to have been fairly old. Houris, the women of paradise, are sweet-smelling and do not menstruate. Faṭima is compared to them, and she and her grave are fragrant, as is the Prophet Muhammad. Soufi, "Image of Fatima in Classical Muslim Thought," 163–64, 166.

157. Van Gelder, *God's Banquet,* 23.

158. See, e.g., "La lettre polémique d'Aréthas," 363. *Risalat al-Kindi,* in *Dialogue islamo-chrétien sous le Calife al-Ma'mun (813–834),* 166; Eulogius, *Memoriale Sanctorum,* in *CSM,* 2:414; Norman Daniel, *Islam and the West,* 104–6; Tolan, *Saracens,* 62, 92–93, 125, 140, 142, 150, 168, 181; Tolan, "Un cadavre mutilé."

159. *Qur'an* 2:173; 5:3; Bukhari, *Ṣaḥiḥ,* 1.9.490; 3.29.5; 3.36.482; 3.39.515–16; 4.54.448, 450; 5.59.338; 7.67.389, 391; 7.72.829; Muslim, *Ṣaḥiḥ,* 002.0549–51; 007.2717–31; 010.3809–11.

160. Tolan, "Un cadavre mutilé."

161. Stroumsa and Lasker, introduction to *Polemic of Nestor,* 1:15–19.

162. תקול אן לי אלאה סכן פי אלאחשא ופי וסך אלחיצה וציק אלבטן (*Polemic of Nestor,* para. 5 [Judeo-Arabic 2:28; English 1:98]). For a parallel passage in the Hebrew version, see Hebrew 2:95, English 1:98.

163. For instances of the use of דנס in the *Qiṣṣat Mujādalat,* see *Polemic of Nestor,* paras. 74, 76 (Judeo-Arabic 2:51, English 1:67); para. 111 (Judeo-Arabic 2:62, col. 1; English 1:73).

164. תעבד אלאה סכן פי אלרחם פי דנס אלחיצה (*Polemic of Nestor,* para. 82 [Judeo-Arabic 2:54, col. 1; English 1:68]).

165. פחמלתה פי ציק אלבטן ואלטלמה ואלדנס ואלחיץ תסעה אשהר (ibid., para. 74 [Judeo-Arabic 2:51, English 1:67]).

166. ואמא זעמכם בדימאר אללאהות ודימאר אלנא[סו]ת, ואנה צעד אלי אלסמא בדימאר אלנאסות וא[ללאהות תא]מין גיר נאקצין, פאסתוא בדלך מע אלאב עלי אלער[ש], פאדא כאן אלאמר כדלך פקד אסתוא עלי אלערש אלכוף ואלפזע ואלהול ואלגזע ואלנום ואלגוע ואלעטש ואלתג[ויט], לאן דימאר אלנאסות ליס לה קיאם אלא באלטעאם ואלשראב ואלתגיוט. אכברני: הו כאן פי אלסמא אן כאן יגיה אלטעאם וירמי תגויטה? פיאהלך מן תלך אלפציחה אלעטימה! (ibid., para. 28 [Judeo-Arabic 2:34, English 1:67]). For other critiques of Jesus' need to eat and defecate or feel emotions, see paras, 5, 59, 60, 85, 95, 96.

167. "Alas and woe to anyone who says that his God became intoxicated from wine-drinking, that he ate smelly fish, salted sprats and sardines. . . .": אלתעס ואלתבר ולאויל לאטויל למן יקול אן אלאהה סכר מן שרב אלכמר ואנה אכל אלסמך אלמנתן ואלציר ואלצחנה. . . . (ibid., para. 60 [Judeo-Arabic 2:44, col. 1; English 1:64]). In this same passage Jesus is "sullied by sins" (דנס מן אלכטייה) and requires John's baptism to cleanse him. Note that a verb from the same root as the word designating filth in the abdomen is used here. See also para. 94 (Hebrew 2:104, English 1:116) and paras. 114–15 (Judeo-Arabic 2:64, English 1:74; Hebrew 2:106, 125, English 1:121). In the Hebrew texts of these baptismal texts Jesus is "impure" (טמאה), not "dirty," because of his sojourn in Egypt.

168. פגעלכם כלכם קלף נגסין, אבדא לם יתם לכם טהר מן גנאבה . . . תם אמרכם באכל אלכנזיר ואן תקרבו אלכבז ואלכמר יציר פי אגואפכם רגיע מנתן (ibid., para. 127 [Judeo-Arabic 2:69, English 1:77]).

169. Cf. para. 171 in which Christians are said to eat the "foul flesh of mice" (לחם אלרגס ואלפאר) (Judeo-Arabic 2:84, English 1:86) and Sargis, *Disputation,* XIII.1, p. 34, where the Jew also attacks the Christians for eating pork and other vermin. Mice qualified as "vermin" (*sherez̦*) in the Jewish system.

170. On the symbolism of odor, see chapter 1 and above.

171. Contrast with Eutychius of Alexandria, *The Book of the Demonstration (Kitāb al-Burhān),* pt. 1, Arabic p. 154, English p. 125, where the Christian author argues that the Eucharist is not expelled from the body as other waste matter from nourishment would be, but rather is completely absorbed by the bodies of those who consume it in faith.

172. *Polemic of Nestor,* paras. 114–15, 131 (Judeo-Arabic 2:64, 71; English 1:74, 78).

173. On the similarity between the *Qiṣṣat* and early Pagan anti-Christian polemic, see Joel Edward Rembaum, "The New Testament in Medieval Jewish Anti-Christian Polemics." Unfortunately Rembaum was unaware that the Hebrew, European version of this text was based on a Judeo-Arabic tradition. However, he was correct to see this text as an important link between Pagan and later Jewish anti-Christian polemics (see 62–64).

174. The *Qiṣṣat* shares many themes with Muslim refutations of Christianity, raising questions of who originated or resuscitated this form of polemic. Jews may have borrowed arguments from the Muslims. However, indications of Jewish critiques of God-as-Jesus in the womb and Christian diet in very early Christian disputation texts from Europe and the Middle East, such as Sergius the Stylite and Gregory of Tours (on these texts see above), support Lasker and Stroumsa's tentative hypothesis that Muslims gained some of these arguments from Jews. One of the primary objections that

Lasker and Stroumsa raised to a Jewish origin for these arguments was the early date of Muslim disputations containing similar themes in contrast to the *Qiṣṣat.* The appearance of certain common topoi in both Jewish and Muslim attacks against Christianity may have resulted from a growing oral tradition of Jewish anti-Christian invective that combined the late antique filth-based polemic against the incarnation with Jewish impurity polemic, which the Muslims then adopted. However, one should not forget early Muslims' strong interest and cultivation of Christian philosophical and disputational literature as part of this equation. For a discussion of the Muslim background of the *Qiṣṣat,* see *Polemic of Nestor,* introduction, 1:19, 21–26; Daniel Lasker, "The Jewish Critique of Christianity under Islam in the Middle Ages"; idem, "*Qiṣṣat Mujādalat al-Usquf* and *Nestor ha-Komer.*"

175. *Polemic of Nestor,* paras. 5, 74, 76, 82, 111.

176. On the composite nature of the *Qiṣṣat,* see *Polemic of Nestor,* 1:23–24.

177. On the fear, antagonism, and even violence Jews felt toward Christians under Byzantine rule and even during the early stages of the Islamic conquests, see *Doctrina Jacobi nuper baptizati;* Jacob of Edessa, *La Didascale de Jacob;* and especially Olster's analysis of the text in *Roman Defeat,* 158–79. On Byzantine persecutions of the Jews from Heraclius to 1204, see Joshua Starr, *The Jews in the Byzantine Empire,* 1–10. On the increasingly negative Christian attitude toward Jews beginning in the fifth century, see Margaret Miles, "Santa Maria Maggiore's Fifth-Century Mosaic."

178. اذ يقول في انجيله : ان الكلمة هي الله و التحمت. فاذا كانت هي الله, و الكلمة التحمت في مشيمة مريم فالله تعالى هو نفسه التحم في مشيمة مريم فعلى هذا فالاب و الابن و الكلمة كلهم البحموا في مشيمة مريم و في امانتهم : ان الابن هو الذى التحم في مشيمة مريم ('Alī ibn Aḥmad Ibn Ḥazm, *al-Faṣl fī al-milal wa al-ahwā' wa al-niḥal,* 1:119).

179. Cf. ibid., 1:110–11, 114–18, 195–96. On this passage, see Burman, *Religious Polemic,* 160–61. Likewise, the *Liber Denudationis,* a Mozarab Christian text originally written in Arabic, now extant only in Latin, insists that Mary "gave birth, and was (still) clean and holy; and there was no filth or uncleanliness mixed with her" (*Liber Denudationis,* 10.4, in Burman, *Religious Polemic,* 342/343). Cf. *Liber Denudationis,* 10.6, 10.14, 10.18–19, pp. 344/345, 354/355, 358/359.

180. For examples from the *Qiṣṣat,* see *Polemic of Nestor,* chap. 2. On Andalusian discussions of the incarnation, see Burman, *Religious Polemic,* 73, 112–20, 158–62. The author of the *Liber Denudationis* also attempted to refute the indignity of the crucifixion: 10.18–22, Burman, 359–63.

181. Alvaro de Córdoba, *Liber Epistolarum Albari,* in *Epistolario,* ed. José Madoz, epistle 18:10–12, pp. 254–60. On this text, also see Heinz Löwe, "Die Apostasie des Pfazdiakons Bodo (838) und das Judentum der Chasaren"; Heinz Schreckenberg, *Die christlichen Adversus-Judaeos-Texte und ihr literarisches und historisches Umfeld (1: 11 Jh.),* 484–500; Bernhard Blumenkranz, "Un pamphlet juif médio-latin de polémique antichrétienne," in his *Juifs et Chrétiens;* Merchavia, *ha-Talmud,* 85, 91. Bodo, who was originally the chaplain of King Louis the Pious, caused considerable consternation among his former coreligionists; see Schreckenberg and Merchavia and Madoz's introduction to the epistles, *Epistolario,* pp. 56–61. One should approach Blumenkranz's "reconstruction" of Bodo-Eleazar's arguments with care.

182. Alvaro, *Epistolario,* 18:11, pp. 256–57. Madoz points out that Alvaro's use of rays versus dirt *(cloaca)* strongly resembles language used in Diogenes Laertius, Tertullian, Hildefonsis, and Pseudo-Hildefonsis; see 256 n. 89.

183. Audi, sceleste, et omnium execrationum vet abominationum replete, spiritus immunde et honende, atque per te Deum vivum blasfemare es ausus . . . (Alvaro, *Epistolario,* 257).

184. See, e.g., epistles 16:3, p. 227; 18:1, 10, 17, pp. 241, 255, 264 respectively.

185. Clamate ei voce maiore, quia forsitan alvum vester Mesias purgat, aut vesicam effusione urine laxat, aut fimi putorem tacite ex ano exhalat, aut certe inflatione ventris instripida digerit et ideo gemitus tam diuturnos vestros non audit (epistle 16:11, p. 238).

186. The association of the Jewish Messiah with human excrement has parallels in Jerome's commentary on Isaiah, bk. 13, chap. 47. See Alvaro, *Epistolario,* 238 n. 57; and Madoz's introduction, 20–22, 58–59.

187. Madoz, introduction to Alvaro, *Epistolario,* 60.

188. Amulo, *Liber contra Judaeos, PL* 116, 39–40, cols. 168–69. On Amino, see Merchavia, *ha-Talmud,* 85–92, esp. 91 on this passage.

189. Both Amulo and his teacher and predecessor, Agobard, are known as being among the first western European Christians in the Middle Ages to discuss potentially real customs of the Jews of their time and to be familiar with some of the *Toledot Yesu* traditions. However, Merchavia argues that much of their material comes from Jerome. See Merchavia, *ha-Talmud,* 41–42, 71–92; Schreckenberg, *Die christlichen Adversus-Judaeos Texte,* 445; Sapir Abulafia, "Invectives," 68; Reuben Bonfil, "'Edoto shel Agobard million 'al 'olamam ha-ruḥani shel yehudei 'iro be-me'a ha-tesh'it." Another possible source for Amulo are the arguments of Eleazar. Amulo knew of and commented on Bodo's (Eleazar's) conversion (Amulo, *Contra ludaeos,* in *PL,* 116, col. 171; and Alvaro, *Epistolario,* 57–58) and thus may have been familiar with some of the arguments that led to Eleazar's decision.

190. Sapir Abulafia argues for the oral nature of the *Toledot Yesu* stories, language, and critiques against Christianity: "Invectives," 68. Regarding the communication of such motifs between Jews in the East and West note the remark by Amulo, *Epistolario,* col. 147.

191. Yanai, *Maḥzor piyuṭe,* vol. 2, poem 109 (Num. 8:1), l. 22, p. 38; poem 119 (Num. 20:14), l. 78, p. 87; poem 135 (Deut. 2:2), ll. 46, 48, p. 127; poem for Yom Kippur, ll. 145–46, p. 221. For pig and other animal imagery, see my discussion in the section on Jewish polemic in this chapter. Also see Bekkum, "Anti-Christian Polemics." On *piyyuṭim* as popular, oral literature, see introduction to Yanai, *Maḥzor piyuṭe,* 74–76. Rabinovitz's arguments are rendered somewhat problematic in the context of early *piyyuṭim* since much of the evidence of his argument comes from the late Middle Ages.

192. All of the extant manuscripts of the Hebrew version of the *Qiṣṣat,* titled *Sefer Nestor ha-Komer,* date from the late fifteenth century. However, Jacob b. Reuben, in his *Milḥamot ha-Shem,* composed in 1170, refers specifically to a Nestor the priest, a convert to Judaism, and the arguments Jacob b. Reuben attributes to this Nestor correspond to arguments in the *Qiṣṣat* and the later Hebrew versions of *Sefer Nestor ha-Komer.*

Lasker and Stroumsa, *Polemic of Nestor,* 1:27–29; Jacob b. Reuben, *Sefer Milḥamot ha-Shem,* 154–56.

193. See, e.g., Muḥammad ibn Abī Bakr Ibn Qayyim al-Jawzīyah, *Kitāb Hadāyat al-ḥayārā fī 'ajwibah al-yahud wa-al-naṣara,* 191. My thanks to Hava Lazarus-Yafeh for passing this reference on to me. Later Byzantine polemicists such as Euthymius Zigabenus (11th century) and Nicetas Choniates (ca. 1140–1214) repeated earlier Christian arguments that the Muslims' paradise was filled with human waste. See Khoury, *Théologiens,* 247, 253. For evidence of these continued as issues in Jewish-Christian polemic in Byzantium and the Muslim world, see Nicetas Pectoratus, *Traité contre les Juifs accusant des le début leur indocilité et leur in fidélité,* in *Opuscules et Lettres,* esp. 416–19 (Nicetas lived ca. 1000–ca. 1090) *[Dissertatio contra Judaeos] Anonymi Auctoris Theognosiae,* 3.530–50, pp. 54–55.

194. Many scholars maintain that the Cathars were derived directly from the Bogomils, though Catharism developed in new directions once established in western Europe. *Christian Dualist Heresies,* 43–52; Henri Puech, "Catharisme médiéval et Bogomilisme." But see *Heresies of the High Middle Ages,* 18–19, where the authors argue that while Catharism was strongly influenced by ideas from the Balkans along with merchants and crusaders returning from the East, it was not a mere import from these lands.

195. On these, see Parkes, *Conflict,* 291–97; Rubin, *Gentile Tales,* 7–11.

196. Aaron Mirsky, *ha-Piyyut,* 689–93; Yuval, "ha-Naqam ve-ha-qlila." Not all *piyyuṭim* either from the land of Israel or from medieval northern Europe denigrated Christianity. Indeed, most did not. However, only those with polemical content are relevant to this project.

Chapter 3. **Twelfth- and Thirteenth-Century Contexts**

1. R. I. Moore, *The Formation of a Persecuting Society,* 1–99.

2. John Boswell, *Christianity, Social Tolerance and Homosexuality,* 3–39, 269–302.

3. Brundage, *Law, Sex, and Christian Society,* 176–324.

4. Penelope Johnson, *Equal in Monastic Profession,* esp. 248–66. She argues for a number of other factors as well, such as the rise of the mendicant orders that were not willing to accord women the same active roles in their orders as men and that funneled donations which once may have been granted to monasteries (male and female) to their new orders.

5. Moore, *Formation,* 1–99, esp. 66–97.

6. Ibid., 102–53. On the shifting economy as a key factor in changing, negative attitudes toward certain sectors of society, see also Little, *Religious Poverty;* Sapir Abulafia, *Christians and Jews,* 51–62.

7. Moore, *Formation,* 100–101.

8. Ibid., 102–53.

9. Mellinkoff, *Outcasts.* Also see William Chester Jordan, "The Medieval Background."

10. Rafael Ocasio, "Ethnic Underclass Representation in the *Cantigas*."

11. Bauchau, "Science et racisme"; Goldberg, "Two Parallel Medieval Commonplaces."

12. Sara Lipton, *Images of Intolerance.*

13. Robert Chazan, *Medieval Jewry in Northern France;* Jordan, *French Monarchy and the Jews;* Gavin I. Langmuir, "'Judei Nostri' and the Beginning of Capetian Legislation"; H. G. Richardson, *The English Jewry under the Angevin Kings.*

14. Browe, *Judenmission*; Merchavia, *Talmud;* Yerushalmi, "Inquistition and the Jews"; Jordan, "Marian Devotion"; Cohen, *Friars;* idem, "Scholarship and Intolerance"; Chazan, *Daggers*. Also see Smalley, *Study of the Bible;* James Kritzeck, *Peter the Venerable and Islam;* Kedar, *Crusade and Mission.*

15. Tolan, *Saracens,* 105–69; Daniel, *Islam and the West,* 80–89, 94, 166, 184–88, 191–92, 273, 276, 283; Alexandra Cuffel, "'Henceforward All Generations Will Call Me Blessed.'" More work needs to be done on the impact of Christian missionizing on Iberian Muslims.

16. Gavin Langmuir, *History, Religion, and Antisemitism.* He differentiates between rational, nonrational, and irrational belief, the last of these deriving from confrontation and conflict between rational and nonrational belief.

17. Sapir Abulafia, *Christians and Jews;* Langmuir, *History, Religion, and Antisemitism;* idem, *Toward a Definition of Antisemitism.*

18. Chazan, *Medieval Jewry;* Efraim Urbach, *Ba'ale ha-tosafot;* Israel Ta-Shma, *Halakhah, minhag u-Mitzi'ut be-Ashkenaz, 1000–1350,* 28–35, provides a good overview of scholarly work and opinion on this subject.

19. Shatzmiller, *Jews, Medicine, and Medieval Society.*

20. Amos Funkenstein, *Perceptions of Jewish History,* esp. 169–219; Berger, "Mission to the Jews"; idem, Introduction to *Jewish-Christian Debate;* Daniel Lasker, *Jewish Philosophical Polemics against Christianity in the Middle Ages.*

21. Elliot Wolfson, "Woman—The Feminine as Other in Theosophic Kabbalah"; idem, "Ontology, Alterity, and Ethics in Kabbalistic Anthropology."

22. On the legal status of women during this period, see Yom-Tov Assis, "Sexual Behavior in Medieval Hispano-Jewish Society"; Cohen, "Purity and Piety"; Dinari, "Hillul ha-qodesh"; idem, "Minhagei ṭum'at ha-niddah"; Avraham Grossman, "The Status of Jewish Women in Germany (10th–12th Centuries)"; Shlomo Riskin, *Women and Jewish Divorce,* 91–111; Kenneth Stow, "The Jewish Family in the Rhineland in the High Middle Ages"; Cheryl Tallan, "The Position of the Medieval Jewish Widow as a Function of Family Structure." One needs to be careful about generalizations, however. The laws and customs regulating Jewish women's behavior varied depending on the geographic and cultural location of the community. On negative literary depictions of Jewish women, see Tova Rosen, *Unveiling Eve;* idem,"Sexual Politics in a Medieval Hebrew Marriage Debate"; Norman Roth, "The 'Wiles of Women' Motif in Medieval Hebrew Literature of Spain." For comparable examples in Christian literature, see R. Howard Bloch, *Medieval Misogyny and the Invention of Western Romantic Love;* Katharina M. Wilson and Elizabeth M. Makowski, *Wykked Wyves and the Woes of Marriage.*

23. Einbinder, "Jewish Women Martyrs."

24. Rubin, *Gentile Tales*, 73–77; Eibinder, "Jewish Women Martyrs."

25. On business and trade relations in Europe and the Near East, see S. D. Goitein, *A Mediterranean Society,* 1:72, 85, 124; 3:292–96, 330; Constable, *Muslim Traders;* Cohen, *Under Crescent and Cross.* On shared religious festivities and saints, see Josef Meri, *The Cult of Saints among Muslims and Jews in Medieval Syria;* N. J. G. Kaptein, *Muhammad's Birthday Festival;* Fernando de la Granja, "Fiestas cristianas en al-Andalus (Materiales para su estudio) I" and "Fiestas cristianas en al-Andalus (Materiales para su estudio) II"; Cohen, *Under Crescent and Cross;* R. I. Burns, *Islam under the Crusaders,* 196–97. Such rituals were not devoid of interfaith tensions and even violence, however. See Nirenberg, *Communities of Violence,* 198–99, 206; and Cuffel " 'Henceforward All Generations Will Call Me Blessed.' "

26. Cohen, *Under Crescent and Cross.*

27. Jordan, *French Monarchy and the Jews.*

28. Chazan, *European Jewry and the First Crusade;* idem, *God, Humanity, and History.*

29. Marcus, *Rituals of Childhood;* idem, "A Jewish-Christian Symbiosis"; Marc Epstein, *Dreams of Subversion in Medieval Jewish Art and Literature;* idem, " 'The Ways of Truth are Curtailed and Hidden' "; Susan Einbinder, *A Beautiful Death;* idem, "Pucellina of Blois"; idem, "The Troyes Elegies"; idem, "Jewish Women Martyrs"; idem, "The Jewish Martyrs of Blois, 1171"; idem, "Signs of Romance"; David Biale, "Counter-History and Jewish Polemics against Christianity."

30. That Jewish, Christian, and Muslim society and culture were deeply integrated in Iberia and to a lesser extent in other parts of southern Europe has long been noted and studied. The scholarship on this subject is legion. See, e.g., Robert I. Burns, *Muslims, Christians and Jews in the Crusader Kingdom of Valencia;* Yitzhak Baer, *A History of the Jews in Christian Spain; Convivencia,* ed. Vivian B. Mann, Thomas F. Glick, and Jerrilynn D. Dodds; Eliyahu Ashtor, *The Jews of Moslem Spain;* Ross Brann, *Power in the Portrayal;* Nirenberg, *Communities of Violence.*

31. Sahar Amer, *Esope au féminin;* Menocal, *The Arabic Role in Medieval Literary History;* Metlitzki, *The Matter of Araby in Medieval England;* Thomas E. Burman, *Religious Polemic and the Intellectual History of the Mozarabs, c. 1050–1200;* Alice E. Lasater, *Spain to England.*

32. Mercantile traffic also played a role in the transmission of texts. See Monica Greene, "The *De Genecia* attributed to Constantine the African," reprinted in her *Women's Healthcare in the Medieval West.*

33. Jordan, "Marian Devotion"; Rubin, *Corpus Christi,* 116–29, 287, 289; idem, *Gentile Tales;* Ellen M. Ross, *The Grief of God;* Kathleen Biddick, "Genders, Bodies, Borders."

34. Usamah ibn Munqidh, *Memoirs of an Arab-Syrian Gentleman,* 130, 163–65, 169.

35. Hillenbrand, *Crusades,* 331–33.

36. On Christian Hebraicists, see Smalley, *Study of the Bible;* Cohen, *Friars;* Chazan, *Daggers.*

37. Christian: "Everyone ought to believe / the populous rejoices: / Our redemption, / was born a little child / flesh was put on / in the belly of a virgin / And by flesh is touched / the majesty of divinity." Jew: "They do not understand you because of this obfuscation of words. Speak to me in French and explain your words! . . . What you say in Latin, gloss them for me in French!" ("La desputoison du Juyf et du Crestien," 459).

38. See esp. "Textual and Visual Communities" in this chapter.

39. See below in this chapter.

40. Hava-Lazarus Yafeh, *Intertwined Worlds;* Dimitri Gutas, *Greek Thought, Arabic Culture.*

41. Burman, *Religious Polemic,* 14–15, 34–36. The text is quoted in the Muslim response by al-Khazrajī. Some have doubted the authenticity of al-Qutī, but on this, see Burman, 62–70.

42. Burman, *Religious Polemic,* 70–80.

43. Ibid., 119–20, 194–95.

44. Ibid., 125–55; Lazarus-Yafeh, *Intertwined Worlds.*

45. Ramon Lull also used Muslim and Jewish traditions in his disputational texts but in very different ways from Ramond Marti. Burman, *Religious Polemic,* 200–209. On the use of Jewish traditions in Christian polemic, see Cohen, *Friars;* Chazan, *Daggers*. For Ramond Marti in particular, see Cohen, *Friars,* 129–69. Of course, Christians in the Latin West such as Ramond Marti had to be curious enough to learn Arabic in the first place so as to read such texts. Thus some of the impetus remains in Western hands.

46. Burman, *Religious Polemic,* 37–62, 95–96, Daniel, *Islam and the West,* 1–6. On the dating of *Liber denudationis,* see 50–53, 62. It is unclear when the text was translated into Latin, in part because we do not know in which language Ramond Marti read it.

47. *Jewish-Christian Debate,* 29–31. For biographical data, see Rosenthal's introduction to Jacob b. Reuben, *Milḥamot ha-shem*, ix–x. Rosenthal suggests that Jacob fled from Spain to southern France during the Almohad persecutions and then eventually returned to Spain.

48. *Polemic of Nestor*, 1:27; Jacob b. Reuben, *Milḥamot ha-shem*, 154–56.

49. One need only compare the use of Christian Scripture in Jacob b. Reuben, *Milḥamot ha-shem,* or even in *Sefer Nestor ha-Komer* to that in the *Niẓẓaḥon Yashan*. On this, see *Jewish-Christian Debate*, 29–32.

50. *Polemic of Nestor*, 1:27–32.

51. On Jacob b. Reuben's potential authorship of the Hebrew translation of the *Qiṣṣat,* see *Polemic of Nestor*, 1:31. Lasker and Stroumsa have rejected the suggestion that he was its translator. On Jacob b. Reuben as translator of Gilbert Crispin, see Berger, "Gilbert Crispin." Berger does note the possibility that the quotations, along with those of Alan of Lille, came not directly from Gilbert Crispin but from an abridged version that contained a collection of Latin polemical texts, including sections of Gilbert's work. This possiblity does not diminish Jacob b. Reuben's unusual endeavor—namely, to read and dispute a Latin Christian polemical work.

52. For a brief discussion of this problem, see Lasker, *Jewish Philosophical Polemics,* 164–65. Lasker notes that Judah Aryeh de Modena seems to have read Thomas Aquinas, but Judah is writing at a much later date (1571–1648) than Jacob b. Reuben.

53. *Jewish-Christian Debate,* 29–32; Berger, "Mission to the Jews."

54. D'Alverny, "Translations and Translators," esp. 430–31; Peter Classen, *Burgundio von Pisa;* John of Damascus, *De fide orthodoxa,* 10, 13, 14, 46–47, 49–56, 70–72; Eligius M. Buytaert, "Another Copy of Cerbanus' Version of John Damascene"; Lasker, *Jewish Philosophical Polemics,* 131.

55. D'Alverny, "Translations and Translators"; Antoine Dondaine, "Hughes Etherien et Léon Toscan"; Nikolaus M. Haring, "The *Liber de differentia naturae et personae* by Hugh Etherian and the Letters Addressed to Him by Peter of Vienna and Hugh of Honau." For further evidence of Latin interest in Greek theological differences, see the quodlibet of Alexander of Hales (d. 1245) in Palémon Glorieux, *La littérature quodlibétique,* vol. 2, 1.2 (p. 57).

56. Ron Barkai, *A History of Jewish Gynaecological Texts in the Middle Ages,* 20–32. On the *Art of medicine* (*Ars medicinae*), also known as the *Articella,* see Nancy Siraisi, *Medieval and Early Renaissance Medicine,* 58, 71; Cornelius O'Boyle, *The Art of Medicine.*

57. Shatzmiller, *Jews, Medicine, and Society,* 36–42, 52–55. Moses b. Daniel of Romano (1292–1350) translated some of the works of Albertus Magnus, Thomas Aquinas, and Aegidius Romanus. On him, see Catherine Rigo, "Yehudah ben Mosheh Romano traduttore degli Scolastici latini"; idem, "Un'antologia filosofica di Yehuda b. Mosheh Romano"; idem, "Un passo sconosciuto di Alberto Magno nel 'Sefer Etsem ha-Shamayim' di Yehudah b. Mosheh"; Joseph [Giuseppe] Sermoneta, "Jehudah ben Mošeh ben Dani'el Romano Romano, traducteur de Saint Thomas." In the fourteenth century Abraham Avigdor (on whom briefly, see Charles H. Manekin, "When Jews Learned Logic from the Pope") and Yekutiel b. Salamon translated Bernard Gordon's *Lilium medicinae* and Gui de Chauliac's *Chirurgia* and the works of Arnold of Villanova (Shatzmiller, *Jews, Medicine, and Society,* 53). Knowledge of Latin was not a requirement for passing state or city medical examinations; individuals had to be familiar with the standard texts and theories, but they could have obtained that familiarity in any language.

58. For example, Ron Barkai notes that in the Hebrew translation of Soranus, the passage encouraging perpetual virginity is altered so that the text merely advocates prolonging that state. While perpetual virginity was in accord with medieval Christian ideals, it ran counter to Jewish law. Barkai, *History*, 33.

59. Marjorie Chibnall, "Pliny's *Natural History* and the Middle Ages"; Danielle Jacquart and Claude Thomasset, *Sexuality and Medicine in the Middle Ages,* 73; Joan Cadden, *Meanings of Sex Difference in the Middle Ages,* 41–43. Siraisi notes that Celsus's compendium also remained available but was not frequently used because of its length and complexity: *Medieval and Early Renaissance Medicine,* 161.

60. Jacquart and Thomasset, *Sexuality and Medicine*, 11–15; Cadden, *Meanings of Sex Difference,* 49–53.

61. This preference of Aristotle over Galen contrasted with the approach taken in *al-Qānūn*, Ibn Sina's medical compendium, in which the Muslim author presented the differing theories without taking sides. Basim F. Musallam, *Sex and Society in Islam,* 46–49; see also Avicenna, *al-Qānun fī al-tibb;* idem, *Liber canonis;* idem, *al-Shifā.* Musallam remarks that Ibn Rushd (=Averroes 1136–98), who was also important for the formation of medieval Western medical thought, was a much more stringent Aristotelian. Gerrit Bos and Resianne Fontaine argue that Ibn Rushd was much more conciliatory in his approach than scholars have characterized him. See Gerrit Bos and Resianne Fontaine, "Medico-Philosophical Controversies in Nathan b. Yo'el Falaquera's *Sefer Sori ha-Guf.*" It should also be noted, however, that the division between Aristotelian and Galenic theories is not perhaps as strong as some have maintained. Anthony Preus has shown that Galen was undecided as to whether female seed was menstruation, fluid excreted during arousal, or some other fluid. Preus, "Galen's Criticism." Also, Galen retains some of the matter-spirit, passive-active duality so prevalent in Aristotle.

62. Musallam, *Sex and Society,* 48–49; Cadden, *Meanings of Sex Difference,* 106–14.

63. Owsei Temkin, *Galenism,* 77–78; Rosner's introduction to Maimonides, *Treatises on Poisons,* 4, 10; Barkai, *History,* 64–67.

64. Moses Maimonides, *The Guide of the Perplexed,* 3.12. For the relationship between Maimonides' thought and that of Aristotle, see very generally Pines's introduction, 1.lvii–lxxv, to Galen, lxxvii–lxxviii: Galen, *The Art of the Cure.* For Judeo-Arabic, see Maimonides, *Les guides des égares;* for medieval Hebrew, see idem, *Moreh nevukhim;* Galen, *De usu partium*, 3.10.

65. Cadden, *Meanings of Sex Difference,* 58–66. Constantinus Africanus, *De genitalibus membris*, in Green, "*De Genecia.*" The edited text is on 312–23, esp. 315–21. This text was, according to Green, excerpted from the *Pantegni* and circulated as a separate gynecological treatise. See *Constantine the African and 'Alī ibn al 'Abbās al-Magūsī,* ed. Charles Burnett and Danielle Jacquart.

66. On Nathan b. Yo'el Falaquera's harmonizing tendencies in *Sefer Sori ha-Guf,* see Bos and Fontaine, "Medico-Philosophical Controversies"; Yehudah b. Solomon ha-Kohen ibn Matka, *Midrash ha-Hokhma,* articles 15–18, *sub* "Be-toldetet"/("On Generation"); Albertus Magnus, [*De Animalibus*] *On Animals*, 15.2.6, 11; Taddeo Alderotti, *Thaddei Florentini Expositiones in arduum aphorismo[rum] Ipocratis volumen,* fol. 357, as cited in Cadden, *Meanings of Sex Difference*, 122. My thanks to Tzvi Langerman of Bar Ilan University, who first showed me Ibn Matka's text and worked with me on the sections dealing with his theories of generation. On the mixture of classical theories of generation in medieval writings generally, see Cadden, *Meanings of Sex Difference*, 106–65; Jacquart and Thomasset, *Sexuality and Medicine*, 48–86, Barkai, *History*, 38–79. On the prevalance of Soranus's gynecology before and after the "medical revolution" of the twelfth and thirteenth centuries, see Monica Green, "Transmission"; idem, "Obstetrical and Gynecological Texts in Middle English," reprinted in her *Women's Healthcare.*

67. Musallam, *Sex and Society*, 52.

68. Indeed, whether Musallam's statement holds true for medieval Islam needs to be explored further. Women in general were believed unable to attain the status of prophet because menstruation hindered them from praying as much as men. Those two women who were sometimes believed to have the status of prophet, Mary, mother of Jesus, and Fatima, daughter of the Prophet Muhammad, were often described by other theologians as not menstruating. Their greater physical and spritual purity was a prerequisite to an exhalted status equal to that of male prophets. See Denise L. Soufi, "The Image of Fatima in Classical Muslim Thought"; Smith and Haddad, "The Virgin Mary"; Stowasser, *Women in the Qur'an,* 76–80. To support his arguments, Musallam cites Ibn Qayyim al-Jawzīya's *Tuḥfat,* a treatise on pregnancy and the upbringing of young children using both medical and religious sources, as partial proof of his arguments. But even in this text, Ibn Qayyim al-Jawzīya alludes to the prohibition against prayer and fasting during menstruation, which need not necessarily be an argument about women's inherent inferiority; but it certainly seems to have been weighted in that way among some authors. Musallam, *Sex and Society,* 55–57; Muḥammad ibn Abī Bakr ibn Qayyim al-Jawzīya, *Tuḥfat al-mawdūd bi-aḥkām al-mawlūd,* 149.

69. Pseudo-Nahmanides, *Igeret ha-qodesh,* in Nahmanides, *Kitve Rabenu Mosheh ben Naḥman;* Aristotle, *On dreams [=Peri enupnion],* 32 Ibn Matka, chaps. 16–18.

70. Pseudo-Nahmanides, *Igeret*; Moses b. Naḥman of Barcelona, *Commentary on Leviticus,* in *Torat Ḥayim Ḥamshah Humshe Torah; The Prose Salernitan Questions,* ed. Brian Lawn, *Vayiqr'a,* para. 16 (pp. 10–11), para. 19 (p. 12), para. 228 (pp. 115–16) ; [Pseudo-]Nahmanides, "Discourse on the Law," in *Writings and Discourses,* 1:109–12; Nahmanides, *Perushe ha-Torah be-Rabenu Mosheh ben Naḥman;* idem, *Commentary on the Torah,* ed. and trans. Charles B. Chavel, Lev. 12:2, 18:9; Abraham b. Meir Ibn Ezra, *Perushe ha-Torah;* idem, *The Commentary of Abraham Ibn Ezra on the Pentateuch,* Lev. 12:2.

71. Pseudo-Albertus Magnus, *Women's Secrets,* 88–89; Avicenna, *De animalibus;* idem, *al-Shifā'.*

72. Pseudo-Albertus Magnus, *Women's Secrets,* 60. There is no critical modern edition of the Latin text. Most readily available is *De secretis mulierum libellus cum scholiis*. Cf. Albertus Magnus, *Quaestiones super de animalibus*, bk. 9, quest. 8–10; Thomas Aquinas, [*Summa Theologica*] *Summa theologiae,* la 117, 3.2; Nahmanides, *Commentary on Leviticus,* 18:19; Claude Thomasset, "La femme au Moyen Âge"; Sharon F. Koren, " 'The Woman from Whom God Wanders,' " 223–24.

73. Pseudo-Albertus Magnus, *Women's Secrets;* Thomas Aquinas, *Summa Theologica,* la 117, 3.2; Jacquart and Thomasset, *Sexuality and Medicine,* 74–76, 191–93.

74. Quaestio texts, texts organized around a series of questions and answers with their "proofs," frequently raised the problem of why women did not contract leprosy during sex with an infected person. Consider, for example, the *Prose Salernitan Questions,* 9, quest. 14. Also see pp. 18, 185, 249; Adelard of Bath, *Die Quaestiones naturales*, 42–43, quest. 41; Brian Lawn, *The Salernitan Questions,* 38, 46, nn. 1, 53; Jacquart and Thomasset, *Sexuality and Medicine*, 188–91.

75. Ultimately the author cites various works of Aristotle against Ibn Sina. The commentators refrained from critiquing Avicenna's position, presumably because they agreed with him. Pseudo-Albertus Magnus, *Women's Secrets,* 96–97.

76. *Prose Salernitan Questions,* 119–20, quest. 239.

77. For medieval texts that link the moon's cycle to menstruation, see *Prose Salernitan Questions*, 344, quest. 11; Albertus Magnus, *Quaestiones super de animalibus,* bk. 9, quest. 7. Note that according to Albertus, not everyone adhered to this theory. Also see discussion and references in Koren, "'Woman from Whom God Wanders,'" 159–62.

78. Koren, "'Woman from whom God wanders,'" 139–42, 150–77, 181–98; Wolfson, "The Image of Jacob Engraved upon the Throne"; idem, "Left Contained in the Right."

79. See, e.g., the poetic depictions of hell in a thirteenth-century Middle English manuscript, *An Old English Miscellany: Containing a Bestiary, Kentish Sermons, Proverbs of Alfred, Religious Poems of the Thirteenth Century,* ed. Richard Morris, 73, 78, 92, 147–51, 224, 227, 228–29, in which foul smell and devouring worms are frequently evoked; and in [Judah ben Samuel] *Sefer Ḥasidim,* ed. Reuven Margolies, 439, para. 705, in which a righteous man is buried next to an unrighteous. The righteous man cannot rest in his grave because of the foul smell and smoke and is obliged to appear in a dream to the inhabitants of the city and plead that they move his body. The author of *Sefer ha-Yashar*, a moralizing Hebrew text whose geographic and chronological origins are uncertain (probably thirteenth century), refers to the fire and worms of hell but no stench. Zerahyah ha-Yevani, *Sefer ha-Yashar,* 220/221.

80. See Jacquart and Thomasset's observations: *Sexuality and Medicine,* 193. Judith R. Baskin links laws of avoidance and restriction in "normative" rabbinic literature to anxiety about menstruation. See her "Woman as Other in Rabbinic Literature." For medieval men's discomfort not only with women's bodies but also with their own sexual, potentially polluting bodies, see Dyan Elliott, *Fallen Bodies,* 14–60; Vern L. Bullough, "On Being a Man in the Middle Ages." Biale suggests that Sephardi attitudes toward sexuality were much more restrictive than Ashkenazi, since in Spain neo-Platonic and Maimonidean influences, both of which take a negative view of sexual pleasure, or even of sex generally, prevailed. Biale, *Eros and the Jews,* 60–120. Koren has likewise argued that Kabbalists adopted older mystical traditions that demanded eschewing the company of women during mystical preparation. See Koren, "'Woman from Whom God Wanders,'" 25–30, 47–135, 157–64, 195–97, 223–39. In Zerahya ha-Yevani's *Sefer ha-Yashar* (pp. 76/77, 118/119–120/121, 130/131, 170/171–172/173, 248/249) those who wish to cleave to the Creator must avoid women, among others. The author does advocate marriage, however; see 142/143, 214/215, 240/241.

81. Cadden, *Meanings of Sex Difference,* 68–69, 107–65; Jacquart and Thomasset, *Sexuality and Medicine,* 54–79.

82. Ottavia Niccoli, "*Menstruum quasi monstruum:* Monstrous Births and Menstrual Taboo in the Sixteenth Century."

83. Jacquart and Thomasset, *Sexuality and Medicine,* 177–88; Horst Müller-Bütow, *Lepra,* 55–133; Michael Dols, "Leprosy in Medieval Arabic Medicine"; idem,

"The Leper in Medieval Islamic Society"; J. N. Hays, *The Burdens of Disease,* 18–29; Oribasius, *Oeuvres d'Oribase,* 45.27–29 (5:59–82), 7.48 (6:189–93); Joseph ben Meir Ibn Zabara, *Sefer sha'ashu'im,* chap. 12; idem, *The Book of Delight,* chap. 12 (p. 155).

84. The standard work is Françoise Bériac, *Histoire des lépreux au Moyen Âge.* Claudine Dauphin, "Leprosy, Lust and Lice"; Luke Demaitre, "The Description and Diagnosis of Leprosy by Fourteenth-Century Physicians"; idem, "The Relevance of Futility"; Douglas, "Witchcraft and Leprosy," in idem, *Risk and Blame*; Stephen R. Ell, "Blood and Sexuality in Medieval Leprosy"; idem, "Reconstructing the Epidemiology of Medieval Leprosy"; Hermann Hörger, "Krankheit and religoses Tabu"; Keith Manchester and Christopher Knüsel, "A Medieval Sculpture of Leprosy in the Cistercian Abbaye de Cadouin"; William McNeill, *Plagues and Peoples,* 176–80; Vilhelm Moller-Christensen, "Evidence of Leprosy in Earlier Peoples"; Mark Gregory Pegg, "Le corps et l'autorité"; Peter Richards, *The Medieval Leper and His Northern Heirs;* Egon Schmitz-Cliever, "Das mittelalterliche Leprosorium Melaten bei Aachen in der Diozese Luttich (1230–1550)." For a good overview of the historiography, see Hays, *Burdens,* 20–36.

85. Bartholomaeus Anglicus, *De rerum proprietatibus,* bk. 4, chap. XI, pp. 111–14; bk. 5, chap. XIII, pp.142–43; bk. 7, chaps. XXII, XXIII, XLIX, LIII, LXI–LXV, pp. 301–2, 332–33, 337, 348–55; Petrus de Abano, *Consiliator controversarium,* Differentia XX, fols. 32r–33r; Differentia XXXIII, fol. 52v ff.; Differentia CLXVII, fol. 233v; Differentia CLXXVI–CLXXVII, fols. 244r–245v. Also see fol. 267r; Thomas of Cantimpré, *Liber de natura rerum,* 45–46, 55–61; Taddeo Alderotti, *Consilia*, XXXII, pp. 200–202; XL, pp. 218–22; XLVI, pp. 252–58; LXII, pp. 298–308; CXLII, pp. 424–28; CXLIII, pp. 434–36; CXLVII, pp. 111–18; CLXVII, pp. 518–22; Johannes Aegidius Zamorensis, *Historia naturalis,* 1: 356–58, 418–22, 488–92. Compare with his discussion of the Ass (2:1226–1234), Pseudo-Albertus Magnus, *Women's Secrets*, 72–74; *Problemata varia anatomica,* ed. L. R. Lind, 11, 13–14, 21, 28, 38, 54–55, 83; Avicenna, *Liber canonis*, Liber III, Fen. I, Tractatus, I, p. 168; 'Abd al-Aziz ibn 'Uthman al-Qabisi, *Alchabitius cum commento,* fol. 9r–v; Ramond Klibansky, Erwin Panofsky, and Fritz Saxl, *Saturn and Melancholy,* 3, 18, 21, 47, 53, 66, 131–32, 146–47.

86. Bartholomaeus Anglicus, *De rerum proprietatibus*, bk. 7, chap. LXIIII, pp. 351–52; Petrus de Abano, *Conciliator*, Differentia CLXXVII, fol 245v. Also see Demaitre, "Relevance of Futility."

87. Albertus Magnus, *Quaestiones super de animalibus*, bk. IX, quest. 6–7; Bartholomaeus Anglicus, *De rerum proprietatibus*, bk. 5, chap. XII, p. 143; bk. 7, chap. XXII, p. 301; Bernard Gordon, *Lilium Medicinae, sub verbo* "emmorroidas" as quoted in Willis Johnson, "Myth of Jewish Male Menses," 289; Johannes Aegidius Zamorensis, *Historia naturalis,* 1:420; Pseudo-Albertus Magnus, *Women's Secrets*, 73–74; *Problemata varia,* 14, 38–39; Yehudah ha-Kohen ibn Mattqa, *Midrash ha-Ḥokhmah,* MS Parma de Rossi 421, "Be-Mahot Zar'a ha-'Ishah u-be-dam niddah." Willis Johnson argues that while "in medieval medical theory menses and haemorrhoidal bleeding were functionally interchangeable," "[t]o read thirteenth-century accounts of men with bleeding anuses as feminizing slurs is to read them with modern sensiblities" ("Myth of Jewish Male Menses," 290). Cf. Irven Resnick, "Medieval Roots of the Myth of Jewish Male Menses"; Peter Biller, "A 'Scientific' View of Jews from Paris around 1300."

88. Laurence Wright, "'Burning' and Leprosy in Old French." Children of menstruating women were also often "red." See chap. 5.

89. Klibansky, *Saturn and Melancholy,* 114–33, 146, 158–59, 186–88, 191, 290; Resnick, "Medieval Roots"; al-Qabīsī, *Alchabitius cum Commento,* fols. 9–10r; *Problemata varia*, 54–55; Bartholomaeus Anglicus, *De rerum proprietatibus,* bk. 4, chap. XI, p. 113.

90. al-Qabīsī, *Alchabitius cum commento,* fol. 9r–v. The majority of the relevant passage is translated in Klibansky, *Saturn and Melancholy,* 131–32, and reproduced and discussed in Biller, "A 'Scientific' View." On negative views of peasants, see Paul Freedman, *Images of the Medieval Peasant.*

91. For example, in one thirteenth-century sermon for Epiphany from Kent, leprosy is used as a symbol for deadly sin and scabs for "little sins," whereas the leper is to be equated with a sensual, sinful person. The preacher is speaking allegorically, but leprosy was a sign of sin all could understand. *An Old English Miscellany,* 31. On leprosy as a sign of sinfulness in the high Middle Ages, see Saul N. Brody, *The Disease of the Soul;* Jacquart and Thomasset, *Sexuality and Medicine,* 184–86; Peter Allen, *The Wages of Sin,* 33–37.

92. Flandrin, *Sexe et l'occident,* 163, 193, 361 (nn. 108–9).

93. *Prose Salernitan Questions,* 98, quest. 179; Flandrin, *Sexe et l'occident,* 151–211. Similar tendencies among Muslim medical writers led Michael Dols to argue that Muslims did not add a moral dimension to leprosy as the Christians did. Dols, "Leprosy" and "The Leper in Medieval Islamic Society."

94. *Prose Salernitan Questions,* Unicorn: 78–79, quest. 161; 91–92, quest. 173; Phoenix: 278–80, quest. 5. How the lion can resurrect its cubs after three days is also addressed: 26–27, quest. 58; as to why a man loses his voice when he sees a wolf: 137, quest. 284. Michael Camille, "Bestiary or Biology?"

95. Koren, "'Woman from Whom God Wanders,'" esp. 102–26; Dinari, "Hilul ha-Qodesh"; idem, "Minhagei ṭum'at ha-niddah"; Israel Ta-Shma, "haraḥaqot niddah," 163–70, repeated in his *Halakhah,* 280–88. Ta-Shma disagrees with Dinari's suggestion that these attitudes differed in Ashkenazi and Sephardi communities. See Ta-Shma, "haraḥaqot," 164; idem, *Halakhah,* 281. Koren suggests that the *Baraita de Niddah* was known and used first by mystical circles in Italy and from there passed to Germany and northern France and thence to Spain and Provence.

96. *Zohar* 1:190b, 3:79a. Koren, "'Woman from Whom God Wanders,'" 251–53; Aristotle, *Gen. an.* 53.

97. Koren, "'Woman from Whom God Wanders,'" 111–12; Dinari, "Hilul ha-Qodesh"; idem, "Minhagei ṭum'at ha-niddah"; Ta-Shma, "haraḥaqot niddah"; idem, *Halakhah*, 280–88; Cohen, "Menstruants and the Sacred"; idem, "Purity and Piety."

98. Hebrew in Meir b. Baruch of Rothenburg, *Sefer She'elot u-teshuvot Maharam bar Baruch,* vol. 2, no. 124, trans. Irving A. Agus, *Rabbi Meir of Rothenberg,* 1:231, no. 150.

99. Koren, "'Woman from Whom God Wanders.'"

100. Judith R. Baskin, "From Separation to Displacement"; Koren, "'Woman from Whom God Wanders,'" 117–18.

101. Dinari, "Minhagei"; Ta-Shma, "haraḥaqot niddah"; idem, *Halakhah*, 280–88. Ta-Shma cautions that not all legal arguments were tied to popular fear of the menstruant as dangerous. See Ta-Shma, "haraḥaqot," 166; idem, *Halakhah*, 283.

102. Koren cites two examples, one from *Megillat Aḥima'ats* (ca. 1054) and the other from a sixteenth-century tradition about the thirteenth-century rabbi Judah ha-Hasid of Speyer. In *Megillat Aḥima'ats* a menstruating woman lights the Sabbath candles and approaches the *Sefer Merkavah*, whereas in the story of Judah ha-Hasid his menstruating wife accidentally touched a case containing notebooks of "holy mysteries." In the first instance most of the *niddah*'s family perished from disease and misfortune. In the second, R. Judah was forced into exile from his home city. See Koren, "'Woman from Whom God Wanders,'" 103–15. In Spanish Kabbalah, the menstruating or bleeding postpaturient Shekhinah became the producer of demons and the source of divine punishment against men. See above.

103. Eleazar ben Judah of Worms, *Perushe sidur ha-Tefilah la-Rokeaḥ;* Koren, "'Woman from Whom God Wanders,'" 133–34.

104. Nahmanides, *Commentary on Leviticus,* in *Kitve Rabenu Mosheh ben Naḥman.* For a discussion of some of these texts, see Koren, "'Woman from Whom God Wanders,'" 222–25.

105. Koren, "'Woman from Whom God Wanders.'" Her entire thesis is based on this premise; see esp. "Chapter 6. Kabbalistic Physiology," 209–47.

106. See Moshe Idel, "Abraham Abulafia on the Jewish Messiah and Jesus," in idem, *Studies in Ecstatic Kabbalah,* 45–61.

107. Brian Stock, *The Implications of Literacy,* 7.

108. Ibid., 90–91. Quotation on 91.

109. On the concept of linguistic shorthand and its cultural context, see James Scott, *Weapons of the Weak,* 138–39. Cf. his discussion of trickster tales and euphemisms in *Domination*, 34–36, 152–66; and Michael Camille, *Image on the Edge,* 26–36, esp. 36.

110. Some Muslims were quite familiar with the Bible, however, and used it for polemical and other purposes. See Hava Lazarus-Yafeh, *Intertwined Worlds.*

111. E.g., see Petrus Alfonsi, *The Disciplina Clericalis of Petrus Al fonsi; Die Disciplina clericalis des Petrus Alfonsi (das älteste novellenbuch des Mittelalters) nach allen bekannten handschriften,* ed. Alfons Hilka and Werner Soderhjelm; on medieval medical discourse on lovesickness, see Allen, *Wages of Sin,* 1–24; Jaques Ferrand, *A Treatise on Lovesickness.* Ferrand wrote later than the period under discussion; however, Beecher and Ciavolella's introduction is useful for earlier periods. Mary Frances Wack, *Lovesickness in the Middle Ages.* Ibn Zabara, *Sefer Sha'ashu'im* and *Book of Delight,* uses medical debate throughout his work to enliven his narrative, as does Isaac ibn Sahula, *Meshal ha-Qadmoni,* and a variety of Muslim writers of autobiographies or literature to entertain: Usamah Ibn Munqidh, *Memoirs;* Ibn Buluggīn al-Zīrī, *Mudhakkirāt al-amīr 'Abd Allāh, al-musammāt bi-Kitāb al-Tibyān;* idem, *The Tibyan,* trans. Amin T. Tibi; *Sefer ha-Zohar*, ed. Re'uven Margolies, 2:149b, 242b–244b; see also Tishby's discussion in *The Wisdom of the Zohar,* Heb. trans. Fischel Lachower and Isaiah Tishby, ed. Isaiah Tishby, Eng. trans. David Goldstein, 2:459–64, 475–82, 488–89.

112. Green, *Women's Healthcare.*

113. See, e.g., *The Book of the Thousand Nights and One Night,* trans. Powys Mathers, vol. 2: Tale of Sympathy the Learned, 156–62. For medicine in Jewish literature, see n. 111 above.

114. Monica Green has found a thirteenth-century vernacular sermon focused on theories of generation. Green, *Women's Healthcare,* 164. Again, this process began earlier in the Muslim world.

115. Muḥammad ibn Aḥmad ibn Jubayr, *Riḥlat,* 34–35; *The Travels of Ibn Jubayr,* trans. R. J. C. Broadhurst, 52.

116. Oderic Vitalis, *Ecclesiastical History,* vol. 5, bk. 9, pp. 166/167–168/169.

117. Hillenbrand, *Crusades,* 308, citing Al-'Umarī, *Masālik al-abṣār,* partially translated in E. R. Lundquist, *Saladin and Richard the Lionhearted,* 34.

118. Tolan, *Saracens,* 116–17.

119. Berger, "Mission to the Jews"; *Jewish-Christian Debate,* 29–32. Berger notes that individual Jewish polemicists differed in the behavior they recommended for their coreligionists around Christians. Some such as the author of the *Nizzaḥon Yashan* extolled an aggressive approach, whereas others such as Jacob b. Reuben and Solomon de Rossi encouraged avoidance and restraint. *Jewish-Christian Debate,* 21–23.

120. On this exchange, see Smalley, *Study of the Bible*. Smalley is primarily interested in Christian Hebraicists rather than the effects of this exchange on medieval Jewish culture.

121. In the Tosafot commentary to BT Shabbat 116b the author prohibits reading "war tales in the vernacular" (literally "in the language of idol worship" [בלשון עבודה זרה]). Chazan interprets this as a prohibition against reading *chansons de geste* and similar literature and a hint that Jews did indeed read Christian adventure stories. Chazan, *European Jewry*, 327 n. 34. The discovery of a Judeo-German *Ritterroman* in the Cairo Geniza strengthens this impression. *Dukus Horant*, ed. P. F. Ganz, F. Norman, and W. Schwarz. Much of Susan Einbinder's research on *piyyuṭim* and Hebrew Crusade Chronicles shows that French and German Jews used similar literary tropes in their texts: Einbinder, "Jewish Women Martyrs"; idem, "Pucellina of Blois." On Jewish awareness and even adaptation of Christian religious rituals, see Marcus, *Rituals of Childhood.* Indeed Nirenberg (*Communities*, 14) has argued for the fourteenth century that Jews and Muslims actively sought and adapted Christian modes of discourse.

122. On Jewish religious poetry in Romance vernacular, see Einbinder, "Troyes Laments"; Arsène Darmesteter, "Deux elegies du Vatican"; idem, "L'auto du fé de Troyes"; *Sefer Ḥasidim,* nos. 209, 220, 238, 428.

123. Ross, *Grief of God*, 53–55, 61. Also, cf. Beryl Rowland and Debra Hassig's discussions of the didactic function of animal images in Christian art: Debra Hassig, *Medieval Bestiaries,* 175–78; Beryl Rowland, "The Art of Memory and the Bestiary."

124. Hassig, *Medieval Bestiaries,* 18–26.

125. Epstein, *Dreams;* Marcus, *Rituals,* 88–101. Also see chap. 6. Regarding the issue of whether the images in Jewish illuminated manuscripts were in fact painted by Jews and the difference authorship would make in the interpretation, see Epstein, *Dreams,* 4–9 and notes.

126. Giles Constable, "The Ideal of the Imitation of Christ."

127. Ross, *The Grief of God,* 5.

128. See discussion of these themes below.

129. See chap. 2; Scheffczyk, *Mariengeheimnis,* 143; Jaroslav Pelikan, *Mary through the Centuries,* 192.

130. See Elliot's discussion in *Fallen Bodies*, 108–10.

131. Walter Delius, *Geschichte der Marienverehrung,* 139–40, 173–77. Also, cf. anonymous quodlibet (30.5) in Glorieux, *Littérature,* 2:306.

132. Anselm of Canterbury, *De Conceptu virginali et de originali peccato*, in *S. Anselmi opera omnia,* vol. 2, chaps. 7–14, 17, 18; Peter Lombard, *Sententiae in IV libris distinctae,* vol. 2, Lib. III, Dist. III, cap. 1–4; Dist. V, cap. 1.5; Bernard of Clairvaux, *In purificatione B. Mariae sermo III* in *Sämtliche werker,* 7:418–24; Thomas Aquinas, *Summa Theologica,* 3a.27.1–6; idem, [*Summa contra gentiles*] *Summe gegen die Heiden,* English: *Summa contra gentiles,* 4.61.3; Delius, *Geschichte,* 173–79; Elliot, *Fallen Bodies,* 112–13. Cf. the quodlibets of William of Ockham, 3.10–11; John of Baconthorpe (fl. 1330), 2.13; Jean of Naples, 6.11; anon., 21.5 in Glorieux, *Littérature,* 120, 151.

133. "Post concessum autem sanctae Virginis, Spiritus Sanctus praevenit in ipsam, secundum verbum Domini quod dixit angelus, purgans ipsam, et potentiam deitatis Verbi receptivam preparans, simul autem et generativam. Et tunc obumbravit ipsam Dei altisimi per se Sapientia et Virtus existens, id est Filius Dei, Patri homousios, id est consubstantialis, sicut divinum semen; et copulavit sibi ipsi ex sanctissimis et purissimis ipsius Virginis sanguinibus carnem animatam" (Peter Lombard, *Sententiae,* Lib. III, Dist. III, cap. I. 3). Peter Lombard is quoting from John of Damascus, *De fide orthodoxa,* III. 2.

134. Albertus Magnus, *De annuntiatione,* in *Opera omnia,* vol. 26, Tract. II, quest. 3, art. 2, and art. 4.3 in *Opera Omnia*, XXVI. Also, cf. his *De Incarnatione,* Tract. III, quest. 2, art. 3. On Albertus's use of Aristotelian biological theories in his theological works, see Henryk Anzulewicz, "Die Aristotelische Biologie in den Frühwerken des Albertus Magnus." For another example of the equation of Mary and Jesus' flesh and the problems therewith, see Richard Knapwell (fl. 1284/85), Quodlibet 1.5 in Glorieux, *Littérature,* 2:56.

135. Albertus Magnus, *De annuntiatione*, Tract. II, quest. 2, art. 7.7. Cf. Tract. II, quest. 1, art. 6, solutio. In this view he was followed by his student, Thomas Aquinas, but Aquinas primarily refers to this "preparation" in terms of purification from original sin and lust, not physical purification. Aquinas, *Summa Theologica,* 3, 24, 2; 3a, 27, 4, 5.2; Delius, *Geschichte,* 182–83.

136. John Duns Scotus, *Reportata Parisiensia,* Distinctio 3, quest. 1–2, pp. 959–65; Pseudo-Albertus Magnus, *Mariale,* quest. 127, 139; Aquinas, *Summa Theologica,* 3a.27.1–2; Delius, *Geschichte,* 183–88; Hubertus P. J. M. Ahsmann, *Le culte de la Sainte Vierge et la littérature française profane du moyen âge,* 36–37, 41–46, 49; Marina Warner, *Alone of All Her Sex,* 241–42; Pelikan, *Mary,* 194–98; Mirella Levi D'Ancona, *The Iconography of the Immaculate Conception in the Middle Ages and Early Renaissance,* 39–43.

137. Warner, *Alone,* 252–54. Carolyn Walker Bynum has emphasized the importance of the female origns of Jesus' humanity in a number of her writings. See her "The

Body of Christ in the Later Middle Ages" and "'. . . And Woman His Humanity'" in *Fragmentation and Redemption.* Bynum was primarily interested in exploring how the feminine origins of Jesus' humanity became a positive avenue for religious contemplation and symbolism. I do not dispute her findings but must agree with Warner that however much Christians may have revered Mary as vessel and source of Christ's humanity, the conjunction of divinity and flesh bothered European Christians enough that they, like the "gnostics" of late antiquity, sought to separate Jesus, and therefore Mary, from the human body. Also see Ross, *Grief,* 50–51. Most of Ross's sources are later than the chronological scope of this work. On Mary's not needing purification after childbirth, see Scheffczyck, *Mariengeheimnis*, 145; and chap. 2. For a twelfth-century example, see Bernard of Clairvaux, *In Purificatione Beatae Mariae,* sermo I, in *Sämtliche Werke,* 7:404–12.

138. Charles T. Wood, "The Doctor's Dilemma," quotation on 718.

139. Ibid., 718.

140. See *Contributions to the Apocryphal Literature of the New Testament,* ed. and trans. William Wright; Pseudo-Melito of Sardis, *"Transitu Mariae" des Pseudo-Melito;* Warner, *Alone,* 81–89; Rubin, *Gentile Tales,* 7–11; Parkes, *Conflict,* 291–97; chap. 2.

141. "Mariae anima claritate fruitur Christi, et gloriosis conspectibus eius . . . excellentiori quadam specialique praerogativa a Filio honoratur: possidens in Christo corpus suum quod genuit, clarificatum in dextera Patris . . . Thronum Dei, thalamum coeli Domini, domum atque tabernaculum Christi dignum est ibi esse ubi ipse est. Tam pretiosum enim thesearum dignius est coelum servare quam terra; tantam integritatem merito incorruptibilitas, non putredinis ulla resolutio sequitur. Illud ergo sacratissimum corpus, de quo Christus carnem assumpsit, et divinam naturam humanae univit. . . . escam vermibus traditum. . . . dicere pertimesco communi sorte putredinis et futuri de vermibus pulveris. De quo si nihil altius sentirem quam de proprio, nihil dicerem nisi quemadmodum de proprio. Quod absque ulla ambiguitate solvendum in mortem, post mortem est futurum putredo, post putredinem vermis, post vermem, ut dignum est, abjectissimus pulvis. Quod de Maria credendum non videtur consentibile; quia aestimationem procul propellit incomparabilis gratiae munis" (Pseudo-Augustine, *"Ad interrogata," De Assumptione Beatae Mariae Virginis,* in *PL* 40, col. 1146, chap. 6. This passage may also be found in Walter Delius, *Texte zur Mariologie un Marienverehrung der mittelalterlichen Kirche,* 21. Cf. Guibert of Nogent, *De pignoribus sanctorum epistola nuncupatoria*, 1.1, in *PL* 156, cols. 623–24; Hildebertus Lavardin, *Opera omnia,* in *PL* 181, col. 627. See discussions in Delius, *Geschichte,* 189–90; Warner, *Alone,* 81–102.

142. Warner, *Alone,* 90–102. On views of death, decay, and resurrection in general, see Bynum, *Resurrection*; and chap. 1.

143. A graphic illustration of Mary as victor not only over death but also over putrescence is Giovanni del Biondo's painting from the fourteenth century in which the haloed Virgin, holding the infant Jesus and being adored by a variety of saints, stands above a worm-eaten skeleton. However, Giovanni is late for our purposes. Reproduced and discussed in Levi D'Ancona, *Iconography,* 26, 32–33 (fig. 10).

144. I cite but a small selection of examples: Rutebeuf, *Le neuf joies Nostre Dame,* in *Oeuvres completes de Rutebeuf,* ed. Edmond Faral and Julia Bastin, 2:249, 11.79–88; John

of Garland, *The Stella Maris of John of Garland,* 121, 11.472–83; Gautier de Coincy, *Les miracles de Nostre Dame,* 1:21, 29, 32–33, 44–45; 2:23; 3:19, 137, 393; "De Beata Maria Virgine," in [*Analecta liturgica*] *Thesauris hymnologicis,* and in Delius, *Texte,* 15; Adam of St. Victor, "Salve, mater Salvatoris," in *Sequentiae,* in *PL* 196, trans. in C. A. Maurin, *Les saluts d'amour,* 1:228–30. Also see Maurin's discussion of his flower imagery, *Les Saluts d'amour,* 1:196; Amedeus of Clermont-Tonnerre, *Epistola ad filios suos ecclesiae Lausannensis,* in *PL* 188, col. 1338, also in Maurin, *Les Saluts d'amour*, 1:216; Albertus Magnus, *De Incarnatione;* Hildegard, *Symphonia,* 112–37; Warner, *Alone,* 99–100, 198–99; Ahsmann, *Culte,* 14; Levi D'Ancona, *Iconography,* 54–55.

145. "Et egredietur virga de radice Jesse et flos de radice eius ascendet. Et requiescet super eum spiritus Domini, spiritus sapientiae et intellectus, spiritus consilii et fortitudinis, spiritus scientiae et pietatis. Et replebit eum spiritus timoris Domini." The translation from Latin is my own.

146. On the flower of Jesse and Marian symbolism, see Anita Guerreau-Jalabert, "L'arbre de Jesse et l'ordre chretien de la parenté"; Levi D'Ancona, *Iconography,* 18, 46–50, 54–55, 65–68. Many of the floral allegories in Hildegard of Bingen's poetry about Mary and Jesus posit Jesus as the flower that bloomed from the branch of Jesse. Hildegard, *Symphonia,* 120/121, 124/125, 126–37.

147. Fulbertus of Chartres, "Sermo I de Nativitate Beatissimae Virginis," in *Opera omnia,* in *PL* 141, col. 322; Levi D'Ancona, *Iconography,* 54.

148. See, e.g., the story of the man with a cancerous foot in Hugo Farsitus, *Libelus de miraculis B Mariae virginis in urbe Suessionensi,* in *PL* 179, miracle 31, cols. 1799–1800.

149. Gautier de Coincy, *Miracles,* 3:398–483, esp. 398–404. Cf. John of Garland, *Stella Maris,* no. 14, pp. 109–13.

150. Gautier de Coincy, *Miracles*, 3:406–9; cf. 422–37.

151. Ibid., 3:475–83.

152. On Mary "Mediatrix," see Delius, *Geschichte,* 188–89; Ahsmann, *Culte,* 65–103; Pelikan, *Mary,* 125–36; Levi D'Ancona, *Iconography,* 33–35.

153. "Tu as sour lui commandement / Con sour celui, haute pucele, / Que nourresis de to mamele" (Gautier de Coincy, *Miracles,* 3:230). Also see the text that follows, 230–33. Cf. 1:32–33, 3:147, 284. On nursing as a fundamental aspect of Mary's power as an intercessor and as a symbol of Christ's human aspect, see Warner, *Alone,* 192–205; Ahsmann, *Culte,* 77, 137; Levi D'Ancona, *Iconography,* 34–35 and fig. 18 from a thirteenth-century psalter in which Mary shows her bare breast to Christ while seated above the tortured souls of hell; Ross, *Grief,* 50–51; Marilyn Yalom, *A History of the Breast,* 36, 40–45. Many of the examples these authors cite date from the fourteenth and fifteenth centuries or later. However, the examples from Gautier de Coincy and the Psalter (British Museum, Add. MS 17868, fol. 31, as cited in Levi D'Ancona) demonstrate that this trope was already being used by the thirteenth century in France.

154. Gautier de Coincy, *Miracles,* 3:25, 139; John of Garland, *Stella Maris,* no. 7, p. 106 (both this and the miracle told by Gautier in vol. 3, p. 25, describe oil oozing from the breast of a statue of Mary and converting a Muslim); Adam de Perseigne, *The Letters of Adam of Perseigne,* vol. 1, Letter 3 (17), pp. 66–89, esp. 77–78; idem, *Lettres;*

Warner, *Alone,* 192–205; Bynum, "The Body of Christ in the Later Middle Ages," in *Fragmentation;* Yalom, *History,* 46–48.

155. Ross, *Grief.* This argument is fundamental to her entire book but is most clearly outlined in her introduction, 3–14, esp. 6.

156. "Christum vorari fas dentibus non est" (Paschasius Radbertus, *De corpore et sanguine domini,* 4.14). For continued identification of the divine presence in the Eucharist and the incarnation, see Peter Damian, *Sermones,* 267; see discussion by Rubin, *Corpus Christi,* 14–22.

157. Berengar of Tours, *Berengarius Turonensis Rescriptum contra Lanfrancum,* 1:941ff.; Rubin, *Corpus Christi,* 6–35; Sapir Abulafia, *Christians and Jews,* 35–39; R. W. Southern, *Saint Anselm,* 44–51. On the influence of ancient philosophy on theological metaphysics in the Middle Ages generally, see Stephen Gersh, "Platonism-Neoplatonism-Aristotelianism."

158. Others attempted to allegorize the Eucharist to a greater degree. Peter Lombard, *Sententiae,* 4.9.2.1, 3; Rubin, *Corpus Christi,* 24–25; Gary Macy, *The Theologies of the Eucharist in the Early Scholastic Period,* 122–26.

159. Bonaventure, *Sententiae,* IV, d. 9, a I, quest. 2–3, in *Opera omnia,* 4:204; also see Albertus Magnus, *Sententiae,* IV, d. 9 a. 5 *in fine* in which he explains that the substance (Christ) only remained until the accidents (the bread) had been digested. Rubin, *Corpus Christi,* 67, 338.

160. Alan of Lille, *Liber poenitentialis,* Lib. 3, cap. 24, p. 141; Rubin, *Corpus Christi,* 69. Other examples of continued theological discomfort with the doctrine of substantiation are quodlibets of Bernard Lombardi (fl. 1331), 1.13; Bertrand de la Tour (fl. 1311–12), 1.8; Durand de Saint Pourçain (fl. 1312–13), 2.1–2, 4.4; William of Ockham (d. 1349), 4.13–35; Jean Peckham (fl. 1277), 3.40–41; Peter Olivi (fl. 1288), 4.23–24; Peter of England (fl. 1305), 3.3; Peter of Trabibus (fl. 1295), 1.1–8; Raymond Rigauld (fl. 1280–95), 3.9–11, 5.23; Roger Marston (fl. 1283), 2.9, 3.23; Anon. 26.1–2; Guillaume Pierre de Falegar (d. 1297), 1.11–12, in Glorieux, *Littérature,* 2:65, 68, 71, 74, 121–22, 126, 178, 209, 214, 229–30, 243, 246.

161. Pope Alexander III, *Sententiae,* in *Die Sentenzen Rolands nachmals Papstes Alexander III,* 232–33. Rubin, *Corpus Christi,* 37, 337–38. On the mistaken identity of "Roland" Bandinelli, see John T. Noonan, "Who Was Rolandus?"; Rudolph Weigand, "Magister Rolandus and Papst Alexander III." On saintly women (and men) living from the Eucharist, see Bynum, *Holy Feast, Holy Fast,* 120, 337. See also John of Naples, Quodlibet (10.16), and Jean Peckham (fl. 1269), Quodlibet 4.3 in Glorieux, *Littérature,* 2:169, 179.

162. The best known of these *exempla* collections is that of Caesarius of Heisterbach. Rubin, *Corpus Christi,* 111–29, 344–45; idem, *Gentile Tales.*

163. Rubin, *Corpus Christi,* 119.

164. Elliot also sees a strong connection between Marian theology and the Eucharist, but her point seems more to contrast the purity of the Virgin and her value as a substitute "wife" (Mary is also the source of eucharistic milk, cleansed of all pollutative associations) to clerical wives who rendered the priests unworthy to give the Eucharist. *Fallen Bodies,* 107–26.

Chapter 4. **Filthy Womb and Foul Believers**

1. In saying that Christians were reacting to discoveries regarding Jewish attitudes toward Mary and her son, I do not mean to suggest that Christian responses were not violent or aggressive. Officially "sponsored debates" such as the Paris Talmud Trial may be seen as an aggressive Christian measure. Nevertheless, it was in response to rumors of Jewish invective. See Grayzel, *The Church and the Jews*, 79–82, no. 116 (pp. 268–71), no. 118 (pp. 274–75).

2. Jean-Paul Sauvage, "Le massacre des Juifs a Blois en 1171"; Robert Chazan, "The Blois Incident of 1171"; H. Wagenaar-Nolthenius, "Der 'Planetus Judei' and der [Alenu-] Gesang judischer Martyrer in Blois anno 1171."

3. On shifting attitudes toward Mary, the incarnation, medical theory, and purity laws in both Jewish and Christian thought during the twelfth and thirteenth centuries, see chap. 3 above.

4. Tolan, *Saracens,* 54, 61–62, 86, 93, 238; idem, "Un cadavre mutilé"; Penny J. Cole, "'God the Heathen Have Come into Your Inheritence,' (Ps. 78:1)"; John of Damascus, *Heresy of the Ishmaelites,* 136–37; *Risalat al-Kindi,* trans. Tartar, 148–53; Theophanes, *Chronicle,* trans. Turtledove, 35; Guibert of Nogent, *Dei gesta per Francos, CCCM,* 127 A: 96; Roger Bacon, *Opus maius pars septima seu moralis philosophia,* 211, 219, 221; idem, *The Opus Majus of Roger Bacon,* 2:814; Rodrigo Jiménez de Rada, *Historia Arabum*, 5–6, 18.

5. Carole Hillenbrand, *The Crusades,* 266, 270–74, 276, 285, 298, 301–3, 317–18; Emmanuel Sivan, *L'Islam et la Croisade,* 61–64, 85, 111, 113, 116, 134; Al-Shams al-Dīn Muḥammad ibn Abī Ṭālib al-Anṣārī al-Dimashqī, *Kitāb Nukhbat al-dahr fī 'ajā'ib al-barr wa'l-baḥr,* 275; Ibn Khallikan, *Wafāyāt al-a'yān,* 4:231; idem, *Ibn Khallikan's Biographical Dictionary,* 2:635; idem, "Extraits de la vie du Sultan Salah ed-Din"; 'Imād al-Dīn Muḥammad ibn Muḥammad al-Kātib al-Iṣfaḥnī, *Al-fatḥ al-qussī fī- 'l-fatḥ al-Qudsī,*116, 118, 135–36, 142–43, 198, 346–49 (portions of this text are in Francesco Gabrieli, *Arab Historians of the Crusades,* 147, 163, 170–72, 204–7); Abd al-Raḥman ibn Isma'il Abī Shamah, *Kitāb al-Rawḍatayn [Livre des deux jardins],* 4:321–22, 338.

6. Odo of Tournai, *De disputation contra iudaeum Leonem nomine de Adventu Christi fillii Dei*, *PL* 160, cols. 1103, 1112 (for an English translation see Odo of Tournai, *On Original Sin and a Disputation with the Jew, Leo, concerning the Advent of Christ the Son of God,* 85, 97); Guibertus of Nogent, *Tractatus de Incarnatione contra Judaeos,* in *Opera omnia*, *PL* 156, cols. 489–90; Alanus de Insulis, *Contra haereticos*, lib. I, cap. 18–22, 33–34, 57–62, *PL* 210, cols. 321–24, 335–37, 359–65. On the Christian sense of Jewish threat, both spiritual and physical, see Chazan, *Medieval Stereotypes*.

7. Joseph ben Nathan Official, *Yosef ha-Mekane'*, 69.

8. "Bar Simson Chronicle," in *Sefer Gezerot*, 24, 31–32; Chazan, *European Jewry*, 244, 255, 265; "Mainz Anonymous," in *Sefer Gezerot*, 101, 104; Chazan, *European Jewry*, 237, 241; R. Yehudah b. R. Kalonymous, "'El 'Evel 'Ekra," in *Sefer Gezerot*, 156; *Penguin Book of Hebrew Verse*, 258; Dalman, *Jesus Christ*, 21–26, 41–47; Sapir Abulafia, "Invectives."

9. On the *Toledot* and its relationship to the Hebrew chronicles and *piyyuṭim,* see Intimations of sexual promiscuity was extended to include all Christians. Joseph K[Q]imḥi, *Sefer ha-Berit,* 26 (English translation: Id *The Book of the Covenant,* 33); and the poems by David b. Meshullam and R. Joshua b. R. Menahem in *Sefer Gezerot 'Ashkenaz ve-Tsarfat,* 70 and 214 respectively.

10. Jehiel b. Joseph of Paris, *Vikuaḥ Rabenu Yeḥi'el mi-Paris,* 5; Guibertus of Nogent, *De Incarnatione, PL* 156, col. 489; Moises Orfali, "El 'Dialogus pro Ecclesia contra Synagogam,'" 691, 698; Jordan, "Marian Devotion"; Yerushalmi, "Inquisition"; Merchaviah, *ha-Talmud,* 274–76, 427, 453.

11. *Jewish-Christian Debate,* paras. 215, 220, Heb. 146, 150, Eng. pp. 209, 214–15; Pseudo-David K[Q]imḥi, *Vikuaḥ Radak 'im ha-Naẓrut,* 91; Orfali, "Dialogus," 712.

12. Pseudo-Guillaume de Champeaux, *Dialogus inter Christianum et Judaeum de fide Catholicae, PL* 163, cols. 1053–54. For further examples of this kind of argument, see Gilbert Crispin, *Disputatio Iudei et Christiani* in *Works,* paras. 83, 89, pp. 28, 30; Odo of Tournai, *Disputatione contra iudaeum, PL* 160, cols. 1110–12 (Eng. pp. 95–97); Guibertus of Nogent, *Tractatus de Incarnatione contra Judaeos, PL* 156, cols. 497–98; Martin of Leon, *Sermones 4, In natale domini, PL* 208, col. 163; Guillaume de Bourges, *Livre des guerres du seigneur et deux homilies,* 120/121; *Desputoison du juyf et du crestien,* 460, 463–64. For further discussion and more sources on this issue, see below. On Pseudo-Guillaume de Champeaux, see Sapir Abulafia, *Christians and Jews,* 46, 74, 81–82.

13. Peccatum autem concupiscentia est (Guibert of Nogent, *De Incarnatione, PL* 156, col. 497). Hildegard, *Scivias,* Vision 6.54, p. 267; idem, *Hildegardis Scivias.*

14. For examples outside the Jewish-Christian encounter, see Adam de Perseigne, *Letters*, Letter 14, pp. 177–79; Alan of Lille's sample sermons on the various sins in Alanus de Insulis, *De Arte Praedicatoria, PL* 210, cols. 119–34; Peter of Blois, *Sermones*, Serm. 24, "In die Pentecostes," *PL* 207, col. 630. In a nonpolemical context some medieval Jewish authors also spoke of the "filth" *(tinuf)* or "impurity" *(miṭuma'h)* of sin, though without denying the uncleanness of ritual impurity. Zerahyah ha-Yevani, *Sefer ha-Yashar*, 34/35, 46/47, 80/81, 170/171–172/173, 248/249. Conversion, willing or otherwise, was also often refered to in terms of uncleanness; see below. On medieval Jewish concepts of original sin, see Dorith Cohen-Aloro, "Me-hokhmata' 'ail'ah li-hokhmata' de-trefei 'ailona'"; Deborah Shechterman, "Sugit ha-heta' ha-qadmon ve-ha-parshanut le-devrei ha-Rambam ba-hagut ha-yehudit ba-me'ot ha-shalosh-'asrah ve-ha-'arba'-'asrah."

15. Chastity within marriage, even Mary and Joseph's, was sometimes problematized in Christian texts; see Dyan Elliot, *Spiritual Marriage,* 142–83. It is possible that medieval Christian discomfort with the legal status of chaste marriage (i.e., whether it was really a marriage) fueled some of the Jewish and Christian protestations in this regard.

16. Talmage, "Hebrew Polemical Treatise"; Berger, "Christian Heresy"; Joseph ben Nathan Official, *Sefer Yosef ha-Mekane',* 104; Pseudo-David Kimḥi, *Vikuaḥ ha-Radak,* 86; *Jewish-Christian Debate,* para. 145 (Heb. p. 96, Eng. p. 153).

17. Talmage, "Hebrew Polemical Treatise."

18. Berger, "Christian Heresy." This is not to say that Jews were unaware of Cathar anti-Catholic polemic, or did not occasionally avail themselves of it, as Berger shows. This argument probably stemmed from internal Christian discourse, however.

19. Hassig, *Medieval Bestiary,* 29–39.

20. Guibert of Nogent, *De Incarnatione, PL* 156, cols. 499–500; St. Martin of Leon, Sermon 34, *In Festo S. Trinitatis, PL* 208, col. 1327; Guillaume de Bourges, *Livre des Guerres,* 248/249; Jacob b. Reuben, *Milḥamot ha-Shem,* 66. Guibert of Nogent describes some unusual "scientific" analogies, that cats generate from catnip and goats from bushes, that were not part of the normal bestiary or scientific discourse. For a brief discussion of this trope, see Lasker, *Jewish Philosophical Polemics,* 157.

21. Sapir Abulafia, *Christians and Jews,* 82–87; Gilbert Dahan, *Les intellectuels chrétiens et les juifs au Moyen Age,* 427–34; Jacob b. Reuben, *Milḥamot ha-shem,* 66–67.

22. לא נאמר דבר זה כי אם בלשון ביזוי (Jacob b. Reuben, *Milḥamot ha-Shem,* 67).

23. Jacob b. Reuben, *Milḥamot ha-Shem,* 11; *Jewish-Christian Debate,* para. 145 (Heb. pp. 96–97, Eng. pp. 153–54); Pseudo-David Kimhi, *Vikuaḥ le-Radaq,* 91–92; Crispin, *Disputatio Iudei,* 28–29; Alan of Lille, *Contra Haereticos, PL* 210, col. 415; Pseudo-Guillelmus of Champeaux, *Dialogus inter Christianum et Judaeum, PL* 163, cols. 1054–55; Guillaume de Bourges, *Livre des guerres,* 98/99; Orfali, "Dialogus," 706, 710–11; *Desputoison du juyf et du crestien,* 460; "quem [mater] non perperit carnali commercio; immo virgo permanens mater est ex filio," "Ludus de Nativitate (Benediktbeuren)," 196.

24. Jacob b. Reuben, *Milḥamot ha-Shem,* 11; Alan de Insulis, *Contra haereticos, PL* 210, col. 415; Pseudo-Guillaume de Champeaux, *Dialogus inter Christianum et Judaeum, PL* 163, cols. 1054–55; Orfali, "Dialogus," 706, 710–11; *Desputoison du juyf et du crestien,* 460; "Ludus de Nativitate (Benediktbeuren)," 178–201. For a discussion of this imagery, see Lasker, *Jewish Philosophical Polemics,* 157–59.

25. Pseudo-Albertus Magnus, *Mariale,* 213.

26. Lev. 12. The second half of Gen. 3:16 ("I will greatly multiply your pain") was "yet your desire shall be for your husband." Thus Mary's lack of pain in birth was an important corollary to her freedom from sexual desire. If she was free of both aspects of Eve's curse, then she must have been free of the original sin that inspired the curse, making her pure in the metaphysical sense so important to Christian theologians.

27. *Jewish-Christian Debate,* para. 6 (Heb. pp. 5–6, Eng. p. 44). Also see Pseudo-David Kimḥi, *Vikuḥei Radak,* 92. The author of this second text argues that if Mary did not need such a sacrifice, then she lied about herself by implying that she did. Hardly fitting behavior for the sinless mother of God.

28. On the Lichtmess, see Berger's note, *Jewish-Christian Debate,* 237, n. 26.

29. Odo of Tournai, *Disputatio contra iudaeum, PL* 160, cols. 1110–12 (trans. *A Disputation,* pp. 95–97); Guibert of Nogent, *De Incarnation, PL* 156 cols. 495, 499–500.

30. On sexual passion and other emotions as biological phenomena, see Petrus Alfonsi, *Dialogo contra los Judios,* 24–28; Sapir Abulafia, *Christians and Jews,* 91–92; Orfali, "Dialogus," 694; Allen, *Wages,* 1–24; Wack, *Lovesickness.*

31. On the impurity of semen, Lev. 15:1–18; Cohen, "Women and the Sacred"; idem, "Purity and Piety"; Koren, "Woman from Whom God Wanders."

32. ולאחר שבא ונראה לעולם, אתם מאמינים כי הוא אלוהים חיים ומלך עולם. ואני תמה ואיני יכול להאמין דבר זה, כי [הוא] אל גדול ונורא אשר עין לא ראתה: ואין לו דמות ואין לו צורה, והוא אמר יתעלה שמו "כי לא יראני האדם וחי" ואיך אאמין באל הגדול, נעלם ונכסה, שנכנס בבטן אישה במעי נקובה, מטר־ נפים מוסרחים בלא צורך בהכרח, ובאלוהים חיים שיהיה ילוד אישה (Joseph Kimḥi, *Sefer ha-Berit*, p. 29, Eng. p. 36). My translation differs slightly from Talmage's.

33. . . . quo audito cogitavit turpiditudinem quam emittunt mulieres pariendo, et cum videret elevari in altari corpus Domini, habuit cogitationem ex illa turpitudine quod esset infectum corpus Domini, et quod ex hoc incidit in dictum errorem credentie videlicet quod non esset ibi corpus Domini Ihesu Christi (testimony of Aude, wife of Guillaume Fauré of Merviel, in *Le Registre d'inquisition de Jacques Fournier*, 2:94, no. 1). Very similar language to describe childbirth, also in connection with a woman's struggle with Catharism, is found in Jacques de Vitry, *Die Exempla, aus den Sermones feriales et communes*. See Carolyn Muessig, *Faces of Women in the Sermons of Jacques de Vitry*, no. 25.2, pp. 30–31, 38–40, 160. Unfortunately, Muessig does not provide the full exemplum and thus the exact context for this remark is missing.

34. See chap. 3; Koren, "The Woman from Whom God Wanders."

35. See the objections of Aude, quoted above, and the arguments of the Cathars regarding the incarnation as presented by Alanus de Insulis, *Contra haereticos*, lib. 1, cap. 23–24, *PL* 210, cols. 335–37; Moneta of Cremona (fl. 1241), *Adversus Catharos et Valdenses*, in *Heresies of the High Middle Ages*, 311, 313; Rainerius Sacconi (fl. 1245–62), *Summa d Catharis et Pauperibus de Lugduno*, 338 but also 344.

36. Cathars, obviously, had other ideas, and on occasion Jews incorporated or addressed aspects of their theology. On this, see above and also Berger, "Christian Heresy."

37. Gilbert Crispin, *Disputatio Iudei*, para. 89, p. 30. Cf. Odo of Tournai, *Disputatio*, *PL* 160, cols. 1111–12 (Eng. pp. 96–97); Martin of Leon, *Sermones*, Serm. 4, "In Natale Domini," *PL* 208, cols. 129–30.

38. דע כי דם הווסת הוא כמעט סם המות. ואילו שותה אדם ממנו כוס אחד, היה מת במעת ימים או היה חוזר מצורע, כי הוא דם מטונף ומלוכלך עד בלי דיי. נפלאות השם יתעלה הם כך גדולים שהעובר ניזון מאותו הדם תשעה חודשים ואינו ניזוק, רק נותן לו חלישות כוח. וכשיוצא מרחם אמו אין לו כוח להלוך על רגליו מפני היזונו מאותו הדם כל אותם החודשים הידועים שעמד ברחם. לא כן הבהמות שמיד שיוצא מרחם הוא הולך על רגליו. למה? מפני שהבהמות והחיות כולן אין להם דם נידות, והעובר שלהן הוא ניזון מדם הלב שהוא דם טוב ובריא ונקי. לכן כשיוצא ממעי אמו הוא הולך על רגליו מיד. אם כן ישו [ש]נתעברה אמו ממנו מרוח הקודש ולא ניזון במעי אמו מאותו דם הטינופת, ראוי היה להלוך על רגליו מאותו יום שנולד ולדבר ולהיות משכיל בכמו שהיה כשהגיע לשלושים שנה (Pseudo-David Kimḥi, *Vikuḥei Radak*, 87).

39. Adelard of Bath, *Questiones naturales*, quest. 38–39, pp. 41–42; *Prose Salernitan Questions*, ques. 228, pp. 115–16; Aquinas, *Summa Theologica*, Ia, 99, 1; Lawn, *Salernitan Questions*, 37–39, 52–53.

40. The author may have been drawing from one of the two versions of Berechiah ha-Nakdan's Hebrew translation of Adelard of Bath's *Questiones naturales*. However, Pseudo-Radak's explanation, that human infants cannot walk because they are fed from

menstrual blood, in contrast to the purer blood from which the young of animals are nourished, follows the explanation given in the *Salernitan Questions* rather than in Adelard of Bath's or Berechiah's version. Yet Adelard's and Berechiah's discussion of milk is closer to the one found in Pseudo-Radak than the one in the *Salernitan Questions*. Also, at least in the version edited by Lawn, the *Salernitan Questions* does not mention the role of the heart. Of course, the idea that milk derived from menstrual blood was a common theory and one present in Jewish religious texts as well as medical ones, so the discussion here need not have derived from the same medical text from which the author drew the argument about infants not walking. However, in Adelard of Bath and the Hebrew translations of his text, the two issues are juxtaposed. Thus the possibilities seem to be (1) Pseudo-Radak read the *Salernitan Questions* or some other Christian medical text in Latin that posits this theory; (2) he knew of it orally; (3) he read of it in a Hebrew or Old French translation or orginal text that is now lost or unknown to me. See *Prose Salernitan Questions,* quest. 115, p. 195; quest. 228, pp. 115–16; Berechiah b. Natronai ha-Nakdan, *Dodi ve-nechdi*, Heb. quest. 40, 41, pp. 28–30, 55; Eng. quest. 40–41, pp. 42–44; quest. 24–25, pp. 78–79. On vernacular texts, see Lawn, *Salernitan Questions*, 111–12; Gollancz, Introduction to *Dodi ve-nechdi*, i–xix.

41. This assumption, along with his argument about Jesus being conceived through Mary's ear, presents questions about the nature of the Christianity familiar to the author since Catholic Christians accepted that Mary menstruated and Jesus derived from Mary's blood. Did the author, intentionally or unintentionally, misunderstand Christian theology?

42. I am not assuming that the text was intended for a Christian audience of any kind, although given the degree to which Jews and Christians seem to have exchanged verbal argumentation or that Christians began investigating Jewish texts, the Christian reaction to any Jewish invective during this period needs to be taken into account.

43. אין דבר צח ונקי בכל העולם כזהב ושמא רוח המקום נוצצה בו ויש בו רוח הקודש (*Jewish-Christian Debate,* para. 39 [Heb. p. 27, Eng. p. 67]). The parallel comment in Joseph ben Nathan Official, *Yosef ha-Mekane',* 50, is a little muddled: לא היו יכולין לומר: שנכנס רוח הקדש בדבר טהור יותר מזהב.

44. Joseph ben Nathan Official, *Yosef ha-Mekane',* 50–51.

45. *Polemic of Nestor,* para. 74, Heb. 2:102, 125, Eng. 1:113; *Jewish-Christian Debate,* para. 152, Heb. p. 104, Eng. p. 165; Guibertus of Nogent, *De Incarnatione, PL* 156, col. 494; Orfali, "Dialogus," 700; Odo of Tournai, *Disputatio, PL* 160, cols. 1110–11, Eng. pp. 95–96; Pseudo-Guillelmus of Champeaux, *Dialogus, PL* 163, cols. 1060–62.

46. omni corpori praeponimus mundius lima [should read "luna"; see Resnick's translation p. 129 n. 31] sole praetiosius (Odo of Tournai, *Disputatio, PL* 160, col. 1111 [discussion begins at col. 1110 and continues to col. 1112] and Eng. p. 96 (discussion begins at p. 95 and continues to p. 97]). On the argument that angel's bodies are also corruptible and thus unworthy, see Guibert of Nogent, *De Incarnatione,* col. 494; Orfali, "Dialogus," 700. Of the two, Guibert uses the strongest language.

47. Odo discusses peasants at cols. 1110–11, Eng. pp. 95–96. On peasants' coarseness and irrationality, see Freedman, *Images,* 137–39, 150–54; on this passage in Odo of Cambrai, see Sapir Abulafia, "Bodies."

48. *Jewish-Christian Debate,* para. 39, Heb. p. 27, Eng. p. 68.

49. In the verse's original context, the concern was probably that the men would render themselves and their wives impure by seminal emission (see Lev. 15:16–18) or that sexual intercourse itself was unacceptable so close to an encounter with God. However, Joseph Official seems to be placing the onus of potential contamination entirely on the woman in this text, even though presumably the women were ritually clean (neither *zavah* or *niddah*). The emphasis on women's impurity, rather than men's, follows along with the arguments of Koren that medieval Jewish mystics were more worried about menstrual than seminal pollution as a barrier to the divine. Koren, "The Woman from Whom God Wanders," 67–85, 116.

50. According to biblical and talmudic law, men could also be *zav.*

51. On male disgust for their own genitalia and semen as a force that both feminizes and makes women repellent to men, see Miller, *Anatomy,* 101–5; Dyan Elliott, "Pollution, Illusion, and Masculine Disarray"; idem, *Fallen Bodies,* 14–34; *Sefer ha-Zohar,* I, 53b–54b. However, supernal semen was also equated with the purifying waters of the *mikvah.* Koren, "Woman from Whom God Wanders," 166–69.

52. Joseph Kimḥi, *Sefer ha-berit,* 29, Eng. p. 36; Jacob b. Reuben, *Milḥamot ha-Shem,* 13–15; Joseph ben Nathan Official, *Yosef ha-Mekane',* 49–50, 65, 119, 125; *Polemic of Nestor,* paras. 5, 74, 75, 82, Heb. 2:95, 102–3, 112–13, 125, Eng. 1:98–99, 113–15 respectively; Pseudo-David Kimḥi, *Vikuḥei Radak,* 86–88, 91–92; *Jewish-Christian Debate,* paras. 6, 39, 143, 145, 152, 173, Heb. pp. 5–6, 27, 91–93, 94–97, 103–4, 121, Eng. pp. 43–44, 67–68, 147–48, 150–55, 164–65, 183–84; R. Meir b. Simon of Narbonne, *Milḥemet Miẓvah,* partially edited in William Herskowitz, "Judaeo-Christian Dialogue in Provence as Reflected in *Milḥemet Miẓvah* of R. Meir hameili," as cited in Robert Chazan, "Polemical Themes in the *Milḥemet Miẓvah,*" esp. 179. The actual text [Mordechai b. Josef of Avignon, *Disputation Montpellier,* was edited by Adolph Posnanski in MS. Jerusalem. Hebrew University. Heb 80, 769, which has remained unavailable to me]. On this text generally, see Chazan, *Daggers,* 103–14; idem, "Chapter Thirteen of the *'Maḥazik Emunah'*"; On the womb and incarnation polemic, see *Jewish-Christian Debate,* 350–54; Lasker, *Jewish Philosophical Polemics,* 105–14; Idel, *Studies in Ecstatic Kabbalah.* There are exceptions. Nahmanides, for example, does not record that this issue, along with the graphic verbal illustrations that can be found in most texts from the period, played much of a role in the Barcelona debate.

53. "Bar Simson Chronicle," in *Sefer Gezerot,* 24, 31–32; Chazan, *European Jewry,* 244, 255, 265; "Mainz Anonymous," in *Sefer Gezerot,* 101, 104; Chazan, *European Jewry,* 237, 241; R. Yehudah b. R. Kalonymous, "'El 'Evel 'Ekra," in *Sefer Gezerot,* 156; *Penguin Book of Hebrew Verse,* 258; Dalman, *Jesus Christ,* 21–26, 41–47; Sapir Abulafia, "Invectives."

54. In quodam vos valde ridemus et insanos judicamus. Dicitis enim Deum, in maternis visceribus obsceno carcere fetidi ventris clausum, novem mensibus pati, et tandem pudendo exitu (qui intuitum sine confusione non admittit), decimo mense progredi, inferentes Deo tantum dedecus, quantum de nobis, quamvis vere, sine magna tamen verecundia non dicimus (Odo of Tournai, *Disputatio, PL* 160, col. 1110; idem.,

Disputation, trans. Resnick, p. 95). Also see Crispin, *Disputatio Iudei,* para. 81, p. 27; Guibert of Nogent, *De Incarnatione, PL* 156, cols. 489, 492, 495; Orfali, "Dialogus," 712; Pseudo-Guillelmus of Champaux, *Dialogus, PL* 163, col. 1053 (this author is more interested in the stain of original sin); Martin of Leon, *Sermone IV,* in *Natale Domini, PL* 208, cols. 129–34; *Desputoison du juyf et du crestien,* 461–62; "Ludus de Nativitate (Benediktbeuren)." Cf. Anselm, *Cur Deus Homo?* 1.3, in *Opera omnia* and in *Basic Writings,* 196 (Anselm's interlocuter was not Jewish, however). Many of these Christian texts were closely related. Both Guibert of Nogent and Gilbert Crispin knew and/or worked with Anselm. Others were members of the same study circles or consciously drew from Crispin's text in particular, and most scholars agree that Crispin's arguments are based on contact with real Jews. One should not make the error of assuming that these Christian disputations were simply carbon copies of Crispin's model, however. Sapir Abulafia, *Christians and Jews,* 81–85, 107–9; idem, "Bodies"; idem, "Jewish Carnality in Twelfth-Century Renaissance Thought"; idem, "Jewish-Christian Disputations"; idem, "An attempt by Gilbert Crispin, Abbot of Westminster, at Rational Argument in the Jewish-Christian Debate"; and see her introduction to Crispin's *Disputatio,* in *Works,* xxvii–xxxv; *Jewish-Christian Debate,* 350–54; Dahan, *Intellectuels chretiens,* 429–30; Pflaum, "Shirei ha-nitsuah"; Avrom Saltman, "Gilbert Crispin as a Source of the Anti-Jewish Polemic of the *Ysagoge in Theologiam.*"

55. Odo of Tournai, *Disputatio, PL* 160, col. 1112; *Jewish-Christian Debate,* no. 39, Heb. p. 27, Eng. p. 68; Joseph Kimḥi, *Sefer ha-Berit,* 29. See also Guibertus of Nogent, *Tractatus de Incarnatione, PL* 156, cols. 493–95; Jacob ben Reuben, *Milḥamot ha-shem,* 13–19; Innocent III, *De miseria humane conditionis,* 1.2–4; idem, *On the Misery of the Human Condition,* 1.2–4; Jacques de Vitry, *Exempla aus den sermones,* sermon 25, sec. 2; and "Sermones feriales et communes," sermon 25, sec. 2, in Carolyn Muessig, *The Faces of Women in the Sermons of Jacques de Vitry,* 30–31, 160.

56. Koren, "Woman from Whom God Wanders," 161 n. 27; *Sefer ha-Zohar I,* 190b. Also see *Sefer ha-Zohar II,* 219a–b; *III,* 97b–98b.

57. Sometimes the writers specify that Mary's abdomen is dirty because of urine and excrement, and sometimes it is merely called a place of filth, which may refer to menstrual blood or excreta or both. Authors frequently call it a place of filth *and* menstrual blood, which may imply both excrement and menstrual blood, or the authors were repeating what they considered synonyms to emphasize their point. For the sake of brevity, I list only those passages that seem to make direct reference to Mary's intestines or excreta (outside of menstrual blood): Joseph Kimḥi, *Sefer ha-berit,* Heb. p. 29, Eng. pp. 36–37; *Polemic of Nestor,* para. 82, Heb. 2:103, Eng. 1:115; *Jewish-Christian Debate,* paras. 6, 39, Heb. pp. 5, 27, Eng. pp. 44, 68. For other references to the abdomen's filth, see note to those evoking menstrual impurity above. On Jesus' excremental productions, see below.

58. Joseph ben Nathan Official, *Yosef ha-Mekane',* sec. 33, 53, 86, 94, 133, 2, 16, p. 52 and note 1, and pp. 65, 82, 88, 119, 125, 129 respectively. Unlike other epithets, such as *ben niddah,* which came from the *Toledot* tradition, *hari'a* seems to be a later nickname. See also *Jewish-Christian Debate,* para. 145 (Heb. pp. 94, 95, 97; Eng. pp. 150, 151, 154).

59. הלא הוא הנולד מגוש עפר מחריא (Joseph ben Nathan Official, *Yosef ha-Mekane'*, 65).

60. Martin of Leon, *Sermones, Serm. 34 In Festo S. Trinitatis, PL* 208, cols. 1314–15; Orfali, "Dialogus," 713. Cf. Guibertus of Nogent, *De incarnatione, PL* 156, cols. 492–94, which makes a similar argument but without an analogy to light. Jews were aware of this argument: Jacob b. Reuben's Christian makes precisely this argument in *Milḥamot ha-Shem,* 15. Jacob rejected that analogy: light, like God, has no body or form. But according to the Christians, God took on an actual body and form in the person of Jesus and therefore filth did stick; see 17; Lasker, *Jewish Philosophical Polemics,* 112.

61. Guibertus of Nogent, *De Incarnatione, PL* 156, cols. 492–98; Odo of Tournai, *Disputatio, PL* 160, cols. 1110–12, Eng. pp. 95–97.

62. Guibertus of Nogent, *De Incarnatione, PL* 156, col. 498. This is typical of the language throughout his tractate.

63. On this generally, see Bynum, *Resurrection.*

64. *Polemic of Nestor,* para. 59, Heb. 2:101 (also see 123 for alternate version), Eng. 1:110. Cf. Pseudo-David Kimḥi, *Vikuḥei Radak,* 87.

65. Joseph Kimḥi, *Sefer ha-berit,* Heb. p. 29, Eng. pp. 36–37.

66. Ibid. Qimḥi (Kimḥi) may also have been thinking of ignorance, weeping, and dependency, states and characteristics that he mentions along with defecating and urinating just prior to the passage quoted above.

67. Bynum, *Resurrection,* 136, 224. Food, especially in excess, was seen as a sinful hindrance to holiness and related to rot in Judaism as well. See, e.g., *Sefer ha-Yashar,* 52/52, 118/119, 134/135–136/137, 148/149–150/151, 170/171–172/173, 206/207–208/209. The dating of this text is uncertain. Editor and translator Seymour Cohen suggests that it was composed during the thirteenth century; see his introduction, xi–xvii.

68. See above, pp. 108–13, 124–31.

69. See especially, however, Guibertus of Nogent, *De Incarnatione, PL* 156, col. 494.

70. See chaps. 2 and 3 and also the vision of Saint Ida of Louvain and its discussion in Shahar, *Childhood,* 96.

71. *Polemic of Nestor*, para. 28, Heb. 2:97, 116, Eng. 1:103.

72. On the association of excrement with hell and demons see above and chaps. 1, 6.

73. On excrement as a tool for depicting individuals as coarse and ridiculous, see Freedman's discussion of the representation of peasants in *Images,* 150–56.

74. On Christianity as a polluting force, see below.

75. Jacob b. Reuben, *Milḥamot ha-Shem,* 150; Joseph ben Nathan Official, *Yosef ha-Mekane',* paras. 119, 125, pp. 110, 114 respectively; *Jewish-Christian Debate,* para. 176, Heb. pp. 123–24, Eng. pp. 185–87.

76. *Jewish-Christian Debate,* para. 202, Heb. p. 141, Eng. p. 202. For more on this, see Lasker, *Jewish Philosophical Polemics,* pp. 131–32.

77. The anonymous author of *Dialogus pro Ecclesia contra Synagogam,* edited by Orfali, contains a whole section regarding Jewish objections to the crucifixion and resurrection, but this text seems to be something of an exception; see 721–25. Crispin

seems to allude to these problems but never deals with them at length: *Disputatio Judei,* paras. 74, 80, pp. 25, 27 respectively. The author of the Old French disputation based on Crispin's work has more numerous references, yet the Jews' primary objections seem to be (1) that Jesus died at all; (2) that he rose from the dead, something Jews find difficult to believe; (3) that he was hung from a cross. *Desputoison du juyf et du crestien,* 467–73. On the texts' supposed derivation from Crispin's *Disputatio Judei,* see Pflaum, "Shirei ha-Nizuah," which accompanies his edition of the dialogue.

78. For examples of Jews denigrating the crusaders' mission because they were traveling to the Holy Sepulchre, see above in this section.

79. חי עולמים בצל כנפיך אנו בורחים כי נשארנו עגונים ואנוחים \\ מבלי להשתתף לתלוי שוחחים פגר מובס, יבושו כל אליו בוטחים (*Sefer Gezerot*, 62). Other examples of the use of "trampled corpse" or similar terminology to refer to Jesus: *"Mainz Anonymous,"* 93, 101; Chazan, *European Jewry*, 225, 237, 238; *Chronicle of Solomon bar Simson*, in *Sefer Gezerot,* 31; Chazan, *European Jewry*, 255; *Chronicle of R. Eliezar bar Nathan*, in *Sefer Gezerot,* 80. Eidelberg translates the term as "decaying carcass," as if the text read *peger muv'ash,* in *The Jews and the Crusaders*, 90. The two terms sound similar, and both were applied to Jesus. It is possible that Jewish writers, playing on the similarity, intended for their audience to think of both words and their meanings.

80. *"Mainz Anonymous,"* in *Sefer Gezerot*, 92, 98; Chazan, *European Jewry*, 229, 234; *Chronicle of Solomon bar Simson*, in *Sefer Gezerot*, 29, 34–36, 39, 47–48; Chazan, *European Jewry*, 251, 260, 261, 266, 280; *Chronicle of R. Eliezer bar Nathan*, in *Sefer Gezerot*, 74, 77; *Jews and the Crusaders*, 82, 86.

81. *Chronicle of Solomon bar Simson,* in *Sefer Gezerot,* 34, 43; Chazan, *European Jewry,* 258, 272.

82. *Jewish-Christian Debate,* para. 145, Heb. p. 96, Eng. p. 153. Also see para. 125, Heb. p. 82, Eng. p. 134.

83. On fragrance and incorruptiblity as an indication of holiness in the twelfth and thirteenth centuries, see Bynum, *Resurrection,* 210–25; on Christ's own body, see 264. The evil nature of individual Christians could also be indicated by pointing to their decay in death. In *Sefer Zekhirah* a Christian who had murdered two Jewish boys not only died after his punishment at the hands of Christian authorities, he "turned into a corpse" (ויפגר): *Sefer Zekhirah,* in *Sefer Gezerot*, 117). Eidelberg, *Jews and the Crusaders*, 124, translates this as "he . . . turned into a putrid corpse," which perhaps follows the spirit of the author's intention; however, there is no adjective in the text to give this additional emphasis. Also see Guibert of Nogent, *De pignoribus, PL* 156, cols. 623–30; Bynum's discussion of the text in *Resurrection*, 206 n. 20.

84. Crispin, *Disputatio Iudei*, 25, 30, 48–50; Guibertus of Nogent, *De Incarnatione*, *PL* 156, cols. 509–11, 519–22; *Desputoison,* 467–70; Orfali, "Dialogus," 721–22; Guillaume de Bourges, *Livre des guerres*, 120/121; Aquinas, *Summa Theologica*, 3a, 52.3; Bynum, *Resurrection*, 264.

85. Tolan, *Saracens,* 61–63, 85–95; idem, "Un cadavre mutilé"; chap. 2.

86. For twelfth- and thirteenth-century examples of this theme, see Petrus Alfonsi, *Dialogus,* 102–3; Alfonso the Wise, *Primera Crónica general de España,* vol. 1, sec.

494, p. 274; Alexandre du Pont, *Le Roman de Mahomet,* ll. 1889–1900, p. 203; Fidentius of Padua, *Liber de recuperatione terrae sanctae,* in *Biblioteca bio-bibliographica della terra santa e dell'oriente francescano,* 2:19.

87. *Jewish-Christian Debate,* para. 227, Heb. pp. 152–53, Eng. pp. 217–18.

88. For Jewish law on this subject, see chap. 2. For Islamic law, see *Qur'an* 5:3. On Christian belief that Muḥammad was worshiped by Muslims, or that Islam was a polytheistic religion, see Tolan, *Saracens,* 105–34.

89. Raoul de Caen, *Gesta Tancredi,* in *RHC occidentaux,* 3:695–96; *La chanson d'Antioche,* ll. 6616–21; 9107–16, pp. 327, 447–48 respectively; *Chanson de Roland,* ll. 2580–91, 3661–65, pp. 186, 252; *The Song of Roland,* 150, 190; *Le Jeu de Saint Nicolas,* ll. 134–43; Tolan, *Saracens,* 105, 119–23.

90. Tolan, *Saracens,* 119–23.

91. Alexandre du Pont, *Roman de Mahomet,* ll. 1876–95, p. 203. Compare *Estoire du Saint Graal,* para. 62, p. 42.

92. "quoniam immunditiam praedicaverat et spurcitiam, a porcis quae immunda animalia reputantur, est devoratus" (Gerald of Wales, *De Principis instructione,* distinctio I, p. 68).

93. Tolan, "Un cadavre mutilé."

94. On synagogues' association with Islam and mosques, see, e.g., *Chanson de Roland,* l. 3662, ed. Jenkins, p. 252, Sayers, p. 190.

95. Bacon, *Opus Majus, moralis philosophae, part 7*; Burke, 2:814. See Peter the Venerable, who compares the fables of the Muslims (*fabulas Mahumeti*) and the fables of the Talmud (*fabulas Talmud*). Petrus Venerabilis, *Schriften zum Islam*, 208/209.

96. Fidentius of Padua, *Liber de recuperatione,* 21–26.

97. ובגיהנם אתם נידונים עם אלוה שלכם, ובצואה רותחת, שהוא בן הזונה. (*Chronicle of Solomon bar Simson*, in *Sefer Gezerot*, 36; Chazan, *European Jewry*, 262).

98. להבאיש ריחינו (Jehiel ben Joseph, *Vikuaḥ*, 4, 6). On Donin and the Paris trial, see Chazan, *Daggers*, 33–37; Jordan, "Marian Devotion."

99. Jehiel ben Joseph, *Vikuaḥ,* 4–6.

100. Isidore Loeb, "La Controverse de 1240 sur le Talmud," 3:48–50, nos. 26–29); Judah M. Rosenthal, "The Talmud on Trial," esp. 160–62; Grayzel, *The Church and the Jews,* no. 119 (pp. 274–80); Merchaviah, *ha-Talmud,* 291–315, 328–30, 347–48, 446–48; Jordan, "Marian Devotion."

101. Sivan, *Islam et la Croisade,* 67, 106, 199; Cole, "Religious Pollution."

102. Jacobus de Voragine, *Legenda Aurea,* 2:182; idem, *The Golden Legend,* 2:386–88. Thanks to Dawn Hayes of Iona College for suggesting this text.

103. Ibid., 385–86, 388.

104. Ibid., 391–95. Cf. Alan of Lille's Sermon on the Annunciation in which the bodies of Mary, Jesus, and Christian believers are equated with the Temple of Solomon. Alanus de Insulis, "Sermo II, In annuntiatione Beatae Mariae, quando evenit Dominica in Palmis," in *Opera Omnia, PL* 210, cols. 202–3. Following the brief comparison of the Temple of Solomon to Christ, the text continues to make a rather detailed comparison between the soterological functions of Christ and the ancient temple cult: col. 202.

105. See texts and discussions in *Wisdom of the Zohar,* 2:447–560; Wolfson, "Crossing Gender Boundaries in Kabbalistic Ritual and Myth"; Koren, "Woman from Whom God Wanders," 47–149, 181–94.

106. Both Jacobus of Voragine and Alan of Lille seem very concerned with the possibility that the church or believers will become polluted and thus lose their status as an appropriate "house" of God.

107. For examples of the uses of *mishuqaẓ* and related terms, see *Sefer Gezerot,* 31, 33, 46, 113, 116, 119, 159, 199; Chazan, *European Jewry,* 255, 258, 277; *Jews and the Crusaders,* 123, 127.

108. On the grave as a frequent habitation for demons and impure spirits, see Koren, "Woman from Whom God Wanders," 52.

109. הלך לבקש טמאה בדרך רחוקה \ הצלוב הקבור ונתון בשוחה עמקה This poem, titled אלהים זדים קמו עלינו, is by R. Eliezar b. Nathan, the author of the poetic chronicle of the first crusade (though this poem is not part of his chronicle) and may be found in *Sefer Gezerot,* 85.

110. נלך גם אנו עמהם, כי כל איש אשר ילך בדרך זה ויפנה דרך לעלות לקבר טמאות הצלוב, יהיה מתוקן ומזומן לתפתה. (*Mainz Anonymous,* in *Sefer Gezerot,* 94; Chazan, *European Jewry,* 226). My translation differs from Chazan's. Other examples of Hebrew chroniclers and poets using cognates of *tam'e* (טמא) to indicate Christians or aspects of the Christian faith may be found in *Sefer Gezerot,* 35, 45, 48, 55, 85, 103, 118, 199; Chazan, *European Jewry,* 260, 276, 281, 291, 240; *Jews and the Crusaders,* 126.

111. Aḥmad ibn Ali al-Qalqashandī, *Ṣubḥ al-a'sha fī ṣinā'at al-inshā,* vol. 7, sec. 7, p. 128; Abū l'Hasan 'Ali b. Abi Bakr al-Harawi, *Kitāb al-ishārāt 'ilā ma'rifat al-ziyārāt,* 27–28; idem, *Guide des Lieux de Pèlerinage,* 68–69; Abū Shama, *Kitāb al-Rawḍatayn,* 321; Imād al-Dīn al-Iṣfahānī, *al-Fatḥ al-qussī,* 118–21; Gabrielli, *Arab Historians,* 148–51; Hillenbrand, *Crusades,* 266, 317–19; Sivan, *Islam et la Croisade,* 113, 182–83.

112. اهل الرجس, اهل الضلال, اهل الغدر (Imād al-Dīn al-Iṣfahānī, *al-Fatḥ al-qussī,* 154, 197).

113. و نسمح بلارواح شحا بمحل الروح. فهذه قمامتنا, فيها مقامتنا , و منها تقوم قيماتنا (Imād al-Dīn al-Iṣfahānī, *al-Fatḥ al-qussī,* 118). Thanks to Anne Broadbridge of the University of Massachusetts for help with this passage. All errors are my own. The description of the other functions or contents of the church are also on this page. Also see Gabrielli, *Arab Historians,* 148, though my translation differs from his.

114. *maḥall* (place) is the more natural reading, though given how Imad al-Din plays with language, it does not seem impossible that he had both words in mind.

115. Al-Harawi, *ma'rifat al-ziyārāt,* 27–28; idem, *Guide,* 68–69.

116. לא רצו ליכנס בעבודה זרה שלהם להריח ריח העורותת, תועבה. (*Chronicle of Solomon bar Simson,* in *Sefer Gezerot,* 38; Chazan, *European Jewry,* 265–66). The Hebrew is somewhat confused here. *'Orot,* (skins) in the printed text is not set up to be in construct state with *to'avah* (abomination) as I have translated it here. The text reads *ha-'orot to'avah* instead of *'orot ha-to'avah.* Chazan declines to translate the phrase, and Eidelberg translates the sentence, "[T]hey refused to enter the edifice of idolatry, rooting their feet on the threshold, unwilling to enter and inhale the odor of the offensive incense."

Jews and the Crusaders, 42. While Eidelberg's translation makes sense in English and in the context of the sentence (what in a church has smell? incense) it is hard to see how or why *'orot* should be translated as "incense." My translation assumes that the scribe misplaced the definite article, attaching it to *'orot* as opposed to *to'avah.*

117. BT Berakhot 6b, 60b, 62a. Koren, "Woman from Whom God Wanders," 50–52. See also chap. 1.

118. *Jewish-Christian Debate,* sec. 41, Heb. pp. 28–29, Eng. pp. 68–69. My translation differs slightly from Berger's. Instead of "shit," Berger wrote "filth," but the word in Hebrew is *zo'ah,* meaning "excrement."

119. *Jewish-Christian Debate*, sec. 41 (Heb. 29, Eng. 69).

120. For the discussion of the tales in *Pesiqta' Rabbati* and *Mishnah 'Avodah Zarah,* see chap. 2. For the need for Jews to create "verbal victories" against the Christians, see Ivan Marcus, "Hierarchies, Religious Boundaries, and Jewish Spirituality in Medieval Germany," which argues that in creating and defending community boundaries, in the Hebrew Crusade Chronicles invectives such as "putrid corpse" and "son of harlotry" were a way of "defiantly erecting a new kind of ritualized boundary between themselves and their Christian attackers" (quotation on 11). Through language Jews could create victory from defeat. This story, along with the invectives discussed above, functions in precisely this way, although *ritualized* might not be the best adjective.

121. לדמם ארבו טמאים וחזירים נקיים לאבדם כתרום \ אכזרים לפיד אש אשר עבר בין הגזרים (from the poem אשאג מנהמת לבי, in *Sefer Gezerot,* 238). Habermann suggests that the poem is either Ashkenazi or English. The specific events to which the poet was referring are unclear.

122. Herman of Scheda, *Hermanus quondam Judaeus,* 2:73–76, 14:110, 19:120 (where he describes the Holy Spirit purifying him from a leprous soul). In describing Rupert of Deutz's arguments in support of Christianity, Herman says Rupert dwells on the idea of the Jews as shedders of their brothers' blood (3–4:76–83). See Rupert of Deutz, *Opera omnia.*

123. "Altaria suis foeditatibus iniquitata subvertunt, Christianos circumcidunt, cruoremque circumcisionis aut super altaria fundunt aut in vasis bapitisterii immergunt" (Robert of Rheims, *Historia Hierosolimitana,* in *RHC occidentaux,* 3:727). Cole "Religious Pollution."

124. *De Expugnatione terrae sanctae per Saladinum, libellus,* 66:246.

125. Sivan, *Islam et la Croisade,* 104.

126. Bauldri of Dol, *Historia de peregrinatione Hierosolimitana,* in *RHC occidentaux,* vol. 4, bk. 1.2, p. 12; Oderic Vitalis, *The Ecclesiastical History of Oderic Vitalis,* vol. 5, bk. 9, pp. 16/17; *Chanson d'Antioche,* ll. 276–80, 329–30, pp. 31, 34 respectively; Cole, "Religious Pollution."

127. Imād al-Dīn al-Iṣfahānī, *al-Fatḥ al-qussī,* 141; Gabrielli, *Arab Historians,* 169; 'Ali ibn Muḥammad ibn al-Nabih, *Diwan,* 458; Ibn Khallikan, *Extraits de la vie du Sultan Salah ed-Din,* in *RHC orientaux,* 3:416; Abū Shama, *Kitāb al-Rawḍatayn,* in *RHC orientaux,* 4:333. In the case of Abū Shama, though he is drawing from Imād al-Dīn, it is not clear whether he means pictures of pigs or actual ones. Also see Hillenbrand, *Crusades,* 285–91; Sivan, *Islam et la Croisade,* 61–63, 81, 85, 111.

128. زفرة قذرة, مملوء كلها رجسا وعذرة (Muḥammad ibn Aḥmad ibn Jubayr, *Riḥlat,* 276; idem, *The Travels of Ibn Jubayr,* 318).

129. *The Book of the Thousand Nights and One Night,* 1:442; Hillenbrand, *Crusades,* 294–95.

130. Muslim writers frequently used the verb طهر (*ṭahara*) "to purify" in reference to ridding the Holy Land of crusaders, much as Christians used the Latin equivalent *mundare* in reference to the Muslims. In terms of pollution and dirt, Muslim authors used cognates of رجس (*rajasa*) "to be dirty, filthy, to commit a shameful act." Christians used terms such as *cloacam, sorditatem, fetidam, immundus.* Imād al-Dīn al-Iṣfahānī, *al-Fatḥ al-qussī,* 116–21, 135–36, 141–44, 153–54, 198; Gabrielli, *Arab Historians,* 146–51, 162–63, 169–70; idem, [*Al-Barq al-shami*] *Der Syrische Blitz,* sec. XIII-6, Arabic p. 68, German p. 353; Ibn al-Nabīh, *Diwan,* 121; Ibn Khallikan, *Wafāyāt al-a'yān,* 4:230–36; idem, *Extraits,* in *RHC orientaux,* 3:416–17; Muḥammad ibn Ahmad ibn Jubayr, *Riḥlat,* 282; idem, *The Travels of Ibn Jubayr,* 324; Guibert of Nogent, *Dei Gesta per Francos,* 5:207, 217, 220; Fulchre of Chartres, *Historia Iherosolymitana,* in *RHC occidentaux,* 3:357; Bauldri of Dol, *Historia,* in *RHC occidentaux,* 4:11–13; Robert of Rheims, *Historia,* in *RHC occidentaux*, 3:728, 745, 869; Gerald of Wales, *De Principis Instructione,* distinction II, pp. 204–5; Oderic Vitalis, *Ecclesiastical History,* vol. 5, bk. 9, pp. 4/5, 172/173; Fidentius of Padua, *Liber de recuperatione,* 18, 26; *De Expugnatione terrae sanctae,* 66:226, 239, 248–50; Hillenbrand, *Crusades,* 276–85, 294, 301–4; Cole, "Religious Pollution."

131. Imād al-Dīn al-Iṣfahānī, *al-Fatḥ al-qussī,* 142–44; Gabrielli, *Arab Historians,* 170–73; Ibn Khallikan, *Wafāyāt al-a'yān,* 4:234; idem, *Biographical Dictionary,* trans. Slane, 2:638–39; Abū Shama, *Kitāb al-Rawḍatayn,* in *RHC orientaux,* 4:333–34.

132. Debra Higgs Strickland, *Saracens, Demons, and Jews,* 174.

133. Hillenbrand, *Crusades,* 285, 298.

134. See, e.g., Guibert of Nogent, *Dei Gesta Francorum,* 101–2, 122; Fidentius of Padua, *Liber recuperationis,* 22; Ibn Jubayr, *Riḥlat,* 279–81; idem, *Travels,* trans. Broadhurst, 321–22; Usamah ibn Munqidh, *Memoirs,* 100, 148, 153–54.

135. On animalistic behavior and cruelty, see, e.g., Abū Shama, *Kitāb al-Rawḍatayn,* in *RHC orientaux,* 4:322; Riccold de Monte Crocce, *Pérégination en Terre Sainte et au Proche Orient,* 120/121, 232–33; Peter the Venerable, *Schriften,* pp. 90/91.

136. "fuit in peccato luxurie fetidissimus" (Fidentius of Padua, *Liber recuperationis,* 18). The theme continues onto p. 19.

137. Fidentius of Padua, *Liber recuperationis,* 21–23.

138. Roger Bacon, *Opus Majus, moralis philosophiae, part 7*, trans. Burke, 2:814.

139. Fidentius of Padua, *Liber recuperationis,* 14.

140. On Christian women's participation in the crusades, see *Gendering the Crusades.*

141. وسيف قاطع ودم صبيب \ وكم من مسلم امسى سليبا \ ومسلمة مها حرم سليب \ وكم من مسجد جعلوه ديرا \ على محرابه نصب الصليب \ دم الخنزير فيه لهم خلوق \ و تحريق المصاحف فيه طيب (Abū Maḥāsin Yūsuf ibn Taghrībirdī, *Al-Nujūm al-zāhira fī mulūk Miṣr, wa al-Qāhirah,* 5:151–52, trans. in Hillenbrand, *Crusades,* 297–98; and see Hillenbrand's analysis there).

142. *Homoeroticism in Classical Arabic Literature*; *Islamic Homosexualities;* Khaled el-Rouayheb, *Before Homosexuality in the Arab-Islamic World,* 13–25.

143. اصجت الارض المقدسة الطاهرة و كانت الطامث (Ibn Khallikan, *Extraits,* in *RHC orientaux,* 3:416). The translation is mine.

144. Hillenbrand, *Crusades*, 303.

145. On prohibitions regarding intercourse during menstruation, see *Qur'an* 2:222; Lazarus-Yafeh, "Some Differences between Judaism and Islam as Two Religions of Law." One of the reasons I think this dual meaning was intentional is that *tamith* is not the most commonly used word for menstruation. Authors often employed حيض (*ḥaiḍ*), the term that appears in the Qur'an.

146. Hillenbrand, *Crusades,* 274–80, 285, 313.

147. Imād al-Dīn al-Iṣfahānī, *al-Fatḥ al-qussī,* 347–49; Gabrielli, *Arab Historians,* 204–6.

148. Imad al-Dīn al-Iṣfahānī, *al-Fatḥ al-qussī,* 349; Garbrielli, *Arab Historians,* 206–7.

149. *Gendering the Crusades*; Helen Solterer, "Figures of Female Militancy in Medieval France"; Rosen, *Unveiling Eve,* 162–64; Remke Kruk, "Warrior Women in Arabic Popular Romance"; M. C. Lyons, *The Arabian Epic*.

150. וציוה אתכם להטביל במי הצחנה ולקנות עץ ריקבון ולעשות צלם אשר אין בו הנייה ולאכול בשר החזיר וכל שרץ ולהקריב לחם ויין, קומוניקטו בלעז, בגופכם ויעשה ממנו צואה וביאוש (*Polemic of Nestor,* para. 127, Heb. 2:107, Eng. 1:123). Note that in the phrase *qomuniqaṭo bila'az,* which Lasker and Stroumsa translate as "*communio* in Latin" the word *la'az* can mean either "foreign language" (thus "Latin" is not specified in the Hebrew text) or "slander." The author of the text was, I suspect, playing on the double meaning of *la'az.* Compare this and the poetic and historical texts to Joseph ben Nathan Official, *Yosef ha-Makane',* sec. 56, p. 66; *Jewish-Christian Debate,* secs. 64, 73, 157, 196, 231, Heb. pp. 43, 49, 109–10, 139, 155, Eng. pp. 85, 92, 171–73, 201, 219.

151. בלחם המגאל הנתעב והמגעל \ התנכלו מזמתם ויוסיפו מעל \ לאמר לבחירי עם הקדש והמועל \ גנבתם אלהיהם ההולך חשכים \ ויהי לאבל כנורי ועגבי לקול בוכים (With bloodstained, abhorrent and nauseating bread / they have conspired from their licentiousness and they have added betrayal / to say to the young men of the people of the Holy and Elevated One / you have stolen their god who walks in darkness / And my harp will be for mourning and my flute for a voice of weeping), *Sefer Gezerot,* 230. The poem in which this passage may be found is titled אבכה לקשה יום. Cf. Joseph ben Nathan Official, *Yosef ha-Makane',* para. 91, p. 85; *Jewish-Christian Debate,* para. 231, Heb. p. 155, Eng. p. 219.

152. Jacob b. Reuben, *Milḥamot ha-Shem,* 114; Joseph ben Nathan Official, *Yosef ha-Makane',* 21, secs. 12, 85, pp. 38, 82; *Jewish-Christian Debate,* secs. 210, 217, Heb. pp. 144, 148, Eng. pp. 206, 211. Cf. *Jewish-Christian Debate,* sec. 212, Heb. p. 145, Eng. p. 207; and Jehiel b. Joseph, *Vikuaḥ,* 9.

153. Citing Isa. 64:1–4 was also intended as a criticism of the Christian cult of the saints. To Jews, the reference to "burning incense on bricks" and "sitting in tombs" depicted and condemned Christian rituals designed to revere and beseech the dead. (See, e.g., *Jewish-Christian Debate,* sec. 103, Heb. p. 69, Eng. p. 118.) Not only did "worshiping" the dead go against biblical law, Christian willingness to be near or touch the dead rendered Christians impure and polluted the churches that housed the bodies of

saints with the strongest level of impurity extant in Jewish law. For examples of Jewish polemicists explicitly arguing this point, see *Jewish-Christian Debate,* sec. 217, Heb. pp. 147–48, Eng. pp. 210–11; *Polemic of Nestor,* secs. 128–30, Heb. 2:127–28, Eng. 1:123–124; also see Lasker and Stroumsa's notes, 1:161.

154. Aude, the young woman who rejected the incarnation because of her recollection of the filth expelled by women at birth, also seems to have been worried about the contamination of God in the form of the host; see above. Alan of Lille specifically addressed the heretical belief that the doctrine of transubstantiation implied that Christ was broken and divided by the believer's digestive system. Alanus de Insulis, *Contra haereticos, PL* 210, cols. 361–63.

155. Martin of Leon, *Sermones, Serm. IV In Natale Domini, PL* 208, cols. 397–98; also see cols. 279–80.

156. Guillaume de Bourges, *Livre des guerres,* 194/195. On Guillaume and his relationship to Judaism, see Dahan, *Les intellectuels chrétiens,* 410–11.

157. Parkes, *Conflict*, 291–97; Rubin, *Gentile Tales*, 1–10; Kenneth Parry, *Depicting the World,* 22–33, 70–88, 99–124, 178–201; Patricia Crone, "Islam, Judeo-Christianity and Byzantine Iconoclasm"; Daniel J. Sahas, *Icon and Logos,* 16–22; Stephan Gero, *Byzantine Iconoclasm during the Reign of Leo III*, 59–84.

158. I thank David Burr of Virginia Polytechnic Institute and State University for his comments on this matter. All errors are my own.

159. For example, in the Old French version of the *Vie des anciens pères* a crucifix struck by Jews issues blood and water. This text is from the thirteenth century. *Catalogue of the Romances of the Department of Manuscripts in the British Museum,* 3:342–43, no. 19.

160. See Stephen of Bourbon, *Anecdotes historiques légendes et apologues,* 328, no. 371; *Catalogue of the Romances,* 3:576, no. 29; p. 543, no. 13; *Liber exemplorum ad usum Praedicantium,* no. 99; Caesarius of Haesterbach, *Die Wundergeschichten*, 9:9, 52; *Catalogue*, 3:46, no. 42; p, 362, no. 142.

161. On tales of Christians desecrating the host, see note 160 above. On Jewish abuse of Christian holy objects and the host, see discussion below. On the discourse of violence against Jews, see Rubin, *Gentile Tales.*

162. Thomas of Monmouth, *The Life and Miracles of St. William of Norwich,* I.6, pp. 23–24.

163. *Sources and Analogues of Chaucer's "Canterbury Tales,"* 467, 474–75; Gavin I. Langmuir, "The Knight's Tale of Hugh of Lincoln," esp. 246. Cf. a report to Innocent III of Jews having killed a Christian scholar and cast his body into a latrine: Langmuir, "Knight's Tale," 241.

164. In Thomas of Monmouth, *Life,* the language of the text and some of the miracles William performs after death make this parallel clear. *Sources and Analogues,* 467. Not all versions include the detail about a cross being cut into the child's stomach.

165. Thomas of Monmouth, *Life,* I.12, 13, 18, II.3, III.6, pp. 37, 39, 52, 66, 132; Langmuir, "Knight's Tale," p. 244.

166. Rigord, *Gesta Philippi Augusti,* in *Oevres de Rigord et Guillaume le Breton historiens de Philippe Auguste,* vol. 1, 13, 14, pp. 25–27.

167. Matthew Paris, *Chronica majora,* 5:114–15; Langmuir, "Knight's Tale," 242; Little, *Religious Poverty,* 52–53.

168. Gautier de Coincy, *Miracles,* 2:101–4.

169. Jew feeding host to dog: *Le Speculum laicorum,* no. 369b; Henmannus Bononiensis, *Das Viaticum,* no. 70; *Catalogue of the Romances,* 3:448, no. 39; 719, no. 10 (late fifteenth century but drawing from earlier souces). On Jew feeding host to swine: *Catalogue of the Romances,* 3:389; Jew with host in his shoe: 3:576, no. 32. This tale is from the mid- to late fourteenth century. Examples of non-Jews abusing the host: Stephen of Bourbon, *Anecdotes historiques,* 328, no. 371; *Catalogue of Romances,* 3:576, no. 29; 543, no. 13; *Liber Exemplorum,* no. 99; Caesarius of Haesterbach, *Wundergeschichten,* 9:17–21, 25.

170. Rudolf von Schlettstadt, *Historiae Memorabiles,* 51; *Catalogue of Romances,* 389, nos. 268–69; 543, no. 95.

171. Rubin, *Gentile Tales; Catalogue of the Romances,* 3:389, no. 268; 5, no. 95.

172. Sara Lipton makes some similar observations. Lipton, *Images,* 36–37, 138.

173. Chazan, *Medieval Stereotypes.*

174. Lipton, *Images,* 24–25, 64–99, 120, 138; David Burr, "The Apocalyptic Element in Olivi's Critique of Aristotle"; idem, "Petrus loannis Olivi and the philosophers."

175. On language as a form of violence, see Butler, *Excitable Speech,* 1–52.

176. See references above to *exempla* depicting Christian abuse or "testing" of the Eucharist.

177. Bynum, "Women Mystics and Eucharistic Devotion in the Thirteenth Century"; Piero Camporesi, "The Consecrated Host."

178. On the meaning of Mary's milk in Christian texts, see chap. 3.

179. Bynum, "Women Mystics and Eucharistic Devotion"; idem, "And Woman His Humanity."

180. Freedman, *Images,* 157–59.

181. Koren, "Woman from Whom God Wanders," 47–149, 181–94; Wolfson, "Crossing Gender Boundaries."

Chapter 5. **Impure, Sickly Bodies**

1. See David K[Q]imḥi's interpretation of Isa. 53:7: *The Fifty-third Chapter of Isaiah, according to Jewish Interpreters,*1:51; 2:53. On self-feminization of Jewish men outside the medieval context, see Daniel Boyarin, *Unheroic Conduct.*

2. Flandrin, *Sexe et l'Occident,* 193–211; Biller, "Views of Jews"; idem, "A 'Scientific' View."

3. George Saliba, "Paulus Alexandrinus in Syriac and Arabic"; idem, *A History of Arabic Astronomy*; Gilbert Dagron, "Histoire et civilisation du monde bysantini"; 'Ali ibn Ridwan, *Medieval Islamic Medicine*; Hillenbrand, *Crusades,* 268–73.

4. Hillenbrand, *Crusades,* 271–73, 295, 303.

5. J. D. North, "Medieval Concepts of Celestial Influence"; Graziella Federici Vescovini, "Peter of Abano and Astrology"; Richard Lemay, "The True Place of

Astrology in Medieval Science and Philosophy"; Doris Ruhe, "Le 'Roe d'astronomie'"; Moshe Idel, "Saturn and Sabbatai Tzevi"; Strickland, *Saracens, Demons, and Jews,* 34–39; John Kirtland Wright, *Geographical Lore at the Time of the Crusades.*

6. Miller, *Anatomy,* 26.

7. Lawrence I. Conrad, "A Ninth-Century Muslim Scholar's Discussion of Contagion"; Touati, "Contagion and Leprosy"; Hays, *Burdens,* 24–25.

8. On the blood libel's relationship to "Jewish remedies," see below.

9. Douglas, *Risk,* 83–101.

10. Ibid., 98. Mark Pegg makes the same argument specifically in relation to the changing targets of medieval accusations of leprosy. Pegg, "Le corps et l'autorité."

11. Scott, "Gender." See also Chaviva Levine, "Jewish Conversion to Christianity in Medieval Northern Europe, 1000–1300."

12. Miller, *Anatomy,* 155–56.

13. See below.

14. Strickland argues, however, that using geographic lore, Christians increasingly identified Muslims and Jews with the monstrous races of antiquity during this period, making them horrific in another way. Strickland, *Saracens, Demons, and Jews.* On concepts of contagion during this period, see *Contagion.*

15. Sander Gilman, *The Jew's Body*; Klaus Hödl, *Die Pathologisierung des jüdischen Körpers*; Trachtenberg, *Devil*, 47–52; Eric Zafran, "Saturn and the Jews"; idem, "The Iconography of Anti-Semitism, 1400–1600."

16. Johnson, "Myth," esp. 287–88. Throughout his article Johnson uses other early modern editions of thirteenth- and early-fourteenth-century texts, as does Resnick in "Medieval Roots," though in a private communication, Resnick underscored the problematic potential that some of the evidence for Jewish male menses were later additions.

17. Andreas Angerstorfer, "Jüdische Reaktionen auf die mittelalterlichen Blütbeschuldigungen vom 13. bis zum 16. Jahrhundert," esp. 133–36; Hödl, *Pathologisierung,* 36–39; Johnson, "Myth"; Langmuir, "Ritual Cannibalism"; Resnick, "Medieval Roots"; Israel Yuval, *Shene goyim be-vitneakh,* 283–93.

18. Athanasias of Alexandria, *Sermon of the Miracle of Beirut,* in *PG* 28, cols. 797/798–805/806; *Synaxaire armenien,* 104–6. By contrast, see Agapius, *Kitāb al-'Unwan,* pt. 2, 439–40, in which no miracle occurs, the Jews do not repent, and the Jews are expelled by the emperor Maurice. For similar stories of Jewish healing and conversion, see *Les légends syriaques,* 709–10; *Sermon sur la Pénitence attribue a St. Cyrille d'Alexandrie*, 6:493–528; *Martyrianus,* in *Acta sanctorum*, 4:442.

19. Sigebertus Gemblacensis, *Chronica*, 333; *Legenda Aurea*, no. 137, Eng. 2:168–73, esp. 171; [*Seelentrost*] *Der grosse Seelentrost*, 4.27, 146–47; Jean Gobi, *La Scala Coeli*, no. 378, p. 327; *Recull de eximplis e miracles, gestes e faules e altres ligendes ordenades per A-B-C*, no. 175, 1:159–60; *Catalogue of Romances*, 342, 517, 537, 605. For more sources, see Frederic C. Tubach, *Index exemplorum*, no. 1373.

20. *Synaxaire arménien*, 106. I am dependent on Bayan's translation of the text into French.

21. Caesarius of Heisterbach, *Dialogus*, 8.27, Latin pp. 102–3; Eng. 2:27–28.

22. Caesarius of Heisterbach, *Dialogus,* 8.23. For further *exempla,* see below.

23. Mellinkoff, *Outcasts,* 1:122–30; William Chester Jordan, "The Last Tormentor of Christ"; idem, "Erosion of the Stereotype of the Last Tormentor of Christ."

24. Jordan, "Last Tormentor"; idem, "Erosion."

25. For this tendency in western European thought, see Pegg, "Corps et l'autorité." He is primarily concerned with leprosy.

26. Colin Richmond, "Englishness and Medieval Anglo-Saxon Jewry"; Christoph Cluse, "'Fabula ineptissima' Die Ritualmordlegende um Adam von Bristol nach der Handschrift London, British Library, Harley 957"; Joe Hillaby, "The Ritual Child-Murder Accusation"; Langmuir, "Thomas of Monmouth"; John M. McCulloh, "Jewish Ritual Murder"; Yuval, "Ha-Nakam"; idem, *Shene goyim.* Most of Juval's book relates at least indirectly to the blood libel, but see esp. chaps. 4, 6.

27. Rubin in her *Gentile Tales* and Yuval in his *Shene goyim* have also looked to earlier legends of host or holy object desecration from Byzantine and Near Eastern Christians as a source for some of the tales adopted and then developed into child-murder stories, though they do not discuss the potential significance of the "Cross of Beirut," also known as the life or story of Saint Nicodemus in Western sources.

28. *The Image of the Black in Western Art,* vol. 2, pt. 1, 16–19, 21–22, 27–31; Thomas Hahn, "The Difference the Middle Ages Makes."

29. For example, in one tale from the *Vitae Patrum (PL* 73, col. 879) a stinking Ethiopian woman appears before a struggling monk and claims God will not allow her to tempt him; all she can do is torment him by her foul odor. For other examples and discussions of this trope and the Ethiopian as a sinner in late antique Christian literature, see *Image,* 2/1:16–21; Dorothy Hoogland Verkerk, "Black Servant, Black Demon."

30. Hrotsvitha, *Dulcitius,* acts 4–5, in *Opera omnia;* English in *The Dramas of Hrosvit of Gandersheim.*

31. For positive or neutral interpretations of dark skin, see *Image,* 2/1:38–46, 119–205; Hahn, "Difference." Note that Verkerk disagrees with Devisse's more benign interpretations of the Ashburnham Pentateuch. Verkerk, "Black Servant, Black Demon."

32. Hahn, "Difference."

33. Freedman, *Images,* 134–56. Like their depictions of Africans, European literary and artistic views of the peasant were not universally negative, a point Freedman is careful to make.

34. Ibid., 86–104; David Goldenberg, *The Curse of Ham,* 79–92, 118–21, 158–77. Both Freedman and Goldenberg warn, however, that Ham was not associated only with Africa and that Africans were not thought of as always black any more than dark-skinned peoples were always viewed as slaves. Also see Bernard Lewis, *Race and Slavery in the Middle East.*

35. Freedman, *Images,* 133–37, 150–54; see Hrotsvitha, *Dulcitius.*

36. Hahn, "Difference." For deformity and grotesqueness of the dark Saracen in some Christian texts, also see Jeffrey Jerome Cohen, "On Saracen Enjoyment."

37. On leprosy and other skin diseases as a result of sin, see Brody, *Disease of the Soul;* and chaps. 1, 3, and below. According to Verkerk, black skin was from Roman times one of several physiological indications of adulterous parents. She also cites Prudentius (ca. 348–410) as saying that the serpent's venom "blackened" the formally

"white" Eve and so stained Adam. Verkerk, "Black Servant, Black Demon." Cf. *Kallah Rabbati* discussed in chap. 2, in which bastard children or children of *niddah* are described as having specific negative characteristics (albeit blackness is not among them).

38. Especially see the passage in *Cursor Mundi* (ca. 1325) cited by Hahn in which four Saracens, black and repulsively deformed, according to the Christian author, draw a parallel between physical loathsomeness and a sinful soul. King David allows them to kiss his staff whereupon their entire appearance changes, including their color. Hahn, "Difference," 14. Other similar examples, both earlier and later, are also presented in Hahn's article. Also cf. the reference to the stench of unbaptized Jews in Caesarius of Heisterbach, *Dialogus,* 2.25, Latin pp. 95; Eng. pp. 107–9. Muslims sometimes used color symbolism of black vs. white to indicate sin, virtue, and transformation. Lewis, *Race and Slavery,* 35–36.

39. See, e.g., Bernard of Clairvaux, *On the Song of Songs,* sermon 25 (2:51–56); *The Letters of Abelard and Heloise,* 138–39; Pseudo-Albertus Magnus, *Mariale,* quest. 15–16, pp. 36–44; Hahn, "Difference," esp. 20–23; Frank M. Snowden, *Blacks in Antiquity,* 198–99, nn. 17–18; Goldenberg, *Curse of Ham,* 48.

40. Jordan, "Medieval Background"; Mellinkoff, *Outcasts,* 1:122–30; Strickland, *Saracens, Demons, and Jews,* 165–82.

41. La maladie del viel lacob senefie la maladie del vieax gieus ceque Ioseph vint devant lacob et lacob la monesta de bien faire senefie Iehsu Christ qi vint devant les gieus et les amonesta de bien faire (*Bible moralisée,* l4rd, trans. on 68).

42. Ibid. For a similar dichotomy of "bad" dark Muslim/"good" white Christians, see fol. 36; and discussion in Strickland, *Saracens, Demons, and Jews,* 171.

43. The *Bible moralisée* and illuminations in other types of manuscripts do not consistently portray Jews or Muslims as dark, though this is not the only instance. See Lipton, *Images,* 105; Strickland, *Saracens, Demons, and Jews,* 72–73.

44. Cf. the carvings of African executioners on the tympanums of the cathedrals of Chartres, Rouen, and Paris and the west facade of the cathedral of Saint Etienne in Auxerre (reproduced in *Image,* 2/1, figs. 30, 31, 32, 33 respectively, pp. 73–75) with the executioners in *Images de la vie de Christ et des saints,* fols. 37v and 76r, and in the Chichester Psalter, fol. 150v (reproduced in *Image,* figs. 36, 34, 35 respectively, pp. 76–77; and in Mellinkoff, *Outcasts,* 2:figs. 1.12, 7.34). For a discussion of the black as executioner or tormentor, see *Image,* 2/1:728; Mellinkoff, *Outcasts,* 1:129–30; Jordan, "Last Tormentor."

45. Chichester Psalter, fols. 150v, 151r (reproduced in Mellinkoff, *Outcasts,* 2:figs. 7.34, 7.35). The Chichester Psalter is in the John Rylands Library in Manchester, MS Lat. 24); *Evangelistary* from Marbach-Scwarzenthann in Laon, Bibliothèque Municipale, vol. 6r (reproduced in *Image,* 2/1:fig. 29, p. 73). Cf. the Salvin Hours, fol. 29r (ca. 1270), in which some of the individuals who arrest Jesus are black-skinned. They share the same distorted features of the other white Jews arresting and judging Jesus (reproduced in Mellinkoff, *Outcasts,* 2:fig. 6.26; the manuscript is in the British Library MS Add. 48985). Jordan has argued that Jews were the primary sufferers from the stereotypes about blackness in the Middle Ages. William Chester Jordan, "Why Race?"

46. *Image,* 2/1:58; Strickland, *Saracens, Demons, and Jews,* 98, 136, 172.

47. Mellinkoff, *Outcasts,* 1:147–57. See, e.g., the portrayal of Judas in the Last Supper in the Liutold Gospels (twelfth-century Germany, located in Vienna, Osterreichische Nationalbibliothek MS Cod. 1244, fol. 176v, reproduced in Mellinkoff, *Outcasts,* 2:fig. 7.2). In the Chichester Psalter (fol. 150v, Mellinkoff fig. 7.34) though Judas does not have dark skin like the other Jews, he has red hair.

48. Gow, *Red Jews,* 7–12, 23–130; Strickland, *Saracens, Demons, and Jews,* 192–200, 232.

49. Daz waz du rott Judschaitt, / Von den man noch in landen saitt. / Die waren och vergifte wol. / . . . / Tugende and beschaidenhaitt / Waz in allen tiirre. / Gross and ungehiirre / Warend sy all unraine, /Wer it ze rechtt nam war, / Des libe must erschreken gar. (Text and translation in Gow, *Red Jews,* 192, 194–95 respectively). Gow translates *unraine* as "foul and unnatural." I have chosen to translate the word more literally. For twelfth-century examples of the Jews of Gog and Magog as ferocious and cannibalistic, see the examples Gow presents on p. 303.

50. Jacobus de Vitriaco, *La traduction de l'Historia Orientalis,* chap. 81, p. 129. This is from the medieval French translation of *Historia Orientalis,* which was probably composed during the second half of the thirteenth century. See Buridant's introduction, 14–17.

51. Li autre Juu des quels lor pere crierent si com li Evangiles dist: "Li sans Jhesu Crist soit sor nos et sor nos enfans," ki sunt espars par tout le monde, serf et treüagier, et ensi com li prophete dist: "Lor force est tornee en flamesque" et si ne sevent aidier d'armes, et ausi come les femes en cascunne lunison soefrent, et por ce est escrit: "Percussit eos dominus in posteriora et obprobrium sepiternum dedit illis"—ce est a dire: Deus les a ferus en membres veroingnous et lor a donne reproce perpetuel—car puis il ocisent lor frere, le vrai Abel, Jhesu Crist, il sunt fait vage et decacié par les terres ausi com li maudis Chaynes et si on les ciés tramblans, ce est a dire les cuers paorus, cremetous par jor et par nuit, et si ne croient mie a lor vie meïsme (Jacques de Vitry, *Traduction,* 129). On the dating and relation to the Latin text, see Beridant's introduction, 12–25; for the Latin text, see Beridant, *Libri Duo quorum prior orientalis, sive Hierosolymitanae,* 159–60. The Old French "lor force et tornee en flamesque" is odd. The Latin reads "fortitudo eorum . . . conversa est in favillam," and I have taken my cue from that. Also, the Latin associates the unwarlike weakness with being like women, not bleeding like women as in the French. The tie between the bleeding and female physiology remains strong because of the juxtaposition of the two sentences, however, and the use of *lunationibus* (= *lunison*). On this text, see Resnick, "Medieval Roots," esp. 259 n. 64; Biller, "A Scientific View." This passage was also discussed by Willis Johnson in an unpublished paper, "Jewish Melancholy: A Christian Trope?" presented at the 35th International Medieval Congress at Kalamazoo, MI, May 2000.

52. On late antique and early medieval interpretations of Matt. 25:25, see Rainer Kampling, *Das Blut Christi und die Juden,* esp. 36, 46, 55, 72, 74–78, 100–101, 109–13, 122, 128, 131, 146–47, 151–60, 177–79, 197, 200. Also see Rupert of Deutz, *In opus Gloria et Honore Filii Homiis super Mattaeum,* in *PL* 168, cols. 1574–77.

53. Jerome, *Commentaire sur S. Matthieu,* 4.25, 2:282/283.

54. Johnson, "Myth"; Resnick, "Medieval Roots"; Kamplin, *Blut Christi,* 193–94 n. 279.

55. Resnick, in examining many of the same sources, came to the same conclusion regarding the feminization of the Jews: "Medieval Roots." Also see Koren, "Woman from Whom God Wanders," 295–300.

56. Despite Jacques de Vitry's championship of Marie d'Oignies, this highly negative portrayal of feminine nature in *Historia Orientalis* is consistent with de Vitry's depiction of women in other works, such as his *Sermones feriales et Communes.* See Muessig, *Faces of Women,* 34–45.

57. Rupert of Deutz, *De Sancta Trinitate et operibus eius,* vol. 2, *In Leviticum* II.16, p. 873.

58. Ibid., vol. 1, *In Genesim,* III.23, p. 261.

59. Ibid., vol. 2, *In Exodum,* I.6, p. 588.

60. For the synagogue as Delilah, see Rupert, *De Sancta Trinitate,* vol. 2, *Libros Regnum* V.7, 9, 14, pp. 1414–15, 1419–23, 1429–33.

61. Hiezabel, quod interpretatur *fluxus sanguinis*, synagoga eiusdem populi est, quae ex quo sic locuta est: *Sanguis eius super nos et super filios nostros,* nunc usque sanguine fluere non desinit (Rupert, *De Sancta Trinitate,* vol. 2, *In Libros Regnum* V.7, 1415). Also see V.9–10, pp. 1419–23; V.14, pp. 1429–32; V.38, p. 1451; and cf. *In Librum Iudicum,* 22, pp. 1181–82.

62. See Willis Johnson's discussion of Rupert in "Myth," 286. He saw this passage as a precusor to thirteenth-century texts that attributed illness and anal bleeding to Jews and those like them.

63. Rupert, *De Sancta Trinitate,* vol. 1, *In Genesim,* VII.5–7, pp. 433–37; vol. 2, *In Librum Iudicum* XXI.8, pp. 1161–62.

64. Ibid., vol. 2, *In Leviticum* II.28, pp. 890–92.

65. Rupert specifically refers to the belief that leprosy was caused in children by coitus with a menstruating woman in vol. 2, *In Leviticum* II.29, p. 892. In this passage, however, he carefully argues that menstruating women are not impure so much as the men who have intercourse with them. Despite common custom to the contrary, women should not be deprived of the opportunity to enter the church while menstruating. He uses the story of the woman with a flux of blood who was cured by touching Jesus' garments (Matt. 9:20–22) to support his argument.

66. Rupert, *De Sancta Trinitate,* vol. 2, *In Leviticum* II.17–27, pp. 874–90.

67. *Mitte,* inquit, *manum tuam in sinum tuum. Quam cum misisset in sinum protulit leprosam albam instar nivis.* Nempe manus protracta de sinu leprosa synagoga est a gratia Dei proiecta. Ex quo latus salvatoris sui lancea rupit, retracta est manus illa de sinu eius, peccatorum suorum lepra candente perfusa. . . . Ecce videmus populum illum a castris Dei segregatum et ad arbitrium summi sacerdotis Christi haud dubie leprae condemnatum, habentem vestimenta dissuta, caput nudum, os veste contectum, clamantem, id est diffiteri non valentem, contaminatum se ac sorditum (ibid., vol. 2, *In Exodum* I.17, p. 605).

68. Jacquart and Thomasset, *Sexuality and Medicine,* 73–74; Bartholomaeus Anglicus, *De rerum proprietatibus,* bk. 7, chap. 61, pp. 348–49. For the continuation of some of these beliefs into the present day, see Febre-Vassas, *Singular Beast,* 49–53.

69. In his unpublished paper, Johnson was careful to point out the limited scope of Jacques de Vitry's accusation.

70. Both authors tell of a Jewess of Louvain (?) who converts to Christianity, joins a monastery, and refuses to see her parents. Caesarius of Heisterbach, *Dialogus,* 2.26; Thomas de Cantimpré, *Bonum universale de apibus,* 2.29.21, pp. 295–99. On the potential links between Caesarius, Thomas, Jacques de Vitry, and Albertus Magnus, see Biller, "A 'Scientific' View."

71. Caesarius of Heisterbach, *Dialogus,* 2.24.

72. Ibid., 2.25, 26 respectively. Cf. the second tale to Thomas de Cantimpré, *Bonum universale,* 2.29. 21, pp. 300–303.

73. Thomas de Cantimpé, *Bonum universale,* 2.29.13, pp. 288–89; 2.29.22, pp. 303–4.

74. In cruce, innuere videtur, quod ex maledictione parentum currat adhuc in filios vena facinoris, per maculam sanguinis: ut per hanc importune fluidam proles impia inexpiabiliter crucietur, quousque se ream sanguinis Christi recognoscat poenitens, et sanetur. Praeterea audivi quemdam litteratissimum Iudaeorum nostris temporibus conversum ad fidem, dixisse: quemdam quasi prophetam eorum in extremo vitae prophetasse Iudaeis, dicentem: Certissime vos, inquit, scitote nullo modo sanari vos posse ab illo, quo punimini verecundissimo cruciatu, nisi solo sanguine Christiano. Quod verbum caeci semper Iudaei et impii rapientes, induxerunt omni anno in omni provincia fundendum sanguinem Christianum, ut tali sanguine convalescant (Thomas de Cantimpré, *Bonum universale,* 2.29.23, pp. 304–5, quotation on 305). Thomas plays on the words for cross and crucifixion, implying that the Jews are crucified for their role in crucifying Jesus. Thomas also attributes the beginning of the passage to Augustine; however, neither I nor the early modern editor was able to find the passage in any of Augustine's or Pseudo-Augustine's sermons. On this passage, see Johnson, "Myth"; Resnick, "Medieval Roots," esp. 249.

75. See notes by Margot King, Miriam Marsolais, and Hugh Feiss in *Two Lives of Marie d'Oignies,* 11. 203–207.

76. Yuval argues for a connection between Christian awareness that Jews killed their children during the first crusade rather than allow them to be baptized and Christian beliefs that Jews "sacrificed" Christian children. Yuval, "Ha-nakqm ve ha-klilah." On the issue of blood vengeance and the Jews in Thomas of Cantimpré, also see Christopher Ocker, "Ritual Murder and the Subjectivity of Christ."

77. Caesarius of Heisterbach, *Dialogus,* 2.23.

78. Eudes de Cheriton, *Fabulis Addita,* in Léopold Hervieux, *Les fabulistes latins depuis le siècle d'Auguste jusqu'à la fin du Moyen Âge,* "Eudes de Cheritons et ses dérivés," no. 21, pp. 374–75.

79. On the importance and meanings of these symptoms, see Resnick, "Medieval Roots."

80. The Vulgate version of Lev. 15:19 and Matt. 9:20 and Luke 8:43–44 all use this term either in reference to a menstruating woman or to the woman who was healed of continual genital bleeding.

81. Giovanni Balbi, *Catholicon,* v. *digitus.* Also see Willis's discussion of this text in "Myth."

82. *Annales Marbacensis,* 17.178.

83. Ibid. On this and related accounts, see Ocker, "Ritual Murder"; Langmuir, "Ritual Cannibalism," in his *Toward a Definition;* Hödl, *Pathologisierung,* 37.

84. *Hermanni Althahensis Annales,* in *MGH Scriptores,* 17.415. See discussion by Ocker, "Ritual Murder."

85. On the Rindfleisch massacres generally, see Rubin, *Gentile Tales,* 45–55. On Rudolf von Schlettstadt in particular, see Rubin, *Gentile Tales,* 53; Erich Kleinschmidt, "Introduction," in Rudolf von Schlettstadt, *Historia memorabiles,* 18–21.

86. Rudolf von Schlettstadt, *Historia memorabiles,* no. 5, pp. 48–49; no. 16, pp. 64–66. Also cf. no. 39, pp. 99–101, although in this example it is not clear if the Jews drained the young Christian furrier of his blood for medical reasons or not.

87. Ibid., no. 16, p. 65.

88. Ibid., 65–66.

89. For a discussion of this tale, see chap. 6; and Rubin, *Gentile Tales,* 7–28. On the tendency of Christian writers to favor the conversion of Jewish women over Jewish men, see Levine, "Jewish Conversion to Christianity."

90. Johnson, "Myth."

91. On the early roots and meaning of this tradition, see chap. 1; Johnson, "Myth." Medieval texts discussing Judas's bowels include Guillaume de Bourges, *Livre des guerres,* 128/129–130/131; Jacobus de Voragine, *Legenda aurea;* idem, *Golden Legend,* 168–69. In the *Glossa Ordinaria* for Acts 1:18–19, the commentator explains that intestinal pains were the most appropriate vehicle of death. Of these William of Bourges makes the explicit connection between Judas and other Jews. For further references, see Johnson, "Myth"; Maccoby, *Judas Iscariot.*

92. Guillaume de Bourges, *Livre des guerres,* 128/129–130/131.

93. On this trend generally, see chap. 3. Regarding the Jews in this context, see Biller "Views of Jews"; idem, "A 'Scientific' View"; Johnson, "Myth"; Resnick, "Medieval Roots"; Zafran, "Saturn and the Jews."

94. *Problemata Varia,* 38–39. Also cf. *Women's Secrets,* 74. For a discussion of these two texts, see Biller, "Views of Jews"; idem, "A 'Scientific' View." Resnick and Johnson ("Medieval Roots" and "Myths" respectively) discuss the exegetical traditions surrounding Ps. 77:66, linking it to Jewish anal bleeding.

95. Johnson, "Myth," quotation on 290; Resnick, "Medieval Roots"; Biller, "A 'Scientific' View." Koren summarizes their arguments in the afterword of her dissertation, "Woman from Whom God Wanders," 295–99. Sander L. Gilman has addressed the implications of these accusations but is not a specialist in medieval sources. Sander L. Gilman, *Jewish Self-Hatred,* 74–75. Of course, most scholars of medieval medical theory recognize the connection between hemorrhoids and menstruation. See, e.g., Jacquart and Thomasset, *Sexuality and Medicine,* 74.

96. Resnick, "Medieval Roots." Albertus Magnus, *Quaestiones super de animalibus,* Liber IX, quest. 7. This quaestio and those surrounding it are primarily devoted to some aspect of menstruation. Also cf. the quodlibet of Henry of Brussels of Henry

of Germany edited and discussed in Biller, "Views of the Jews" and "A 'Scientific' View."

97. Resnick, "Medieval Roots"; Bernard Gordon, *Lilium Medicinae* (1480), sub verbo emorroidibus, as quoted in Johnson, "Myth," 289; *Problemata Varia,* 39. Also see Biller's discussion of Cecco d'Ascoli and a medieval interpolator of Michael Scot, in "Views of the Jews," 199, or "A 'Scientific' View," 141. Each of the last two bluntly state that Jewish men menstruate.

98. Resnick, "Medieval Roots." For discussions of melancholy and Jews, also see Biller, "Views of Jews"; idem, "A 'Scientific' View"; Zafran, "Saturn and the Jews"; Idel, "Saturn and Sabbatai Tzevi."

99. Albertus Magnus, *Quaestiones super de Animalibus,* Liber IX, quest. 7. Cf. Pseudo-Albertus Magnus, *Women's Secrets,* 73–74, in which Jews are described as being more melancholic than most and thus prone to anal bleeding. This author compares menstruation to hemorrhoids but also notes that women as well as men could suffer from the condition.

100. Albertus Magnus, *De Animalibus* 15.114; 9.21 respectively. Also see Resnick's discussion of all these texts, including the one quoted from *Quaestiones Animalibus* above, in "Medieval Roots," 253–54.

101. See, e.g., Bartholomaeus Anglicus, *De Rerum proprietatibus,* bk. 4, chap. 7, pp. 104–7; bk. 7, chap. 63, pp. 35–55.

102. *Prose Salernitan Questions,* p. 9; quest. 14, p. 18; quest. 33. They were also protected from leprosy and similar diseases because they purged their bodies through monthly bleeding. *Problemata Varia,* 38. See also Jacquart and Thomasset, *Sexuality and Medicine,* 188–93; Nirenberg, *Communities,* 96. Of course, medieval Christian literature is full of female lepers, so Christian thought was not always consistent on this issue.

103. Peter of Poitiers, *"Summa de Confessione" Compilatio presens,* 17. My thanks to Irven Resnick for giving me this reference. Also see *Die Chirurgie des Heinrich von Mondeville,* 1:422, as cited in Malcom Barber, "Lepers, Jews and Moslems," esp. 13. The author of *Problemata Varia Anatomica* suggests that those suffering from a hemorrhoidal flux, like menstruants, rarely suffer from infirmities such as dropsy and leprosy. He does not talk about the Jews until after that statement, but presumably they would be included. If so, for this Christian author at least, Jewish and female immunity from leprosy and related diseases was based on the same biological priniciple.

104. Barber, "Lepers, Jews, and Moslems." Nirenberg relates the "conspiracy" of Jews and lepers to popular fears in France of royal immorality (which would cause the king to lose his ability to heal people of scrofula and leprosy), which he argues was linked directly to the king's support of the Jews. In Aragon, animosity was directed toward foreigners. Nirenberger, *Communities,* 48–124.

105. Arnau de Villanova, *Regimen Sanitatis ad Regem Aragonum,* in *Opera medica omnia,* 10:1 (pp. 454–55); Taddeo Alderotti *Consilia,* chap. 40, p. 218 (he does say that lightly salted pork in small quantities can be beneficial for melancholy). Albertus Magnus seems to identify rabbits as melancholic themselves rather than causing melancholy: *Quaestiones* I.34–37; Biller, "A 'Scientific' View," 159; Luke Demaitre, "Relevance of Futility"; Kenneth Albala, "Southern Europe," in *The Cambridge World*

History of Food, esp. 2:1206, col. 2. For Jews and rabbits, see Epstein, *Dreams,* 16–38; chap. 6 here.

106. Resnick assumes the former. He translates the relevant sentence: "This occurs according to nature especially among people who thrive on gross and salty nourishment, *like the Jews,* and because this blood is gross and has an earthy nature its flow is not governed by the moon as is the menses ("Medieval Roots," 253; original emphasis).

107. Sed ille qui multum est melancolicus multum habet de sanguine melancolico, et inde debet habere fluxum sanguinis, sed iudei sunt huiusmodi. Probo quia utuntur alimentis assatis et non elixatis non coctis, et hec sunt difficile digestibilia, ut dicitur Me[teorum]. Item, utuntur assarem [should be "assatam"] pinguedinem scilicet in oleo etc. et hec sunt difficile indigestibilia [should be "digestibilia"], ut patet manifestum sens[i], ideo, etc. Alia causa huius est quia digestio per vinum [erasure in MS] quod [blank in MS], ergo illi qui non habent bibere vinum habent multos superfluos humores indigestos; ipsi sunt huiusmodi, ergo, etc. (Biller, "Views of Jews," Latin text 206, his translation 192–94). The Latin text may also be found in Biller's "A 'Scientific' View," 161. In this second version the word *difficile* is missing from the second sentence. My translation mostly follows his, with a few minor alterations. Note that not all wine was seen as beneficial to melancholics. See Taddeo Alderotti, *Consilia,* chap. 32, p. 200.

108. *Problemata Varia,* 39.

109. Resnick also notes that *Problemata Varia,* also known as *Omnes Homines,* places the blame on Jews' lifestyle and diet. "Medieval Roots."

110. Note Charlemagne's physicians' insistence that he give up roast for his heals in Einhard, *Vita Karoli Magni,* chap. 22; idem, *The Life of Charlemagne,* chap. 22, in *Two Lives of Charlemagne*; Albala, "Southern Europe," 1207, col. 2.

111. Arnau de Villanova, *Regimen Sanitatis,* esp. 453–55.

112. The literature on this subject is vast. However, see Jordan, *French Monarchy.*

113. *Women's Secrets,* 129.

114. Ibid., 129, 131.

115. Of course, Jews and old women were also often depicted as working together to obtain either a host or a young child, whom the Jews would then wound or kill. For example, in Thomas de Cantimpré, *Miraculorum,* 2.29.22, p. 303, it is a *malignissima vetula* who gives the little girl to the Jews. Thus old women, like Jews, go from being more or less helpless victims of their own bodies in medical texts to being malicious child murderers in *exempla.*

116. Sed iste [istis in MS] magis habundat in iudeis quia ipsi sunt melancolici ut in pluribus. Quia melancolicus fugit cohabitacionem et congregacionem et diligit loca secretaria vel solitaria; sed iudei naturaliter retrahunt se a societate et coniuncti [possibly coniungi] cum aliis ut patet, ergo sunt melancolici. Item pallidi sunt, ergo sunt melancolice complexionis. Item timidi sunt naturaliter et hec tria sunt [supra? MS] accidencia propria melancolicorum, ut dicit Ipocras (Biller, "Views of Jews," Latin p. 206, Eng. p. 192). Latin also in Biller's "A 'Scientific' View," 160. My translation mostly follows Biller's, with a few minor alterations.

117. *Problemata Varia,* 39. Cf. Bernard Gordon, *Lilium Medicinae,* 5.21, fol. 77r, as quoted in Resnick, "Medieval Roots," 257.

118. Though as Mark Pegg indicates in a very different context, in medieval thought the body's sufferings, whether as a result of illness or as a result of torture, ultimately reflected the person's innocence or guilt. Pegg, "Corps et l'autorité."

119. Resnick, "Medieval Roots."

120. 'Abd al-'Aziz ibn 'Uthman al-Qabīṣī, *The Introduction to Astrology,* 2.2–6; for an alternate version in Latin, see *Alchabitius cum commento,* fol. 9r. A translation of a slightly different version of the text exists in Klibansky, *Saturn and Melancholy,* 131–32. The latter contains an even longer list of lowly trades and negative characteristics. Also see Biller, "A 'Scientific' View," 155–56.

121. al-Qabīṣī, *Introduction to Astrology: Alchabatius cum commento*; Klibansky, *Saturn and Melancholy*. On the scorn in which peasants were sometimes held, at least in Latin Europe, see Freedman, *Images.*

122. *Women's Secrets,* 91.

123. al-Qabīṣī, *Introduction to Astrology*, 2:2–3; *Alchabatius cum commento,* vol. 9r; Klibansky, *Saturn and Melancholy,* 131. Cf. Johannes Aegidii, Zamorensis, *Historia naturalis,* 3:1372–74.

124. *Mariale,* quest. XIX.II.5, p. 44. My thanks to Irven Resnick for this reference.

125. Ibid., quest. XIX.II.1, p. 43.

126. *Women's Secrets,* 91. Cf. *Alchabatius cum commento,* fol. 9r–10r; Klibansky, *Saturn and Melancholy,* 131–32. The early modern edition of Alcabitius that I have examined is slightly more positive in tone than the manuscript translated in *Saturn and Melancholy.* However, the Arabic and Latin versions of al-Qabīṣī (*Introduction to Astrology*, 2:6), edited by Burnett, Yamamoto, and Yano, make the person dark, sickly, and possessing undesirable personality traits: cunning, seductiveness, murderousness. Also see Zafran, "Saturn and the Jews," though much of his source material is later than the period under examination here. Black hair and eyes could be considered beautiful in Western Christian estimation. The author of the *Mariale* ultimately concluded that Mary had to be both beautiful and have a perfect balance of humors. The manifestation of that for this author was black hair and eyes and pale skin. *Mariale* quest. XV–XIX, pp. 36–44.

127. See Chazan, *Medieval Stereotypes.*

128. Lewis, *Race and Slavery*, 43–47; idem, *Race and Color in Islam,* 9, 22; Hillenbrand, *Crusades,* 268–73.

129. Sa'id ibn Aḥmad al-Andalusi, *Al-ta'rīf bi-ṭabaqāt al-umam,* 146–47; *Science in the Medieval World,* 7. Sa'id was referring to the Slavs and Bulgars, but these characteristics were applied by other authors to all those living in the North, including France, England, Germany, and Scandanavia, as well as Slavs and Bulgarians, as Hillenbrand points out, *Crusades,* 271.

130. Shams al-Dīn Muḥammad ibn Abī Ṭālib al-Dimashqī, *Nukhbat al-Dahr fī 'Ajā'ib al-Barr wa al-Baḥr,* 275–76; Zakarīyā ibn Muḥammad al-Qazwīnī, *Āthār al-Bilād al-'ibād,* 610; Hillenbrand, *Crusades,* 271–76.

131. Ibn al-Faqīh al-Hamadānī, *Mukhtaṣar Kitāb al-Buldān,* 5:162; *The Thousand Nights and One Night,* trans. Mathers, 2:278.

132. Michael Dols, "The Leper in Medieval Islamic Society"; idem, "Leprosy in Medieval Arabic Medicine." Hillenbrand (*Crusades,* 295) says that Imād al-Dīn al-Isfahānī emphasized Baldwin IV's leprosy and blue eyes in *Der Syrische Blitz.* However, I have been unable to find the passage.

133. al-Qabīṣī, *Introduction to Astrology,* 2:2–7; idem, *Alchabatius cum commento,* vol. 9r; Ibn Buluggīn, *Kitāb al-Tibyān,* 188–89; idem, *The Tibyān,* 181–82; Brann, *Power in the Portrayal,* 58.

134. Ibn Buluggīn, *Kitāb al-Tibyān,* 189; idem, *The Tibyān,* 182.

135. اليس هم زهريين؟ و الزهرة دالة على الدين, و النظافة, و المروءة, و الضوء, و الطهر من الجنابة, و اباحة النكاح, و الاماء, و الطيب و الزينة؟ (ibid.). I suspect he is playing on the similarity of the word *zuharah* (Venus) and the word *ṭuhr* (purity). Abu Ma'shar also links Muslims and Venus: Biller, "A 'Scientific' View," 154.

136. John of Damascus, 136–37; Petrus Alfonsi, *Dialogus,* 97, 98; Bacon, *Opus Maius,* pt. 4, mathematics, trans. Burke, 1:278–79, and pt. 7, moral philosophy, 2:791–92; Khoury, *Polémique contre l'Islam,* 60–62, 240–42, 275–79; Tolan, *Saracens,* 44, 53–54, 73, 226; Norman Daniel, *Islam and the West,* 217, 371; Bernard Septimus, "Petrus Alfonsi on the Cult of Mecca." My thanks to Irven Resnick for alerting me to Septimus's article and reminding me of Petrus Alfonsi's discussion of astrology and Islam. Note that both Petrus and Bacon are writing after Ibn Buluggīn, but they are drawing from earlier traditions.

137. Not all areas of the Mediterranean were ideal in this schema, however. See Ibn Ridwan, *Medieval Islamic Medicine.*

138. Guibert of Nogent, *Der Gesta per Francos,* bk. 1, pp. 89–90; idem, *Deeds of God through the Franks,* 30.

139. Guibert of Nogent, *Der Gesta per Francos,* 90–101; Tolan, *Saracens,* 145.

140. William of Malmesbury, *Gesta regum anglorum,* 4.347.8; *William of Malmesbury Gesta regum anglorum,* 1:600–603.

141. Strickland, *Saracens, Demons, and Jews,* 178.

142. Petrus Alfonsi, *Dialogus,* 99; Septimus, "Petrus Alfonsi on the Cult of Mecca." Septimus shows that Petrus was drawing from a rather mangled understanding of Jewish traditions regarding Muslim idolatry and the origins of the Ka'ba.

143. Petrus Alfonsi, *Dialogus,* 98.

144. Bacon, *Opus maius,* pt. 4, mathmatics, 1:278; Gerald of Wales, *De Principis Instructione*, distinctio 1, p. 70; Tolan, *Saracens,* 73, 226; Strickland, *Saracens, Demons, and Jews,* 179.

145. Petrus Alfonsi, *Dialogus,* 97.

146. Tacitus, *Histories* 5.2. Again, my thanks to Irven Resnick for this reference.

147. Idel, "Saturn."

148. Abraham Abulafia, *Sefer Gan Na'ul,* MS München, 58, fol. 327, as quoted in Idel, "Saturn," 179.

149. Roger Bacon, *Opus Maius,* pt. 4, mathematics, in Burke 1:278. Bacon is paraphrasing or partially quoting from the Latin translation of Abu Ma'shar. See Biller, "A 'Scientific' View," 154–55.

150. Idel, "Saturn," esp. 185–86. In theosophic Kabbalah, God is made up of 10 *sefirot* that are divided into masculine and feminine. *Ḥokhmah*, meaning wisdom, is the highest paired *sefirot* on the masculine side of God.

151. As cited in Idel, "Saturn," 185–86. The passage is from Joseph b. Shalom Ashkenazi, *Commentary on Sefer Yetzirah* (Jerusalem, 1961), fols. 516–52a, which I have been unable to obtain.

152. Isaac ibn Sahula takes a less direct but similar approach without the mystical connotations; in his collection of tales, Saturn is portrayed as powerful, noble, and righteously destructive. Isaac ibn Sahula, *Meshal ha-Qadmoni,* vol. 2, gate 5, pp. 576/577, 580/581, 600/601–604/605.

153. Johnson made this connection between Christian beliefs about Jews' sickness or darkness and Jewish exegesis of this chapter in "Jewish Melancholy." On Song of Songs and the darkness of Jews as redemptive, see Goldenberg, *Curse of Ham,* 48–50, 87–89. Goldenberg points out that Christians applied this tradition to themselves and to the Church.

154. BT Sanhedrin 98b; Michael Fishbane, "Midrashic Theologies of Messianic Suffering," in his *The Exegetical Imagination,* 73–85.

155. See Rashi on Isa. 52:13–53:12, in *Fifty-third Chapter of Isaiah,* Heb. 1:37–39, Eng. 2:37–39, 136.

156. כאשר שממו כאשר תמהו עליכם עמים רבים בראותם שפלותכם ואמרו זה לזה כן משחת מאיש מראהו ראו מה תארם חשוך משאר בני אדם כן כאשר אנחנו רואים בעינינו . . . מרוב בשתם ושפלותם היו כמסתירי פנים ממנו חבושי פנים בטמון כדי שלא נראה כאדם מנוגע שמסתיר פניו וירא מהביט (*Fifty-third Chapter of Isaiah,* 2:37–38). The translation here differs slightly from that of Driver and Neubauer. See Isa. 52:14; 53:3.

157. See, e.g., Gen. 12:17; Lev. 13:51. Neubauer and Driver translate: "And as a result of their shame and depression they were as men hiding their faces from us—like a person striken [with leprosy], who is afraid to look up, they had their faces bound up that we might not see them." *Fifty-third Chapter of Isaiah,* 2:37.

158. See discussion of blackness and leprosy above. Also cf. *Mariale,* quest. XV–XVIII, pp. 36–42, in which the Christian author toys with the idea that Jesus or Mary must have been black or deformed as a sign of their great humility.

159. שאין לך אומה בעולם שהגיע אליה מכאובים כמכאובה וחולי כחוליה (R. Joseph Qara, on Isa. 53:3, in *Fifty-third Chapter of Isaiah,* 1:41–42; 2:42). My translation differs slightly from the one given there.

160. Abraham ibn Ezra, on Isa. 52:14, in *Fifty-third Chapter of Isaiah,* Heb. 1:44, Eng. 2:44. The theology of Jewish suffering in contrast to the Gentiles' freedom from it is essentially the same as Rashi's, though Ibn Ezra seems to suggest that the Gentiles will be punished for their treatment of the Jews but also that the Gentiles will ultimately convert. Ibid., 1:44–47; 2:45–48.

161. ודמיון השה הוא לענוי הגוף ולתמותתו ודמיון הרחל הוא לנגישת הממון שהוא בדמיון הגז ודמה אותו לרחל ולא לכבש לחולשתה יותר כי בכל המינין הנקבה חלושה מהזכר כן ישראל בגלות הם חלושים מאד. (David K[Q]imḥi in *Fifty-third Chapter,* 1:51; 2:52–53; and see Isa. 53:7. My translation differs considerably from the one given by Neubauer and Driver. In the first set of similes they confuse the lamb and the ewe. They translate תמותו as having to do

with bodily affliction. However, this word can be interpreted as either "his perfection/completeness" or "his harmlessness."

162. The issue of monetary extortion seems to have been an important one to David Qimḥi as he refers to it throughout the passage.

163. Cf. Joseph ben Nathan Official, *Yosef ha-Mekane'*, no. 84, pp. 79–82; also in *Fifty-third Chapter,* 1:64–67; 2:71–74.

164. MS Oppenheim 757, Neubauer Catalogue MS 2289 (6), pp. 50–51, as cited in Joseph ben Nathan Official, *Yosef ha-Mekane'* 95 n. 1 to para. 104.

165. וגם אני נתתי אתכם נבזים ושפלים לכל (העמים) [העם]' א"ל משומד אחד לה"ר נתן: אתם מכוערים יותר מכל אדם אשר על פני האדמה, ובני עמינו יפים מאד. השיבו: אותן שויסקי שקורין פרונילש הגדלים בסנאים איזה פרח היה בהם? א"ל: לבן. ופרח התפוח מהו? א"ל: אדום. א"ל: כך אנו מזרע נקי ולבן לכך פנינו שחורים אבל אתם מזרע האדום מן הנדות לכך אתם תארכם צהוב ומאדם. אבל הטעם: לפי שאנו בגלות, כמו שאמר בשיר השירים: אל תראוני שאני שחרחרת ששזפתני השמש, בני אמי נחרו בי, שמוני נוטרה את הכרמים, כרמי שלי לא נטרתי, אבל כשנטרתי כרמי הייתי יפה מאד, כדכתיב: ויצא לך שם בגוים ביופיך (Official, *Yosef ha-Mekane',* no. 104, p. 95).

166. וזה עדות לישראל שהם טהורים מדם נידות ואין כאן שום אודם בראשונה, אבל הגוים שאינם מוזהרים מנידות ובועלים בשעת ראיית דמיהן ויש אודם בראשות לפיכך הפרי הבא ממנו, הם הבנים, הם לבנים (*Jewish-Christian Debate,* no. 238, Heb. p. 159, Eng. p. 224).

167. Lawn, *Salernitan Questions,* 80; *Prose Salernitan Questions,* 302–3, nos. 38–39; Cf. pp. 85–86, no. 167, on the coloration of animals' fur. The botanical theory behind these two Hebrew texts continues to elude me, however.

168. See chapter 3 above; Jacquart and Thomasset, *Sexuality and Medicine,* 73–74; Fabre-Vassas, *Singular Beast,* 49–53, 150.

169. Brundage, *Law, Sex, and Christian Society,* 155–56. It has been suggested to me that in the *Nizzahon Yashan* passage Christians were not being accused of having intercourse with their menstruant wives per se, but since Christian women did not purify themselves after their flux was over, they were by rabbinic standards always impure (though theoretically non-Jewish women did not convey *niddah* impurity). The term בועלים בשעת ראית דמיהן (bo'alim besha'at re'iyat dameihen), "they [masc.] have intercourse at the hour of seeing their [fem.] blood," belies that interpretation.

170. Of course, being darkened by external forces did not necessarily counter the negative connotations associated with darkness. See my discussion above and Freedman, *Images.* Technically, even Africans were dark only because they were "overcooked" by the sun, even as the Slavs were "undercooked."

171. Isaac Polgar, *'Ezer ha-Dat,* 36. I am indebted to Joel Kenny for giving me this reference.

172. הצילנו הקב"ה שאין אנו זבים ומצעורים ושרופי אש כמותם כי ה, רופאינו. (*Jewish-Christian Debate,* no. 217, Heb. p. 148, Eng. p. 211).

173. On male gonorrhea and nightly emissions as a manifestation of corrupt humors, see Elliot, "Pollution"; Jacquart and Thomasset, *Sexuality and Medicine,* 120–21.

174. *Jewish-Christian Debate,* nos. 18, 19, 49, 123, 145, 146, 156; Heb. pp. 16, 33, 81, 96, 97–98, 108–9; Eng. pp. 55, 73–74, 133–34, 153, 155, 170–71 respectively.

175. Ibid., nos. 18–19, Heb. p. 16, Eng. p. 55.

176. דא מזוהמא דדהבא אתעביד (*Zohar* III. 51a). See the beginning of the passage on 50b.

177. *Zohar* II.149b, 167a–b, 236a–237b. Cf. *Zohar* II.219b–220a, III.104b; Koren, "Woman from Whom God Wanders," 287, 292–94. On pp. 192–93 n. 59 Koren says that another Jewish mystic from this period, Joseph Hamadan, maintained in his *Sefer Ta'mei ha-Miẓvot* that gentiles' souls derived from God's union with his impure (menstruating) concubine. On the Shekhinah as a menstruating woman, equivalent to an "alien woman," see Koren's discussion on the same pages. In general, also see *Wisdom of the Zohar,* 3:529–32; Wolfson, "The Feminine as Other"; idem, "Erasing the Erasure"; idem, "Re/membering the Covenant."

178. For the formation of tumors or other types of "formless flesh" in the womb in a Jewish text, see "A Record of the Diseases in the Genital Members," in Barkai, *History,* Heb. pp. 115–16, Eng. pp. 133–34.

179. In the *Zohar* the Serpent, the one who tempted Eve, is also the product of supernal waste. See *Zohar* II.236b.

180. Ruth Mellinkoff, *Antisemitic Hate Signs in Hebrew Illuminated Manuscripts from Medieval Germany.*

181. Epstein, *Dreams.* Both Mellinkoff and Epstein, but especially Epstein, are largely concerned with animal iconography.

182. Being like a woman was beginning to acquire positive associations, especially in the Cistercian world. See Caroline Walker Bynum, "Jesus as Mother."

Chapter 6. **Signs of the Beast**

1. Sahar Amer, *Ésope au feminine,* 92; Scott, *Domination,* 162–66; Epstein, *Dreams,* 8–9.

2. Rowland, "Art of Memory"; Hassig, *Medieval Bestiaries,* 175–78; Epstein, *Dreams.* Hassig (18–26) cautions that images and their signification were not subservient to the text and sometimes the images conveyed very different meanings, theological and otherwise, than the texts they accompanied; nor were the interpretations static or fixed.

3. Remke Kruk, "Traditional Islamic Views of Apes and Monkeys"; Uri Rubin, *Between the Bible and the Qur'an*; Helga Venzlaff, *Al-Hudhud*; Peter Schienerl, *Tierdarstellung im Islam.* More research needs to be done on this subject.

4. An excellent example of this is how early Eastern Christian tales of Jewish malice toward Christians, icons, and the host were transformed in late medieval Western Europe. On this, see Rubin, *GentileTtales.*

5. Epstein, *Dreams.* Also see Epstein's "'The Ways of the Truth'"; Therese Metzger and Mendel Metzger, *Jewish Life in the Middle Ages,* 19–37.

6. Epstein, *Dreams;* idem., "'The Ways of the Truth.'"

7. Bernard O'Kane, *Early Persian Painting*; Esin Atil, *Kalila wa Dimna*; Sofie Walzer, "The Mamluk Illuminated Manuscripts of Kalila wa-Dimna"; Richard Ettinghausen, *Arab Painting*; Thomas W. Arnold, *Painting in Islam.*

8. For example, Muslim authors objected most strenuously to the sculptures and paintings of animals that the Christians placed in the Dome of the Rock. See Imād al-Dīn al-Iṣfahānī, *al-Fatḥ al-qussī,* 141; Gabrielli, *Arab Historians,* 169.

9. This point is explored in greater detail in this chapter, but see Sapir Abulafia, *Christians and Jews*, 105–17; Peter the Venerable, *Adversus iudeorum inveteratam duritiem*, I.340–45; V.1–29, 936–70, 1981–90, pp. 13, 125, 151–52, 181 respectively; Friedman's introduction, viii; Gautier de Coincy, *Miracles*, 2:16; *Sefer Gezerot*, 82, 158, 168–69, 177, 191, 220, 238.

10. Ruth Mazo Karras, *From Boys to Men,* 100–108.

11. Ibid., 67–108; Ephraim Kanarfogel, *Jewish Education and Society in the High Middle Ages*; Marcus, *Rituals of Childhood*; Jonathan Berkey, *Transmission of Knowledge in Medieval Cairo.* Berkey's research shows that Muslim women had greater access to certain kinds of formal higher learning than many of their Jewish and Christian counterparts. However, women were still considered less rational and more emotional than men. See, e.g., the comments of ʿAli ibn ʿAbd al-Kāfī Taqī al-Dīn al-Subkī, *Shifāʾ al-Saqām fī ziyārat khayr al-Anām,* 84.

12. Sapir Abulafia, "Twelfth-Century Renaissance Theology and the Jews"; idem, *Christians and Jews,* 44–47, 72–122; idem, "Bodies"; idem, "Attempt by Gilbert Crispin"; Funkenstein, *Perceptions,* 172–89; Tolan, *Petrus Alfonsi,* 14–15, 22–41.

13. Sapir Abulafia, *Christians and Jews,* 23–47.

14. Tolan, *Petrus Alfonsi,* 14–15. For examples of Moses' evocation of reason, see Petrus Alfonsi, *Dialogo contra los Judios,* Prologue, p. 8; chap. 1, p. 12; chap. 3, pp. 76–77; chap. 6, p. 104. Anselm's thought was also a key factor in the emphasis on rationality in religious debates with Jews and other groups; however, he is not an important source for accusations of animalistic mentality. See Sapir Abulafia, *Christians and Jews,* 42–47; idem, "Attempt by Gilbert Crispin."

15. Nos sane per bestias illas, que rapina et carne vivunt, impios homines intelligimus et raptores, per reliquas vero pecudes mansuetos et simplices, et de illis propheta dixit, quod Christus eos simul habitare hac pacem habere preciperet. Quod autem de hominibus intelligi voluerit, in sequentibus insinuat propheta, cum subiungit "quia repleta est terra scientia domini." Neque enim hoc propter pecudes dixit, que cum nec animam habeant rationalem, nec domini scientiam habere possunt, id est domini cognitionem (Petrus Alfonsi, *Dialogo,* chap. 9, pp. 146–47). Alfonsi is playing with the meanings of *rapina* and *raptor. Rapina* can mean robbery and plunder as well as prey. The customary meaning of *pecudes* is "cattle," but it can also refer to sheep and, more rarely, horses. Cf. Alfonsi's discussion of these verses with that of the thirteenth-century writer of *Dialogus pro Ecclesia contra Synagogam:* Orfali, "Dialogus," esp. 708.

16. Petrus Alfonsi, *Dialogo,* chap. 1, pp. 14–15, 24–50; Sapir Abulafia, *Christians and Jews,* 91–93; Tolan, *Petrus Alfonsi,* 22–27.

17. Peter Abelard, *Dialogus inter philosophum, Judaeum et Christianum,* 90 (English: *A Dialogue of a Philosopher with a Jew and a Christian*, 39); Jacob b. Reuben, *Milḥamot ha-Shem,* 66, 67. Also see Yvonne Friedman's introduction to Peter the Venerable, *Adversus iudeorum,* xxii; Sapir Abulafia, "Bodies," esp. 130; idem, *Christians and Jews*, 105, 113, 116–17.

18. Peter the Venerable, *Adversus iudeorum,* 4. Many scholars have remarked on Peter the Venerable's application of animal imagery to the Jews. See Dominique Iogna-Prat, *Order and Exclusion,* 292, 305, 315, 318; Sapir Abulafia, *Christians and Jews,* 116–17, 128; idem, "Bodies"; Friedman, Introduction to *Adversus iudeorum,* viii; Tolan, *Petrus Alfonsi,* 116–17; Jean Paul Torrell, "Les Juifs dans l'oeuvre de Pierre le Venerable."

19. On the brutishness of Jews and their intellect, see Peter the Venerable, *Adversus iudeorum*, 13, 33, 42, 125, 144, 167, 169, 181, 186. For comparisons to various "stupid" farm animals, see Peter the Venerable, *Adversus indeorum,* 43, 61–62, 125; Iogna-Prat, *Order and Exclusion,* 295–316. Nearly a century after Peter the Venerable's death, Thibaut of Sézanne derided the Talmud for its "insane blasphemies" and intimated that Jews were like animals: Orfali, "Dialogus," 691, 693, 703. This text was part of a collection known by various names: *Excerpta de erroribus iudeorum in Talmuth*; *Talmud obiectiones*. The author seems to have borrowed from Petrus Alfonsi but developed the material according to his own inclinations. See Orfali's discussion, 679–89; and also Tolan, *Petrus Alfonsi*, 117–19, on Theobald of Saxony's *Pharetra Fidei.*

20. Peter the Venerable, *Schriften zum Islam,* 78/79–80/81; Iogna-Prat, *Order and Exclusion,* 340. Cf. Aquinas, *Summa Contra Gentiles*, 1:6.

21. *Jewish-Christian Debate,* Heb. p. 27, Eng. pp. 67–68.

22. Ibid., Heb. p. 95, Eng. p. 152, and see Berger's note 1 to p. 152 on p. 302.

23. This observation is common to nearly all who have worked on Peter the Venerable, but see esp. Sapir Abulafia, *Christians and Jews*; Torrell, "Juifs."

24. See Lasker, *Jewish Philosophical Polemics.*

25. Peter the Venerable, "Adversus Quendam Furiosum Apollinaristam Hereticum," vol. 1, letter 37, pp. 117–18, 120, 122; Petrus Alfonsi, *Dialogo,* chap. 5, p. 96; Gautier de Coincy, *Miracles,* 3:132; 4:168; *Bible moralisée Codex Vindobonensis 2554, Vienna, Osterreichische Nationalbibliothek,* 85 (28va), 86 (28vc and d; 29ra and b), 96 (59rc); Camille, *Image on the Edge,* 72; Lipton, *Images of Intolerance,* 49, 83, 89; Torrell, "Juifs," esp. 338; Freedman, *Images,* esp. chap. 6; André le Chapelain, *On Love,* 1.12, where he compares the loving of peasants to that of mules and horses.

26. On oxen and horses in the Middle Ages, see Jordan, *Great Famine,* 33.35–36.

27. On Peter the Venerable's views of how Jews should be "used" for the service of Christianity, see his letter to King Louis: "Ad Ludovicum Francorum Regem," letter 130, in *Letters,* pp. 327–30; Torrell, "Juifs." On their servile status generally, see Iogna-Prat, *Order and Exclusion,* 278–84, 290–95.

28. For Ashkenazi Jews' desire for the defeat of the Christians, see Yuval's discussion in his "Ha-Naqam ve-ha-qlilah."

29. Gautier of Coincy (1177/78–1236) was part of the community of the abbey of Saint Médard de Soissons. For bibliographic information, see Frederic Koenig's introduction to his edition of Gautier's *Miracles,* 1:xviii–xxx.

30. Gautier de Coincy, *Miracles,* 2:16.

31. "Diex, to les dois corn un viel chien/ Ferir dou pie et dire fi." Gautier de Coincy, *Miracles,* 2:21.

32. *Evangelia infantiae apocrypha* = *Apocryphe Kindheitsevangelien*; *The Old French Evangile de l'Enfance*, 76–80, ll. 1761–1888. Jesus states that the beasts are

wiser than the oldest of the Jews, 80, ll. 1872–75; *Les enfaunces de Jesu Crist*, 71–73, ll. 1385–1467, esp. 73, ll. 1452–55.

33. Peter the Venerable, *Adversus iudeorum,* V:132.

34. Philippe de Thaün, *Le Bestiare,* CIII, 2–5, ll. 25–108; Hassig, *Medieval Bestiaries,* 152.

35. On the *Physiologus,* see Florence McCulloch, *Mediaeval Latin and French Bestiaries,* 15–44. On the ant, see McCulloch, *Mediaeval Latin and French Bestiaries*; *Bestiary being an English version of the Bodleian Library, Oxford MS 764,* 115; *The Bestiary,* ed. James; *The Bestiary,* trans. White, 97; Pierre de Beauvais, *Le bestiaire de Pierre de Beauvais version course,* 67–68. Not all bestiaries include this detail. See, e.g., the Old English bestiary published in *Old English Miscellany,* 8–10; Brunetto Latini, *Libro del tesoro,* 90; idem, *Li livres dou tresor.*

36. Guillaume le Clerc, *Le Bestiaire das Thierbuch des normanischen Dichters Guillaume le Clerc*, 263, ll. 950–56; idem, *The Bestiary of Guillaume le Clerc*, 33–34.

37. Guillaume le Clerc is well known for being much more virulent in his polemic against the Jews than other compilers of bestiaries. See Lipton, *Images of Intolerance,* 88. Also see *Bestiary,* trans. White, 16.

38. On the patrons of bestiaries, see Hassig, *Medieval Bestiaries,* 5, 175–76, 217–18 n. 31. For the relationship among bestiaries, *exempla,* and miracle collections, see Lilian Randall, "*Exempla* as a Source of Gothic Marginal Illumination."

39. For an example of how Muslim victories could cause differences in Christian polemic directed at Muslims and Jews, see Alexandra Cuffel, " 'Henceforward All Generations Will Call Me Blessed.' "

40. Oderic Vitalis, *Ecclesiastical History,* vol. 5, bk. 9, pp. 16/17.

41. Ibid. Women did in fact participate in the crusades. See *Gendering the Crusades.*

42. Oderic Vitalis, *Ecclesiastical History,* vol. 5, bk. 9, pp. 18/19.

43. Epstein, " 'The Ways of the Truth' "; idem, *Dreams.*

44. Isaac ibn Sahula, *Meshal Haqadmoni,* vol. 1, prologue, ll. 5–7, 11; Heb. p. 5, Eng. pp. 6–7 and p. 6 n. 3. On Ibn Sahula's life, see Loewe's introduction, xv–xxiv.

45. Ibid., vol. 1, preface, ll. 25–35, pp. 22/23; gate 1, ll. 36–39, 93–95, 530–760, 1239–41, pp. 46/47, 50/51, 88/89–108/109, 150/151; vol. 2, gate 3, ll. 57–75, 354–99, pp. 336/337, 362/363–366/367; gate 4, ll. 330–48, pp. 448/449–450/451.

46. 'Abd Allāh ibn Muqaffa', *Kitāb Kalīlah wa-Dimnah,* 116–96; idem, *The Fables of Kalīlah and Dimnah,* 79–117. In Ibn Sahula's version a number of details are changed and no names are given, including for the fox (as opposed to the jackal in the Arabic version). It is not unreasonable to assume that Ibn Sahula read *Kalīlah wa-Dimnah.* See Loewe's introduction, l–lvi.

47. Ibn Sahula, *Meshal Haqadmoni,* vol. 1, gate 1, ll. 176–277, pp. 58/59–66/67. See Num. 13:27.

48. Ibn Sahula, *Meshal Haqadmoni,* vol. 1, gate 1, ll. 278–810, pp. 68/69–112/113.

49. Ibid., ll. 265–77, 283–309, pp. 66/68–70/71.

50. Epstein, " 'The Ways of Truth,' " esp. 216–17; idem, *Dreams,* 43–66, 107–12.

51. McCulloch, *Medieval Latin and French Bestiaries,* 137–40; *Bestiary,* ed. White, 8–9; Pierre de Beauvais, *Bestiare,* 37; bestiary in an *Old English Miscellany,* 1–2; *Bestiary* . . . MS Bodley 764, 24–25. Of course, to the Christians the lion was also symbolic of the tribe of Judah and the one whom they claimed sprang from it, namely, Jesus Christ. See McCulloch, *Medieval Latin and French Bestiaries,* 137; *Bestiary,* ed. White, 8; *Bestiary* . . . MS Bodley 764, 24; John of Garland, *Stella Maris,* 104–5, ll. 196–201; *Jewish-Christian Debate*, sec. 29, Heb. pp. 22–23, Eng. pp. 62–63.

52. Epstein, *Dreams,* 16–38, 102–12.

53. Ibn Sahula, *Meshal Haqadmoni,* vol. 1, gate 1, l. 786, pp. 110/111.

54. הצורה הראשון היא הנפש הצומחת, יחד על עפר נחת. הצורה השניה היא הנפש הבהמית המתאוה, כל היום דוה (ibid., ll. 649–52, p. 99). My translation differs from Loewe's.

55. בהיות הנפש בבצע הגופות טבועה, ומכל חכמה ושכל גדועה, וזלזלה לכבוד קונה, לרצונה ושלא רצונה היתה לזונה. ותטמא בטמאת המדות, ותענגות בני אדם שדה ושדות, והגאוה והסכלות תרעינה, ופריץ חיות יעלנה, ואיש אחר ישכבנה. (ibid., gate 1, ll. 696–702, p. 103). My translation differs from Loewe's. The phrase "the pleasures of men a concubine and concubines" (ותענגות בני אדם שדה, ושדות) is from Eccles. 2:8. The meaning of *shidah* (שדה) is debated. It can either mean "coffer, chest" or "pretty woman, mistress." In the context of this passage, Ibn Sahula seems to be taking the second of these meanings. The reference to a wild beast is a play on Isa. 35:9 in which Israel is promised that wild beasts shall *not* walk over her. In this passage, however, the beasts have free rein. The passage may also refer to the talmudic tradition that marrying a daughter to a commoner is like giving her to a lion (a lion is also mentioned in Isa. 35:9) or wild beast (see chap. 2). Ibn Sahula may have been playing with the fact that the "woman" in question is the soul of a lion (a wild beast), ravaged by her own master. Finally, "another man shall lie with her" comes from Deut. 28:30. In that chapter one of the threats for Israel's disobedience is that another man shall lie with an Israelite's new bride. The cumulative effect of the last two biblical citations is that the "bad" soul is like Israel gone astray, removed from God's promises of protection and doomed to suffer punishment.

56. Ibid., ll. 711–33, 750, pp. 104/105, 106/107.

57. Ibid., ll. 288–309, pp. 68/69–70/71.

58. אבי היה נבון לחשים, יועץ וחכם חרשים (ibid., ll. 763–64, pp. 108/109).

59. Berechiah ben Natronai ha-Naqdan, *Mishle Shu'alim,* fable 47 (pp. 55–56). English: *Fables of a Jewish Aesop,* fable 47, pp. 87–88.

60. הנה מלכך יבוא לך צדיק ונושע הוא עני ורוכב על חמור ועל עיר בן אתנות The Hebrew differs slightly from the standard English translation: rather than "triumphant and victorious," "righteous and saved" might be more accurate. Also see Matt. 21:1–10; Mark 11:1–10; Luke 19:29–38; John 12:12–15. The Gospels of Matthew and John refer most explicitly to Zechariah. Donkeys were also messianic symbols in Jewish illuminated manuscripts; see Epstein, *Dreams,* 99–102, 148 n. 31.

61. . . . זדון לבך השיאך Berechia ben Natronai ha-Naqdan, *Mishlei Shu'alim*, fable 47 (p. 56); *Fables of a Jewish Aesop*, p. 88.

62. See the commentary of R. David K[Q]imḥi, especially for verses 15, 16, and 21. Also see *Mainz Anonymous*, which begins by citing Obad. 1:4 in reference to the crusaders. Hebrew text in *Sefer Gezerot,* 93. English translation in Chazan, *European*

Jewry, 225; see 336 n. 3. On anti-Christian polemic in biblical commentaries generally, see E. I. J. Rosenthal, "Anti-Christian Polemic in Medieval Biblical Commentaries." See Eliezer of Beaugency, *Perush.*

63. Berechiah b. Natronai ha-Naqdan, *Mishlei Shu'alim,* fable 47 (p. 55); *Fables of a Jewish Aesop,* p. 88.

64. Of course, whether Jesus really claimed to be either is a matter of debate. Important for our purposes is that medieval Jews and Christians thought he did.

65. Ezek. 28:11–19. Berechiah b. Natronai ha-Naqdan, *Mishlei Shu'alim,* fable 47 (p. 55); *Fables of a Jewish Aesop*, p. 88. The language in *Mishlei Shu'alim* is not identical to that in Ezek. 28:11–19, though the themes are similar. Note that the men who propose to hunt the ass-lion (see p. 71 of *Mishlei* and p. 87 of *Fables*) draw from Exod. 32:27. The context of this command is the aftermath of the incident of the golden calf. Berechiah thus hints that the hunters seek to destroy an idol worshiper, or one who leads Israel astray, which again is quite apt as part of an anti-Christian invective. See also *Jewish-Christian Debate*, paras. 80–81 (Heb. pp. 53–54, Eng. pp. 98–99).

66. Berechiah b. Natronai ha-Naqdan, *Mishlei Shu'alim,* fable 47 (p. 54); *Fables of a Jewish Aesop,* p. 87.

67. Berechiah b. Natronai ha-Naqdan, *Mishlei Shu'alim,* fable 47 (p. 55); *Fables of a Jewish Aesop,* p. 88.

68. וכארי יטרוף להם ארב וצדה, האדם והבהמה אשר ימצא בשדה (And like a lion he hunted and tracked man and beast in the field). Berechiah b. Natronai ha-Naqdan, *Mishlei Shu'alim*, fable 47 (p. 55); *Fables of a Jewish Aesop*, p. 87.

69. Berechiah b. Natronai ha-Naqdan, *Mishlei Shu'alim,* fable 47 (p. 55); *Fables of a Jewish Aesop,* p. 88.

70. Joseph K[Q]imḥi argues that Christian society is much more violent than that of Jews. *Sefer ha-berit,* Heb. pp. 25–26, Eng. pp. 32–33. Jewish polemicists also argued that Jesus could not have been the Messiah based on Isa. 2:4. This messianic prophecy had clearly not been fulfilled since Christians were even more violent than other nations. See Nahmanides, *Vikuaḥ ha-Ramban,* in *Kitvei,* 1:311; Joseph ben Nathan Official, *Yosef ha-Mekane',* para. 80, p. 77; Mordechai b. Joseph, *Mahzik Emunah,* in Chazan, *Daggers,* 110–11.

71. On Jewish expectations or calls for divine vengeance against Christians, see Yuval, "Ha-naqam ve-ha-qlilah." Berechiah has most often been discussed as being Norman or English (from Oxford), where he has been identified with the Oxford scribe Benedictus le Puncteur.

72. Epstein, *Dreams,* 16–38, 102–12; Hassig, *Medieval Bestiaries,* 88–89. See Worms Maḥzor I, MS. Jerusalem, JNUL MS Heb. 4 78111 fol. 170v (Worms 1272); and the Brabant Pentatuch from 1310, MS Hamburg Staats-und Universitatsbibliotek, Cod. Levy 19, fol. 97r, reproduced in Epstein, *Dreams, 2*0, 106, figs. 6, 41 respectively; Lisbon, Biblioteca Nacional, MS Il. 72, fol. 305r (Spain, ca. 1300) and Oxford Bodleian Library, MS Mich. 619, fol. 201r (Germany, ca. 1325), reproduced in Metzger, *Jewish Life,* 215, 275, figs. 320, 394, information, 212, 277 respectively. The one clear Christian example in which Jews are the hunters represents Christians as the beaver. Further study of Christian iconography may reveal more instances. Another nonhunting example of

Jewish “threat” to the “Christian” animal is in MS Cambridge. University Library Ii. 4.26, fol. 7, reproduced in Hassig, *Medieval Bestiaries,* fig. 144. In this manuscript a large Jew beats an elephant and its Christian riders. On the symbolism of the elephant in Christian and Jewish art, see Hassig, *Medieval Bestiaries,* 129–44; Epstein, *Dreams,* 39–69; idem, “‘The Ways of the Truth.’” Muslims do not seem to have incorporated such symbolism into their manuscript illuminations, but it is clearly evident in textual discussions of Christians.

73. See, e.g., *Bible moralisée,* 28va–29rb, trans. on pp. 85–86; 62vb, trans. p. 101. Sara Lipton has shown that heretics were linked with cats: *Images,* 82–111.

74. *Bible moralisée,* 22va, trans. p. 78; 28vd, trans. p. 86; 29rb, trans. p. 86; 30rc, trans. p. 88; Pigs are also associated with usurers and greedy people; see 28va, trans. p. 85; 59rc, trans. p. 96. See Lipton's discussion, *Images,* 31–53.

75. Ili vienent li fil israel et aportent aigneax tigneus et tachelez qi ont les menbres brisiez et font offrande a deu et Dex la refuse. Et qu li fil israel fistrent offrande de lors aigneax tigneus et tachelz et Dex le refusa senefie cels qi font offrande de tigne du luxe et de convoitise et de symonie et dex refuse cele offrande et detorne dels (*Bible moralisée,* 30rC and c; trans. p. 88). My thanks to Penelope Johnson for her assistance with this passage. The citation prior to the longer quotation is from 30ra, which in the original reads: “Li tigneus senefie lusurier qi est plains de tigne dusure et de malaventure et Dex le maudist.”

76. *Bible moralisée*, 30r. On this image, see Lipton, *Images,* 35, and 168 n. 30.

77. Lipton, *Images,* 33. The manuscript in which Lipton found the text and image is MS Vienna, Osterreichische Nationalbibliothek Cod. 1179: *Bible moralisée* (Latin) fol. 51b. See Lipton's fig. 13.

78. Lipton, *Images,* 33; cod. 1179, fol. 74a. See Lipton's fig. 12 and pp. 43–44. The association of Jews with the raven may derive in part from a melding of the characteristics of the regular crow or raven with those of the screech owl, known as the *niticorax,* or night raven. On the night raven and the Jews, see below; and Hassig, *Medieval Bestiaries,* 97–102.

79. *Bible moralisée,* 28vA and a, 28vD and d; trans. pp. 85–86.

80. Pigs: Lev. 11:7; ravens: Lev. 11:15; creatures that travel on their bellies and “swarm”: Lev. 11:42–43.

81. The view of usurers or Jews as being full of worms, toads, or poisonous creatures is similar to depictions of heretics, bad rulers, and Judas having their innards devoured by rot and worms.

82. The harshest depiction of the raven or crow that I have encountered in the bestiary tradition comes from Hugh of Fouilloy's (d. 1172) *Avarium.* Hugh of Fouilly, *The Medieval Book of Birds,* chap. 40, pp. 174/175–180/181. Hugh also provides positive symbolic associations for the raven.

83. See the section on food in chap. 1 above and my discussion of *Clementine Recognitions, Epistle of Barnabas,* and Novitian's *On Jewish Meats.*

84. Lipton, *Images,* 31–53, esp. 36; Little, *Religious Poverty,* 51–57, 73; Chazan, *Medieval Jewry.* Money and those involved with it were also frequently associated with excrement and stench.

85. "Li gros poisson senefie les gros usurers qi mainiuent les petis ce runt la pouvre gent" (*Bible moralisée,* 1 rc; trans. p. 54). Also cited and discussed in Lipton, *Images,* pp. 34–35, 167 n. 27.

86. "La colueure qi est vemineuse et poignanz senefie les gieus et les mesciranz qi mentienent la viex loi et it runt point et envelimei de coleure" (*Bible moralisée,* 18ra; trans. p. 71).

87. *Bible moralisée,* 18ra; trans. p. 71. Illustration of the serpent biting the foot of Christ is on 18rA.

88. On the increasing sense of Jewish "malice of intent" during the crucifixion, see Cohen, "Jews as the Killers of Christ."

89. Lipton, *Images,* 66–68 and illustrations there.

90. [MS 6, John Rylands Library, Manchester, England] *The Rylands Haggadah,* fols. 16a–b.

91. Frogs, which also sometimes figure as symbols of greed, usury, and Jews, attack the Egyptians on fol. 16a. In this plague, the *haggadah* simply follows the biblical story.

92. Epstein, *Dreams,* 27–38. (Rabbits' uncleanness was associated with Jews and homosexuals).

93. *Rylands Haggadah,* fols. 29b, 33a; [MS Add. 14761 British Library] *Haggadah (Ms. Barcelona Haggadah),* fol. 18r (pl. 9). Snails would fall into the category of *sherez̤* and are thus impure. On owls, see discussion below. The exact dating of this *Barcelona haggadah* has been debated. See Beit Arié's discussion in the introductory volume to the facsimile edition, pp. 12–14, 21; and Margouliouth, *Catalogue of Hebrew and Samaritan Manuscripts in the British Library,* vol. 2.

94. In this manuscript Jewish men tend to be bearded, whereas individuals who seem to be gentiles often are not. But this is a general, not an absolute, rule.

95. Lilian Randall, "The Snail in Gothic Marginal Warfare."

96. Derek Pearsall, "Strangers in Late Fourteenth-Century London."

97. That the snails were meant to represent Jews is strongly suggested by the illumination on fol. 29b of the *Rylands haggadah.* There the "snail" has a human face that is bearded and a head covering similar to Jews in the main panels.

98. عدوك كالذباب له طنين (Imād al-Dīn al-Iṣfahānī, *Syrische Blitz,* no. VI-6, verse 81). Cf. Ibn Khallikan, in *RHC orientaux,* 3:417–18, in which the Franks are compared to reptiles and butterflies.

99. Imād al-Dīn al-Iṣfahānī, *Syrische Blitz,* no. VI-8, verses 66, 69.

100. Remke Kruk, "A Frothy Bubble."

101. Imād al-Dīn al-Iṣfahānī, *Syrische Blitz,* VI-6, ll. 69, 82–83.

102. See Harry Norris's and Lena Jayyusi's introductory articles to *The Adventures of Sayf Dhi ben Yazan.*

103. See the summary of *Sīrat al-Ẓāhir Baybars* in M. C. Lyons, *The Arabian Epic,* 3:78, 81–83, 129, 151, 158, 205; *Sīrat al-Amīra Dhāt al-Himma,* in Lyons, *The Arabian Epic,* 313, 381, 409.

104. Ibn Jubyar, *Riḥlah,* 264; idem, *Travels,* 314; Hillenbrand, *Crusades,* 296.

105. For ḥadith regarding dogs, see note 159, chap. 2 above.

106. *Sīrat al-Ẓāhir Baybars,* in Lyons, *The Arabian Epic,* 133, 224.

107. That calling someone a son of a dog prompted immediate, fatal retaliation in *Sīrat al-Ẓāhir Baybars* (Lyons, *The Arabian Epic,* 227) points to the severity of the insult.

108. *Sīrat al-Ẓāhir Baybars,* in Lyons, *The Arabian Epic,* 129.

109. Usamah ibn Munqidh, *Memoirs,* 161; Hillenbrand, *Crusades,* 273–74.

110. al-Dimashqī, *Nukhbat al-Dahr,* 275.

111. See Hillenbrand's discussion of Muslims' perception that the Franks were completely lacking in culture. *Crusades,* 268–82.

112. Abū Shama, *Kitāb al-Rawdatayn,* in *RHC orientaux,* 3:322.

113. Peter the Venerable, *Adversus iudeorum,* III, p. 57. Cf. Gonzalo de Berceo, *Duelo de la Virgen,* st. l6cd, in *El duelo de la virgen,* in which Judas is equated with a wolf who leads the crowd to the "Lamb"; and Dwayne E. Carpenter, "Social Perception and Literary Portrayal," esp. 63.

114. Deficiunt verba ad tantam absurditatem, tam bestialem crudelitatem, tam nefandam nequitiam confutandam. Vere avida humani sanguis bestia Satanas hoc invenit (Peter the Venerable, *Schriften zum Islam,* pp. 45/46); Riccoldo de Monte Croce's description of Kurds: *Peretrination,* pp. 120/121. Also in his letters he calls Muḥammad "the beast" in reference to his cruelty. See his *Lettres,* 215, 227.

115. *De expurgatione terrae sanctae,* 210; Oderic Vitalis, *Ecclesiastical History,* vol. 5, bk. 9, pp. 84/85, 166/167. In this text the Muslims are compared to predators or wolves. Cf. Riccoldo de Monte Croce's description of Kurds: *Péregrination,* pp. 110/111; Cole, "Religious Pollution."

116. Jew as stinking dog: Gautier de Coincy, *Miracles,* 4:56, l. 347. On Mary's sweet smell, flavor, and purity: 1:20–21, ll. 20–50; p. 29, ll. 1–9; p. 32. ll. 9–17; p. 35, ll. 77–80; 2:102, ll. 22–25; 3:19, ll. 196–208; p. 137, ll. 93–98; p. 301, ll. 25–40. Other types of sinful or undesirable people also stink; see 1:81, l. 516; 2:52, l. 1229; p. 54, ll. 1266–76; 3:409, ll. 2685–86; and Peter-Michael Spangenberg, "Judenfeindlichkeit in den altfranzosischen Marienmirakeln," esp. 159–61. On canine imagery applied to Jews in Gautier de Coincy, see Gilbert Dahan, "Les Juifs dans les *Miracles* de Gautier de Coincy."

117. *De expurgatione terrae sanctae,* 210.

118. Gautier de Coincy, *Miracles,* 4:47, ll. 140, 142; p. 52, ll. 257–58. Also see Dahan, "Juifs."

119. Gautier of Coincy, *Miracles,* 2:98, l. 84. Also see p. 97, l. 62; and Dahan, "Juifs," 3:42–45. For the background and uses of this story, see Rubin, *Gentile Tales,* 7–39. Compare Gautier's depiction of the father in this story to that of the father of the Jewish child who befriends Jesus in *Old French Evangile,* pp. 53–56, ll. 1003–1108; *Enfaunces,* pp. 55–57, ll. 769–845.

120. "A Madre do que livrou / dos legs Daniel / essa do fogo guardou / un menyo d'Irrael" (Alfonso X, *Cantigas de Santa Maria,* 1:63, cantiga 4, ll. 3–6).

121. Dan. 6.

122. Dan. 3:15; *Cantigas,* 1:65, cantiga 4, l. 65. For direct reference to Daniel's companions, to whom Alfonso refers by their Hebrew names Hananiah (Ananias in the Vulgate), Mishael, and Azariah, see p. 65, ll. 84–86.

123. Ibid., p. 65, ll. 62, 68.

124. Dan. 4:28–33.

125. *Cantigas*, 1:66, cantiga 4, ll. 101–4. On the depiction of Jews in the Cantigas generally, see Albert I. Bagby Jr., "The Figure of the Jew in the *Cantigas* of Alfonso X."

126. Dahan, "Juifs"; Jordan, "Marian Devotion"; Rubin, *Gentile Tales,* 12–15; Sprangenberg, "Judenfeindlichkeit." Dahan's study is particularly thorough, so there is no need to repeat his work here. Taking but one example, compare Gautier's version of the Jewish glassmaker's son to that of John of Garland in *Stella Maris* (pp. 95–96, ll. 76–99).

127. Dahan, in "Juifs," was primarily interested in comparing Gautier to other French or Anglo-Norman authors of miracle tales prior to or contemporary with Gautier. For other linguistic and cultural milieux, see J. N. Hillgarth, *The Spanish Kingdoms, 1250–1516,* 1:140–41, 152, 210–14.

128. Rubin, *Gentile Tales,* 7–11; Parkes, *Conflict,* 291–97.

129. Thomas of Monmouth, *Life and Miracles of St. William,* I.4–5, pp. 18–19. Monmouth completed the *Life* in its full form between 1155 and 1173, although book 1, which relates William's life and death, was finished in 1150. On this text, see Gavin Langmuir, "Thomas of Monmouth," in his *Toward a Definition,* 209–36; Yuval, "ha-naqam ve-ha-qlilah," and the collection of articles and Yuval's responses in *Tsiyon* 59/2–3 (1994).

130. Thomas of Monmouth, *Life,* I.11, 15, pp. 34–35, 42 respectively. Compare with Rudolf von Schlettstadt, *Historiae memorabiles,* #17, p. 67; Gautier de Coincy, *Miracles,* 4:52.

131. Thomas of Monmouth, *Life,* I.10, 12, 13, 18, II.3, III.6, pp. 33–34, 37, 39, 52, 54, 66, 132 respectively.

132. Ibid., II.14, p. 99.

133. For examples of the saint's ability to defend himself, see Thomas of Monmouth, *Life,* III.12, IV.9, V.5, VII.18, pp. 136–45, 174–77, 192–93, 279–82 respectively.

134. For examples, see *Rylands Haggadah,* fols. 27b, 29a, 33b, 41a, 42b, 46b (the last three are later additions to the manuscript); *Barcelona Haggadah,* fols. 17v, 20v, 24r, 31r, 31v, 41r, 82r; MS Michael 617 Bodleian Library, Oxford, fols. 4v, 34r, 73v, 117r; MS Laud Or. 321 Bodleian Library, fols. 38v; Cervera Bible MS II 72 Biblioteca Nacional, Lisbon, fol. 154v; MS Heb. 36 Bibliotèque Nationale, Paris, fol. 1r; Brabant Pentateuch, Cod. Levy 19, Staats und Universitats Bibliotek, Hamburg, fols. 11v, 72v.

135. *Barcelona Haggadah,* fols. 24r, 26v, 30v, 31r. 26v, 30v; also reproduced in Epstein, *Dreams,* 32, 30, figs. 12, 11 respectively; also p. 63, pl. 4. Compare these folios with 20v, in which a dog hands a naked, capped man a robe.

136. Epstein, *Dreams,* 29, 31.

137. Randall, "The Snail in Gothic Marginal Warfare."

138. See, e.g., the tale of the fox and the fish and the spider and the king in Berechiah b. Natronai ha-Naqdan, *Mishle Shu'alim,* fable 6; Heb. pp. 14–15, 123–24, Eng. pp. 16–18, 209–11 respectively. On the role or image of the fox as a deceiver, heretic, or Jew in Christian literature, see Hassig, *Medieval Bestiaries,* 62–71; Amer, *Ésope au féminin,* 133, 136–38, 157–66, 179; Epstein, *Dreams,* 9.

139. Berechiah b. Natronai ha-Naqdan, *Mishle Sch'alim,* fable 3; Heb. pp. 10–11, Eng. pp. 12–13. Alexander Neckam, *Novus Aesopus,* X, in *Recueil general des Isopets,* 1:9–10; Walter l'Anglais, *Romulus,* II, in *Recueil general,* 2:8–9; *Isopet de Lyon,* II, in *Recueil general,* 2:87–89; *Isopet I–Avionnet,* II, in *Recueil general,* 2:206–7. On *Isopet* literature and its relation to other types of medieval fable and bestiary collections, also see Amer, *Ésope au féminin,* 34–37, 66–67.

140. Eilberg-Schwartz, *Savage;* also see chaps. 1 and 2 above.

141. *Sefer Gezerot,* 82, 158, 168–69, 177, 191, 220, 238. Also see pp. 133, 85 (stanza 7 of that poem uses the verb לטרוף), and 204; S. Bernfeld, *Sefer Dema'ot,* 1:268, 271, 272. All these examples are from *piyyuṭim.* The Hebrew crusade chronicles also contain such language. In the long prose version of the first crusade chronicle, the crusaders "stood ready to swallow them (the Jews) alive, body and flesh" (ועמדו לבלעם חיים, הגוף עם הבשר). *Chronicle of Solomon bar Simson,* in *Sefer Gezerot,* 54; trans. Chazan, *European Jewry,* 290.

142. Isa. 9:11 (12 in English translations); Jer. 5:6; Zeph. 3:3. See *Chronicle of Solomon bar Simson,* in *Sefer Gezerot,* 25, 52; Chazan, *European Jewry,* 245, 272; *Chronicle of Rabbi Eliezer bar Nathan,* in *Sefer Gezerot,* 72, (trans., *Jews and the Crusaders,* 81).

143. For other instances of predatory language or language likening Jews to slaughtered sheep in the chronicles, see *Mainz Anonymous,* in *Sefer Gezerot,* 95, 101 (trans. Chazan, *European Jewry,* 229, 237); *Chronicle of R. Eliezer bar Nathan,* in *Sefer Gezerot,* 81 (trans. Eidelberg, *Jews and the Crusaders,* 92). For Jews taking care to slaughter one another according to the laws of kashrut (ritually clean food) or linking the communal suicides with eating, see, e.g., *Chronicle of Solomon bar Simson,* in *Sefer Gezerot,* 45, 48–49 (trans. Chazan, *European Jewry,* 276–77, 281–82), where the community is instructed to recite the customary prayer said after meals. See Chazan's n. 273, p. 349. In general, see Shalom Spiegel, *The Last Trial,* esp. 17–27, 127–38. Also see Jeremy Cohen, "A 1096 Complex"; Chazan, *European Jewry,* 50–84.

144. *Chronicle of Solomon bar Simson,* in *Sefer Gezerot,* 29, 33, 34, 39, 47–48 (Chazan, *European Jewry,* 251, 258, 260, 266–67, 280); *Mainz Anonymous,* in *Sefer Gezerot,* 95, 97, 99, 101 (Chazan, *European Jewry,* 229, 231–32, 234, 238); *Chronicle of Eliezer bar Nathan,* in *Sefer Gezerot,* 74, 77; *Jews and the Crusaders,* 82, 84; and the *piyyuṭim* in *Sefer Gezerot,* 71, 82, 84–88, 133, 159, 168–69, 176–77, 191, 195–97, 216–17, 220. As Einbinder rightly notes, the fate of the Torah and that of the martyrs desecrated and dragged through mud are portrayed in a similar fashion. Einbinder, "Jewish Women Martyrs." Also see *Mainz Anonymous,* in *Sefer Gezerot,* 102–3 (Chazan, *European Jewry,* 240); *Chronicle of R. Eliezer bar Nathan,* in *Sefer Gezerot,* 73, 76; *Jews and the Crusaders,* 81, 85; *Sefer Zekhirah,* in *Sefer Gezerot,* 121; *Jews and the Crusaders,* 130.

145. *Mainz Anonymous* and *Chronicle of Solomon bar Simson,* in *Sefer Gezerot,* 99, 29 (Chazan, *European Jewry,* 234, 251) respectively.

146. יראה יראה פעלת בנות בוטחות \ בחם היום ערמות לשמש נשטחות \ יפות בנשים מבקעות כרס אלהים שליה ולד מפריחות \ מבין רגליהם שליה ולד מפריחות \ ומפלחות (*Sefer Gezerot,* 71). The poem is titled אלהים אל-דמי לדמי (God Do Not Be Silent regarding My Blood). Also see Einbinder's discussion of this poem in "Jewish Women Martyrs," esp. 116–18.

147. Einbinder, "Jewish Women Martyrs."

148. ואל כל המקום אשר שמה, דיבר רע על כל היהודים אשר בארץ ושיסה בנו את הנחש ואת הכלבים (R. Ephraim of Bonn, *Sefer Zekhirah,* in *Sefer Gezerot,* 115 [*Jews and the Crusaders,* 122]).

149. אנא יי אלהים, למה עזבת את עמך ישראל ללעג ולביזה ולחרפה לאבדנו בידי העמים הטמאים כחזיר, שאוכלים אותנו (*Sefer Gezerot,* 55). My translation differs slightly from Chazan's. He translates the text: "Woe, O Lord God! Why have you abandoned your people Israel to calumny, plunder and shame, destroying us through the hands of a people as impure as the pig they eat" (*Jews and the Crusaders,* 291). His translation in fact supports my point that Jews particularly associated Christians with the pig because pigs were an important part of the medieval Christian diet, argued below. However, given that poetic accounts of the first crusade or other persecutions do use the image of the pig eating, tearing, or gnawing the Jews, having the piglike Christians eating the Jews is probably the idea that the chronicler was trying to convey here.

150. Jordan, *Great Famine,* 55–56; Barbara Hanawalt, *The Ties That Bound,* 51–52; Fabre-Vassas, *Singular Beast.*

151. For examples of evocations of the pig in *piyyuṭim,* see *Sefer Gezerot,* 82, 168, 177, 220.

152. *Sefer Gezerot,* 168. Poem titled זולתך אין אל צדיק ומושיע (Apart from You There Is No Righteous and Saving God). Also see p. 82.

153. Candles, for example. See Hanawalt, *Ties,* 53.

154. On Christian symbolic meanings assigned to pigs and the use of these associations against the Jews in the Middle Ages, see Shachar, *Judensau.* Also see Israel Yuval, "ha-naqam ve-ha-qlilah."

155. והחזיר הכביד לבו ויקש ערפו (Berechiah b. Natronai ha-Naqdan, *Mishle Shu'alim,* fable 105; Heb. pp. 113–14, citation on 113; Eng. pp. 191–93, citation on 191).

156. ויבט צבי אחד בחזירה, הנגאלת ובטיט פערה, פיה אשר אשפות חתר, תאכל ותשבע ותותר (Berechiah b. Natronai ha-Naqdan, *Mishle Shu'alim,* fable 49; Heb, p. 57, Eng. p. 91). For deer as symbols of the Jewish people in Jewish illuminated manuscripts and poetry, see Epstein, *Dreams,* 22–25.

157. Berechiah b. Natronai ha-Naqdan, *Mishle Shu'alim,* fables 49, 105; Heb. pp. 57, 113; Eng. pp. 191, 192 respectively.

158. *Sefer Ḥasidim,* paras. 193, 198, 209, 219, 221, 427, 806, 1017.

159. The phrase *nokhriah 'avodato* appears once in the Bible in Isa. 28:21: "For the Lord will rise up as on Mount Perazim, he will be angry as in the valley of Gibeon; to do his deed—strange is his deed! and to work his work—alien is his work!" (כי כהר פרצים יקום יהוה כעמק בגבעון ירגז לעשות מעשהו זר מעשהו ולעבד עבדתו נכריה עבדתו). That God is the one doing this "strange work" in the verse would seem to work against my interpretation. Yet the "work" God is doing is explained in 28:16: "Behold I am laying in Zion for a foundation a stone, a tested stone, a precious cornerstone, of a sure foundation." This verse was understood by Christians as a prophesy of Jesus. Thus the choice of phrase in Berachiah's tale may perhaps be understood as a subtle mockery of Christian belief.

160. *Chronicle of Solomon bar Simson.* Hebrew in *Sefer Gezerot*, 34, 35, 39, 45; English in Chazan, *European Jewry*, 258, 260, 276. *Mainz Anonymous,* in *Sefer Gezerot*,

103 (Chazan, *European Jewry*, 240). "Anonymous account of the persecution at Blois," in *Sefer Gezerot*, 144.

161. Moses Hadas in Berechiah b. Natronai ha-Naqdan, *Fables of a Jewish Aesop,* v–xi; Epstein, " 'The Ways of the Truth' "; Amer, *Ésope au feminin,* 34–37.

162. Shachar, *Judensau,* 4–11.

163. *Bestiary,* trans. Barber, 84. On this text (MS Oxford, Bodleian 764), also see Shachar, *Judensau,* 7–8.

164. *Bestiary,* trans. Barber, 84–86. The distorted version of Ps. 16:14 reads as follows: "Their belly is filled with your hidden treasure: they are filled with pork, and leave what remains to their children" (De absconditis tuis adimpletus est venter eorum, saturati sunt porcina et reliquentur que superfuerunt parvulis suis"). In the printed version of the Vulgate, the verse reads as follows: "De abscondis tuis adimpletus est venter eorum. Saturati sunt filiis, et dimiserunt reliquias suas parvulis suis" or "Et quorum ventrem imples opibus tuis; Quorum filii saturantur et relinquunt, quod eis superest, parvulis suis" ("Their belly is filled with your hidden treasure, their sons are satisfied / filled and they leave what remains to their little ones"). There is no mention of pigs in this verse. See Shachar, *Judensau,* 6–12; Barber translates "saturati sunt porcina" as "they are filled like swine." The other biblical texts cited are 2 Peter 2:22; Matt. 7:6; Matt. 27:25. Both Ps. 16:14 and Matt. 27:25 were used to show that sinners and Jews passed on their "uncleanness," i.e. sin, to their children. The discussion of the sow in bestiary, MS Harley 4751, fols. 20r–21r, also evokes Matt. 27:25.

165. Tolan, "Un cadavre mutilé"; Strickland, *Saracens, Demons, and Jews,* 159–60, 181–82, 190–92, 223–24.

166. *Sīrat al-Ẓāhir Baybars,* in Lyons, *The Arabian Epic,* 151, 172, 182, 205; *Sīrat al-Amīra Dhāt al-Himma,* in Lyons, *The Arabian Epic,* 315.

167. *Sīrat al- Amīra Dhāt al-Himma,* in Lyons, *The Arabian Epic,* 315.

168. *Sīrat al-Ẓāhir Baybars,* in Lyons, *The Arabian Epic,* 182.

169. Ibid., 149; *Sīrat al-Amīra Dhāt al-Himma,* in Lyons, *The Arabian Epic,* 326, 329.

170. Oderic Vitalis, *Ecclesiastical History,* vol. 5, bk. 9, pp. 98/99, 140/141.

171. Pigs seem to have remained the premier symbol for Muslims in Christian writing and art, however.

172. McCulloch, *Mediaeval Latin and French Bestiaries,* 147; Hassig, *Medieval Bestiaries,* 97–98; *Bestiary,* trans. White, 133–34; *Bestiary,* trans. Barber, 147–48; Pierre de Beauvais, *Bestiare,* 64; Philippe de Thaün, *Bestiare,* 111–12; Guillaume le Clerc, *Bestiary,* 25–26; idem, *Bestiaire,* 247–49, ll. 615–56; *Physiologus,* chap. 7. MS Harley 4751, fol. 46v; MS Add. 11283, fols. 20r–v. Cambridge MS Ii. 4.46, fols. 38v–39r. Cf. Hugh of Fouilloy, *Avarium,* 172–75, in which the *niticorax is* compared alternatively to Christ and to sinners but not to Jews. Closer to the traditional entry for *niticorax* is Hugh's discussion of the regular owl *(bubo),* 216–19, but again he does not liken the creature to Jews.

173. Guillaume le Clerc, *Bestiary,* 25–26, ll. 615–25; idem, *Bestiaire,* ed. Reinsch, 247–49, ll. 615–56; *Bestiary,* trans. Barber, 148–49; Philippe de Thaün, *Bestiaire,* 101, ll. 2789–2842; MS Harley 4751, fols. 46v–47v; McCulloch, *Mediaeval Latin and*

French Bestiaries, 146–47; Hassig, *Medieval Bestiaries,* 97–98. Also see discussion above concerning ravens. Hugh of Fouilloy provides a similar list of characteristics for the owl *(bubo)* but does not mention the Jews; see his *Avarium,* 216–19.

174. McCulloch, *Mediaeval Latin and French Bestiaries,* 130–32; Hassig, *Medieval Bestiaries,* 145–55; *Bestiary,* trans. White, 30–32; *Bestiary,* trans. Barber, 45–47; Pierre de Beauvais, *Bestiaire,* 73; Guillaume le Clerc, *Bestiary,* 48–50, ll. 1567–1642; idem, *Bestiaire,* 290–92, ll. 1567–1642. MS Add. 11283, fols. 5r–v; MS Cambridge Ii. 4.26, fols. 9r–10r. Also see Philippe de Thaün, *Bestiaire,* 44–45, ll. 1177–1216; and Latini, *Libro de tesoro,* capitulo 189, p. 90, who discuss the properties of the hyena but without connecting the animal to Jews.

175. Camille, *Image*. Most of Camille's book deals with these issues for medieval manuscripts. For architectural marginalia on monasteries and cathedrals, see pp. 56–97. Not all of the marginalia depicted animals, nor does all of it seem to be related to the texts. As Camille has pointed out, scribal doodles often seem to have no relation to the text at all; see 42–47. Epstein argues that Camille's arguments also hold true for the illuminated marginalia of Hebrew manscripts: *Dreams*, 10–11.

176. Ibid., 26–55; Lilian M. C. Randall, "Humor and Fantasy in the margins"; idem, "Exempla."

177. See Suger, *On the Abbey Church of St. Denis,* 73–77, and commentary, 211–16. Suger was born in 1081, became abbot of St. Denis in 1122, and died in 1151 (1).

178. Shachar, *Judensau,* 1–2 and notes, 4–12; G. C. Druce, "The Sow and Pigs." See also Bernhard Blumenkranz, *Le Juif médiéval au miroir de l'art chrétien,* 67, where he notes Jews sucking on sows' teats on a chapel in Upsala, Sweden (late thirteenth–early fourteenth century).

179. Shachar, *Judensau,* 25–26.

180. For the story of Steven, see Acts 7. On the legend of Saint Helen and the cross: *Finding of the True Cross.*

181. I do not mean to imply, however, that anti-Judaism was the only message these carvings were intended to convey.

182. A wakeful Ecclesia and a blindfolded Synagoga stand on either side of the southern portal; many of the stained-glass windows contain portrayals of Jews arguing with, trying, or otherwise harming Jesus; the main tympanum of the cathedral shows the Jews tormenting and executing Jesus; also decorating the main portal, beneath the lions that occupy the stairs of the "couronment," are a variety of grotesques and animals associated with Jews, such as boars, rabbits, and an owl (?); in the bas-relief sculpture along both aisles of the cathedral is a Jew's head suckling a sow and a Jew grabbing a demon or gryphon. The Jews are marked in these carvings or images by their hats. Some of these elements were added later than the friezes, but this need not deter from the cumulative effect. On the sculpture of the Strasbourg cathedral as a whole, see Haug et al., *La Cathédrale de Strasbourg*; Otto Schmitt, *Gotische Skulpturen des Strassburger Münsters.* Other churches, such as those in Bad Wimpfen and Xanten, which Shachar identified as having a *Judensau* or other identifications of Jews and pigs also possess other potentially anti-Jewish imagery (blind Synagoga, Bad Wimpfen; misericord owls and apes, Xanten). On owls and apes, see Mariko Miyazaki, "Misericord

Owls and Medieval Anti-Semitism"; Elaine Block, "Judaic Imagery on Medieval Choir Stalls"; idem, *Corpus of Medieval Misericords—France XIII–XVI Cent.*

183. Shachar, *Judensau,* 4–6.

184. Ibid., 7–8.

185. Little, *Religious Poverty,* 42–57, 73–75; Lipton, *Images,* 31–53; and see discussion of the *Bible moralisée* at the beginning of this section.

186. MS Harley 4751, fols. 20r–21r; *Bestiary,* trans. Barber, 84–86.

187. Lipton, *Images,* 21–29, 83–111; Moore, *Formation.* Lipton does not agree with some of Moore's assessments; see *Images,* 51–52.

188. *Bestiary,* trans. Barber, 84–86. The text makes explicit this connection between eating and inherited sin.

189. These images occur in Brandenburg, Xanten, Wimpfen, Magdeburg, Heiligenstadt, Cologne, and Metz. See Shachar, *Judensau,* pls. 5, 6, 9, 10, 12, 13, 14, 16a, 16b, 17, and 18a and discussion pp. 15–25. Block has identified similar imagery in Iberian misericords, but they tend to be later than similar images in northern Europe. Block, "Judaic Imagery."

190. Kissing pigs: Schachar, *Judensau.* See the Marienkirch in Lemgo, pls. 7 and 8 and discussion pp. 16–17; and the church of St. Maria Magdalena in Eberswald, pl. 11, discussion p. 18. Touching pigs' hindquarters: pls. 5a, 5b (Brandenburg), discussion p. 15; and possibly pls. 13, 14 (Magdeburg), discussion pp. 19–20. Jews' touching or kissing swines' anuses became more common as a motif in later centuries. Block, "Judaic Imagery."

191. Lipton, *Images,* 40–45, 49, 88–91, 95–96, 104–5, and illustrations there; *Bible moralisée,* 25vA and a, translated text p. 82; 37rd, translated text p. 110. Frogs are also occasionally included in this repertoire of wrongfully adored animals. *Images,* 43–45.

192. Jacobus de Voragine, *Golden Legend,* 2:52.

193. Miyazaki, "Misericord Owls"; Block, "Judaic Imagery."

194. Also see *Rylands Haggadah,* fol. 27a; *Barcelona Haggadah*, fol. 32v; MS Heb. 8, Bibliothèque Nationale, Paris, fol. 63v.

195. McCulloch, *Mediaeval Latin and French Bestiaries,* 148–50, 104–5; *Bestiary,* trans. White, 14–17, 122–23; *Bestiary,* trans. Barber, 30–33, 138; *Bestiary,* in *An Old English Miscellany,* 23–25; Guillaume le Clerc, *Bestiaire,* ed. Reinisch, 308–10, ll. 1965–2028; idem, *Bestiary,* 58–64; Pierre de Beauvais, *Bestiaire,* 76–78; Philippe de Thaün, *Bestiaire,* 18–22, 99–101; Latini, *Libro de tesoro,* 91 (no moral likening of the panther to Christ is provided in this text).

196. Petrus Alfonsi, *Disciplina clericalis,* chap. 8; idem, *"Disciplina Clericalis" of Petrus Alfonsi,* chap. 8, pp. 118–19. Cf. Peter Damian's condemnation of women: "You I address, you harem of the ancient enemy, you hoopoes, screech owls, night owls, she-wolves, horse leeches" (Vos, inquam, alloquor gineca hostis antique, upupae, ululae, noctuae, lupae, sanguisugae). Peter Damian, *Epistolae, MGH, Die briefe de Deutschen Kaiserzeit,* 4, Ep. 112, 3:278. Cited and discussed in Iogna-Prat, *Order and Exclusion,* 134–35.

197. Hassig, *Medieval Bestiaries,* 97–98.

198. Circulus aureus in naribus suis, mulier pulchra et fatua (*Bestiary,* trans. Barber, 86).

199. McCulloch, *Mediaeval Latin and French Bestiaries,* 106–8. She states that the dung can be used to make someone beautiful; she does not mention the gender or associated moralization that often accompanies this feature of the crocodile. *Bestiary,* trans. White, 49–51; *Bestiary,* trans. Barber, pp. 61–63; Guillaume le Clerc, *Bestiaire,* ed. Reinisch, 293–97; idem, *Bestiary,* ll. 1643–1728, esp. ll. 1677–84, pp. 50–52; MS Add 11283 (British Library) fol. 8r.; MS Harley 3244 (British library) fol. 43r. See (Pseudo) Hugo of St. Victor in *PL* 177, cols. 15–164, esp. 3.55.

200. Richard de Fornival, *Li bestiaires d'amours di maistre Richart de Fornival e Li reponse du Bestiaire,* 86–88; Jeanette Beer, "Duel of Bestiaries." Also see *Bestiaire d'amour rime,* ll. 2757–87, pp. 90–91; however, this author, while making the comparison with the hoopoe, leaves out derogatory remarks about the bird's or woman's filth. Also cf. Odo of Cheriton, in Leopold Hervieux, *Les fabulistes latins,* vol. 4, "Odonis de Ceritona Fabulae"; Odo of Cheriton, *The Fables of Odo of Cheriton,* chap. 41; Hassig, *Medieval Bestiaries,* 101. In Odo's fable, the woman is merely lustful, not old.

201. McCulloch, *Mediaeval Latin and French Bestiaries,* 126–27; *Bestiary,* trans. White, 150; *Bestiary,* trans. Barber, 171–72; Guillaume le Clerc de Normandie, *Le Bestiaire*; idem, *The Bestiary of Guillaume le Clerc,* ll. 821–70; Isidore of Seville, *Isidori Hispalensis Episcopi,* xii, 7.66; *Physiologus,* 37. MS Harley 4751, fol. 55r; MS Add. 11283, fol.23r–v; MS Cambridge Ii. 4. 26, fol. 47v. Hassig, *Medieval Bestiaries,* 93–103.

202. Shulamith Shahar, *Growing Old in the Middle Ages*; George Minois, *History of Old Age,* 113–208, esp. 118–28, 162–63, 191–93, 200–204. Unfortunately, Minois's study is focused on men, with few observations on old women. The association of old women with filth goes back to Roman literature. See Richlin, *Garden,* 114–23.

203. McCulloch, *Mediaeval Latin and French Bestiaries,* 130–32; *Bestiary,* trans. White, 30–32; *Bestiary,* trans. Barber, 45–47; Pierre de Beauvais, *Bestiaire,* 73; *Physiologus,* chap. 37; Isidore of Seville, 16.25.25; MS Harley 4751, fols. 10r–v; MS Add. 11283, fols. 5r–v; MS Harley 3244, fol. 40v; MS Cambridge Ii. 4.26, fols. 9r–10r.

204. See Scott, "Gender."

205. Philippe de Thaün, *Bestiaire,* ll. 1193–1204, pp. 44–45.

206. Ceste beste, ne dotez mie / Lee fiz Israel signefie / Qui be crurent premerement / El verai pere omnipotent / E lealment a lui se tindrent / Mes apres femele devindrent / Quant it furent suef norri / E as delices adenti / A la char e a la luxure (Guillaume le Clerc, *Bestiaire,* 292; idem, *Bestiary,* ll. 1607–15, p. 49).

207. Brown, *Body and Society*, 9–13; Ross Shepard Kraemer, *Her Share of the Blessings,* 157–78; Bernadette J. Brooten, *Love between Women,* 42–60; John Chrysostom, *Commento alla prima lettera a Timoteo*, homily XVII, on 1 Tim. 6:12; Augustine, *Confessions*, 9.4. For late antique and early medieval examples of "masculine" women, see "Pelagia of Antioch," "Mahya," "Anastasia," and "Febriona," in *Holy Women of the Syrian Orient,* 40–62, 109–11, 142–49, 150–76; Karen Jo Torjensen, "Martyrs, Ascetics and Gnostics"; J. H. Welch, "Cross Dressing and Cross Purposes"; Kraemer, "Other as Woman." For a similar phenomenon in a different context in the Jewish tradition, see Eilberg-Schwartz, *God's Phallus;* Elliot Wolfson, "Crossing Gender Boundaries"; idem, "Woman—The Feminine as Other."

208. In the twelfth-century Christian tradition, not all feminizing was seen as spiritually negative. See Caroline Walker Bynum, "Jesus as Mother and Abbot as Mother, Some Themes in Twelfth-Century Cistercian Writing," in *Jesus as Mother,* 110–69.

209. Hassig, *Medieval Bestiaries,* 149–52. For a hyena with exaggerated genitalia (both male and female), see Aberdeen University MS 24, fol. IIV, reproduced in Hassig, fig. 148. There is an element of sexual violation implied here, since the hyena bites the corpse's breast. The corpse seems to be male, given its short hair, but lacks distinguishing biological markers. For a hyena biting a dead woman near her genital region, see MS Harley 4751, fol. 10r (= pl. 10). Also reproduced in Hassig, fig. 158.

210. C. S. Lewis, *Prince Caspian,* 107.

211. On the Christian sense of danger or threat from medieval Jews at this period, see Chazan, *Medieval Stereotypes,* 1–18, 41–73.

212. Eilberg-Schwartz, *Savage,* 115–40.

213. Such worries are reflected in characters such as Uqba in *Sīrat al-Amīra Dhāt al-Himma* who continually change their religion. See, e.g., Lyons, *The Arabian Epic,* 228–335.

Conclusion

1. *Blood Magic.*

2. Julia Kristeva, *Powers of Horror,* 4.

3. I do not mean to suggest that orality was not equally important in exchanges among the Byzantine world, Latin Christendom, and the Muslim world; I have not accumulated enough evidence to say one way or another. It is an area that bears further research.

4. See Nirenberg's analysis of the meaning of prostitution laws in medieval Iberia: David Nirenberg, "Conversion, Sex, and Segregation." Kristeva makes similar observations regarding the modern French author Céline's anti-Semitism: *Powers of Horror,* 182.

5. Kristeva, *Powers of Horror;* Scott, "Gender."

6. Joseph W. Esherick, *The Origins of the Boxer Uprising,* 235, 297–98.

7. Ben Okri, *Songs of Enchantment,* 138–41. Being familiar with the Western literary tradition and a resident at Trinity College, Cambridge, Okri would have been well aware of the effect of such images on a Nigerian audience as well as on a Western, English-speaking one.

Bibliography

Manuscript Sources

Ibn Matka, Yehudah b. Solomon ha-Kohen. *Midrash ha-Hokmah.* MS Parma. Biblioteca Palatina Parm. 2769 [De Rossi 421].

MS II. 72 [Cervera Bible], Biblioteca Nacional, Lisbon.

MS Mich. 619, Bodleian Library, Oxford.

MS Laud Or. 321, Bodleian Library, Oxford.

MS Cambridge Ii. 4.26, Cambridge University Library.

MS Harley 4751, British Library, London.

MS Heb. 36, Bibliothèque Nationale, Paris.

Brabant Pentateuch, Codex Levy 19, Staats und Universitats Bibliotek, Hamburg.

Primary Sources

Abelard, Peter. *Dialogus inter philosophum, Iudeorum et Christianum.* Ed. Rudolf Thomas. Stuttgart–Bad Cannstatt: F. Frommann, 1970.

———. [*Dialogus inter philosophum, Judeorum et Christianum.*] *A Dialogue of a Philosopher with a Jew and a Christian.* Trans. Pierre J. Payer. Mediaeval Sources in Translation, 20. Toronto: Pontifical Institute of Mediaeval Studies, 1979.

———. [*Letters.*] *The Letters of Abelard and Heloise.* Trans. Betty Radice. Penguin Classics. Harmondsworth: Penguin, 1974.

Abū ʻĪsā al-Warrāq. *Abū ʻĪsā al-Warrāq Yahyā ibn ʻAdī: De l'incarnation.* Ed. E. Platti. 2 vols. Corpus scriptorum Christianorum Orientalium. Scriptores Arabici, 46–47. Louvain: E. Peeters, 1987.

Abū Shama. *Kitāb al-Rawd)atayn.* In *Recueil des historiens des croisades orientaux.* Vol. 3 of 5. Paris: Imprimerie Nationale, 1872–1906.

Acta sanctorum quotquot toto orbe coluntur: Vel a catholicis scriptoribus celebrantur. 61 vols. Paris: Apud Victorem Palme, 1863–67.

Adam de Perseigne. *Lettres.* Ed. and trans. Jean Bouvet. Sources chrétiennes, 66. Paris: Éditions du Cerf, 1960– .

———. [*Lettres.*] *The Letters of Adam of Perseigne.* Trans. Grace Perigo. Cistercian Fathers, 21. Kalamazoo: Cistercian Publications, 1976– .

Adam of St. Victor. "Salve, mater Salvatoris." In Adam of St. Victor, *Sequentiae.* In Migne, *Patrologiae . . . latina*, 196. Paris: s.n., 1855.

Adelard of Bath. *Die Quaestiones naturales des Adelardus von Bath.* Ed. Martin Müller. Münster: W. Aschendorff, 1934.

The Adventures of Sayf Dhi ben Yazan: An Arabic Folk Epic. Ed. and trans. Harry Norris and Lena Jayyusi. Bloomington: Indiana University Press, 1996.

Agapius, Bishop of Hieropolis. *Kitāb al-'Unwan.* Trans. Alexander Vasiliev. Patrologia Orientalis, 5:4, 7:4, 8:3, 11:1. Paris: Firmin-Didot, 1908–15.

Agobard, Saint. *De insolentia Judaeorum.* In *Agobardi Lugdunensis Opera omnia*, ed. L. van Acker. Corpus Christianorum. Continuatio medievalis, 52. Turnholt: Brepols, 1981.

———. *De Judaicis superstitionibus.* In *Agobardi Lugdunensis Opera omnia*, ed. L. van Acker. Corpus Christianorum. Continuatio medievalis, 52. Turnholt: Brepols, 1981.

———. *Opera omnia.* In Migne, *Patrologiae . . . latina*, 116. Paris: s.n., 1852.

Aḥimaaz ben Paltiel. *Megilat Aḥima'ats: Ve-hu megilat yohasim le-Rabi Aḥima'ats be Rabi Palti'el avotav ve-khol ma'ase tokpam . . .* Ed. Benjamin Klar. Jerusalem: Tarshish, 1973–74.

Alan of Lille. *Contra haereticos.* In *Opera omnia.* In Migne, *Patrologiae . . . latina*, 210. Paris: s.n., 1855.

———. *De Arte Praedicatoria.* In *Opera omnia.* In Migne, *Patrologiae . . . latina*, 210. Paris: s.n., 1855.

———. *Liber poenitentialis.* Ed. Jean Longère. 2 vols. Analecta mediaevalia Namurcensia, 17–18. Louvain: Éditions Nauwelaerts, 1965.

Albertus Magnus, Saint. [*De animalibus.*] *On Animals: A Medieval Summa Zoologica.* Trans. Kenneth F. Kitchell Jr. and Irven Michael Resnick. 2 vols. Foundations of Natural History. Baltimore: Johns Hopkins University Press, 1999.

———. *De annuntiatione.* In *Opera omnia: Ad fidem codicum manuscriptorum edenda apparatus critico notis prolegomenis indicibus instruenda.* Vol. 26. Cologne: Monasterii Westfalorum in Aedibus Aschendorff, 1951– .

———. *De incarnatione.* In *Opera omnia: Ad fidem codicum manuscriptorum edenda apparatus critico notis prolegomenis indicibus instruenda.* Vol. 26. Cologne: Monasterii Westfalorum in Aedibus Aschendorff, 1951– .

———. *Quaestiones super De Animalibus.* In *Opera omnia: Ad fidem codicum manuscriptorum edenda apparatu critico notis prolegomenis indicibus instruenda*, vol. 12. Ed. Berhard Geyer. Cologne: Monasterii Westfalorum in Aedibus Aschendorff, 1951– .

———. *Sententiae.* In *Opera Omnia*: *B. Alberti Magni Ratisbonensis episcopi, ordinis Praedicatorum*, vols. 25–30. Ed. Auguste Borgnet and Émile Borgnet. Paris: Louis Viros, 1890–95.

——— [Pseudo]. *De secretis mulierum libellus cum scholiis.* Lyons: s.n., n.d.

——— [Pseudo]. [*De secretis mulierum.*] *Women's Secrets: A Translation of Pseudo-Albertus Magnus's* De secretis mulierum *with Commentaries*. Trans. Helen Rodnite Lemay. SUNY Series in Medieval Studies. Albany: State University of New York Press, 1992.

——— [Pseudo]. *Mariale*. In *Opera omnia: B. Alberti Magni Ratisbonensis episcopi, ordinis Praedicatorum,* vol. 37. Ed. Auguste Borgnet and Émile Borgnet. Paris: Louis Viros, 1890–95.

Alderotti, Taddeo. *Consilia*. Ed. Piero P. Giorgi and Gian Franco Pasini. Opere dei maestri (Università di Bologna, Istituto per la storia), 8. Bologna: Istituto per la storia dell'Universitá di Bologna, 1997.

Alexander III, Pope. *Die Sentenzen Rolands nachmals Papstes Alexander III*. Ed. Ambrosius M. Gietl. Freiburg-im-Breisgau: Herder, 1891.

Alexandre du Pont. *Le Roman de Mahomet*. Ed. Yvan G. LePage. Paris: Klincksieck, 1977.

Alfonso X, King of Castile and Leon. *Cantigas de Santa Maria*. Ed. Walter Mettmann. 3 vols. Clásicos Castalia, 134, 172, 178. Madrid: Castalia, 1986–89.

———. *Primera crónica general de España*. Ed. Ramón Menéz Pidal. 2 vols. Madrid: Editorial Gredos, 1977.

Alvaro de Córdoba. *Epistolario*. Ed. José Maduz. Madrid: Consejo Superio de Investigaciones Científicas, Instituto Francisco Suárez, 1947.

Amedeus of Clermont-Tonnerre, Bishop of Lausanne. *Epistola ad filios suos ecclesiae Lausannensis: Homiliae de Maria Virgine*. In Migne, *Patrologiae . . . latina*, 188. Paris: s.n., 1855.

'Ammār al-Baṣrī. *Kitāb al-burhān*. Ed. Michel Hayek. Recherches. Nouvelles série B. Orient chrétien, 5. Beirut: Dar el-Machreq, 1977.

Amulo, Bishop of Lyons. *Epistolae: Opuscula duo [etc.]*. In Migne, *Patrologiae . . . latina,* 116. Paris: s.n., 1852.

[*Analecta liturgica.*] *Thesauris hymnologicis . . .* 2 parts in 3 vols. Lille: Societatis S. Augustini, 1888–92.

André le Chapelain. [*De amore et amoris remedio.*] *Andreas Capellanus on Love*. Ed. and trans. P. G. Walsh. Duckworth Classical, Medieval, and Renaissance Editions. London: Duckworth, 1982.

Annales Marbacensis qui dicuntur. Ed. Hermann Bloch. Monumenta Germaniae historica; Scriptores rerum Germanicarum in usum scholarum separatim editi, 9. Hannover/Leipzig: Hahn, 1907; reprint Hannover: Hahn, 1979.

Anselm, Saint, Archbishop of Canterbury. *De conceptu virinali et originali peccato*. In *S. Anselmi cantuarensis archiepiscopi opera omnia*. Ed. Franciscus Salesius Schmitt. Seckau, 1938– .

———. [Selections.] *Basic Writings: Proslogium, Monologium, Cur Deus homo, Gaunlion's "On Behalf of the Fool."* Trans. S. N. Deane. 2d ed. La Salle, IL: Open Court, 1962.

The Ante-Nicene Fathers: Translations of the Writings of the Fathers Down to A.D. 325. Ed. Alexander Roberts and James Donaldson. 10 vols. Grand Rapids, MI: W. B. Eerdmans, 1986.

Apocryphon of John. Trans. Frederick Wisse. In [*Nag Hammadi Codices*. English] *The Nag Hammadi Library in English,* 103–7. Gen. ed. James Robinson. San Francisco: Harper and Row, 1981.

[*Apostolic Constitutions*.] *Constitutiones Apostolicae: Textum graecum recognovit, praefatus est, annotationes criticas et indices subiecit*. Ed. Wilhelm Ültzen. Suerinus: Sumtibus Stillerianis, 1853.

Apuleius. *Opuscules philosophiques (Du dieu de Socrate, Platon et sa doctrine, Du monde) et fragments*. Ed. and trans. Jean Beaujeu. Collection des universités de France. Paris: Belles Lettres, 1973.

Aristotle. *Aristotle on Sleep and Dreams*. Ed. and trans. David Gallop. Warminster: Aris & Phillips, 1996.

———. [*De animalium generatione*.] *Generation of Animals*. Trans. A. L. Peck. Rev. ed. Loeb Classical Library, 366. Cambridge, MA: Harvard University Press; London: Heinemann, 1953.

———. *Historia animalium*. 3 vols. Loeb Classical Library. Cambridge, MA: Harvard University Press; London: Heinemann, 1965– .

———. *Metereologica*. Loeb Classical Library. Cambridge, MA: Harvard University Press, 1952.

———. *The Nicomachaean Ethics*. New and rev. ed. Loeb Classical Library. London: Heinemann, 1956.

Arnau de Villanova. [*Opera medica omnia*.] *Arnaldi de Villanova Opera medica omnia*. 16 vols. Granada: Seminarium Historiae Medicae Granatensis, 1981–2000.

Arnobius of Sicca. *Adversus nations libri VII*. Ed. C. Marchesi. 2d ed. Corpus scriptorum latinorum Paravianum. Turin: In aedibus Io. Bapt. Paraviae, 1953.

———. *The Case against the Pagans*. Ed. and trans. George E. McCracken. 2 vols. Ancient Christian Writers; the Works of the Fathers in Translation, 7–8. Westminster, MD: Newman Press, 1949.

Athanasius, Saint, Patriarch of Alexandria. *Contra gentes; and De incarnatione*. Ed. and trans. Robert W. Thomson. Oxford Early Christian Texts. Oxford: Clarendon Press, 1971.

——— [Pseudo]. "Sermon on the Miracle of Berut." In *Opera omnia* . . . 4 vols. In Migne, *Patrologiae* . . . *graeca*, 25–28. Paris: s.n., 1857.

Athenagoras. [*Apologia pro Christianis*.] *Supplique au sujet des chrétiens; et, Sur la résurrection des morts*. Ed. and trans. Bernard Pouderon. Sources chrétiennes, 379. Paris: Cerf, 1992.

Augustine, Saint, Bishop of Hippo. *Contra Faustum*. In *Sancti Aureli Augustini hipponensis episcopi Opera omnia* . . . 11 vols. in 15. In Migne, *Patrologiae* . . . *latina*, 32–46.

———. [*De civitate Dei*.] *Concerning the City of God against the Pagans*. Trans. Henry Bettenson. Pelican Classics. Harmondsworth: Penguin Books, 1972.

———. *In Evangelium Iohannis tractatus*. In *Sancti Aureli Augustini hipponensis episcopi Opera omnia* . . . 11 vols. in 15. In Migne, *Patrologiae* . . . *latina*, 32–46.

———. [*In Evangelium Iohannis tractatus.*] *Tractates on the Gospel of John.* Trans. John W. Rettig. 5 vols. Fathers of the Church, 78–79, 90, 92. Washington, DC: Catholic University of America Press, 1988–95.

———. *Oeuvres de Saint Augustin.* Bibliothèque augustinienne. Paris: Desclée de Brouwer, 1949– .

———. *The Works of Aurelius Augustine.* 15 vols. Edinburgh: s.n., 1872–1934.

——— [Pseudo]. *"Ad interrogata," De assumptione Beata Mariae Virginis.* In *Sancti Aureli Augustini hipponensis episcopi Opera omnia . . .* 11 vols. in 15. In Migne, *Patrologiae . . . latina*, 32–46.

Autpertus, Ambrosius. *Ambrosii Autperti Opera.* Ed. Robert Weber. 3 vols. Corpus Christianorum. Continuatio medievalis, 27–27A–27B. Turnholt: Brepols, 1975–79.

[*Avesta.* English.] *The Zend-Avesta.* Trans. James Darmesteter and Lawrence Heyworth Mills. 3 vols. Sacred Books of the East, 4, 23, 31. Oxford: Clarendon Press, 1880–87.

The Bahir. Trans. Aryeh Kaplan. York Beach, ME: S. Weiser, 1979–89.

Balbi, Giovanni. *Catholicon.* Mainz: s.n., 1640; reprint Westmead: Gregg International, 1971.

Bāqillāni, Muḥammad ibn al-Ṭayyib. *Kitāb al-tamhīd.* Ed. Richard Joseph McCarthy. Manshūrat Jāmi'at al-Hikmah fī Baghdād Silsilat 'ilm al-kalām, 1. Beirut: al-Maktabah al-Sharqīyah, 1957.

Bartholomaeus Anglicus. *De rerum proprietatibus.* Frankfurt: Minerva, 1964. [Reprint of *De genuinis rerum coelestium, terrestrium et inferarum proprietatibus libri XVIII.* Frankfurt: W. Richter, 1601.]

Bate midrashot: 'esrim va-hamishah midreshe Hazal 'al pikitve yad mi-genizat Yerushalayim u-Miẓrayim. Ed. Solomon Aaron Wertheimer. 2 vols. Jerusalem: Ketav va-sefer, 1979–80.

Bauldri of Dol. *Historia de peregrinatione Hierosolimitana.* In *Recueil des historiens occidentaux.* Vol. 4 of 5. Paris: Imprimerie Royale, 1844–95.

Berceo, Gonzalo de. *El duelo de la virgen; los himnos; los loores de nuestra señora; los signos del Juicio final.* Ed. Brian Dutton. Colección Timesis: Serie A, monografías, 18. London: Timesis Books, 1975.

Berechiah ben Natronai ha-Naqdan. *Dodi ve-nechdi (Uncle and Nephew): The Work of Berachya Hanakdan.* Ed. and trans. Hermann Gollancz. London: Oxford University Press, 1920.

———. *Mishle shu'alim.* Ed. Abraham Meir Habermann. Jerusalem: Shoken, 1945–46.

———. [*Mishle shu'alim.*] *Fables of a Jewish Aesop.* Trans. Moses Hadas. New York: Columbia University Press, 1967.

Berengar of Tours. *Berengarius Turonensis Rescriptum contra Lanfrannum.* Ed. R. B. C. Huygens. 2 vols. Corpus Christianorum. Continuatio medievalis, 84–84A. Turnhout: Brepols, 1988.

Bernard of Clairvaux, Saint. "In purificatione B. Mariae sermo I." In *Sämtliche Werke: Lateinisch/deutsch,* 7:404–12. 10 vols. Innsbruck: Tyrolia-Verlag, 1990– .

———. "In purificatione B. Mariae sermo III." In *Sämtliche Werke: Lateinisch/deutsch,* 7:418–24. 10 vols. Innsbruck: Tyrolia-Verlag, 1990– .

———. *On the Song of Songs*. Trans. Kilian Walsh. 4 vols. Works of Bernard of Clairvaux, vols. 2–3. Cistercian Fathers, 4, 7, 31, 40. Spencer, MA: Cistercian Publications, 1971–80.

Berthold, von Regensburg. *Berthold von Regensburg*. 2 vols. Berlin: De Gruyter, 1965.

Bestiaire d'amour rimé: Poème inédit du XIIIe *siècle*. Ed. Arvid Thordstein. Études romanes de Lund, 2. Lund: G. W. K. Gleerup, 1941.

The Bestiary. Ed. Montague Rhodes James. Oxford: J. Johnson, 1928.

The Bestiary: A Book of Beasts. Trans. T. H. White. Capricorn Books, 26. New York: Putnam, 1960.

Bestiary: Being an English Version of the Bodleian Library, Oxford MS Bodley 764. Trans. Richard Barber. Woodbridge: Boydell Press, 1993.

[Bible.] *Biblia Latina cum glossa ordinaria: Facsimile Reprint of the Editio princeps, Adolph Rusch of Strassburg, 1480/81*. Vulgate. 4 vols. Turnholt: Brepols, 1992.

[Bible.] *Épītre de Barnabé*. Ed. Robert A. Kraft. Trans. Pierre Prigent. Sources chrétiennes, 172. Paris: Éditions du Cerf, 1971.

[Bible.] *The Holy Bible*. Rev. Standard. Ed. Herbert G. May and Bruce M. Metzger. New York: Oxford University Press, 1971.

[Bible.] *Leviticus 1–16: A New Translation with Introduction and Commentary*. Ed. and trans. Jacob Milgrom. Anchor Bible, vol. 3. New York: Doubleday, 1991.

[Bible.] *Torat Hayim: Hamishah humshe Torah: Mugahim 'al-pi ha-nusah vehamesorah shel Keter Aram Tsovah ve-khitve-yad ha-kerovim lo, 'im Targum Onkelos mugah ,'al-pi ha-Tag'; 'im perushe Rasag, Rah, Rashi . . . ; yots'im la-or 'al-pi kitve-yad u-defusim rishonim 'im tsiyune mekorot, he'arot u-ve'urim*. 7 vols. Jerusalem: Mosad ha-Rav Kuk, 1986–93.

Bible moralisée: Codex Vindobonensis 2554, Vienna, Österreichischen Nationalbibliothek. Trans. Gerald B. Guest. London: Harvey Miller, 1995.

Bodel, Jean. *Le Jeu de Saint Nicolas*. Ed. Albert Henry. Geneva: Droz, 1981.

Bonaventure, Saint, Cardinal. *Sententiae*. In *Doctoris seraphici S. Bonaventurae . . . Opera omnia*. 10 vols. in 9. Quaracchi: Ex Typographia Colegii S. Bonaventurae, 1882–1902.

The Book of the Thousand Nights and One Night. Trans. J. C. Mardrus and Powys Mathers. 4 vols. London: Routledge & Kegan Paul, 1986.

Caesarius of Arles, Saint. [*Sermons*.] *Sanct Caesarii Arelatensis Sermones: Nunc primum in unum collecti et ad leges artis criticae ex innumeris mss. Recogniti*. Ed. Germain Morin. 2 vols. 2d ed. Corpus Christianorum. Series Latina, 103–4. Turnholt: Brepols, 1953.

Caesarius of Heisterbach. [*Dialogus miraculorum*.] *Die Wundergeschichten des Caesarius von Heisterbach*. Ed. Alfons Hilka. 3 vols. Publikationen der Gesellschaft für rheinische Geschichtskunder, 43. Bonn: P. Hanstein, 1933–37.

Cartulaire de l'abbaye de Saint-Père de Chartres. Ed. M. Guérard. 2 vols. Collection des cartularies de France, 1–2. Paris: Impr. De Crapelet, 1840.

Catullus, Gaius Valerius. *Catullus, Tibullus, and Pervirgilium Veneris*. Loeb Classical Library. Cambridge, MA: Harvard University Press; London: Heinemann, 1962.

La chanson d'Antioche. Ed. Suzanne DuParc-Quioc. 2 vols. Paris: P. Geuthner, 1976.

Chanson de Roland. Ed. T. Atkinson Jenkins. Boston: American Life Foundation, 1977.

Christian Dualist Heresies in the Byzantine World, c. 650–c. 1450: Selected Sources. Trans. Janet Hamilton and Bernard Hamilton, with Yuri Stoyanov. Manchester: Manchester University Press, 1998.

Cicero, Marcus Tullius. [*De natura deorum*.] *M. Tulli Ciceronis De natura deorum*. Ed. Arthur Stanley Pease. 2 vols. Latin Texts and Commentaries. Cambridge, MA: Harvard University Press, 1955–58.

———. [*De natura deorum*.] *The Nature of the Gods*. Trans. Horace C. P. McGregor. Penguin Classics, L265. Harmondsworth: Penguin, 1972.

———. [*Somnium Scipionis*.] *Laelius on Friendship (Laelius de amicitia); and The Dream of Scipio (Somnium Scipionis)*. Ed. and trans. J. G. F. Powell. Classical Texts. Arminster: Aris & Phillips, 1990.

Clement I, Pope. *Épītre aux Corinthiens*. Ed. and trans. Annie Jaubert. Sources chrétiennes, 167. Paris: Éditions du Cerf, 1971.

Clement I [Pseudo]. [*Homilies*.] *Die Pseudoklementinen*. 2 vols. Griechischen christlichen Schriffsteller der ersten 3 Jahrhundete. Berlin: Akademie Verlag, 1953– ; reprint 1992.

Clement of Alexandria, Saint. *La pédagogue*. 3 vols. Sources chrétiennes, 70, 108, 158. Paris: Éditions du Cerf, 1960–70.

[*Cologne Mani codex*.] *The Cologne Mani Codex (P. Colon. Inv. Nr. 4780): Concerning the Origin of His Body*. Trans. Ron Cameron and Arthur J. Dewey. Missoula, MT: Scholars Press, 1979.

[*Cologne Mani codex*.] *Der Kölner Mani-Kodex. Über das Werden seines Leibes*. Ed. Ludwig Kuenen and Cornelia Römer. Opladen: Westdeutscher Verlag, 1988.

[*Consultationes Zacchei Christiani et Apollonii philosophi*.] *Questions d'un païen à un chrétien (Consultationes Zacchei christiani et Appollonii philosophi)*. Ed. and trans. Jean Louis Feiertag with Werner Steinmann. 2 vols. Sources chrétiennes, 401–2. Paris: Éditions du Cerf, 1994.

Contributions to the Apocryphal Literature of the New Testament. Ed. and trans. William Wright. London: Williams and Norgate, 1865.

Corpus Hermeticum. Ed. A. D. Nock. Trans. A.-J. Festugière. 4 vols. Collection des universités de France. Paris: Société d'édition "Les Belles lettres," 1945–54.

Cyril, Saint, Patriarch of Alexandria. *Cyrille d'Alexandrie: Deux dialogues christologiques*. Ed. and trans. G. M. de Durand. Sources chrétiennes, 97. Paris: Éditions du Cerf, 1964.

——— [Pseudo]. *Sermon sur la penitence attribué à Saint Cyrille d'Alexandrie*. Ed. and trans. P. M. Chaine. In *Mélanges de la faculté orientale*, 7 vols., 6:492–528. Beirut: Impr. Catholique, 1906–14/21.

Cyril, Saint, Bishop of Jerusalem. *Catéchèses mystagogiques*. Ed. Auguste Piédagnel. Trans. Pierre Paris. Sources chrétiennes, 126. Paris: Éditions du Cerf, 1966.

———. *The Works of Saint Cyril of Jerusalem*. Trans. Leo P. McCauley and Anthony A. Stephenson. 2 vols. Fathers of the Church, a New Translation, 61, 64. Washington, DC: Catholic University of America Press, 1969–70.

De Expugnatione terrae sanctae per Saladinum, libellus. Ed. Joseph Stevenson. In *Radulphi de Coggeshall Chronicon anglicanum*. Rerum britannicanum medii aevi scriptores, 66. London: Longman, 1875.

The Dead Sea Scrolls in English. Ed. and trans. Géza Vermès. Harmondsworth: Penguin, 1975.

The Dead Sea Scrolls of St. Mark's Monastery. Ed. Millar Burrows. 2 vols. New Haven: American Schools of Oriental Research, 1950– .

The Dead Sea Scrolls Translated: The Qumran Texts in English. Ed. Florentino García Martinez. Trans. Wilfred G. E. Watson. Leiden: E. J. Brill, 1994.

[*Dead Sea Scrolls. 4Q*. Selections.] *A Preliminary Edition of the Unpublished Dead Sea Scrolls: The Hebrew and Aramaic Texts from Cave Four*. Ed. Ben Zion Wacholder and Martin G. Abegg. 4 vols. Washington, DC: Biblical Archaeology Society, 1991–96.

[*Dead Sea Scrolls. 4Q*. Selections.] *Qumrān Cave 4*. 21 vols. Discoveries in the Judaean Desert of Jordan, 5– . Oxford: Clarendon Press, 1968–2000.

[*Dead Sea Scrolls. 4Q*. Polyglot. Selections.] *The Dead Sea Scrolls Uncovered: The First Complete Translation and Interpretation of 50 Key Documents Withheld for over 35 Years*. Ed. Robert H. Eisenman and Michael Wise. Shaftesbury, MA: Element, 1992.

La desputoison du Juyf et du Crestien. In Hiram Pflaum, "Shirei ha-nitsuah ha-dati'im shel yamei ha-benaim ('im tekst she 'aino yedu'a be-tsarfatit yashanah)." *Tarbits* 2–3 (1931): 459–75.

Didascalia apostolorum; The Syriac Version Translated and Accompanied by the Verona Latin Fragments. Trans. R. Hugh Connolly. Oxford: Clarendon Press, 1929.

[al-Dimashqī] Al-Shams al-Dīn Muḥammad ibn Abī Ṭālib al-Anṣārī al-Dimashqī. *Kitāb Nukhbat al-dahr fī 'ajā'ib al-barr wa'l-baḥr*. Ed. A. F. Mehren. St. Petersburg, 1865.

[*Dissertatio contra Judaeos*]. *Anonymi auctoris Theognosiae (saec. IX/X). Dissertatio contra Judaeos*. Ed. Michiel Hostens. Corpus Christianorum. Series Graeca, 14. Turnholt: Brepols; Leuven: University Press, 1986.

Doctrina Iacobi nuper baptizati. Ed. G. N. Bonwetsch. Abhandlungen der Könglichen Gesellschaft der Wissenschaften zu Göttingen, Philologisch-Historische Klasse, n.s. 13. Berlin: Weidmannische Buchhandlung, 1910.

Dukus Horant. Ed. P. F. Ganz, F. Norman, and W. Schwarz. Altdutsche Textbibliothek. Ergänzungsreihe, 2. Tübingen: M. Niemeyer, 1964.

Duns Scotus, John. *Opera theologica*. Ed. Giovanni Lauriola. 2 vols. Quaderno/Centro studi personalisti "Giovanni Duns Scotto," 12. Alberobello: Edizioni A.G.A., 1998– .

Durand, Guillaume. *Guillelmi Duranti rationale divinorum officiorum*. Ed. Anselmus Davril and T. M. Thibodeau. 3 vols. Corpus Christianorum. Continuatio medievalis, 140. Turnholt: Brepols, 1995– .

———. *The Symbolism of Churches and Church Ornaments: A Translation of the First Book of the* Rationale divinorum officium. Ed. John Mason Neale and Benjamin Webb. 3d ed. London: Gibbings, 1906.

Einhard. *Vita Karoli Magni: The Life of Charlemagne*. Ed. and trans. Evelyn Scherabon Firchow and Edwin H. Zeydel. Coral Gables: University of Miami Press, 1972.

Eleazar ben Judah of Worms. *Perushe sidur ha-tefilah ha-Rokeaḥ: perush ha-tefilah ve-sodoteha le-khol yermot ha-shanah*. Ed. Moshe Hershler and Yehudah A. Hershler. 2 vols. Jerusalem: Mekhon ha-Rav Hershler, 1992.

Eliezer of Beaugency. *Perush ʻal Yeḥezq'el u-Tere ʻashar.* Ed. Samuel Abraham Poznanski. Sefarim ha-yots'im la-or be-fa'am rishonah 'al yede hevrat Mekitse nirdamim. Warsaw: H. Epfelberg, 1913.

Les enfaunces de Jesu Crist. Ed. Maureen Boulton. Anglo-Norman Texts, 43. London: Anglo-Norman Text Society, 1985.

Ephraem Syrus, Saint. *Ephrem the Syrian: Hymns*. Trans. Kathleen E. McVey. Classics of Western Spirituality. New York: Paulist Press, 1989.

———. [Works. Selections.] *S. Ephraim's Prose Refutations of Mani, Marcion, and Bardaisan: Of which the greater part has been transcribed from the Palimpsest B.M. add. 14623 and is now first published.* Ed. C. W. Mitchell. 2 vols. Text and Translation Society. London: Williams and Norgate, 1912–21.

Epiphanius, Saint, Bishop of Constantia in Cyprus. *Epistula Luciani*. In Migne, *Patrologiae . . . graeca,* 41. Paris: s.n., 1863–64.

———. *The Panarion*. Trans. Frank Williams. 2 vols. Nag Hammadi Studies, 35–36. Leiden: E. J. Brill, 1987– .

———. [Works.] *Epiphanius*. Ed. Karl Holl. Die Griechischen christlichen Schriftsteller der ersten Jahrhunderte. Berlin: Akademie Verlag, 1980– .

Epistola Luciani. In Migne, *Patrologiae . . . latina*, 41. Paris: s.n., 185?.

Estoire du Saint Graal. Ed. Jean-Paul Ponceau. Paris, 1997.

Eugnostos the Blessed and the Sophia of Jesus Christ. Trans. Douglas Parrott. In *The Nag Hammadi Library in English,* 220–43. Gen. ed. James Robinson. San Francisco: Harper and Row, 1981.

Eusebius of Caesaria. *Adversus Helvidium de Mariae Virginitate Perpetua.* In *Opera omnia*. In Migne, *Patrologiae . . . latina,* 23. Paris: s.n., 1857.

Euthymius, Zigabanus. *Panoplia*. In *Opera omnia*. In Migne, *Patrologiae . . . graeca,* 130. Paris: s.n., 1865.

Eutychius, Patriarch of Alexandria. *The Book of the Demonstration (Kitāb al-burhān)*. Ed. Pierre Cachia. Trans. W. Montgomery Watt. 4 vols. in 2. Corpus scriptorum Christianorum Orientalium. Scriptores Arabici, 20–23. Louvain: Secrétariat du Corpus SCO, 1960–61.

Evangelia infantiae apocrypha = Apocryphe Kindheitsevangelien. Trans. Gerhard Schneider. Fontes Christiani, 18. Freiburg im Breisgau: Herder, 1995.

[*Évangile de l'Enfance.*] *The Old French Évangile de l'Enfance: An Edition.* Ed. Maureen Barry McCann Boulton. Studies and Texts, 70. Toronto: Pontifical Institute of Mediaeval Studies, 1984.

Ferrand, Jacques. *A Treatise on Lovesickness.* Ed. and trans. Donald A. Beecher and Massimo Ciavolella. Syracuse: Syracuse University Press, 1990.

Fidentius of Padua. *Liber de recuperatione terrae sanctae.* In *Biblioteca biobibliographica della terra santa e dell'oriente francescano,* vol. 2 of 5. Ed. Girolamo Golubovich. Quaracchi: Collegio dis Bonaventura, 1906–27.

The Fifty-third Chapter of Isaiah, according to the Jewish Interpreters. Comp. Adolf Neubauer. Trans. S. R. Driver. 2 vols. Oxford, 1876–77; reprint New York: Ktav Publications, 1969.

Finding of the True Cross: The Judas Kyriakos Legend in Syriac. Ed. and trans. H. J. W. Drijvers and Jan Willem Drijvers, 565–93. Corpus scriptorum Christianorum Orientalium. Louvain: Peeters, 1997.

Fortunatus, Venantius Honorius Clementianus. *Poèmes.* Ed. and trans. Marc Reydellet. 2 vols. Collection des universités de France. Paris: Belles Lettres, 1994– .

Fulbert, Saint, Bishop of Chartres. "Sermo I de Nativitate Beatissimae Virginis." In *Opera omnia.* In Migne, *Patrologiae . . . latina,* 141. Paris: s.n., 1853.

Fulchre of Chartres. *Historia Iherosolymitana.* In *Recueil des historiens des croisades occidentaux,* vol. 3 of 5. Paris: Imprimerie Royale, 1844–95.

Gabrieli, Francesco. *Arab Historians of the Crusades.* Trans. E. J. Costello. Berkeley: University of California Press, 1969.

Galen. [*De naturalibus facultatibus.*] *Galen On the Natural Faculties.* Loeb Classical Library. London: Heinemann; New York: Putnam, 1916.

———. [*De semine.*] *On Semen.* Ed. and trans. Philip De Lacy. Corpus medicorum Graecorum, V.3.1. Berlin: Akademie Verlag, 1992.

———. [*De usu partium corporis humani.*] *Galen On the Usefulness of the Parts of the Body. Peri chreias morión/De usu partium.* Trans. Margaret Tallmadge May. 2 vols. Cornell Publications in the History of Science. Ithaca: Cornell University Press, 1968.

———. [Selections.] *The Art of Cure: Extracts from Galen.* Judeo-Arabic trans. Moses Maimonides. English trans. Uriel S. Barzel. Maimonides' Medical Writings, 5. Haifa: Maimonides Research Institute, 1992.

———. *Opera omnia.* Ed. Karl G. Kühn. 20 vols. in 22. Medicorum Graecorum opera quae exstant, 1–20. Leipzig: K. Knobloch, 1821–33.

Gautier de Coincy. *Les miracles de Nostre Dame.* Ed. Fréderic Koenig. 4 vols. Textes littéraires français. Geneva: Droz, 1955–70.

Georgius, Monachus, surnamed Hamartolus. *Chronicon breve.* In Migne, *Patrologia . . . graeca,* 110. Paris: s.n., 1863.

Gerald of Wales. *De Principis instructione.* Ed. George F. Warner. *Rerum Britannicarum Medii Aevi Scriptores,* vol. 21. London: Kraus Reprint, 1964.

Gilbert Crispin. *The Works of Gilbert Crispin, Abbot of Westminster.* Ed. Anna Sapir Abulafia and G. R. Evans. Auctores Britannici Medii Aevi, 8. London: Oxford University Press, 1986.

Ginze Midrash: le-tsuratam ha-kedumah shel midreshe Hazal lefi kitve yad min ha-Genizah. Ed. Zvi Meir Rabinowitz. Tel Aviv: Bet ha-sefer le-mada'e ha-Yahadut 'a. sh. Hayim Rozenberg, Universitat Tel Aviv, 1976.

Ginze Shekhter: qeṭ'et midrash ve-haggadah min ha-Genizah she-be-miẓraim. Ed. Louis Ginzberg. 3 vols. Texts and Studies of the Jewish Theological Seminary of America, 7–9. New York: Bet midrash ha-rabanim asher ba-Amerika, 1928–29.

Gobi, Jean. *La Scala Coeli de Jean Gobi*. Ed. Marie-Anne Polo de Beaulieu. Sources d'histoire médievale. Paris: Édition di Centre Nationale de la Recherché Scientifique, 1991.

Greek and Latin Authors on Jews and Judaism. Ed. Menahem Stern. 3 vols. Fontes ad res Judaicas spectantes. Jerusalem: Israel Academy of Sciences and Humanities, 1974–80.

Gregentius, Saint, Bishop of Taphar. *Homeritarum Leges; Disputatio cum Herbano Judaeo*. In Migne, *Patrologiae . . . graeca*, 86:1. Paris: s.n., 1865.

Gregory of Nyssa, Saint. *Traité de la virginité*. Ed. and trans. Michel Aubineau. Sources chrétiennes, 119. Paris: Éditions du Cerf, 1966.

Gregory, Saint, Bishop of Tours. *De virtutibus sanct Martini*. In *Opera omnia*. In Migne, *Patrologiae . . . latina*, 71. Paris: s.n., 185?.

———. *The History of the Franks*. Trans. Lewis Thorpe. Penguin Classics. Harmondsworth: Penguin, 1974.

———. *Vita Patrum: The Life of the Fathers*. Platina, CA: St. Herman of Alaska Brotherhood, 1988.

Guibert of Nogent. *De pignoribus sanctorum epistola nuncupatoria*. In *Opera omina*. In Migne, *Patrologiae . . . latina*, 156. Paris: s.n., 1853.

———. *Dei gesta per Francos*. Ed. R. B. C. Huygens. Corpus Christianorum. Continuatio medievalis, 127A. Turnholt: Brepols, 1996.

———. *Tractatus de Incarnatione contra Judaeos*. In *Opera omnia*. In Migne, *Patrologiae . . . latina*, 156. Paris: s.n., 1853.

Guillaume de Bourges. [*Liber bellorum Domini*.] *Livre des guerres du Seigneur et deux homélies*. Ed. and trans. Gilbert Dahan. Sources chrétiennes, 288. Paris: Éditions du Cerf, 1981.

Guillaume le Clerc de Normandie. *Le Bestiaire: Das Thierbuch des normannischen Dichters Guillaume le Clerc . . .* Ed. Robert Reinsch. Altfranzösische Bibliothek, 14. Leipzig: O. R. Reisland, 1892.

———. [*Le bestiaire*.] *The Bestiary of Guillaume le Clerc, Originally Written in 1210–11*. Ed. George Claridge Druce. Ashford: privately published, 1936.

Guillaume of Champeaux [Pseudo]. *Dialogus inter Christianum et Judaeum* in *De sacramento altaris; Chartae*. In Migne, *Patrologiae . . . latina*, 163. Paris: s.n., 1854.

al-Harawī, Abū l'Hasan 'Alī b. Abī Bakr. *Kitāb al-ishārāt ilā ma'rifat al-ziyārat*. Ed. J. Sourdel-Thomine. Damascus: Institut Français de Damas, 1953.

———. *Guide des Lieux de Pèlerinage*. Trans. J. Sourdel-Thomine. Damascus: Institut Français de Damas, 1957.

Hegemonius. *Hegemonius: Acta Archelai*. Ed. Charles Henry Beeson. Leipzig: J. C. Hinrichs, 1906.

Henmannus Bononiensis. *Das viaticum narrationum des Henmannus Bononiensis*. Ed. Alfons Hilka. Beiträge zur lateinischen Erzählungsliteratur des Mittelalters,

3. Abhandlungen—Gesellschaft der Wissenschaften zu Göttingen. Philologisch-historische Klasse. Dritte Folge, 16. Berlin: Weidmannsche Buchhandlung, 1935; reprint Nendeln: Kraus Reprint, 1972.

Hermanni Althahenses annales. Ed. Hermann Bloch. Monumenta Germaniae historica. Scriptores rerum Germanicarum in usum scholarum separatim editi, 9. Hannover: Hahn, 1907; reprint Hannover: Hahn, 1979.

Heresies of the High Middle Ages. Trans. Walter L. Wakefield and Austin P. Evans. Rev. ed. Records of Civilization: Sources and Studies, 81. New York: Columbia University Press, 1991.

Herman of Scheda. *Hermanus quondam Judaeus: Opusculum de conversione sua*. Ed. Gerlinde Niemeyer. Monumenta Germanica historiae. Die deutschen Geschichtsquellen des Mittelalter, 500–1500. Quellen zur Geistesgeschichte des Mittelalters, 4. Weimar: H. Böhlau, 1963.

Hermetica: The Greek Corpus Hermeticum and the Latin Aesclepius in a New English Translation. Trans. Brian P. Copenhaver. Cambridge: Cambridge University Press, 1992.

Hidelfonsus, Saint, Bishop of Toledo. *De virginitate perpetua SS. Mariae, adversus tres infideles; De cognitione baptismi [etc.]*. In Migne, *Patrologiae . . . latina*, 96. Paris: s.n., 1862.

——— [Pseudo]. *Sermones*. In *De virginitate perpetua SS. Mariae, adversus tres infideles; De cognitione baptismi [etc.]*. In Migne, *Patrologiae . . . latina*, 96. Paris: s.n., 1862.

Hildebert, Bishop of Lavardin. *Opera omnia*. In Migne, *Patrologiae . . . latina*, 171. Paris: s.n., 1854.

Hildegard, Saint. *Hildegardis Scivias*. Ed. Adelgundis Führkötter with Angela Carlevaris. 2 vols. Corpus Christianorum. Continuatio medievalis, 43. Turnholt: Brepols, 1978.

———. *Scivias*. Trans. Columba Hart and Jane Bishop. Classics of Western Spirituality. New York: Paulist Press, 1990.

———. *Symphonia: A Critical Edition of the* Symphonia armonie celestium revelationum *[Symphony of the Harmony of Celestial Revelations]*. Ed. and trans. Barbara Newman. Ithaca: Cornell University Press, 1988.

Hippocrates. *Hippocrates*. 8 vols. Loeb Classical Library. New York: Putnam; London: Heinemann, 1923–95.

Hippolytus, Antipope. *Refutatio omnium haeresisium*. Ed. Miroslav Marcovich. Patristische Text und Studien, 25. Berlin: De Gruyter, 1986.

Holy Women of the Syrian Orient. Trans. Sebastian P. Brock and Susan Ashbrook Harvey. The Transformation of the Classical Heritage, 13. Berkeley: University of California Press, 1987.

Hrotsvitha. *The Dramas of Hrosvit of Gandersheim*. Trans. Katharina M. Wilson. Matrologia latina. Saskatoon: Peregrina, 1985.

———. *Opera omnia*. Ed. Walter Berschin. Bibliotheca scriptorum Graecorum et Romanorum Teubneriana. Munich: K. G. Saur, 2001.

Hugh of Fouilloy. *The Medieval Book of Birds: Hugh of Fouilloy's* Aviarium. Ed. and trans. Willene B. Clark. Medieval and Renaissance Texts and Studies, 80. Binghamton: Medieval and Renaissance Texts and Studies, 1992.

Hugh of St. Victor. *On the Sacraments of the Christian Faith.* Trans. Roy J. Deferrari. Medieval Academy of America Publications, 58. Cambridge, MA: Medieval Academy of America, 1951.

———. *Opera omnia.* 3 vols. In Migne, *Patrologiae . . . latina*, 175–77. Paris: s.n., 1854.

Hugo Farsitus. *Libellus de miraculis B. Mariae virginis in urbe Suessionensi.* In Migne, *Patrologiae . . . latina*, 179. Paris: s.n., 1855.

The Hypostases of the Archons. Trans. Bentley Layton. In *The Nag Hammadi Library in English.* Gen. ed. James Robinson. San Francisco: Harper and Row, 1981.

Ibn al-Nabīh, 'Alī ibn Muḥammad. *Diwan.* Beirut, 1969.

Ibn Buluggīn al-Zīrī, 'Abd Allāh. *Mudhakkirāt al-amīr 'Abd Allāh, al-musammāt bi-Kitāb al-Tibyān.* Ed. E. Levi-Provençal. Cairo: Dar al-Ma'arif, 1955.

———. *The Tibyan: Memoires of 'Abd Allah b. Buluggin Last Zirid Amir of Granada.* Trans. Amin T. Tibi. Leiden: E. J. Brill, 1986.

Ibn Ezra, Abraham ben Meïr. *Perushe ha-Torah le-rabenu Avraham Ibn 'Ezra: 'al-pi k.t.y. u-defusim rishonim.* Ed. Asher Weiser. 3 vols. Jerusalem: Hotsa'at Mosad ha-rav Kuk, 1976.

———. [*Perush ha-Torah.*] *The Commentary of Abraham Ibn Ezra on the Pentateuch.* Trans. Jay F. Shachter. 5 vols. Hoboken, NJ: Ktav, 1986– .

Ibn Ḥazm, 'Alī ibn Aḥmad. *al-Faṣl fī al-milal wa-al-ahwā' wa-al-niḥal.* Ed. Muḥammad Ibrāhīm Nasr and 'Abd al-Raḥmān 'Umayrah. 5 vols. Jiddah: 'Ukāz, 1982.

Ibn Jubayr, Muḥammad ibn Aḥmad. *Riḥlat.* Beirut: Dar Sadir lil-Tiba'ah wa-al-Nashr, 1964.

———. *The Travels of Ibn Jubayr.* Trans. R. J. C. Broadhurst. London: J. Cape, 1952.

Ibn Khallikan. *Wafāyāt al-a'yān.* 8 vols. Beirut: Dar Assakafa, 1968–72.

———. *Ibn Khallikan's Biographical Dictionary.* 4 vols. Paris, 1843–71.

———. "Extraits de la vie du Sultan Salah ed-Din." In *Recueil des historiens des croisades orientaux,* vol. 3. Paris, 1884.

Ibn Muqaffa', 'Abd Allāh. *Kitāb Kalīlah wa-Dimnah.* Introd. Faruq S'ad. Beirut: Dar al-Afaq al-Jaddah, 1977.

———. *The Fables of Kalilah and Dimnah.* Trans. Saleh Sa'adeh Jallad. London: Melisende, 2002.

Ibn Qayyim al-Jawzīyah, Muḥammad ibn Abī Bakr. *Kitāb ḥidāyat al-hayārā fī ajwibat al-yahūd wa-al-Nasārā.* Ed. Muḥammad Alī Abū Abbas. Cairo: s.n., 1990.

———. *Tuḥfat al-mawdūd bi-aḥkām al-mawlūd.* Ed. 'Abd al-Karīm Sharaf al-Dīn. Bombay: al-Matba'ah al-Hindīyah al- 'Arabiyah, 1961.

Ibn Ridwan. *Medieval Islamic Medicine: Ibn Ridwan's Treatise "On the Prevention of Bodily Ills in Egypt."* Trans. and introd. Michael Dols. Ed. Adil S. Gamal. Berkeley: University of California Press, 1984.

Ibn Sahula, Isaac. *Meshal haQadmoni: Fables from the Distant Past.* Ed. and trans. Raphael Loewe. 2 vols. Oxford: Littman Library of Jewish Civilization, 2004.

Ibn Sina. [*al-Ḥayawān.*] *De animalibus*. Venice: Johannes et Gregorius de Gregorius, 1500.

———. *al-Qānūn fī al-ṭibb*. 3 vols. Beirut, 1999.

———. [*al-Qānūn fī al-ṭibb.*] *Liber canonis*. 1507; reprint Hildesheim: G. Olms, 1998.

———. *al-Shifā'*. Ed. Ibrāhīm Madkūr, Georges Anawati, Maḥmūd Muḥammad Khudayrī, and Aḥmad Fu'ād Ahwānī. 4 in 21 vols. Cairo: Wizarat al-Ma'arif 1952–83.

Ibn Taghrībirdī, Abū Maḥāsin Yūsuf. *Al-Nujūm al-zāhira fī mulūk Miṣr, wa al-Qāhirah*. Vol. 5 of 16. Cairo, 1929–72.

Ibn Zabara, Joseph ben Meir. *Sefer sha'ashu'im*. Ed. Israel Davidson. Berlin: Eshkol, 1925.

———. [*Sefer sha'ashu'im.*] *The Book of Delight*. Trans. Moses Hadas. Records of Civilization: Sources and Studies, 16. New York: Columbia University Press, 1932.

'Imād al-Dīn Muḥammad ibn Muḥammad al-Kātib al-Iṣfahānī. *Al-fatḥ al-qussī fī-'l-fatḥ al-Qudsī*. n.p., 1969.

———. [*Al-Barq al-shami.*] *Der Syrische Blitz: Sala dins Sekretär zwischen Selbstdarstellung und Geschichtsscreibung*. Ed. and trans. Lutz Richter-Berenburg. Beirut: Franz Steiner, 1998.

Innocent, III, Pope. [*De contemptu mundi.*] *On the Misery of the Human Condition: De miseria humane conditionis*. Ed. Donald R. Howard. Trans. Margaret Mary Dietz. Library of Liberal Arts, 132. Indianapolis: Bobbs-Merrill, 1969.

———. *De miseria humane conditionis*. Ed. Michele Maccarrone. Thesaurus mundi. Zurich: Thesaurus mundi, 1955.

Irenaeus, Saint, Bishop of Lyons. [*Adversus haereses.*] *St. Irenaeus of Lyons against the Heresies*. Trans. Dominic J. Unger and John J. Dillon. Ancient Christian Writers, 55– . New York: Paulist Press, 1992– .

———. [*Adversus haereses.*] *Contre les hérésies*. 5 vols. in 10. Sources chrétiennes, 34, 100, 152–53, 210–11, 263–64, 293–94. Paris: Éditions du Cerf, 1952– .

Isidore of Seville, Saint. [*Etymologiae*]. *Isidori Hispalensis Episcopi Etymologiarum sive originvm libri XX*. Ed. W. W. Lindsay. 2 vols. Scriptorum classicorum bibliotheca Oxoniensis. Oxford: Clarendon Press; New York: Oxford University Press, 1911. Reprint 1985.

———. *Quaestiones in Vet. Testamentum*. In Migne, *Patrologiae . . . latina*, 83. Paris: s.n., 1850–62.

Ivo, Saint, Bishop of Chartres. *Opera omnia*. In Migne, *Patrologiae . . . latina*, 162. Paris: s.n., 1854.

Jacob ben Reuben. *Milḥamot ha-shem*. Ed. Yehuda Rosenthal. Sifiryat Mekorot, 18. Jerusalem: Mosad ha-Rav Kuk, 1963.

Jacob of Edessa. *La didascale de Jacob: Texte grec, original du argis d'Aberga (P.O. III 4)*. Ed. F. Nau. Patrologia Orientalis, 8:5. Paris: s.n., 1912.

Jacob de Voragine. *Legenda aurea*. Ed. Giovanni Paulo Maggioni. 2d ed. 2 vols. Millennio medievale, 6; Testi 3. Taramuzze: SISMEL/Edizioni del Galluzzo, 1998.

———. [*Legenda aurea.*] *The Golden Legend: Readings on the Saints.* Trans. William Granger Ryan. 2 vols. Princeton: Princeton University Press, 1993.

Jacques de Vitry, Cardinal. *Libri duo. Quorum prior Orientalis, sive Hierosolymitanae: Alter, Occidentalis Historiae nominee inscribitur.* Ed. Francisco Moschi. Douai: Balthazar Beller, 1597.

———. *Die Exempla, aus den Sermones feriales et communes des Jakob von Vitry.* Ed. Joseph Greuen. Sammlung mittellateineischer Texte, 9. Heidelberg: C. Winter, 1914.

———. *The Exempla, or Illustrative Stories from the* Sermones vulgares *of Jacques de Vitry.* Ed. Thomas Frederick Crane. Folk-lore Society Publications, 26. London: D. Nutt, 1890.

———. *La traduction de l'Historia Orientalis de Jacques de Vitry.* Ed. Claude Buridant. Bibliothèque française et romane. Série B, Editions critiques de texts, 19. Paris: Klincksieck, 1986.

al-Jāḥiẓ, Abī 'Uthmān 'Amr ibn Baḥr. *al-Mukhtār fī al-radd 'alā al-Naṣāra.* Ed. Muḥammad 'Abd Allāh al-Sharqāwī. Cairo: Dār al-Sahwah, 1984.

Jean le Marchant. *Miracles de Notre-Dame de Chartres.* Ed. Pierre Kunstmann. Publications médiévales de l'Université d'Ottawa, 1. Ottawa: Éditions de l'Université d'Ottawa, 1973.

Jerome, Saint. [*Commentariorum in Evangelium Matthei libri quatuor.*] *Commentaire sur S. Matthieu.* Ed. and trans. Émile Bonnard. 2 vols. Sources chrétiennes, 242, 259. Paris: Éditions du Cerf, 1977–79.

———. [Correspondence.] *Lettres.* Ed. and trans. Jérôme Labourt. 8 vols. Collection des universités de France. Paris: Belles Lettres, 1949–63.

———. [Works.] *S. Hieronymi presbyteri opera.* 3 vols. in 11. Corpus Christianorum. Series Latina, 72–75A, 77–80. Turnholt: Brepols, 1958–2000.

"The Jewish Martyrs of Blois." Ed. and trans. Susan Einbinder. In *Medieval Hagiography: An Anthology*, ed. Thomas Head, 537–60. Garland Reference Library of the Humanities, 1942. New York: Garland, 2000.

The Jews and the Crusaders: The Hebrew Chronicles of the First and Second Crusades. Ed. and trans. Shlomo Eidelberg. Madison: University of Wisconsin Press, 1977.

Jiménez de Rada, Rodrigo. *Historia Arabum.* Ed. Jose Lozano Sanchez. Seville: Secretariado de Publicaciones de la Universidad de Sevilla, 1993.

Joannes Aegidius, Zamorensis. *Historia naturalis.* Ed. and trans. Avelíno Domínguez and Luis García Ballester. 3 vols. Estudios de historia de la ciencia y de la técnica, 11. Salamanca: Junta de Castilla y León, Consejería de Cultura y Turismo, 1994.

John Chrysostom, Saint. *Commento alla prima lettera a Timoteo.* Ed. and trans. Gerardo Di Nola. Collana di testa pastristici, 124. Rome: Città Nuova, 1995.

John of Damascus. *Against the Heresy of the Nestorians.* In [*Works.* Greek. 1864.] *Opera omnia.* In Migne, *Patrologiae . . . graeca*, 95. Paris: s.n., 185?.

———. *De fide orthodoxa: Versions of Burgundio and Cerbanus.* Ed. Eligius M. Buytaert. Franciscan Institute Publications, Text Series, 8. St. Bonaventure, NY: Franciscan Institute, 1955.

———. *Dispute of an Orthodox with a Nestorian.* In [*Works.* Greek. 1864.] *Opera omnia.* In Migne, *Patrologiae . . . graeca*, 96. Paris: s.n., 185?.

John of Garland. *The Stella Maris of John of Garland . . .* Ed. Evelyn Faye Wilson. Medieval Academy of America Publications, 45. Cambridge, MA: Medieval Academy of America, 1946.

Joseph ben Nathan Official. *Yosef ha-mekane*. Ed. Judah Rosenthal. Sefarim ha-yotẓ'im le-'or 'al yede Hevrat Mekitse nirdamim. Jerusalem: Mekitse nirdamim, 1970.

Josephus, Flavius. [*Antiquitates Judaicae.*] *Les antiquités juives*. Ed. and trans. Étienne Nodet. 3 vols. Paris: Éditions du Cerf, 1990.

———. *The New Complete Works.* Trans. William Whiston. Rev. and exp. ed. Grand Rapids, MI: Kregel Publications, 1999.

Judah ben Barzillai al-Bargeloni. *Sefer ha-'itim: kolel pisqe ha-Shas va-halakhot gam ḥidushim u-teshuvot meha-ge'onim qadmonim.* Ed. Jacob Schor. Krakow: Y. Fisher, 1903.

[Judah ben Samuel]. *Sefer Ḥasidim.* Ed. Reuben Margolies. Jerusalem: Mosad ha-Rav Kuk, 1969–70.

Julianus, Emperor of Rome. *The Works of the Emperor Julian.* 3 vols. Loeb Classical Library. London: Heinemann, 1913– .

Justin Martyr, Saint. *Apologies*. Ed. and trans. André Wartelle. Paris: Études Augustiniennes, 1987.

———. [*Dialogus cum Tryphone.*] *Dialogue avec Tryphon.* Ed. and trans. Georges Archambault. 2 vols. Textes et documents pour l'étude historique du christianisme, 8, 11. Paris: A. Picard, 1909.

———. [Works. Selections.] *Saint Justin Martyr: The First Apology, The Second Apology, Dialogue with Trypho, Exhortation to the Greeks, Discourse to the Greeks, The monarchy, or, the Rule of God.* Trans. Thomas B. Falls. New York: Christian Heritage, 1949.

K[Q]imḥi, David [Pseudo]. *Vikuḥe Radaq.* In Joseph Kimḥi, *Sefer ha-Berit, u-vikuhe Radak 'im ha-Natsrut.* Ed. Frank Talmage. Sifiryat 'Dorot'. Jerusalem: Mosad Byalik, 1974.

K[Q]imḥi, Joseph, *Sefer ha-Berit, u-vikuḥe Radaq 'im ha-Naẓrut.* Ed. Frank Talmage. Sifiryat 'Dorot'. Jerusalem: Mosad Byalik, 1974.

———. [*Sefer ha-Berit.*] *The Book of the Covenant of Joseph Kimḥi.* Trans. Frank Talmage. Toronto: Pontifical Institute of Mediaeval Studies, 1972.

[*Koran.*] *Al-Qur'ān: A Contemporary Translation.* Trans. Aḥmed Ali. Rev. ed. Princeton: Princeton University Press, 1984.

Lactantius. *Lactanti De ave phoenice*. Ed. and trans. Mary Cletus FitzPatrick. Philadelphia: s.n., 1933.

Latini, Brunetto. *Li livres dou tresor*. Ed. François Adrien Polycarpe Chabaille. Paris: Imprimerie Impériale, 1863.

———. [*Livres dou tresor.*] *Libro del tesoro: Versión castellana de Li livres dou tresor*. Ed. Spurgeon Baldwin. Spanish Series, 46. Madison: Hispanic Seminary of Medieval Studies, 1989.

Les légendes syriaques: d'Aaron de Saroug, de Maxime et Domèce, d'Abraham, maître de Barsoma et de l'empereur Maurice. Ed. and trans. François Nau and L. Leroy. Patrologia Orientalis, 5. Paris: Firmin-Didot, 1910.

Leo VI the Wise, Emperor of the East. *Opera omnia*. In Migne, *Patrologiae . . . graeca*, 107. Paris: s.n., 1863.

Leontius Byzantinus. *Against the Nestorians and the Eutychians*. In *Opera omnia*. In Migne, *Patrologiae . . . graeca*, 86. Paris: s.n., 1865.

——— [Pseudo]. *On the Sects*. In *Opera omnia*. In Migne, *Patrologiae . . . graeca*, 86. Paris: s.n., 1865.

Liber exemplorum ad usum praedicantium saeculo xiii compositus a quodam fratre minore anglico de provincia Hiberniae. Ed. A. G. Little. British Society of Franciscan Studies, 1. Abedeen: Typis Academicis, 1908.

"Ludus de Nativitate (Benediktbeuren)." In *Medieval Drama,* comp. David Bevington. Boston: Houghton Mifflin, 1975.

Lyons, M. C. *The Arabian Epic: Heroic and Oral Story-telling*. 3 vols. Cambridge: Cambridge University Press, 1995.

Maimonides, Moses. [*Dalālat al-ḥā'irīn*.] *Le guide des égarés: Traité de théologie et de philosophie*. Ed. and trans. Salomon Munk. 3 vols. Paris: A. Franck, 1856–66; reprint Osnabrück: O. Zeller, 1964.

———. [*Dalālat al-ḥā'irīn*.] *The Guide of the Perplexed*. Trans. Shlomo Pines. Chicago: University of Chicago Press, 1963.

———. [*Dalālat al-ḥā'irīn*.] *Moreh nevukhim*. Trans. Shmuel Ibn Tibbon. Vilna: Yitshak Funk, 1914.

———. [*Pirqe Moshe bi-refu'ah*.] *The Medical Aphorisms of Moses Maimonides*. Trans. Fred Rosner and Süssmann Muntner. 2 vols. Studies in Judaica, 3–4. New York: Yeshiva University Press, 1970.

———. [Selections.] *Treatises on Poisons; Hemorrhoids; Cohabitation*. Trans. Fred Rosner. Maimonides' Medical Writings, 1. Haifa: Maimonides Research Institute, 1984.

A Manichaean Psalm-book. Ed. C. R. C. Allberry. Manichaean Manuscripts in the Chester Beatty Collection, 2. Stuttgart: W. Kohlhammer, 1938.

Marcus Aurelius, Emperor of Rome. [*Meditations*.] *The Communings with Himself of Marcus Aurelis Antonius, Emperor of Rome, Together with His Speeches and Sayings*. Loeb Classical Library. London: Heinemann; New York: Putnam, 1916– .

Martial. [*Epigrammata*. Selections.] *Sixty Poems of Martial, in Translation*. Trans. Dudley Fitts. New York: Harcourt, Brace and World, 1967.

Martin, Saint, of Leon. *Sermones*. In *Opera omnia*. In Migne, *Patrologiae . . . latina*, 208–9. Paris: s.n., 1855.

Maximus, Confessor, Saint. [Works. Selections.] *Opuscules théologiques et polémiques*. Trans. Emmanuel Ponsoye. Sagesses chrétiennes. Paris: Éditions du Cerf, 1998.

Meir ben Baruch of Rothenburg. *Sefer She'elot u-teshuvot Maharam bar Barukh*. 5 vols. Bene Berak: Sifiryah Haredit 'olamit, 1996/7–98/9.

———. [*Sefer She'elot u-teshuvot Maharam bar Barukh*. Selections.] In Irving A. Agus, *Rabbi Meir of Rothenburg, His Life and His Works as Sources for the*

Religious, Legal and Social History of the Jews of Germany in the Thirteenth Century. 2 vols. Philadelpha: Dropsie College for the Study of Hebrew and Cognate Learning, 1947.

[*Mekhilta of Rabbi Ishmael.*] *Mekhilta de-Rabi Yishma'el.* Ed. Jacob Lauterbach. 3 vols. Schiff Series of Jewish Classics. Philadelphia: ha-Hevrah ha-Yehudit le-hotsa'at sefarim asher ba-Amerika, 1949.

Melito, Saint, Bishop of Sardis [Pseudo]. [German and Latin.] *"Transitu Mariae" des Pseudo-Melito: Text-kritische Ausgabe und Darlegung der Bedeutung dieser ursprunenglicheren fassung fuer Apokryphenforschubung und lateinische und deutsche Dichtung des Mittelalters.* Ed. Monika Haibach-Reinisch. Bibliotheca assumptionis B. Virginis Mariae, 5. Rome: Pontificia Academia Mariana Internationalis, 1962.

Midrash Rabbah. Ed. and trans. H. Freedman and Maurice Simon. 10 vols. 3d ed. London: Soncino Press, 1983.

[*Midrash Rabbah Deuteronomy.* 1974.] *Midrash Devarim rabah: yotse la-or pa'am rishonah 'al pi ketav yad Oksford kovez̩ 147.* Ed. Saul Lieberman. 3d ed. Jerusalem: Sifre Vahrman, 1974.

[*Midrash Rabbah Genesis.*] *Bereshit Rabba.* Ed. J. Theodor and Ch. Albert. 3 vols. Veröffentlichungen der Akademie für die Wissenschaft des Judentums. Jerusalem: Wahrmann Books, 1965.

[*Midrash Rabbah Leviticus.*] *Midrash Vayikra Rabbah: A Critical Edition Based on Manuscripts and Genizah Fragments with Variants and Notes.* Ed. Mordecai Margulies. 5 vols. Jerusalem: s.n., 1953–60.

Midrash Tanḥuma'. In *Ginze Midrash: le-z̩uratam ha-qedumah shel midreshe Hazal lefi kitve yad min ha-Genizah,* ed. Zvi Meir Rabinowitz, 66–71. Tel Aviv: Bet ha-sefer le-mada'e ha-Yahadut 'a. sh. Hayim Rozenberg, Universitat Tel Aviv, 1976.

Migne, J. P. *Patrologiae cursus complete . . . Series graeca.* 161 in 166 vols. Paris: s.n., 1857–66.

———. *Patrologiae cursus completes . . . Series latina.* 221 vols. Paris: s.n., 1844–64.

Minucius Felix, Marcus. *Octavius.* Ed. and trans. Bernhard Kytzler. 2d ed. Universal-Bibliothek, 9860. Stuttgart: Reclam, 1983.

[*Mishnah. Avot.*] *Pirqe Avot.* In *Shishah sidre Mishnah.* Ed. Chanokh Albeck. 6 vols. Jerusalem: Mosad Byalikl; Tel Aviv: Deviri, 1952–59.

[*Mishnah. Ohalot.*] *The Mishnah Tratise Ohaloth/Masekhet Mishnah Ohalot.* Ed. Abraham Goldberg. Jerusalem: s.n., 1955.

Nahmanides. *Kitve Rabenu Mosheh ben Naḥman: yoz̩'im la-or 'al-pi kitve yad u-defusim rishonim 'im mar'e meqamot, he'arot u-mevo'ot.* Ed. Hayim Dov Chavel. 2 vols. Jerusalem: Mosade ha-Rav Kuk, 1976/7–77/8.

———. *Perushe ha-Torah le-Rabenu Mosheh ben Naḥman.* Ed. Hayim Dov Chavel. 2 vols. Jerusalem: Mosad ha-Rav Kuk, 1959–60.

———. [*Perushe ha-Torah.*] *Commentary on the Torah.* Ed. and trans. Charles B. Chavel. 5 vols. New York: Shilo, 1971–76.

——— [Pseudo]. "Discourse: The Law of the Eternal is Perfect." In *Writings and Discourses,* vol. 1. Trans. Charles B. Chavel. New York: Shilo, 1978.

——— [Pseudo]. *Igeret ha-qodesh.* In *Kitve Rabenu Mosheh ben Naḥman: yoẓ'im la-or 'al-pi kitve yad u-defusim rishonim 'im mar'e meqamot, he'arot u-mevo'ot,* ed. Hayim Dov Chavel. 2 vols. Jerusalem: Mosade ha-Rav Kuk, 1976/7–77/8.

A Nestorian Collection of Christological Texts, Cambridge University Library Ms. Oriental 1319. Ed. and trans. Luise Abramowski and Alan E. Goodman. 2 vols. Cambridge: University Press, 1972.

Nestorius. *The Bazaar of Heracleides*. Ed. and trans. G. R. Driver and Leonard Hodgson. Oxford: Clarendon Press, 1925.

———. *The Sermons of Nestorius*. Trans. Ford Lewis Battle with Daniel Sahas. Pittsburgh: s.n., 1973.

[*Neutestamentliche Apokryphen.*] *New Testament Apocrypha.* Ed. Wilhelm Schneemelcher. Trans. R. McL. Wilson. 2 vols. Philadelphia: Westminster Press, 1963–66.

Nicetas Byzantinus. *Refutation of the False Book which Muḥammad the Arab Wrote.* In *Opera omnia.* In Migne, *Patrologiae . . . graeca*, 105. Paris: s.n., 1862.

Nicetas Pectoratus [Nicetas Stêthatos]. *Traité contre les Juifs accusant dès les début leur indocilité et leur infidelité*. In *Opuscules et lettres,* ed. and trans. J. Darrouzès. Sources chrétiennes, 81. Paris: Éditions du Cerf, 1961.

Novatianus. [Works.] *Opera quae supersunt: Nunc primum in unum collecta ad fidem codicum qui adhuc extant necnon adhibitis editionibus veteribus*. Ed. G. F. Diercks. Corpus Christianorum. Series Latina, 4. Turnholt: Brepols, 1972.

Odo of Cheriton. *Fabulae*. In Léopold Hervieux, *Les fabulistes latins depuis le siècle d'Auguste jusqu'à la fin du Moyen Âge*. 5 vols. Burt Franklin Research and Source Works, 99. Paris: Firmin-Didot, 1893–99; reprint New York: Burt Franklin, 1985.

———. [*Fabulae.*] *The Fables of Odo of Cheriton*. Ed. and trans. John C. Jacobs. Syracuse: Syracuse University Press, 1985.

———. *Parabolae*. In Léopold Hervieux, *Les fabulists latins depuis le siècle d'Auguste jusqu'à la fin du Moyen Âge*. 5 vols. Burt Franklin Research and Source Works, 99. Paris: Firmin-Didot, 1893–99; reprint New York: Burt Franklin, 1985.

Odo of Tournai. *De disputatione contra iudaeum Leonem nomine de Adventu Christi filii Dei*. In Migne, *Patrologiae . . . latina*, 160. Paris: s.n., n.d.

———. [*De disputatione contra iudaeum Leonem nomine de Adventu Christi filii Dei.*] In *On Original Sin; and A Disputation with the Jew, Leo, concerning the Advent of Christ the Son of God: Two Theological Treatises*. Trans. Irven M. Resnick. Middle Ages series. Philadelphia, University of Pennsylvania Press, 1994.

Okri, Ben. *Songs of Enchantment.* New York: Doubleday, 1993.

An Old English Miscellany: Containing a Bestiary, Kentish Sermons, Proverbs of Alfred, Religious Poems of the Thirteenth Century, from Manuscripts in the British Museum, Bodleian Library, Jesus College Library, etc. Ed. Richard Morris. Early English Text Society, o.s., 49. London: EETS, 1872; reprint Millwood, NY: Kraus Reprint, 1988.

The Old Testament Pseudepigrapha. Ed. James H. Charlesworth. 2 vols. Garden City, NY: Doubleday, 1983–85.

On the Origin of the World. Trans. Gebhard Baethge and Orval S. Wintermute. In *The Nag Hammadi Library in English,* 162–67. Gen. ed. James Robinson. San Francisco: Harper and Row, 1981.

Ordericus Vitalis. *The Ecclesiastical History of Orderic Vitalis*. Ed. and trans. Marjorie Chibnall. 6 vols. Oxford: Clarendon, 1975.

Oribasius. *Oeuvres d'Oribase*. Ed. and trans. Charles Daremberg and Ulco Cats Bussemaker. 6 vols. Collection des medicines grecs et latins. Paris: Imprimérie Nationale, 1851–76.

Origen. *Contra Celsum*. Trans. Henry Chadwick. Cambridge: Cambridge University Press, 1980.

———. *Contre Celse*. Ed. and trans. Marcel Borret. 5 vols. Sources chrétiennes, 132, 136, 147, 150, 217. Paris: Éditions du Cerf, 1967–76.

———. [*Homeliae in Ezechielem*.] *Homélies sur Ezéchiel*. Ed. and trans. Marcel Borret. Sources chrétiennes, 352. Paris: Éditions du Cerf, 1989.

The Paraphrase of Shem. Trans. Frederick Wisse. In *The Nag Hammadi Library in English,* 309–25. Gen. ed. James Robinson. San Francisco: Harper and Row, 1981.

Paris, Matthew. *Matthei Parisiensis, monachi Sancti Albani, Chronica majora*. Ed. Henry Richards Luard. 7 vols. Rerum Britannicarum medii aevi scriptores, 57. London: Her Majesty's Stationery Office, 1872–83.

Paschasius Radbertus, Saint. *De corpore et sanguine domini*. Ed. B. Paulus. Corpus Christianorum. Continuatio medievalis, 16. Turnholt: Brepols, 1969.

———. *De nativitate Christi*. In Migne, *Patrologiae . . . latina*, 96. Paris: s.n., 185?.

———. *Paschasii Radberti De partu virginis*. Ed. E. Ann Matter. Corpus Christianorum. Continuatio medievalis, 56C. Turnholt: Brepols, 1985.

———. *Sermones*. In Migne, *Patrologiae . . . latina,* 96. Paris: s.n., 185?.

Penguin Book of Hebrew Verse. Ed. and trans. T. Carmi. New York: Penguin Books, 1981.

Pesiqta de-Rav Kahana ʻal pi ketav yad Oksford, ve-shinuye nusha'ot mi-khol kitve ha-yad u-sheride ha-genizah. Ed. Bernard [Dov] Mandelbaum. 2 vols. New York: Bet ha-midrash le-Rabenu sheba-Amerikah, 1962.

[*Pesiqta rabbati*.] *Pesikta rabbati, Discourses for Feasts, Fasts, and Special Sabbaths*. Trans. William G. Braude. 2 vols. Yale Judaica, 18. New Haven: Yale University Press, 1968.

Peter Damian, Saint. *Epistolae*. Ed. Kurt Reindel. 4 vols. In *Monumenta Germaniae Historica: Die Briefe de Deutschen Kaiserzeit,* 4. Munich, 1983–93.

———. [*Sermones*.] *Sancti Petri Damiani sermones*. Ed. Giovanni Lucchesi. Corpus Christianorum. Continuatio medievalis, 57. Turnholt: Brepols, 1983.

Peter Lombard, Bishop of Paris. [*Sententiarum libri IV*.] *Sententiae in IV libris distinctae*. 3 vols. Grottaferrata: Editiones Collegii S. Bonaventurae ad Claras Aquas, 1971–81.

Peter of Blois. *Sermones*. In Migne, *Patrologiae . . . latina*, 207. Paris: s.n., 1855.

Peter of Poitiers. *Summa de confessione Compilatio presens*. Ed. Jean Longére. Corpus Christianorum. Continuatio medievalis, 51. Turnholt: Brepols, 1980.

Peter the Venerable. [*Contra Judeos.*] *Petri Venerabilis Adversus iudeorum inveteratam duritiem*. Ed. Yvonne Friedman. Corpus Christianorum. Continuatio medievalis, 58. Turnholt: Brepols, 1985.

———. *The Letters of Peter the Venerable*. Ed. Giles Constable. 2 vols. Harvard Historical Studies, 78. Cambridge, MA: Harvard University Press, 1967.

———. *Schriften zum Islam*. Ed. and trans. Reinhold Glei. Altenberg: CIS-Verlag, 1985.

Petrus Alfonsi. [*Dialogus contra Judaeos.*] *Diálogo contra los judios*. Ed. Klaus-Peter Mieth. Trans. Esperanza Ducay. Larumbe, 9. Huesca: Instituto de Estudios Altoaragonienses, 1996.

———. *Die Disciplina clericalis des Petrus Alfonsi (das älteste Novellenbuch des Mittelalters) nach alten bekannten Handschriften*. Ed. Alfons Hilka and Werner Söderhjolm. Sammlung mittellateinischer Texte, 1. Heidelberg: C. Winter, 1911.

———. *The Disciplina clericalis of Petrus Alfonsi*. Ed. and trans. Eberhard Hermes. The Islamic World Series. Berkeley: University of California Press, 1977.

Petrus de Abano. *Conciliator controversarium, quae inter philosophos et medicos versantur . . . Libellus De venenis eodem auctore. Petri Cararii Quaestio de venenis ad terminum. Symphoriani Chaperii Lugdunensis In Conciliatorem cribationes. Quae omnia nuperrime . . . accuratissime sunt recognitia, variisque annotationibus, ac indice locupletiori illustrati*. Venice: Juntas, 1548.

Petrus Siculus. *Historia Manichaeorum; Adversus anichaeos sermons tres*. In Migne, *Patrologiae . . . graeca*, 104. Paris: s.n., 1860.

Philippe de Thaun. *Le bestiaire de Philippe de Thaun*. Ed. Emmanuel Walberg. Lund: H. Møller, 1900.

Philo of Alexandria. *Philo*. 10 vols., 2 suppl. Loeb Classical Library. London: Heinemann; New York: Putnam, 1929– .

———. *The Works of Philo: Complete and Unabridged*. New updated ed. Peabody, MA: Hendrickson, 1993.

Physiologus latinus versio y. Ed. Francis J. Carmody. University of California Publications in Classical Philology, 12:7. Berkeley: University of California Press, 1941.

Pierre de Beauvais. *Le bestiare de Pierre de Beauvais, version courte*. Ed. Guy R. Mermier. Paris: A. G. Nizet, 1977.

Pirqe de Rabi Eli'ezer—mahad mada 'it. Ed. Chaim Meir Horowitz. Jerusalem: Makor, 1972.

[*Pirqe de Rabi Eli'ezer.*] *Pirke de Rabbi Eliezer (The Chapters of Rabbi Eliezer the Great) according to the Text of the Manuscript Belonging to Abraham Epstein of Vienna*. Trans. Gerald Friedlander. New York: Hermon Press, 1970.

Pistis Sophia. Ed. Carl Schmidt. Trans. Violet Macdermot. Nag Hammadi Studies, 9. Leiden: E. J. Brill, 1978.

Plato. *Timaeus*. In *The Collected Dialogues of Plato, including the Letters*. Ed. Edith Hamilton and Huntington Cairns. Trans. Lane Cooper et al. Bollingen Series, 71. New York: Pantheon Books, 1961.

Pliny the Elder. [*Naturalis historia.*] *Natural History.* 10 vols. Loeb Classical Library. Cambridge, MA: Harvard University Press, 1938– .

Plotinus. [*Enneads.*] *Plotinus.* Trans. A. H. Armstrong. 7 vols. Loeb Classical Library. Cambridge, MA: Harvard University Press; London: Heinemann, 1966–88.

Plutarch. *Plutarch's Lives.* 11 vols. Loeb Classical Library. Cambridge, MA: Harvard University Press; London: Heinemann, 1914– .

The Polemic of Nestor the Priest: Qiṣṣat Mujādalat al-usquf and Sefer Nestor ha-Komer. Ed. and trans. Daniel J. Lasker and Sarah Stroumsa. 2 vols. Jerusalem: Ben-Zvi Institute for the Study of Jewish Communities in the East, 1996.

Polgar, Isaac. *'Ezer ha-dat.* Ed. Ya'akov Levinger. Tel-Aviv: Bet ha-sefer le-mada'e ha-Yahadut 'a. sh. Ḥayim Rozenberg, Universitat Tel-Aviv, 1984.

Porphyry. [*Against the Christians.*] *Porphyrius "gegen die christen," 15 Bücher.* Ed. Adolf von Harnack. Abhandlungen der Königlich preussischen Akademie der Wissenschaften. Jahr. 1916. Philosophisch-historische Klasse, 1. Berlin: Verlag der Königl. Akademie der Wissenschaften im Kommission bei Georg Reiner, 1916.

———. *Porphyry's Against the Christians: The Literary Remains.* Ed. and trans. R. Joseph Hoffmann. Amherst, NY: Prometheus Books, 1994.

Problemata varia anatomica: The University of Bologna, MS. 1165. Ed. L. R. Lind. University of Kansas Publications. Humanistic Studies, 38. Lawrence: University of Kansas, 1968.

The Prose Salernitan Questions: Edited from a Bodleian manuscript (Auct. F.3.10): An anonymous collection dealing with science and medicine written by an Englishman c. 1200, with an appendix of ten related collections. Ed. Brian Lawn. Auctores Britannici Medii Aevi, 5. London: Oxford University Press, 1979.

Puech, Émile. "Un hymne essènien en partie retrouvé et le béatitudes: 1QH V 12–VI 18 (+ col. XIII–XIV 7) et 4Q Béat." *Revue des Qumran* 49–52.13 (1988): 59–88.

[al-Qabīṣī] 'Abd al-'Aziz ibn 'Uthman al- Qabīṣī. *Alchabitius cum commento.* Noviter impresso. Venice: Melcior Sessa, 1512.

———. *The Introduction to Astrology: Editions of the Arabic and Latin Texts and an English Translation.* Ed. Charles Burnett, Keiji Yamamoto, and Michio Yano. London: Warburg Institute, 2004.

[al-Qalqashandī] Aḥmad ibn Alī al-Qalqashandī. *Ṣubḥ al-a'sha fī ṣina'at al-insha.* Vol. 7 of 14. Ed. M. A. Ibrahim. Cairo, 1913–20.

Al-Qazwinī, Zakarīyā ibn Muḥammad ibn Maḥmud. *Āthār al-bilād wa akhbār al-'ibād.* Beirut: Dar Sadir, 1960.

Rabanus Maurus. *De rerum naturis.* In *Opera omnia.* 6 vols. In Migne, *Patrologiae . . . latina*, 111. Paris, s.n., 1852–86.

Raoul de Caen. *Gesta Tancredi.* In *Recueil des historiens des croisades occidentaux,* vol. 3. Paris, 1866.

Ratramnus, Monk of Corbie. *Liber de Nativitate Christi.* In *Opera omnia.* In Migne, *Patrologiae . . . latina*, 121. Paris: s.n., 1852.

Recueil général des Isopets. Ed. Julia Bastin. 2 vols. Société des anciens textes français. Paris: H. Champion, 1929–30.

Recull de eximplis e miracles, gestes e faules e altres ligendes ordenades per A-B-C tretes de un manuscrit en pergami del començament del segle XV. Ed. Mariano Aguiló y Fuster. 2 vols. Barcelona: Verdaguer, 1904.

Le Registre d'inquisition de Jacques Fournier, évêque de Pamiers (1318–1325) (Manuscrit no. Vat. Latin 4030 de la Bibliothèque vaticane). Ed. Jean Duvernoy. 3 vols. Toulouse: É. Privat, 1965.

Richard de Fournival. *Li bestiaires d'amours di maistre Richart de Fornival e Li response du Bestiaire*. Ed. Cesare Segre. Documenti di filologia, 2. Milan: R. Ricciardi, 1957.

Ricoldo da Monte Croce. *Pérégination en Terre Sainte et au Proche Orient / Lettres sur la chute de Saint Jean d'Acre*. Ed. and trans. René Kappler. Paris: Champion, 1997.

Rigord. [*Gesta Philippi Augusti.*] *Oeuvres de Rigord et de Guillaume le Breton, historiens de Philippe Auguste*. Ed. H.-François Delaborde. 2 vols. Société de l'histoire de France. Publications in Octavo, 210, 224. Paris: Libraire Renouard, 1882–85.

Robert of Rheims. *Historia Hierosolimitana*. In *Recueil des historiens des croisades occidentaux* vol. 3. Paris, 1866.

Roger Bacon. *Opus maius pars septima seu moralis philosophiae*. Ed. Eugenio Massa Turin, 1953.

———. *The Opus Majus of Roger Bacon*. 2 vols. Trans. Robert Belle Burke. Bristol: Thoemmes Press, 2000.

Rudolf von Schlettstadt. *Historiae memorabiles: Zur Dominikanerliteratur u. Kulturgeschichte d. 13. Jahrhunderts*. Ed. Erich Kleinschmidt. Archiv für Kulturgeschichte; Beihefte, 10. Cologne: Bölau, 1978.

Rufinus. *Historia Ecclesiasticae*. In *Eusebius Werke*. 13 vols. Die Griechischen christlichen Schriftsteller der ersten drei Jahrhundete. Leipzig: J. C. Hinrichs, 1902– .

Rufinus of Aquileia. *Opera*. Ed. Manlio Simonetti. Corpus Christianorum. Series Latina, 20. Turnholt: Brepols, 1961.

Rufus of Ephesus. *Quaestiones medicinales*. Ed. Hans Gärtner. Bibliotheca scriptorum Graecorum et Romanorum Teubneriana [Scriptores Graeci]. Leipzig: Teubner, 1970.

Rupert of Deutz. *Ruperti Tuitensis De Sancta Trinitate et operibus eius*. Ed. Rhabanus Maurus Haacke. 4 vols. Corpus Christianorum. Continuatio medievalis, 21–24. Turnholt: Brepols, 1971–72.

———. *Opera omnia*. In Migne, *Patrologiae . . . latina*, vols. 167–70. Paris: s.n., 1854.

Rutebeuf. *Le neuf joies Nostre Dames*. In *Oeuvres completes de Rutebeuf*, 2. Ed. Edmond Faral and Julia Bastin. Paris: A. & J. Picard, 1960.

The Rylands Haggadah: A Medieval Sephardi Masterpiece in Facsimile. New York: Abrams, 1988.

Sargis Istunaya de-Gusit. *The Disputation of Sergius the Stylite against a Jew*. Ed. and trans. A. P. Hayman. 2 vols. Corpus scriptorum Christianorum Orientalium. Scriptores Syri, 152–53. Louvain: Secretariat di Corpus SCO, 1973.

Scot, Michael. [*Liber physiognomiae.*] *Liber phisionomie*. Venice: Giacopo Penicio de Leuco, 1505.

[*Seelentrost.*] *Der grosse Seelentrost: Ein niederdeutsches Erbauungsbuch des vierzehnten Jahrhunderts*. Ed. Margaret Schmitt. Miederdeytsche Studien, 5. Cologne: Böhlau Verlag, 1959.

Sefer Gezerot Ashkenaz ve-Ẓarfat: divre zikhronot mi-bene ha-dorot she bi-tequfot mas'e ha-ẓelav u-mivḥar piyuṭehem. Ed. Abraham Meir Habermann. Jerusalem: Sifre Tarshish be-siyu'a Mosad ha-Rav Kuk, 1945.

[*Sefer niẓẓaḥon ha-yashan.*] *The Jewish-Christian Debate in the High Middle Ages: A Critical Edition of the* Niẓẓaḥon vetus. Ed. and trans. David Berger. Philadelphia: Jewish Publication Society of America, 1979.

Seifried Helbling [*Werke*]. In *Satire*. Ed. Thomas Cramer. Spätmittelalterliche Texte, 5. Munich: W. Fink, 1981.

Seneca, Lucius Annaeus. [*Epistulae morales ad Lucilium.*] *Ad Lucilium epistolae morales*. 3 vols. Loeb Classical Library. London: Heinemann; New York: Putnam's Sons, 1917– .

———. *Seneca in Ten Volumes*. 10 vols. Loeb Classical Library. London: Heinemann; Cambridge, MA: Harvard University Press, 1917–72.

Severus Sozopolitanus. *La polémique antijulianiste*. Ed. Robert Hespel. 8 vols. Corpus scriptorum Christianorum Orientalium. Scriptores syri, 104–5, 124–27, 136–37. Louvain: Secrétariat du Corpus SCO, 1964– .

Sigebertus Gemblacensis. *Chronica*. Ed. Ludwig C. Bethmann. In *Scriptores rerum germanicarum*, 6/9. Hannover: Imprensis Bibliopolii Hahniani, 1844.

The Song of Roland. Trans. Dorothy L. Sayers. New York: Penguin Books, 1957.

Soranus, of Ephesus. [*Gynaecia.*] *Gynecology*. Trans. Owsei Temkin. Publications of the Institute of the History of Medicine, the Johns Hopkins University. 2d ser. Texts and Documents, 3. Baltimore: Johns Hopkins University Press, 1956.

———. [*Gynaecia.*] *Maladies des femmes*. Ed. and trans. Paul Burguière, Danielle Gourevitch, and Yves Malinas. Collection des universités de France. Paris: Belles Lettres, 1988– .

Sources and Analogues of Chaucer's Canterbury Tales. Ed. William Frank Bryan and Germaine Dempster. Chicago: University Press, 1941.

"Les sources grecques pour l'histoire des Pauliciens d'Asie Mineur. IV. Les formules d'abjurations." *Travaux et mémoires (Centre de Recherché d'Histoire et Civilization Byzantines)* 4 (1970): 190–208.

Le Speculum laicorum, édition d'une collection d'exempla, composée en Angleterre à la fin du XIIIe siècle. Ed. J. Th. Welter. Paris: A. Picard, 1914.

Stephan de Borbone. *Anecdotes historiques, légendes et apologues, tirés du recueil inédit d'Étienne de Bourbon, Dominicain du XIIIe siècle*. Ed. A. Lecoy de La Marche. Société de l'histoire de France. Publications in Octavo, 185. Paris: Librairie Renouard, H. Loones, successeur, 1877.

Suger, Abbot of Saint Denis. [Selections. English and Latin.] *Abbot Suger on the Abbey Church of St.-Denis and Its Treasures*. Ed. and trans. Erwin Panofsky. 2d ed., ed. Gerda Panofsky-Soergel. Princeton: Princeton University Press, 1971.

Le synaxaire arménien de Ter Israel. Ed. and trans. G. Bayan. 12 vols. in 3. Patrologia orientalis, 5:3, 6:2, 15:3, 16:1, 18:1, 19:1, 21:1–6. Paris: Firmin-Didot, 1910–30.

Tacitus, Cornelius. *Tacitus in Five Volumes.* 5 vols. Loeb Classical Library. London: Heinemann; Cambridge, MA: Harvard University Press, 1968–70.

[Talmud.] *The Babylonian Talmud.* Ed. Isidore Epstein. 18 vols. London: Soncino Press, 1961–90.

[Talmud.] *Talmud Bavli.* 20 vols. Jerusalem: ha-Makhon, 1972– .

[Talmud.] *The Talmud = [Talmud Bavli]: The Steinsaltz Edition.* Ed. Adin Steinsaltz. 1st Amer. ed. New York: Random House, 1989– .

[Talmud.] *Talmud Yerushalmi.* Krotishin, 1866; reprint Jerusalem, 1969.

[Talmud. Minor Tractates.] *The Minor Tractates of the Talmud: Massekhoth Ketannoth.* Ed. and trans. Abraham Cohen. 2 vols. London: Soncino Press, 1965.

[Talmud. Minor Tractates. Avot de Rabbi Nathan.] *Abhoth de Rabbi Nathan = Masekhot Avot de-Rabi Natan.* Ed. Solomon Schechter. 3d ed. Vienna: Ch. D. Lippe, 1887; reprint Hildesheim: G. Olms, 1979.

[Talmud. Minor Tractates. Avot de Rabbi Nathan.] *The Fathers according to Rabbi Nathan.* Trans. Judah Goldin. Yale Judaica, 10. New Haven: Yale University Press, 1955.

[Talmud. Minor Tractates. Kallah.] *Masekhtot kalah, ve-hen, masekhet kalah min sekhet kalah rabbati.* Ed. Michael Higger. New York: Debe Rabanan, 1936.

[Talmud. Minor Tractates. Kallah rabbati.] *Masekhet Kalah rabbati: 'im perush Lehem she'arim.* Ed. Hayim M. Mendel. Jerusalem: M. Safra, 1982–83.

[*Tanna debe Eliyahu.*] *Sefer Tana de-be Eliyahu.* Ed. Shmu'el mi-Shinovi. Warsaw, 1881–1908; reprint Jerusalem: Levin-Epshtein, 1965–66.

Tanna de be Eliyahu = The Lore of the School of Elijah. Trans. William G. [Gershon Zev] Braude and Israel J. Kapstein. Philadelphia: Jewish Publication Society of America, 1981.

Tatian. *Oratio ad Graecos and Fragments.* Ed. and trans. Moly Whittaker. Oxford: Clarendon Press, 1982.

[*Temple Scroll.*] *Megilat ha-miqdash = The Temple Scroll.* Ed. Yigael Yadin. 3 vols. Jerusalem: Israel Exploration Society, 1977–83.

Tertullian. [*Adversus Judaeos.*] *Q.S.F. Tertulliani Adversus Judaeos: Mit Einleitung und kritischen Kommentar.* Ed. Hermann Tränkle. Wiebaden: Steiner, 1964.

———. [*Adversus Marcionem.*] *Contre Marcion.* Ed. and trans. René Braun. 4 vols. Paris: Éditions du Cerf, 1990– .

———. [*Adversus Valentianos.*] *Contre les valentiniens.* Ed. and trans. Jean-Claude Fredouille. 2 vols. Sources chrétiennes, 280–81. Paris: Éditions du Cerf, 1980–81.

———. [*Apologeticum.*] *Apology; De spectaculis . . .* Loeb Classical Library. London: Heinemann; New York: Putnam's Sons, 1931.

———. [*De anima*]. *Quinti Septimi Florentis Tertulliani De anima.* Ed. J. H. Waszink. Amsterdam: J. M. Meulenhoff, 1947.

———. *De baptismo.* Ed. Bruno Luiselli. 2d ed. Corpus scriptorum Latinorum Paravanium. Turin: In aedibus Io. Bapt. Paraviae, 1968.

———. [*De carne Christi.*] *La chair du Christ.* Ed. and trans. Jean-Pierre Mahé. 2 vols. in 1. Sources chrétiennes, 216–17. Paris: Éditions du Cerf, 1975.

———. *De Ieiunio adversa psychicos*. In *Opera omnia, cum selectis praecedentium editionum lectionibus variorumque commentariis*. 2 vols. Turnholt: Brepols, 1956–71.

———. *De resurrectione mortuorum*. In *Opera omnia, cum selectis praecedentium editionum lectionibus variorumque commentariis*. 2 vols. Turnholt: Brepols, 1956–71.

Theodor Abū Qurra. *Opuscula*. In *Schriften zum Islam: Johannes Damaskenos und Theodor Abū Qurra,* ed. and trans. Reinhold Glei and Adel Théodore Khoury. Corpus Islamo-Christianum. Series Graeca, 3. Würzburg: Echter; Altenberge: Oros, 1995.

———. [Works.] *Theodori Abucaræ Carum Episcopi scripta tum historica, tum ascetica quæ supersunt*. In Migne, *Patrologiae . . . graeca*, 97. Paris: s.n., 1865.

Theodore, Bishop of Mopsuestia. [*Catechetical Homilies.*] *Les homélies catéchétiques, reproduction phototypique du MS Mingnana Syr. 561*. Trans. Raymond Tonneau and Robert Devreesse. Studi e Testi, 145. Rome: s.n., 1849.

Theophanes the Confessor. *Theophanus Chronographia*. Ed. Carl de Boor. 2 vols. Leipzig: Teubner, 1883–85; reprint Hildesheim: G. Olms, 1963.

Theophylact Lecapenus. [*Letter to Tsar Peter of Bulgaria on the Bogomils.*] "L'epistola sui Bogomili del patriarca constantinopolitano Teofilatto." In *Mélanges Eugène Tisserant*, 7 vols., 2:88–91. Studie Testi, 231–37. Vatican City: Biblioteca Apostolica Vaticana, 1964.

Thomas Aquinas, Saint. *Summa contra gentiles*. 4 in 5 vols. Garden City, NY: Hanover House, 1955–57; reprint Notre Dame: University of Notre Dame Press, 1975.

———. [*Summa contra gentiles.*] *Summe gegen die Heiden*. Ed. and trans. Karl Albert and Paulus Engelhardt. 5 vols. Texte zur Forschung, 15–19. Darmstadt: Wissenschaftliche Buchgesellschaft, 1974– .

———. [*Summa theologica.*] *Summa theologiae*. 60 vols. Cambridge: Blackfriars; New York: McGraw-Hill, 1964– .

Thomas de Cantimpré. *Bonum universale de apibus*. Ed. Georges Colvener. Douai: B. Belleri, 1627.

———. *Liber de natura rerum*. Berlin: De Gruyter, 1973.

Thomas of Monmouth. *The Life and Miracles of St. William of Norwich*. Ed. and trans. Augustus Jessopp and Montague Rhodes James. Cambridge: University Press, 1896.

Three Middle English Sermons from the Worcester Chapter Manuscript F.10. Ed. D. M. Grisdale. Kendal: T. Wilson, 1939.

[*Toldoth Jesu.*] *Das Leben Jesu nach jüdischen Quellen*. Ed. and trans. Samuel Krauss. Berlin: S. Calvary, 1902; reprint New York: s.n., 1978.

Tosfata 'atikata = Uralte Tosefta's (Borajta's): Oder, die tanaitische und amoräische Literatur aus den ersten fünf Jahrhunderten. Ed. Chaim Meir Horowitz. 5 parts in 1 vol. Frankfurt-am-Main: Horowitz, 1889–90.

The Trotula: A Medieval Compendium of Women's Medicine. Ed. and trans. Monica H. Green. Middle Ages series. Philadelphia: University of Pennsylvania Press, 2001.

Two Lives of Charlemagne. Trans. Lewis Thorpe. Penguin Classics. Harmondsworth: Penguin, 1969.

Two Lives of Marie d'Oignies. Ed. Margot H. King, Hugh Feiss, and Miriam Marsolais. 4th ed. Toronto: Peregrina, 1998.

A Valentinian Exposition. Trans. John Turner. In *The Nag Hammadi Library in English,* 481–87. Gen. ed. James Robinson. San Francisco: Harper and Row, 1981.

Vitae patrum, sive, Historia eremitica. In Migne, *Patrologiae . . . latina,* 73. Paris: s.n., 1860.

Warrāq, Muḥammad ibn Hārūn. [*Radd 'alā al-thalāth firaq min al-Naṣārā.*] *Anti-Christian Polemic in Early Islam: Abū 'Isā al-Warrāq's "Against the Trinity."* Ed. and trans. David Thomas. University of Cambridge Oriental Publications, 45. Cambridge: Cambridge University Press, 1992.

Yannai. [*Maḥazor Yanai.*] *Maḥazor piyyuṭe Rabi Yanai la-Torah vela-mo'adim*. Ed. Zvi Meir Rabinovitz. 2 vols. Jerusalem: Mosad Byalik, 1985–87.

Yeḥiel ben Joseph of Paris. [*Vikuaḥ de Rabi Yeḥi'el 'im Nikola'ush.*] *Vikuaḥ Rabenu Yeḥi'el mi-Paris*. Thorn: s.n., 1873.

Zerahyah ha-Yevani. *Sefer ha-Yashar: The Book of the Righteous*. Ed. and trans. Seymour J. Cohen. New York: Ktav, 1973.

[*Zohar.*] *Sefer ha-Zohar 'al ḥamishah ḥumshe Torah me-ha-tanna Shim'on ben Yoḥai*. Ed. Re'uven Margolies. 4 vols. in 3. Jerusalem: Mosad ha-Rav Kuk, 1964.

[*Zohar*. Selections.] *The Wisdom of the Zohar*. Hebrew trans. Fischel Lachower and Isaiah Tishby. Ed. Isaiah Tishby. English trans. David Goldstein. 3 vols. Littman Library of Jewish Civilization. Oxford: Oxford University Press, 1989.

Secondary Sources

Abel, A. "Le chapitre sur le christianisme dans le 'Tamhîd' d'al-Bâqillâni." In *Études d'orientalisme dédiées à la mémoire de Lévi-Provençal,* 1:1–11. 2 vols. Paris: G.-P. Maisonneuve et Larose, 1962.

———. "La lettre polémique 'd'Aréthas' à l'émir de Damas." *Byzantion: Revue Internationale des Études Byzantines* 24.2 (1954): 343–70.

———. "La polémique damascénienne et son influence sur les origins de la théologie musulmane." In *L'Elaboration de l'Islam: Colloque de Strasbourg, 12–13–14 juin 1959,* 61–85. Travaux du Centre d'Études Supérieures Specialize d'Histoire des Religions de Strasbourg. Paris: Presses Universitaires de France, 1961.

Ahsmann, Hubertus Petrus Johannes Maria. *Le culte de la Sainte Vierge et la littérature française profane du moyen âge*. Utrecht-Nijmegen: N.V. Dekker & Van de Vegt en J. W. Van Leeuwen; Paris: A. Picard, 1930.

Alcalay, Reuben. *The Complete Hebrew-English Dictionary*. Jerusalem: Massada, 1981.

Alexander-Frizer, Tamar. *The Pious Sinner: Ethics and Aesthetics in the Medieval Hasidic Narrative*. Texts and Studies in Medieval and Early Modern Judaism, 5. Tübingen: J. C. B. Mohr (P. Siebeck), 1991.

Allen, Peter L. *The Wages of Sin: Sex and Disease, Past and Present.* Chicago: University of Chicago Press, 2000.

Alon, Gedalia. "The Levitical Uncleanness of Gentiles." In [*Mehkarim be-Toldot Yi'srae'el.*] *Jews, Judaism, and the Classical World: Studies in Jewish History in the Times of the Second Temple and Talmud,* trans. Israel Abrahams, 146–89. Jerusalem: Magnes Press, 1977.

d'Alverny, Marie Thérèse. "Translations and Translators." In *Renaissance and Renewal in the Twelfth Century,* ed. Robert L. Benson and Giles Constable, with Carol D. Lanham, 421–62. Cambridge, MA: Harvard University Press, 1982.

Amer, Sahar. *Ésope au feminine: Marie de France et la politique de l'interculturalité.* Faux titre, 169. Amsterdam: Rodopi, 1999.

———. "Lesbian Sex and the Military: From the Medieval Arabic Tradition to French Literature." In *Same-Sex Love and Desire among Women in the Middle Ages,* ed. Francesca Canadé Sautman and Pamela Sheingorn, 179–98. New York: Palgrave, 2000.

Andrews, E. A. *A Latin Dictionary Founded on Andrews' Edition of Freund's Latin Dictionary*. Rev. and enl. Ed. Charlton T. Lewis and Charles Short. Oxford: Clarendon Press, 1879.

Angerstorfer, Andreas. "Jüdische Reaktion auf die mittelalterlichen Blutbeschuldingen vom 13. bis zum 16. Jahrhundert." In *Die Legende vom Ritualmord: Zur Geschichte der Blütbeschuldigung gegen Juden,* ed. Rainer Erb, 133–56. Reihe Dokumente, Texte, Materialien, 6. Berlin: Metropol, 1993.

Anzulewicz, Henryk. "Die Aristotelische Biologie in dem Frühwerken des Albertus Magnus." In *Aristotle's Animals in the Middle Ages and the Renaissance,* ed. Carlos Steel, Guy Guldentops, and Pieter Beullens, 159–88. Mediaevalia Lovaniensia, ser. 1, studia 27. Leuven: Leuven University Press, 1999.

Arnold, Thomas W. *Painting in Islam: A Study of the Place of Pictorial Art in Muslim Culture.* Oxford: Clarendon Press, 1928; reprint New York: Dover Press, 1965.

Assis, Yom Tov. "Sexual Behavior in Medieval Hispano-Jewish Society." In *Jewish History: Essays in Honour of Chimen Abramsky,* ed. Ada Rapoport-Albert and Steven J. Zipperstein, 25–59. London: Halban, 1988.

Astrology, Science and Society: Historical Essays. Ed. Patrick Curry. Woodbridge: Boydell Press, 1987.

Atil, Esin. *Kalila wa Dimna: Fables from a Fourteenth-Century Arabic Manuscript.* Washington, DC: Smithsonian Institution Press, 1981.

Bagby, Arthur I., Jr. "The Figure of the Jew in the *Cantigas* of Alfonso X." In *Studies on the* Cantigas de Santa María*: Art, Music and Poetry: Proceedings of the International Symposium on the* Cantígas de Santa María *of Alfonso X, el Sabio (1221–1284) In Commemoration of Its 700th Anniversary Year (New York, November 19–21),* ed. Israel J. Katz and John E. Keller, 235–45. Madison, WI: Hispanic Seminary of Medieval Studies, 1987.

Barber, Malcolm. "Lepers, Jews and Moslems: The Plot to Overthrow Christendom in 1321." *History* 66 (1991): 1–17.

Barkai, Ron. *A History of Jewish Gynaecological Texts in the Middle Ages*. Brill's Series in Jewish Studies, 20. Leiden: Brill, 1998.

Baron, S. W. *A Social and Religious History of the Jews*. 2d ed. 18 vols. New York: Columbia University Press, 1957– .

Barton, Carlin. *Sorrows of the Ancient Romans: The Gladiator and the Monster.* Princeton: Princeton University Press, 1993.

Baskin, Judith. "From Separation to Displacement: The Problem of Women in *Sefer Hasidim.*" *AJS Review* 19.1 (1994): 1–18.

———. "Woman as Other in Rabbinic Literature." In *Judaism in Late Antiquity* 3/2. ed. Jacob Neusner and Alan J. Avery-Peck, 177–96. Handbuch der Orientalistik. Erste Abteilung, Nahe und Mittlere Osten, 53. Leiden: E. J. Brill, 1999.

Bauchau, Benedicte. "Science et racisme: Les Juifs, la lèpre et la peste." *Stanford French Review* 13 (1989): 21–35.

Baumgarten, Albert I. "The Temple Scroll, Toilet Practices, and the Essenes." *Jewish History* 10.1 (1996): 9–20.

Baumgarten, Joseph. "Halakhic Polemics in New Fragments from Qumran Cave 4." In *Biblical Archaeology Today: Proceedings of the International Congress on Biblical Archaeology, Jerusalem, April 1984,* 390–99. Jerusalem: Israel Exploration Society, 1985.

———. "The Laws about Fluxes in 4Q Tohora a (4Q 274)." In *Time to Prepare the Way in the Wilderness: Papers on the Qumran Scrolls,* ed. Devorah Dimant and Lawrence H. Schiffman, 1–8. Studies on the Texts of the Desert of Judah, 16. Leiden: E. J. Brill, 1995.

———. "The Purification Rituals in DJD 7." In *The Dead Sea Scrolls: Forty Years of Research,* ed. Devorah Dimant and Uriel Rappaport, 199–209. Studies on the Texts of the Desert of Judah, 10. Leiden: E. J. Brill; Jerusalem: Magnes Press, 1992.

———. "Zab Impurity in Qumran and Rabbinic Law." *Journal of Jewish Studies* 45.2 (1994): 273–77.

Beer, Jeanette. "Duel of Bestiaries." In *Beasts and Birds of the Middle Ages: The Bestiary and Its Legacy,* ed. Willene B. Clark and Meradith T. McMunn, 96–105. Middle Ages series. Philadelphia: University of Pennsylvania Press, 1989.

Bekkum, Wout J. C. van. "Anti-Christian Polemics in Hebrew Liturgical Poetry *(piyyut)* of the Sixth and Seventh Centuries." In *Early Christian Poetry: A Collection of Essays*, ed. J. Den Boeft and A. Hillhorst, 297–308. Supplements to Vigilae Christianae, 22. Leiden: E. J. Brill, 1993.

Berger, David. "Christian Heresy and Jewish Polemic in the Twelfth and Thirteenth Centuries." *Harvard Theological Review* 68 (1975): 287–303.

———. "Gilbert Crispin, Allan of Lille, and Jacob ben Reuben," *Speculum* 49 (1974): 34–47.

———. "Mission to the Jews and Jewish-Christian Contacts in the Polemical Literature of the High Middle Ages." *American Historical Review* 91 (1986): 576–91.

Berger, Michael S. *Rabbinic Authority*. New York: Oxford University Press, 1998.

Bernfeld, Simon. *Sefer ha-dema'ot: me'ora'ot ha-gezerot veha-redifot ve-hashmadot.* 3 vols. Berlin: Eshkol, 1923–26.

Biale, David. "Counter-History and Jewish Polemics against Christianity: The 'Sefer toledot yeshu' and the 'Sefer zerubavel.'" *Jewish Social Studies* 6.1 (1999): 130–45.

———. *Eros and the Jews: From Biblical Israel to Contemporary America*. Berkeley: University of California Press, 1997.

Biale, Rachel. *Women and Jewish Law: The Essential Texts, Their History, and Their Relevance for Today.* New York: Schocken Books, 1995.

Biddick, Kathleen. "Genders, Bodies, Borders: Technologies of the Visible." *Speculum* 68 (1993): 389–418.

Biller, Peter. "A 'Scientific' View of Jews from Paris around 1300." *Micrologus: Natura, Scienze e Società Medievali*, 9 (2001): 137–68.

———."Views of Jews from Paris around 1300: Christian or 'Scientific'?" In *Christianity and Judaism: Papers Read at the 1991 Summer Meeting and the 1992 Winter Meeting of the Ecclesiastical History Society,* ed. Diana Wood, 187–207. Cambridge, MA: Ecclesiastical History Society, 1992.

Bloch, R. Howard. *Medieval Misogyny and the Invention of Western Romantic Love.* Chicago: University of Chicago Press, 1991.

Block, Elaine. "Bell the Cat and Gnaw the Bone: Animals and Proverbs on Misericords." *Reinardus: Yearbook of the International Reynard Society* 4 (1991): 41–50.

———. *Corpus of Medieval Misericords in France XIII–XVI Century.* Turnhout: Brepols, 2003.

———. "Judaic Imagery on Medieval Choirstalls," *Reinardus: Yearbook of the International Reynard Society* 8 (1995): 26–47.

———. "Half Angel–Half Beast: Images of Women on Misericords." *Reinardus: Yearbook of the International Reynard Society* 5 (1992): 17–34.

Blood Magic: The Anthropology of Menstruation. Ed. Thomas Buckley and Alma Gottlieb. Berkeley: University of California Press, 1988.

Blumenkranz, Bernhard. *Le Juif médiéval au miroir de l'art chrétien.* Paris: Études augustiniennes, 1966.

———. *Juifs et Chrétiens: Patristique et Moyen Âge.* Variorum Reprint, CS 70. London: Variorum Reprints, 1977.

Bonfil, Reuben. "Edoto shel Agobard mi-Leon 'al 'olamam ha-ruchani shel yehude 'iro beme'a ha-tesh'it." In *Mehkarim ba-kabalah, be-filosofyah yehudit uve-sifrut ha-musar vehe-hagut: mugashim li-Yesh'ayah Tishbi bi-milot lo shiv'im vi-hamesh sharim,* ed. Joseph Dan and Joseph Hecker, 327–48. Jerusalem: Magnes Press, 1986.

Borchers, Susanne. *Judisches Frauenleben im Mittelalter: Die Texte des Sefer Chasidim.* Judentum und Umwelt, 68. Frankfurt-am-Main: Peter Lang, 1998.

Bos, Gerrit, and Resianne Fontaine. "Medico-Philosophical Controversies in Nathan b. Yo'el Falaquera's *Sefer Sori ha-Gut.*" *Jewish Quarterly Review* 90.1–2 (1999): 27–60.

Boswell, John. *Christianity, Social Tolerance, and Homosexuality: Gay People in Western Europe from the Beginning of the Christian Era to the Fourteenth Century.* Chicago: University of Chicago Press, 1980.

Bouhdiba, Abdel wahab. La sexualité en Islam. Paris: 1979.

Boyarin, Daniel. *Carnal Israel: Reading Sex in Talmudic Culture.* New Historicism: Studies in Cultural Poetics, 25. Berkeley: University of California Press, 1993.

———. *Dying for God: Martyrdom and the Making of Christianity and Judaism.* Figurae. Stanford, CA: Stanford University Press, 1999.

———. "The Great Fat Massacre: Sex, Death, and the Grotesque Body in the Talmud." In *People of the Body: Jews and Judaism from an Embodied Perspective,* ed. Howard Eilberg-Schwartz, 69–100. Body in Culture, History, and Religion. Albany: State University of New York Press, 1992.

———. *Intertextuality and the Reading of Midrash*. Indiana Studies in Biblical Literature. Bloomington: Indiana University Press, 1990.

———. *Unheroic Conduct: The Rise of Heterosexuality and the Invention of the Jewish Man*. Contraversions, 8. Berkeley: University of California Press, 1997.

Boyce, Mary. *Zoroastrians: Their Religious Beliefs and Practices*. Library of Religious Beliefs and Practices. London: Routledge and Kegan Paul, 1979.

Brandenburg, Dietrich. *Priesterärzte und Heilkunst im alten Persien*. Stuttgart: J. Fink, 1969.

Brann, Ross. *Power in the Portrayal: Representations of Jews and Muslims in Eleventh- and Twelfth-Century Islamic Spain*. Princeton: Princeton University Press, 2002.

Breuer, Mordechai. "Dimonio shel ha-historion ve-ha-'emet ha-historit." *Tsiyon* 59.2–3 (1994): 317–25.

Brody, Saul Nathaniel. *The Disease of the Soul: Leprosy in Medieval Literature*. Ithaca: Cornell University Press, 1974.

Brooten, Bernadette J. *Love between Women: Early Christian Responses to Female Homoeroticism*. Chicago Series on Sexuality, History and Society. Chicago: University of Chicago Press, 1996.

Browe, Peter. *Die Judenmission im Mittelalter und die Päpste*. Rome: SALER, 1942.

Brown, Peter [Robert Lamont]. "Bodies and Minds: Sexuality and Renunciation in Early Christianity." In *Before Sexuality: The Construction of Erotic Experience in the Ancient Greek World,* ed. David M. Halperin, John J. Winkler, and Froma I. Zeitlin, 479–93. Princeton: Princeton University Press, 1990.

———. *The Body and Society: Men, Women, and Sexual Renunciation in Early Christianity*. Lectures on the History of Religions, n.s., 13. New York: Columbia University Press, 1988.

———. *The Cult of the Saints: Its Rise and Function in Latin Christianity*. Haskell Lectures on the History of Religions, n.s., 2. Chicago: University of Chicago Press, 1981.

Le brûlement du Talmud à Paris: 1242–1244. Ed. Gilbert Dahan with Elie Nicolas. Nouvelle Gallia Judaica. Paris: Éditions du Cerf, 1999.

Brundage, James A. *Law, Sex, and Christian Society in Medieval Europe*. Chicago: University of Chicago Press, 1987.

Büchler, Adolf. "The Levitical Impurity of the Gentile in Palestine before the Year 70." *Jewish Quarterly Review*, n.s., 17 (1926/7): 1–81.

Buckley, Jorunn Jacobsen. "Tools and Tasks: Elchasaite and Manichaean Purification Rituals." *Journal of Religion* 66 (1986): 399–411.

Bulliet, Richard W. *Conversion to Islam in the Medieval Period: An Essay in Quantitative History*. Cambridge, MA: Harvard University Press, 1979.

Bullough, Vern L. "On Being a Man in the Middle Ages." In *Medieval Masculinities: Regarding Men in the Middle Ages,* ed. Clare A. Lees, with Thelma Fenster and Jo Ann McNamara, 31–46. Medieval Cultures, 7. Minneapolis: University of Minnesota Press, 1994.

Burman, Thomas E. *Religious Polemic and the Intellectual History of the Mozarabs, c. 1050–1200.* Brill's Studies in Intellectual History. Leiden: E. J. Brill, 1994.

Burr, David B. "The Apocalyptic Element in Olivi's Critique of Aristotle." *Church History* 40 (1971): 15–29.

———. "Petrus Ioannis Olivi and the Philosophers." *Franciscan Studies* 34 (1971): 41–71.

Butler, Judith. *Excitable Speech: A Politics of the Performative.* New York: Routledge, 1997.

Buytaert, Eligius M. "Another Copy of Cerbanus' Version of John Damascene." *Antonianum* 40 (1965): 303–10.

Bynum, Caroline Walker. *Fragmentation and Redemption: Essays on Gender and the Human Body in the Middle Ages.* New York: Zone Books, 1991.

———. *Holy Feast and Holy Fast: The Religious Significance of Food to Medieval Women.* New Historicism: Studies in Cultural Poetics. Berkeley: University of California Press, 1987.

———. *Jesus as Mother: Studies in the Spirituality of the High Middle Ages.* Publications of the Center for Medieval and Renaissance Studies, UCLA, 16. Berkeley: University of California Press, 1982.

———. *The Resurrection of the Body in Western Christianity, 200–1336.* Lectures on the History of Religions, n.s., 15. New York: Columbia University Press, 1995.

Cadden, Joan. *Meanings of Sex Difference in the Middle Ages: Medicine, Science, and Culture.* Cambridge History of Medicine. Cambridge: Cambridge University Press, 1993.

The Cambridge World History of Food. Ed. Kenneth F. Kiple and Kriemhild Coneè Ornelas. 2 vols. Cambridge: Cambridge University Press, 2000.

Cameron, Averil. "Sacred and Profane Love: Thoughts on Byzantine Gender." In *Women, Men, and Eunuchs: Gender in Byzantium,* 1–23. London: Routledge, 1997.

Camille, Michael. "Bestiary or Biology? Aristotle's Animals in Oxford Merton College, MS 271." In *Aristotle's Animals in the Middle Ages and the Renaissance,* ed. Carlos Steel, Guy Guldentops, and Pieter Beullens, 355–96. Mediaevalia Lovaniensia, ser. 1, studia 27. Leuven: Leuven University Press, 1999.

———. *Image on the Edge: The Margins of Medieval Art.* Essays in Art and Culture. Cambridge, MA: Harvard University Press, 1992.

Camporesi, Piero. "The Consecrated Host: A Wondrous Excess." In *Fragments for a History of the Human Body,* ed. Michel Feher, with Ramona Naddaff and Nadia Tazi, 1:220–37. 3 vols. New York: Urzone, 1989.

Carpenter, Dwayne E. "Social Perception and Literary Portrayal: Jews and Muslims in Medieval Spain." In *Convivencia: Jews, Muslims, and Christians in Medieval Spain,* ed. Vivian B. Mann, Thomas F. Glick, and Jerrilyn D. Dodds, 61–81. New York: G. Braziller, 1992.

Carson, Anne. "Putting Her in Her Place: Women, Dirt and Desire." In *Before Sexuality: The Construction of Erotic Experience in the Ancient Greek World,* ed. David M. Halperin, John J. Winkler, and Froma I. Zeitlin, 135–69. Princeton: Princeton University Press, 1990.

Carter, K. Codell. "An Illustration of the Religious Foundations of Talmudic Medicine; Tractate Megillah, fol. 27b–28a." *Korot* 9.1–2 (1985): 92–98.

Catalogue of the Romances in the Department of Manuscripts in the British Museum. 3 vols. Ed. J. A. Herbert. London: British Museum, 1883–1910.

Chadwick, Henry. *The Early Church.* Pelican History of the Church, 1. London: Penguin Books, 1967.

Chazan, Robert. "The Barcelona 'Disputation' of 1263: Christian Missionizing and Jewish Response." *Speculum* 52 (1977): 824–42.

———. "The Blois Incident of 1171: A Study in Jewish Intercommunal Organization." In *Medieval Jewish Life: Studies from the Proceedings of the American Academy of Jewish Research,* ed. Robert Chazan, 334–52. New York: Ktav, 1976.

———. "Chapter Thirteen of the '*Mahazik Emunah*': Further Light on Friar Paul Christian and the New Christian Missionizing." *Michael* 12 (1991): 9–26.

———. "The Condemnation of the Talmud Reconsidered (1239–1248)." *Proceedings of the American Academy of Jewish Research* 55 (1989): 11–30.

———. "Confrontation in the Synagogue of Narbonne: A Christian Sermon and a Jewish Reply." *Harvard Theological Review* 67 (1974): 437–57.

———. *Daggers of Faith: Thirteenth-Century Christian Missionizing and Jewish Response.* Berkeley: University of California Press, 1989.

———. *European Jewry and the First Crusade.* Berkeley: University of California Press, 1987.

———. "From Friar Paul to Friar Raymond: The Development of Innovative Missionizing Argumentation." *Harvard Theological Review* 76 (1983): 289–306.

———. "Maestro Alfonso of Valladolid and the New Missionizing." *Revue des Études Juives* 143 (1984): 83–94.

———. *Medieval Jewry in Northern France: A Social and Political History.* Johns Hopkins University Studies in Historical and Political Science, 91st ser., 2. Baltimore: Johns Hopkins University Press, 1973.

———. *Medieval Stereotypes and Modern Antisemitism.* Berkeley: University of California Press, 1997.

———. "Polemical Themes in the *Milhemet Mizvah.*" In *Les Juifs au regard de l'histoire: Mélanges en l'honneur de Bernhard Blumenkranz,* ed. Gilbert Dahan, 169–84. Paris: A. Picard, 1985.

Chibnall, Marjorie. "Pliny's *Natural History* and the Middle Ages." In *Empire and Aftermath: Silver Latin II,* ed. T. A. Dorey, 57–77. Greek and Latin Studies: Classical Literature and Its Influence. London: Routledge and Kegan Paul, 1975.

Choksy, Jamsheed K. *Purity and Pollution in Zoroastrianism: Triumph over Evil.* Austin: University of Texas Press, 1989.

Christian Arabic Apologetics during the Abbasid Period, 750–258. Ed. Salil Khamir Salil and Jorgen Nielsen. Leiden: E. J. Brill, 1994.

Classen, Peter. *Burgundio von Pisa: Richter, Gesandter, Übersetzer*. Sitzungsberichte der Heidelberger Akademie der Wissenschaften: philosophisch-historische Klasse; Jahr. 1974, Abh. 4. Heidelberg: C. Winter, 1974.

Cluse, Christoph. "'*Fabula ineptissima*': Die Ritualmordlegende um Adam von Bristol nach der Handschrift London, British Library, Harley 957." *Aschkenas* 5 (1995): 293–330.

Cohen, Jeffrey Jerome. "On Saracen Enjoyment: Some Fantasies of Race in Late Medieval France and England." *Journal of Medieval and Early Modern Studies* 31.1 (2001): 113–46.

Cohen, Jeremy. "The Christian Adversary of Solomon ben Adret." *Jewish Quarterly Review* 71 (1980–81): 48–55.

———. *The Friars and the Jews: The Evolution of Medieval Anti-Judaism*. Ithaca: Cornell University Press, 1982.

———. "Gezirot 1096: ha-me'or'ot ve ha-'alilot sipurei kidush ha shem be heksharam ha tarbuti-ha hevrati." *Tsiyon* 59.2–3 (1994): 169–208.

———. "The Jews as Killers of Christ in the Latin Tradition, from Augustine to the Friars." *Traditio* 39 (1983): 1–27.

———. "Scholarship and Intolerance in the Medieval Academy: The Study and Evaluation of Judaism in European Christendom." *American Historical Review* 91 (1986): 592–613.

———. "A 1096 Complex? Constructing the First Crusade in Jewish Historical Memory, Medieval and Modern." In *Jews and Christians in Twelfth-Century Europe,* ed. Michael A. Signer and John van Engen, 9–26. Notre Dame Conference in Medieval Studies, 10. Notre Dame: University of Notre Dame Press, 2001.

Cohen, Mark R. *Under Crescent and Cross: The Jews in the Middle Ages*. Princeton: Princeton University Press, 1994.

Cohen, Shaye. "Menstruants and the Sacred in Judaism and Christianity." In *Women's History and Ancient History,* ed. Sarah B. Pomeroy, 273–99. Chapel Hill: University of North Carolina Press, 1991.

———. "Purity and Piety: The Separation of Menstruants from the Sancta." In *Daughters of the King: Women and the Synagogue, a Survey of History, Kalakhah, and Contemporary Realities,* ed. Susan Grossman and Rivka Haut, 103–15. 1st ed. Philadelphia: Jewish Publication Society, 1992.

Cohen-Aloro, Dorith. "Me-hokhmata' 'ail'ah li-hokhmata' de-trefei 'ailona': ha-kishuf be-sefer ha-zohar ke-po'al yotse' shel heta' ha-'adam ha-rishon." *Da'at* 19 (1987): 31–65.

Cole, Penny J. "'God the Heathen Have Come into Your Inheritance' (Ps. 78:1): The Theme of Religious Pollution in Crusade Documents, 1095–1188." In *Crusaders and Muslims in Twelfth-Century Syria,* ed. Maya Shatzmiller, 84–111. Leiden: E. J. Brill, 1993.

Constable, Giles. "The Ideal of the Imitation of Christ." In *Three Studies in Medieval Religious and Social Thought,* 143–248. Cambridge: Cambridge University Press, 1995.

Constantine the African and 'Alî ibn al-'Abbâs al-Magûsî: The Pantegni *and Related Texts*. Ed. Charles Burnett and Danielle Jacquart. Studies in Ancient Medicine, 10. Leiden: E. J. Brill, 1994.

Contagion: Perspectives from Pre-modern Societies. Ed. Lawrence I. Conrad and Dominik Wujastyk. Aldershot: Ashgate, 2000.

Corbeill, Anthony. "Dining Deviants in Roman Political Invective." In *Roman Sexualities,* ed. Judith P. Hallett and Marilyn B. Skinner, 99–128. Princeton: Princeton University Press, 1997.

Crone, Patricia. "Islam, Judeo-Christianity and Byzantine Iconoclasm." *Jerusalem Studies in Arabic and Islam* 2 (1980): 1–11.

Crone, Patricia, and Michael Cook. *Hagarism: The Making of the Islamic World*. Cambridge: Cambridge University Press, 1977.

Cuffel, Alexandra. " 'Henceforward All Generations Will Call Me Blessed': Medieval Christian Tales of Non-Christian Marian Devotion." *Mediterranean Studies* 12 (2002): 37–60.

Dahan, Gilbert. *Les intellectuels chrétiens et les Juifs au Moyen Âge*. Patrimoines Judaïsme. Paris: Éditions du Cerf, 1990.

———. "Les Juifs dans les *Miracles* de Gautier de Coincy." *Archives Juives* 16 (1980): 3:41–49, 4:59–68.

Dagron, Gilbert. "Histoire et civilisation du monde bysantini: Aux frontières du domaine chrétien; gens de savoire, philosophes astrologues." *Annuaire du College de France* 80 (1979): 665–73.

Dalman, Gustaf. [*Jesus Christ im Talmud*. English and Hebrew.] *Jesus Christ in the Talmud, Midrash, Zohar and the Liturgy of the Synagogue*. Cambridge: Deighton Bell, 1893.

Daniel, Norman. *Islam and the West: The Making of an Image*. Rev. ed. Oxford: Oneworld, 1993.

Darmesteter, Arsène. "L'auto de fé de Troyes." *Revue des Études Juives* 2 (1881): 199–247.

———. "Deux elegies du Vatican." *Romania* 3 (1874): 1–46.

Dauphin, Claudine. "Leprosy, Lust and Lice: Health and Hygiene in Byzantine Palestine." *Bulletin of the Anglo-Israel Archaeological Society* 15 (1996–97): 55–80.

Davies, Philip R. *The Damascus Covenant: An Interpretation of the "Damascus Document."* Journal for the Study of the Old Testament, suppl. Ser., 25. Sheffield: JSOP Press, 1983.

Dean-Jones, Lesley. *Women's Bodies in Classical Greek Science*. Oxford: Clarendon Press; New York: Oxford University Press, 1994.

Delacampagne, Christian. *L'invention du racisme: Antiquité et Moyen Âge*. Paris: Fayard, 1983.

Delius, Walter. *Geschichte der Marienverehrung*. Munich: E. Reinhardt, 1963.

———. *Texte zur Mariologie und Marienverehung der mittelalterlichen Kirche*. Kleine Texte für Vorlesungen und Übungen, 184. Berlin: De Gruyter, 1961.

Demaitre, Luke. The Description and Diagnosis of Leprosy by Fourteenth-Century Physicians." *Bulletin of the History of Medicine* 59 (1985): 327–44.

———. "The Relevance of Futility: Jordanus de Turre (fl. 1313–1335) on the Treatment of Leprosy." *Bulletin of the History of Medicine* 70 (1996): 25–61.

Detienne, Marcel. [*Jardins d'Adonis.*] *The Gardens of Adonis: Spices in Greek Mythology*. Trans. Janet Lloyd. Mythos. Princeton: Princeton University Press, 1994.

Dinari, Yedidya. "Hilul ha-kodesh 'al-yadei niddah ve-takanat 'Ezra.'" *Te'udah* 3 (1983): 17–37.

———. "Minhagei ṭum'at ha-niddah-mekoram ve-hishtalshelutam." *Tarbits* 49 (1979–80): 302–24.

Dodds, E. R. *Pagan and Christian in an Age of Anxiety: Some Aspects of Religious Experience from Marcus Aurelius to Constantine*. Wiles Lectures, 1963. Cambridge: University Press, 1965.

Dols, Michael W[alters]. "The Leper in Medieval Islamic Society." *Speculum* 58 (1983): 891–916.

———. "Leprosy in Medieval Arabic Medicine." *Journal of the History of Medicine and Allied Sciences* 34 (1979): 314–33.

Dondaine, Antoine. "Hughes Etherien et Leon Toscan." *Archives d'Histoire Doctrinale et Littéraire du moyen Âge* 19 (1952): 67–134.

Douglas, Mary. *Implicit Meanings: Essays in Anthropology*. London: Routledge and Kegan Paul, 1975.

———. *Natural Symbols: Explorations in Cosmology*. 1st Amer. ed. New York: Pantheon Books, 1970.

———. *Purity and Danger: An Analysis of the Concepts of Pollution and Taboo*. London: Routledge and Kegan Paul, 1966.

———. *Risk and Blame: Essays in Cultural Theory*. London: Routledge, 1992.

Druce, G. C. "The Sow and the Pigs: A Study in Metaphor." *Archaeologia Cantiana* 46 (1934): 1–6.

Dunn, Thomas Franklin, Jr. *The* facetiae *of the* Mensa philosophica. Washington University studies, n.s., Language and Literatue, 5. St. Louis: s.n., 1934.

Dupont, Florence. [*Vie quotidienne du citoyen romain sous la République.*] *Daily Life in Ancient Rome*. Trans. Christopher Woodall. Oxford: Blackwell, 1993.

Eilberg-Schwartz, Howard. *God's Phallus and Other Problems for Men and Monotheism*. Boston: Beacon Press, 1994.

———. "The Problem of the Body for the People of the Body." In *People of the Body: Jews and Judaism from an Embodied Perspective,* ed. Howard Eilberg-Schwartz, 17–46. Body in Culture, History, and Religion. Albany: State University of New York Press, 1992.

———. *The Savage in Judaism: An Anthropology of Israelite Religion and Ancient Judaism*. Bloomington: Indiana University Press, 1990.

Einbinder, Susan L. *Beautiful Death: Jewish Poetry and Martyrdom in Medieval France*. Princeton: Princeton University Press, 2002.

———. "The Jewish Martyrs of Blois." In *Medieval Hagiography: An Anthology,* ed. Thomas Head. New York: Garland, 2000.

———. "Jewish Women Martyrs: Changing Models of Representation," *Exemplaria* 12.1 (2000): 105–27.

———. "Pucellina of Blois: Romantic Myths and Narrative Conventions." *Jewish History* 12.1 (1998): 29–46.

———. "The Troyes Laments: Jewish Martyrology in Hebrew and Old French." *Viator* 30 (1999): 201–30.

Elbogen, Ismar. [*Jüdische Gottesdienst in seiner geschichtlichen Entwicklung.*] *Jewish Liturgy: A Comprehensive History*. Trans. Raymond P. Scheindlin. Philadelphia: Jewish Publication Society; New York: Jewish Theological Seminary of America, 1993.

Ell, Stephen. "Blood and Sexuality in Medieval Leprosy." *Janus* (1984): 153–64.

———. "Reconstructing the Epidemiology of Medieval Leprosy: Preliminary Efforts with Regard to Scandinavia." *Perspectives in Biology and Medicine* 31 (1988): 496–506.

Elliott, Dyan. *Fallen Bodies: Pollution, Sexuality and Demonology in the Middle Ages*. Middle Ages series. Philadelphia: University of Pennsylvania Press, 1999.

———. "Pollution, Illusion, and Masculine Disarray: Nocturnal Emissions and the Sexuality of the Clergy." In *Constructing Medieval Sexuality,* ed. Karma Lochrie, Peggy McCracken, and James A. Schultz, 1–23. Medieval Cultures, 11. Minneapolis: University of Minnesota Press, 1997.

———. *Spiritual Marriage: Sexual Abstinence in Medieval Wedlock*. Princeton: Princeton University Press, 1993.

Encyclopaedia Judaica. 17 vols. Corrected ed. Jerusalem: Encyclopaedia Judaica, 1982–93.

Epstein, Marc Michael. *Dreams of Subversion in Medieval Jewish Art and Literature*. University Park: Pennsylvania State University Press, 1997.

———. "'The Ways of Truth Are Curtailed and Hidden': A Medieval Hebrew Fable as a Vehicle for Covert Polemic." *Prooftexts* 14.3 (1994): 205–31.

Escherick, Joseph W. *The Origins of the Boxer Uprising*. Berkeley: University of California Press, 1987.

Ettinghausen, Richard. *Arab Painting*. Geneva: Skira, 1962.

Fabre-Vassas, Claudine. [*Bête singulière.*] *The Singular Beast: Jews, Christians, and the Pig*. European Perspectives. New York: Columbia University Press, 1997.

Ficker, Gerhard. *Die Phundagiagiten: Ein Beitrag zur Ketzergeschichte des byzantischen Mittelalters*. Leipzig: J. A. Barth, 1908.

Fine, John V. A., Jr. *The Early Medieval Balkans: A Critical Survey from the Sixth to the Late Twelfth Century*. Ann Arbor: University of Michigan Press, 1983.

Fishbane, Michael A. "Midrashic Theologies and Messianic Suffering." In *The Exegetical Imagination: On Jewish Thought and Theology,* 73–85. Cambridge, MA: Harvard University Press, 1998.

Flandrin, Jean-Louis. *Le sexe et l'Occident: Évolution des attitudes et des comportements*. L'Univers historique. Paris: Seuil, 1981.

Fleischer, Ezra. "Yahasei Notsrim-Yehudim be-yamei ha-benaim be ra'i 'akom.'" *Tsiyon* 59.2–3 (1994): 267–316.

Fowden, Garth. *The Egyptian Hermes: A Historical Approach to the Late Pagan Mind.* Mythos. Princeton: Princeton University Press, 1993.

Freedman, Paul H. *Images of the Medieval Peasant*. Stanford, CA: Stanford University Press, 1999.

Frey, Jörg. "Different Patterns of Dualistic Thought in the Qumran Library: Reflections on Their Background and History." In *Legal Texts and Legal Issues: Proceedings of the Second Meeting of the International Organization for Qumran Studies, Cambridge, 1995: Published in Honor of Joseph M. Baumgarten,* ed. Moshe Bernstein, Florentino García Martínez, and John Kampen. Studies on the Texts of the Desert of Judah, 23. Leiden: E. J. Brill, 1997.

Funkenstein, Amos. *Perceptions of Jewish History*. Berkeley: University of California Press, 1993.

Gager, John G. "Body-Symbols and Social Reality: Resurrection, Incarnation and Asceticism in Early Christianity." *Religion* 12 (1982): 345–63.

Gendering the Crusades. Ed. Susan B. Edgington and Sarah Lambert. Cardiff: University of Wales Press, 2001.

Gero, Stephen. *Byzantine Iconoclasm during the Reign of Leo III; With Particular Attention to the Oriental Sources*. Corpus scriptorum Christianorum Orientalium, 346. Subsidia, t. 41. Louvain: Secrétariat du Corpus, 1973.

Gersh, Stephen. "Platonism-Neoplatonism-Aristotelianism: A Twelfth-Century Metaphysical System and Its Sources." In *Renaissance and Renewal in the Twelfth Century,* ed. Robert L. Benson and Giles Constable, with Carol D. Lanham, 512–34. Cambridge, MA: Harvard University Press, 1982.

Gerson, L. P. *God and Greek Philosophy: Studies in the Early History of Natural Theology*. Issues in Ancient Philosophy. London: Routledge, 1990.

Gilman, Sander L. *Jewish Self-Hatred: Anti-Semitism and the Hidden Language of the Jews*. Baltimore: Johns Hopkins University Press, 1986.

———. *The Jew's Body*. New York: Routledge, 1991.

Glorieux, Palémon. *La littérature quodlibétique*. 2 vols. Bibliothèque thomiste. La Saulchoir: Revue des Sciences Philosophiques et Théologiques, 1935.

Goldberg, Harriet. "Two Parallel Medieval Commonplaces: Antifeminism and Anti-Semitism in Hispanic Literary Tradition." In *Aspects of Jewish Culture in the Middle Ages: Papers of the Eighth Annual Conference of the Center for Medieval and Early Renaissance Studies, State University of New York at Binghamton, 3–5 May 1974,* ed. Paul E. Szarmach, 85–119. Albany: State University of New York Press, 1979.

Goldenberg, David M. *The Curst of Ham: Race and Slavery in Early Judaism, Christianity, and Islam.* Princeton: Princeton University Press, 2003.

Goldstein, Morris. *Jesus in the Jewish Tradition*. New York: Macmillan, 1950.

Goshen-Gottstein, Alon. "The Body as Image of God in Rabbinic Literature." *Harvard Theological Review* 87.2 (1994): 171–95.

Gow, Andrew Colin. *The Red Jews: Antisemitism in an Apocalyptic Age, 1200–1600.* Studies in Medieval and Reformation Thought, 55. Leiden: E. J. Brill, 1995.

Grabmayer, Johannes. "Rudolf von Schlettstadt und das aschkenasische Judentum um 1300." *Aschkenas: Zeitschrift für Geschichte und Kultur der Juden* 4 (1994): 301–36.

Grayzel, Solomon. *The Church and the Jews in the XIIIth Century: A Study of Their Relations during the Years 1198–1254, Based on the Papal Letters and the Conciliar Decrees of the Period.* Philadelphia: Dropsie College for Hebrew and Cognate Learning, 1933.

Green, Monica H. "The Transmission of Ancient Theories of Female Physiology and Disease through the Early Middle Ages." Ph.D. dissertation, Princeton University, 1985.

———. *Women's Healthcare in the Medieval West: Texts and Contexts*. Variorum Collected Studies Series, CS680. Aldershot: Ashgate, 2000.

Greenberg, Moshe. "The Etymology of *nidah* 'Menstrual Impurity.'" In *Solving Riddles and Untying Knots: Biblical, Epigraphic, and Semitic Studies in Honor of Jonas C. Greenfield,* ed. Ziony Zevit, Seymour Gitin, and Michael Sokoloff, 69–77. Winona Lake, IN: Eisenbrauns, 1995.

Gregg, Joan Young. *Devils, Women, and Jews: Reflections of the Other in Medieval Sermon Stories*. SUNY Series in Medieval Studies. Albany: State University of New York Press, 1997.

Grmek, Mirko D. *Diseases in the Ancient Greek World.* Trans. Mireille Muellner and Leonard Muellner. Baltimore: Johns Hopkins University Press, 1991.

Grossman, Avraham. "'ha Ge'ulah ha-megayet': be mishnatim shel hakhamei 'ashkenaz ha-ri'shonim," *Tsiyon* 59.2–3 (1994): 325–42.

———. "The Status of the Jewish Women in Germany (10th–12th Centuries." In *Zur Geschichte der jüdischen Frau in Deutschland,* ed. Julius Carlebach, 17–35. Berlin: Metropol, 1993.

Grubmüller, Klaus. "Fabel, Exempel, Allegorese: Über Sinnbildungsverfahren und Verwendungzusammenhänge." In *Exempel und Exempelsammlungen,* ed. Walter Haug and Burghart Wachinger, 58–76. Fortuna vitrea, 2. Tübingen: M. Niemeyer, 1991.

Gruenwald, Ithamar. "The Problem of the Anti-Gnostic Polemic in Rabbinic Literature." In *Studies in Gnosticism and Hellenistic Religions: Presented to Gilles Quispel on the Occasion of His 65th Birthday,* ed. R. van den Broek and M. J. Vermaseren, 171–89. Études preliminaries aux religions orientales dans l'Empire romain, 91. Leiden: E. J. Brill, 1981.

Güdemann, Moritz. *Geschichte des Erziehungswesens und der Cultur der abenländischen Juden während des Mittelalters und der neueren Zeit.* 3 vols. 1880–88; reprint Amsterdam: Philo Press, 1966.

Guerreau-Jalabert, Anita. "L'arbre de Jessé et l'ordre chrétien de la parenté." In *Marie: Le culte de la Vierge dans la société médiévale,* ed. Dominique Iogna-Prat, Eric Palazzo, and Daniel Russo, 137–70. Paris: Beauchesne, 1996.

Haas, Peter. "The *Am Ha'Arets* as Literary Character." In *Formative Judaism: New Series,* ed. Jacob Neusner, 139–53. 2 vols. South Florida Studies in the History of Judaism, 113, 145. Atlanta: Scholars Press, 1996–97.

Hahn, Thomas. "The Difference the Middle Ages Makes: Race before the Modern World." *Journal of Medieval and Early Modern Studies* 31.1 (2001): 1–37.

Halbertal, Moshe. "Coexisting with the Enemy: Jews and Pagans in the Mishnah." In *Tolerance and Intolerance in Early Judaism and Christianity,* ed. Graham N. Stanton and Guy G. Stroumsa, 159–72. Cambridge: Cambridge University Press, 1998.

Hanawalt, Barbara. *The Ties That Bound: Peasant Family Life in Medieval England.* New York: Oxford University Press, 1986.

Hanson, Anne Ellis. "Conception, Gestation, and the Origins of Female Nature in the *Corpus Hippocraticum.*" *Helios* 19.1–2 (1992): 31–71.

———. "The Medical Writer's Woman." In *Before Sexuality: The Construction of Erotic Experience in the Ancient Greek World,* ed. David M. Halperin, John J. Winkler, and Froma I. Zeitlin, 309–37. Princeton: Princeton University Press, 1990.

Häring, Nikolaus M. "The *Liber de differentia naturae et personae* by Hugh Etherian and the Letters Addressed to Him by Peter of Vienna and Hugh of Honau." *Mediaeval Studies* 24 (1964): 1–34.

Harrington, Hannah K. *The Impurity Systems of Qumran and the Rabbis: Biblical Foundations.* Dissertation Series, 143. Atlanta: Scholars Press, 1993.

Hassig, Debra. *Medieval Bestiaries: Text, Image, Ideology.* RES Monographs on Anthropology and Aesthetics. Cambridge: Cambridge University Press, 1995.

"Haug, Hans. *La Cathédrale de Strasbourg.* Strasbourg: Éditions des Dernières Nouvelles, 1957.

Hayes, Christine. *Gentile Impurities and Jewish Identities: Intermarriage and Conversion from the Bible to the Talmud.* Oxford: Oxford University Press, 2002.

Hays, J. N. *The Burdens of Disease: Epidemics and Human Response in Western History.* New Brunswick: Rutgers University Press, 1998.

Herford, R. Travers. *Christianity in Talmud and Midrash.* London: Williams and Norgate, 1903.

Herrin, Judith. *The Formation of Christendom.* Princeton: Princeton University Press, 1989.

Hervieux, Léopold. *Les fabulistes latins depuis le siècle d'Auguste jusqu'à la fin du Moyen Âge.* 5 vols. Paris: Firmin-Didot, 1893–99; reprint New York: Burt Franklin, 1965.

Hillaby, Joe. "The Ritual-Child-Murder Accusation: Its Dissemination and Harold of Gloucester." *Jewish Historical Studies* 34 for 1994–95 (1997): 69–104.

Hillenbrand, Carole. *The Crusades: Islamic Perspectives.* Edinburgh: Edinburgh University Press, 1999.

Hillgarth, J. N. *The Spanish Kingdoms, 1250–1516.* 2 vols. Oxford: Clarendon Press, 1976–78.

Hödl, Klaus. *Die Pathologisierung des jüdischen Körpers: Antisemitismus, Geschlecht und Medizin im Fin de Siècle.* Vienna: Picus Verlag, 1997.

Hollender, Elisabeth. *Synagogale Hymnen: Qedushta'ot des Simon b. Isaak im Amsterdam Mahsor.* Judentum und Umwelt, 55. Frankfurt-am-Main: P. Lang, 1994.

———. "Zwei hebräische Klagedichtungen aus der Zeit nach dem Zweiten Kreuzzug." *Aschkenas: Zeitschrift für Geschichte und Kultur der Juden* 6 (1996): 11–54.

Horbury, William. "The Benediction of the *minim* and Early Jewish-Christian Controversy." *Journal of Theological Studies,* n.s., 33.1 (1982): 19–61.

———. "The Trial of Jesus in the Jewish Tradition." In *The Trial of Jesus: Cambridge Studies in Honour of C. F. D. Moule,* ed. Ernst Bammel. Studies in Biblical theology, 2d ser., 13. London: Students Christian Movement Press, 1970.

Hörger, Hermann. "Krankheit und religiöses Tabu—die Lepra in der mittelalterlich-früneuzeitlichen Gesellschaft Europas." *Gesnerus* 1 (1982): 53–70.

Horowitz, Alimelch. "Ve-nahafokh hu': yehudim mol sona'eihem be-hagigot ha-purim." *Tsiyon* 59 (1994): 129–68.

Horst, Pieter Willem van der. "Two Notes on Hellenistic Lore in Early Rabbinc Literature." *Jewish Studies Quarterly* 1 (1993–94): 252–62.

Hsia, R. Po-chia. *The Myth of Ritual Murder: Jews and Magic in Reformation Germany*. New Haven: Yale University Press, 1988.

———. *Trent 1475: Stories of a Ritual Murder Trial*. New Haven: Yale University Press, 1992.

Idel, Moshe. "Saturn and Sabbatai Tzevi: A New Approach to Sabbateanism." In *Toward the Millenium: Messianic Expectations from the Bible to Waco,* ed. Peter Schäfer and Mark Cohen, 173–202. Leiden: E. J. Brill, 1998.

———. *Studies in Ecstatic Kabbalah*. SUNY Series in Judaica. Albany: State University of New York Press, 1988.

Iogna-Pratt, Dominique. *Order and Exclusion: Cluny and Christendom Face Heresy, Judaism and Islam (1000–1150)*. Trans. Graham Robert Edwards. Ithaca: Cornell University Press, 2002.

The Image of the Black in Western Art. 4 vols. Fribourg: Office du Livre, 1976–89.

Jacquart, Danielle, and Claude Thomasset. *Sexuality and Medicine in the Middle Ages*. Trans. Matthew Adamson. Cambridge: Polity Press, 1988.

Janowitz, Naomi. "Rabbis and Their Opponents: The Construction of the *min* in Rabbinic Anecdotes." *Journal of Early Christian Studies* 6.3 (1998): 449–62.

Jastrow, Marcus. *A Dictionary of the Targumim, the Talmud Babli and Yerushalmi, and the Midrashic Literature*. New York: Jastrow, 1967.

Jeffery, Arthur. "Gherond's Text of the Correspondence between 'Umar II and Leo III." *Harvard Theological Review* 37.4 (1949): 269–332.

Johnson, Penelope D. *Equal in Monastic Profession: Religious Women in Medieval France*. Women in Culture and Society. Chicago: University of Chicago Press, 1991.

Johnson, Willis. "Before the Blood Libel: Jews in Christian Exegesis after the Massacres of 1096." M.Phil. Thesis, University of Cambridge, 1994.

———. "Jewish Melancholy: A Christian Trope?" Paper presented at the 35th International Congress on Medieval Studies, Kalamazoo, MI, May 2000.

———. "The Myth of Jewish Male Menses." *Journal of Medieval History* 24 (1998): 273–95.

Jordan, William Chester. "Adolescence and Conversion in the Middle Ages: A Research Agenda." In *Jews and Christians in Twelfth-Century Europe,* ed. Michael A. Signer and John van Engen, 77–93. Notre Dame Conference in Medieval Studies, 10. Notre Dame: University of Notre Dame Press, 2001.

———. "Erosion of the Stereotype of the Last Tormentor of Christ." *Jewish Quarterly Rview* 81.1–2 (1990): 13–44.

———. *The French Monarchy and the Jews: From Philip Augustus to the Last Capetians*. Philadelphia: University of Pennsylvania Press, 1989.

———. *The Great Famine: Northern Europe in the Early Fourteenth Century*. Princeton: Princeton University Press, 1996.

———. "Jews on Top: Women and the Availability of Consumption Loans in Northern France in the Mid-Thirteenth Century." *Journal of Jewish Studies* 29 (1978): 39–56.

———. "The Last Tormentor of Christ: An Image of the Jew in Ancient and Medieval Exegesis, Art and Drama." *Jewish Quarterly Review* 77.1–2 (1987): 21–47.

———. "Marian Devotion and the Talmud Trial of 1240." In *Religionsgespräche im Mittelalter,* ed. Bernard Lewis and Friedrich Niewöhner, 61–76. Wolfenbütteler Mittelalter-Studien, 4. Wiesbaden: Harrassowitz, 1992.

———. "The medieval background." In *Struggles in the Promised Land: Towards a History of Black-Jewish Relations in the United States,* ed. Jack Salzman and Cornel West, 53–64. New York: Oxford University Press, 1997.

———. "Why Race?" *Journal of Medieval and Early Modern Studies* 31.1 (2001): 165–73.

Kalman, Richard. "Christians and Heretics in Rabbinic Literature of Late Antiquity." *Harvard Theological Review* 87.2 (1994): 155–69.

Kam, J. C. van der, and J. T. Milik. "A Preliminary Publication of a Jubilees Manuscript from Qumran Cave 4: 4Qjub d (4Q 219)." *Biblica* 73.1 (1992): 62–83.

Kampling, Rainer. *Das Blut Christi und die Juden: Mt 27, 25 bei den lateinischsprachigen christlichen Autoren bis zu Leo dem Grossen*. Münster: Aschendorff, 1984.

Karras, Ruth Mazo. *From Boys to Men: Formations of Masculinity in Late Medieval Europe.* Philadephia: University of Pennsylvania, 2003.

Katz, Jacob. *Exclusiveness and Tolerance: Jewish-Gentile Relations in Medieval and Modern Times.* New York: Behrman House, 1961.

Katz, Marion Holmes. *Body of the Text: Emergence of Sunnī Law of Ritual Purity.* Albany: SUNY Press, 2002.

Kedar, B. Z. *Crusade and Mission: European Approaches toward the Muslims*. Princeton: Princeton University Press, 1984.

———. "Tafsīr and Translation: Traditional Arabic Qur'ān Exigesis and the Latin Qur'āns of Robert of Ketton and Mark of Toledo." *Speculum* 73.3 (1998): 703–32.

Khoury, Adel Théodore. *Les théologiens byzantins et l'Islam. Textes et auteurs VIIIe–XIIIe s.* 2nd ed. Louvain: Editions "Nauwelaerts"; Paris: Beatrice-Nauuwelaerts, 1969.

Khvol'son, D. A. *Die Blutanklage und sonstige mittelalterliche Beschuldigungen der Juden eine historische Untersuchung nach den Quellen.* Frankfurt-am-Main: J. Kauffmann, 1901.

Klawans, Jonathan. *Impurity and Sin in Ancient Judaism.* Oxford: Oxford University Press, 2000.

Klibansky, Raymond, Erwin Panofsky, and Fritz Saxl. *Saturn and Melancholy: Studies in the History of Natural Philosophy, Religion, and Art.* New York: Basic Books, 1964.

Kohlberg, Etan. "The Position of the *walad zina* in Imami Shi'ism." In *Belief and Law in Imami Shi'ism,* 237–66. Brookfield, VT: Variorum, Gower, 1991.

Kolbaba, Tia M. *The Byzantine Lists: Errors of the Latins.* Illinois Medieval Studies. Urbana: University of Illinois Press, 2000.

Koren, Sharon Faye. "'The Woman from Whom God Wanders': The Menstruant in Medieval Jewish Mysticism." Ph.D. dissertation, Yale University, 1999.

Kottek, Samuel J. "Concepts of Disease in the Talmud." *Korot* 9.1–2 (1985): 7–33.

Kraemer, Ross Shepard. *Her Share of the Blessings: Women's Religions among Pagans, Jews, and Christians in the Greco-Roman World.* New York: Oxford University Press, 1992.

———. "The Other as Woman: An Aspect of Polemic among Pagans, Jews, and Christians in the Greco-Roman World." In *The Other in Jewish Thought and History: Constructions of Jewish Culture and Identity,* ed. Laurence J. Silberstein and Robert L. Cohn, 121–44. New Perspectives on Jewish Studies. New York: New York University Press, 1994.

Krauss, Samuel. *The Jewish-Christian Controversy from the Earliest Times to 1789.* Ed. William Horbury. Texte und Studien zum antiken Judentum, 56. Tübingen: J. C. B. Mohr, 1996.

Kristeva, Julia. *Powers of Horror, an Essay on Abjection.* Trans. Leon S. Roudiez. New York: Columbia University Press, 1982.

Kritzeck, James. *Peter the Venerable and Islam.* Princeton Oriental Studies, 23. Princeton: Princeton University Press, 1964.

Kruk, Remke. "A Frothy Bubble: Spontaneous Generation in the Medieval Islamic Tradition." *Journal of Semitic Studies* 35.2 (1990): 265–82.

Lamoreaux, John C. "Early Eastern Christian Responses to Islam." In *Medieval Christian Perceptions of Islam: A Book of Essays,* ed. John Victor Tolan, 3–31. Garland Reference Library of the Humanities, 1768; Garland Medieval Casebooks, 10. New York: Garland, 1996.

Lane Fox, Robin. *Pagans and Christians.* New York: Knopf, 1987.

Langmuir, Gavin I. *History, Religion, and Antisemitism.* Berkeley: University of California Press, 1990.

———. *Toward a Definition of Antisemitism.* Berkeley: University of California Press, 1990.

Lasker, Daniel J. "The Jewish Critique of Christianity under Islam in the Middle Ages." *Proceedings of the American Academy of Jewish Research* 57 (1991): 121–53.

———. *Jewish Philosophical Polemics against Christianity in the Middle Ages.* New York: Ktav, 1977.

———. "*Qissat Mujâdalat al-Usquf* and *Nestor ha-Komer:* The Earliest Arabic and Hebrew Jewish Anti-Christian Polemics." In *Genizah Research after Ninety Years: The Case of Judaeo-Arabic: Papers Read at the Third Congress of the Society for Judaeo-Arabic Studies,* ed. Joshua Blau and Stefan C. Reif, 112–59. University of

Cambridge Oriental Publications, 47. Cambridge: Cambridge University Press, 1992.

Lawn, Brian. *The Salernitan Questions: An Introduction to the History of Medieval and Renaissance Problem Literature*. Oxford: Clarendon Press, 1963.

Lazarus-Yafeh, Hava. *Intertwined Worlds: Medieval Islam and Bible Criticism*. Princeton: Princeton University Press, 1992.

———. "Some Differences between Judaism and Islam as Two Religions of Law." *Religion* 14 (1984): 175–91.

Levi, Israel. "Le Juif de la légende," *Revue des Études Juives* 20 (1890): 49–52.

Levi D'Ancona, Mirella. *The Iconography of the Immaculate Conception in the Middle Ages and Early Renaissance*. Monographs on Archaeology and Fine Arts, 7. New York: College Art Association, 1957.

Levine, Chaviva M. "Jewish Conversion to Christianity in Medieval Northern Europe: 1000–1300." Ph.D. dissertation, New York University, forthcoming.

Lewis, Bernard. *Race and Slavery in the Middle East: A Historical Enquiry.* New York: Oxford University Press, 1990.

Lewis, C. S. *Prince Caspian, the Return to Narnia*. Suffolk: Macmillan, 1951; reprint 1972.

Lipton, Sara. *Images of Intolerance: The Representation of Jews and Judaism in the* Bible moralisée. S. Mark Taper Foundation Imprint in Jewish Studies. Berkeley: University of California Press, 1999.

Little, Lester K. *Religious Poverty and the Profit Economy in Medieval Europe*. Ithaca: Cornell University Press, 1978.

Liu, Benjamin. "'Affined to the Love of the Moor': Sexual Misalliance and Cultural Mixing in the *Cantigas d'escarnho e de la dizer*." In *Queer Iberia: Sexualities, Cultures, and Crossings from the Middle Ages to the Renaissance,* ed. Josiah Blackmore and Gregory S. Hutcheson, 48–72. Durham: University of North Carolina Press, 1999.

Loeb, Isidore. "La controverse de 1240 sur le Talmud." *Revue des Études Juives* 1 (1880): 247–61; 2 (1881): 248–70; 3 (1881): 39–57.

———. "Le Juif de l'histoire et le Juif de la légende." *Revue des Études Juives* 20 (1890): 33–51.

Löwe, Heinz. "Die Apostasie des Pfalzdiakons Bodo (838) und des Judentum der Chasaren." In *Person und Gemeinschaft im Mittelalter: Karl Schmid zum fünf und sechzigsten Geburstag,* ed. Gerd Althoff et. al., 157–69. Sigmaringen: Thorbecke, 1988.

Maccoby, Hyam. "Corpse and the Leper." *Journal of Jewish Studies* 49 (1998): 280–85.

———. *Judas Iscariot and the Myth of Jewish Evil*. 1st Amer. ed. New York: Free Press, 1992.

Macy, Gary. *The Theologies of the Eucharist in the Early Scholastic Period: A Study of the Salvific Function of the Sacrament According to the Theologians, 1080–1220.* Oxford: Clarendon Press, 1984.

Maloy, R. "The Sermonary of St. Idelphonsus of Toledo." *Classical Folia* 25 (1971): 137–99, 243–301.

Malti-Douglass, Fedwa. "Tribadism/Lesbianism and the Sexualized Body in Medieval Arabo-Islamic Narratives." In *Same-Sex Love and Desire among Women in the Middle Ages*. Ed. Francesca Canadé Sautman and Pamela Sheingorn, 123–41. New York: Palgrave, 2000.

———. *Women's Body, Women's Word: Gender and Discourse in Arabo-Islamic Writing*. Princeton: Princeton University Press, 1991.

Manchester, Keith, and Christopher Knüsel. "A Medieval Sculpture of Leprosy in the Cistercian Abbaye de Cadouin." *Medical History* 38.2 (1994): 204–6.

Manekin, Charles H. "When the Jews Learned Logic from the Pope: Three Medieval Hebrew Translations of the *Tractatus* of Peter of Spain." *Science in Context* 10.3 (1997): 395–430.

Mann, Max Friedrich. *Der Bestiaire divin des Guillaume le Clerc*. Französisch Studies, 6/2. Heilbronn: Henninger, 1888; reprint Nandeln: Sändig, 1976.

Marcus, Ivan G. "Hierarchies, Religious Boundaries, and Jewish Spirituality in Medieval Germany." *Jewish History* 1.2 (1986): 7–26.

———. "Images of the Jews from the *Exempla* of Caesarius of Heisterbach." In *From Witness to Witchcraft: Jews and Judaism in Medieval Christian Thought*. Wolfenbütteler Mittelalter-Studien, 11. Wiesbaden: Harrassowitz, 1996.

———. "A Jewish-Christian Symbiosis: The Culture of Early Ashkenaz." In *Cultures of the Jews: A New History*, ed. David Biale, 449–516. New York: Schocken Books, 2002.

———. "Jews and Christians Imagining the Other in Medieval Europe." *Prooftexts* 15.3 (1995): 209–26.

———. *Rituals of Childhood: Jewish Culture and Acculturation in the Middle Ages*. New Haven: Yale University Press, 1996.

Margulies, Mordecai. *Ha-Hilukim she-ben anshe Mizrah u-vene Erets Yi'srael Yots'im le-or 'al pi kol ha-nusha'ot ha-nidpasot ve-kamah kitve yad'im mavo u-berur mekorot*. Jerusalem: Hotsa'at Re'uven Mas, 1937.

Marmorstein, Arthur. *The Old Rabbinic Doctrine of God*. 2 vols. Jews' College Publications, 10, 14. London: Oxford University Press, 1927–37.

Masoret ha-piyyuṭ. Ed. Binyamin Bar Tikvah and Efrayim Hazan. 2 vols. Sidrat pirsumim, 1–2. Ramat-Gan: Universitat Bar-Ilan, 1996– .

Maurin, C. A. *Les saluts d'amour: Les troubadours de Notre-Dame*. 2 vols. Geneva: Slavkine Reprints, 1977.

McCulloch, Florence. *Mediaeval Latin and French Bestiaries*. Rev. ed. University of North Carolina Studies in Romance Languages and Literatures, 30. Chapel Hill: University of North Carolina Press, 1962.

McCulloh, John M. "Jewish Ritual Murder: William of Norwich, Thomas of Monmouth, and the Early Dissemination of the Myth." *Speculum* 72 (1997): 698–740.

McNeill, William H. *Plagues and Peoples*. Garden City, NY: Anchor Press, 1976.

Meacham, Tirzeh. "An Abbreviated History of the Development of the Jewish Menstrual Laws." In *Women and Water: Menstruation in Jewish Life and Law,* ed. Rahel R. Wasserfall, 23–39. Hanover, NH: University Press of New England, 1999.

———. "Mishnat masekhet Nida'im mavo ma hadurah bikortit 'im he'arot be-nusah, be-farsharit ure-'arikah u-ferakim be-toldot he-halakhah uve-re'alyah." Ph.D. dissertation, Hebrew University of Jerusalem, 1989.

Melinkoff, Ruth. *Antisemitic Hate Signs in Hebrew Illuminated Manuscripts from Medieval Germany*. Jerusalem: Center for Jewish Art, Hebrew University of Jerusalem, 1999.

———. *Outcasts: Signs of Otherness in Northern European Art of the Late Middle Ages*. 2 vols. California Studies in the History of Art, 32. Berkeley: University of California Press, 1993.

Menocal, Maria Rosa. *The Arabic Role in Medieval Literary History: A Forgotton Heritage.* Philadelphia: University of Pennsylvania Press, 1987.

Mentgen, Gerd. "ha-yavitzrotah shel ha-badutah 'al 'alitat ha dam." *Tsiyon* 54.2–3 (1994): 343–50.

Merchavia, Ch. *ha-Talmud be-re'i ha-Natsrut: ha-yahas lesafrut yisra'el sheleahar ha-mikra'beolam ha-notsri be-yemai-ha-baynayyim (500–1248)*. Jerusalem: Mosad Byalik, 1970.

Meri, Josef. *The Cult of Saints among Muslims and Jews in Medieval Syria.* Oxford: Oxford University Press, 2002.

Metlitzki, Dorothee. *The Matter of Araby in Medieval England.* New Haven: Yale University Press, 1977.

Metzger, Thérèse, and Mendel Metzger. [*Vie juive au Moyen Âge.*] *Jewish Life in the Middle Ages: Illuminated Hebrew Manuscripts of the Thirteenth to the Sixteenth Centuries*. New York: Alpine Fine Arts Collection, 1982.

Meyendorff, John. *Byzantine Theology: Historical Trends and Doctrinal Themes*. New York: Fordham University Press, 1974.

Miles, Margaret. "Santa Maria Maggiore's Fifth-Century Mosaics: Triumphal Christianity and the Jews." *Harvard Theological Review* 86.2 (1993): 155–75.

Milgrom, Jacob. "4Q Tohora a: An Unpublished Qumran Text on Purities." In *Time to Prepare the Way in the Wilderness: Papers on the Qumran Scrolls,* ed. Devorah Dimant and Lawrence H. Schiffman, 56–68. Studies on the Texts of the Desert of Judah, 16. Leiden: E. J. Brill, 1995.

———. "The Paradox of the Red Cow (Numbers XIX)." *Vetus Testamentum* 31 (1981): 62–72.

———. "Sin Offering or Purification Offering." *Vetus Testamentum* 21 (1971): 237–39.

———. "Studies in the Temple Scroll." *Journal of Biblical Literature* 97 (1978): 501–23.

———. "Two kinds of Hatta't." *Vetus Testamentum* 26 (1976): 333–37.

Milik, J. "*Milki-sedek et milki-resa'* dans les anciens écrits Juifs et Chrétiens." *Journal of Jewish Studies* 23 (1972): 95–144.

Miller, Stuart S. "The *minim* of Sepphoris Reconsidered." *Harvard Theological Review* 86.4 (1993): 377–402.

Miller, William Ian. *The Anatomy of Disgust*. Cambridge, MA: Harvard University Press, 1997.

Mimouni, Simon C. "La '*Birkat ha-minim*': Une prière juive contre le Judéo-Chrétiens." *Revue des Sciences Réligieuses* 71.3 (1997): 275–98.

Minois, George. [*Histoire de la viellesse*.] *History of old age*. Trans. Sarah Hanbury Tenison. Cambridge: Polity Press, 1989.

Mirsky, Aaron. *ha-Piyut: hipathuto be Erets-Yi'sra'el uva-golah Sifriyat "kinus."* Jerusalem: Magnes Press, 1990.

Miyazaki, Mariko. "Misericord Owls and Medieval Anti-Semitism." In *The Mark of the Beast: The Medieval Bestiary in Art, Life, and Literature,* ed. Debra Hassig, 23–49. New York: Garland, 1999.

Moller-Christensen, Vilhelm. "Evidence of Leprosy in Earlier Peoples." In *Diseases in Antiquity: A Survey of the Diseases, Injuries, and Surgery of Early Populations*. Compl. and ed. Don Brothwell and A. T. Sandison, 295–306. Springfield, IL: C. C. Thomas, 1967.

Moore, R. I. *The Formation of a Persecuting Society: Power and Deviance in Western Europe, 950–1250*. Oxford: Blackwell, 1987.

Moos, Peter von. "Die Kunst der Anwort; Exempla und *dicta* im lateinischen Mittelalter." In *Exempel und Exempelsammlungen,* ed. Walter Haug and Burghart Wachinger, 23–57. Fortuna vitrea, 2. Tübingen: M. Niemeyer, 1991.

Moulinier, Louis. *Le pur et l'impur dans la pensée des Grecs d'Homère à Aristote*. Études et commentaires, 11. Paris: C. Klincksieck, 1952.

Muessig, Carolyn. *The Faces of Women in the Sermons of Jacques de Vitry*. Peregrina Translations Series. Toronto: Peregrina, 1999.

Müller-Bütow, Horst. *Lepra: Ein medizinhistorischer Überblick unter besonderer Berücksichtigung der mittelalterlichen arabischen Medizin*. Europäische Hochschulschriften. Reihe VII, Medizin. Abt. B, Geschichte der Medizin, 3. 1936; reprint Frankurt-am-Main: P. Lang, 1981.

Muntner, Süssmann. *Mavo' le-sefer Asaf ha-rofe*. Jerusalem: s.n., 1957.

Musallam, B[asim] F. *Sex and Society in Islam: Birth Control before the Nineteenth Century*. Cambridge Studies in Islamic Civilization. Cambridge: Cambridge University Press, 1983.

Mussies, Gerard. "Identification and Self-Identification of Gods in Classical and Hellenistic Times." In *Knowledge of God in the Graeco-Roman World,* ed. R. van den Broek, T. Baarda, and J. Mansfeld, 1–18. Études preliminaries aux religions orientales dans l'Empire romain, 112. Leiden: E. J. Brill, 1988.

Neusner, Jacob. "*Genesis Rabbah* as Polemic: An Introductory Account." *Hebrew Annual Review* 9 (1985): 253–65.

———. *A History of the Mishnaic Law of Purities*. 3 vols. Studies in Judaism in Late Antiquity, 6. Leiden: E. J. Brill, 1974– .

———. *The Incarnation of God: The Character of Divinity in Formative Judaism*. Philadelphia: Fortress Press, 1988.

———. *What Is Midrash?* Guides to Biblical Scholarship. Philadelphia: Fortress Press, 1987.

Newmyer, Stephen. "Talmudic Medicine and Greek Sources." *Korot* 9.1–2 (1985): 34–57.

Niccoli, Ottavia. "*Menstruum quasi monstruum*: Monstrous Births and Menstrual Taboo in the Sixteenth Century." In *Sex and Gender in Historical Perspective,* ed. Edward Muir and Guido Ruggiero, 1–25. Trans. Margaret A. Gallucci. Baltimore: Johns Hopkins University Press, 1990.

Nieto, María Dolores. *Estructura y función de los relatos medievales*. Biblioteca de Filiologiá Hispánica, 9. Madrid: Consejo Superior de Investigaciones Científicas, 1993.

Nirenberg, David. *Communities of Violence: Persecution of Minorities in the Middle Ages*. Princeton: Princeton University Press, 1996.

———. "Conversion, Sex, and Segregation: Jews and Christians in Medieval Spain." *American Historical Review* 107.4 (2002): 1065–93.

Noonan, John T. "Who Was Rolandus?" In *Law, Church, and Society: Essays in Honor of Stephan Kuttner*, ed. Kenneth Pennington and Robert Somerville, 21–48. Philadelphia: University of Pennsylvania Press, 1977.

Obscenity: Social Control and Artistic Creation in the European Middle Ages. Ed. Jan M. Ziolkowski. Cultures, Beliefs, and Traditions, 4. Leiden: E. J. Brill, 1998.

Ocasio, Rafael. "Ethnic Underclass Representation in the *Cantigas*: The Black Moro as a Hated Character." In *Estudios alfonsinos y otros escritos*, ed. Nicolás Toscano, 183–88. New York: National Endowment for the Humanities and the Hispanic Foundation for the Humanities, 1991.

Ocker, Christopher. "Ritual Murder and the Subjectivity of Christ: A Choice in Medieval Christianity." *Harvard Theological Review* 91.2 (1998): 153–92.

O'Kane, Bernard. *Early Persian Painting: Kalila and Dimna Manuscripts from the Late Fourteenth Century*. London: I. B. Tauris, 2003.

Olster, David M. *Roman Defeat, Christian Response, and the Literary Construction of the Jew*. Middle Ages series. Philadelphia: University of Pennsylvania Press, 1994.

O'Murray, Stephen, and Will Roscoe. *Islamic Homosexualities: Culture, History, and Literature.* New York: 1997.

Orfali, Moïsés. "El *Dialogus pro Ecclesia contra Synagogam*: Un tratado anónimo de polemica antijudía." *Hispania* 54.2 (1994): 679–732.

Ostrogorski, Georgije [Ostrogorsky, George]. [*Geschichte des byzantinischen Staates.*] *History of the Byzantine State.* Trans. Joan Hussey. 1st pbk. ed. Oxford: Blackwell, 1980.

Parker, Robert. *Miasma: Pollution and Purification in Early Greek Religion*. Oxford: Clarendon Press, 1983.

Parkes, James William. *The Conflict of the Church and the Synagogue: A Study in the Origins of Antisemitism*. Cleveland: World; Philadelphia: Jewish Publication Society of America, 1964.

Parry, Kenneth. *Depicting the Word: Byzantine Iconophile Thought of the Eighth and Ninth Centuries*. Medieval Mediterranean, 12. Leiden: E. J. Brill, 1996.

Passover and Easter: Origin and History to Modern Times. Ed. Paul Bradshaw and Lawrence A. Hoffman. Two Liturgical Traditions, 5. Notre Dame: University of Notre Dame Press, 1999.

Peers, Glenn. *Subtle Bodies: Representing Angels in Byzantium*. Transformation of the Classical Heritage, 32. Berkeley: University of California Press, 2001.

Pelikan, Jaroslav Jan. *The Christian Tradition: A History of the Development of Doctrine*. 5 vols. Chicago: University of Chicago Press, 1971–89.

———. *Mary through the Centuries: Her Place in the History of Culture*. New Haven: Yale University Press, 1996.

Pegg, Mark Gregory. "Le corps et l'autorité: la lèpre de Baudoin IV." *Annales, Économies, Sociétés, Civilisations,* vols. 4–5 (1990): 265–87.

Petuchowski, Jakob Josef. *Theology and Poetry: Studies in Medieval* piyyuṭ. Littman Library of Jewish Civilization. London: Routledge and Kegan Paul, 1977.

Pflaum, H. "Shirei ha-nitsuah ha-dati'm shel yamei ha-benaim ('im tekst she 'aino yedu'a be-tsarfaht yashanah)." *Tarbits* 2.3 (1931): 443–76.

Pines, Shlomo. "Points of Similarity between the Exposition of the Doctrine of Sefirot in the *Sefer Yezira* and a Text of the Pseudo-Clementine Homilies: The Implications of this Resemblance." *Proceedings of the Israel Academy of Sciences and the Humanities* 7 (1989): 63–141.

Poliakov, Léon. *Histoire de l'antisémitisme*. 4 vols. Liberté de l'esprit. Paris: Calmann-Lévy, 1955– .

Prêcher d'examples: Récits de prédicateurs du Moyen Âge. Ed. Jean-Claude Schmitt. Série "Moyen Âge." Paris: Stock, 1985.

Preus, Anthony. "Galen's Criticism of Aristotle's Conception Theory." *Journal of the History of Biology* 10 (1977): 65–85.

Preuss, Julius. [*Biblisch-talmudische Medizin.*] *Biblical and Talmudic Medicine*. Ed. and trans. Fred Rosner. New York: Sanhedrin Press, 1978.

Puech, Henri. "Catharisme médiéval et Bogomilisme." In *Convegno di scienze morali storici e filologiche: Oriente ed occidente nel medio evo*. Fondazione Alessandro Volta. Atti dei convegni, 12. Rome: s.n., 1957.

———. "Un hymne Essénien en parte retrouvé et le beatitudes: 1QH V12–VI 18 (+ col. XIII–XIV 7) et 4Q Béat." *Revue de Qumran* 49–52.13 (1988): 59–88.

Randall, Lilian M. C. "*Exempla* as a Source of Gothic Marginal Illumination." *Art Bulletin Quarterly* 39.2 (1957): 97–107.

———. "Humor and Fantasy in the Margins." *Apollo* 84 (1966): 482–88.

———. "The Snail in Gothic Marginal Warfare." *Speculum* 37.3 (1962): 358–67.

Reinhart, A. Kevin. "Impurity/No Danger." *History of Religions* 30.1 (1990): 1–24.

Rembaum, Joel Edward. "The New Testament in Medieval Jewish Anti-Christian Polemics." Ph.D. dissertation, University of California, Los Angeles, 1975.

Resnick, Irven. "Medieval Roots of the Myth of Jewish Male Menses." *Harvard Theological Review* 93.3 (2000): 241–63.

Richards, Peter. *The Medieval Leper and His Northern Heirs*. Cambridge: D. S. Brewer; Totowa, NJ: Rowman and Littlefield, 1977.

Richardson, H. G. *The English Jewry under Angevin Kings*. London: Methuen, 1960.

Richlin, Amy. *The Garden of Priapus: Sexuality and Aggression in Roman Humor*. Rev. ed. New York: Oxford University Press, 1992.

———. "Pliny's Brassiere." In *Roman Sexualities,* ed. Judith P. Hallett and Marilyn B. Skinner, 197–220. Princeton: Princeton University Press, 1997.

Richmond, Colin. "Englishness and Medieval Anglo-Saxon Jewry." In *The Jewish Heritage in British History,* ed. Tony Kushner, 42–59. London: F. Cass, 1992.

Rigo, Caterina. "Un'antologia filosofica di Yehudah b. Mosheh Romano." *Italia: Studi e Ricerche sulla Storia, la Cultura e la Letteratura degli Ebrei d'Italia* 10 (1993): 73–104.

———. "Un passo sconosciuto di Alberto Magno nel '*Sefer Etsem ha-Shamayim*' di Yehudah b. Mosheh." *Henoch: Studi Storicofilologici sull'Ebraismo* 11.2–3 (1989): 295–318.

———. "Yehudah ben Mosheh Romanp traduttore degli Scolastici latini." *Henoch: Studi Storicofilologici sull'Ebraismo* 17.1–2 (1995): 141–70.

Riskin, Shlomo. *Women and Jewish Divorce: The Rebellious Wife, the* agunah*, and the Right of Women to Initiate Divorce in Jewish Law, a Halakhic Solution*. Hoboken, NJ: Ktav, 1989.

Rokeah, David. *Jews, Pagans and Christians in Conflict*. Studia Post-Biblica, 33. Jerusalem: Magnes Press, 1982.

Rose, Eugen. *Die manichäische Christologie*. Studies in Oriental Religions, 5. Wiesbaden: Harrassowitz, 1979.

Rose, Tricia. *Black Noise: Rap Music and Black Culture in Contemporary America*. Music Culture. Hanover, NH: University Press of New England, 1994.

Rosen, Tova. "Sexual Politics in a Medieval Hebrew Marriage Debate." *Exemplaria* 12.1 (2000): 157–84.

———. *Unveiling Eve: Reading Gender in Medieval Hebrew Literature*. Philadelphia: University of Pennsylvania Press, 2003.

Rosenthal, E. I. J. "Anti-Christian Polemic in Medieval Biblical Commentaries." *Journal of Jewish Studies* 11 (1960): 115–35.

Rosenthal, Judah M. "The Talmud on Trial: The Disputation of Paris in the Year 1240." *Jewish Quarterly Review* 47 (1956–57): 58–76, 145–69.

Ross, Ellen M. *The Grief of God: Images of the Suffering Jesus in Late Medieval England*. New York: Oxford University Press, 1997.

Roth, Norman. "The 'Wiles of Women' Motif in Medieval Hebrew Literature of Spain." *Hebrew Annual Review* 2 (1978): 145–65.

Rouayheb, Khaled el-. *Before Homosexuality in the Arab-Islamic World, 1500–1800*. Chicago: University of Chicago Press, 2005.

Rowland, Beryl. "The Art of Memory and the Bestiary." In *Beasts and Birds of the Middle Ages: The Bestiary and Its Legacy,* ed. Willene B. Clark and Meradith T. McMunn, 12–25. Middle Ages series. Philadelphia: University of Pennsylvania Press, 1989.

Rozin, Paul, and April Fallon. "A Perspective on Disgust." *Psychological Review* 94 (1987): 23–41.

Rubin, Miri. *Corpus Christi: The Eucharist in Late Medieval Culture*. Cambridge: Cambridge University Press, 1991.

———. *Gentile Tales: The Narrative Assault on Late Medieval Jews*. New Haven: Yale University Press, 1999.

———. "The Person in the Form: Medieval Challenges to Bodily Order." In *Framing Medieval Bodies,* ed. Sara Kay and Miri Rubin, 100–122. Manchester: Manchester University Press, 1994.

Rubin, Nissan. "Body and Soul in Talmudic and Mishnaic Sources." *Korot* 9 (1988): 151–64.

Ruhe, Doris. "Le' Roe d'Astronomie': Le livre de Sidrac et les Encyclopédies françaises du Moyen Age." *L'Enciclopedismo Medievale* (1994): 293–310.

Sahas, Daniel J. *Icon and Logos: Sources in Eighth-Century Iconoclasm*. Toronto: University of Toronto Press, 1986.

———. *John of Damascus on Islam: The "Heresy of the Ishmaelites."* Leiden: E. J. Brill, 1972.

Saliba, George. *A History of Arabic Astronomy: Planetary Theories during the Golden Age of Islam*. New York: New York University Press, 1994.

———. "Paulus Alexandrinus in Syriac and Arabic." *Byzantion* 62.2 (1995): 440–54.

Saltman, Avrom. "Gilbert Crispin as a Source of the Anti-Jewish Polemic of *Ysagoge in Theologiam*." In *Confrontation and Coexistence,* 89–99. Bar-Ilan Studies in History, 2. Ramat-Gan: Ban-Ilan University Press, 1984.

Sapir Abulafia, Anna. "An Attempt by Gilbert Crispin, Abbot of Westminster, at Rational Argument in the Jewish-Christian Debate." *Studia Monastica* 26.1 (1984): 55–74.

———. "Bodies in the Jewish-Christian Debate." In *Framing Medieval Bodies,* ed. Sara Kay and Miri Rubin, 123–37. Manchester/New York: Manchester University Press, 1994.

———. "Christian Imagery of the Jews in the Twelfth Century: a Look at Odo of Cambrai and Guibert of Nogent." *Theoretische Geschiedenis* 16 (1989): 383–91.

———. *Christians and Jews in the Twelfth-Century Renaissance*. New York: Routledge, 1995.

———. "Invectives against Christianity in the Hebrew Chronicles of the First Crusade." In *Crusade and Settlement: Papers Read at the First Conference of the Society for the Study of the Crusades and the Latin East and Presented to R. C. Smail,* ed. Peter W. Edbury, 66–77. Cardiff: University College Cardiff Press, 1985.

———. "Jewish Carnality in Twelfth-Century Renaissance Thought." In *Christianity and Judaism: Papers Read at the 1991 Summer Meeting and the 1992 Winter Meeting of the Ecclesiastical History Society,* ed. Diana Wood, 59–78. Cambridge, MA: Ecclesiastical History Society, 1992.

———. "Jewish-Christian Disputations and the Twelfth-Century Renaissance." *Journal of Medieval History* 15/2 (1989): 102–25.

———. "Twelfth-Century Renaissance Theology and the Jews." In *From Witness to Witchcraft: Jews and Judaism in Medieval Christian Thought,* 125–39. Wolfenbütteler Mittelalter-Studien, 11. Wiesbaden: Harrassowitz, 1996.

Satlow, Michael L. *Tasting the Dish: Rabbinic Rhetorics of Sexuality*. Brown Judaic Series, 303. Atlanta: Scholars Press, 1995.

Sauvage, Jean-Paul. "Le massacre des Juifs à Blois en 1171." *Mémoires de la Société des Sciences et Lettres du Loir-et-Cher* 49 (1994): 5–22.

Schäfer, Peter. *Judeophobia: Attitudes toward the Jews in the Ancient World*. Cambridge, MA: Harvard University Press, 1997.

Schechter, S. *Documents of Jewish Sectaries: Edited from Hebrew MSS. In the Cairo Genizah Collection, Now in the Possession of the University Library, Cambridge*. 2 vols. in 1. Library of Biblical Studies. New York: Ktav, 1970.

Scheffczyk, Leo. *Das Mariengeheimnis in Frömmigkeit und Lehre der Karolingerzeit*. Erfurter theologische studien, 5. Leipzig: St. Banno-Verlag, 1959.

Schiffman, Lawrence H. *Who Was a Jew? Rabbinic and Halakhic Perspectives on the Jewish Christian Schism*. Hoboken, NJ: Ktav, 1985.

Schimmel, Annemarie. *My Soul Is a Woman: The Feminine in Islam*. Trans. Susan Ray. New York: Continuum, 1977.

Schipperges, Heinrich. *Die Assimilation der arabischen Medizin durch das lateinische Mittelalter*. Sudhoffs Archiv für Geschichte der Medizin und der Naturwissenschaften. Beihefte, 3. Wiesbaden: F. Steiner, 1964.

Schirmann, Jefim. "Hebrew Liturgical Poetry and Christian Hymnology." *Jewish Quarterly Review* 64.2 (1953): 123–61.

Schleifer, Aliah. *Mary the Blessed Virgin of Islam*. Louisville, KY: Fons Vitae, 1998.

Schmitt, Otto. *Gotische Skulpturen des Strassburger Münsters*. 2 vols. Frankfurt am Main: Frankfurter Verlags-Anstalt,1924.

Schmitz-Cliever, Egon. "Das mittelalterliche Leprosarium Melalten bei Aachen in der Diozese Lüttich (1230–1550)." *Clio Medica* 7 (1972): 13–34.

Scholem, Gershom Gerhard. [*Von der mystischen Gestalt der Gottheit*.] *On the Mystical Shape of the Godhead: Basic Concepts in the Kabbalah*. Trans. Joachim Neugroschel. Ed. and rev. Jonathan Chipman. 1st Amer. ed. New York: Schocken Books, 1991.

Schreckenberg, Heinz. *Die christlichen Adversus-Judaeos-Texte und ihr literarisches und historisches Umfeld (1.-11. Jh.)*. Europäische Hochschulschriften. Reihe XXIII, Theologie, 172. Frankfurt: P. Lang, 1982.

Schultz, Joseph. "Angelic Opposition to the Ascension of Moses and the Revelation of the Law." *Jewish Quarterly Review* 61 (1970–71): 282–307.

Schwartz, Joshua. "Gallus, Julian and anti-Christian Polemic in *Pesikta Rabbati*." *Theologische Zeitschrift* 46.1 (1990): 1–19.

Scott, James C. *Domination and the Arts of Resistance: Hidden Transcripts*. New Haven: Yale University Press, 1990.

———. *Weapons of the Weak: Everyday Forms of Peasant Resistance*. New Haven: Yale University Press, 1985.

Scott, Joan Wallach. "Gender: A Useful Category of Historical Analysis." In *Gender and the Politics of History*, 28–50. Gender and Culture. New York: Columbia University Press, 1989.

Scribner, Robert W. *For the Sake of Simple Folk: Popular Propaganda for the German Reformation*. Cambridge Studies in Oral and Literate Culture, 2. Cambridge: Cambridge University Press, 1981.

———. *Popular Culture and Popular Movements in Reformation Germany*. London: Hambledon Press, 1987.

Segal, Alan F. *Two Powers in Heaven: Early Rabbinic Reports about Christianity and Gnosticism*. Studies in Judaism in Late Antiquity, 25. Leiden: E. J. Brill, 1977.

Septimus, Bernard. *Hispano-Jewish Culture in Transition: The Career and Controversies of Ramah*. Harvard Judaic Monographs, 4. Cambridge, MA: Harvard University Press, 1982.

Sermoneta, Joseph [Giuseppe] B. "Jehudah ben Mošeh ben Daniel Romano: Traducteur de St. Thomas." In *Hommage à Georges Vajda; Études d'histoire et de pensée juives*, ed. Gérard Nahon and Charles Touati, 235–62. Louvain: Peeters, 1980.

Shachar, Isaiah. *The Judensau: A Medieval Anti-Jewish Motif and Its History*. London: Warburg Institute, 1974.

Shahar, Shulamith. [*Yoledet be-yemei ha-benaim*.] *Childhood in the Middle Ages*. Trans. Chaya Galai. London: Routledge, 1990.

———. [*Horef ha-'oteh otanu*.] *Growing Old in the Middle Ages: "Winter Clothes Us in Shadow and Pain."* London: Routledge, 1997.

Shatzmiller, Joseph. *Jews, Medicine, and Medieval Society*. Berkeley: University of California Press, 1994.

Shechterman, Deborah. "Sugit ha-heta' ha-kadmon ve-ha-parshanut le-divre ha-Rambam ba-hagut ha-yehudit be-me'ot ha-shalush-'asrah ve-ha-'aruba'-'asah." *Da'at* 20 (1988): 65–90.

Simon, Marcel. [*Verus Israel*.] *Verus Israel: A Study of the Relations between Christians and Jews in the Roman Empire (135–425)*. Trans. H. McKeating. Littman Library of Jewish Civilization. New York: Oxford University Press, 1986.

Siraisi, Nancy G. *Medieval and Early Renaissance Medicine: An Introduction to Knowledge and Practice*. Chicago: University of Chicago Press, 1990.

Sivan, Emmanuel. *L'Islam et la Croisade: Idéologie et propagande dans les réactions musulmanes aux Croisades*. Paris: Librairie d'Amérique et d'Orient, 1968.

Smalley, Beryl. *The Study of the Bible in the Middle Ages*. Notre Dame: University of Notre Dame Press, 1964.

Smith, Jane, and Yvonne Y. Haddad. "The Virgin Mary in Islamic Tradition and Commentary." *Muslim World* 79.3–4 (1989): 161–87.

Snowden, Frank M. *Blacks in Antiquity; Ethiopians in the Greco-Roman Experience*. Cambridge, MA: Belknap Press, 1970.

Soloveitchik, Haym. "Three Themes in the Sefer Hasidim." *AJS Review* 1 (1976): 311–57.

Soufi, Denise L. "The Image of Fâtima in Classical Muslim Thought." Ph.D. dissertation, Princeton University, 1997.

Sourdel, Dominique. "Un pamphlet musulman anonyme d'époque 'abbâside contre les Chrétiens." *Revue des Études Islamiques* 34 (1966): 2–34.

Southern, R. W. *Saint Anselm: A Portrait in a Landscape*. Cambridge: Cambridge University Press, 1990.

Spangenberg, Peter-Michael. "Judenfeindlichkeit in den altfranzösischen Marienmirakeln: Stereotypen oder Symptome der Veränderung der kollektiven Selbsterfahrung?" In *Die Legende vom Ritualmord: zur Geschichte der Blütbeschuldigung gegen Juden,* ed. Rainer Erb, 157–77. Reihe Dokumente, Texte, Materialien, 6. Berlin: Metropol, 1993.

Spiegel, Shalom. [*Me-agadot ha-'akedah.*] *The Last Trial: on the Legends and Lore of the command to Abraham to offer Isaac as a Sacrifice: The Akedah*. Trans. Judah Goldin. New York: Pantheon, 1967.

Stacey, Robert. "The Conversion of Jews to Christianity in Thirteenth-Century England." *Speculum* 67 (1992): 263–83.

Starr, Joshua. *The Jews in the Byzantine Empire, 641–1204.* Texte und Forschungen zur byzantinisch-neugriechischen Philologie, zwanglose Beihefte zu den "Byzantinisch-neugriechischen Jahrbüchern," 30. Athens: Verlag der "Byzantinisch-Neugriechischen Jahrbücher," 1939.

Stern, David. "Midrash and the Language of Exegesis: A Study of *Vayikra Rabbah*, chapter 1." In *Midrash and Literature*, ed. Geoffrey H. Hartman and Sanford Budick, 105–24. New Haven: Yale University Press, 1986.

Stock, Brian. *The Implications of Literacy: Written Language and Models of Interpretation in the Eleventh and Twelfth Centuries*. Princeton: Princeton University Press, 1983.

Stow, Kenneth. "The Jewish Family in the Rhineland in the High Middle Ages: Form and Function." *American Historical Review* 92.4 (1987): 1085–1110.

Stowasser, Barbara Freyer. *Women in the Qur'an: Traditions and Interpretation*. New York: Oxford University Press, 1994.

Strack, H. L., and G. Stemberger. [*Einleitung in Talmud und Midrasch.*] *Introduction to the Talmud and Midrash*. Trans. Markus Bockmuehl. 1st Fortress Press ed. Minneapolis: Fortress Press, 1992.

Strickland, Debra Higgs. *Saracens, Demons, and Jews: Making Monsters in Medieval Art.* Princeton: Princeton University Press, 2003.

Strousma, Sarah. "Jewish Polemics against Islam and Christianity in Light of Judeo-Arabic Texts." In *Studies in Muslim-Jewish Relations* 3, ed. Norman Golb, 241–50. Amsterdam: Harwood, 1997.

Sukenik, Eleazar Lipa. *The Dead Sea Scrolls of the Hebrew University*. Jerusalem: Magnes Press, 1955.

Swartz, Michael D. "'Like the Ministering Angels': Ritual and Purity in Early Jewish Mysticism and Magic." *AJS Review* 19/2 (1994): 135–67.

———. *Scholastic Magic: Ritual and Revelation in Early Jewish Mysticism*. Princeton: Princeton University Press, 1996.

Symposium on Byzantine Medicine. Ed. John Scarborough. Dumbarton Oaks Papers, 38. Washington, DC: Dumbarton Oaks Research Library and Collection, 1985.

Synopse zur Hekhalot-Literatur. Ed. Peter Schäfer. Texte und Studien zum antiken Judentum, 2. Tübingen: J. C. B. Mohr, 1981.

Tallan, Cheryl. "The Position of the Medieval Jewish Widow as a Function of Family Structure." In *Proceedings of the Tenth World Congress of Jewish Studies, Jerusalem, August 16–24, 1989,* 2:91–98. Jerusalem: World Union of Jewish Studies, 1990.

Talmage, Frank. "A Hebrew Polemical Treatise: Anti-Cathar and Anti-Orthodox." *Harvard Theological Review* 60 (1967): 323–48.

Ta-Shma, Israel M. *Halakhah, minhag u-metsi'ut be-Ashkenaz, 1000–1350.* Jerusalem: Magnes Press, 1996.

———. "haraḥaqot niddah be-Ashkenaz ha-qodem: ha-haim ve-ha-sifrut," *Sidra* 9 (1993): 163–70.

Temkin, Owsei. *Galenism: Rise and Decline of a Medical Philosophy.* Cornell Publications in the History of Science. Ithaca: Cornell University Press, 1973.

———. *Hippocrates in a World of Pagans and Christians.* Baltimore: Johns Hopkins University Press, 1991.

Thomasset, Claude. "La femme au Moyen Âge: Les composantes fondamentales de sa representation-immunité impunité." *Ornicar* 22–23 (1981): 223–38.

Tolan, John. "Anti-Hagiography: Embrico of Mainz's *Vita Mahumeti.*" *JMH* 22 (1996): 25–41.

———. *Saracens: Islam in the Medieval European Imagination.* New York: Columbia University Press, 2002.

———. "Peter the Venerable on the 'Diabolical Heresy of the Saracens.'" In *The Devil, Heresy, and Witchcraft in the Middle Ages: Essays in Honor of Jeffrey B. Russell,* ed. Alberto Fereiro, 345–67. Leiden: E. J. Brill, 1998.

———. *Petrus Alfonsi and His Medieval Readers.* Gainesville: University Press of Florida, 1993.

———. "Un cadavre mutilé: Le déchirement polémique de Mahomet." *Le Moyen Âge* 104 (1998): 53–72.

Torjensen, Karen Jo. "Martyrs, Ascetics and Gnostics: Gender Crossing in Early Christianity." In *Gender Reversals and Gender Cultures: Anthropological and Historical Perspectives,* ed. Sabrina Petra Ramet, 79–91. London: Routledge, 1996.

Torrell, Jean Paul. "Les Juifs dans l'oeuvre de Pierre le Vénérable." *Cahiers de Civilization Médiévale* 30.4 (1987): 331–46.

Trachtenberg, Joshua. *The Devil and the Jews: The Medieval Conception of the Jew and Its Relation to Modern Antisemitism.* 2d pbk. ed. Philadelphia: Jewish Publication Society, 1983.

Trafton, Joseph L. *The Syriac Version of the Psalms of Solomon: A Critical Evaluation.* Septuagint and Cognate Studies, 11. Atlanta: Scholars Press, 1985.

Transmitting Jewish Traditions: Orality, Textuality, and Cultural Diffusion. Ed. Yaakov Elman and Israel Gershon. Studies in Jewish Culture and Society. New Haven: Yale University Press, 2000.

Tubach, Frederic C. *Index exemplorum: A Handbook of Medieval Religious Tales.* FF Communications, 86:204. Helsinki: Suomalainen Tiedeakaternia, 1969.

Urbach, Efraim Elimelech. *Ba`ale ha-tosafot: toldotehem, hiburehem, shitatam.* 2 vols. Jerusalem: Mosad Biyalik, 1980.

van Gelder, Geert Jan. *God's Banquet: Food in Classical Arabic Literature.* New York: Columbia University Press, 2000.

Vana, Liliane. "Les rélations sociales entre juifs et païens à l'époque de la Mishna: la question du Banquet privé ("mishteh shel goyim")." *Revue des Sciences Religieuses* 71.2 (1997): 147–70.

Verkerk, Dorothy Hoogland. "Black Servant, Black Demon: Color Ideology in the Ashburn Pentateuch." *Journal of Medieval and Early Modern Studies* 31.1 (2001): 57–77.

Visotzky, Burton L. "Anti-Christian Polemic in *Leviticus Rabbah.*" *Proceedings of the American Academy for Jewish Research* 56 (1990): 83–100.

Von Staden, Heinrich. "Women and Dirt." *Helios* 19.1–2 (1992): 7–30.

Wagenaar-Nolthenius, H. "Der 'Planetus Judei' und der [Alenu-]Gesang judischer Martyrer in Blois anno 1171." In *Mélanges offerts à René Crozet à l'occasion de son soixante-dixième anniversaire,* ed. P. Gallais and Y.-J. Riou, 881–85. 2 vols. Poitiers: Société d'Études Médiévales, 1966.

Wack, Mary Frances. *Lovesickness in the Middle Ages: The* Viaticum *and Its Commentaries*. Middle Ages series. Philadelphia: University of Pennsylvania Press, 1990.

Walz, Rainer. "Die Verfolgungen von 1096 und die Ritualmordlegende: Die Debatte über die Thesen Israel J. Yuval." *Aschkenas* 9.1 (1999): 189–232.

Walzer, Sofie. "The Mamluk Illuminated Manuscripts of Kalila wa-Dimna." In *Aus de Welt der Islamischen Kunst: Festschrift für Ernst Kühnel zum 75. Geburstag am 26.10.1957,* ed. Richard Ettinghausen, 195–206. Berlin: Gebr. Mann, 1959.

Warner, Marina. *Alone of All Her Sex: The Myth and Cult of the Virgin Mary*. 1st Amer. ed. New York: Knopf, 1976.

Wasserstein, Abraham. "Normal and Abnormal Gestation Periods in Humans: A Survey of Ancient Opinion (Greek, Roman, and Rabbinic)." *Korot* 9.1–2 (1985): 221–29.

Weigand, Rudolph. "Magister Rolandus und Papst Alexander III." *Archiv für Katholisches Kirchenrecht* 149 (1980): 3–44.

Welch, J. L. "Cross Dressing and Cross Purposes." In *Gender Reversals and Gender Cultures: Anthropological and Historical Perspectives,* ed. Sabrina Petra Ramet, 66–78. London: Routledge, 1996.

Welter, J.-Th. *L'Exemplum dans la littérature religieuse et didactique du Moyen Âge*. Paris: E. H. Guitard, 1927.

Williams, A. V. "Zoroastrian and Judaic Purity Laws: Reflections on the Viability of a Sociological Interpretation." *Irano-Judaica* 3 (1994): 72–89.

Williams, Michael A. *Rethinking "Gnosticism": An Argument for Dismantling a Dubious Category*. Princeton: Princeton University Press, 1996.

Wilson, Katharina M., and Elizabeth M. Makowski. *Wykked Wyves and the Woes of Marriage: Misogamous Literature from Juvenal to Chaucer*. SUNY Series in Medieval Studies. Albany: State University of New York Press, 1990.

Wolf, Kenneth Baxter. *Christian Martyrs in Muslim Spain.* Cambridge: Cambridge University Press, 1988.

Wolfson, Elliot R. "Crossing Gender Boundaries in Kabbalistic Ritual and Myth." In *Ultimate Intimacy: The Psychodynamics of Jewish Mysticism,* ed. Mortimer Ostrow, 255–337. London: Karnac Books, 1995.

———. "Erasing the Erasure/Gender and the Writing of God's Body in Kabbalistic Symbolism." In *Circle in the Square: Studies in the Use of Gender in Kabbalistic Symbolism,* 49–78. Albany: State University of New York Press, 1995.

———. "The Image of Jacob Engraved upon the Throne: Further Reflection on the Esoteric Doctrine of the German Pietists." In *Along the Path: Studies in Kabbalistic Myth, Symbolism, and Hermeneutics,* 1–62. Albany: State University of New York Press, 1995.

———. "Images of God's Feet: Some Observations on the Divine Body in Judaism." In *People of the Body: Jews and Judaism from an Embodied Perspective,* ed. Howard Eilberg-Schwartz, 143–81. Body in Culture, History, and Religion. Albany: State University of New York Press, 1992.

———. "Left Contained in the Right: A Study of Zoharic Hermeneutics." *AJS Review* 11 (1986): 27–52.

———. "Ontology, Alterity, and Ethics in Kabbalistic Anthropology." *Exemplaria* 12.1 (2000): 129–55.

———. "Re/membering the Covenant: Memory, Forgetfulness, and the Construction of History in the Zohar." In *Jewish History and Jewish Memory: Essays in Honor of Yosef Hayim Yerushalmi,* ed. Elisheva Carlebach, John M. Efron, and David N. Myers, 214–46. Hanover, NH: University Press of New England, 1998.

———. *Through a Speculum That Shines: Vision and Imagination in Medieval Jewish Mysticism*. Princeton: Princeton University Press, 1994.

———. "Woman—The Feminine as Other in Theosophic Kabbalah: Some Philosophical Observations on the Divine Androgyne." In *The Other in Jewish Thought and History: Constructions of Jewish Culture and Identity,* ed. Lawrence J. Silberstein and Robert L. Cohn, 166–204. New Perspectives on Jewish Studies. New York: New York University Press, 1994.

Women in the Medieval Islamic World: Power, Patronage, and Piety. Ed. G. Hambly. New York: St. Martin's Press, 1998.

Women, Men and Eunuchs: Gender in Byzantium. Ed. Liz James. London: Routledge, 1997.

Wood, Charles T. "The Doctor's Dilemma: Sin, Salvation, and the Menstrual Cycle in Medieval Thought." *Speculum* 56.4 (1981): 710–27.

Wright, John Kirtland. *Geographical Lore at the Time of the Crusades: A Study in the History of Medieval Science and Tradition in Western Europe.* New York: American Geographical Society, 1925; reprint New York: Dover, 1965.

Wright, Laurence. "'Burning' and Leprosy in Old French." *Medium Aevum* 56.1 (1987): 101–11.

Yalom, Marilyn. *A History of the Breast*. New York: Knopf, 1997.

Yassif, Eli. [*Sipur ha-'am ha-'Ivri.*]. *The Hebrew Folktale: History, Genre, Meaning.* Trans. Jacqueline S. Teitelbaum. Folklore Studies in Translation. Bloomington: Indiana University Press, 1999.

———. "ha-Sipur ha-eksemplari be-Sefer Hasidim." *Tarbits* 57.2 (1988): 217–55.

Yerushalmi, Yosef Hayim. "The Inquisition and the Jews in the Time of Bernard Gui." *Harvard Theological Review* 63 (1970): 317–76.

———. *Zakhor: Jewish History and Jewish Memory*. Samuel and Althea Stroum Lectures in Jewish Studies. Seattle: University of Washington Press, 1982.

Yuval, Israel Jacob. "Easter and Passover as Early Jewish-Christian dialogue." In *Passover and Easter: Origin and History to Modern Times,* ed. Paul Bradshaw and Lawrence A. Hoffman, 98–124. Two Liturgical Traditions, 5. Notre Dame: University of Notre Dame Press, 1999.

———. "Nakam Adonai hi' nikamat hekhal': historia lelo' Haro ve-lelo' maso' panim." *Tsiyon* 59.2–3 (1994): 351–414.

———. "ha-Nakam ve-ha-k'lilah ha-dam ve-ha-'alilah me-'alilot kedushim le-'alilot dam." *Tsiyon* 58 (1993): 33–89.

———. "Passover in the Middle Ages." In *Passover and Easter: Origin and History to Modern Times,* ed. Paul Bradshaw and Lawrence A. Hoffman, 127–60. Two Liturgical Traditions, 5. Notre Dame: University of Notre Dame Press, 1999.

———. "ha-Poshim 'al shtei ha-sa'ifuim: ha haggadah shel pesah ve-ha-pasha' ha-notsrit." *Tarbits* 65 (1995): 5–28.

———. *Shene goyim be-vitnekh: Yehudim ve-Nosrim, dimuyim hadadiyim.* Tel Aviv: 'Alma: 'Am 'oved, 2000.

Zafran, Eric. "The Iconography of Antisemitism: A Study of the Representation of Jews in the Visual Arts of Europe, 1400–1600." 2 vols. Ph.D. dissertation, New York University, 1973.

———. "Saturn and the Jews." *Journal of the Warburg and Coutauld Institutes* 42 (1979): 16–27.

Index

abomination, 49, 51, 56, 81, 139, 143, 317n116
accusation(s), 1, 2, 3, 6, 9, 10, 15, 67, 120, 122, 151, 162, 176, 177, 191, 194, 196, 219, 220, 225, 238. *See also* blood libel; desecration; host, desecration of; murder, child
—of disease, 5, 12, 13, 42, 54, 156, 158–60, 166, 174, 191, 195, 240, 323n10
—of filth/impurity, 12, 47, 48, 55–56, 66, 76, 78, 79, 82, 120, 122, 143, 145, 152, 154, 156, 194, 269n1, 287n155
activity, sexual, 25, 34, 184
adulterer(s), 59, 60, 82, 324n37
adultery, 41, 45, 57, 120, 137
ailments, skin, 30, 40, 41, 157
Alan of Lille, 114, 119, 294n51, 317n106, 321n154
Albertus Magnus, 99, 109, 175, 176, 178
—Pseudo-Albertus Magnus, *De Secretis Mulierum*, 100, 179, 195
am(mei) ha-'areẓ, 51, 52, 53, 56, 259n66, 271nn28, 29, 30
Amulo, 81, 82, 290n189
Andalusi, Said al-, 183, 332n129
angel(s), 22, 36, 39, 62, 109, 128
anger, 8, 9, 13, 68, 80, 88, 93, 102, 130, 135, 138, 144, 154, 161, 171, 193, 219, 242, 243
animals
—despised, 44, 76, 152, 216, 245n1
—images of, 14, 45, 198, 199, 200–239
—impure/unclean, 10, 13, 43–46, 50–54, 59, 60, 67, 76, 134–36, 145, 177, 211, 212, 219, 226, 227, 233, 267n145, 268n149, 270n17
—wild, 203, 210, 219, 222
—*See also specific animal name*
Anselm, 109, 312n54, 337n14
anthropomorphic, 22–24, 33, 253n22
antibiographies, 77, 134, 147, 154
anti-Islam/Muslim, 87, 88, 95, 96, 186, 217, 247n45
anti-Judaism, 2, 3, 8, 10, 15, 88, 90, 91, 94, 97, 119, 123, 151, 154, 158, 182, 187, 196, 198, 200, 205, 208, 217, 224, 229, 230, 232, 234, 243, 349nn181, 182
anxiety/ies, 6, 46, 78, 90, 93, 200, 211, 212, 219, 236, 238, 239, 240, 242
Aquinas, Thomas, 109, 295n52, 303n135
Arabic, 4, 12, 74, 77, 82, 88, 91, 94–99, 101, 110, 115, 159, 205, 216, 243, 284n142, 294n45, 332n126
Aristotle/Aristotelian, 26, 27, 29, 99–101, 104, 105, 109, 110, 113, 119, 157, 180, 195, 214, 255n37, 296n61
Arnobius of Sicca, 21, 24–26, 59, 60, 61, 63, 64, 65

ALEXANDRA CUFFEL is assistant professor of history at Macalester College. She has published a number of articles and reviews on medieval and early modern studies.